12-87

D1706261

-87

Early
KENTUCKY
HOUSEHOLDERS

—————— ➤ 1787–1811 ◄ ——————

Early
KENTUCKY HOUSEHOLDERS

1787–1811

Compiled by
JAMES F. SUTHERLAND

GENEALOGICAL PUBLISHING CO., INC.
Baltimore 1986

Copyright © 1986 by James F. Sutherland
All Rights Reserved
Published by Genealogical Publishing Co., Inc.
Baltimore, Maryland 1986
Library of Congress Catalogue Card Number 86-80831
International Standard Book Number 0-8063-1159-2
Made in the United States of America

INTRODUCTION

"Ye'll not find MY name in any books published 200 years from now!" is very likely a prophecy uttered by many of the early Kentucky settlers listed in this book. Most of them were hard-working farmers and they were simply too busy keeping their families alive in the harsh surroundings of the frontier to be very much concerned about future posterity. Today, we are indeed fortunate to have simultaneous access to the old records and to modern computer-based processing tools. By combining them, we can give the early pioneers their deserved place in history even though the county tax commissioners, compiling their annual tax lists based on phonetic spelling, almost succeeded in making the early householders' prophecy come true.

Early tax commissioners used their imagination when entering the names of their district householders into annual tax lists. Conversion of spoken surnames into handwritten entries was not consistant from year to year, even if the same tax commissioner entered the data for both years. In the 1700's they were not working under ideal conditions, and it is doubtful that we could have done a better job under the same circumstances. The tax commissioners were a very select group because they could read and write at a time when many people could only mark their name with an "X".

By the time the eight-year project of compiling this data was nearly completed, many possible book titles had come to mind. One of them, "4495 WAYS TO SPELL 1614 EARLY KENTUCKY SURNAMES" seemed particularly appropriate. It had been a struggle to untangle the early tax records of Lincoln County, Kentucky, and the frustration of dealing gracefully with 3.5 million characters of computer files, full of misspelled surnames, was a real test of the author's patience. However, careful and persistent use of a personal computer finally produced a rationalized data base from which this book was extracted.

TAX RECORDS AS A RESOURCE

Tax records provide a better sampling of the householders than federal census records because the pioneers were mobile during the westward movement of the frontier. Some settlers moved into Kentucky after a census was taken, and then moved out of the state before the next census. They could be missed in the tax list for one year, such as 1790 or 1800, from which the federal census has been reconstructed, but it is unlikely that they could evade the tax commissioner every year for twenty-three years and thereby be omitted from this book.

WHY LINCOLN COUNTY, KENTUCKY?

Forty-six counties of the 54 Kentucky counties which existed in the year 1811 are mentioned in the descriptions of landholdings claimed by the Lincoln County householders for the years 1787-1811. Many of the persons living in Lincoln County claimed land in other counties when there were only three counties in the state, or they lived in an area of the parent county which was eventually split off to form a new county. That information is lost if a researcher does not know that information relating to his subject is available in an "unrelated" county tax list. There are no landholdings listed with the householders in this book because that additional information would have expanded the book beyond what may be published and marketed in a single volume. A second volume, identifying early Kentucky landholders, may be extracted from the data base and published in the future if a need is established .

THE INCENTIVE

The task of reading more than 34,000 Lincoln County tax list entries for the 1787-1811 period began in 1977 when I purchased two reels of microfilm from the Kentucky Historical Society in Frankfort. I was looking for information about my ancestor, URIAH SUTHERLAND, who lived in Kentucky from 1789 until 1804, when his will was probated in Lincoln County. The tax records for Lincoln County had never been indexed before, and I believed that I could use my H-89 computer to sort the entries for Uriah and his neighbors. I wanted to find precisely where URIAH had lived in the county prior to moving to a farm 12 miles south of

Liberty, in what is now Casey County. As a by-product of that project, this index has been produced which may help you determine where your ancestor lived as a householder in the broad region of Kentucky covered by Lincoln County records.

DATA PROCESSING

A microfiche viewer was used to read 35mm microfilmed pages which had been cut apart and individually mounted on aparture cards, 1600 in all. The extra magnification provided by the microfiche viewer made the task of deciphering each record entry much easier. The surnames were enlarged to fill the entire screen so that the dot of the "i" or the crossing of the "t" were more clearly seen and distinguished from an "e" or an "l". The structure of the data on the work sheets was modified several times during the project in order to accommodate tax list information which varied from year to year. For example, in some years the landholdings were not shown, and occasionally the number of white males 16-21 was not enumerated. After completing the worksheet for the final year, 1811, it was easy to determine how many characters should be reserved for each field of each record in the computer data base.

Only information useful in correlating entries or for genealogical purposes was transcribed. The number of slaves, horses, cattle, or 4-wheeled carriages was not transcribed, but the location and acreage of landholdings along with the name of prior land-assignees were carefully recorded.

If a landholding was included in the original records, the details were copied into the data base and that information was used to connect the various spellings of surnames. The householder's first name was usually spelled consistently if it was a Biblical name, implying that the Bible was used as a dictionary. The surnames, on the other hand, could be spelled many different ways, depending on how the commissioner heard it pronounced. I wrote a program to calculate the SOUNDEX code for each surname so that similar codes might help me connect the various spellings, but I found that it didn't automatically consolidate the misspelled surnames. A better method of sorting was developed by doing a preliminary sort on the householders' first names. From a listing of the alphabetized first names, it was easy to make a comparison of the surnames and land holdings and assign a new field in each householder's data base record to contain a rationalized surname group. The final computer sort was executed using the descending keys of surname group, original surname, first name, and year-date of entry, with some manual adjustments made in the placement of those records which contained slightly misspelled first names.

The spelling of householder names as found in the tax lists was carefully preserved through each stage of computer processing. In the Index which makes up the rest of this book, an alphabetic listing of householders has been extracted from the data base. Householders are listed under surname group headings to make it easier for you to find the yearly entries for each householder.

USAGE GUIDELINES

The Surname Directory at the end of this Introduction should be consulted BEFORE searching the Index. It will tell you which surname group contains the particular surname you are tracing. For instance, if you are looking for the surname "Aaronton", the Surname Directory will help you find it in the "HERRINGTON" group in the Index. This eliminates the time needed to search through all of the Aaronton, Aronton, Arrington, Harrington, Herrington, and Herington surnames which unfortunately would have been scattered through the Index if the computer had been simply used to alphabetically sort the phonetically spelled surnames.

The date shown for each householder in the Index is the date of entry into the tax list by the commissioner. Neighbors were usually listed together in the same tax book with the same date of entry.

Each tax commissioner was responsible for compiling a list of householders in his assigned district of Lincoln County. Even though he might serve as official tax commissioner for the same region for several years, the numbers assigned to his tax book each year depended upon when he returned it to the clerk of the county court for recording. Therefore, the householders in a particular region of the county might be found in book number 1 for one year, and in book number 2 the next. William Bryant, for instance, was assigned the "upper district" of Lincoln County for 1794, 1795, and 1797, but different tax book numbers were assigned to his lists for each of those years.

The following table lists each of the Lincoln County tax commissioners along with tax book numbers before their names. In the tax records, the book number appears on the cover-page, and the commissioner's name is normally written at the top of the first page. The microfilmed tax lists do not always preserve the numerical order of the tax books for each year, so it may be necessary to use the commissioner-name rather than just the book number to locate an entry. Once the proper tax book has been found in the original records, the rest of the search is easy. Page numbers were always prominently written or stamped in the upper left corner of each page.

The three tax lists for the year 1789 are microfilmed in duplicate sets. One set of the lists is available in "negative" form and the other set is "positive". Since the "positive" microfilm is more distinct, the book numbers for 1789 in the table which follows are for the "positive" microfilm records.

Year	Bk	Commissioner	Bk	Commissioner	Bk	Commissioner
1787	(1)	William ---	(2)	William Lewis	3.	John Bryant
1788	(1)	Joseph Bledsoe		(missing)		(missing)
1789	2.	Charles Campbell	5.	* Joseph Bledsoe	6.	William Reed
1790	1.	William Reed	(2)	Young Ewing		(missing)
1791	1.	Abraham Miller	2.	William Reed	3.	William Pawling
1792	1.	William Reed	2.	George Davidson	3.	William Pawling
1793	1.	George Davidson	(2)	-.Pawling	3.	William Reed
1794	1.	George Davidson	2.	Urbin Ewing	3.	William Bryant
1795	1.	William Bryant	2.	George Davidson	3.	Urbin Ewing
1796	1.	George Davidson	2.	Urbin Ewing	4.	---
1797	1.	James Berry	2.	William Bryant	3.	---
1798	-No 1798 tax list found in microfilmed records for Lincoln County-					
1799	1.	Joseph Davis Jr	2.	Henry Baughman	3.	James Berry
1800	1.	Henry Baughman	2.	George McRoberts	3.	John Jones
1801	1.	Henry Baughman	2.	George McRoberts	3.	Hugh Magill
1802	1.	Henry Baughman	2.	Hugh Magill	3.	George McRoberts
1803	1.	Henry Baughman	2.	# George McRoberts	3.	John Jones
1804	1.	Henry Baughman	2.	Hugh Magill	3.	G.M. 4. Buford Peyton
1805	1.	Henry Baughman	2.	George McRoberts	3.	Hugh Magill
1806	1.	Henry Baughman	2.	George McRoberts	3.	Hugh Magill
1807	1.	Nudeget Owsley	2.	Hugh Magill		
1808	1.	---	2.	Hugh Magill		
1809	1.	John Shanks	2.	Thomas Owsley		
1810	-No 1810 tax list found in microfilmed records for Lincoln County-					
1811	1.	---				

*   Page 3 of 1789 list for Joseph Bledsoe appears to belong between
     pages 2 and 3 of Bledsoe's 1788 tax list.

Page 0 missing from Book 2, 1803.

(n) Parentheses enclose book numbers which were inferred by their
     order in the microfilmed records.

--- Commissioner's name was not written on first page of the tax book.

The "TM" columns basically show the number of white males living in the region covered by the Lincoln County tax commissioners. The Taxpayer Status (T) column indicates the number of white males above 21 years of age living in the household. Column (M) shows the number of white males 16-21 years of age living in the household. This information can give the researcher a clue to parent/son relationships which should be corroborated further from other sources. For example, Elijah Bell appears as a householder above 21 years of age the same year that William Bell's 16-21 year old son disappears from the records after having been listed for four years, so Elijah Bell was very likely the son of William Bell.

In addition, column (T) shows the status of certain non-voters by the following letter-codes:

   Female (F)   Minor (M)   Free Black (B)   Exempt (0)   Deceased (D)
                                                 or
                                              Deceased

The following householders, not counted as voters in the tax list, were entered as "free black":

Ned Bright	Thomas Cannon	Isaac Connor	Frank Craig
Isam Davis	Adam Evans	William Gowen	Isaac Gumm
Jack Hart	William Hinton	Jack ---	Michael Jackson
Jupiter ---	Isaac Majors	Adam Martin	Solomon Martin
Bristoe Mathews	Edward Mathews	Michael ---	Darby Penman
John Rock	Ruth ---	Stepp ---	William Williams
Peter Worser			

The requirements for tax-exempt status are not known to the author, but an exemption may have been given because the householder held a county office or served the county in some other way. "Exempt from county levy" was noted for the following householders:

James Bailey	Samuel Blevins	David Blythe	Nathan Buley
John Christison	John Sr Collier	Moses Collier	William Crum
Moses Cummins	Joseph Elliot	James Sr Farris	Joseph Hall
William Irvin	John Murphy	William Wells	

It is my sincere hope that this index will help you find new clues in your search for hard-to-find early Kentucky householders. This book is intended to be a beginning rather than an end to your search. If you find your subject here, go back to the original records, or to their microfilmed copies, and focus your research efforts on the actual entries as they were recorded almost 200 years ago.

If you own a personal computer and you have found it to be extremely helpful in organizing your data, you may be interested in using it for further sorting of the householder information contained in this book. If so, write the author asking for information about availability and price of the "Early Kentucky Householders 1787-1811" data base on flexible data diskettes.

James F. Sutherland
4857 Havana Drive
Pittsburgh, PA   15239

SURNAME DIRECTORY

searching	find in	searching	find in	searching	find in
Aarenton	HERRINGTON	Arnet	ARNETT	Barber	BARBER
Aaronton	HERRINGTON	Arnett	ARNETT	Bardett	BURDETT
Abbot	ABBOTT	Arnitt	ARNETT	Barger	BARKER
Abott	ABBOTT	Arnold	ARNOLD	Barkee	BARKER
Abrell	ABRELL	Arnott	ARNETT	Barker	BARKER
Achman	AIKMAN	Arrington	HERRINGTON	Barley	BOSLEY
Achols	ECHOLS	Artgas	ORKEES	Barnes	BARNES
Acklin	ACTON	Arther	ARTHUR	Barnet	BARNETT
Acles	ECHOLS	Arthur	ARTHUR	Barnett	BARNETT
Acres	ACRES	Arven	IRVIN	Barns	BARNES
Acton	ACTON	Arvin	IRVIN	Bartes	BARTES
Acuss	ACRES	Asberry	ASBURY	Barton	BURTON
Adams	ADAMS	Ashberry	ASBURY	Bateast	BATISTE
Aderson	ANDERSON	Ashby	ASHBY	Bates	BATES
Adkens	ATKINSON	Asher	ASHER	Batest	BATISTE
Adkins	ATKINSON	Ashley	ASHLEY	Batey	BEATY
Adkinson	ATKINSON	Ashlock	ASHLOCK	Bathuram	BETHURAM
Agenew	AGNEW	Ashly	ASHLEY	Bathuren	BETHURAM
Agnew	AGNEW	Ashmore	ASHMORE	Bathurum	BETHURAM
Aikman	AIKMAN	Atkens	ATKINSON	Bathuurum	BETHURAM
Aines	HAYNES	Atkenson	ATKINSON	Batist	BATISTE
Airs	AYERS	Atkerson	ATKINSON	Batiste	BATISTE
Akells	ECHOLS	Atkins	ATKINS	Battees	BATISTE
Akeman	AIKMAN	Atkins	ATKINSON	Battes	BATISTE
Aken	AKIN	Atkinson	ATKINSON	Battesste	BATISTE
Akens	AKIN	Atkison	ATKINSON	Battest	BATISTE
Akers	ACRES	Attkins	ATKINS	Battis	BATISTE
Akes	ACRES	Atwood	ATWOOD	Baughman	BAUGHMAN
Akin	AKIN	Austen	AUSTIN	Baunty	BAUNTY
Akis	ACRES	Austin	AUSTIN	Bause	BOST
Albertson	ALBERTSON	Averly	ABRELL	Baust	BOST
Alcorn	ALCORN	Ayers	AYERS	Baverly	BEVERLY
Alcorne	ALCORN	B-11	BALL	Bavers	BAVERS
Alder	ELDER	Baber	BABER	Bawers	BOWERS
Alderson	ALDERSON	Backster	BAXTER	Bawl	BALL
Alexander	ALEXANDER	Baden	BADEN	Baxter	BAXTER
Alferd	ALFORD	Baen	BEAN	Baxton	BAXTER
Alford	ALFORD	Baggs	BAGGS	Baxtor	BAXTER
Alfred	ALFORD	Bailey	BAILEY	Baylor	BAYLOR
Allbough	ALLBOUGH	Bailley	BAILEY	Baynice	BAYNICE
Allbuck	ALLBOUGH	Bailor	BAYLOR	Bays	BAYS
Allcorn	ALCORN	Bails	BAILEY	Bazel	BAZEL
Allen	ALLEN	Baily	BAILEY	Beacon	BEACON
Allin	ALLEN	Bain	BEAN	Beadels	BEADLES
Allsop	ALSOP	Bainbridge	BAINBRIDGE	Beadles	BEADLES
Allspach	ALSPAW	Baird	BEARD	Beaker	BAKER
Allspaw	ALSPAW	Baker	BAKER	Bealey	BAILEY
Allston	ALLSTON	Baldock	BALDOCK	Bealy	BAILEY
Allstot	ALSTOTT	Baldridge	BALDRIDGE	Beam	BEAM
Alsoup	ALSOP	Balenger	BALLENGER	Beamer	BEAMER
Alspach	ALSPAW	Baley	BAILEY	Beams	BEAN
Alspaugh	ALSPAW	Balinger	BALLENGER	Bean	BEAN
Alspaw	ALSPAW	Ball	BALL	Beanett	BENNETT
Alspen	ALSPAW	Ballard	BALLARD	Beard	BEARD
Alstadt	ALSTOTT	Ballden	BALLDEN	Bearris	BURROUGHS
Alstot	ALSTOTT	Balldock	BALDOCK	Beattey	BEATY
Alstott	ALSTOTT	Ballenger	BALLENGER	Beavens	BLEVINS
Altstott	ALSTOTT	Ballinger	BALLENGER	Beaver	BEAVERS
Amberson	EMERSON	Ballow	BALLOW	Beavers	BEAVERS
Amonds	AMONDS	Balor	BAYLOR	Beavis	BEAVERS
Amoureux	AMOUREUX	Bambridge	BAMBRIDGE	Beaxler	BIGSLER
Ample	ANTLE	Bancks	BANKS	Beck	BECK
Anderson	ANDERSON	Bankhead	BANKHEAD	Beckley	BECKLEY
Andrews	ANDREWS	Banks	BANKS	Beddles	BEADLES
Anthony	ANTHONY	Bannon	BANNON	Bedles	BEADLES
Antle	ANTLE	Banta	BAUNTY	Beedels	BEADLES
Aranhart	ARANHART	Bantee	BAUNTY	Beedler	BEADLES
Arbuckel	ARBUCKLE	Banten	BANTON	Beedles	BEADLES
Arbuckle	ARBUCKLE	Banton	BANTON	Beem	BEAM
Aris	AYERS	Bantton	BANTON	Been	BEAN
Armstrong	ARMSTRONG	Bantun	BANTON	Begar	BAKER
Arnald	ARNOLD	Barbee	BARBEE	Beidles	BEADLES

searching	find in	searching	find in	searching	find in
Beigles	BEADLES	Blackiston	BLACKSTONE	Bowerman	BOWMAN
Beleu	BALLOW	Blackledge	BLACKLEDGE	Bowers	BOWYERS
Bell	BELL	Blacklidge	BLACKLEDGE	Bowin	BOWEN
Bellimon	BELLIMON	Blackston	BLACKSTONE	Bowlen	BOWLIN
Belshe	BELSHE	Blackstone	BLACKSTONE	Bowler	BOWLER
Benadick	BENEDICT	Blackwell	BLACKWELL	Bowles	BOWLES
Benedic	BENEDICT	Blackwood	BLACKWOOD	Bowlin	BOWLIN
Benedick	BENEDICT	Blain	BLAIN	Bowman	BOWMAN
Benedict	BENEDICT	Blaine	BLAIN	Bowyer	BOWYERS
Bengaman	BINGAMAN	Blair	BLAIR	Bowyers	BOWYERS
Benjamin	BINGAMAN	Blakey	BLAKEY	Boyd	BOYD
Benley	BAILEY	Blaky	BLAKEY	Boyder	BOYDER
Benly	BENTLEY	Bland	BLAND	Boyers	BOWYERS
Bennadick	BENEDICT	Blane	BLAIN	Boyle	BOYLES
Bennedeck	BENEDICT	Blank	BLANKS	Boyles	BOYLES
Bennedick	BENEDICT	Blankenship	BLANKENSHIP	Bozley	BOSLEY
Bennedict	BENEDICT	Blanks	BLANKS	Brackinridg	BRACKINRIDG
Bennet	BENNETT	Blare	BLAIR	Braden	BRADEN
Bennett	BENNETT	Bleaky	BLAKEY	Bradford	BRADFORD
Bennit	BENNETT	Blear	BLAIR	Bradley	BRADLEY
Benny	BURDETT	Bledsoe	BLEDSOE	Bradly	BRADLEY
Bentley	BENTLEY	Bleven	BLEVINS	Brady	BRADY
Bently	BENTLEY	Blevens	BLEVINS	Brailes	BRILES
Berdit	BURDETT	Blevin	BLEVINS	Branon	BRANON
Beriman	BERREMAN	Blevins	BLEVINS	Branton	BRUMPTON
Berks	BURK	Blith	BLYTHE	Brasfield	BRASFIELD
Berksler	BIGSLER	Bliven	BLEVINS	Bray	BRAY
Bernard	BERNARD	Blivens	BLEVINS	Breadon	BREEDING
Bernaugh	BRONAUGH	Blivins	BLEVINS	Bready	BRADY
Berney	BIRNEY	Bloid	BLOID	Breden	BREEDING
Berreman	BERREMAN	Bly	BLYTHE	Bredger	BRIDGES
Berriman	BERREMAN	Blythe	BLYTHE	Bredin	BREEDING
Berrimon	BERREMAN	Boatman	BOATMAN	Breeden	BREEDING
Berry	BERRY	Bodry	BOWDRY	Breedin	BREEDING
Beryman	BERREMAN	Boen	BOWEN	Breeding	BREEDING
Best	BOST	Bogard	BOGARD	Brehner	BREHNER
Bethuram	BETHURAM	Boldock	BALDOCK	Brenaugh	BRONAUGH
Bettes	BETTIS	Bolen	BOWLIN	Bresh	BRUSH
Bettis	BETTIS	Boles	BOWLES	Brewer	BREWER
Beverly	BEVERLY	Boley	BOLEY	Brian	BRYANT
Bevery	BEVERLY	Bolton	BOLTON	Briant	BRYANT
Bevis	BEAVERS	Bolue	BALLOW	Bride	BRIGHT
Bexler	BIGSLER	Booford	BUFORD	Bridges	BRIDGES
Bias	BIAS	Boon	BOON	Brient	BRYANT
Bibb	BIBB	Boran	BOREN	Briggs	BRIGGS
Bibbs	BIBB	Borand	BOREN	Bright	BRIGHT
Bigg	BIGGS	Boren	BOREN	Brigs	BRIGGS
Biggs	BIGGS	Boress	BURROUGHS	Briles	BRILES
Bigham	BIGHAM	Boring	BOREN	Brinton	BRUMPTON
Bigs	BIGGS	Borman	BOWMAN	Brisco	BRISCOE
Bigsler	BIGSLER	Borrand	BOREN	Briscoe	BRISCOE
Bingaman	BINGAMAN	Bosht	BOST	Brish	BRUSH
Bingamin	BINGAMAN	Boslee	BOSLEY	Bristoral	BRISTORAL
Bingamon	BINGAMAN	Bosler	BOSLEY	Briton	BRITON
Binler	BIGSLER	Bosley	BOSLEY	Brock	BROCK
Binney	BIRNEY	Bost	BOST	Broiler	BRILES
Birch	BURCH	Bostick	BOSTICK	Broiles	BRILES
Bird	BIRD	Bouarn	BOREN	Broils	BRILES
Birney	BIRNEY	Boudrey	BOWDRY	Bronaugh	BRONAUGH
Birns	BURNS	Bouford	BUFORD	Bronough	BRONAUGH
Birt	BURT	Boughman	BAUGHMAN	Brook	BROCK
Birtt	BURT	Boular	BOWLER	Brook	BROOKS
Bishop	BISHOP	Boulin	BOWLIN	Brooks	BROOKS
Bisshop	BISHOP	Boulten	BOLTON	Broos	BRUCE
Bivens	BLEVINS	Boulton	BOLTON	Broughnah	BRONAUGH
Bixler	BIGSLER	Bouren	BOREN	Brounlee	BROWNLEE
Black	BLACK	Bowden	BOWDEN	Brounts	BROUNTS
Blackaby	BLACKABY	Bowdery	BOWDRY	Brown	BROWN
Blackborn	BLACKBURN	Bowdry	BOWDRY	Browning	BROWNING
Blackbourn	BLACKBURN	Bowels	BOYLES	Brownlee	BROWNLEE
Blackburn	BLACKBURN	Bowen	BOWEN	Broyles	BRILES
Blackburne	BLACKBURN	Bower	BOWYERS	Broyls	BRILES

searching	find in	searching	find in	searching	find in
Bruce	BRUCE	Butcher	BUTCHER	Caten	CATTON
Bruer	BREWER	Butler	BUTLER	Catewill	COTRILL
Bruks	BROOKS	Bybe	BYBE	Cathey	CATHEY
Brumingham	BRUMINGHAM	Byers	BYERS	Catlive	CATLIVE
Brumpton	BRUMPTON	Byrd	BIRD	Catnoy	COURTNEY
Brumston	BRUMPTON	Byrns	BURNS	Caton	CATTON
Brumton	BRUMPTON	Cabbell	CAVELL	Catton	CATTON
Brunk	BRUNK	Cabble	CAVELL	Caudrey	CAUDREY
Brush	BRUSH	Cadis	CADIS	Caufman	COFFMAN
Bryan	BRYANT	Cagle	CAGLE	Cauhorn	CAUHORN
Bryant	BRYANT	Cail	CALE	Caumley	CAUMLEY
Brydon	BRYDON	Cain	CAIN	Cavanaugh	KAVANAGH
Bryent	BRYANT	Caise	KEY	Cavel	CAVELL
Bryon	BRYANT	Calahan	CALAHAN	Cavell	CAVELL
Bryson	BRYANT	Caldwell	CALDWELL	Cavenar	KAVANAGH
Bucher	BUTCHER	Cale	CALE	Cavender	KAVANAGH
Buck	BUCK	Calekorn	CALEKORN	Cavil	CAVELL
Buckanan	BUCHANAN	Calfee	CALFEE	Cavill	CAVELL
Buckanon	BUCHANAN	Calhoon	CALHOON	Cayton	CATTON
Buckhanan	BUCHANAN	Calison	CALLISON	Ceaser	CEASER
Buckhann	BUCHANAN	Callemees	CALLEMEES	Cembroo	CEMBROO
Buckhannon	BUCHANAN	Caller	CALLER	Certain	CERTAIN
Buckhanon	BUCHANAN	Callicut	CALLICUT	Chadwell	CHADWELL
Buckhonon	BUCHANAN	Callicut	CALLISON	Chamberlain	CHAMBERLAIN
Buckner	BUCKNER	Callison	CALLISON	Chambers	CHAMBERS
Bucknor	BUCKNER	Calp	COPE	Champman	CHAPMAN
Buford	BUFORD	Calverd	CALVERT	Chanc	CHANCE
Bufort	BUFORD	Calvert	CALVERT	Chance	CHANCE
Buley	BULEY	Calvin	COLVIN	Chandler	CHANDLER
Bull	BULL	Cambell	CAMPBELL	Chanler	CHANDLER
Bullock	BULLOCK	Camdem	CAMDEN	Chanse	CHANCE
Bunch	BUNCH	Camden	CAMDEN	Chapell	CHAPPEL
Bunday	BUNDY	Camdun	CAMDEN	Chapill	CHAPPEL
Bunder	BUNDY	Camel	CAMPBELL	Chapman	CHAPMAN
Bundy	BUNDY	Cameron	CAMDEN	Chappel	CHAPPEL
Bunsh	BUNCH	Camlin	CAMDEN	Chappell	CHAPPEL
Buntch	BUNCH	Cammel	CAMPBELL	Chappill	CHAPPEL
Bunting	BUNTON	Camp	CAMP	Chapple	CHAPPEL
Bunton	BUNTON	Campbell	CAMPBELL	Charteen	CHARTEEN
Buntting	BUNTON	Campble	CAMPBELL	Charter	CHARTER
Burch	BURCH	Campden	CAMDEN	Cheatam	CHEATAM
Burcher	BURCHWELL	Camper	KEMPER	Cheek	CHEEK
Burchwell	BURCHWELL	Campis	CAMPIS	Chelse	CHILDS
Burck	BURK	Canifax	CANIFAX	Chelton	CHILTON
Burd	BIRD	Cannifax	CANIFAX	Chesney	CHESNEY
Burdet	BURDETT	Cannon	CANON	Chevue	CHEVUE
Burdett	BURDETT	Canon	CANON	Chiels	CHILDS
Burdit	BURDETT	Cape	COPELAND	Childers	CHILDERS
Burditt	BURDETT	Capell	CAVELL	Childress	CHILDRESS
Burford	BUFORD	Caplen	COPELAND	Chilton	CHILTON
Burges	BURGESS	Car	KERR	Chism	CHISM
Burgess	BURGESS	Carleson	CARLESON	Christall	CHRISTILL
Burk	BURK	Carley	KERLEY	Christason	CHRISTISON
Burkes	BURK	Carman	CARMAN	Christeson	CHRISTISON
Burks	BURK	Carns	CARNS	Christian	CHRISTISON
Burnes	BURNS	Carpenter	CARPENTER	Christill	CHRISTILL
Burnett	BARNETT	Carr	KERR	Christipher	CHRISTOPHER
Burney	BIRNEY	Carrier	CARRIER	Christison	CHRISTISON
Burns	BURNS	Carsen	CARSON	Christman	CHRISTMAN
Burnside	BURNSIDE	Carsey	CARSEY	Christopher	CHRISTOPHER
Burnsides	BURNSIDE	Carson	CARSON	Christosen	CHRISTISON
Burres	BURRIS	Carter	CARTER	Christy	CHRISTY
Burris	BURRIS	Cartright	CARTWRIGHT	Chrittenden	CRITTENDEN
Burroughs	BURROUGHS	Cartwright	CARTWRIGHT	Chronick	CHRONICK
Burt	BURCH	Carver	CARVER	Chrystil	CHRISTILL
Burtch	BURCH	Casaday	CASSADY	Chrystill	CHRISTILL
Burtchfield	BURCHWELL	Casey	CASEY	Chuck	CHUCK
Burten	BURTON	Cash	CASH	Church	CHURCH
Burtin	BURTON	Casill	CASILL	Churchill	CHURCHWELL
Burton	BURTON	Casity	CASSADY	Churchwell	CHURCHWELL
Bush	BRUSH	Cassady	CASSADY	Cimble	KIMBLE
Busley	BOSLEY	Caswell	CASWELL	Cirkpatrick	KIRKPATRICK

searching	find in	searching	find in	searching	find in
Clampel	CLAMPETT	Colven	COLVIN	Coye	COY
Clampell	CLAMPETT	Colvin	COLVIN	Coyer	COLLIER
Clampet	CLAMPETT	Colwell	CALDWELL	Coyler	COLLIER
Clampett	CLAMPETT	Colyar	COLLIER	Cozzey	COSSY
Clark	CLARK	Colyear	COLLIER	Crabb	CRAIG
Clarke	CLARK	Colyer	COLLIER	Crabile	CRABILE
Clarkson	CLARKSON	Comb	COMBS	Craddock	CRADDOCK
Clarry	CLARY	Combes	COMBS	Crafford	CRAWFORD
Clary	CLARY	Combs	COMBS	Craford	CRAWFORD
Claybrok	CLAYBROOK	Comer	COMER	Crafort	CRAWFORD
Claybrook	CLAYBROOK	Comes	COMBS	Craftan	CRAFTON
Cleark	CLARK	Commer	COMER	Crafton	CRAFTON
Clearkson	CLARKSON	Commins	CUMMINS	Craftsman	CRAFTON
Clemens	CLEMENTS	Commons	CUMMINS	Crag	CRAIG
Clement	CLEMENTS	Compoten	CAMDEN	Crage	CRAIG
Clements	CLEMENTS	Conchright	CRONKRIGHT	Craig	CRAIG
Clemmens	CLEMENTS	Conder	CONDER	Craimer	CRAMER
Clemmon	CLEMENTS	Condiff	CUNDIFF	Crainshaw	CRAINSHAW
Clemmons	CLEMENTS	Condon	CONDON	Cramer	CRAMER
Clemonds	CLEMENTS	Conkright	CRONKRIGHT	Cranock	CHRONICK
Clemons	CLEMENTS	Conley	CONLEY	Craven	CRAVENS
Clepole	CLEPOLE	Connally	CONLEY	Cravens	CRAVENS
Clery	CLARY	Connel	CONWILL	Cravins	CRAVENS
Clifton	CLIFTON	Conner	CONNOR	Crawfford	CRAWFORD
Clinton	CLINTON	Connor	CONNOR	Crawford	CRAWFORD
Cloid	CLOYD	Conwill	CONWILL	Crawfort	CRAWFORD
Clonsh	CLONSH	Cooch	COUCH	Crawley	CRAWLEY
Clore	CLORE	Cook	COOK	Creasy	CREASY
Cloyd	CLOYD	Cooley	COOLEY	Creed	CREED
Clury	CLARY	Cooly	COOLEY	Creel	CREEL
Clyer	COLLIER	Coons	KOONS	Crews	CREWS
Clyne	CLYNE	Coope	COOPER	Cristil	CHRISTILL
Coal	COLE	Cooper	COOPER	Critchfield	CRUTCHFIELD
Coalman	COLEMAN	Coos	COOS	Crittenden	CRITTENDEN
Coatney	COURTNEY	Cop	COPE	Crittendon	CRITTENDEN
Cockeril	COCKRELL	Cope	COPE	Crocket	CROCKET
Cockerl	COCKRELL	Copeland	COPELAND	Crockett	CROCKET
Cockral	COCKRELL	Copelin	COPELAND	Crofford	CRAWFORD
Cockram	COCKRAM	Coplen	COPELAND	Cromer	COMER
Cockrel	COCKRELL	Coplin	COPELAND	Cronic	CHRONICK
Cockril	COCKRELL	Cord	CORD	Cronick	CHRONICK
Cockrum	COCKRAM	Corder	CORDER	Cronkright	CRONKRIGHT
Cocks	COX	Cordon	CORDON	Cronnick	CHRONICK
Coddington	CODINGTON	Corkrum	COCKRAM	Cronock	CHRONICK
Codington	CODINGTON	Cornett	CORNETT	Croock	CROOK
Coffee	COFFEY	Cornit	CORNETT	Crook	CROOK
Coffey	COFFEY	Cosbey	COSBEY	Cross	CROSS
Coffman	COFFMAN	Cosey	COSSY	Crossgrove	CROSSGROVE
Coffy	COFFEY	Cosse	COSSY	Crouch	CROUCH
Coghill	COGHILL	Cossy	COSSY	Croucher	CROUCHER
Cogswell	COGHILL	Cotes	COTES	Crousuch	CHRONICK
Cogwell	COGHILL	Cotington	CODINGTON	Crout	CROUT
Cole	COLE	Cotner	COTNER	Croutch	CROUCH
Coleman	COLEMAN	Cotral	COTRILL	Croutcher	CROUCHER
Coleney	COURTNEY	Cotrill	COTRILL	Crow	CROW
Coleson	CALLISON	Cotter	COULTER	Crowder	CROWDER
Coleson	COLSON	Cottinton	CODINGTON	Crowt	CROUT
Coley	COOLEY	Cottrele	COTRILL	Crucher	CROUCHER
Colgate	COLGATE	Couch	COUCH	Crum	CRUM
Collans	COLLINS	Couls	COUCH	Crumb	CRUM
Colleir	COLLIER	Coulter	COULTER	Crumton	CHAPMAN
Collens	COLLINS	Coun	COWAN	Crutcher	CROUCHER
Coller	COULTER	Counts	COUNTS	Crutchfield	CRUTCHFIELD
Collet	COLLET	Courtney	COURTNEY	Culberson	CULBERTSON
Collett	COLLET	Coutch	COUCH	Culbertson	CULBERTSON
Collicutt	CALLICUT	Couteny	COURTNEY	Culp	COPE
Collier	COLLIER	Couts	COUCH	Culton	CULTON
Collins	COLLINS	Covington	COVINGTON	Culwell	CALDWELL
Colman	COLEMAN	Cowan	COWAN	Cumbel	COMBS
Colp	COPE	Cowhorn	CAUHORN	Cumins	CUMMINS
Colson	COLSON	Cox	COX	Cummens	CUMMINS
Colter	COULTER	Coy	COY	Cummings	CUMMINS

searching	find in	searching	find in	searching	find in
Cummins	CUMMINS	Delanah	DELANY	Donley	DONLEY
Cummons	CUMMINS	Delany	DELANY	Donnaldson	DONNALDSON
Cundiff	CUNDIFF	Demory	DEMORY	Donnally	DONLEY
Cundoff	CUNDIFF	Demoss	DEMOSS	Donnaly	DONLEY
Cunnagame	CUNNINGHAM	Denis	DENNIS	Donnan	DONAN
Cunningham	CUNNINGHAM	Denney	DENNY	Donnelly	DONLEY
Curd	CURD	Dennis	DENNIS	Donner	DONAN
Curren	CURREN	Denny	DENNY	Donton	DENTON
Currey	CURRY	Denton	DENTON	Donton	DUNTON
Curry	CURRY	Depau	DEPAUW	Doolen	DOOLEY
Cuting	CUTTING	Depaugh	DEPAUW	Dooley	DOOLEY
Cuttan	CULTON	Depauw	DEPAUW	Doolin	DOOLEY
Cutting	CUTTING	Depaw	DEPAUW	Dooling	DOOLEY
Cutton	CULTON	Depawed	DEPAUW	Dooly	DOOLEY
Dadderman	DADISMAN	Depeau	DEPAUW	Dorrel	DOYLE
Dadisman	DADISMAN	Depow	DEPAUW	Dorrell	DOYLE
Dafferen	DAFFRON	Deveee	DEVEEE	Dorrey	DORREY
Daffron	DAFFRON	Dever	DEVER	Dorril	DOYLE
Dailey	DAILEY	Devin	DEVINE	Dorsey	DORSEY
Daily	DAILEY	Devine	DEVINE	Doss	DOSS
Daisey	DAILEY	Devion	DEVINE	Dossin	DAWSON
Damrel	DAMREL	Dewitt	DEWITT	Dotson	DODSON
Damron	DAMRON	Dey	DAY	Dougherty	DAUGHERTY
Daniel	DANIEL	Dezarnett	DEJARNETT	Doughlas	DOUGLASS
Danier	DANNER	Dickason	DICKSON	Douglas	DOUGLASS
Danner	DANNER	Dicken	DICKEN	Douglass	DOUGLASS
Darlington	DARLINGTON	Dickerson	DICKSON	Douil	DOYLE
Darnal	DARNELL	Dickeson	DICKSON	Douthat	DOUTHIT
Darnald	DARNELL	Dickin	DICKEN	Douthet	DOUTHIT
Darnel	DARNELL	Dicking	DICKEN	Douthit	DOUTHIT
Darnell	DARNELL	Dickinson	DICKSON	Dove	DOVE
Datisman	DADISMAN	Dickison	DICKSON	Dowell	DOWELL
Daugherty	DAUGHERTY	Dickson	DICKSON	Downey	DOWNEY
Davenport	DAVENPORT	Dicky	DICKY	Downing	DOWNEY
Davice	DAVIS	Dieiment	DIERMON	Doyel	DOYLE
Davids	DAVIS	Dierman	DIERMON	Doyl	DOYLE
Davin	DEVINE	Diermon	DIERMON	Drake	DRAKE
Davis	DAVIS	Dillingham	DILLINGHAM	Dreskel	DRESKEL
Davise	DAVIS	Dinwidda	DINWIDDIE	Drew	DREW
Davison	DAVIDSON	Dinwiddie	DINWIDDIE	Dreyden	DRYDEN
Daviss	DAVIS	Dinwidie	DINWIDDIE	Drummin	DRUMMOND
Dawsen	DAWSON	Dinwidy	DINWIDDIE	Drummind	DRUMMOND
Dawson	DAWSON	Dinwoode	DINWIDDIE	Drummon	DRUMMOND
Day	DAY	Dirmon	DIERMON	Drummond	DRUMMOND
Dayer	DYER	Dismuke	DISMUKES	Drummonds	DRUMMOND
Dayhoff	DAYHOFF	Dismukes	DISMUKES	Drumond	DRUMMOND
Dayhoof	DAYHOFF	Diven	DEVINE	Dry	DRY
Dayhuff	DAYHOFF	Divenport	DAVENPORT	Dryden	DRYDEN
Daynor	DAYNOR	Divenporty	DAVENPORT	Drydon	DRYDEN
De Journett	DEJARNETT	Dives	DAVIS	Dudarar	DUDDERAR
DeFoor	DEFOE	Divin	DEVINE	Dudderar	DUDDERAR
DeJarnett	DEJARNETT	Divine	DEVINE	Dudderer	DUDDERAR
Dean	DEAN	Division	DEVINE	Dudderoo	DUDDERAR
Dear	DEER	Dixon	DICKSON	Dudderrar	DUDDERAR
Dearman	DIERMON	Dixson	DICKSON	Duddoran	DUDDERAR
Deavenport	DAVENPORT	Doboard	DEBOARD	Duderer	DUDDERAR
Deboard	DEBOARD	Dobsen	DOBSON	Dudgan	DUDGEON
Deboe	DEBOE	Dobson	DOBSON	Dudgen	DUDGEON
Debord	DEBOARD	Dodd	DODDS	Dudgens	DUDGEON
Deen	DEAN	Dodds	DODDS	Dudgeon	DUDGEON
Deer	DEER	Dodson	DODSON	Dudgin	DUDGEON
Deffern	DAFFRON	Dolen	DOLLINS	Dudgon	DUDGEON
Defoe	DEFOE	Dolens	DOLLINS	Dudgons	DUDGEON
Defoo	DEFOE	Dolins	DOLLINS	Duel	DOYLE
Defoor	DEFOE	Dollens	DOLLINS	Dueray	DUDDERAR
Defore	DEFOE	Dollins	DOLLINS	Dugeon	DUDGEON
Defow	DEFOE	Dolton	DOLTON	Duggans	DUGAN
Dehart	DEHART	Donald	DONALD	Duggin	DUGAN
Deir	DEER	Donally	DONLEY	Duggins	DUGAN
Dejarne	DEJARNETT	Donan	DONAN	Duglas	DOUGLASS
Dejarnett	DEJARNETT	Doner	DANNER	Duglass	DOUGLASS
Dejournett	DEJARNETT	Donier	DANNER	Dugles	DOUGLASS

searching	find in	searching	find in	searching	find in
Dugless	DOUGLASS	Ely/King	ELY/KING	Fenley	FINLEY
Duke	DUKE	Emberson	EMERSON	Fenton	FENTON
Dulen	DOOLEY	Embre	EMBREE	Fepps	PHIPPS
Dunaway	DUNAWAY	Embree	EMBREE	Ferigo	FERIGO
Dunbar	DUNBAR	Embrey	EMBREE	Ferral	FERRELL
Duncan	DUNCAN	Embrie	EMBREE	Ferrel	FERRELL
Duncin	DUNCAN	Embry	EMBREE	Ferrell	FERRELL
Dungan	DUNCAN	Emerson	EMERSON	Ferril	FERRELL
Dunkin	DUNCAN	Emery	EMBREE	Ferrill	FERRELL
Dunn	DUNN	Emmerson	EMERSON	Fewel	FEWELL
Dunton	DUNTON	Emmery	EMBREE	Fichpatrick	FITZPATRICK
Dunwiddie	DINWIDDIE	Emmons	EMMONS	Field	FIELDS
Dunwiddy	DINWIDDIE	Emrey	EMBREE	Fielden	FELAND
Dunwodde	DINWIDDIE	Emry	EMBREE	Fielding	FELAND
Dunwoddie	DINWIDDIE	England	ENGLAND	Fields	FIELDS
Dunwoodie	DINWIDDIE	Engleman	ENGLEMAN	Fillips	PHILLIPS
Dupeau	DEPAUW	English	ENGLISH	Fillwell	FOLLOWELL
Durham	DURHAM	Ennes	ENNIS	Fincounty	VANCOUNTY
Durrsey	DORSEY	Ennis	ENNIS	Findley	FINLEY
Dwan	DWAN	Enniss	ENNIS	Finley	FINLEY
Dyar	DYER	Eoff	EOFF	Finly	FINLEY
Dyer	DYER	Eperson	EPPERSON	Finn	FINN
Dyre	DYER	Epperson	EPPERSON	Finncounty	VANCOUNTY
Dysert	DYSERT	Erls	EARLE	Finney	FOURNEY
Eaden	EDENS	Erven	IRVIN	Fipps	PHIPPS
Eadens	EDENS	Ervin	IRVIN	Fips	PHIPPS
Eades	EADES	Erwin	IRVIN	Fisher	FISHER
Eakman	AIKMAN	Estace	ESTES	Fitzgarrel	FITZGERALD
Earle	EARLE	Estep	ESTES	Fitzgerald	FITZGERALD
Earles	EARLE	Estes	ESTES	Fitzgerrel	FITZGERALD
East	EAST	Estice	ESTES	Fitzjarrel	FITZGERALD
Easter	EASTER	Estis	ESTES	Fitzpatrick	FITZPATRICK
Eastes	ESTES	Estridge	ESTES	Flack	FLACK
Eastice	ESTES	Estus	ESTES	Flacker	FLETCHER
Eastis	ESTES	Eton	ETON	Flake	FLACK
Echols	ECHOLS	Eubanks	EUBANKS	Flasher	FLETCHER
Ecton	ACTON	Evan	EVANS	Flatcher	FLETCHER
Edden	EDENS	Evans	EVANS	Fleck	FLACK
Eden	EDENS	Evens	EVANS	Fleece	FLEECE
Edens	EDENS	Everhart	EVERHART	Fleese	FLEECE
Ederington	EDERINGTON	Every	EVERY	Fleming	FLEMING
Edes	EADES	Evins	EVANS	Fletcher	FLETCHER
Edon	EDENS	Eweing	EWING	Flinn	FLINN
Edons	EDENS	Ewing	EWING	Flint	FLINT
Edward	EDWARDS	Ewings	EWING	Flock	FLACK
Edwards	EDWARDS	Fair	FAIR	Floid	FLOYD
Eggnew	AGNEW	Fairis	FARRIS	Floro	FLURRY
Ekman	AIKMAN	Falcomberry	FALCONBERRY	Flory	FLURRY
Elder	ELDER	Falin	FELAND	Flourney	FOURNEY
Elders	ELDER	Fantrees	VANTREESE	Floyd	FLOYD
Eley	ELY	Faris	FARRIS	Fluch	FLETCHER
Eli	ELY	Farrel	FERRELL	Flurry	FLURRY
Elinwood	ELINWOOD	Farrell	FARRELL	Fluse	FLEECE
Eliott	ELLIOTT	Farril	FERRELL	Followay	FOLLOWELL
Elison	ELLISON	Farris	FARRIS	Followell	FOLLOWELL
Elles	ELLIS	Farthing	FARTHING	Forbes	FORBIS
Ellett	ELLIOTT	Faulen	FELAND	Forbis	FORBIS
Elliot	ELLIOTT	Fawlen	FELAND	Forbus	FORBIS
Elliott	ELLIOTT	Fawling	FELAND	Forbush	FORBIS
Ellis	ELLIS	Fealand	FELAND	Forcomberry	FALCONBERRY
Ellison	ELLISON	Fealden	FELAND	Ford	FORD
Elliston	ELLISON	Fealen	FELAND	Foreman	FOREMAN
Ellmore	ELMORE	Fear	FEAR	Forest	FORREST
Ellot	ELLIOTT	Feeland	FELAND	Forguson	FORGUSON
Ellott	ELLIOTT	Feiral	FERRELL	Forker	FORKER
Elmar	ELMORE	Felan	FELAND	Forkner	FORKER
Elmore	ELMORE	Feland	FELAND	Forrest	FORREST
Elott	ELLIOTT	Felin	FELAND	Forsaythe	FORSYTHE
Ely	ELY	Femaster	FEMISTER	Forscythe	FORSYTHE
Ely/Craig	ELY/CRAIG	Femester	FEMISTER	Forseythe	FORSYTHE
Ely/Forbis	ELY/FORBIS	Femister	FEMISTER	Forsithe	FORSYTHE
Ely/Forbus	ELY/FORBUS	Fendley	FINLEY	Forsyth	FORSYTHE

searching	find in	searching	find in	searching	find in
Forsythe	FORSYTHE	Gastion	GASTON	Goggin	GOGGIN
Fort	FORD	Gaston	GASTON	Goggins	GOGGIN
Fosith	FORSYTHE	Gately	GATELY	Goggon	GOGGIN
Foster	FOSTER	Gathwright	GATHWRIGHT	Gogin	GOGGIN
Fourney	FOURNEY	Gatley	GATELY	Gogins	GOGGIN
Fowler	FOWLER	Gatliff	GATLIFF	Goin	GOWEN
Fox	FOX	Gau	GOFF	Goldsby	GOLDSBY
Frame	FOURNEY	Gaudes	GADDIS	Goldsmith	GOLDSMITH
Frances	FRENCH	Gaudus	GADDIS	Goliher	GALLAGHER
Francis	FRANCIS	Gauldon	GAULDON	Golson	GOLSON
Franklin	FRANKLIN	Gault	GAULT	Gooch	GOOCH
Frazer	FRAZIER	Gaven	GARVIN	Good	GOOD
Freeland	FELAND	Gawin	GARVIN	Goode	GOOD
Freeman	FREEMAN	Gay	GAY	Gooden	GOODWIN
French	FRENCH	Geary	GEARY	Gooding	GOODWIN
Frentch	FRENCH	Geary	GERRY	Goodknight	GOODNIGHT
Fresh	FRESH	Gee	GEE	Goodnight	GOODNIGHT
Friend	FRIEND	Geery	GEARY	Goodnite	GOODNIGHT
Friley	FRILEY	Gelespie	GILLESPIE	Goodwin	GOODWIN
Fristo	FRISTO	Gell	GILL	Goosh	GOOCH
Frizzle	FRIZZLE	Gellaspie	GILLESPIE	Goph	GOFF
Froggit	FRISTO	Gellet	GILLETT	Gorden	GORDON
Frush	FRESH	Genings	JENNINGS	Gordon	GORDON
Fry	FRY	Genkens	JENKINS	Goss	GOSS
Fuil	FEWELL	Gennings	JENNINGS	Gosset	GOSSETT
Fuill	FEWELL	Gentrey	GENTRY	Gossett	GOSSETT
Fukeway	FUKEWAY	Gentry	GENTRY	Gotner	GOTNER
Fullen	FELAND	Gesford	GESFORD	Gough	GOFF
Fullin	FELAND	Getwood	GETWOOD	Gowen	GOWEN
Funck	FUNK	Gibbs	GIBBS	Gowin	GOWEN
Funcounty	VANCOUNTY	Gibs	GIBBS	Graceham	GRESHAM
Funk	FUNK	Gibsen	GIBSON	Graham	GRAHAM
Furnay	FOURNEY	Gibson	GIBSON	Graham	GRIMES
Furr	FAIR	Gicor	GREER	Gravel	GRAVEL
Furway	FOURNEY	Gidcom	GIDCOM	Gravell	GRAVEL
Gaary	GEARY	Gilbert	GILBERT	Graves	GRAVES
Gaary	GERRY	Gilbrath	GILBREATH	Gray	GRAY
Gabbert	GABBERT	Gilbreath	GILBREATH	Grayham	GRAHAM
Gabert	GABBERT	Gileland	GILELAND	Grayville	GRAVEL
Gabriel	GABRIEL	Giles	GILES	Greeham	GREER
Gad	GADD	Gilford	GESFORD	Green	GREEN
Gadberry	GADBERRY	Gill	GILL	Greenlee	GREENLEE
Gadd	GADD	Gillanwater	GILLANWATER	Greenup	GREENUP
Gaddes	GADDIS	Gillaspie	GILLESPIE	Greenwood	GREENWOOD
Gadus	GADDIS	Gillespe	GILLESPIE	Greenwoode	GREENWOOD
Gaines	GAINES	Gillet	GILLETT	Greer	GREER
Gains	GAINES	Gillett	GILLETT	Greeves	GRAVES
Galbrath	GILBREATH	Gillitt	GILLETT	Gregory	GREGORY
Galbreath	GILBREATH	Gillmore	GILMORE	Greham	GRAHAM
Galbreth	GILBREATH	Gillot	GILLETT	Grerham	GRESHAM
Galeley	GATELY	Gilmer	GILMORE	Gresham	GRESHAM
Gallan	GALLAN	Gilmore	GILMORE	Greshom	GRESHAM
Galloway	GALLOWAY	Ginings	JENNINGS	Grey	GRAY
Garad	GARRARD	Ginnings	JENNINGS	Greyville	GRAVEL
Garland	GARLAND	Gipson	GIBSON	Griffen	GRIFFIN
Garner	GARNER	Givens	GIVENS	Griffin	GRIFFIN
Garrant	GARRANT	Givins	GIVENS	Griffon	GRIFFIN
Garrard	GARRARD	Gladon	GLADON	Grigg	GRIGGS
Garrat	GARRETT	Glaisbrook	GLAZEBROOK	Griggs	GRIGGS
Garret	GARRETT	Glazebrook	GLAZEBROOK	Griham	GRESHAM
Garrison	GARRISON	Glazebrooks	GLAZEBROOK	Grindstaff	GRINDSTAFF
Garten	GARTEN	Glazerooks	GLAZEBROOK	Grisham	GRESHAM
Garton	GARTEN	Gleeson	GLEESON	Grisom	GRESHAM
Garvan	GARVIN	Glen	GLENN	Grison	GRESHAM
Garven	GARVIN	Glenn	GLENN	Grissham	GRESHAM
Garvey	GARVEY	Glens	GLENN	Grissom	GRESHAM
Garvin	GARVIN	Glore	GLORE	Grisson	GRESHAM
Garvine	GARVIN	Glover	GLOVER	Grissum	GRESHAM
Gasford	GESFORD	Glover	GROVER	Grove	GROVE
Gass	GASS	Goan	GOWEN	Grubb	GRUBB
Gasten	GASTON	Goard	GOOD	Grunter	GRUNTER
Gaster	GASTON	Goff	GOFF	Guin	GUINN

searching	find in	searching	find in	searching	find in
Guinn	GUINN	Hansford	HANSFORD	Hauskins	HAWKINS
Gum	GUMM	Hansley	HENSLEY	Havord	HAVORD
Gumm	GUMM	Hants	HENSLEY	Hawker	HOCKER
Gunn	GUNN	Happer	HOPPER	Hawkins	HAWKINS
Gutherie	GUTHRIE	Har	HAR	Hay	HAYS
Guthrey	GUTHRIE	Harbart	HARBERT	Haynes	HAYNES
Guthrie	GUTHRIE	Harber	HARBERT	Haynor	HANNA
Gutrey	GUTHRIE	Harberd	HARBERT	Hays	HAYS
Gutry	GUTHRIE	Harberson	HARBISON	Hayse	HAYS
Guttery	GUTHRIE	Harbert	HARBERT	Hazelwood	HAZELWOOD
Hacker	HOCKER	Harbeson	HARBISON	Hazlewood	HAZELWOOD
Hackley	HACKLEY	Harbison	HARBISON	Headrick	HEADRICK
Hackney	HACKNEY	Harbour	HARBERT	Headspath	HEADSPATH
Hackor	HOCKER	Hardedge	HARDRIDGE	Headspeath	HEADSPATH
Haddon	HADDON	Harden	HARDIN	Heanor	HANNA
Hadrick	HEADRICK	Harder	HARDIN	Hearn	HERRIN
Hadspeath	HEADSPATH	Hardey	HARDY	Heart	HART
Hagard	HAGGARD	Hardgrave	HARGROVE	Heasly	HEASLY
Hagart	HAGGARD	Hardgrove	HARGROVE	Heaten	HEATON
Hagen	HAGEN	Hardin	HARDIN	Heaton	HEATON
Haggard	HAGGARD	Harding	HARDRIDGE	Heatt	HYATT
Haggart	HAGGARD	Hardridge	HARDRIDGE	Heatton	HEATON
Hagwood	HAGWOOD	Hardry	HARDRIDGE	Hederick	HEADRICK
Hail	HALE	Hardwich	HARDRIDGE	Hedgepeth	HEADSPATH
Haild	HALE	Hardwick	HARDRIDGE	Hedreck	HEADRICK
Hailey	HALEY	Hardwitch	HARDRIDGE	Hedrich	HEADRICK
Haines	HAYNES	Hardy	HARDY	Hedrick	HEADRICK
Hains	HAYNES	Harghfield	HARGHFIELD	Heesley	HEASLY
Hairis	HARRIS	Hargnod	HARGNOD	Hegans	HIGGINS
Hais	HAYS	Hargrove	HARGROVE	Height	HITE
Hales	HALE	Harington	HERRINGTON	Heisley	HEASLY
Haley	HALEY	Harison	HARRISON	Hellacost	HELLACOST
Hall	HALL	Harkley	HARKLEY	Hellams	HELMS
Haly	HALEY	Harlan	HARLAN	Hellem	HELMS
Ham	HAM	Harland	HARLAN	Hellemns	HELMS
Hambleton	HAMILTON	Harlen	HARLAN	Hellet	HELLET
Hamelton	HAMILTON	Harley	HARLEY	Hellett	HELLETT
Hamer	HAMMER	Harlin	HARLAN	Hellicosh	HELLACOST
Hamhilton	HAMILTON	Harling	HARLAN	Helloms	HELMS
Hamilton	HAMILTON	Harlon	HARLAN	Helm	HELMS
Hammar	HAMMER	Harlow	HARLOW	Helms	HELMS
Hammelton	HAMILTON	Harly	HARLEY	Helton	HILTON
Hammer	HAMMER	Harman	HARMON	Hendeman	HINDMAN
Hammet	HAMMOND	Harmer	HARMON	Henderson	HENDERSON
Hammilton	HAMILTON	Harmin	HARMON	Henen	HANNA
Hammon	HAMMOND	Harmon	HARMON	Hener	HANNA
Hammond	HAMMOND	Harness	HARNESS	Henery	HENRY
Hammonds	HAMMOND	Harnish	HARNESS	Henner	HANNA
Hammons	HAMMOND	Harper	HARPER	Henor	HANNA
Hamond	HAMMOND	Harrad	HARROD	Henry	HENRY
Hampton	HAMPTON	Harran	HERRIN	Hensel	HENSLEY
Hamsberry	HANSBROUGH	Harrington	HERRINGTON	Hensley	HENSLEY
Hanah	HANNA	Harris	HARRIS	Hensly	HENSLEY
Hanceford	HANSFORD	Harrison	HARRISON	Henton	HINTON
Hanceley	HENSLEY	Harrisson	HARRISON	Herbert	HARBERT
Hancock	HANCOCK	Harrod	HARROD	Herington	HERRINGTON
Handgrave	HARGROVE	Hart	HART	Herman	HARMON
Handlin	HANLEN	Hartgrave	HARGROVE	Hern	HERRIN
Handsmore	HANDSMORE	Hartgrove	HARGROVE	Herns	HERRIN
Haner	HANNA	Harveu	HARVEY	Herren	HERRIN
Hanes	HAYNES	Harvey	HARVEY	Herrick	HERRICK
Hanlen	HANLEN	Harvy	HARVEY	Herrin	HERRIN
Hanley	HANLEY	Harwood	HARWOOD	Herring	HERRIN
Hanna	HANNA	Hasher	HASHER	Herrington	HERRINGTON
Hannah	HANNA	Hashfield	HASHFIELD	Herrod	HARROD
Hanner	HANNA	Hashwood	HASHWOOD	Herron	HERRIN
Hannon	SHANNON	Haslewood	HASLEWOOD	Hess	HESS
Hanor	HANNA	Hatchitt	HATCHITT	Hete	HITE
Hansberry	HANSBROUGH	Hatfield	HATFIELD	Hetin	HEATON
Hansborough	HANSBROUGH	Hatter	HATTER	Heynor	HANNA
Hansbrough	HANSBROUGH	Hatwood	HATWOOD	Hiat	HYATT
Hansel	HENSLEY	Hauk	HOUK	Hiatt	HYATT

searching	find in	searching	find in	searching	find in
Hickason	HICKISON	Horien	HORINE	Hunphrey	HUMPHREYS
Hickerson	HICKISON	Horine	HORINE	Hunsley	HENSLEY
Hickeson	HICKISON	Horodeshell	HOWDESHELL	Hunsman	HUNTSMAN
Hickison	HICKISON	Horoine	HORINE	Hunt	HUNT
Hickman	HICKMAN	Horrel	HORINE	Hunter	HUNTER
Hickmond	HICKMAN	Horrin	HORINE	Huntsman	HUNTSMAN
Hicks	HICKS	Hoskins	HOSKINS	Hurberd	HARBERT
Higans	HIGGINS	Houchangs	HOUCHINS	Hurley	HURLEY
Higdon	HIGDON	Houchins	HOUCHINS	Hurly	HURLEY
Higgans	HIGGINS	Houck	HOUK	Hurst	HURST
Higgens	HIGGINS	Houghfman	HUFFMAN	Husband	HUSBAND
Higginbotom	HIGINBOTHAM	Houghman	HUFFMAN	Husbands	HUSBAND
Higgins	HIGGINS	Houk	HOUK	Huse	HUGHES
Highat	HYATT	Hounsellor	HENSLEY	Husk	HUSK
Highatt	HYATT	Hounslee	HENSLEY	Huston	HUSTON
Highens	HIGGINS	Hounsler	HENSLEY	Huston/Lewi	HUSTON
Hight	HITE	Hounsly	HENSLEY	Huston/Lewi	HUSTON/LEWI
Higinbotham	HIGINBOTHAM	House	HOUSE	Hutchason	HUTCHISON
Higins	HIGGINS	Howard	HOWARD	Hutchens	HUTCHINS
Hilk	HILL	Howdashall	HOWDESHELL	Hutchenson	HUTCHISON
Hill	HILL	Howdershell	HOWDESHELL	Hutcherson	HUTCHISON
Hilla	HILLEY	Howdeshall	HOWDESHELL	Hutcheson	HUTCHISON
Hilley	HILLEY	Howdeshalt	HOWDESHELL	Hutchings	HUTCHINS
Hillicost	HELLACOST	Howdeshel	HOWDESHELL	Hutchins	HUTCHINS
Hilly	HILLEY	Howdeshell	HOWDESHELL	Hutchinson	HUTCHISON
Hilton	HILTON	Howdyshell	HOWDESHELL	Hutchison	HUTCHISON
Hind	HINDS	Howel	HOWELL	Hutchons	HUTCHINS
Hindman	HINDMAN	Howell	HOWELL	Hutsman	HUNTSMAN
Hinds	HINDS	Howert	HOWARD	Hutson	HUDSON
Hineman	HINDMAN	Howerton	HOWARD	Hyat	HYATT
Hines	HINDS	Howkes	HOUK	Hyatt	HYATT
Hinton	HINTON	Hoxsey	HOXSEY	Hyette	HYATT
Hise	HISE	Huchens	HUTCHINS	Hynes	HINDS
Hitch	HITCH	Huchings	HUTCHINS	Ilkins	ILKINS
Hite	HITE	Huchins	HUTCHINS	Ingham	INGHAM
Hixt	HICKS	Huckeby	HUCKEBY	Ingleman	ENGLEMAN
Hobbs	HOBBS	Hudgance	HUDGENS	Ingram	INGRAM
Hobs	HOBBS	Hudgans	HUDGENS	Inman	INMAN
Hocker	HOCKER	Hudgeance	HUDGENS	Innes	ENNIS
Hockings	HAWKINS	Hudgeanes	HUDGENS	Innis	ENNIS
Hodge	HODGES	Hudgen	HUDGENS	Innman	INMAN
Hodges	HODGES	Hudgens	HUDGENS	Innys	ENNIS
Hoeback	HOEBACK	Hudgeons	HUDGENS	Irvin	IRVIN
Hoffman	HUFFMAN	Hudgiance	HUDGENS	Irvine	IRVIN
Hog	HOGG	Hudgins	HUDGENS	Isaac	ISAACS
Hogan	HOGAN	Hudson	HUDSON	Isaacs	ISAACS
Hogg	HOGG	Hudspeth	HEADSPATH	Isable	ISBELL
Holand	HOLLAND	Huff	HUFF	Isbell	ISBELL
Holaway	HOLLOWAY	Huffman	HUFFMAN	Isbels	ISBELL
Holderman	HOLDERMAN	Huffmans	HUFFMAN	Jack	JACK
Holdiman	HOLDERMAN	Hufman	HUFFMAN	Jackman	JACKMAN
Holland	HOLLAND	Hufmond	HUFFMAN	Jackmon	JACKMAN
Hollet	HELLET	Hufner	HUFNER	Jackmond	JACKMAN
Holley	HOLLEY	Hugans	HIGGINS	Jackson	JACKSON
Holliday	HOLLIDAY	Hugans	HUDGENS	Jacob	JACOBS
Holloway	HOLLOWAY	Hugeon	HUDGENS	Jacobs	JACOBS
Holmes	HOLMES	Huggens	HUDGENS	James	JAMES
Holms	HOLMES	Hughbank	EUBANKS	Jameson	JAMISON
Holsy	HOLSY	Hughes	HUGHES	Jamesson	JAMISON
Holt	HOLT	Hughs	HUGHES	Jamison	JAMISON
Holte	HOLT	Hukebee	HUCKEBY	January	JANUARY
Holton	HOLTON	Hults	HULTS	Jee	GEE
Holts	HOLT	Humber	HUMBER	Jeffries	JEFFRIES
Holtzclaw	HOLTZCLAW	Humble	HUMBLE	Jekes	JEKES
Homes	HOLMES	Humley	HUNDLEY	Jeles	GILES
Hon	HAR	Humphras	HUMPHREYS	Jenkings	JENKINS
Hood	HOOD	Humphrey	HUMPHREYS	Jenkins	JENKINS
Hopkins	HOPKINS	Humphreys	HUMPHREYS	Jennings	JENNINGS
Hopper	HOPPER	Hundley	HUNDLEY	Jentry	GENTRY
Hopwood	HOPWOOD	Huneman	HUNTSMAN	Jerves	JERVES
Hord	HORD	Hunley	HUNDLEY	Jestes	JESTES
Horenes	HORINE	Hunn	HUNN	Jillett	GILLETT

searching	find in	searching	find in	searching	find in
Jillot	GILLETT	Kenney	KINNEY	Lacefield	LASEFIELD
Jimmerson	JAMISON	Kenny	KINNEY	Lackey	LACKEY
Jinings	JENNINGS	Kenor	KEENOR	Lacky	LACKEY
Jinkens	JENKINS	Ker	KERR	Lae	LEE
Jinkenson	JINKENSON	Kerey	KEREY	Lain	LAIN
Jinnens	JENNINGS	Kerkendall	KERKENDALL	Lair	LAIR
Jnyard	JNYARD	Kerkland	KIRKLAND	Laird	LAIR
Jnyart	JNYARD	Kerley	KERLEY	Lamb	LAMME
Joanes	JONES	Kerly	KERLEY	Lambert	LAMBERT
Job	JOB	Kerr	KERR	Lamm	LAMME
John	JOHNS	Kertley	KERTLEY	Lamme	LAMME
Johns	JOHNS	Kertly	KERTLEY	Lamone	LAMME
Johnson	JOHNSTON	Kesoner	KISSINGER	Lancaster	LANCASTER
Johnston	JOHNSTON	Kester	KISTER	Lanceford	LUNSFORD
Jones	JONES	Ketcham	KETCHEM	Landes	LANDIS
Jonson	JOHNSTON	Ketchem	KETCHEM	Landess	LANDIS
Joslen	JOSLIN	Key	KEY	Landis	LANDIS
Joslin	JOSLIN	Keys	KEY	Landsdown	LANDSDOWN
Josling	JOSLIN	Kidd	KIDD	Laney	LANEY
Josselling	JOSLIN	Kilbern	KILBURN	Lang	LANEY
Josslen	JOSLIN	Kilbourn	KILBURN	Langdan	LANGDON
Jossling	JOSLIN	Kilbraith	GILBREATH	Langden	LANGDON
Journey	JOURNEY	Kilbreath	GILBREATH	Langdon	LANGDON
Juman	INMAN	Kilbreth	GILBREATH	Langdon	LANGFORD
Jump	JUMP	Kilburn	KILBURN	Langford	LANGFORD
Jupiter	JUPITER	Kiler	KELLER	Langla	LANGLEY
Kamper	KEMPER	Killbraith	GILBREATH	Langley	LANGLEY
Kannada	KENNEDY	Killburn	KILBURN	Lankford	LANGFORD
Kannady	KENNEDY	Killen	KILLIN	Lansdon	LANDSDOWN
Kanon	CANON	Killin	KILLIN	Lansdown	LANDSDOWN
Kar	KERR	Killum	KELLAM	Lany	LANEY
Karr	KERR	Kilpatrick	KIRKPATRICK	Lapesley	LIPSEY
Kass	KERR	Kimberland	KIMBERLAND	Lapley	LIPSEY
Kaster	KISTER	Kimberlin	KIMBERLAND	Lapsley	LIPSEY
Katen	CATTON	Kimble	KIMBLE	Larance	LAWRENCE
Kavaughna	KAVANAGH	Kimple	KIMBLE	Lare	LAIR
Kavonaugh	KAVANAGH	Kincaid	KINCAID	Larfield	LASEFIELD
Kean	KEAN	Kindrick	KENDRICK	Larger	LARGER
Keany	KEANY	Kindricks	KENDRICK	Larker	LARGER
Kearly	KERLEY	King	KING	Larrance	LAWRENCE
Keasy	CASEY	Kinley	KENLY	Larrence	LAWRENCE
Kee	KEY	Kinney	KINNEY	Larriman	LARRIMAN
Keech	COUCH	Kinny	KINNEY	Lasefield	LASEFIELD
Keen	KEAN	Kirby	KIRBY	Lasewell	LASEFIELD
Keene	KEAN	Kirkland	KIRKLAND	Lasswell	LASEFIELD
Keenly	KENLY	Kirkpatrick	KIRKPATRICK	Laswell	LASEFIELD
Keenor	KEENOR	Kirktley	KERTLEY	Laughlin	LAUGHLIN
Kelbern	KILBURN	Kirtley	KERTLEY	Laurance	LAWRENCE
Kellam	KELLAM	Kishinger	KISSINGER	Laurence	LAWRENCE
Kelland	KELLAND	Kishner	KISSINGER	Law	LAIR
Kellason	KELLISON	Kisinger	KISSINGER	Law	LOWE
Keller	KELLER	Kisler	KISLER	Lawles	LAWLESS
Kelley	KELLY	Kislinger	KISSINGER	Lawless	LAWLESS
Kellison	KELLISON	Kissah	KISSAH	Lawrance	LAWRENCE
Kellow	KELLER	Kissinger	KISSINGER	Lawrence	LAWRENCE
Kellum	KILBURN	Kister	KISTER	Lawsen	LAWSON
Kelly	KELLY	Knary	KNARY	Lawson	LAWSON
Kellyson	KELLISON	Knight	KNIGHT	Lay	LEE
Kemp	CAMP	Knoax	KNOX	Lea	LEE
Kemper	KEMPER	Knoble	NOBLE	Leach	LEECH
Kenaday	KENNEDY	Knoel	NOEL	Leaper	LEEPER
Kenady	KENNEDY	Knowe	NOE	Lear	LAIR
Kenary	KNARY	Knox	KNOX	Leas	LEE
Kendrick	KENDRICK	Konckright	CRONKRIGHT	Lease	LEESE
Kendricks	KENDRICK	Koons	KOONS	Leasun	LEASURE
Keneday	KENNEDY	Kosey	COSSY	Leasure	LEASURE
Kenly	KENLY	Kronkkright	CRONKRIGHT	Leathan	LEATHAN
Kennady	KENNEDY	Kronkright	CRONKRIGHT	Leavill	LEAVILL
Kenneday	KENNEDY	Krout	CROUT	Lee	LEE
Kennedy	KENNEDY	Kunce	KOONS	Leece	LEESE
Kennely	KENLY	Kutch	COUCH	Leecefield	LEESE
Kennerly	KENLY	Laach	LEECH	Leecewell	LASEFIELD

searching	find in	searching	find in	searching	find in
Leech	LEECH	Lucky	LACKEY	Masey	MASSEY
Leeper	LEEPER	Lucus	LUCAS	Mash	NASH
Leese	LEESE	Ludin	LUCAS	Mason	MASON
Lefoe	LEFOE	Lukis	LUCAS	Massey	MASSEY
Legg	LEESE	Lukus	LUCAS	Massie	MASSEY
Leice	LEESE	Lumkin	LUMPKINS	Masterson	MASTERSON
Leigh	LEE	Lumkins	LUMPKINS	Mastison	MASTERSON
Leiper	LEEPER	Lumpkin	LUMPKINS	Mathas	MATTHEWS
Lendis	LANDIS	Lumpkins	LUMPKINS	Matheney	MATHERLY
Lenn	LYON	Lunsford	LUNSFORD	Matherly	MATHERLY
Leoperd	LEOPERD	Lusk	LUSK	Mathes	MATTHEWS
Lepsey	LIPSEY	Luteral	LUTTRELL	Mathew	MATTHEWS
Lester	LESTER	Luthrell	LUTTRELL	Mathews	MATTHEWS
Levelle	LEAVILL	Lutral	LUTTRELL	Mathias	MATTHEWS
Lever	LEWIS	Lutrell	LUTTRELL	Mathis	MATTHEWS
Levi	LEVI	Lutteral	LUTTRELL	Matocks	MADDOX
Levil	LEAVILL	Lutterell	LUTTRELL	Matthew	MATTHEWS
Levy	LEVI	Lutterol	LUTTRELL	Matthews	MATTHEWS
Lewis	LEWIS	Luttrell	LUTTRELL	Matthias	MATTHEWS
Ligget	LIGGET	Lyn	LYON	Mattocks	MADDOX
Likens	LIKENS	Lyne	LYON	Mattox	MADDOX
Likings	LIKENS	Lynim	LYON	Maugey	MASSEY
Limbro	CEMBROO	Lynn	LYON	Mauk	MAUK
Limeberry	LINEBERRY	Lyon	LYON	Maum	MAUM
Lin	LYON	Mackey	MACKEY	Mawzy	MASSEY
Linch	LINK	Macksbury	MACKSBERRY	Maxberry	MACKSBERRY
Line	LYON	Macky	MACKEY	Maxbury	MACKSBERRY
Linebarger	LINEBERRY	Macomb	MC COMBE	Maxel	MAXWELL
Lineberere	LINEBERRY	Maddox	MADDOX	Maxey	MAXEY
Lineberry	LINEBERRY	Maddux	MADDOX	Maxill	MAXWELL
Linesbarger	LINEBERRY	Made	MEADE	Maxwell	MAXWELL
Link	LINK	Mades	MEADE	May	MAY
Linn	LYON	Madlock	MADLOCK	Mayberry	MAYBERRY
Linsey	LINDSEY	Maffett	MOFFETT	Mayburry	MAYBERRY
Linthecomb	LINTHICUM	Maggard	MAGGERT	Maybury	MAYBERRY
Linticome	LINTHICUM	Maggert	MAGGERT	Mayfield	MAYFIELD
Linum	LYON	Magil	MAGILL	Maysen	MASON
Lion	LYON	Magill	MAGILL	Mayson	MASON
Lipsey	LIPSEY	Magraw	MC GRAW	Mazee	MASSEY
Lipsy	LIPSEY	Mahonney	MAHONY	McAfferty	MC CAFFERTY
Literal	LITLER	Mailom	MILAM	McAin	MC CAIN
Litler	LITLER	Main	MAIN	McAlester	MC ALLISTER
Litten	LITTEN	Maiourity	MAIOURITY	McAlexander	MC ALEXANDE
Litter	LITLER	Majors	MAJORS	McAllester	MC ALLISTER
Little	LITTLE	Majures	MAJORS	McAndlass	MC CANDLESS
Littlejohn	LITTLEJOHN	Malond	MALONEY	McAndless	MC CANDLESS
Littler	LITLER	Malone	MALONEY	McAnelly	MC ANELLY
Littrell	LUTTRELL	Maloney	MALONEY	McAninch	MC ANINCH
Lock	LOCK	Man	MANN	McAnless	MC CANDLESS
Loe	LOWE	Manefee	MENEFEE	McAnne	MC CANN
Logan	LOGAN	Manifee	MENEFEE	McArel	MC CARROLL
Logans	LOGAN	Mankspile	MANSFIELD	McAther	MC ATHER
Logwood	LOGWOOD	Mann	MANN	McBride	MC BRIDE
Long	LONG	Mannah	MANNERS	McCabe	MC CABE
Longden	LONGDON	Manner	MANNERS	McCaferty	MC CAFFERTY
Longdon	LONGDON	Manners	MANNERS	McCaffary	MC CAFFERTY
Lorance	LAWRENCE	Mansfield	MANSFIELD	McCafferty	MC CAFFERTY
Lorger	LARGER	Mansfile	MANSFIELD	McCaffrey	MC CAFFERTY
Lotterell	LUTTRELL	Manson	MANSON	McCagee	MC CAGEE
Lotthell	LUTTRELL	Manspile	MANSFIELD	McCain	MC CAIN
Lottrell	LUTTRELL	Manzy	MASSEY	McCairell	MC CARROLL
Love	LOVE	Mark	MARK	McCalf	MC CALF
Lovin	LOVIN	Marks	MARKS	McCampbell	MC CAMPBELL
Low	LOWE	Marksberry	MACKSBERRY	McCan	MC CANN
Lowe	LOWE	Marshal	MARSHALL	McCanlass	MC CANDLESS
Lower	LOWER	Marshall	MARSHALL	McCanless	MC CANDLESS
Lowery	LOWRY	Marshell	MARSHALL	McCanliss	MC CANDLESS
Lowrey	LOWRY	Martain	MARTIN	McCann	MC CANN
Lowry	LOWRY	Marten	MARTIN	McCarland	MC CARLAND
Lucas	LUCAS	Martial	MARSHALL	McCarley	MC CARLEY
Luckey	LACKEY	Martin	MARTIN	McCarrel	MC CARROLL
Luckie	LACKEY	Masen	MASON	McCarrell	MC CARROLL

searching	find in	searching	find in	searching	find in
McCarrill	MC CARROLL	McFarrin	MC FERRIN	McMichel	MC MICHAEL
McCarter	MC CARTER	McFarson	MC PHERSON	McMillen	MC MULLEN
McCarty	MC CARTY	McFearson	MC PHERSON	McMorne	MC MORNE
McCay	MACKEY	McFerren	MC FERRIN	McMullen	MC MULLEN
McCinney	MC KINNEY	McFerrin	MC FERRIN	McMurray	MC MURRAY
McCinnsey	MC KINNEY	McFerron	MC FERRIN	McMurrey	MC MURRAY
McClanahan	MC CLANAHAN	McFerson	MC PHERSON	McMurry	MC MURRAY
McClemore	MC ELMORE	McGeehe	MC GEEHE	McNally	MC ANELLY
McClewee	MC ELWEE	McGill	MAGILL	McNeal	MC NEAL
McCluer	MC CLURE	McGinnis	MC GINNIS	McNealey	MC NEELY
McClure	MC CLURE	McGlachlan	MC LAUGHLIN	McNeally	MC NEELY
McClurr	MC CLURE	McGlocklin	MC LAUGHLIN	McNealy	MC NEELY
McColastor	MC ALLISTER	McGloughlin	MC LAUGHLIN	McNeeley	MC NEELY
McColester	MC ALLISTER	McGluchlin	MC LAUGHLIN	McNeely	MC NEELY
McColister	MC ALLISTER	McGraw	MC GRAW	McNella	MC NEELY
McCollester	MC ALLISTER	McHaddin	MC HATTON	McNely	MC NEELY
McColley	MC CULLOCH	McHatton	MC HATTON	McNight	MC KNIGHT
McCollister	MC ALLISTER	McHenally	MC ANELLY	McNinch	MC ANINCH
McColliston	MC ALLISTER	McHenry	MC HENRY	McNinih	MC ANINCH
McCollistr	MC ALLISTER	McIlwee	MC ELWEE	McOlister	MC ALLISTER
McCollom	MC COLLOM	McInnely	MC ANELLY	McPharlin	MC FARLAND
McCombe	MC COMBE	McIntosh	MC INTOSH	McPherren	MC FERRIN
McConn	MC COWN	McIntouch	MC INTOSH	McPhersin	MC PHERSON
McConnal	MC CONNELL	McKabe	MC CABE	McPherson	MC PHERSON
McConnell	MC CONNELL	McKaffordy	MC CAFFERTY	McQuary	MC QUARY
McCorkle	MC CORKLE	McKain	MC CAIN	McQuene	MC QUEEN
McCormac	MC CORMACK	McKane	MC CAIN	McQuerrey	MC QUARY
McCormack	MC CORMACK	McKanlas	MC CANDLESS	McQuerry	MC QUARY
McCormick	MC CORMACK	McKarell	MC CARROLL	McQuerter	MC WHORTER
McCoun	MC COWN	McKay	MACKEY	McQuire	MC QUIRE
McCown	MC COWN	McKean	MC CAIN	McRae	MC REA
McCoy	MC COY	McKee	MACKEY	McRobards	MC ROBERTS
McCray	MC REA	McKeney	MC KINNEY	McRoberds	MC ROBERTS
McCruchin	MC CUTCHEN	McKenlas	MC CANDLESS	McRoberts	MC ROBERTS
McCulla	MC CULLOCH	McKenley	MC KINLEY	McSwain	MC SWAIN
McCuller	MC CULLOCH	McKenly	MC KINLEY	McVay	MC VAY
McCulley	MC CULLOCH	McKenney	MC KINNEY	McWaters	MC WHORTER
McCulloch	MC CULLOCH	McKenny	MC KINNEY	McWherter	MC WHORTER
McCullock	MC CULLOCH	McKensey	MC KINNEY	McWhertor	MC WHORTER
McCully	MC CULLOCH	McKenzie	MC KINNEY	McWhorter	MC WHORTER
McCutchen	MC CUTCHEN	McKenzy	MC KINNEY	McWhortor	MC WHORTER
McCutcheon	MC CUTCHEN	McKey	MACKEY	McWhoter	MC WHORTER
McCutchin	MC CUTCHEN	McKiney	MC KINNEY	McYuly	MC YULY
McCutheon	MC CUTCHEN	McKinley	MC KINNEY	Mclarning	MC LARNING
McDale	MC DALE	McKinley	MC KINNEY	Mead	MEADE
McDaneld	MC DONALD	McKinly	MC KINLEY	Meade	MEADE
McDaniel	MC DONALD	McKinney	MC KINLEY	Medlock	MADLOCK
McDonald	MC DONALD	McKinney	MC KINNEY	Meek	MEEK
McDonnell	MC DONALD	McKinny	MC KINNEY	Meens	MEANS
McDonold	MC DONALD	McKinsey	MC KINNEY	Meginnis	MC GINNIS
McDoogle	MC DOUGAL	McKintee	MC KINNEY	Melner	MILNER
McDowel	MC DOWELL	McKinzey	MC KINNEY	Melon	MALONE
McDowell	MC DOWELL	McKinzy	MC KINNEY	Melone	MALONE
McElewee	MC ELWEE	McKnight	MC KNIGHT	Meloney	MALONEY
McElhaney	MC ELHANEY	McKnite	MC KNIGHT	Menefee	MENEFEE
McElhany	MC ELHANEY	McKonally	MC CONNELL	Menfee	MENEFEE
McElheney	MC ELHANEY	McLaning	MC LARNING	Menifee	MENEFEE
McElheny	MC ELHANEY	McLardy	MC LARDY	Merret	MERRITT
McElmore	MC ELMORE	McLarning	MC LARNING	Merrit	MERRITT
McElwain	MC ELWAIN	McLaughlen	MC LAUGHLIN	Merritt	MERRITT
McElwee	MC ELWEE	McLaughlin	MC LAUGHLIN	Mershon	MERSHON
McEnelley	MC ANELLY	McLearning	MC LARNING	Mesur	MASSEY
McEvoy	MC EVOY	McLure	MC CLURE	Metle	METLE
McEwen	MC EWEN	McMahan	MC MAHAN	Mi-ers	MYERS
McFadden	MC FADDEN	McMamis	MC MANNIS	Michael	MC MICHAEL
McFadgen	MC FAGGIN	McMannes	MC MANNIS	Michael	MICHAEL
McFaggin	MC FAGGIN	McMannis	MC MANNIS	Michal	MITCHELL
McFall	MC FALL	McManus	MC MANNIS	Michel	MITCHELL
McFarland	MC FARLAND	McMerry	MC MURRAY	Michelltree	MITCHELLTREE
McFarling	MC FARLAND	McMical	MC MICHAEL	Micheltree	MITCHELTREE
McFarran	MC FERRIN	McMichael	MC MICHAEL	Mickeleboro	MICKELBORO
McFarren	MC FERRIN	McMicheal	MC MICHAEL	Middleton	MIDDLETON

searching	find in	searching	find in	searching	find in
Mideleton	MIDDLETON	Mourton	MOURTON	Nickleson	NICHOLSON
Midleton	MIDDLETON	Mouser	MOUSER	Nickolds	NICHOLS
Mikesel	MIKESEL	Moyers	MYERS	Nickum	NICKEN
Milam	MILAM	Mtres	MYERS	Nicleson	NICHOLSON
Mileham	MILAM	Mudy	MOODY	Nicoleson	NICHOLSON
Miles	MILES	Muerhead	MOREHEAD	Niel	NEAL
Millar	MILLER	Muirhead	MOREHEAD	Niele	NEAL
Miller	MILLER	Mulhy	MULHY	Nifeong	NIFONG
Miller	MILNER	Mullican	MULLICAN	Niff	NEFF
Millinear	MILNER	Mullin	MULLINS	Nifong	NIFONG
Millner	MILNER	Mulvaney	MULVANEY	Night	KNIGHT
Millnor	MILNER	Mulveny	MULVANEY	Nikes	KNOX
Millor	MILLER	Mumford	MUMFORD	Nilson	NELSON
Mills	MILLS	Munrony	MUNRONY	Nimo	NINO
Milner	MILNER	Murell	MURRELL	Nino	NINO
Milnor	MILNER	Murfey	MURPHY	Noaker	KNOX
Miner	MINOR	Murfy	MURPHY	Noakes	KNOX
Minor	MINOR	Murphey	MURPHY	Noaks	KNOX
Minter	MINTER	Murphy	MURPHY	Noax	KNOX
Mires	MYERS	Murral	MURRELL	Nobill	NOBLE
Misener	MIZENER	Murrel	MURRELL	Noble	NOBLE
Mitcham	MITCHAM	Murrell	MURRELL	Noc	NOE
Mitchel	MITCHELL	Murren	MURREN	Nocks	KNOX
Mitchell	MITCHELL	Murril	MURRELL	Noe	NOE
Mitcheltree	MITCHELTREE	Murrin	MURREN	Noel	NOEL
Mizener	MIZENER	Murron	MURREN	Noele	NOEL
Mlone	MALONE	Murry	MURRY	Noelin	NOLAND
Moberley	MOBERLY	Musick	MUSICK	Noell	NOEL
Moberly	MOBERLY	Myers	MYERS	Nokes	KNOX
Mobley	MOBERLY	Myors	MYERS	Noland	NOLAND
Moderel	MODREL	Myres	MYERS	Norcut	NORTHCUTT
Modral	MODREL	Naff	NEFF	Norcutt	NORTHCUTT
Modral	MURRELL	Nall	NAUL	Norrel	NORVELL
Modreal	MODREL	Nansteel	NANSTEEL	Norrell	NORVELL
Moffet	MOFFETT	Narvill	NORVELL	Northcut	NORTHCUTT
Moffett	MOFFETT	Nash	NASH	Northcutt	NORTHCUTT
Moffit	MOFFETT	Navel	NEVILL	Norton	NORTON
Mohon	MOHON	Naylor	NAYLOR	Norvell	NORVELL
Moirick	MORRICK	Neal	NEAL	Norvil	NORVELL
Monday	MONDAY	Neale	NEAL	Norvill	NORVELL
Monfort	MONFORT	Neall	NEAL	Norwell	NORVELL
Montgomery	MONTGOMERY	Nealy	NEALY	Novel	NOEL
Moody	MOODY	Neavell	NEVILL	Nowel	NOEL
Mooney	MOONEY	Neel	NEAL	Nowell	NOEL
Moony	MOONEY	Neele	NEAL	Nowlen	NOLAND
Moor	MOORE	Neely	NEALY	Nowlin	NOLAND
Moore	MOORE	Neff	NEFF	Nowvell	NORVELL
Moorhead	MOREHEAD	Nelson	NELSON	Nudgen	NUGENT
Mophet	MOFFETT	Neugen	NUGENT	Nugen	NUGENT
Mophett	MOFFETT	Neugent	NUGENT	Nugent	NUGENT
Moppen	MOFFETT	Nevel	NEVILL	Nugin	NUGENT
Mordock	MORDOCK	Nevil	NEVILL	Nutt	KNIGHT
More	MOORE	Nevill	NEVILL	O'Hara	O'HARA
Morehead	MOREHEAD	New	NEW	O'Neal	O'NEAL
Morgain	MORGAN	Newal	NEWAL	O'Neall	O'NEAL
Morgan	MORGAN	Newcom	NEWCOMB	O'Neel	O'NEAL
Moris	MORRIS	Newcomb	NEWCOMB	Oakes	OAKS
Morison	MORRISON	Newgan	NUGENT	Oateman	OATMAN
Moriss	MORRIS	Newgart	NUGENT	Oathis	ORKEES
Morres	MORRIS	Newgent	NUGENT	Oatman	OATMAN
Morrice	MORRIS	Newlin	NEWLAND	Obannon	O'BANNON
Morrick	MORRICK	Newman	NEWMAN	Ocah	OCAH
Morris	MORRIS	Newton	NEWTON	Odam	ODAM
Morrison	MORRISON	Nezbit	NEZBIT	Oglesby	OGLESBY
Morrisson	MORRISON	Niccun	NICKEN	Ohlan	OHLAR
Morrow	MORROW	Nice	NICE	Oins	OWENS
Mosely	MOSELY	Niceleson	NICHOLSON	Oleahy	OLEAHY
Mosley	MOSELY	Nicholasson	NICHOLSON	Oliver	OLIVER
Moss	MOSS	Nicholison	NICHOLSON	Ollever	OLIVER
Motesed	MOTESED	Nicholson	NICHOLSON	Onstat	ONSTOTT
Mounce	MOUNTS	Nicken	NICKEN	Onstot	ONSTOTT
Mounts	MOUNTS	Nickle	NICKLE	Orient	ORIENT

searching	find in	searching	find in	searching	find in
Orkees	ORKEES	Payton	PAYTON	Peteate	PETTIT
Orkeese	ORKEES	Peak	PEAK	Peters	PETERS
Orkies	ORKEES	Peake	PEAK	Petitt	PETTIT
Ormsby	ORMSBY	Pearce	PIERCE	Pettes	PETTUS
Ortgiss	ORKEES	Pearl	PEARL	Pettet	PETTIT
Ortgiz	ORKEES	Pearrel	PEARL	Pettir	PETTIT
Orthis	ORKEES	Pearson	PEARSON	Pettit	PETTIT
Ortkies	ORKEES	Peasant	PLEASANT	Pettitt	PETTIT
Ortkis	ORKEES	Peaw	PEW	Pettus	PETTUS
Ortkus	ORKEES	Pegg	PIGG	Petty	PETTY
Osburn	OSBURN	Peirce	PIERCE	Pettyjohn	PETTYJOHN
Oshwall	OSWALD	Peke	PEAK	Pew	PEW
Oteman	OATMAN	Pelham	PELHAM	Peyten	PAYTON
Ott	OTT	Pels	PELS	Peyton	PAYTON
Ousley	OWSLEY	Pemberton	PEMBERTON	Philips	PHILLIPS
Overlees	OVERLEESE	Penalton	PENNINGTON	Philis	PHILLIPS
Overleese	OVERLEESE	Pence	PENCE	Phillip	PHILLIPS
Owen	OWENS	Pendergrass	PENDERGRASS	Phillips	PHILLIPS
Owens	OWENS	Pendergress	PENDERGRASS	Phipps	PHIPPS
Owin	OWENS	Pendexter	PENDERGRASS	Phips	PHIPPS
Owings	OWENS	Pendleton	PENDERGRASS	Pickard	PICKARD
Ownsbey	ORMSBY	Pendleton	PENNINGTON	Pickens	PICKENS
Ownsler	OWSLEY	Peneck	PENECK	Piearce	PIERCE
Owsley	OWSLEY	Penelton	PENNINGTON	Pierce	PIERCE
Oxford	OXFORD	Penex	PENECK	Pierse	PIERCE
Ozwald	OSWALD	Peng	PING	Pierson	PEARSON
Ozwell	OSWALD	Penick	PENECK	Pig	PIGG
Packston	PAXTON	Penicks	PENECK	Pigg	PIGG
Page	PAGE	Peniman	PENMAN	Piner	PENCE
Pagget	PADGET	Penington	PENNINGTON	Piner	PENECK
Pagin	PADGET	Peniston	PENNINGTON	Pinex	PENECK
Pain	PAINE	Peniton	PENNINGTON	Ping	PING
Paine	PAINE	Penix	PENECK	Pinkerton	PINKERTON
Painter	PAINTER	Penleton	PENNINGTON	Pinor	PENCE
Pair	PARR	Penman	PENMAN	Pinter	PAINTER
Pankey	PANKEY	Pennal	PENNAL	Pipe	PIPES
Panky	PANKEY	Pennek	PENECK	Piper	PIPER
Pannel	PANNEL	Pennel	PENNAL	Pipes	PIPES
Pantor	PAINTER	Pennell	PENNAL	Pirkens	PERKINS
Paptisthalp	PESTORUP	Pennenton	PENNINGTON	Pirkins	PERKINS
Pardorm	PURDOM	Penneton	PENNINGTON	Pitman	PITMAN
Parie	PERRY	Pennex	PENECK	Pitmon	PITMAN
Parker	PARKER	Pennington	PENNINGTON	Pitmond	PITMAN
Parks	PARKS	Penninton	PENNINGTON	Pittman	PITMAN
Parmelee	PARMELEE	Pennix	PENECK	Pleasant	PLEASANT
Parnal	PURNALL	Penuton	PENNINGTON	Pleasants	PLEASANT
Parneblee	PARMELEE	Penx	PENECK	Plummer	PLUMMER
Parr	PARR	Penyx	PENECK	Plusner	PLUMMER
Parral	PEARL	Perce	PIERCE	Pohon	PAYTON
Parran	PERRIN	Percen	PEARSON	Pointer	POINTER
Parrel	PEARL	Percize	PERSISE	Poke	POKE
Parrett	PARRETT	Periman	PENMAN	Polard	POLLARD
Parron	PERRIN	Perin	PERRIN	Polely	POLEY
Parson	PEARSON	Peringer	PERRIGOE	Poley	POLEY
Parsons	PARSONS	Perkens	PERKINS	Pollard	POLLARD
Passwater	PASSWATERS	Perkins	PERKINS	Polly	POLEY
Passwaters	PASSWATERS	Perl	PEARL	Polston	POLSTON
Paterson	PATTERSON	Pernal	PURNALL	Pope	POPE
Paton	PATTON	Perral	PEARL	Popes	PIPES
Paton	PAYTON	Perran	PERRIN	Porter	POINTER
Pattan	PATTON	Perrel	PEARL	Portman	PORTMAN
Patten	PATTON	Perren	PERRIN	Posey	POSEY
Pattern	PATTON	Perrigo	PERRIGOE	Poteet	PETTIT
Patterson	PATTERSON	Perrigoe	PERRIGOE	Pots	POTTS
Pattin	PATTON	Perril	PEARL	Potter	POTTER
Patton	PATTON	Perrin	PERRIN	Pottle	POTTLE
Paul	PAUL	Perry	PERRY	Potts	POTTS
Pawling	PAWLING	Persise	PERSISE	Poulson	POLSTON
Paxton	PAXTON	Person	PARSONS	Powall	POWELL
Payne	PAINE	Person	PEARSON	Powel	POWELL
Paynter	PAINTER	Persons	PEARSON	Powell	POWELL
Payten	PAYTON	Pestorup	PESTORUP	Powers	POWERS

searching	find in	searching	find in	searching	find in
Poynter	POINTER	Ranolds	REYNOLDS	Richardson	RICHARDSON
Prather	PRATHER	Ranuck	RENICK	Richarson	RICHARDSON
Prator	PRATHER	Rass	RASS	Richason	RICHARDSON
Pratt	PRATT	Ratekin	RATEKIN	Richerson	RICHARDSON
Presston	PRESTON	Ratherford	RUTHERFORD	Richeson	RICHARDSON
Preston	PRESTON	Ratliff	RATLIFF	Richey	RICHEY
Prevo	PROVO	Rauls	ROLES	Richie	RICHEY
Prewit	PRUITT	Raulston	RAULSTON	Richison	RICHARDSON
Prewitt	PRUITT	Rawls	ROLES	Rickets	RICKETTS
Price	PRICE	Ray	RAY	Ricketts	RICKETTS
Pridmore	PRIDMORE	Raybirn	RAYBURN	Rickits	RICKETTS
Priest	PRIEST	Raybourn	RAYBURN	Riddle	RIDDLE
Prince	PRINCE	Rayburn	RAYBURN	Ridgal	RIDDLE
Prinkle	PRINKLE	Rayder	RAYDER	Ridgel	RIDDLE
Printy	PRINTY	Raynolds	REYNOLDS	Ridgeton	RIGDON
Prise	PRICE	Read	REED	Ridgeway	RIDGEWAY
Procise	PERSISE	Ready	READY	Ridgle	RIDDLE
Procter	PROCTER	Reaney	RAINEY	Ridgway	RIDGEWAY
Proctor	PROCTER	Reanolds	REYNOLDS	Ridgwell	RIDGEWAY
Prosis	PERSISE	Reany	RAINEY	Ried	REED
Prosithe	PERSISE	Reas	REES	Rife	RIFFE
Prosythe	PERSISE	Reatherford	RUTHERFORD	Riffe	RIFFE
Protzman	PROTZMAN	Reburn	RAYBURN	Rigdon	RIGDON
Protzmon	PROTZMAN	Reddiford	RUTHERFORD	Riggle	RIDDLE
Proutzman	PROTZMAN	Redick	REDICK	Riggs	RIGGS
Provin	PROVIN	Redy	READY	Right	WRIGHT
Provo	PROVO	Reed	REED	Rigney	RIGNEY
Pruet	PRUITT	Reeder	REEDER	Rigs	RIGGS
Pruett	PRUITT	Rees	REES	Rikons	RIGDON
Pruitt	PRUITT	Reeves	REEVES	Riley	RILEY
Purcifield	PURCIFIELD	Reid	REED	Rilie	RILEY
Purdom	PURDOM	Reidiford	RUTHERFORD	Rimal	RIMAL
Purdon	PURDOM	Reighnerson	REYNIORSON	Rincarson	REYNIORSON
Puriafield	PURCIFIELD	Reighneson	REYNIORSON	Riner	RINER
Purkins	PERKINS	Reiley	RILEY	Rineyarson	REYNIORSON
Purnal	PURNALL	Reily	RILEY	Rise	RICE
Purnall	PURNALL	Ren	WREN	Ritcherson	RICHARDSON
Purnel	PURNALL	Renbry	RUBY	Ritcheson	RICHARDSON
Purnell	PURNALL	Rench	WRENCH	Ritchey	RICHEY
Purtun	PURDOM	Renex	RENICK	Ritchorson	RICHARDSON
Puttett	PETTIT	Renfro	RENFROW	Rite	WRIGHT
Queen	QUEEN	Renfrow	RENFROW	Ritherford	RUTHERFORD
Quin	QUIN	Renick	RENICK	Roach	ROACH
Quinton	QUINTON	Renicks	RENICK	Road	ROACH
R---sey	RAMSEY	Renix	RENICK	Roatch	ROACH
Raburn	RAYBURN	Renn	WREN	Robason	ROBINSON
Radcliff	RATLIFF	Rennalds	REYNOLDS	Robbins	ROBERTS
Radekin	RATEKIN	Rennals	REYNOLDS	Robennight	ROBINET
Ragan	RAGAN	Rennels	REYNOLDS	Roberds	ROBERTS
Ragen	RAGAN	Rennick	RENICK	Roberdson	ROBINSON
Ragland	RAGLAND	Rennicks	RENICK	Roberson	ROBINSON
Raglen	RAGLAND	Rennix	RENICK	Robert	ROBERT
Raglin	RAGLAND	Renolds	REYNOLDS	Roberts	ROBERTS
Ragon	RAGAN	Renox	RENICK	Robertson	ROBINSON
Railey	RILEY	Rentfroe	RENFROW	Robinet	ROBINET
Rainey	RAINEY	Rentfrow	RENFROW	Robins	ROBERTS
Ramsey	RAMSEY	Retheford	RUTHERFORD	Robinson	ROBINSON
Ranax	RENICK	Retherford	RUTHERFORD	Robison	ROBINSON
Randall	RANDALL	Reubey	RUBY	Rock	ROCK
Randolph	RANDOLPH	Reves	REEVES	Rodgers	ROGERS
Ranels	RENICK	Reyburn	RAYBURN	Roe	ROWE
Ranex	RENICK	Reynearson	REYNIORSON	Roger	ROGERS
Raney	RAINEY	Reynierson	REYNIORSON	Rogers	ROGERS
Ranfro	RENFROW	Reyniorson	REYNIORSON	Roles	ROLES
Ranick	RENICK	Reynolds	REYNOLDS	Rolls	ROLES
Ranken	RANKIN	Reynox	RENICK	Romine	ROMINE
Rannack	RENICK	Rhyley	RILEY	Ronion	RONION
Rannak	RENICK	Rial	ROYAL	Ronnalds	REYNOLDS
Rannax	RENICK	Rialtee	ROYALTY	Ronstsan	RONSTSAN
Rannels	REYNOLDS	Rice	RICE	Rooe	ROWE
Rannols	REYNOLDS	Richard	RICHARDS	Roop	ROOP
Ranoalds	REYNOLDS	Richards	RICHARDS	Roope	ROOP

searching	find in	searching	find in	searching	find in
Rose	ROSE	Samson	SAMPSON	Sheffer	SHAFFER
Rosen	ROSEN	Sandadge	SANDRIDGE	Shefner	SHAFFER
Roseon	ROSEN	Sandefer	SANDIFER	Sheill	SHIELDS
Ross	ROSE	Sandeford	SANDIFER	Shelby	SHELBY
Ross	ROSS	Sanders	SANDERS	Shelton	SHELTON
Rossin	ROSEN	Sandidge	SANDRIDGE	Shelts	SHIELDS
Rosson	ROSEN	Sandifer	SANDIFER	Sheltz	SHIELDS
Rotherford	RUTHERFORD	Sandipher	SANDIFER	Shennon	SHANNON
Roundtree	ROUNDTREE	Sandridge	SANDRIDGE	Shephard	SHEPHERD
Rountree	ROUNDTREE	Sapp	SAPP	Shepheard	SHEPHERD
Roupe	ROOP	Sarborugh	SCARBROUGH	Shepherd	SHEPHERD
Rous	ROSS	Sarten	SARTIN	Shepmon	SHIPMAN
Rouse	ROSS	Sartin	SARTIN	Sherley	SHERLEY
Rout	ROUT	Sartrough	SCARBROUGH	Sherroon	SHERROON
Routen	ROUTEN	Sasseen	SPRAGGINS	Sherwood	SHERWOOD
Routon	ROUTEN	Sassimore	SASSIMORE	Shield	SHIELDS
Routten	ROUTEN	Saunders	SANDERS	Shields	SHIELDS
Row	ROWE	Sawyers	SAWYERS	Shiell	SHIELDS
Rowe	ROWE	Sayers	SAWYERS	Shiells	SHIELDS
Rowlon	ROUTEN	Sayers	SAYERS	Shier	SPIRES
Rowls	ROLES	Scarbrough	SCARBROUGH	Shiffer	SHAFFER
Rowsley	ROWSLEY	Scarbrow	SCARBROUGH	Shipley	SHIPLEY
Rowten	ROUTEN	Schmick	SMICK	Shipman	SHIPMAN
Rowton	ROUTEN	Scofield	SCOFIELD	Shmick	SMICK
Royal	ROYAL	Sconce	SCONCE	Shockley	SHOCKLEY
Royalty	ROYALTY	Scons	SCONCE	Shockly	SHOCKLEY
Royston	ROYSTON	Sconts	SCONCE	Shoemaker	SHOEMAKER
Rubarts	ROBERTS	Scoot	SCOTT	Shoemate	SHOEMAKER
Ruberts	ROBERTS	Scott	SCOTT	Shonomore	SPOONAMORE
Rubey	RUBY	Scruggs	SCRUGGS	Shontee	SHAUNTY
Ruby	RUBY	Seacat	SEACAT	Shonty	SHAUNTY
Ruchladge	RUTLEDGE	Seacot	SEACAT	Shook	SHUCK
Rueby	RUBY	Seacott	SEACAT	Shools	SHOULS
Ruffener	RUFFNER	Secat	SEACAT	Short	SHORT
Ruffner	RUFFNER	Seers	SEARS	Shotwell	SHOTWELL
Ruffnor	RUFFNER	Segant	SERGANT	Shough	SHUCK
Rufman	RUFFNER	Selch	SELCH	Shouls	SHOULS
Rufner	RUFFNER	Self	SELF	Show	SHAW
Rufnor	RUFFNER	Sellars	SELLERS	Showers	SHOWERS
Runnels	REYNOLDS	Sellers	SELLERS	Shrons	SRONTS
Rupe	ROOP	Senter	SENTER	Shuck	SHUCK
Rusel	RUSSELL	Sentor	SENTER	Shuder	SLUDER
Rusell	RUSSELL	Sentre	SENTER	Shumake	SHOEMAKER
Rusk	RUSK	Sergant	SERGANT	Shumaker	SHOEMAKER
Rusner	RUFFNER	Seronts	SRONTS	Shunamer	SPOONAMORE
Russel	RUSSELL	Serounce	SRONTS	Shurley	SHERLEY
Russell	RUSSELL	Sertain	SARTIN	Shy	SHY
Russle	RUSSELL	Servant	SERVANT	Shyers	SPIRES
Ruth	RUTH	Sevant	SERVANT	Sidebottom	SIDEBOTTOM
Rutherford	RUTHERFORD	Shackeford	SHACKLEFORD	Sideburn	SIDEBOTTOM
Rutherfore	RUTHERFORD	Shackelford	SHACKLEFORD	Sigall	SIGALL
Ryall	ROYAL	Shackleford	SHACKLEFORD	Silvenny	SWEENEY
Ryalta	ROYALTY	Shaddock	SHADDOCK	Silvers	SILVERS
Ryalty	ROYALTY	Shadock	SHADDOCK	Simmons	SIMMS
Ryan	RYAN	Shaffer	SHAFFER	Simms	SIMMS
Ryant	RYAN	Shanan	SHANNON	Simpson	SIMPSON
Ryenerson	REYNIORSON	Shanklen	SHANKLIN	Sims	SIMMS
Ryle	ROYAL	Shanklin	SHANKLIN	Simson	SIMPSON
Ryley	RILEY	Shanks	SHANKS	Sincleer	SINCLAIR
Rynolds	REYNOLDS	Shannan	SHANNON	Singelton	SINGLETON
Salch	SELCH	Shannon	SHANNON	Singleton	SINGLETON
Sallay	SALLEE	Shanon	SHANNON	Sink	SINK
Sallee	SALLEE	Shapher	SHAFFER	Sissen	SISSON
Sallers	SALYERS	Sharp	SHARP	Sisson	SISSON
Salley	SALLEE	Shaunty	SHAUNTY	Skidmore	SKIDMORE
Salliers	SALYERS	Shaver	SHAFFER	Skillerin	SKILLERN
Sally	SALLEE	Shaw	SHAW	Skilleron	SKILLERN
Salmon	SALMON	Shealds	SHIELDS	Skillerun	SKILLERN
Salsh	SELCH	Sheals	SHIELDS	Skillon	SKILLERN
Salyers	SALYERS	Shearwood	SHERWOOD	Skinear	SKINEAR
Sample	SAMPLE	Sheeks	SHEEKS	Slade	SLADE
Sampson	SAMPSON	Sheels	SHIELDS	Slader	SLUDER

searching	find in	searching	find in	searching	find in
Slanton	SLAYTON	Spragan	SPRAGGINS	Stigall	STIGALL
Slaten	SLAYTON	Spragens	SPRAGGINS	Stigate	STIGALL
Slatin	SLAYTON	Spraggan	SPRAGGINS	Stills	STULTS
Slaton	SLAYTON	Spraggans	SPRAGGINS	Stilts	STULTS
Slattan	SLAYTON	Spraggens	SPRAGGINS	Stincen	STINSON
Slatton	SLAYTON	Spraggin	SPRAGGINS	Stine	STINE
Slaughter	SLAUGHTER	Spraggins	SPRAGGINS	Stinnet	STINNET
Slayton	SLAYTON	Spraggon	SPRAGGINS	Stinnot	STINNET
Sled	SLADE	Spraggons	SPRAGGINS	Stinson	STINSON
Sledd	SLADE	Spragins	SPRAGGINS	Stockdale	STOCKDALE
Sleed	SLADE	Spragons	SPRAGGINS	Stogdon	STOGDON
Sleet	SLEET	Sprat	SPRATT	Stokes	STOKES
Sleight	SLEET	Spratt	SPRATT	Stolts	STULTS
Sleton	SLAYTON	Springate	SPRINGATE	Stone	STONE
Sloan	SLOAN	Springgate	SPRINGATE	Stones	STINE
Slone	SLOAN	Sprot	SPRATT	Stons	STONE
Slonty	SHAUNTY	Sproteman	PROTZMAN	Stoo	STOW
Sloon	SLOAN	Sprotsman	PROTZMAN	Stotes	STOTT
Sluder	SLUDER	Sprotzman	PROTZMAN	Stots	STOTT
Smach	SMICK	Sproul	SPROWL	Stott	STOTT
Smack	SMICK	Sproule	SPROWL	Stotts	STOTT
Small	SMALL	Sprowl	SPROWL	Stow	STOW
Smeck	SMICK	Spurgon	SPURGON	Stowers	STOWERS
Smick	SMICK	Spyers	SPIRES	Strand	STRAND
Smidda	SMIDDY	Squire	SQUIRE	Strange	STRANGE
Smiddy	SMIDDY	Sreet	STREET	Stratin	STRATIN
Smiley	SMILEY	Sronce	SRONTS	Strawbridge	TROWBRIDGE
Smilie	SMILEY	Sronch	SRONTS	Street	STREET
Smily	SMILEY	Sronts	SRONTS	Stringer	STRINGER
Smith	SMITH	Srowder	SOWDER	Stront	SRONTS
Smyth	SMITH	St Leair	SINCLAIR	Strowbridge	TROWBRIDGE
Sneed	SNEED	Stacy	STACY	Stuart	STEWART
Snider	SNIDER	Staff	STOTT	Stuck	STUCK
Snodgrass	SNODGRASS	Stagall	STIGALL	Stuckler	STUCKLER
Snow	SNOW	Stagg	STAGGS	Stukley	STUCKLER
Snuck	SMICK	Staggs	STAGGS	Stull	STULTS
Sockris	SOCKRIS	Stanley	STANLEY	Stuls	STULTS
Sogurner	SOJURNER	Stanton	STANTON	Stults	STULTS
Sojurner	SOJURNER	Stapp	STEPP	Stump	STUMP
Souder	SOWDER	Star	STAR	Sturgel	STURGEL
Souders	SOWDER	Staunton	STANTON	Sturgis	STURGIS
Souseen	SPRAGGINS	Stavens	STEPHENS	Sturret	STEWART
Southard	SOUTHARD	Steagal	STIGALL	Stuts	STULTS
Souther	SOUTHERN	Steal	STEELE	Stutts	STULTS
Southerland	SUTHERLAND	Stean	STINE	Stygall	STIGALL
Southren	SOUTHERN	Steel	STEELE	Stylee	STYLEE
Sowder	SOWDER	Steele	STEELE	Sublet	SUBLETT
Sowell	SOWELL	Steen	STINE	Sublett	SUBLETT
Spann	SPANN	Steene	STINE	Sublick	SUBLETT
Sparkes	SPARKS	Stein	STINE	Suddeth	SUDDETH
Sparks	SPARKS	Stemans	STEMMONS	Sugg	SUGG
Spears	SPEARS	Stemman	STEMMONS	Sulavan	SULLIVAN
Speed	SPEED	Stemmons	STEMMONS	Sulivan	SULLIVAN
Speer	SPEARS	Step	STEPP	Sullivan	SULLIVAN
Speers	SPEARS	Stepe	STEPP	Sully	SALLEE
Spelce	SPELCE	Stephen	STEPHENS	Summers	SUMMERS
Spelman	SPILLMAN	Stephens	STEPHENS	Sumpter	SUMPTER
Spencer	SPENCER	Stephenson	STEPHENS	Sunders	SANDERS
Spenser	SPENCER	Stepher	STEPHENS	Sunn	SUNN
Spillman	SPILLMAN	Stepp	STEPP	Survan	SERVANT
Spilman	SPILLMAN	Sterret	STEWART	Survant	SERVANT
Spires	SPIRES	Sterus	STEWART	Survay	SURVAY
Spohnamore	SPOONAMORE	Stevens	STEPHENS	Surver	SURVAY
Sponamore	SPOONAMORE	Stevenson	STEPHENS	Sutherland	SUTHERLAND
Sponimore	SPOONAMORE	Stever	STEPHENS	Suttels	SUTTELS
Sponomore	SPOONAMORE	Stevinston	STEPHENS	Sutten	SUTTON
Spoonamor	SPOONAMORE	Steward	STEWART	Sutter	SUTTELS
Spoonamore	SPOONAMORE	Stewart	STEWART	Suttle	SUTTELS
Spoonemer	SPOONAMORE	Stewerd	STEWART	Suttles	SUTTELS
Spoonemore	SPOONAMORE	Stewert	STEWART	Sutton	SUTTON
Spoonimer	SPOONAMORE	Stickler	STUCKLER	Swan	SWAN
Spoonimore	SPOONAMORE	Stickley	STUCKLER	Swance	SRONTS

searching	find in	searching	find in	searching	find in
Swarts	SWORTS	Thurmond	THURMAN	Tubbs	TIBBS
Swartson	SWORTS	Thursbey	THURSBY	Tucker	TUCKER
Sweeney	SWEENEY	Thursby	THURSBY	Tull	TULL
Sweeny	SWEENEY	Thurston	THURSTON	Tunget	TUNGATE
Sweney	SWEENEY	Thyrman	THURMAN	Tunstell	TUNSTELL
Swenna	SWEENEY	Tibbs	TIBBS	Turner	TURNER
Swenney	SWEENEY	Ticker	TUCKER	Turney	THURMAN
Swenny	SWEENEY	Tidwell	TIDWELL	Turpen	TURPIN
Swigget	SWIGGETT	Tierney	TIERNEY	Turpin	TURPIN
Swiggett	SWIGGETT	Tig	TIG	Twidwell	TWIDWELL
Swiney	SWEENEY	Tilford	TILFORD	Tyler	TYLER
Swinna	SWEENEY	Tilman	TILMAN	Tylor	TYLER
Swinney	SWEENEY	Timberlake	TIMBERLAKE	Ubank	EUBANKS
Swinny	SWEENEY	Timrell	TIMRELL	Ubanks	EUBANKS
Swisher	SWISHER	Tindel	TINDLE	Ulery	ULREY
Swop	SWOPE	Tindle	TINDLE	Ulrey	ULREY
Swope	SWOPE	Tinkersley	TINKERSLEY	Underwood	UNDERWOOD
Sword	SWORD	Tinkle	TINKLE	Upton	UPTON
Sworde	SWORD	Tinley	TINSLEY	Urls	EARLE
Sworts	SWORTS	Tinly	TINSLEY	Urven	IRVIN
Syephenson	STEPHENS	Tinsley	TINSLEY	Usary	USERY
Tadderman	TOTTISMAN	Tinsly	TINSLEY	Usery	USERY
Tadlock	TADLOCK	Tipton	TIPTON	Ussery	USERY
Talbert	TALBOTT	Tirpin	TURPIN	Utman	UTMAN
Talbot	TALBOTT	Tisdale	TISDALE	Valuzat	VILEZATT
Talbott	TALBOTT	Tisdel	TISDALE	Valuzatt	VILEZATT
Talford	TILFORD	Titous	TITOUS	VanCounter	VANCOUNTY
Tallisman	TOTTISMAN	Tizdale	TISDALE	VanCounty	VANCOUNTY
Tally	TATEM	Todd	TODD	VanMeter	VANMETER
Tanner	TANNER	Toddesman	TOTTISMAN	VanMetre	VANMETER
Tanzey	TANZEY	Tolbart	TALBOTT	VanTreece	VANTREESE
Taps	TAPS	Tolbert	TALBOTT	VanWinkle	VANWINKLE
Tardavan	TARDIVAN	Tolbott	TALBOTT	Vance	VANCE
Tardevau	TARDIVAN	Tollisman	TOTTISMAN	Vancel	VANCE
Tardeveau	TARDIVAN	Tombs	TOMS	Vancounty	VANCOUNTY
Tardevou	TARDIVAN	Tomkins	TOMPKINS	Vandever	VANDIVER
Tardivean	TARDIVAN	Tomlinson	TOMPKINS	Vandicraft	VANDICRAFT
Tardiveau	TARDIVAN	Tompkins	TOMPKINS	Vandike	VANDYKE
Tarrant	TARRANT	Tompkun	TOMPKINS	Vandiver	VANDIVER
Tate	TATE	Tomplin	THOMPSON	Vanisdale	VANASDALE
Tatem	TATEM	Tompson	THOMPSON	Vann	VANN
Tatern	TATEM	Toms	TOMS	Vansil	VANCE
Tatisman	TOTTISMAN	Toney	TONEY	Vanton	VOTAW
Tattisman	TOTTISMAN	Tottesman	TOTTISMAN	Vantrase	VANTREESE
Taylor	TAYLOR	Tottisman	TOTTISMAN	Vantreece	VANTREESE
Tebb	TIBBS	Tounsin	TOWNSEND	Vantrees	VANTREESE
Tebbs	TIBBS	Townsend	TOWNSEND	Vantreese	VANTREESE
Tebo	TEBO	Trap	TRAP	Vantreez	VANTREESE
Teboe	TEBO	Travis	TRAVIS	Vantress	VANTREESE
Tedlerson	TEDLERSON	Tresner	TRESNER	Vantrise	VANTREESE
Templeman	TEMPLIN	Tressner	TRESNER	Vanwinkle	VANWINKLE
Templen	TEMPLIN	Triplette	TRIPLETTE	Vardaman	VARDEMAN
Templin	TEMPLIN	Triumph	TRUMP	Vardeman	VARDEMAN
Tensly	TINSLEY	Trobridge	TROWBRIDGE	Vardiman	VARDEMAN
Terill	TERRELL	Trocksel	TROCKSEL	Vardimon	VARDEMAN
Terrel	TERRELL	Troter	TROTTER	Vardymon	VARDEMAN
Teter	TETER	Trotter	TROTTER	Vattaw	VOTAW
Thacker	THACKER	Trotty	TROTTY	Vaugh	VAUGHN
Tharman	THURMAN	Troughtman	TROUTMAN	Vaughen	VAUGHN
Tharp	THARP	Troup	TROUP	Vaughn	VAUGHN
Therman	THURMAN	Troutman	TROUTMAN	Vaught	VAUGHN
Thermon	THURMAN	Trowbridge	TROWBRIDGE	Vaughtes	VOTAW
Thirmon	THURMAN	Trowsel	TROWSEL	Vaun	VAUGHN
Thomas	THOMAS	Troyer	TROYER	Vawn	VAUGHN
Thomeson	THOMPSON	Truby	TINSLEY	Vawtre	VOTAW
Thompson	THOMPSON	Truelove	TRUELOVE	Vazy	VAZY
Thomson	THOMPSON	Trumball	TRUMBALL	Veach	VEACH
Thornton	THORNTON	Trumbow	TRUMBOW	Vellezette	VILEZATT
Thorton	THURMAN	Trump	TRUMP	Venasdale	VANASDALE
Thrumond	THURMAN	Trusner	TRESNER	Vencounty	VANCOUNTY
Thurman	THURMAN	Tub	TIBBS	Vendevere	VANDIVER
Thurmon	THURMAN	Tubb	TIBBS	Verdiman	VARDEMAN

searching	find in	searching	find in	searching	find in
Vest	VEST	Wear	WARE	Wilkenson	WILKERSON
Vigers	VIGUS	Wearen	WARREN	Wilkerson	WILKERSON
Vigrus	VIGUS	Weather	WEATHERFORD	Wilkeson	WILKERSON
Vigus	VIGUS	Weatherford	WEATHERFORD	Wilkins	WILKERSON
Vilezat	VILEZATT	Weatheringt	WEATHERFORD	Wilkinson	WILKERSON
Vilezatt	VILEZATT	Weathers	WITHERS	Wilkison	WILKERSON
Viluzette	VILEZATT	Webb	WEBB	Willeby	WILLOUGHBY
Viluzott	VILEZATT	Webber	WEBER	Willes	WILLIS
Vinegarden	VINEGARDEN	Weber	WEBER	Willey	WILEY
Vineyard	VINEYARD	Webster	WEBSTER	Willhite	WILHOIT
Vinson	VINSON	Weeland	WELAND	Willhoit	WILHOIT
Vontreese	VANTREESE	Weir	WARE	Willhort	WILHOIT
Voris	VORRUS	Weire	WARE	William	WILLIAMS
Vorrus	VORRUS	Weithers	WITHERS	Williams	WILLIAMS
Vorus	VORRUS	Weland	WELAND	Williamson	WILLIAMSON
Votau	VOTAW	Welch	WELSH	Willibough	WILLOUGHBY
Votaw	VOTAW	Welcher	WILCHER	Williby	WILLOUGHBY
Votta	VOTAW	Welden	WELDON	Willis	WILLIS
Waddel	WADDEL	Weldon	WELDON	Willoughby	WILLOUGHBY
Waddle	WADDEL	Wellch	WELSH	Willoughsby	WILLOUGHBY
Wade	WADE	Welldon	WELDON	Willson	WILSON
Waggoner	WAGGONER	Welles	WELLS	Wilson	WILSON
Waggonner	WAGGONER	Wells	WELLS	Wilye	WILEY
Wagner	WAGGONER	Welsh	WELSH	Winant	WINANT
Wagonar	WAGGONER	Weltch	WELSH	Wincounty	VANCOUNTY
Wagoner	WAGGONER	Wenant	WINANT	Winegarden	WINEGARDNER
Waid	WADE	Wenfrey	WINFREY	Winegardner	WINEGARDNER
Wain	WAIN	Weron	WARREN	Winford	WINFORD
Waken	WALKER	Werthers	WITHERS	Winfree	WINFREY
Walace	WALLACE	Werzer	WISER	Winfrey	WINFREY
Walch	WELSH	Wese	WESE	Winkle	WINKLE
Wald	WALD	West	WEST	Winscot	WINSCOT
Walden	WALDON	Westervill	WESTERVILL	Wintem	WINTEM
Waldon	WALDON	Wetherford	WEATHERFORD	Winters	WINTERS
Wales	WALES	Wethers	WITHERS	Wise	WISE
Walker	WALKER	Wheatley	WHITLEY	Wiser	WISER
Walkup	WALKUP	Wheeland	WHELAN	Wisher	WISHER
Wall	WALL	Wheeldon	WELDON	Wisor	WISER
Wallace	WALLACE	Wheeler	WHEELER	Wite	WHITE
Wallen	WALLACE	Wheetley	WHITLEY	Witham	WITHAM
Walles	WALLACE	Wheldon	WELDON	Witheroe	WITHEROE
Wallis	WALLACE	Wheles	WHELES	Witherow	WITHEROE
Walls	WALL	Whight	WHITE	Withers	WITHERS
Wals	WELSH	Whitaker	WHITAKER	Withors	WITHERS
Walsh	BARNETT	White	WHITE	Withroe	WITHEROE
Walsh	WELSH	Whitehead	WHITEHEAD	Withum	WITHAM
Wamuch	WAMUCK	Whitehouse	WHITEHOUSE	Witt	WITT
Wamuck	WAMUCK	Whiteside	WHITESIDES	Witthorst	WILHOIT
Ward	WARD	Whitesides	WHITESIDES	Wizer	WISER
Warden	WARDEN	Whitley	WHITLEY	Wolf	WOLF
Ware	WARE	Whitsid	WHITESIDES	Wolfe	WOLF
Warner	WARNER	Whitten	WHITTON	Woner	WARNER
Warran	WARREN	Whitticar	WHITAKER	Wood	WOODS
Warren	WARREN	Whitting	WHITTING	Woodall	WOODALL
Warrin	WARREN	Whittle	WHITTLE	Wooddy	WOODS
Warring	WARREN	Whitton	WHITTON	Woode	WOODS
Warthington	WORTHINGTON	Wiatt	WYATT	Woodfin	WOODFIN
Warton	WARTON	Wiggason	WIGGASON	Woodfork	WOODFORK
Wash	WASH	Wilburn	WILBURN	Woodram	WOODRUM
Wason	WASSEN	Wilcher	WILCHER	Woodrom	WOODRUM
Wassen	WASSEN	Wilcock	WILCOX	Woodruf	WOODRUF
Water	WATERS	Wilcot	WILCOTT	Woodrum	WOODRUM
Waters	WATERS	Wilcott	WILCOTT	Woods	WOODS
Watherford	WEATHERFORD	Wilcox	WILCOX	Woodson	WOODSON
Watkins	WATKINS	Wiles	WILLIS	Woodward	WOODWARD
Watley	WATLEY	Wiley	WILEY	Woolen	WOOLFORK
Wats	WATTS	Wilhite	WILHOIT	Woolford	WOOLFORK
Watson	WATSON	Wilhoit	WILHOIT	Woolfork	WOOLFORK
Watt	WATTS	Wilhort	WILHOIT	Woollen	WOOLFORK
Watters	WATERS	Wilis	WILLIS	Woolsey	WOOLSEY
Watts	WATTS	Wilkans	WILKERSON	Word	WARD
Wayet	WYATT	Wilkens	WILKERSON	Worley	WORLEY

searching	find in	searching	find in	searching	find in
Wornell	WORNELL				
Worner	WARNER				
Worser	WORSER				
Wortham	WORTHAM				
Worthing	WORTHINGTON				
Worthington	WORTHINGTON				
Wray	RAY				
Wright	WRIGHT				
Wuthington	WORTHINGTON				
Wyatt	WYATT				
Wyett	WYATT				
Wyette	WYATT				
Wyland	WELAND				
Wyle	WILEY				
Wyler	WILLIS				
Wyles	WILLIS				
Wyley	WILEY				
Wylie	WILEY				
Wynant	WINANT				
Wyzer	WISER				
Yager	YAGER				
Yagor	YAGER				
Yancey	YANCY				
Yancy	YANCY				
Yandeirs	YANTES				
Yansey	YANCY				
Yantes	YANTES				
Yantice	YANTES				
Yantise	YANTES				
Yantus	YANTES				
Yarberer	YARBROUGH				
Yarborough	YARBROUGH				
Yarbrough	YARBROUGH				
Yates	YATES				
Yeager	YAGER				
Yeandus	YANTES				
Yearly	YEARY				
Yearry	YEARY				
Yeary	YEARY				
Yeats	YATES				
Yeger	YAGER				
Yegor	YAGER				
Yency	YANCY				
Yerry	YEARY				
Yocom	YOCUM				
Yocum	YOCUM				
Yonders	YOUNG				
Yongue	YOUNG				
Yont	YOUNT				
York	YORK				
Young	YOUNG				
Younger	YOUNGER				
Younse	YOUNT				
Yount	YOUNT				
Zachariah	ZACHARIAS				
Zacharias	ZACHARIAS				
Zacheheus	ZACHARIAS				
Zacherias	ZACHARIAS				
Zackerias	ZACHARIAS				
Zecharias	ZACHARIAS				
Zeklidge	ZEKLEDGE				
Zimmerman	ZIMMERMAN				
Zukledge	ZEKLEDGE				

EARLY KENTUCKY HOUSEHOLDERS
1787-1811

surname	name	date	bk.pg	TM	surname	name	date	bk.pg	TM
ABBOTT					Adams	Hugh	21AUG04	2.01	1
Abbot	Mary	21OCT92	2.01	F	Adams	Hugh	24AUG05	3.01	11
Abott	Mary	07AUG93	1.01	F1	Adams	Larken	13JUL07	2.01	1
ABRELL					Adams	Lewis	18JUL06	2.01	1
Averly	Jacob	16MAY97	1.01	1	Adams	Lewis	13JUL07	2.01	1
Abrell	Jacob	28MAY99	1.01	1	Adams	Matthew	12AUG89	2.01	1
Abrell	Jacob	24MAY00	2.01	11	Adams	Nathaniel	22MAY97	3.01	1
ACRES					Adams	Nathan	-----11	1.01	1
Akes	Frederick	22JUN03	1.01	1	Adams	Peter	12MAY89	6.01	1
Akis	Frederick	02AUG04	1.01	1	Adams	Peter	23MAY90	1.01	1
Acres	Frederick	30JUL05	1.01	1	Adams	Richard	22APR95	1.01	0
Acres	Frederick	31JUL06	1.01	1	Adams	Robert	02JUN97	3.02	1
Akers	Frederick	02JUN08	1.01	1	Adams	Silvester	12MAR95	1.01	1
Akis	Frederick	14JUN09	2.01	1	Adams	Sil	26JUL96	1.01	1
Akis	Frederick	14JUN09	2.01	1	Adams	Soloman	30MAY01	3.01	1
Acuss	Henry	-----11	1.01	1	Adams	Solomon	12JUL02	2.01	1
Acres	Peter	31JUL06	1.01	1	Adams	Solomon	06JUN03	3.01	1
Akers	Peter	02APR08	1.01	1	Adams	Thomas	11JUN02	1.01	1
Akers	Peter	14JUN09	2.01	1	Adams	Thomas	04JUL03	1.01	1
ACTON					Adams	Thomas	03AUG04	2.01	1
Acton	Aaron	-----96	1.01	1	Adams	Thomas	17JUN05	1.01	1
Ecton	Aron	20MAR97	2.01	1	Adams	Thomas	20JUN06	1.01	1
Acklin	Christopher	09OCT94	2.01	0	Adams	Thomas	13JUN07	1.01	1
ADAMS					Adams	Thomas	02MAY09	2.01	1
Adams	Abraham	-----96	1.01	1	Adams	Thomas	-----11	1.01	2
Adams	Abraham	04MAY07	1.01	1	Adams	William	26JUN87	1.01	1
Adams	Abraham	12JUN09	2.01	1	Adams	William Sr	30MAY89	6.01	2
Adams	Absolam	31MAY90	2.01	1	William Jr Adams listed with him				
Adams	Absolam	25MAR91	1.01	1	Adams	William Jr	30MAY89	6.01	
Adams	Absolam	30JUL00	2.01	1	Listed with William Sr Adams				
Adams	Absolam	20JUL01	3.01	1	Adams	William	05APR90	1.01	1
Adams	Absolom	05JUN02	2.01	1	Adams	William	21MAY97	3.02	1
Adams	Allen	26MAY97	1.01	11	Adams	William	25JUN00	1.01	1
Adams	Allen	09MAY99	1.01	11	AGNEW				
Adams	Allen	28JUL00	1.01	1	Eggnew	George	25JUN00	2.09	11
Adams	Allen	20JUL01	3.01	1	Agnew	George	13JUL01	3.01	11
Adams	Allen	02JUN02	2.01	11	Agnew	George	05AUG02	2.01	11
Adams	Allen	10JUN03	3.01	11	Eggnew	George	14JUN03	3.08	11
Adams	Allen	04AUG04	3.01	11	Agenew	George	16JUN04	2.01	1
Adams	Allen	19JUL05	2.01	11	Agnew	George	14AUG05	3.01	1
Adams	Allen	23JUL06	3.01	12	Agnew	George	08AUG06	3.01	1
Adams	Allen	13JUL07	2.01	11	Agenew	James	16JUN04	2.01	1
Adams	Charles	13JUL07	2.01	1	Agnew	James	14AUG05	3.01	1
Adams	Charles	03JUN08	2.01	1	Agnew	James	08AUG06	3.01	1
Adams	Charles	04JUN09	1.01	1	AIKMAN				
Adams	Charles	-----11	1.01	11	Akeman	Adam	06JUN96	1.01	1
Adams	Coonrod	13MAY94	1.01	1	Aikman	Jane	14MAY89	6.01	
Adams	Coonrod	20JUN95	2.01	1	W.Main listed as taxpayer				
Adams	Daniel	-----96	1.01	1	Aikman	Jane	14MAY89	6.01	F
Adams	Daniel	10MAR97	2.01	1	Aikman	Jane	18MAY90	1.01	F
Adams	Daniel	17JUN00	2.01	1	Aikman	Jane	14MAY91	2.01	F
Adams	Daniel	04JUN01	2.01	1	Eakman	Jane	19OCT92	2.03	F
Adams	Daniel	14JUN02	1.01	1	Akeman	Jane	15AUG93	1.01	F
Adams	Daniel	04JUL03	1.01	1	Ekman	Jane	02JUN95	2.04	F
Adams	Daniel	01AUG04	2.01	1	Akeman	John	16AUG93	1.01	1
Adams	Daniel	17JUN05	1.01	1	Akeman	John	28MAY94	1.01	1
Adams	Daniel	18MAY07	1.01	1	Ekman	John	02JUN95	2.04	1
Adams	Daniel	08JUN07	1.01	1	Achman	John	10APR97	3.01	1
Adams	Daniel	27APR08	1.01	1	Aikman	Joseph	19APR94	2.01	1
Adams	Daniel	30MAY09	2.01	1	Aikman	Joseph	20MAR95	3.01	1
Adams	Daniel	02MAY09	2.01	1	Aikman	Joseph	26APR96	2.01	1
Adams	Daniel	-----11	1.01	1	AKIN				
Adams	Daniel	-----11	1.01	1	Akens	James	17JUN07	2.01	11
Adams	David	26JUN87	1.01	1	Akens	James	25JUN08	2.01	11
Adams	David	09JUN89	6.01	1	Aken	John	26JUN09	1.01	1
Adams	David	05APR90	1.01	1	Akin	John	-----11	1.01	1
Adams	David	14MAY91	2.01	1	Aken	Joseph	16OCT92	2.01	0
Adams	Elijah	28MAY01	1.01	1	Akens	William	29JUL06	3.01	1
Adams	Elijah	11AUG02	2.01	1	ALBERTSON				
Adams	Elijah	25JUN03	3.01	1	Albertson	Airley	31JUL05	1.01	11
Adams	Elijah	11AUG04	3.01	1	ALCORN				
Adams	Hugh	17JUN03	3.01	1	Allcorn	George	21MAY90	1.01	1

1

surname	name	date	bk.pg	TM	surname	name	date	bk.pg	TM
Allcorn	George	17MAY91	2.01	1	Allen	James	-----05	3.38	1
Allcorn	George	20SEP92	1.01	1	Allen	James	13---04	2.01	11
Allcorn	George	08AUG93	3.01	1	Allen	James	06AUG05	3.01	1
Allcorn	George	21APR94	2.01	1	Allen	James-heirs	10JUN05	3.01	02
Alcorn	James	25MAY99	3.01	11	Allen	James	30JUL06	3.01	1
Allcorn	James	19JUN00	3.01	13	Allen	James	17JUL06	3.01	02
Alcorne	James	19JUN01	3.01	12	Allen	James	13JUL07	2.01	12
Allcorn	James	31JUL02	3.01	11	Allen	James(heirs	25JUN08	2.01	
Allcorn	James	09JUN04	4.01	11	Taxes paid by Rebekah Allen				
Allcorn	James	10JUN05	2.01	1	Allen	James	21AUG09	1.01	1
Allcorn	James	12MAY06	2.01	1	Allen	John	21JUN87	2.01	1
Alcorn	James	13JUL07	2.01	12	Allen	John	29OCT88	1.01	1
Alcorne	James	03JUN08	2.01	11	Allin	John	19MAY89	6.01	1
Alcorn	James	13JUL09	1.01	1	Allen	John	23JUN89	5.01	1
Alcorn	James	-----11	1.01	1	Allen	John	31MAR90	2.01	1
Alcorn	Thomas	03JUL99	3.01	M1	Allen	John	15APR90	1.01	1
ALDERSON					Allin	John	03OCT92	1.01	1
Alderson	James	27JUN96	1.01	1	Allen	John	02NOV92	2.01	1
Alderson	James	17APR97	3.01	1	Allen	John	07AUG93	3.01	1
Alderson	James	22MAY99	1.01	1	Allin	John	10AUG93	1.01	1
Alderson	John	30JUN00	3.01	1	Allen	John	23MAY94	2.01	1
Alderson	Nancy	17APR97	3.01	F	Allin	John	24MAY94	1.01	1
Alderson	Simon	31MAY08	1.01	1	Allen	John	-----95	2.26	
Alderson	Simon	09JUN09	2.01	1	One lot in Stanford				
ALEXANDER					Allen	John	10JUN95	2.01	1
Alexander	George	30JUN07	1.01	1	Allin	John	14JUN96	1.01	1
Alexander	George	27APR08	1.09	1	Allin	John Sr	09JUN96	1.01	1
Alexander	Gidian	20JUN07	2.01	1	Allin	John	14JUN96	1.13	
Alexander	James	25JUL89	2.01	1	One town lot in Stanford				
Alexander	John	16MAY97	3.01	1	Allen	John	13APR97	3.01	1
Alexander	William	27JUN89	2.01	1	Allen	John	07JUN97	1.01	1
ALFORD					Allen	John	13JUN97	3.01	1
Alferd	Charles	27JUN09	1.01	1	Allen	John	13JUN97	3.33	
Alferd	Charles	-----11	1.02	1	One town lot in Stanford				
Alford	John	18NOV88	1.01	1	Allen	John	13MAY99	3.01	1
Alford	John	29JUN89	5.01	1	Allen	John	29MAY99	2.01	1
Alford	John	01JUN90	2.01	1	Allen	John	26JUN99	1.01	1
Alfred	John	25MAR91	1.01	1	Allen	John	19JUN00	2.01	1
Alfred	John	09OCT92	2.01	1	Allen	John	20JUN00	1.01	1
Alford	John	07AUG93	1.01	1	Allen	John	21JUN00	3.01	1
Alford	John	16MAY94	1.01	1	Allen	John	05MAY01	3.01	1
Alferd	John	-----11	1.02	1	Allen	John	23JUN01	1.01	1
ALLBOUGH					Allen	John	25JUL01	2.01	1
Allbuck	John	25JUL04	1.01	1	Allen	John	04JUN02	1.01	1
Allbough	John	23JUL05	2.01	1	Allen	John	02AUG02	2.01	1
ALLEN					Allen	John	17JUN03	3.01	1
Allen	Benjamin	13MAY90	1.01	1	Allen	John	23JUN03	1.01	1
Allin	Benjamin	20APR91	2.01	11	Allen	John	03AUG04	2.01	11
Allin	Benjamin	06OCT92	1.01	11	Allen	John	16JUN06	1.01	1
Allen	Benjamin	09AUG93	3.01	11	Allen	John	13JUN07	1.01	1
Allen	Benjamin	12MAY94	2.01	1	Allen	Rebekah	25JUN08	2.01	F1
Allen	Benjamin	09APR95	3.01	1	Paid taxes for James Allen (heirs				
Allen	Benjamin	15JUN96	2.01	1	Allen	Rebecca	04JUN09	1.01	F
Allen	Benjamin	13JUL97	1.01	11	Allen	Rebeca	-----11	1.01	F
Allen	Benjamin	26JUN99	1.01	12	Allen	Robert	06SEP87	1.01	1
Allen	Benjamin	25JUL00	2.01	12	Allin	Robert	19MAY89	6.01	1
Allen	Benjamin	28MAY01	3.01	12	Allen	Robert	15APR90	1.01	1
Allen	Benjamin	11AUG02	2.01	12	Allin	Robert	30APR91	2.01	11
Allen	Benjamin	26JUL03	3.01	11	Allin	Robert	03OCT92	1.01	11
Allen	Benjamin	08AUG04	3.01	11	Allen	Robert	07AUG93	3.01	11
Allen	Benjamin	06AUG05	3.01	11	Allen	Robert	10JUN94	2.01	11
Allen	Benjamin	20AUG06	3.01	1	Allen	Robert	09APR95	3.01	M1
Allen	Karr	26MAY99	3.01	11	Allen	Robert	18JUL97	1.01	1
Allen	Carr	24JUN00	3.01	1	Allen	Robert	26JUN99	1.01	1
Allen	Churchwell	04JUN09	1.01	1	Allen	Robert	25JUL00	2.01	1
Allen	Churchwell	-----11	1.01	1	Allen	Robert	28MAY01	3.01	1
Allen	James	15APR90	1.01	M1	Allen	Robert	12AUG02	2.01	1
Allen	James	28MAY01	3.01	1	Allen	Robert	04JUN03	3.01	1
Allen	James	11AUG02	2.01	1	Allen	Robert	04JUN04	3.01	1
Allen	James	26JUL03	3.01	1	Allen	Robert	14AUG05	3.01	1
Allen	James	-----05	3.38		Allen	Robert	21AUG06	3.01	1
1804 tax info in 1805 tax list					Allen	Thomas	08AUG04	3.01	1

surname	name	date	bk.pg	TM	surname	name	date	bk.pg	TM
Allen	Thomas	06AUG05	3.01	1	Allstot	Polly	19JUN05	3.01	F
Allen	Thomas	21AUG06	3.01	1	Alstott	Polly	30JUL06	3.01	F
Allen	Tobias	05DEC92	3.01	1	AMONDS				
Allen	Tobias	22APR95	1.01	1	Amonds	Josiah	06AUG02	3.01	1
Allen	Tobias	-----96	1.01	1	AMOUREUX				
Allen	Tobias	10MAR97	2.01	1	Amoureux	Michael	29JUN97	1.01	1
Allen	Tobias	16JUN00	1.01	1	ANDERSON				
Allen	Tobias	04JUN01	1.01	1	Anderson	Abraham	29JUN04	4.01	1
Allen	Tobias	24JUN02	1.01	1	Anderson	Abraham	31MAY05	2.01	2
Allen	Tobies	16JUL03	1.01	1	Anderson	Abraham	09AUG06	2.01	1
Allen	Tobias	15AUG04	1.01	1	Anderson	Charles	14MAY90	1.01	1
Allen	Tobias	04MAY07	1.01	1	Anderson	Charles	20JUN91	2.01	1
Allen	William	15NOV88	1.01	1	Anderson	Charles	24SEP92	1.01	1
Allen	William	19JUN89	5.01	1	Anderson	Charles	05AUG93	3.01	1
Allen	William	24JUN89	5.01	1	Anderson	Charles	12AUG93	3.01	00
Allen	William	21APR90	2.01	1	Anderson	Charles	12MAY94	2.01	M1
Allen	William	30MAR91	1.01	1	Anderson	Charles	19MAY94	2.01	1
Allen	William	14APR91	1.01	1	Anderson	Charles	09APR95	3.01	1
Allen	Will	09OCT92	2.01	1	Anderson	Charles	18JUN00	3.01	M1
Allen	William	14OCT92	2.01	1	Anderson	Francis	29MAR94	3.01	M1
Allin	William	13AUG93	1.01	1	Anderson	George	-----96	1.01	1
Allin	William	14AUG93	1.01	1	Anderson	James	07AUG89	2.01	1
Allin	William	21MAY94	1.01	1	Anderson	James	01JUN97	3.02	1
Allin	William	22MAY94	1.01	1	Anderson	John	27JUN89	2.01	1
Allen	William	06JUN95	2.01	1	Anderson	John	07MAY91	3.01	1
Allin	William	06JUN95	1.01	1	Anderson	John	04DEC92	3.01	1
Allin	William	21JUN96	1.01	1	Anderson	John	29MAR94	3.01	1
Allin	William	29JUN96	1.01	1	Anderson	John	04JUN00	2.01	1
Allen	William	10APR97	3.01	1	Anderson	John	10JUN02	2.01	1
Allen	William	15APR97	3.01	1	Anderson	John	04AUG03	3.01	1
Allen	William	13APR97	3.01	1	Anderson	John	06APR04	4.01	1
Allen	William	29MAY99	2.01	1	Anderson	John	19JUN05	3.01	1
Allen	William	20JUN00	1.01	11	Anderson	John	30JUL06	3.01	1
Allen	William	23JUN01	1.01	11	Anderson	John	02JUN08	1.01	1
Allen	William	29JUN05	2.01	1	Anderson	Nathan	23JUL05	2.01	1
Allen	William	31JUL06	2.01	1	Anderson	Nathan	16JUL06	2.01	1
Allen	William D.	20AUG06	3.01	1	Anderson	Robert	06MAY90	1.01	2
ALLSTON						S.Cimble listed with him			
Allston	Michael	19MAY91	2.01	1	Anderson	Robert	19MAY91	2.01	1
ALSOP					Anderson	Robert	24SEP92	1.01	1
Allsop	William	23JUN02	1.01	1	Anderson	Robert	15AUG93	3.01	1
Allsop	William	22JUN03	1.01	1	Anderson	Robert	16APR94	2.01	1
Allsop	William	03AUG04	1.01	1	Anderson	Robert	24MAR95	3.01	1
Allsop	William	31JUL05	1.01	1	Aderson	Robert	04JUN96	2.01	1
Allsop	William	01AUG06	1.01	1	Anderson	Robert	18MAY97	3.01	1
Alsoup	William	09MAY07	1.01	1	Anderson	Stephen	26JUL02	3.01	M1
Alsoup	William	-----08	1.01	1	Anderson	Vardiman	30JUN96	1.01	1
Alsoup	William	11JUL09	2.01	1	Anderson	Vardeman	12APR97	3.01	1
ALSPAW					Anderson	Vardiman	-----11	1.01	1
Allspach	Barbara	21AUG93	3.01	F	Anderson	Walter	29JUL00	2.01	1
Allspaw	Barberry	30APR94	2.01	F	Anderson	Walter	21JUL01	3.01	1
Allspaw	Barbiry	01APR95	3.01	F	Anderson	Walter	05JUN02	2.01	1
Alspach	David	09JUN89	6.01	1	Anderson	Walter	06AUG03	3.01	1
Alspach	David	18MAY91	2.01	1	Anderson	Walter	04AUG04	3.01	1
Alspach	David	08OCT92	1.01	1	Anderson	Walter	19JUN05	3.01	11
Alspen	David	25JUN08	2.01	1	Anderson	Walter	14JUL06	3.01	11
Alspaw	David	22JUN09	1.01	1	Anderson	Walter	13JUL07	2.01	11
Allspaw	David	-----11	1.02	1	Anderson	Walter	31MAY08	2.01	11
Alspaugh	Isaac	23MAY97	1.01	1	Anderson	Walter	11JUL09	1.01	1
ALSTOTT					Anderson	Walter	-----11	1.01	1
Alstadt	Daniel	30APR91	2.01	1	Anderson	William	21AUG04	3.01	1
Alstadt	Daniel	09AUG93	3.01	1	Anderson	William	16AUG05	3.01	M1
Allstot	Daniel	10JUN94	2.01	1	Anderson	William	08AUG06	3.01	M1
Allstot	Daniel	10APR95	3.01	1	Anderson	William	13JUL07	2.01	1
Alstot	Daniel	05JUL96	2.01	1	Anderson	William	31MAY08	2.01	1
Altstott	Daniel	31MAY97	1.01	1	Anderson	William	25JUN08	2.01	1
Allstot	Daniel	13MAY99	3.01	1	Anderson	William	16AUG09	1.01	1
Allstot	Daniel	18JUN00	3.01	1	Anderson	William	23AUG09	2.01	1
Alstott	Daniel	17JUN01	3.01	1	ANDREWS				
Alstott	Daniel	10JUN02	2.01	1	Andrews	James	29MAR94	3.01	1
Alstott	Daniel	05AUG03	3.01	1	ANTHONY				
Altstott	Daniel	06APR04	4.01	1	Anthony	Abram	16MAY97	3.01	1

surname	name	date	bk.pg	TM	surname	name	date	bk.pg	TM
Anthony	William	17MAY97	1.01	1	Arnald	Rubin	19APR91	3.01	1
Anthony	William	19MAY01	3.01	1	Arnold	Reuben	26NOV92	3.01	1
Anthony	William	13AUG02	3.01	1	Arnold	Reuben	29MAR94	3.01	1
ANTLE					Arnold	Rubin	10MAR95	1.01	1
Ample	Henry	26NOV92	3.01	1	Arnold	Reuben	-----96	1.01	1
Antle	Henry	26AUG93	1.01	1	Arnold	Samuel	22APR95	1.01	1
Antle	Henry	21MAY94	1.01	1	Arnald	William	07MAY91	3.01	1
Antle	Henry	11JUN95	2.01	1	Arnold	William	29MAR94	3.01	1
Antle	Henry	14JUN96	1.01	11	ARTHUR				
Antle	Henry	13JUN97	3.01	11	Arthur	Ambros	29JUN99	2.01	1
ARANHART					Arther	Dillen	20JUN99	2.01	1
Aranhart	James	-----11	1.01	1	Arthur	Elias	04MAY08	1.01	1
ARBUCKLE					Arthur	Elias	15JUN09	2.01	1
Arbuckle	John	20AUG87	1.01	1	Arthur	Samuel	-----08	1.01	1
Arbuckle	John	12MAY89	6.01	1	Arther	Thomas	29JUN99	2.01	1
Arbuckle	John	15APR90	1.01	1	ASBURY				
Arbuckle	John	19APR91	2.01	1	Ashberry	Joseph	18OCT92	1.01	1
Arbuckle	John	04DEC92	1.01	1	Asberry	Joseph	13AUG93	3.01	1
Arbuckle	John	14AUG93	3.01	1	ASHBY				
Arbuckle	John	10MAY94	2.01	1	Ashby	Silas	12MAY89	6.01	1
Arbuckel	John	10MAY94	2.01	1	Ashby	Silas	10APR90	1.01	1
Arbuckle	Samuel	28AUG87	1.01	1	Ashby	Silas	30APR91	2.01	1
Arbuckle	Samuel	02AUG90	1.01	1	ASHER				
Arbuckle	Samuel	01AUG91	2.01	1	Asher	Dinell	20MAY97	3.01	1
Arbuckle	Samuel	14SEP92	1.01	1	Asher	John	30JUN99	2.01	1
Arbuckle	Samuel	14AUG93	3.01	1	ASHLEY				
Arbuckel	Samuel	10MAY94	2.01	1	Ashley	Mary	15AUG06	2.01	F
Arbuckel	Samuel	10APR95	3.01	1	Ashly	Robert	08AUG93	3.01	1
ARMSTRONG					Ashley	Robert	21APR94	2.01	1
Armstrong	Henry	03JUN08	2.01	1	ASHLOCK				
Armstrong	John Jr	26JUN87	3.01	1	Ashlock	John	31MAY06	2.01	1
Armstrong	John Sr	26JUN87	3.01	1	Ashlock	John	13JUL07	2.01	1
Armstrong	John	01JUL89	2.01	1	Ashlock	John	02JUN08	1.01	1
Armstrong	John	26NOV92	3.01	1	Ashlock	John	-----11	1.01	1
Armstrong	John	29MAR94	3.01	1	Ashlock	Richard	25JUN04	1.01	12
Armstrong	John	22APR95	1.01	1	Ashlock	Richard	20JUN05	1.01	12
Armstrong	John	-----96	1.01	1	Ashlock	Richard	23JUN06	1.01	11
Armstrong	John	08JUL99	3.01	1	Ashlock	Richard	08JUN07	1.01	1
Armstrong	Ralph	30APR08	1.01	1	Ashlock	Richard	02JUN08	1.01	1
ARNETT					Ashlock	Richard	15AUG09	2.01	1
Arnet	David	26JUN87	2.01	1	Ashlock	Richard	-----11	1.01	1
Arnett	David	29OCT88	1.01	11	Ashlock	William	30MAY90	2.01	1
Arnett	David	29JUN89	5.01	11	Ashlock	William	28JUL04	2.01	1
Arnett	David	07APR91	1.01	1	Ashlock	William	26JUL05	1.01	1
Arnet	David	02NOV92	2.01	1	Ashlock	William	16JUL06	1.01	1
Arnitt	David	07AUG93	1.01	1	Ashlock	William	30JUN07	1.01	1
Arnett	David	15MAY94	1.01	1	Ashlock	William	13JUN07	1.01	M1
Arnitt	David	18JUN95	2.01	1	Ashlock	William Sr	02JUN08	1.01	1
Arnitt	David	10JUN96	1.01	1	Ashlock	William	02JUN08	1.01	1
Arnett	David	08MAY97	3.01	1	Ashlock	William	16AUG09	2.01	1
Arnett	David	27MAY99	1.01	1	Ashlock	William	-----11	1.01	1
Arnett	David	09JUL00	2.01	1	ASHMORE				
Arnett	David	13JUL01	2.01	1	Ashmore	Robert	16MAY94	1.01	1
Arnett	David	14JUN02	3.01	1	Ashmore	Robert	13JUN96	1.01	1
Arnet	David	24JUL04	1.01	11	ATKINS				
Arnett	David	02MAY05	2.01	1	Atkins	Anderson	06JUN95	2.01	1
Arnett	David	09JUN06	2.01	11	Atkins	Anderson	10JUN96	1.01	1
Arnott	David	13JUL07	2.01	11	Attkins	Anderson	10MAY97	3.01	11
Arnet	David	09AUG08	1.01	2	Atkins	Anderson	15JUL99	1.01	1
Arnett	David	24AUG09	2.01	1	Atkins	Bengamin	31MAY97	3.01	1
Arnet	David	-----11	1.01	1	Atkins	William	27JUN89	2.01	1
ARNOLD					Atkins	William	05DEC92	3.01	1
Arnold	Humphrey	26JUN87	3.01	11	Atkins	William	10MAR94	3.01	1
Arnold	Humphrey	27JUN89	2.01	1	Atkins	Wyatt	25JUN96	1.01	1
Arnald	Humphry	19APR91	3.01	1	Atkins	Wyette	31MAY97	3.01	1
Arnold	Humphrey	05DEC92	3.01	1	ATKINSON				
Arnold	Humphrey	10MAR94	3.01	1	Adkins	Bartlet	21JUN87	2.01	1
Arnold	Humphrey	22APR95	1.01	1	Adkinson	Bartlett	11NOV88	1.01	1
Arnold	Humphrey	-----96	1.01	1	Atkerson	Henry	30JUN07	1.01	1
Arnold	Nimrod	13JUL07	2.01	1	Adkins	Henry	18AUG09	2.01	1
Arnold	Peter	21JUN97	1.01	1	Adkins	Jesse	21JUN87	2.01	1
Arnold	Reubin	27JUN89	2.01	1	Adkins	Jesse	22NOV88	1.01	1

surname	name	date	bk.pg	TM	surname	name	date	bk.pg	TM
Atkinson	Joel	16JUN89	5.01	1	Bailey	Elisha	06AUG93	3.01	1
Adkinson	Joel	27MAR90	2.01	1	Baily	Elisha	11JUN94	2.02	1
Atkins	Joel	05APR91	1.01	1	Bailey	Elisha	16APR95	3.02	1
Adkens	Joel	01NOV92	2.01	1	Bailey	Elisha	10MAY96	2.01	1
Adkins	Joal	03AUG93	1.01	1	Bailey	Elisha	26MAY97	1.02	1
Adkins	Joal	12MAY94	1.01	1	Bailey	Elisha	29JUL00	2.04	1
Atkins	Joel	10JUN95	2.01	1	Bailey	Elisha	21JUL01	3.05	1
Atkins	Joal	06JUN96	1.01	1	Bailey	James	05AUG89	5.02	1
Atkens	Joel	11JUL97	3.01	1	Bailey	James	30MAY90	2.01	1
Atkison	Joel	01JUN99	2.01	1	Bailey	James	06APR91	1.01	1
Atkinson	Joel	05JUL00	2.01	1	Bailey	James	28OCT92	2.01	1
Atkinson	Joel	05AUG01	2.01	1	Bailey	James	06AUG93	1.01	1
Atkinson	Joel	07JUN02	3.01	1	Bailley	James	14MAY94	1.02	1
Adkinson	Joel	13JUN04	2.01	1	Bailey	James	20MAY95	2.02	1
Atkinson	Joel	31MAY05	2.01	1	Bailey	James	09JUN96	1.02	1
Atkinson	Joel	09AUG06	2.01	1	Bails	James	30JUN96	1.02	1
Atkenson	Joel	13JUL07	2.01	1	Bailey	James	21APR97	3.04	1
Atkenson	Joel	-----08	2.23	D	Bailey	James	29MAY99	1.03	1
Tax pd by Jesse Spragons/Wm. Gooc					Bailey	James	17JUL00	2.03	
Adkinson	John	17JUN05	3.01	1	Exempt from county leavy				
Atkison	Joseph	12JUN02	2.01	1	Bailey	James	28JUL01	2.02	
Atkinson	Joseph	19JUL03	3.01	1	Exempt from County levy				
Adkins	Samuel	-----93	3.01	1	Bailey	James	30JUN02	3.02	
ATWOOD					Exempt from county leavy				
Atwood	James	14SEP93	3.01	1	Bailey	James	26JUL02	3.02	1
AUSTIN					Bailey	James	12AUG03	2.04	1
Austin	Benjamin	23JUL04	1.01	1	Bailey	James	05JUN04	4.04	1
Austen	Benjamin	14JUL06	3.01	1	Baley	James	26JUL04	1.02	1
Austin	Benjamin	14AUG06	3.31	1	Baley	James T.	05JUN05	1.01	1
Austin	Benjamin	08JUN07	2.01	1	Bailey	James	27JUN05	2.03	11
Austen	Benjamin	25JUN08	2.01	1	Bailey	James	31JUL05	2.05	
Austin	David	29JUN04	4.01	12	Exempt from county leavy				
Austin	John	27JUN94	2.16	1	Bailey	James	15JUL06	2.03	11
Austin	John	03APR95	3.01	1	Exempt from paying Cty leavy				
Austin	John	05AUG02	2.01	1	Bailey	James	01AUG06	2.05	1
Austen	Jonas	30JUL06	3.01	11	Bailey	James	-----07	2.03	11
AYERS					Baley	James	20MAY07	1.20	1
Ayers	Joseph	15JUN96	2.01	1	Tax paid by William Peneck				
Airs	Joseph	10AUG97	1.01	1	Bailey	James	04AUG07	2.03	1
Airs	Joseph	11JUL99	3.01	1	Bailey	James	30MAY08	2.01	1
Ayers	Joseph	10JUL00	3.01	1	Baley	James	02JUN08	1.28	0
Aris	Mary	26JUN89	6.01	F	Tax pd by William Penx - Guardean				
Airs	Mary	23JUN90	1.01	F	Bailey	James	11JUL09	1.05	1
Airs	Mary	02AUG91	2.01	F	Baley	James	-----11	1.02	1
Airs	Mary	11JUL99	3.01	F	Bailey	James	-----11	1.08	
Airs	Mary	-----05	2.36	F	Exempt from county levey				
Airs	Robert	-----90	1.01	1	Baley	Jane	02JUN91	3.02	F
BABER					Baley	Jesse	18MAY07	1.02	1
Baber	James	29JUL03	2.03	1	Baley	John	27JUN87	2.01	1
BADEN					Bailey	John	29OCT88	1.01	1
Baden	James	18APR08	1.01	1	Bailey	John	03NOV88	1.01	1
BAGGS					Bailey	John	29JUN89	5.01	11
Baggs	Alexander	23JUN90	1.02	1	Bailey	John	29MAR90	2.01	1
BAILEY					Bailey	John	18MAY90	2.02	11
Baley	Daniel	06MAY07	1.01	M1	Bailey	John	05APR91	1.02	1
Bailey	Edward	-----11	1.03	1	Bailey	John	01OCT91	1.02	11
Bailey	Elijah	03NOV92	2.02	1	Bailey	John	01NOV92	2.02	12
Bailey	Elijah	07AUG93	1.01	1	Bailey	John	04SEP93	1.02	11
Bailey	Elijah	12MAY94	1.01	1	Bailey	John	15MAY94	1.01	11
Bailey	Elijah	12MAY95	2.02	1	Bailey	John	16JUN95	2.14	1
Bailey	Elijah	06JUN96	1.02	1	Bailey	John	13MAY99	3.01	1
Baley	Elijah	25JUL04	1.02	1	Bailey	John	16MAY99	1.02	1
Bailey	Elijah	02MAY05	2.01	1	Bailey	John	03JUN00	2.01	1
Bailey	Elijah	04AUG07	2.03	1	Baley	John	18JUN00	3.01	1
Baley	Elijah	17JUN08	1.04	1	Bealey	John	17JUN01	3.02	1
Paid tax for ---(heirs) Jackman					Bailey	John	26JUL02	3.02	11
Baley	Elijah	21AUG09	2.04	1	Baley	John Sr	10JUN03	3.02	12
Baley	Elijah	-----11	1.08	1	Baley	John Jr	06JUN03	3.02	1
Bailey	Elisha	23MAY89	6.01	1	Bailey	John Jr	12AUG03	2.04	1
Baily	Elisha	13AUG90	1.02	1	Baley	John	05JUL03	1.03	1
Baily	Elisha	21JUN91	2.01	1	Baley	John	13JUN04	1.01	11
Baily	Elisha	03OCT92	1.02	1	Bailey	John	15AUG04	3.03	1

surname	name	date	bk.pg	TM	surname	name	date	bk.pg	TM
Bailey	John	04JUN05	1.01	11	Baker	Abner	07JUN00	1.01	1
Bailey	John	18JUN05	2.02	1	Baker	Absalom	03NOV92	1.01	1
Bailey	John	16AUG05	3.04	1	Baker	Absalom	27AUG93	3.02	1
Baley	John	13JUN06	1.02	11	Baker	Absolam	29MAY94	2.01	1
Bailey	John	02AUG06	2.05	1	Baker	Absolum	10JUL00	3.05	1
Bailey	John	05AUG06	2.05	1	Beaker	Absalom	30JUL01	3.04	1
Baley	John	19MAY07	1.02	11	Baker	Absalom	29JUL02	3.03	1
Baley	John	09JUN07	2.01	1	Baker	Absalom	10AUG03	2.04	1
Baley	John (Rev)	17JUN08	1.04	D1	Baker	Absalom	08JUN04	4.04	1
Baley	John	06JUN08	1.02	1	Baker	Benjamin	30MAY99	2.01	1
Bailey	John	25JUN08	2.02	1	Baker	Benjamin	12JUN99	2.02	1
Baley	John	23MAY09	2.02	1	Baker	Benjamin	19JUN00	1.01	1
Bailey	John	13JUL09	1.05	1	Baker	Benjamin F.	11JUN01	1.01	1
Bailey	John	-----11	1.06	11	Baker	Benjamin	08JUN02	1.01	1
Baley	Lewis	26JUL04	1.02	1	Baker	Benjamin	20JUN03	1.02	1
Baley	Peter J.	11JUN06	1.02	11	Baker	Benjamin	16JUN06	1.02	1
Baley	Peter J.	18MAY07	1.02	11	Baker	Elijah	20JUN87	2.01	1
Baley	Peter J.	10JUN08	1.03	11	Baker	Elijah	06NOV88	1.01	1
Baley	Peter J.	14JUN09	2.02	1	Baker	Elijah	09SEP89	2.02	1
Bailey	Pierce	-----93	3.01	1	Baker	Elijah	22MAY90	2.02	1
Baley	Ralph	18JUN00	3.01	1	Baker	Elijah	05JUL91	1.01	1
Bealy	Realph	18JUN01	3.02	1	Baker	Elijah	02OCT92	2.01	1
Bailey	Ralph	11AUG03	2.04	1	Baker	Elijah	10AUG93	1.01	1
Bailey	Ralph	05JUN04	4.03	1	Baker	Elizabeth	10JUN09	1.03	F
Bailey	Ralph	18JUN05	2.02	1	Baker	Fredrick	13AUG93	1.02	1
Bailey	Ralph	31JUL06	2.04	1	Baker	Henry	-----11	1.03	1
Bailey	Ralph	12JUN07	2.02	1	Baker	Indimion	21MAY94	3.03	1
Bailey	Relph	25JUN08	2.02	1	Baker	Indemon	01MAY95	1.03	1
Baily	Ralph	13JUL09	1.06	1	Baker	James	14SEP91	3.03	1
Benley	Ralph	-----11	1.05	1	Baker	James	29NOV92	3.03	1
Bailey	Rubin	04SEP93	1.02	1	Baker	James	22MAY94	3.04	1
Bailey	Reuben	18MAY95	2.02	1	Baker	James	04APR95	1.02	1
Baley	Rubin	31APR03	3.02	1	Baker	James	-----96	1.03	1
Bailey	Rueben	04AUG04	3.02	1	Baker	John	04JUN01	1.01	1
Bailey	Reuben	16AUG05	3.04	1	Baker	John	07JUN05	1.01	1
Bailey	Reuben	28JUN06	3.02	1	Baker	John	18MAY07	1.02	1
Bailey	Reuben	17JUL06	3.02	1	Baker	John	17JUN08	1.03	1
Bailey	"Bailey"	10JUN07	2.02	1	Baker	Joseph	02JUL99	1.04	1
Bailey	Reuben	-----11	1.06	1	Baker	Joseph	22JUL00	2.03	1
Bailey	Robert	27JUN89	2.01	1	Beaker	Joseph	24JUL01	3.06	1
Bailey	Robert	03APR90	2.02	1	Baker	Joseph	26MAY02	2.02	1
Bailey	Thomas	02AUG90	1.01	1	Baker	Joseph	25JUN03	3.03	1
Baily	Thomas	24APR91	2.01	1	Baker	Joseph	24AUG04	3.03	1
Baily	Thomas	24SEP92	1.01	1	Beaker	Joseph	31MAY05	3.02	1
Baily	Thomas	13AUG93	3.02	1	Baker	Joseph	01AUG06	3.03	1
Baily	Thomas	10MAY94	2.02	11	Baker	Julatha	31MAY97	3.04	F1
Bailey	Thomas	13JUL96	2.02	11	Baker	Julitha	12MAY99	2.02	F
Bailey	Thomas	31MAY97	1.02	11	Baker	Patsy	25AUG08	2.04	F
Bailey	Thomas	13MAY99	3.01	11	Baker	Patsey	-----11	1.08	F
Baley	Thomas	18JUN00	3.01	1	Baker	Patsey(wid)	-----11	1.04	F
Bealey	Thomas	17JUN01	3.02	1	Baker	Patsey	-----11	1.08	
Baley	Thomas	23JUN02	1.02	1	Guardian for Wm Baker Heirs				
Bailey	Thomas	27JUL02	3.03	1	Baker	Richard	20JUN87	2.01	1
Bailey	Thomas	12AUG03	2.04	1	Baker	Richard	16JUN89	5.01	1
Baley	Thomas	05JUN04	4.03	1	Baker	Richard	02JUN90	2.02	1
Bailey	Thomas	18JUN05	2.02	1	Baker	Robert	11JUL96	2.02	1
Bailey	Thomas	02AUG06	2.05	1	Baker	Squire	14SEP92	1.02	1
Bailey	Thomas	04AUG07	2.03	1	Baker	Squire	13MAY94	2.01	1
Bailey	Thomas	03JUN08	2.01	1	Baker	Squire Jr	08APR95	3.01	1
Bailey	Thomas	13JUL09	1.05	1	Baker	William	19APR91	2.01	1
Bailey	Thomas	-----11	1.05	1	Baker	William	17SEP92	1.02	1
Bailey	Urial	08JUL05	2.03	M1	Baker	William	08AUG93	3.01	1
Bailey	Urial	12MAY06	2.02	1	Baker	William	17APR94	2.02	1
Baley	Vincent	19AUG09	2.04	1	Baker	William	23JUN95	3.02	1
Bailey	William	01JUL89	2.02	1	Baker	William	30JUN96	2.02	1
BAINBRIDGE					Baker	William	22MAY97	1.04	1
Bainbridge	Peter	04JUN00	2.02	1	Baker	William	04JUL99	3.02	1
Bainbridge	Peter	24JUN01	2.02	1	Baker	William	25JUN00	3.02	1
BAKER					Beaker	William	07MAY01	3.02	1
Baker	Abner	20MAY96	2.01	11	Baker	William	08JUL02	3.02	1
Baker	Abner	10MAR97	2.01	1	Baker	William	11JUL03	2.02	1
Baker	Abner	16MAY99	2.02	1	Baker	William	29JUN04	4.02	1

surname	name	date	bk.pg	TM	surname	name	date	bk.pg	TM
Baker	William	29MAY05	2.02	1	Baldock	William	02JUN08	1.02	1
Baker	William	07AUG06	2.05	1	Baldock	William	15AUG09	2.02	1
Begar	William	09AUG06	2.05	1	Baldock	William	-----11	1.08	1
Baker	William	25AUG08	2.04	D	BALDRIDGE				
Tax pd by Pearce Wade/Patsy Baker					Baldridge	Robert	24JUN89	5.01	1
Baker	Wm(heirs)	-----11	1.08		Baldridge	Robert	03JUN90	2.02	1
Patsey Baker named as Guardian					Baldridge	Robert	15OCT92	2.01	1
BALDOCK					BALL				
Baldock	Ann	21AUG09	2.04	F	Ball	Benjamin	21JUL89	2.02	12
Baldock	Levi	30JUL87	1.01	11	Ball	Benjamin	26AUG91	3.02	1
Baldock	Levy	03APR90	2.01	1	Ball	Benjamin	01DEC92	3.03	1
Baldock	Levi	07APR91	1.01	11	Ball	Benjamin	22MAY94	3.04	11
Baldock	Levi	10OCT92	2.01	11	Ball	Benjamin	25MAR95	1.01	11
Baldock	Levi	07AUG93	1.01	11	Ball	Daniel	17JUL00	2.03	1
Baldock	Levi	16MAY94	1.01	12	Ball	Daniel	09JUL01	3.03	1
Baldock	Levi	10JUN94	2.02	0	Ball	Daniel	30JUN02	3.02	1
Baldock	Levi	18MAY95	2.01	1	Ball	Daniel	21JUN03	2.02	1
Baldock	Levi	18MAY95	2.02	11	Ball	Daniel	28JUL04	4.01	1
Baldock	Levi	13JUN96	1.02	11	Ball	Daniel	25JUL05	2.05	1
Baldock	Levi	08MAY97	3.03	11	Ball	Daniel	-----07	2.03	1
Baldock	Levi	13JUN97	3.04	1	Ball	Daniel	25AUG08	2.03	1
Baldock	Levi	20MAY99	1.02	11	Ball	Daniel	24JUN09	1.04	1
Baldock	Levi Jr	24MAY99	1.03	1	Ball	Daniel	-----11	1.03	1
Baldock	Levi Sr	08JUL00	2.03	11	Ball	Elizabeth	28OCT88	1.02	F1
Baldock	Levi Jr	21JUN00	2.02	1	Ball	Eliza.	05AUG89	5.02	F
Baldock	Levi Sr	30MAY01	2.01	11	Ball	Elizabeth	06APR91	1.01	F
Baldock	Levi Jr	08JUN01	2.01	1	Ball	Elizabeth	20OCT92	2.01	F
Baldock	Levi Sr	26MAY02	3.01	1	Ball	Elizabeth	06AUG93	1.01	F
Baldock	Levi Jr	26MAY02	3.01	1	Ball	Elizabeth	14MAY94	1.02	F
Baldock	Levi Sr	17JUN03	2.01	1	Ball	Elizabeth	21MAY95	2.02	F
Baldock	Levi Sr	06AUG04	1.03	1	Ball	Elizabeth	09JUN96	1.01	F
Baldock	Levi	25JUL04	1.02	1	Ball	Elizabeth	21APR97	3.04	F
Balldock	Levi Sr	02MAY05	2.01	1	Ball	Elizabeth	02JUL99	1.04	F
Balldock	Levi Jr	02MAY05	2.01	1	Ball	Elizabeth	17JUL00	2.03	F
Balldock	Levi	09JUN06	2.02	1	Ball	Elizabeth	28JUL01	2.02	F
Baldock	Levi	23AUG06	3.04	1	Ball	Isaiah	10JUN08	1.03	1
Baldock	Levi	13AUG07	2.04	1	Ball	James	26JUN87	2.01	1
Baldock	Levi Sr	02JUN08	1.02	1	Ball	James	05AUG89	5.02	1
Baldock	Levy Jr	17JUN08	1.04	1	Ball	James	18MAY90	2.01	1
Baldock	Levi	21AUG09	2.04	1	Ball	James	06APR91	1.01	1
Baldock	Levy	-----11	1.03	1	Ball	James	13JUL91	3.02	1
Baldock	Levy	-----11	1.08	1	Ball	James	28OCT92	2.01	1
For heirs of Levy Baldock					Ball	James	29NOV92	3.03	1
Baldock	Levy	-----11	1.08		Ball	James	06AUG93	1.01	1
Tax pd for heirs by Levy Baldock					Ball	James	14MAY94	1.02	1
Baldock	Rubin	03APR90	2.02	1	Ball	James	02JUN94	3.04	1
Baldock	Rubin	25MAR91	1.01	1	Ball	James	20MAY95	2.02	1
Baldock	Reubin	22MAY99	1.03	1	Ball	James	21MAY95	2.14	1
Baldock	Reuben	08JUN01	2.01	1	Ball	James	-----96	1.02	1
Baldock	Reuben	26MAY02	3.01	1	Ball	James	09JUN96	1.02	1
Baldock	Reuben	14JUN03	2.01	1	Ball	James	21APR97	3.04	1
Baldock	Reuben	25JUL04	1.02	1	Ball	James	29MAY99	1.04	1
Balldock	Reuben	02MAY05	2.01	1	Ball	James	17JUL00	2.03	11
Balldock	Reuben	20MAY06	2.02	1	Ball	James	28JUL01	2.02	11
Balldock	Richard	11JUN89	6.01	1	Ball	James	30JUN02	3.02	11
Baldock	Richard	14MAY90	1.02	1	Ball	John	30OCT88	1.01	1
Baldock	Richard	28OCT92	2.01	1	Ball	John	12MAR97	2.01	1
Baldock	Richard	07AUG93	1.01	1	Ball	John	15MAY99	2.02	1
Baldock	Richard	18MAY95	2.01	1	Ball	John	12JUN00	1.01	1
Baldock	Richard	13JUN96	1.02	1	Bawl	John	03JUN01	1.01	1
Baldock	Richard	13JUN97	3.04	1	Ball	John	18MAY06	2.01	1
Baldock	Richard	17JUN00	2.02	1	B-11	John	-----07	2.02	1
Baldock	Richard	27JUN01	2.02	1	Ball	Lewis	01DEC92	3.03	1
Balldock	Richard	02MAY05	2.01	1	Ball	Lewis	16JUL03	3.03	1
Balldock	Richard	30MAY06	2.02	1	Ball	Lewis	16JUN04	2.01	1
Baldock	Richard	13AUG07	2.04	1	Ball	Lewis	07AUG06	3.04	1
Baldock	Richard	15AUG09	2.02	1	Ball	Lewis	28JUL08	2.02	1
Baldock	William	26MAY02	3.01	M1	Ball	Lewis	08APR09	1.02	1
Baldock	William	17JUN03	2.01	1	Ball	Lewis	-----11	1.09	1
Balldock	William	02MAY05	2.01	1	Ball	Sarah	06AUG93	1.01	F
Balldock	William	20MAY06	2.02	1	Ball	Sarah	14MAY94	1.02	F1
Boldock	William	17AUG07	2.05	1	Ball	Sarah	21MAY95	2.02	F1

surname	name	date	bk.pg	TM	surname	name	date	bk.pg	TM
Ball	Sarah	09JUN96	1.02	F1	Ballenger	Joseph	24MAY99	1.39	
Ball	Sarah	21APR97	3.04	F1	Three lotts in Stanford				
Ball	Thomas	13AUG87	1.01	1	Ballenger	Joseph	18JUN00	2.02	1
Ball	Thomas	18APR89	6.01	1	Ten lots in Standford				
Ball	Thomas	10APR90	1.02	1	Ballenger	Joseph	03AUG01	2.03	1
Ball	Thomas	09JUN91	2.02	1	Ten lots in Standford				
Ball	Thomas	24SEP92	1.01	1	Ballenger	Joseph	09AUG02	3.03	1
Ball	Thomas	17AUG93	3.02	1	Ten lotts in Standford				
Ball	Thomas	16APR94	2.02	1	Balenger	Joseph	22AUG03	1.01	1
Ball	Thomas	22APR95	3.02	1	Ballenger	Joseph	22AUG04	2.02	1
Ball	Thomas	22JUL96	2.03	1	Ballenger	Joseph	05AUG05	2.05	1
Ball	Thomas	29MAY97	1.03	1	Balenger	Richard	19JUN99	2.02	1
Ball	Thomas	15JUL99	3.03	11	Ballenger	Thomas	06JUN06	2.02	M1
Ball	Thomas	25JUN00	3.03	11.	Ballinger	Thomas	-----07	2.03	1
Ball	Thomas	10JUL01	3.03	11	Balinger	Thomas	17JUN08	1.04	1
Ball	Thomas	16AUG02	3.04	12	Balinger	Thomas	23AUG09	2.04	1
Ball	Thomas	27JUL03	2.03	2	Ballenger	Thomas	-----11	1.08	1
Ball	Thomas	24JUL04	4.03	1	BALLOW				
Ball	Thomas	22JUL05	2.04	11	Ballow	Charles	26SEP87	1.01	1
Ball	Thomas	18JUL06	2.04	1	Bolue	Linsey	20MAY97	3.03	1
Ball	Thomas	03AUG07	2.03	1	Bolue	Robert	20MAY97	3.03	1
Ball	Thomas	24AUG08	2.03	1	Beleu	William C.	05JUL96	2.02	1
Ball	Thomas	08JUN09	1.02	1	BAMBRIDGE				
Ball	Thomas	-----11	1.04	1	Bambridge	Abner	13AUG99	1.40	1
Ball	William	05AUG89	5.02	1	BANKHEAD				
Ball	William	30MAY90	2.01	1	Bankhead	Robert	12JUN97	1.03	1
Ball	William	07APR91	1.01	1	Bankhead	Robert	13MAY99	3.01	1
Ball	William	06APR91	1.01	1	BANKS				
Ball	William	19JUL91	1.02	1	Banks	Adam	31MAY97	3.03	1
Ball	William	28OCT92	2.01	1	Banks	John	26AUG91	3.02	1
Ball	William	06AUG93	1.01	1	Banks	John	27NOV92	3.02	1
Ball	William	14MAY94	1.02	1	Banks	John	21MAY94	3.03	1
Ball	William	21MAY94	3.03	1	Banks	Linn	07AUG89	2.02	11
Ball	William	25MAR95	1.01	1	Banks	Linn	26AUG91	3.02	1
Ball	William	20MAY95	2.02	1	Banks	Linn	27NOV92	3.02	1
Ball	William	21MAY95	2.15	1	Bancks	Linn	24APR94	3.02	1
Ball	William	09JUN96	1.01	1	Banks	Linn	13MAR95	1.02	2
Ball	William	21MAY97	3.02	1	Banks	Linn	-----96	1.03	2
Ball	William	29MAY99	1.04	1	Banks	Reubin	07AUG89	2.02	1
Ball	William	17JUL00	2.03	1	Banks	Rubin	24JUN91	3.02	1
Ball	William	28JUL01	2.02	1	Banks	Rubin	14SEP91	3.03	1
Ball	William	30JUN02	3.02	1	Banks	Reuben	30NOV92	3.17	1
Ball	William	14JUN03	2.01	1	Banks	Reuben	22MAY94	3.05	1
Ball	William	03MAY04	3.02	1	Banks	Rubin	25MAR95	1.01	1
Ball	William	26JUL04	1.02	1	Banks	Reubin	-----96	1.02	1
Ball	William	31MAY05	3.02	1	Banks	Richard	05DEC92	3.04	1
Ball	William	31JUL05	2.05	1	Banks	Thomas	15JUN96	1.02	11
Ball	William	15JUL06	2.03	1	Banks	Thomas	31MAY97	3.03	1
Ball	William Jr	18JUL06	2.04	1	Banks	William	01JUL89	2.02	1
Ball	William	03AUG07	2.03	1	Banks	William	27NOV92	3.02	1
Ball	William	24AUG08	2.03	1	Bancks	William	24APR94	3.02	1
Ball	William	29JUN09	1.04	1	Banks	William	13MAR95	1.02	1
Ball	William	-----11	1.09	1	Banks	William	-----96	1.03	1
BALLARD					BANNON				
Ballard	John	30MAY01	1.01	1	Bannon	James	14MAY91	2.01	1
Ballard	Johnston	30MAY01	1.01	1	BAUNTY				
Ballard	Micajah	-----11	1.07	1	Banta	Albert	27JUN87	2.01	11
BALLDEN					Baunty	Albert	28OCT88	1.02	11
Ballden	Joseph	14JUN09	2.02	1	Baunty	Albert	04AUG89	5.02	11
BALLENGER					Bantee	Albert	30MAY90	2.01	12
Ballenger	Achillis	-----96	1.02	1	Baunty	William	10APR90	1.02	1
Ballenger	Achilles	10MAR97	2.01	1	BANTON				
Ballenger	James	09JUN07	2.01	1	Banton	Henry	28JUN02	1.02	1
Balenger	John	19JUN99	2.02	1	Banton	Henry	10JUN03	1.01	1
Ballenger	Joseph	03SEP93	1.02	11	Bantun	John	28MAY91	3.02	1
Ballenger	Joseph	21MAY94	1.02	1	Banton	John	04DEC92	3.03	1
Ballinger	Joseph	-----95	2.26		Banton	John	23MAY94	3.04	1
Two lots in Stanford					Banton	John	13MAR95	1.02	1
Ballenger	Joseph	20JUN95	2.02	1	Banton	John	-----96	1.02	1
Ballenger	Joseph	27JUN96	1.02	1	Banton	John	30JUL01	1.01	1
Balenger	Joseph	13JUN97	3.04	1	Banton	John	28JUN02	1.02	1
Ballenger	Joseph	24MAY99	1.03	1	Banton	John	10JUN03	1.01	11

surname	name	date	bk.pg	TM	surname	name	date	bk.pg	TM
Bantton	Robert	25AUG06	2.06	11	Barnett	James	14MAY90	1.01	1
Bantun	William	02JUN91	3.02	1	Barnett	James	24JUN91	2.01	1
Banton	William	04NOV92	3.01	1	Barnett	James	18OCT92	1.01	1
Banton	William Jr	04NOV92	3.01	11	Barnett	James	13AUG93	3.02	1
Banton	William	17AUG93	3.02	1	Barnet	James	10JUN94	2.02	1
Banten	William	29MAR94	3.01	11	Barnett	James Sr	12JUN94	2.01	0
Banton	William	04APR95	1.02	11	Barnett	James Jr	12JUN94	2.01	0
Banton	William	-----96	1.02	12	Barnet	James	12JUN94	2.02	
Banton	William	15MAR97	2.01	11		Father of John Barnet			
Banton	William	19JUN99	2.02	11	Barnett	James	15APR95	3.02	1
Banton	William	06JUN00	1.01	11	Barnett	James	10MAY96	2.01	1
Banton	William	08JUN01	1.01	1	Barnett	James	22JUN97	1.03	1
Banton	William	28JUL01	1.02	12	Barnett	James	11JUN99	1.02	1
Banton	William	28JUN02	1.02	1	Barnett	James	24JUN99	1.02	1
Banton	William	10JUN03	1.02	1	Barnett	James	29JUL00	2.04	1
Banton	William	13JUN04	1.01	1	Barnett	James Jr	12AUG00	2.04	1
Banton	William	05JUN05	1.01	1	Barnett	James	18JUN01	3.04	1
Banton	William	13JUN06	1.02	1	Barnett	James	21JUL01	3.05	1
Banton	William	19MAY07	1.02	1	Barnett	James	01JUN02	2.02	1
Banton	William	10JUN08	1.03	11	Barnett	James	10JUN03	3.02	1
Banton	William Sr	24MAY09	2.02	21	Barnett	James	04AUG04	3.02	1
Banton	William	-----11	1.06	1	Barnett	James	22JUN05	3.03	1
BARBEE					Barnett	James	22JUL06	3.03	1
Barbee	Elias	30MAY89	6.01	1	Barnett	James	17AUG07	2.05	1
Barbee	Elias	15APR90	1.01	1	Barnett	James	03JUN08	2.01	1
Barbee	Elias	18MAY91	2.01	1	Barnett	James	11JUL09	1.05	1
BARBER					Barnet	James	-----11	1.05	11
Barber	Robert	06JUN97	1.02	2	Barnett	John	06SEP87	1.01	1
BARKER					Barnett	John	13MAY89	6.01	1
Barkee	John	09JUN08	1.03	1	Barnett	John	12JUN89	6.08	1
Barger	John	09JUN09	2.02	1	Barnett	John	20APR90	1.01	1
Barker	Nancy	29SEP92	2.01	F	Barnett	John	13AUG90	1.02	11
BARLOW					Barnett	John	04AUG91	2.01	1
Barlow	Henry	03DEC92	3.03	1	Barnett	John Jr	18MAR91	2.02	12
Barlow	Henry	22MAY94	3.05	1	Barnett	John	03OCT92	1.02	1
Barlow	Henry	10MAR95	1.02	1	Barnett	John	28SEP92	1.02	12
Barlow	Henry	-----96	1.02	1	Barnett	John Jr	13AUG93	3.02	1
BARNES					Barnett	John Sr	12JUN94	2.01	21
Barnes	James	05AUG05	3.03	1	Barnett	John Jr	28JUN94	2.01	1
Barnes	James	01AUG06	3.03	1	Barnet	John	12JUN94	2.02	0
Barnes	John	24APR94	3.02	1		Son of James Barnet			
Barns	John	04APR95	1.02	1	Barnett	John Sr	10APR95	3.03	4
Barns	John	-----96	1.01	1	Barnett	John Jr	15APR95	3.02	1
Barns	Richard	12MAR97	2.01	1	Barnett	John Sr	20MAY96	2.01	3
Barnes	Thomas	16AUG04	3.03	11	Barnett	John Jr	14AUG96	2.03	1
Barnes	Thomas	23AUG05	3.04	1	Barnett	John Sr	11MAY97	1.02	11
Barnes	Thomas	07AUG06	3.04	1	Barnett	John Jr	26MAY97	1.01	1
BARNETT					Barnett	John	24MAY99	1.03	1
Barnett	Alexander	21JUN87	2.01	1	Barnett	John	27JUN99	3.02	2
Barnett	Alexander	22OCT88	1.02	1	Barnett	John Sr	19JUN00	3.02	1
Barnett	Alexander	27JUN99	3.02	1	Barnett	John Jr	01JUL00	3.05	1
Barnett	Alexander	20JUN00	3.02	1	Barnett	John	21MAY01	3.02	1
Barnett	Alexander	21MAY01	3.02	1	Barnett	John	21JUL01	3.05	1
Barnett	Alexander	10AUG02	3.04	1	Barnett	John	02AUG02	2.03	00
Barnett	Alexander	30JUL03	2.03	1	Barnett	John	10AUG02	3.04	1
Barnett	Alexander	30MAY05	2.02	1	Barnett	John	16JUN03	3.02	1
Barnett	Alexander	07AUG06	2.05	1	Barnett	John	30JUL03	2.03	1
Barnett	Alexander	25AUG08	2.03	1	Barnett	John	08JUL04	4.02	1
Barnett	Alexander	05JUN09	1.02	1	Barnett	John	15AUG04	3.03	1
Barnet	Alexander	-----11	1.04	1	Barnett	John(heirs)	17JUN05	3.17	D
Barnet	Eddy	29NOV92	3.03	1		Tax pd by Jos. Hall & John Walsh			
Barnett	Eddy	21MAY94	3.03	1	Barnett	John	30MAY05	2.02	1
Barnet	Eddy	04APR95	1.02	1	Walsh	John(decd)	23AUG06	3.18	
Barnett	Eddy	-----96	1.03	1		John Walsh - Admin.			
Barnet	Edward	01JUL89	2.02	11	Barnett	John(decd)	26AUG06	3.18	D
Barnet	Edward	16SEP91	3.03	1		Joseph Hall & John Wilsh - Adm.			
Barnet	Edmond	29NOV92	3.03	1	Barnett	John	09AUG06	2.05	1
Barnett	Edward	23MAY94	3.04	1	Barnett	John	22JUN07	2.16	D
Barnet	Edward	04APR95	1.02	11		Tax pd by John Walsh & Joseph Hal			
Barnett	Edward	-----96	1.03	11	Barnett	John	18JUL08	2.14	D
Barnett	James	12MAY89	6.08	1		Tax pd by Joseph Hall & John Wels			
					Barnett	John	25AUG08	2.03	1

surname	name	date	bk.pg	TM	surname	name	date	bk.pg	TM
Barnett	John	05JUN09	1.17	D	Batist	John	05AUG06	2.06	1
Barnett	John	05JUN09	1.17	r	Batist	John	15AUG06	2.06	1
Barnett	John	07JUN09	1.02	1	Battees	John	-----07	2.02	1
Barnet	John	-----11	1.04	1	Battees	John	27JUN08	2.02	1
Barnett	John	-----11	1.37	D	Bateast	John	-----11	1.07	1
Tax pd by Joseph Hall					BAUGHMAN				
Barnett	Robert	24AUG87	1.01	1	Baughman	Henry	15MAR97	2.01	1
Barnett	Robert	19MAY89	6.01	1	Boughman	Henry	02JUL99	1.04	1
Barnet	Robert	30JUN89	2.01	11	Baughman	Henry	22AUG00	1.01	1
Barnett	Robert	15APR90	1.02	1	Baughman	Henry	25JUN01	1.02	1
Barnett	Robert	30APR91	2.02	1	Baughman	Henry	06JUN02	1.03	1
Barnett	Robert	01AUG91	2.02	1	Baughman	Henry	19JUL03	1.03	1
Barnett	Robert	25SEP92	1.01	1	Baughman	Henry	13AUG04	1.03	1
Barnett	Robert	14AUG93	3.02	11	Baughman	Henry	04JUN05	1.01	1
Barnett	Robert	12JUN94	2.01	11	Baughman	Henry	12JUN06	1.01	1
Barnett	Robert	29APR95	3.02	11	Baughman	Henry	07JUN08	1.03	1
Barnett	Robert	05JUL96	2.02	11	Baughman	Henry	10MAY09	2.01	1
Barnett	Robert	20JUN97	1.03	11	Baughman	Henry	-----11	1.06	1
Barnett	Robert	20MAY99	3.01	1	Baughman	Jacob	16SEP91	3.03	1
Barnett	Robert	21JUL00	3.06	1	Baughman	Mary	28JUL00	1.06	F
Paid tax for James Wood					Tax paid by William Hamilton				
Barnett	Robert	19MAY01	3.03	1	Baughman	Mary	16JUN01	1.08	F
Barnett	Robert	27JUL02	3.02	1	Tax paid by William Hamilton				
Barnett	Robert	08AUG03	2.04	1	Baughman	Mary	16JUL02	1.11	F
Barnett	Robert	05JUN04	4.03	11	Tax paid by William Hamilton				
Barnett	Robert	28JUN05	2.03	11	BAVERS				
Barnett	Robert	28JUL06	2.04	11	Bavers	Daniel	14AUG93	1.02	1
Burnett	Robert	29JUL06	2.04	1	BAXTER				
Barnett	Robert	04AUG07	2.03	12	Baxter	Charles	07JUN03	3.02	1
Barnett	Robert	01AUG08	2.02	11	Baxter	Grisley	27JUN87	1.01	F
Barnett	Robert	03APR09	1.01	11	Baxter	Grizel	19AUG91	2.02	F1
Barnet	Skilar	-----11	1.05	1	Baxter	Grizza	13OCT92	1.01	F
Barnett	Will	06SEP87	1.01	1	Baxter	Grissel	14SEP93	3.02	F
Barnet	William	12JUN94	2.02	0	Baxtor	Grizle	29MAY94	2.02	F
Barnett	William	29JUL96	2.03	1	Baxter	Grizzy	01MAY95	3.01	F
Barnett	William	20JUN97	1.03	1	Baxter	Grizzy	29JUN96	2.02	F
Barnett	William	21MAY99	1.03	1	Baxter	Grizzy	29JUN97	1.03	F
Barnet	William	04JUN00	2.02	1	Baxter	Grissy	09JUL00	3.05	F
Barnett	William	25JUL01	2.02	1	Baxter	Grisee	29JUL02	3.03	F
Barnett	William	02AUG02	2.03	1	Backster	James	19JUN89	5.01	1
Barnett	William	03AUG03	3.03	1	Backster	James	13SEP91	3.03	1
Barnett	William	13JUN04	2.01	1	Baxton	James	05DEC92	3.04	1
Barnett	William	17JUL06	3.02	1	Baxter	James	29JUN94	2.01	1
Barnett	William	17JUL06	3.02	1	Baxter	James	20MAY95	3.02	1
Barnett	William	21AUG07	2.05	1	Baxter	James	23JUN96	2.02	1
Barnett	William	20JUN08	2.01	1	Baxter	James	10AUG97	1.04	1
Barnett	William	25JUN08	2.02	1	Baxter	James	10JUL99	3.03	1
Barnett	William	05JUN09	1.02	1	Baxter	James	09JUL00	3.05	1
Barnett	William	10JUL09	1.05	1	Baxter	James	04AUG03	3.03	1
BARTES					Backster	James	05APR04	4.03	1
Bartes	John	18AUG09	2.03	1	Baxter	James	19JUN05	3.03	1
BATES					Baxter	James	29JUL06	3.03	1
Bates	James	29MAR94	3.01	1	Baxter	William	02MAY95	3.02	1
Bates	James	01MAY95	1.03	1	Baxter	William	23JUN96	2.02	1
BATISTE					Baxter	William	10AUG97	1.04	1
Bateast	John	27JUN87	1.01	1	Baxter	William	10JUL99	3.03	1
Batest	John	15MAY89	6.01	1	Baxter	William	10JUL00	3.05	1
Batiste	John	15MAY90	1.01	1	Baxter	William	29JUL01	3.04	1
Battest	John	09AUG91	2.02	1	Baxter	William	29JUL02	3.03	1
Battest	John	13OCT92	1.01	1	Baxter	William	10AUG03	2.04	1
Battest	John	14SEP93	3.02	1	Backster	William	07APR04	4.03	1
Batist	John	29MAY94	2.02	1	Baxter	William	20JUN05	2.03	1
Battest	John	01MAY95	3.03	1	Baxter	William	31JUL06	2.04	1
Batist	John	30JUN96	2.02	1	BAYLOR				
Battest	John	28JUN97	1.02	1	Baylor	Robert	28MAY94	1.11	1
Batist	John	12JUL99	3.03	1	Baylor	Robert	01JUN95	2.14	1
Batiste	John	04JUL00	3.05	1	Balor	Walker	14JUN87	2.01	1
Battes	John	19MAY01	3.02	1	Baylor	Walker	18NOV88	1.01	1
Batist	John	12AUG02	3.04	1	Baylor	Walker	08AUG89	5.02	1
Batist	John	28JUL03	2.03	1	Baylor	Walker	02JUN90	2.02	1
Battesste	John	27JUL04	4.01	1	Baylor	Walker	28DEC91	1.02	1
Batist	John	19JUL05	2.04	00	Bailor	Walker	16OCT92	2.01	1

surname	name	date	bk.pg	TM	surname	name	date	bk.pg	TM
Baylor	Walker	28MAY94	1.01	1	BEARD				
Baylor	Walker	28MAY94	1.01	1	Baird	Hardiman	30MAR95	2.14	1
Baylor	Walker	16JUN95	2.02	1	Baird	Henry	30MAR95	2.14	1
BAYNICE					Beard	John	28OCT92	2.02	1
Baynice	Henry	-----93	3.01	1	Beard	John	03AUG93	1.02	1
BAYS					Baird	John	29MAY94	1.01	1
Bays	Isaiah	19JUN05	3.03	1	Beard	John	12MAY97	3.02	1
Bays	Isaiah	30JUL06	3.03	1	Baird	John	27JUL97	1.03	1
Bays	James	14APR91	1.01	1	Beard	John	11JUN99	2.02	1
Bays	Jesse	19JUN05	3.03	1	Beard	John	20JUN00	1.01	1
BAZEL					Beard	Joseph	01JUN97	3.03	1
Bazel	John	-----11	1.09	1	Beard	Samuel	12MAY94	1.01	1
BEACON					Baird	Samuel	11MAY95	2.02	1
Beacon	Jeremiah	09AUG05	3.03	1	Baird	Samuel	11MAY95	2.14	1
Beacon	Jeremiah	22JUL06	3.03	1	Beard	Samuel	06JUN96	1.02	1
BEADLES					Beard	Samuel	15JUN97	3.04	1
Beddles	Edmond	05JUL00	3.05	1	Beard	Samuel	31MAY99	1.04	1
Beadles	Edmond	19MAY01	3.02	1	Beard	Samuel	16JUN00	2.02	1
Beedles	Edmond	12AUG02	3.04	1	Beard	Samuel	27JUN01	2.02	1
Beigles	Edmond	28JUL03	2.03	1	Beard	Samuel	07JUN02	3.01	1
Bedles	Edmund	27JUN04	4.02	1	Beard	Samuel	17JUN03	2.01	1
Beedler	Edmond	19JUL05	2.04	1	Baird	Samuel	22AUG04	2.02	1
Beedles	Edmond	19AUG06	2.06	1	Beard	Samuel	08JUL05	2.03	1
Beadles	John	-----07	2.02	1	Beard	Samuel	09AUG06	2.06	11
Beadles	Wrice	12JUL99	3.03	1	Beard	Samuel	-----07	2.02	12
Beadles	Rice	05JUL00	3.05	1	Baird	Samuel	24JUN08	2.02	12
Beadles	Rice	19MAY01	3.02	1	Beard	Samuel	10MAY09	1.02	12
Beedles	Rice	12AUG02	3.04	1	Beard	Samuel	-----11	1.07	2
Beigles	Rice	28JUL03	2.03	1	Beard	Thomas	08JUL99	3.02	1
Bedles	Rice	27JUN04	4.02	11	Beard	William	27JUN87	2.01	11
Beedles	Rice	19JUL05	2.04	11	BEATY				
Beidles	Rice	19AUG06	2.06	11	Beattey	James	18AUG09	2.04	1
Beadles	Rice	-----07	2.02	11	Batey	William	-----11	1.06	1
Beedels	Rice	29JUN08	2.02	11	BEAVERS				
Beadles	Rice	08JUN09	1.03	1	Beavers	John	28JUN99	3.02	1
Beadles	Rice	-----11	1.07	21	Bevis	John	27JUN00	3.03	1
Bedles	Seaton	24JUL04	4.02	1	Beavis	John	21MAY01	3.02	1
Beedler	Setin	19JUL05	2.04	1	Beaver	John	01JUL02	3.02	1
Beedles	Setin	19AUG06	2.06	1	Beaver	John	01JUL03	2.02	1
Beadels	Seaton	24AUG08	2.03	1	Bevis	John	09AUG04	4.01	1
BEAM					Beaver	John	31MAY05	2.02	1
Beam	Conrod	23JUN09	1.04	1	Beavers	John	09AUG06	2.05	1
Beam	Jacob	03APR90	1.01	1	BECK				
Beam	Jacob	14MAY91	2.01	1	Beck	Frederick	-----96	1.02	1
Beem	Jacob	26NOV92	3.02	1	BECKLEY				
Beam	Nicholas	03APR90	1.01	1	Beckley	James	25AUG08	2.03	1
Beem	Nicholass	16NOV92	3.02	1	BELL				
Beam	Nicholas	04JUL99	3.02	1	Bell	Burrill	25JUN00	2.03	1
Beem	Nicholas	30JUN00	3.04	1	Bell	Burrell	21JUL01	3.05	1
Beam	Nicholas	17JUL01	2.02	1	Bell	Elijah	26MAY07	1.02	1
BEAMER					Bell	Elijah	18APR08	1.01	1
Beamer	Henry	-----96	1.03	00	Bell	Elijah	04JUL09	2.03	1
Beamer	---	03JUL99	3.10		Bell	Henry	31JUL01	2.03	1
Tax paid by Michael Horine					Bell	Henry	24JUN02	2.02	1
Beamer	Henry	22JUN03	2.15	1	Bell	Henry	29AUG03	3.03	1
Tax paid by Michael Horine					Bell	Henry	05AUG05	3.03	1
BEAN					Bell	Henry	07AUG06	3.04	1
Baen	Anney	-----11	1.09		Bell	James	20APR03	3.02	1
By L.Sandridge					Bell	James	06AUG04	3.03	1
Beams	Conrad	22JUN03	2.02	1	Bell	James	16AUG05	3.04	1
Bean	Conrod	25AUG08	2.03	1	Bell	James	01AUG06	3.03	1
Bean	George	20MAY99	2.01	1	Bell	John	13MAY99	1.02	1
Bean	John	21APR97	3.04	11	Bell	John	15JUL99	3.03	1
Been	John	28JUN00	3.03	1	Bell	John	03JUN00	2.01	1
Bean	John	15JUL01	2.02	1	Bell	John	25JUN00	3.02	1
Bean	John	03JUL02	3.02	1	Bell	John	29MAY01	3.04	1
Bean	John	14JUN03	2.01	1	Bell	John	08JUN01	2.02	1
Bean	John	24JUL04	1.01	1	Bell	John	25JUL01	2.02	1
Bean	John	03JUN05	2.02	1	Bell	John	05JUN02	1.01	1
Bean	John	07AUG06	2.05	1	Bell	John	05JUN02	1.01	1
Bean	William	11JUL97	1.03	1	Bell	John	12AUG02	2.03	1
Bain	William	21MAY99	3.02	1	Bell	John	04JUL03	1.03	1

surname	name	date	bk.pg	TM	surname	name	date	bk.pg	TM
Bell	John	03AUG04	2.02	1	Bennedeck	John Sr	19JUL00	3.06	1
Bell	John	17JUN05	1.02	1	Bennedeck	John Jr	19JUL00	3.05	1
Bell	John	20JUN06	1.02	1	Benadick	John Sr	06MAY01	3.01	1
Bell	John	07AUG06	3.04	1	Benadick	John Jr	06MAY01	3.01	1
Bell	John	03JUL07	1.03	1	Benedic	John Sr	06AUG02	3.03	1
Bell	John (T/F)	-----07	2.02	11	Benedic	John	05AUG02	3.03	1
Bell	John	07JUN08	1.03	1	Benedic	John	05AUG03	2.03	1
Bell	John T.	09JUN08	1.03	1	Benedic	John Jr	05AUG03	2.03	1
Bell	John F.	06JUL09	2.03	1	Benadick	John Sr	13JUN04	4.04	1
Bell	John T.	-----11	1.07	1	Benedick	John	09APR04	4.03	1
Bell	Josiah	16JUN96	1.02	1	Benedic	John Sr	27JUN05	2.03	11
Bell	Michael	18APR08	1.01	M1	Benedic	John Jr	27JUN05	2.03	1
Bell	Michael	30JUN09	2.03	1	Benedick	John Sr	13AUG06	2.06	11
Bell	Rachel	05JUL96	2.02	F	Benedick	John Jr	13AUG06	2.06	1
Bell	Rachel	10AUG07	2.28	F	Benadick	John Sr	18AUG07	2.05	11
Tax paid by William Patten					Benadick	John Jr	18AUG07	2.05	1
Bell	Rachel	-----08	2.22	F	Benadick	John	25JUL08	2.02	11
Tax paid by William Patten					Benadick	John	25JUL08	2.02	1
Bell	Rachell	-----09	1.28		Bennedict	John Sr	17JUL09	1.06	1
Tax paid by William Patten					Bennedict	John	13JUL09	1.06	1
Bell	Robert	01JUN95	2.02	1	Benedict	John	-----11	1.10	11
Bell	Robert	16JUN96	1.02	1	BENNETT				
Bell	Sam (Heirs)	29APR95	3.02	0	Beanett	Arthur	07APR95	3.03	0
Bell	Sam.(heirs)	31MAY97	1.19	D	Bennett	John	06JUN99	1.04	1
Tax pd by William Patton					Bennet	John	26JUL00	2.03	1
Bell	Samuel	22JUL99	3.17	D	Bennett	John	18JUL06	2.02	1
Tax paid by William Patton					Bennett	John	13AUG07	2.04	1
Bell	Sam.(heirs)	19JUN01	3.27	D	Bennit	Samuel	16MAY97	1.02	1
Tax paid by William Patton					BENTLEY				
Bell	Thomas	16JUN96	1.02	1	Bentley	James	18JUN05	2.02	1
Bell	Thomas M.	08JUN09	1.02	1	Bentley	James	01AUG06	2.05	1
Bell	William	01JUN95	2.02	1	Bently	James	21AUG07	2.05	1
Bell	William	01JUN95	2.14	1	Benly	James	25JUL08	2.02	1
Bell	William	15JUL99	3.03	1	Bently	James	13JUL09	1.06	1
Bell	William	25JUN00	3.02	1	Bentley	James	-----11	1.09	1
Bell	William	28MAY01	3.04	1	Bently	John	21AUG87	1.01	1
Bell	William	12AUG02	2.03	1	Bently	John	19MAY89	6.01	1
Bell	William	25JUL03	3.03	11	Bentley	John	14MAY90	1.01	11
Bell	William	08AUG04	3.03	11	Bently	John	20APR91	2.01	1
Bell	William	08AUG05	3.03	11	Bently	John	14SEP92	1.02	1
Bell	William	04AUG06	3.04	11	Bently	John	07AUG93	3.01	1
Bell	William	06AUG06	3.04	1	Bently	John	13JUN94	2.01	1
BELLIMON					Bently	John	14APR95	3.02	1
Bellimon	Benjamin	11JUN01	1.02	1	Bently	John	21JUN96	2.02	1
BELSHE					Bently	John	31MAY97	1.02	1
Belshe	Zaceriah	02JUN08	1.02	1	Bentley	John	20MAY99	3.01	1
BENEDICT					Bently	John	24JUN00	3.02	1
Benedick	Benjamin	08MAY95	3.01	01	Bently	John	17JUN01	3.02	11
Benedict	Benjamin	08JUN97	1.02	1	Bentley	John	27JUL02	3.03	11
Benedict	Benjamin	21MAY99	3.02	1	Bentley	John	06AUG03	2.04	11
Bennedeck	Benjamin	19JUL00	3.05	1	Bentley	John	05JUN04	4.04	11
Benedick	Benjamin	13AUG06	2.06	1	Bentley	John	18JUN05	2.02	1
Benadick	Benjamin	04AUG07	2.04	1	Bently	John	01AUG06	2.05	1
Bennedick	Daniel	25JUN00	3.03	1	Bently	John	12JUN07	2.02	1
Bennedict	Jacob	17JUL09	1.06	1	Bently	John	25JUL08	2.02	1
Benedick	John	12JUN89	6.08	1	Bently	John	13JUL09	1.05	1
Benedick	John	21APR90	1.02	11	Bently	John	-----11	1.05	1
Benedict	John Jr	29MAY90	1.02	1	Bentley	Levi	22JUN03	2.02	1
Benedict	John	18MAR91	2.02	1	Bentley	Levi	27JUL04	4.01	1
Bennedict	John	12SEP92	1.02	11	Bentley	Levi	25JUL05	2.05	1
Benedick	John	18OCT92	1.01	1	Bentley	Levi	18JUL06	2.02	1
Bennedict	John	05AUG93	3.01	1	Bently	Levi	13AUG07	2.04	1
Benedict	John	07AUG93	3.02	11	Bently	Levy	-----11	1.03	11
Benedict	John Sr	13MAY94	2.02	11	Bently	Thomas	07AUG93	3.02	1
Benedict	John Jr	13MAY94	2.01	1	Bently	Thomas	13MAY94	2.01	1
Benedick	John Sr	08APR95	3.01	1	Bently	Thomas	14APR95	3.02	1
Benedick	John Jr	08APR95	3.01	1	Bently	Thomas	14MAY96	2.01	1
Bennedick	John	04JUN96	2.01	1	Bentley	Thomas	31MAY97	1.02	1
Bennadick	John Jr	16JUN96	2.02	1	Bentley	Thomas	27MAY99	1.03	1
Benedict	John Sr	08JUN97	1.02	1	Bently	Thomas	24JUL00	2.03	1
Benedict	John Jr	06JUN97	1.03	1	Bently	Thomas	28MAY01	3.04	1
Benedict	John Jr	21MAY99	3.01	1	BERNARD				

surname	name	date	bk.pg	TM	surname	name	date	bk.pg	TM
Bernard	Lerois	-----93	3.01	1	Bathurum	Benjamin	30JUL05	1.02	12
BERREMAN					Bathurum	Benj. Sr	01AUG06	1.03	11
Beryman	Thomas	26JUN87	2.01	1	Bathurum	Benj. Jr	12JUN06	1.01	1
Berriman	Thomas	22OCT88	1.02	1	Bathuurum	Benjamin	07MAY07	1.02	11
Berrimon	Thomas	04AUG89	5.02	1	Bathuurum	Benj. Jr	07MAY07	1.02	1
Beriman	Thomas	25APR90	2.01	1	Bathuram	Benj. Sr	19APR08	1.02	11
Berreman	Thomas	05APR91	1.02	1	Bathurum	Benj. Jr	19APR08	1.02	1
BERRY					Bathurum	Benj. Sr	16JUN09	2.02	21
Berry	Ephraim	-----11	1.07	1	Bathurum	Benj. Jr	15JUN09	2.02	1
Berry	Hannah	23JUN91	2.01	F1	Bathurum	David	12JUN06	1.01	1
Berry	Hannah	25SEP92	1.01	F1	Bathuurum	David	07MAY07	1.02	1
Berry	Hannah	24AUG93	3.02	F1	Bathurum	Isack	13JUN99	2.02	1
Berry	Hannah	09MAY94	2.02	1	Bathurum	Isaac	24JUN01	1.02	1
Berry	Hannah	13MAY97	1.02	F	Bathurum	Isach	23JUN02	1.02	1
Berry	Hanna	13AUG99	1.40	F	Bathurum	Isaac	22JUN03	1.02	1
Berry	Hannah	28JUN00	2.03	F	Bathurum	Isaac	03AUG04	1.02	1
Berry	Hannah	31JUL01	2.03	F	Bathurum	Isaac	30JUL05	1.02	1
Berry	Hannah	23AUG02	2.03	F	Bathurum	Isaac	12JUN06	1.01	1
Berry	Hannah	13JUL03	3.03	F	Bathuurum	Isaac	07MAY07	1.02	1
Berry	James	23JUN91	2.01	1	Bathuram	Isaac	19APR08	1.02	1
Berry	James	18OCT92	1.01	1	Bathurum	Isaac	01JUL09	2.03	1
Berry	James	24AUG93	3.02	1	Bathurum	William	22JUN03	1.02	1
Berry	James	22APR95	3.02	1	Bathurum	William K.	01AUG04	1.02	1
Berry	James	17MAY96	2.01	1	Bathurum	William	30JUL05	1.02	1
Berry	James	08AUG97	1.03	1	Bathurum	William	01AUG06	1.03	1
Berry	James	13AUG99	1.40	1	Bathuurum	William	07MAY07	1.02	1
Berry	Jesse	21AUG07	2.05	1	Bathuram	William	20APR08	1.02	1
Berry	Jesse	20JUN08	2.01	11	Bathurum	William	01JUL09	2.03	1
Berry	Jesse	06APR09	1.01	11	BETTIS				
Berry	Jesse	-----11	1.09	11	Bettis	John	10MAY09	2.01	1
Berry	John	21JUL87	1.01	1	Bettes	John	-----11	1.02	1
Berry	Joseph	02APR95	3.02	1	BEVERLY				
Berry	Joseph	02JUN96	2.01	1	Bevery	John	13OCT92	2.01	1
Berry	Joseph	13MAY97	1.02	1	Beverly	John	27AUG93	1.02	1
Berry	Thomas	12JUN89	6.08	1	Baverly	John	24MAY94	1.01	1
Listed with William Berry					Beverly	John	02JUN95	2.02	1
Berry	William	11JUN89	6.08	1	BIAS				
Berry	William	12JUN89	6.08		Bias	Jeremiah	09SEP89	2.02	1
Listed with Thomas Berry					BIBB				
Berry	William	21JUN91	2.01	1	Bibb	Edmond	22JUN07	2.02	1
Berry	William	25SEP92	1.01	1	Bibb	Martin	11JUL09	1.05	1
Berry	William	24AUG93	3.02	1	Bibbs	Thomas	16APR94	2.02	1
Berry	William	28APR95	3.02	1	Bibbs	Thomas	18MAR95	3.03	1
Berry	William	11MAY96	2.01	1	Bibb	Thomas	21APR96	2.01	1
Berry	William	18JUL97	1.03	1	Bibbs	Thomas	15MAY97	1.02	1
Berry	William	02JUL99	1.04	1	Bibb	Thomas	28JUN99	3.02	1
Berry	William	31JUL00	2.04	1	Bibb	Thomas	27JUN00	3.03	1
Berry	William	22JUL01	3.05	1	Bibb	Thomas	18MAY01	3.02	11
Berry	William	26MAY02	2.02	1	Bibb	Thomas	14JUN02	3.01	11
Berry	William	11JUN03	3.02	1	Bibb	Thomas	01JUL03	2.02	1
Berry	William	24AUG04	3.03	1	Bibb	Thomas	30MAY05	2.02	1
Berry	William	12JUN05	3.02	1	Bibb	Thomas	09AUG06	2.05	1
Berry	William	16JUL06	3.02	1	Bibb	Thomas	13AUG07	2.04	1
Berry	William	10JUL07	2.01	1	Bibb	Thomas	25AUG08	2.04	1
Berry	William	03JUN08	2.01	1	Bibb	Thomas	07JUN09	1.02	1
Berry	William	28JUN09	1.04	1	Bibb	Thomas	-----11	1.05	1
Berry	William	-----11	1.09	1	BIGGS				
BETHURAM					Bigs	John	13JUL87	1.01	1
Bathurum	Benjamin	02OCT92	2.01	1	Biggs	John	12MAY89	6.01	1
Bathuram	Benjamin	15AUG93	1.02	1	Biggs	John	19APR91	2.01	1
Bethuram	Benjamin	23MAY94	1.01	11	Bigs	John	14SEP92	1.02	1
Bethuram	Benjamin	02JUN95	2.02	11	Biggs	John	10AUG93	3.01	1
Bathuren	Bengamin	10MAY97	3.02	12	Biggs	John	13MAY94	2.02	1
Bathurum	Benjamin	13JUN99	2.02	12	Biggs	John	13APR95	3.02	1
Bathurum	Benjamin	23JUL00	1.01	12	Biggs	John	04JUN96	2.01	1
Bathurum	Benjamin	24JUN01	1.02	13	Biggs	John	08JUN97	1.02	1
Bathurum	Benjamin	23JUN02	1.02	12	Biggs	John	21MAY99	3.01	1
Bathurum	Benjamin Jr	23JUN02	1.02	1	Bigg	John	21JUN00	3.02	1
Bathurum	Benjamin	22JUN03	1.02	11	Biggs	John	02MAY01	3.01	1
Bathurum	Benj. Jr	22JUN03	1.02	1	Biggs	John	30JUL02	3.03	1
Bathurum	Benjamin	01AUG04	1.02	12	Biggs	John	06AUG03	2.04	1
Bathurum	Benj. Jr	01AUG04	1.02	1	Bigs	John	12JUN04	4.04	1

surname	name	date	bk.pg	TM	surname	name	date	bk.pg	TM
Biggs	John	27JUN05	2.03	1	Bird	John	02JUN95	2.02	12
Biggs	John	02AUG06	2.05	1	Bird	John	20JUN96	1.01	12
Biggs	John	17AUG07	2.05	1	Bird	Lewis	28MAY05	3.02	1
Biggs	Mary	25JUL08	2.02	F	Bird	Rubin	03APR90	2.01	1
Biggs	Mary	17JUL09	1.06	F	Bird	Rueben	29SEP92	2.01	1
BIGHAM					Bird	Reuben	10AUG93	1.01	1
Bigham	Robert	13JUN96	2.02	1	Bird	Reuben	21MAY94	1.01	1
Bigham	Robert	16MAY97	1.02	1	Bird	Reuben	01JUN95	2.01	1
BIGSLER					Bird	Rubin	20JUN96	1.01	1
Bixler	David	03JUL99	3.02	1	Bird	Rubin	10MAY97	3.03	1
Bigsler	David	21JUN00	2.02	1	Bird	Thomas	20MAY99	1.03	1
Bigsler	David	30JUN01	2.02	1	Bird	Thomas	10AUG01	2.03	1
Bigsler	David	24MAY02	3.01	1	BIRNEY				
Bigsler	David	20JUN03	2.02	1	Berney	James	28OCT92	2.01	1
Bixler	David	25JUL04	1.02	11	Binney	James	10JUN94	2.03	1
Bigsler	David	23JUL05	2.05	1	Birney	James	18MAY95	3.02	1
Bigsler	David	19MAY06	2.02	11	Burney	James	13AUG96	2.03	2
Bexler	David	-----07	2.03	11	BISHOP				
Berksler	David	17JUN08	1.04	21	Bishop	Richard	-----96	1.02	1
Beaxler	David	18AUG09	2.03	1	Bishop	Vatchel	08OCT92	1.02	1
Binler	David	-----11	1.08	1	Bishop	Veachel	30APR94	2.02	1
Beaxler	John	18AUG09	2.03	1	Bishop	Vaschel	29MAR95	3.03	1
Bexler	John	-----11	1.08	1	Bishop	Veacheal	20JUN96	2.02	1
BINGAMAN					Bishop	Vashel	23MAY97	1.02	1
Bingamin	Christian	26MAY97	3.02	1	Bishop	Veashel	03JUL99	3.02	1
Bingamin	Christen	17JUN00	1.01	1	Bishop	Veachel	01JUL00	3.04	1
Bingamin	Christian	03JUN01	1.01	1	Bisshop	Vichel	09JUL01	3.03	1
Bingamin	Henry	31MAR91	1.01	1	Bishop	Vachell	16AUG02	3.05	1
Bengaman	Henry	11OCT92	2.01	1	Bishop	Vachell	-----03	2.01	1
Bingaman	Henry	15AUG93	1.02	1	BLACK				
Bingamin	Henry	23MAY94	1.01	1	Black	Andrew	16AUG05	3.03	1
Bingamin	Henry	02JUN95	2.01	1	Black	Andrew	23AUG06	3.04	1
Bingamin	Henry	27JUN96	1.02	1	Black	Hugh	13JUN87	2.01	11
Bingamin	Henry	26MAY97	3.02	1	Black	Hugh	01NOV88	1.01	11
Bingamin	Henry	13MAY99	1.02	1	Black	Hugh	30JUN89	5.01	11
Bingamin	Henry	17JUN00	1.01	1	Black	Hugh	30JUN90	2.01	11
Bingamin	Henry	18JUN00	2.02	1	Black	Hugh	13APR91	1.01	11
Bingamin	Henry	03JUN01	1.01	1	Black	Hugh	04OCT92	2.01	11
Bingamin	Henry	24JUL01	2.02	1	Black	Hugh	10AUG93	1.01	1
Bingamon	Henry	10JUN02	1.01	1	Black	Hugh	22MAY94	1.01	1
Benjamin	Henry	29JUN03	1.03	1	Black	Hugh	01JUN95	2.01	1
Bengaman	Henry	03AUG04	2.01	11	Black	Hugh	20JUN96	1.02	1
Bingamin	Henry	13JUN05	1.02	11	Black	Hugh	10MAY97	3.03	1
Bingamon	Henry	19JUN06	1.02	11	Black	Hugh	24JUN99	1.04	1
Bengaman	Henry	02JUN07	1.02	1	Black	James	13JUN87	2.01	1
Bengaman	Henry	14MAY08	1.02	11	Black	James	14NOV88	1.01	1
Bingaman	Henry	29MAY09	2.02	1	Black	James	23JUN89	5.01	1
Bingaman	Henry Sr	-----11	1.06	1	Black	James	02JUN90	2.02	1
Bingaman	Henry Jr	-----11	1.06	1	Black	James	13APR91	1.01	1
Bingamin	Jacob	16MAY99	1.02	1	Black	James	02OCT92	2.01	1
Bingamin	Jacob	03JUN00	2.02	1	Black	James	20AUG93	1.01	1
Bingamin	Jacob	24JUL01	2.02	1	Black	James	21MAY94	1.01	1
Bingamon	Jacob	10JUN02	1.01	1	Black	James	29APR95	3.01	2
Bingamin	Lewis	17JUN00	1.01	1	Black	James	01JUN95	2.01	1
Bingamin	Lewis	03JUN01	1.01	1	Black	James	28JUN96	1.01	1
BIRD					Black	James	26APR97	3.03	1
Burd	Andrew	16MAR95	3.03	0	Black	Jeramiah	10AUG93	1.01	1
Bird	James	02JUN95	2.02	1	Black	Jeremiah	21MAY94	1.01	1
Bird	James	20JUN96	1.02	1	Black	Jeremiah	01JUN95	2.01	1
Bird	James	23JUN00	2.02	1	Black	Jeremiah	20JUN96	1.02	1
Bird	James	02JUN01	2.01	1	Black	Jeremiah	10MAY97	3.03	1
Bird	James	12JUL02	2.02	1	Black	John	03JUN95	2.02	1
Bird	James	14JUN04	2.01	1	Black	John	24JUN96	1.02	1
Bird	James	28MAY05	3.02	1	Black	John	10MAY97	3.02	1
Byrd	John	22OCT88	1.02	1	Black	John	24MAY97	1.03	1
Byrd	John	01NOV88	1.02	1	Black	John	22MAY99	2.01	1
Byrd	John	07AUG89	5.02	1	Black	Joseph	28JUN87	1.01	1
Bird	John	03APR90	2.01	1	Black	Joseph	08JUN89	6.01	1
Bird	John	05JUL91	1.01	1	Black	Josias	09AUG90	1.02	1
Bird	John	03NOV92	2.02	11	Black	Josias	18AUG91	2.02	1
Bird	John	10AUG93	1.01	11	Black	Josias	03NOV92	1.01	1
Bird	John	23MAY94	1.01	1	Black	Josiah	23AUG93	3.02	1

surname	name	date	bk.pg	TM	surname	name	date	bk.pg	TM
Black	Josiah	29MAY94	2.02	1	Blain	Alex. Sr	22JUN97	1.03	1
Black	Josiah	02MAY95	3.02	1	Tax paid by John Blain				
Black	Joseph	01JUN95	2.01	1	Blain	Alexander	26MAY97	1.01	11
Black	Joseph	20JUN96	1.01	1	Blaine	Alexander	24JUN99	1.02	12
Black	Josiah	24JUN96	2.02	1	Blane	Alexander	30JUL00	2.04	12
Black	Joseph	24MAY99	2.01	1	Blain	Alexander	22JUL01	3.05	21
Black	Patrick	14JUN87	2.01	1	Blain	Alexander	26MAY02	2.02	21
Black	Peterick	23JUN89	5.01	1	Blain	Alexander	27MAY02	2.02	11
Black	Patrick	02JUN90	2.02	1	Blain	Alexander	12JUL02	2.02	1
Black	Patrick	13APR91	1.01	1	Blane	Alexander	03JUN03	3.02	3
Black	Patrick	29SEP92	2.01	1	Blane	Alex. Jr	16JUN03	3.02	1
Black	Patrick	10AUG93	1.01	1	Blain	Alexander	07AUG04	2.02	2
Black	Patrick	22MAY94	1.01	1	Blane	Alexander	24AUG04	3.03	3
Black	Patrick	01JUN95	2.01	1	Blain	Alex. Sr	19JUN05	3.03	1
Black	Patrick	20JUN96	1.01	1	Blain	Alexander	13JUN05	3.02	2
Black	Shederah	14APR91	1.02	1	Blain	Alexander	19JUN05	3.03	2
Black	Thomas	24AUG87	1.01	1	Blain	Alexander	31JUL06	3.03	3
Black	Thomas	19MAY89	6.01	1	Blain	Alexander	23AUG06	3.04	2
Black	Thomas	13AUG90	1.02	12	Blain	Alexander	-----07	2.02	1
Black	Thomas	03NOV92	1.01	12	Blain	Alexander	17AUG07	2.05	D
Black	Thomas	27AUG93	3.02	12	Blain	Alexander	-----07	2.02	2
Black	Thomas	02MAY95	3.02	12	Blain	Alex	03AUG08	2.03	D
Black	Thomas	24JUN96	2.02	3	Tax pd by Joseph/John Blain				
BLACKABY					Blain	Alexander	20JUN08	2.01	21
Blackaby	Thomas	-----11	1.08	1	Blain	Alexander	25AUG08	2.04	1
BLACKBURN					Blain	Alexander	29JUN09	1.04	2
Blackburne	James	13JUN05	1.01	1	Blain	Alexander	01JUL09	1.05	1
Blackburn	James	19JUN06	1.02	11	Blain	Alexander	12JUL09	1.05	D
Blackburn	James	04JUN07	1.03	1	Paid by John/James Blain-Exec				
Blackburn	James	22APR08	1.02	1	Blane	Alexander	-----11	1.05	0
Blackburn	James	06JUN09	2.02	1	Blane	Alexander	-----11	1.05	0
Blackburn	James	-----11	1.06	1	Blane	Alexander	-----11	1.09	11
Blackburn	William	23MAY94	3.04	1	Blain	Alexander	-----11	1.05	11
Blackborn	William	10APR95	1.03	1	Blane	Alexander	-----11	1.05	
Blackbourn	William	-----96	1.02	1	Executor - John Blane				
BLACKLEDGE					Blain	Isaac	21JUN00	3.02	1
Blackledge	Ichabad	21APR97	3.04	11	Blain	Isaac	18JUN01	3.02	1
Blacklidge	Ichabad	30MAY99	1.04	11	Blane	Isaac	28JUL02	3.03	1
Blacklidge	Ichabod	21JUN00	2.02	11	Blane	Isaac	05AUG03	2.04	1
Blacklidge	Ichabod	04APR01	2.01	11	Blane	Isaac	05JUN04	4.04	10
Blacklidge	Ichabod	27MAY02	3.01	11	Blane	Isaac	28JUN05	2.03	1
Blackledge	Jacob	24OCT92	2.01	1	Blane	Isaac	01AUG06	2.05	1
Blackledge	Jacob	14MAY94	1.01	1	Blain	Isaac	08JUN07	2.01	1
Blacklidge	Jacob	06JUN95	2.01	1	Blain	Isaac	30MAY08	2.10	D
Blackledge	Jacob	08JUN96	1.02	1	Tax paid by Daniel Guthrie				
Blackledge	Jacob	20APR97	3.04	1	Blain	Isaac	21AUG09	1.16	D
Blacklidge	John	21JUN00	2.02	1	Daniel Guthrie Executor				
BLACKSTONE					Blaine	Isaac	-----11	1.30	D1
Blackiston	Ebenezer	10JUL99	3.03	1	Blaine	Isaac(decd)	-----11	1.30	
Blackston	Ebenezer	24JUN00	3.02	1	Daniel Guthrie - Exec.				
Blackstone	Ebenezer	18JUN05	2.02	1	Blane	James	06SEP87	1.01	1
BLACKWELL					Blain	James	16MAY89	6.01	1
Blackwell	Benjamin	-----03	2.01	1	Blain	James	21APR90	1.02	1
BLACKWOOD					Blain	James	30APR91	2.02	1
Blackwood	Joseph	-----07	2.02	1	Blain	James	06AUG93	3.01	1
Blackwood	Joseph	03JUN08	2.01	1	Blain	James	24MAY94	2.02	1
Blackwood	Joseph	07JUL09	1.05	1	Blain	James	23APR95	3.02	1
Blackwood	Joseph	-----11	1.07	1	Blain	James	-----96	1.03	1
Blackwood	Samuel	12AUG89	2.02	1	Blane	James	-----11	1.09	1
Blane	Alex Sr	06SEP87	1.01	1	Blain	John	23MAY89	6.01	1
Blane	Alex Jr	06SEP87	1.01	1	Blain	John	30APR91	2.02	11
Blain	Alexander	19MAY89	6.01	1	Blain	John	03OCT92	1.02	2
Blain	Alex. Jr	23MAY89	6.01	1	Blane	John	06AUG93	3.01	1
Blain	Alexander	14MAY90	1.01	1	Blane	John	24MAY94	2.02	2
Blain	Alex./John	21APR90	1.02	21	Blane	John	08MAY95	3.01	1
Blain	Alexander	30APR91	2.02	1	Blane	John	08MAY95	3.01	2
Blain	Alex.	03OCT92	1.02	1	Blane	John	06JUL96	2.02	2
Blane	Alex. Sr	06AUG93	3.01	1	Blain	John	22JUN97	1.03	2
Blain	Alexander	13AUG93	3.01	1	Paid tax for Alex. Sr Blain				
Blain	Alexander	10JUN94	2.02	1	Blaine	John	06JUN99	1.01	2
Blain	Alexander	15APR95	3.02	1	Blane	John	29JUL00	2.04	2
Blane	Alexander	11MAY96	2.01	11	Blain	John	20JUL01	3.05	2

surname	name	date	bk.pg	TM	surname	name	date	bk.pg	TM
Blain	John	09JUN02	2.02	2	Blanks	Sharach	17MAY99	1.02	1
Blane	John	08AUG03	3.03	2	Blanks	Shedrach	30MAY00	2.01	1
Blane	John	12MAY04	3.02	2	Blanks	Shedrach	21JUL01	2.02	1
Blain	John	19JUN05	3.03	1	Blanks	Shadrack	05JUN02	1.01	1
Blain	John	06AUG06	3.04	1	Blanks	Shadrack	04JUL03	1.03	1
Blain	John	07AUG06	3.04	1	Blanks	Shadrack	20JUN04	1.01	1
Blain	John	17AUG07	2.05	1	Blanks	Shadrack	17JUN05	1.02	1
Blain	John	03AUG08	2.03	1	Blanks	Shadrack	21JUN06	1.02	1
Blain	Jas/John	03AUG08	2.03		Blanks	Shaderich	18JUN07	1.03	1
Paid tax for Alex Blain					Blanks	Shadereck	06JUN08	1.03	11
Blain	John	12JUL09	1.05	1	BLEDSOE				
Blain	John/James	12JUL09	1.05		Bledsoe	Abraham	22MAY94	3.05	1
Exec. for Alexander Blain					Bledsoe	Abraham	-----96	1.03	1
Blane	John	-----11	1.05	1	Bledsoe	Benjamin	04NOV92	3.01	1
Executor for Alexander Blane					Bledsoe	Benjamin	20MAR94	3.03	1
Blain	Michael	-----96	1.03	1	Bledsoe	Bengamin	13MAR95	1.02	1
Blain	Nathan	13MAY97	1.02	1	Bledsoe	Benjamin	-----96	1.03	1
Blain	Robert	12JUL02	2.03	1	Bledsoe	Elijah	04NOV92	3.01	1
Blain	Thomas	01AUG05	3.03	1	Bledsoe	Elijah	21MAY94	3.03	1
Blain	William	30MAY08	2.01	1	Bledsoe	Elijah	13MAR95	1.02	1
Blain	William	20JUN07	2.02	1	Bledsoe	Elijah	-----96	1.03	1
BLAIR					Bledsoe	Joseph	01NOV88	1.02	1
Blare	Alexander	23JUN89	5.01	1	Bledsoe	Joseph	30JUN89	2.02	11
Blair	Alexander	27MAR90	2.01	1	Bledsoe	Joseph	19AUG89	5.02	1
Blair	Alexander	10SEP93	1.01	1	Bledsoe	Joseph Sr	19APR91	3.01	1
Blair	Alexander	21MAY94	1.01	1	Bledsoe	Joseph	19APR91	3.01	1
Blare	John	15JUN03	1.02	1	Bledsoe	Joseph	04NOV92	3.01	1
Blare	John	19JUN04	1.01	1	Bledsoe	Joseph	-----93	3.01	1
Blair	John	20MAY06	2.02	1	Bledsoe	Joseph Sr	29MAY94	3.02	1
Blear	John	29MAY07	1.02	1	Bledsoe	Joseph Jr	13MAR95	1.02	1
Blair	John	17JUN08	1.04	1	Bledsoe	Joseph Jr	01JUN95	1.03	1
Blair	John	12MAY09	2.02	1	Bledsoe	Joseph Sr	-----96	1.03	1
Blair	John	-----11	1.06	1	Bledsoe	Joseph Jr	-----96	1.02	00
Blare	Joseph	20JUN04	1.01	1	Bledsoe	William	19APR91	3.01	1
Blear	Joseph	05JUN07	1.03	1	Bledsoe	William	05DEC92	3.04	1
Blair	Joseph	17JUN08	1.04	1	Bledsoe	William	-----93	3.01	1
Blair	Joseph	12MAY09	2.01	1	Bledsoe	William M.	20MAR94	3.03	1
Blair	Peter	30JUN87	1.01	1	Bledsoe	William	10APR95	1.03	1
BLAKEY					BLEVINS				
Blakey	Pleasant	12MAR95	1.01	1	Blevens	Berry	30APR94	2.01	01
Blakey	Pleasant	-----96	1.01	1	Blevens	Berry	17MAR95	3.03	1
Bleaky	Reuben	25AUG08	2.03	1	Blevin	Berry	23JUL96	2.02	1
Blaky	Reuben	09JUN09	1.03	1	Blevins	Berry	15JUL99	3.03	1
Blakey	Reuben	-----11	1.07	1	Blevens	Daniel	08JUN09	1.03	1
BLAND					Blevens	Daniel	-----11	1.05	1
Blan	Charles	23MAY94	3.04	1	Blevens	Isam	-----11	1.05	1
Blan	Charls	25MAR95	1.01	1	Blevens	James	23JUL05	2.04	1
Bland	Charles	-----96	1.03	1	Bivens	James	04AUG07	2.03	1
BLANKENSHIP					Blevens	James	25AUG08	2.04	1
BlankenshipAsey		10JUN08	1.03	1	Blevens	James	22JUN09	1.04	1
BlankenshipJane		22APR96	2.01	F	Blevins	John	02JUL99	3.02	1
BlankenshipNoah		23JUN02	1.02	1	Blevins	John	01JUL00	3.04	1
BlankenshipNowel		20JUN03	1.02	1	Beavens	John	20MAY01	3.02	1
BlankenshipNoel		03AUG04	2.01	1	Bliven	John	14AUG02	3.04	1
BlankenshipNoah		12JUN05	1.01	1	Bivens	John	26JUL03	2.03	1
BlankenshipNoel		16JUN06	1.01	1	Bivens	John	28JUN04	4.02	1
BlankenshipNowel		31MAY08	1.02	1	Blevens	John	25JUL05	2.05	1
BlankenshipNoel		12MAY09	2.01	1	Blivins	John	25JUL05	2.05	1
BlankenshipNoah		-----11	1.06	1	Blevens	John	18JUL06	2.02	1
BLANKS					Blevens	John	09JUN09	1.03	1
Blanks	Lydia	05JUL09	2.03	F	Blevens	John	21JUN09	1.03	1
Blanks	Lydia	-----11	1.07	F	Blevens	John	-----11	1.03	1
Blanks	Shaderie	27JUN87	2.01	1	Bivens	John	-----11	1.03	1
Blanks	Shadrack	29OCT88	1.01	1	Blevins	Lemuel	25JUL03	2.02	1
Blanks	Shadrack	24JUN89	5.01	1	Blevins	Samuel	10OCT92	1.01	1
Blanks	Shederick	03JUN90	2.02	1	Blevins	Samuel	19AUG93	3.02	11
Blanks	Shederick	10OCT92	2.01	1	Bleven	Samuel	01MAY94	2.02	1
Blanks	Shadrick	20AUG93	1.01	1	Blevens	Samuel	02APR95	3.03	11
Blank	Shedrick	23MAY94	1.01	1	Blevins	Samuel	22JUL96	2.03	11
Blanks	Shadrick	03JUN95	2.01	1	Blevins	Samuel	17MAY97	1.02	11
Blank	Shadrick	16JUN96	1.02	1	Blevins	Samuel	02JUL99	3.02	12
Blanks	Shadrick	11MAY97	3.02	1	Blevins	Samuel	01JUL00	3.04	11

surname	name	date	bk.pg	TM	surname	name	date	bk.pg	TM
Blevins	Samuel	01JUL00	3.04	1	Boulten	Robert	15JUN09	1.03	1
Blevens	Samuel	18JUL06	2.02	1	BOON				
Blevens	Samuel	09JUN09	1.03		Boon	Jeremiah	26JUN87	2.01	1
Exempt from county tax					Boon	Jeremiah	28OCT88	1.02	1
Blevins	William	22JUL96	2.02	1	Boon	Jeremiah	06AUG89	5.02	1
Blevens	William	17MAY97	1.03	1	Boon	Jerry	05APR91	1.02	1
Blevins	William	02JUL99	3.02	1	Boon	Jeremiah	24OCT92	2.01	1
BLOID					Boon	Jeremiah	06AUG93	1.01	1
Bloid	Jacob	15JUN05	1.02	1	Boon	Jeremiah	23MAY94	1.02	1
BLYTHE					Boon	Jeremiah	06JUN95	2.01	1
Blythe	David	13AUG89	2.02	1	Boon	Jeremiah	08JUN96	1.01	1
Blith	David	13SEP91	3.03	1	Boon	Jeremiah	20MAY97	3.02	1
Bly	David	-----96	1.02	1	Boon	Josiah	26JUN87	2.01	1
Blythe	David	12JUN99	2.02	11	BOREN				
Blythe	David	21JUL00	1.01	11	Bouren	Ann	13JUL03	3.03	F
Blythe	David	23JUN01	1.02	1	Bouarn	Anna	07JUL09	1.05	F
Blythe	David	20JUN02	1.01	1	Bouren	David	19JUL03	3.03	M1
Blythe	David	21JUN03	1.02	1	Borand	David	23AUG05	3.04	1
Blythe	David	01AUG04	1.02	1	Boran	James	27JUN00	2.03	1
Blythe	David	29JUL05	1.02	00	Borrand	James	22JUL01	3.05	11
Blythe	David	30JUL06	1.03	1	Bouren	James	13JUL03	3.03	1
Free (of tax)					Boren	John	17MAY97	1.02	1
Bly	David	04MAY07	1.01	0	Boren	John	03JUL99	3.02	1
Free from county levy					Boren	John	01JUL00	3.04	1
Bly	David	10JUN08	1.03	0	Borrand	John	22JUL01	3.05	1
Exempt					Borand	John	13AUG02	2.03	1
Bly	David	17JUN09	2.03	0	Bouren	John	15JUN03	3.02	1
Exempt from county levy					Borand	Nancy	09AUG02	2.03	F1
Blythe	John	12JUN99	2.02	01	Borand	Nancy	23AUG05	3.04	F
Blythe	John	23JUN01	1.02	1	Borrand	Nancy	01AUG06	3.03	F
Blythe	John	20JUN02	1.01	1	Bouren	Nathaniel	09JUN03	3.02	1
Blythe	John	21JUN03	1.02	1	Boring	Thomas	01JUL99	1.04	1
Blythe	John	01AUG04	1.02	1	Boran	Thomas	27JUN00	2.03	1
Blythe	John	29JUL05	1.02	1	Borrand	Thomas	22JUL01	3.05	1
Blythe	John	30JUL06	1.03	1	Borand	Thomas	09AUG02	2.03	1
Bly	John	04MAY07	1.01	1	Bouren	Thomas	03JUN03	3.02	1
Bly	John	10JUN08	1.03	1	Borrand	Thomas	23AUG05	3.04	1
Bly	John	12JUN09	2.02	1	Borand	Thomas	01AUG06	3.03	1
Blythe	Thomas	30MAY99	2.01	1	BOSLEY				
Blythe	William	13JUN01	1.02	1	Bosley	Abraham	28JUN99	3.02	1
Blythe	William	20JUN02	1.02	1	Bosley	Abraham	28JUN00	3.03	1
Blythe	William	29JUL05	1.02	1	Bozley	Abraham	07JUL01	3.03	1
Blythe	William	30JUL06	1.03	1	Bosley	Abraham	17JUN02	3.02	
Bly	William	04MAY07	1.01	1	One lot in Lancaster				
Bly	William	01JUL08	2.02	1	Bosley	Abraham	17JUN02	3.02	1
Bly	William	17JUN09	2.03	1	Bosley	Abraham	20JUN03	2.01	1
BOATMAN					One lot in Lancaster				
Boatman	John	20JUN03	1.02	1	Bosley	Abraham	28JUL04	4.01	1
Boatman	John	01AUG04	1.02	1	Bosley	Abraham	23JUL05	2.04	1
Boatman	John	07JUN05	1.01	1	one lott in Lancaster				
Boatman	John	30JUL06	1.02	1	Bosley	Abraham	17JUL06	2.03	1
Boatman	John	25MAY07	1.02	1	One lott in Lancaster				
Boatman	John	10JUN08	1.03	1	Bosler	Abraham	13AUG07	2.04	1
Boatman	John	12MAY09	2.01	1	Boslee	Abraham	25AUG08	2.03	1
Boatman	John	-----11	1.06	1	Bosley	Abraham	21JUN09	1.03	1
BOGARD					One lott in Lancaster				
Bogard	Daniel	18JUN00	2.02	1	Barley	Abraham	-----11	1.03	2
BOWLIN					Bosley	Gedian	18MAY97	1.02	11
Bolen	Benjamin	19JUN99	2.02	1	Bosley	Gidian	28JUN99	3.02	11
Bolen	James	06JUN02	1.01	1	Bosley	Gidon	28JUN00	3.03	11
BOLEY					Bozley	Gedian	07JUL01	3.03	13
Boley	Isaac	-----11	1.07	1	Bosley	Gideon	17JUN02	3.02	22
BOLTON					Bosley	Gideon	20JUN03	2.01	22
Boulten	James	07JUL09	1.05	1	Boslee	Gedian	03AUG07	2.03	1
Bolton	James	-----11	1.07	1	Boslee	Gidian	25AUG08	2.03	1
Boulton	John	17JUN08	1.04	1	Bosley	Gideon	21JUN09	1.03	1
Bolton	Payton	18JUL08	2.02	1	Bosley	Gideon	-----11	1.09	1
Boulten	Payton	15JUN09	1.03	1	Boslee	James	03AUG07	2.03	1
Bolton	Peyton	-----11	1.07	1	Bosler	James	25AUG08	2.03	1
Boulton	Robert	31MAY05	3.02	11	Bosley	James	21JUN09	1.03	1
Bolton	Robert	22JUN07	2.02	11	Bosley	Sary	25JUL04	4.03	F2
Bolton	Robert	18JUL08	2.02	1	Boslee	Sally	25AUG08	2.03	F

surname	name	date	bk.pg	TM	surname	name	date	bk.pg	TM
Bosley	Sarah	21JUN09	1.03	F	Boulin	John	19JUN05	2.03	1
Bosley	Thomas B.	24JUL05	2.05	2	Boulin	John	29JUL06	2.04	1
Bosley	Thomas B.	28MAR06	2.01	21	BOWMAN				
Boslee	Thomas B.	04AUG07	2.03	1	Bowman	Elisha	16JUN09	2.03	1
Boslee	Thomas B.	25AUG08	2.03	1	Bowman	John	29SEP92	2.01	1
Bosley	Thomas B.	21JUN09	1.03	1	Bowman	Judah	15JUL03	3.03	1
Barley	Thomas B.	-----11	1.02	11	Bowman	Judah	16JUN04	2.01	1
Busley	Willis	-----07	2.02	1	Bowerman	Judah	12JUN05	3.02	1
BOST					Borman	Judah	01AUG06	3.03	1
Baust	David	13AUG07	2.04	1	Bowerman	Judah	21AUG07	2.05	1
Baust	David	24JUN09	1.04	1	BOWYERS				
Bost	David	-----11	1.02	1	Bower	Adam	30JUL04	2.01	1
Bost	Peter	03APR90	1.01	1	Bowyers	Adam	31MAY05	3.02	1
Bosht	Peter	14MAY91	2.01	1	Boyers	John	14MAY89	6.01	1
Bost	Peter	08OCT92	1.02	1	Boyers	John	05APR90	1.01	1
Bosht	Peter	16AUG93	3.02	1	Boyers	John	08OCT92	1.02	1
Bost	Peter	23APR94	2.02	1	Boyers	John	16AUG93	3.02	1
Bost	Peter	28MAR95	3.03	1	Bowyer	Joseph	06AUG04	2.02	1
Bost	Peter	04AUG96	2.03	1	Bowyers	Joseph	31MAY05	3.02	1
Bost	Peter	23MAY97	1.02	1	Bowyer	Joseph	17JUL06	3.02	1
Bost	Peter	03JUL99	3.02	1	Bowyers	Joseph	08JUN07	2.01	1
Bost	Peter	30JUN00	3.04	1	Bowers	Joseph	20JUN08	2.01	1
Bost	Peter	09JUL01	3.03	1	Bowyers	Joseph	05JUN09	1.02	1
Bost	Peter	12AUG02	3.04	1	Bowers	Robert	20JUN08	2.01	1
Bost	Peter	-----03	2.01	1	Bowers	William	19JUL05	2.04	1
Bost	Peter	27JUL04	4.01	11	Bowers	William	19AUG06	2.06	1
Bost	Peter	25JUL05	2.05	12	Bowers	William	20JUN07	2.02	1
Bost	Peter	15JUL06	2.03	12	Bowers	William	24AUG08	2.03	1
Baust	Peter	13AUG07	2.04	11	Bowers	William	08JUN09	1.03	1
Bause	Peter	25AUG08	2.03	1	BOYD				
Baust	Peter	24JUN09	1.04	1	Boyd	Charles	13AUG89	2.02	1
Bost	Peter	-----11	1.02	11	Boyd	Charles	21MAY94	3.03	1
Best	Samuel	13AUG07	2.04	1	Boyd	George	13AUG89	2.02	1
Best	Samuel	25AUG08	2.03	1	Boyd	George	29MAR94	3.01	1
Best	Samuel	18AUG09	2.04	1	Boyd	George	01JUN97	3.04	1
Bost	Samuel	-----11	1.08	1	Boyd	Hugh	28JUL08	2.02	1
Bause	Valentine	25AUG08	2.03	1	Boyd	Hugh	08APR09	1.01	1
Bost	Valuntine	-----11	1.03	1	Boyd	Hugh	-----11	1.09	1
BOSTICK					Boyd	John	21JUL01	2.02	1
Bostick	John	19JUN06	1.01	1	BOYDER				
BOWDEN					Boyder	Nicholas	03JUN90	2.02	1
Bowden	William	05JUN09	2.02	1	BOYLES				
BOWDRY					Bowels	Benjamin	-----07	2.02	1
Bodry	James	29OCT88	1.01	1	Boyles -	David	23JUN90	1.02	1
Bowdery	James	29JUN89	5.01	1	Boyles	James	01JUN97	3.04	1
Bowdry	James	05APR91	1.02	1	Boyles	John	08JUL05	2.03	1
Bowdry	Lewis	05NOV88	1.01	1	Boyles	John	14AUG06	2.06	1
Boudrey	Samuel	27JUN87	2.01	1	Bowels	John	-----07	2.02	1
Bowdry	Samuel	01NOV88	1.02	1	Boyle	Patrick	11AUG01	2.21	
BOWEN						Retail Store			
Bowen	James	04JUL03	1.03	1	Boyles	Patrick	11AUG01	2.21	
Bowin	James	15JUN04	1.01	1		Tax paid by Patrick O'Hara			
Bowin	James	20JUN05	1.02	1	Boyles	Sally	08JUL05	2.03	F1
Bowen	James	21JUN06	1.01	1	Boyles	Sally	14AUG06	2.06	F1
Bowen	James	18JUN07	1.03	1	BRACKINRIDG				
Bowen	James	07JUN08	1.03	1	Brackinridg	George	16NOV92	3.02	1
Bowen	James	05JUL09	2.03	1	BRADEN				
Boen	James	-----11	1.07	1	Braden	John	20JUN01	3.04	1
BOWERS					Braden	John	14JUN03	3.02	11
Bawers	William W.	-----11	1.08	1	Braden	John	03AUG04	3.02	11
BOWLER					BRADFORD				
Boular	Larkin	31JUL06	2.05	1	Bradford	John	04JUN02	1.01	1
Boular	Lucy	01AUG06	2.05	F	Bradford	John	29JUN03	1.03	1
Bowler	Richa	30JUN89	2.01	1	BRADLEY				
BOWLES					Bradley	Daniel	05DEC92	3.04	1
Bowles	John	04AUG04	3.02	1	Bradley	Daniel	23MAY94	3.04	1
Boles	Pleasant	11JUN07	1.03	1	Bradley	Daniel	01JUN95	1.03	1
BOWLIN					Bradley	Daniel	-----96	1.03	1
Bowlen	Benjamin	-----11	1.07	1	Bradley	Daniel	15MAR97	2.01	1
Bowlin	James	10AUG97	1.04	1	Bradley	Daniel	13JUN00	1.01	11
Bowlin	John	10AUG97	1.04	1	Bradley	George	13JUN03	1.02	1
Bowlin	John	10JUL99	3.03	1	Bradley	George	15JUN04	1.01	1

surname	name	date	bk.pg	TM	surname	name	date	bk.pg	TM
Bradley	George	18JUN05	1.02	1	Breeden	John	31MAR90	2.01	1
Bradley	John	12MAY96	2.01	1	Breeding	John Sr	15OCT92	2.01	1
Bradley	John	08JUN97	1.02	1	Breeding	John	29SEP92	2.01	1
Bradley	John	26JUN99	3.02	1	Breeding	John	10AUG93	1.01	1
Bradley	John	13JUN00	1.01	1	Breeding	John	14AUG93	1.02	1
Bradley	John	19JUN00	3.02	1	Breeding	John	14MAY94	1.02	1
Bradley	John	02MAY01	3.01	1	Breeding	John	01JUN95	2.01	1
Bradley	John	27JUL02	3.03	1	Breeding	John	20JUN96	1.01	1
Bradley	John	21JUN03	1.02	1	Breeding	John	10MAY97	3.03	1
Bradley	John	11AUG03	2.04	1	Bredin	John	23JUN97	1.03	1
Bradley	John	05JUN04	4.04	1	Breedin	John	29JUL00	2.04	1
Bradley	John	18JUN04	1.01	1	Breeden	John	01JUN02	2.02	1
Bradley	John	06JUN05	1.01	1	Breadon	John	19JUN05	3.03	11
Bradley	John	27JUN05	2.03	1	Breden	John	17JUL06	3.02	11
Bradley	John	10JUN06	1.01	1	Breeding	Peter	30OCT88	1.01	1
Bradley	John	01AUG06	2.05	1	Breeding	Peter	24JUN89	5.01	1
Bradley	John	-----07	2.02	1	Breeden	Peter	02JUN90	2.02	1
Bradley	John	03JUL07	1.03	1	Breeding	Peter	20JUN96	1.01	1
Bradly	John	03JUN08	2.01	1	Breden	Peter	25JUL04	1.02	1
Bradley	John	11JUL09	1.05	1	BREHNER				
Bradley	John	-----11	1.05	11	Brehner	Jacob	03APR90	1.01	1
Bradley	Joseph	31JUL05	1.02	1	BREWER				
Bradley	Richard	12MAY97	3.02	1	Brewer	Gaits	14MAY08	1.02	1
Bradley	Samuel	20MAY97	3.02	1	Bruer	John	19MAY97	3.03	1
Bradley	Samuel	24JUL04	1.02	1	Brewer	John	21MAY99	2.01	1
Bradley	William	21MAY99	2.01	1	Brewer	John	18JUL06	2.04	1
BRADY					BRIDGES				
Brady	John	28JUL96	2.03	2	Bridges	Absalom	30JUN03	1.03	1
Brady	John	07JUN99	1.04	1	Bridges	Absolom	07AUG04	2.02	1
Brady	Samuel	20MAY95	2.02	1	Bridges	Absalom	15JUN05	1.02	1
Brady	Samuel	01JUN96	1.02	1	Bridges	Absalom	19JUN06	1.02	1
Brady	Samuel	27MAY99	1.03	1	Bridges	Absolom	02JUN07	1.03	1
Brady	Samuel	21JUN00	2.02	1	Bridges	Absalom	30APR08	1.02	1
Brady	Samuel	04APR01	2.01	1	Bridges	Absalom	29MAY09	2.02	1
Brady	Samuel	26JUN02	1.02	1	Bridges	Absalom	-----11	1.06	1
Brady	Samuel	20JUN03	2.02	1	Bridges	James	20MAY94	1.01	1
Brady	Thomas A.	01AUG04	1.02	1	Bridges	Jesse	15JUL01	2.02	1
BRADLEY					Bridges	John L.	18JUL06	2.04	1
Bradley	Thomas A.	30JUL05	1.02	1	Two lotts in Danville				
Bradley	Thomas A.	04AUG07	2.03	1	Bredger	John L.	17AUG07	2.05	1
BRADY					Paid tax for Edward Thursby				
Bready	Thomas A.	03AUG08	2.03	1	Bredger	John L.	17AUG07	2.05	
Brady	Thomas A.	30JUN09	1.05	1	Two town lotts in Danville				
Brady	Thomas A.	-----11	1.05	1	Bridges	John L.	29JUN08	2.02	1
Brady	William A.	30JUN09	1.05	1	Paid tax for Edward Thursby				
BRANON					BRIGGS				
Branon	John	27JUN01	2.02	1	Briggs	Benjamin	14MAY90	1.01	1
BRASFIELD					Briggs	Benjamin	24JUN91	2.01	1
Brasfield	Roy	05DEC92	3.04	1	Briggs	Benjamin	06OCT92	1.01	1
BRAY					Briggs	Benjamin	24AUG93	3.02	1
Bray	Henry	29JUL05	1.02	1	Briggs	Benjamin	12JUN94	2.02	1
BREEDING					Briggs	Benjamin	17APR95	3.02	1
Breden	Abraham	25JUL04	1.02	1	Briggs	Benjamin	12MAY96	2.01	1
Breeding	George	14NOV88	1.01	1	Briggs	Benjamin	23JUN97	1.03	1
Breeding	George	23JUN89	5.01	1	Briggs	Benjamin	05JUN99	1.04	1
Breeden	George	31MAR90	2.01	1	Briggs	Benjamin	28JUN00	2.03	1
Breeden	George	13APR91	1.01	1	Briggs	Benjamin	02AUG02	2.03	1
Breeding	George	04OCT92	2.01	11	Briggs	Benjamin	21JUL03	3.03	1
Breeding	George	10AUG93	1.01	1	Briggs	Benjamin	03MAY04	3.02	1
Breeding	George	21MAY94	1.01	11	Briggs	Benjamin	29JUN05	3.03	1
Breeding	George	01JUN95	2.01	11	Briggs	Benjamin	29JUL06	3.03	1
Breeding	George	20JUN96	1.01	12	Paid tax for Joseph Briggs				
Breeding	George	10MAY97	3.03	1	Briggs	Benjamin	12JUN07	2.02	1
Breeding	George	10MAY97	3.03	11	Paid tax for Joseph Briggs				
Breeding	George Jr	20MAY99	1.03	1	Briggs	Benjamin	30MAY08	2.01	1
Breeding	George Sr	20MAY99	1.03	1	Paid tax for Joseph Briggs				
Breeden	George	04JUN00	2.02	2	Briggs	Benjamin	30JUN09	1.05	1
Breeden	George Sr	10AUG01	2.03	2	Paid tax for Joseph Briggs				
Breeding	George	10MAY02	2.02	2	Briggs	Benjamin	-----11	1.05	1
Breeding	James	20MAY99	1.02	1	Briggs	Benj.	-----11	1.05	
Bredin	James	30JUL05	1.02	1	Paid tax for Jo. Briggs				
Breeding	John	23JUN89	5.01	1	Briggs	Betsey	02JUN08	1.02	F

surname	name	date	bk.pg	TM	surname	name	date	bk.pg	TM
Briggs	John	29MAY90	1.01	1	Broils	Zachariah	24JUL05	2.05	1
Briggs	Joseph	05JUN99	1.01	M1	Broils	Zachariah	28MAR06	2.01	1
Briggs	Joseph	08JUL00	2.03	M1	Broiler	Zacheriah	12AUG07	2.04	1
Briggs	Joseph	29JUL06	3.03	1	Broiles	Zecky	25AUG08	2.03	1
Taxes pd by Benjamin Briggs					Broiles	Zachariah	09JUN09	1.03	1
Briggs	Joseph	12JUN07	2.02		Briles	Zacheriah	01JUL00	3.05	1
Taxes pd by Benjamin Briggs					BRISCOE				
Briggs	Joseph	30MAY08	2.01	0	Briscoe	Edward	26JUN89	6.01	1
Tax pd by Benjamin Briggs					Briscoe	Edward	23JUN90	1.01	1
Briggs	Joseph	30JUN09	1.05	0	Briscoe	Phillip	19MAY97	3.03	1
Paid by Benjamin Briggs					Brisco	William	04JUN02	1.01	1
Briggs	Jo	-----11	1.05	0	Briscoe	William	15JUN03	1.02	1
Briggs	Jo	-----11	1.05	0	Brisco	William	20JUN04	1.01	1
Taxes paid by Benj. Briggs					Brisco	William	17JUN05	1.02	1
Briggs	Mary	24AUG93	3.02	F	Brisco	William	20JUN06	1.01	1
Briggs	Mary	12JUN94	2.02	F	Brisco	William	30JUN07	1.01	1
Briggs	Mary	08AUG97	1.03	F1	Brisco	William	06JUN08	1.02	1
Brigs	Samuel	24AUG87	1.01	12	Brisco	William	05JUL09	2.03	1
Briggs	Samuel	19MAY89	6.02	1	BRISTORAL				
Briggs	Samuel	13AUG90	1.02	1	Bristoral	Matthias	10MAY96	2.01	1
Briggs	Samuel	20APR91	2.01	1	BRITON				
BRIGHT					Briton	Levi	19JUN99	2.02	1
Bright	David	19MAY06	2.02	1	BROCK				
Bright	David	-----07	2.03	1	Brock	Elizabeth	-----11	1.09	F1
Bright	David	17JUN08	1.04	1	Brock	Evan	10JUN03	3.02	1
Bride	David	19AUG09	2.04	1	Brock	Evan	04AUG04	3.02	1
Bright	Elizabeth	10MAR95	1.02	F	Brock	Evan	13JUN05	3.02	1
Bright	George	-----07	2.03	1	Brock	Evan	31JUL06	3.03	1
Bright	George	18AUG09	2.03	1	Brock	Even	10JUN07	2.01	1
Bright	Henry	27JUN89	2.01	1	Brock	Even	03JUN08	2.01	1
Bright	Henry	26NOV92	3.02	1	Brock	Evan	28JUN09	1.04	1
Bright	Henry	05AUG93	1.01	1	Brock	Henry	12JUN07	1.03	1
Bright	Henry	13MAY94	1.01	1	Brook	Joshua	30MAY05	2.02	1
Bright	Henry	20MAY95	2.02	1	Brock	Richard	12JUN97	1.02	1
Bright	Henry	08JUN96	1.01	1	Brook	Richard	08JUL00	2.03	1
Bright	Henry	21MAY97	3.02	1	Brock	Richard	30MAY01	3.04	1
Bright	Henry	29MAY99	1.03	1	Brock	Richard	05AUG02	2.03	1
Bright	Henry	07JUL00	2.03	1	Brock	Richard	18JUL03	3.03	1
Bright	Henry	04APR01	2.01	1	Brock	Richard	24AUG04	3.03	1
Bright	Henry	17JUN02	3.01	1	Brock	Richard	12JUN05	3.02	1
Bright	Henry	14JUN03	2.01	1	Brock	Richard	16JUL06	3.02	11
Bright	Henry	13AUG04	1.03	1	Brock	Thomas	24AUG04	3.03	1
Bright	Henry	13AUG04	1.03	1	BRONAUGH				
Bright	Henry	23JUL05	2.05	1	Bronaugh	Thomas	20JUN96	2.02	1
Bright	Henry	19MAY06	2.02	11	Bronaugh	Thomas	17MAY97	1.03	1
Bright	Henry	09JUN07	2.01	11	Bronaugh	Thomas	16JUL99	3.03	1
Bright	Henry	17JUN08	1.04	11	Bronough	Thomas	28JUN00	3.03	1
Bright	Henry	18AUG09	2.03	21	Bronough	Thomas	07JUL01	3.03	1
Bright	Henry	-----11	1.08	2	Brenaugh	Thomas	20JUN03	2.01	1
Bright	Jacob	27JUN89	2.01	1	Bernaugh	Thomas	28JUL04	4.01	1
Bright	Jacob	09OCT92	1.02	1	Brenaugh	Thomas	24MAY05	2.02	1
Bright	Jacob	17AUG93	3.02	1	Brenaugh	Thomas	04APR06	2.01	1
Bright	John	27JUN89	2.01	1	Bronaugh	Thomas L.	04AUG07	2.03	1
Bright	John	28MAY91	3.01	1	Bronaugh	Thomas	25AUG08	2.03	1
Bright	John	03DEC92	3.03	1	Bronaugh	Thomas	21JUN09	1.04	1
Bright	Michael	08JUN02	3.01	1	Bronaugh	Thomas	-----11	1.02	1
Bright	Michael	17JUN03	2.01	1	Bronaugh	Talifero	20JUN96	2.02	1
Bright	Ned	23AUG09	2.03		Bronaugh	Taliaferro	17MAY97	1.03	1
A free neagro					Bronaugh	Taliferro	16JUL99	3.03	1
Bright	William	26SEP92	1.01	1	Bronough	Tollever	28JUN00	3.03	1
Bright	William	01JUN96	1.02	1	Bronough	Telifaro	07JUL01	3.03	1
Bright	William	29MAY99	1.04	1	Brenaugh	Toliver	24MAY02	3.01	1
Bright	William	24MAY00	2.01	1	Brenaugh	Toliver	20JUN03	2.02	1
BRILES					Bernaugh	Talifero	28JUL04	4.01	1
Briles	Elizabeth	-----11	1.03	F	Brenaugh	Toliver	13MAY05	2.02	1
Briles	Julius	-----11	1.03	1	Brenaugh	Toliver	04APR06	2.01	1
Broyles	Michael	03JUL99	3.02	1	Bronough	Tolliver	13AUG07	2.04	1
Briles	Michael	27JUN00	3.03	1	Bronaugh	Tolliver	25AUG08	2.04	1
Brailes	Thomas	-----11	1.02	1	Bronaugh	Tolliferro	10JUN09	1.03	1
Broiles	Zechariah	20MAY01	3.02	1	Bronaugh	Toliver	-----11	1.02	1
Briles	Zachariah	14AUG02	3.04	1	Bronaugh	William	02JUN94	3.04	1
Briles	Zachariah	25JUL03	2.02	1	Bronaugh	William	28MAR95	3.03	11

surname	name	date	bk.pg	TM	surname	name	date	bk.pg	TM
Bronaugh	William	20JUN96	2.02	1	Brown	Ezekiel	30APR08	1.02	1
Bronaugh	William	17MAY97	1.03	1	Brown	Ezekiel	-----11	1.07	1
Bronaugh	William	16JUL99	3.03	1	Brown	Frances C.	25AUG08	2.03	1
Bronough	William	28JUN00	3.03	1	Brown	Gaffick	28MAY91	3.02	1
Bronough	William	08JUL01	3.03	1	Brown	Garfield	26JUN87	2.01	1
Brenaugh	William	14AUG02	3.04	1	Brown	Garfield	27JUN89	2.01	1
Brenaugh	William	25JUL03	2.02	1	Brown	Henry	07MAY91	3.01	1
Bronaugh	William	26JUL04	4.03	1	Brown	Henry	26NOV92	3.02	1
Brenaugh	William	13MAY05	2.02	1	Brown	Henry Sr	02JUN94	3.04	1
Brenaugh	William	28MAR06	2.01	1	Brown	Henry Jr	22MAY94	3.05	1
Broughnah	William	04AUG07	2.03	1	Brown	Henry Sr	25MAR95	1.01	1
Bronaugh	William	25AUG08	2.04	1	Brown	Henry Jr	25MAR95	1.01	1
Bronaugh	William	21JUN09	1.04	1	Brown	Henry Sr	-----96	1.02	1
Bronaugh	William	-----11	1.02	11	Brown	Henry Jr	-----96	1.02	1
BROOKS					Brown	Horasha G.	24JUN07	1.03	1
Brook	Elisha	24MAY05	2.02	1	Brown	James	28MAY91	3.01	1
Brooks	Elisha	09AUG06	2.05	1	Brown	James	26NOV92	3.02	1
Bruks	George	05MAY94	2.02	1	Brown	James	23JUN00	2.02	1
Brooks	George	31MAR95	3.03	1	Brown	James	23JUL01	3.05	1
Brooks	George	20MAY96	2.01	1	Brown	James	04AUG02	2.03	1
Brooks	George	10MAY97	1.03	1	Brown	James	15JUL03	3.03	M1
Brooks	George	16JUL99	3.03	1	Brown	James	21AUG04	3.03	1
Brooks	George	24JUN00	3.02	1	Brown	James	25JUL05	2.05	1
Brooks	George	24JUN00	3.02	1	Brown	James	14AUG05	3.03	1
Brooks	George	18MAY01	3.02	1	Brown	Jesse	04AUG07	2.04	1
Brooks	George	07AUG02	3.03	1	Brown	John	21JUN87	2.01	1
Brooks	George	30JUL03	2.03	11	Brown	John	24JUN89	5.01	1
Brooks	George	28JUN04	4.02	11	Brown	John	03JUN90	2.02	1
Brooks	George	19JUL05	2.03	11	Brown	John	30MAR91	1.01	1
Brooks	George	14AUG06	2.06	11	Brown	John	05DEC92	3.04	1
Brooks	James	29APR95	3.02	0	Brown	John	29MAY94	1.01	1
Brooks	John	13AUG07	2.04	1	Brown	John	13JUN96	2.02	1
Brooks	Joshua	30JUL03	2.03	1	Brown	John	30JUN96	1.02	1
Brooks	Joshua	28JUN04	4.02	1	Brown	John	16MAY97	1.02	1
Brooks	Joshua	09AUG06	2.05	1	Brown	John	29MAY97	3.03	1
Bruks	William	22MAY94	2.02	1	Brown	John	23JUN02	1.02	1
Brooks	William	18APR95	3.02	1	Brown	John	22JUN03	1.02	1
Brooks	William	-----11	1.06	1	Brown	John	-----04	1.02	1
BROUNTS					Brown	John	31JUL05	1.02	1
Brounts	Hannah	28JUN87	1.01	F	Brown	John	04AUG06	3.04	1
BROWN					Brown	John	04AUG06	3.37	1
Brown	Barola	28MAY91	3.02	1	Brown	John	07MAY07	1.02	1
Brown	Benagah	31MAY97	3.03	1	Brown	John	18APR08	1.01	1
Brown	Benjamin	28MAY91	3.02	1	Brown	John	30APR08	1.02	1
Brown	Benjamin	10NOV92	3.02	1	Brown	John	04JUL09	2.03	1
Brown	Benjamin	29MAR94	3.01	1	Brown	Joseph	27JUN89	2.01	11
Brown	Caleb	21JUL01	3.05	1	Brown	Joseph	28MAY91	3.02	1
Brown	Caleb	04AUG02	2.03	1	Brown	Joseph	28NOV92	3.03	1
Brown	Caleb	18JUN05	2.02	1	Brown	Joseph	22MAY94	3.05	1
Brown	Caleb	02AUG06	2.05	1	Brown	Joseph	25MAR95	1.01	1
Brown	Caleb	-----07	2.02	1	Brown	Joseph	-----96	1.02	1
Brown	Caleb	25JUL08	2.02	1	Brown	Joshua	-----07	2.02	1
Brown	Caleb	13JUL09	1.06	1	Brown	Mathew	26MAY07	1.02	1
Brown	Caleb	-----11	1.09	1	Brown	Mathew	18APR08	1.01	1
Brown	Christopher	02AUG06	2.05	1	Brown	Mathew	04JUL09	2.03	1
Brown	Christopher	-----07	2.02	1	Brown	Morris	19MAY89	6.01	1
Brown	Christopher	25AUG08	2.03	1	Brown	Morris	02JUN90	1.02	1
Brown	Christopher	07JUN09	1.02	1	Brown	Morrice	21JUN91	2.01	1
Brown	Elisha	20JUN03	1.02	1	Brown	Morrice	28SEP92	1.02	1
Brown	Elisha	30JUN04	1.01	1	Brown	Morrice	13AUG93	3.02	1
Brown	Elisha	29JUN05	1.02	1	Brown	Morris	10JUN94	2.02	1
Brown	Elisha	30JUL06	1.02	1	Brown	Morris	10APR95	3.03	1
Brown	Elisha	25MAY07	1.02	1	Brown	Morris	12MAY96	2.01	1
Brown	Elisha	07JUN08	1.03	1	Brown	Morris	12JUN97	1.02	1
Brown	Elisha	20JUN09	2.03	1	Brown	Morris	06JUN99	1.02	1
Brown	Elisha	-----11	1.06	1	Brown	Morris	28JUN00	2.03	11
Brown	Elizabeth	20AUG93	1.01	F	Brown	Morris	20JUN01	3.04	11
Brown	Elliott	19APR91	2.01	1	Brown	Maurice	09JUN02	2.02	12
Brown	Ellis	14JUN05	3.02	1	Brown	Morris	31APR03	3.02	12
Brown	Ellis	16JUL06	3.02	1	Brown	Maurice	31JUL04	3.02	13
Brown	Eake	05JUL06	3.02	11	Brown	Maurice	14JUN05	3.02	12
Brown	Ezekiel	04JUN07	1.03	1	Brown	Mauris	16JUL06	3.02	13

surname	name	date	bk.pg	TM	surname	name	date	bk.pg	TM
Brown	Maurice	10JUN07	2.01	12	Brinton	Bryan	29JUL06	2.04	11
Brown	Maurice	14JUN08	2.01	12	Brumston	James	09AUG03	2.04	1
Brown	Maurice	30JUN09	1.05	3	Brinton	James	-----05	2.36	1
Brown	Morris	-----11	1.05	11	Brumton	James	20JUN05	2.03	1
Brown	Moses	30MAY99	2.01	1	Brinton	James	29JUL06	2.04	1
Brown	Nancy	03DEC92	3.03	F	BRUNK				
Brown	Nathaniel	29JUN08	2.02	1	Brunk	Jacob	30MAY89	6.01	1
Brown	Nathaniel	08JUN09	1.03	1	BRUSH				
Brown	Robert	04JUN00	2.02	M1	Brush	Crain	04JUN95	2.02	1
Brown	Robert	04APR01	2.01	M1	Bush	Crane	30JUN96	1.01	1
Brown	Robert	07JUN02	3.01	M1	Brush	James	04JUN95	2.02	1
Brown	Robert	04JUN03	2.01	M1	Brish	James	30JUN96	1.02	1
Brown	Robert	23JUL04	1.01	1	Brush	Richard	12OCT92	2.02	1
Brown	Robert	03JUN05	2.02	1	Brush	Richard	14AUG93	1.02	1
Brown	Robert	30MAY06	2.02	1	Brush	Richard	30MAY94	1.01	1
Brown	Robert	-----07	2.02	1	Brush	Richard	04JUN95	2.02	1
Brown	Stephen	13JUN05	1.02	1	Bush	Richard	28JUN96	1.01	1
Brown	Stephen	18JUN06	1.01	1	Brush	Richard	13MAY97	3.02	1
Brown	Stephen	11JUN07	1.03	1	Brush	Richard	30MAY99	2.01	1
Brown	Stephen	10JUN08	1.03	1	Brush	Richard	20JUN00	1.01	1
Brown	Stephen	05JUN09	2.02	1	Brush	Richard	10JUN01	1.01	1
Brown	Stephen	-----11	1.06	1	Brush	Richard	28JUN02	1.02	1
Brown	Thomas	15AUG09	1.06	1	Brush	Richard	20JUN03	1.02	1
Brown	Thomas	-----11	1.04	11	Bresh	Richard	20JUN04	1.01	1
Brown	William	13MAR95	1.02	1	Brush	William	04JUN95	2.01	1
Brown	William	24JUN00	3.02	1	BRYANT				
Brown	William	08JUL02	3.02	1	Bryant	Bryan	08JUN04	4.04	11
Brown	William	01AUG03	2.03	1	Bryant	David	04JUL99	3.02	1
Brown	William	19MAY06	2.02	1	Bryan	David	30JUN00	3.03	1
Brown	William	17JUN08	1.04	1	Bryan	David	20MAY01	3.02	1
Brown	Willis	-----11	1.02	1	Bryan	David	16AUG02	3.05	1
BROWNING					Bryan	David	28JUL04	4.01	1
Browning	Luke	13JUN96	2.02	1	Bryan	David	31JUL05	2.05	1
BROWNLEE					Bryan	David	04APR06	2.01	1
Brownlee	Alexander	27JUN87	2.01	1	Briant	David	04AUG07	2.03	1
Brownlee	Alexander	15NOV88	1.01	1	Bryan	David	03AUG08	2.02	1
Brounlee	Alexander	07AUG89	5.02	1	Bryant	David	22JUN09	1.04	1
Brownlee	John	14JUN87	2.01	1	Bryan	David	-----11	1.03	1
BRUCE					Bryan	James	16MAY89	6.01	1
Bruce	Elijah	20MAY06	2.02	1	Bryant	James	21APR90	1.02	1
Bruce	William	16MAY97	1.02	1	Bryan	James	19APR91	2.01	1
Bruce	William	12JUN99	1.02	1	Bryant	James	17SEP92	1.02	1
Bruce	William	17JUL00	2.03	1	Bryan	James	08AUG93	3.01	1
Bruce	William	28JUL01	2.03	1	Brian	James	17APR94	2.02	0
Bruce	William	30JUN02	3.02	1	Bryan	James	25MAR95	1.01	1
Bruce	William	01AUG03	2.03	1	Bryan	James	-----96	1.02	1
Broos	William	25JUL04	1.02	1	Bryent	Jessee	22JUN03	1.02	1
Broos	William	25JUL04	1.02	1	Brient	Jessee	12JUN06	1.01	1
Bruce	William	03JUN05	2.02	1	Bryant	Jesse	10JUN08	1.03	1
Bruce	William	19MAY06	2.02	1	Bryant	Jesse	16JUN09	2.03	1
Bruce	William	-----07	2.03	1	Bryant	John	27JUN89	2.01	1
Broos	William	17JUN08	1.04	1	Bryant	John	01JUL89	2.02	1
Bruce	William	23AUG09	2.04	1	Bryant	John	19APR91	3.01	1
Bruce	William	-----11	1.08	1	Bryant	John	02JUN91	3.02	1
BRUMINGHAM					Bryant	John	13JUL91	3.02	1
Brumingham	Thomas	06APR97	3.03	1	Bryant	John	28NOV92	3.03	1
BRUMPTON					Bryant	John	-----93	3.01	1
Brumpton	Brian	26JUL87	1.01	1	Bryant	John	-----93	2.01	
Brumpton	Bryan	26JUN89	6.01	1	Paid tax for Obediah Garrant				
Brumpton	Bryant	23JUN90	1.02	1	Bryant	John	02JUN94	3.04	1
Brumpton	Bryant	19AUG91	2.02	1	Bryant	John	12MAR95	1.01	1
Brumpton	Bryant	26SEP92	1.01	1	Bryan	John	09APR95	3.01	1
Brumpton	Bryan	08AUG93	3.01	1	Bryant	John	-----96	1.01	1
Brumpton	Bryan	02MAY95	3.02	1	Bryant	John	04JUN96	2.02	1
Brumton	Briant	24JUN96	2.02	1	Bryant	John	07JUN97	1.02	1
Branton	Bryan	10AUG97	1.04	1	Brient	John	20JUN03	1.02	1
Brinton	Bryan	10JUL99	3.03	11	Bryant	Josiah	24MAY99	3.02	1
Brinton	Bryan	10JUL00	3.05	11	Bryant	Josiah	11JUL00	3.05	1
Brumpton	Bryan	31JUL01	3.04	11	Bryan	Josiah	29JUL01	3.04	1
Brumton	Bryant	29JUL02	3.03	21	Bryant	Josiah	10JUN02	2.02	1
Brumston	Bryan	09AUG03	2.04	11	Briant	Josiah	05AUG03	3.03	1
Brumton	Bryant	20JUN05	2.03	11	Bryant	Joseph	06APR04	4.03	1

surname	name	date	bk.pg	TM	surname	name	date	bk.pg	TM
Bryan	Robert	01JUL00	3.05	1	Buckhannon	William	10JUN03	1.01	1
Bryan	Robert	10JUL01	3.03	1	Buckhannon	William	26JUL04	1.02	1
Bryan	Robert	16AUG02	3.05	1	Buckhannon	William	04JUN05	1.01	1
Bryan	Robert	25JUL03	2.03	1	Buckhannon	William	13JUN06	1.02	00
Bryon	Robert	27JUL04	4.01	1	Buckhannon	William	20MAY07	1.02	1
Bryan	Robert	23JUL05	2.04	1	Free from county levy				
Bryan	Robert	13AUG07	2.04	1	BUCK				
Bryan	Robert	03AUG08	2.02	1	Buck	Thomas	30MAR95	3.03	0
Bryant	Robert	09JUN09	1.03	1	BUCKNER				
Bryant	Robert	-----11	1.02	1	Buckner	Thomas	08JUN89	6.05	
Bryant	William	13JUL91	3.02	1	Listed with Jacob Myers				
Bryant	William	01DEC92	3.03	1	Buckner	Thomas	04NOV92	3.02	1
Bryant	William	01DEC92	3.03	1	Buckner	Thomas	10APR95	1.03	1
Brian	William	01MAY94	2.02	21	Buckner	Thomas	-----96	1.02	1
Bryant	William	21MAY94	3.03	1	Bucknor	William	28MAY99	1.04	1
Bryant	William	25MAR95	1.01	1	Buckner	William	24MAY00	2.01	1
Bryan	William	05JUN95	3.01	11	Buckner	William	30JUN01	2.02	1
Bryant	William	-----96	1.01	1	Buckner	William	22JUL01	2.02	1
Bryant	William	13JUL96	2.02	1	Buckner	William	09AUG02	1.03	1
Bryan	William	19AUG96	2.03	26	BUFORD				
Bryan	William	13JUN97	1.01	2	Bufort	Henry	07JUN08	1.03	1
Bryant	William	29JUN99	3.02	1	Buford	Henry	14JUN09	2.02	1
Bryan	William	04JUL99	3.03	2	Burford	James	29OCT92	2.02	12
Bryan	William	30JUN00	3.03	1	Buford	John	01JUL89	2.02	1
Bryan	William	01JUL00	3.04	1	Burford	John	28OCT92	2.02	1
Bryan	William Sr	10JUL01	3.03	1	Buford	Thomas	27MAY99	1.03	1
Bryant	William	14AUG02	3.04	1	Buford	Thomas	09JUL00	2.03	1
Bryan	William	16AUG02	3.04	1	Buford	Thomas	17JUL01	2.02	1
Bryant	William	22JUN03	2.02	1	Buford	Thomas	04AUG02	3.03	1
Bryan	William	25JUL03	2.02	1	Buford	Thomas	18JUN03	2.01	1
Bryant	William	28JUL04	4.01	1	Buford	William	07APR91	1.01	1
Bryan	William	12AUG04	4.02	2	Burford	William	28OCT92	2.02	11
Bryant	William	17JUN05	3.02	1	Booford	William	06AUG93	1.01	11
Bryan	William	23JUL05	2.04	1	Booford	William	20MAY94	1.01	11
Bryant	William	25JUL05	2.05	1	Booford	William	16JUN95	2.02	11
Bryan	William	17JUL06	2.03	1	Bouford	William	10JUN96	1.01	11
Bryant	William	03AUG07	2.03	1	Buford	William	14JUN97	3.04	12
Bryan	William	13AUG07	2.04	1	Buford	William	30MAY99	1.01	11
Bryant	William	01AUG08	2.02	1	Buford	William	18JUL00	2.04	11
Bryan	William	25AUG08	2.04	2	BULEY				
Bryant	William	21JUN09	1.03	1	Buley	Harison	-----11	1.06	1
Bryant	William	22JUN09	1.04	1	Buley	Isaac	-----11	1.06	1
Bryan	William	-----11	1.08	1	Buley	Isaiah	23MAY09	2.02	1
Bryan	William	-----11	1.08	1	Buley	Jesse	17JUN08	1.03	1
Bryant	William Cpt	-----11	1.03	2	Buley	Jesse	23MAY09	2.02	1
BRYDON					Buley	Josiah	-----11	1.06	1
Brydon	Barbara	13AUG89	2.02	F	Buley	Nathan	17JUN08	1.03	21
Brydon	Robert	27JUN89	2.01	1	Buley	Nathan	23MAY09	2.02	
BUCHANAN					Exempt from county levy				
Buckhann	Andrew	22MAY94	3.04	1	Buley	Nathan	-----11	1.06	1
Buckhann	Andrew	10MAY99	2.01	1	BULL				
Buckhannon	Andrew	30JUL00	1.01	1	Bull	Abraham	19AUG91	2.02	1
Buckhannon	Andrew	29MAY01	1.01	1	Bull	Isaiah	31JUL06	1.03	1
Buckhannon	Andrew	28JUN02	1.02	1	Bull	Isaiah Jr	31JUL06	1.03	1
Buckhannon	Andrew	10JUN03	1.01	1	Bull	Isaiah	06MAY07	1.01	1
Buckhanan	James	08JUL05	2.03	1	Bull	Isaiah Jr	06MAY07	1.01	1
Buckhanon	James	13AUG06	2.06	1	Bull	Richard	02OCT92	2.01	1
Buckhannon	John	29MAY01	1.01	1	BULLOCK				
Buckhannon	John	20MAY07	1.02	1	Bullock	James	12MAY97	3.02	1
Buckanan	Nathaniel	24MAY97	3.02	1	Bullock	Richard	12MAY97	3.02	11
Buckhannon	William	04AUG89	5.02	11	BUNCH				
Buckanan	William	03APR90	2.01	11	Bunch	Charles	10JUN02	1.01	1
Buckhonon	William	10NOV92	3.02	1	Buntch	Charles	15JUN05	1.02	1
Buckhannon	William	21MAY94	3.03	1	Buntch	Charles	19JUN06	1.01	1
Buckanon	William	13MAR95	1.02	1	Bunch	Charles	02JUN07	1.02	11
Buckanon	William	-----96	1.02	2	Bunch	Charles	27APR08	1.02	1
Buckanon	William	15MAR97	2.01	1	Bunch	Charles	12MAY09	2.01	1
Buckhann	William	10MAY99	2.01	11	Bunsh	Drury	20MAY97	3.03	1
Buckhannon	William	07JUN00	1.01	1	Bunsh	George	20MAY97	3.03	1
Buckhannon	William	29MAY01	1.01	1	Bunch	George	19JUN99	2.02	1
Buckhannon	William Sr	29MAY01	1.01	1	Bunsh	James	20MAY97	3.03	1
Buckhannon	William	28JUN02	1.02	1	Bunch	James	19JUN99	2.02	1

surname	name	date	bk.pg	TM	surname	name	date	bk.pg	TM
Buntch	James	21JUN06	1.01	1	Burdet	Joseph	10MAR95	1.02	1
Bunch	James	20JUN07	1.01	1	Burdett	Joseph	-----96	1.01	11
BUNDY					Berdit	Joseph	-----11	1.10	1
Bunder	James	28JUN00	3.03	M1	Burdit	Joshua	01JUL89	2.02	1
Bundy	James	30JUN01	2.02	1	Burdet	Joshua	07MAY91	3.01	1
Bunday	Reuben	24MAY99	2.01	1	Burdet	Joshua	16NOV92	3.02	1
Bundy	Reuben	30JUN01	2.02	1	Benny	Joshua	10AUG93	3.01	1
BUNTON					Burditt	Joshua	22MAY94	3.04	1
Buntting	John	17JUN01	3.02	1	Burdet	Joshua	10MAR95	1.02	1
Bunton	William	18APR89	6.01	1	Burdett	Joshua	-----96	1.01	1
Bunton	William	20APR91	2.01	1	BURGESS				
Bunton	William	09OCT92	1.02	1	Burges	Harden	29JUN05	3.03	M1
Bunting	William	30APR94	2.02	1	Burgess	Harden	27JUN08	2.02	1
BURCH					Burgess	Harden	13MAY09	1.02	1
Burch	Benjamin	12MAY89	6.01	1	Burges	William	18AUG06	2.06	12
Burt	Benjamin	29JUN89	5.01	1	Burgess	William Sr	04AUG07	2.04	2
Burch	Benjamin Jr	13MAY89	6.01	1	Burgess	William	27JUN08	2.02	11
Burch	Benjamin	20APR90	1.02	12	Burgess	William	13MAY09	1.02	1
Burch	Benjamin Jr	21APR90	1.02	1	BURK				
Burch	Benjamin	19APR91	2.01	11	Burks	Allen	09AUG93	3.01	1
Burt	Benjamin	05JUL91	1.02	1	Burks	Allin	10APR95	3.03	1
Burch	Benjamin	12SEP92	1.02	11	Burks	Allen	01JUN96	2.01	1
Burch	Benjamin	17SEP92	1.02	1	Burks	Allen	04AUG02	2.03	1
Burt	Benjamin	10OCT92	2.01	1	Burks	Allen	06JUN03	3.02	1
Burch	Benjamin Sr	05AUG93	3.01	11	Burkes	Allen	06AUG04	3.03	1
Burch	Benjamin Jr	20AUG93	3.02	12	Burks	Allen	14AUG05	3.03	1
Burch	Benjamin	05MAY94	2.02	11	Burks	Allen	23AUG06	3.04	1
Burch	Benjamin	30MAR95	3.03	1	Burk	George	28JUN87	1.01	1
Burch	Benjamin	30MAY96	2.01	1	Burks	George	19MAY89	6.01	1
Burch	Benjamin	12MAR97	2.01	1	Burks	George	02JUN90	1.02	1
Burch	Benjamin	14MAY99	2.02	1	Burks	George	23JUN91	2.01	1
Burch	Benjamin	19JUN00	1.01	1	Burks	George	20AUG93	3.02	1
Burch	Benjamin	22JUN01	1.02	1	Burks	George	20MAY94	2.01	1
Burch	Benjamin	02JUN02	1.01	1	Burks	George	19JUL00	2.03	1
Burtch	Benjamin	14JUN03	1.02	1	Burks	George	04AUG02	2.03	1
Burtch	Benjamin	14JUN04	1.01	1	Burks	George	06JUN03	3.02	1
Burtch	Benjamin	07JUN05	1.01	1	Burkes	George	07AUG04	3.03	1
Burtch	Benjamin	11JUN06	1.02	1	Burks	George	08JUL05	3.03	1
Burch	Benjamin	18MAY07	1.02	1	Burks	George	23AUG06	3.04	1
Burch	Benjamin	07JUN08	1.03	1	Burks	Levi	06JUN03	3.02	1
Birch	Benjamin	23MAY09	2.02	1	Burkes	Levi	22AUG04	3.03	1
Birch	Benjamin	-----11	1.06	1	Burks	Levi	16AUG05	3.04	1
Burch	John	25SEP92	1.01	1	Burks	Levi	23AUG06	3.04	1
Burch	John	05AUG93	3.01	1	Burks	Levi	10JUL09	1.05	1
Burt	Moses	17NOV88	1.01	12	Burks	Levy	-----11	1.07	1
Burt	Moses	03JUL89	5.01	12	Burks	Mathew	22JUN09	1.04	1
Burch	Moza	12SEP92	1.02	1	Berks	Matthew	-----11	1.02	1
Burch	Moza	09AUG93	3.01	1	Burks	Rollin	18JUL97	1.03	1
Burch	Moses	12MAY94	2.01	1	Burks	Rolling	02JUL99	1.04	1
Burch	Moses	30MAR95	3.03	1	Burks	Roland	31JUL00	2.04	1
Burch	Moses	12MAR97	2.01	1	Burks	Roland	13JUL01	3.04	1
Burch	Moza	14MAY99	2.02	1	Burks	Roland	26MAY02	2.02	1
Burch	Moza	17JUN00	1.01	1	Burks	Rolen	18JUN03	3.03	1
Burch	Moza	04JUN01	1.01	1	Burkes	Rolling	04AUG04	3.02	1
Burch	Moses	-----11	1.05	1	Burks	Roland	16AUG05	3.04	1
BURCHWELL					Burks	Roland	28JUN06	3.04	1
Burchwell	Isaac	31JUL00	2.04	1	Burk	William	24AUG87	1.01	12
Burchwell	Isaac	02JUN01	2.01	1	Burks	William	19MAY89	6.01	1
Burtchfield	Isaac	04JUL03	1.03	1	Burks	William	02JUN90	1.02	1
Burcher	Isach	30JUN02	1.02	1	Burks	William	21JUN91	2.01	1
Burcher	John	29JUL06	2.04	1	Burks	William	28SEP92	1.02	1
BURDETT					Burks	William	10AUG93	3.01	1
Burdet	Featherick	16NOV92	3.02	1	Burck	William	04JUL99	3.02	1
Burdett	Frederick	-----93	3.01	1	Burks	William	09JUL01	3.03	1
Bardett	Frederick	29MAY94	3.02	1	Burk	William	12AUG02	3.04	1
Burdet	Fredrick	10MAR95	1.02	1	Burk	William	-----03	2.01	1
Burdett	Frederick	-----96	1.01	1	Burks	William	07JUN03	3.02	1
Burdet	James	16NOV92	3.02	1	Burkes	William	07AUG04	3.03	11
Burdett	John	-----96	1.01	1	Burks	William	16AUG05	3.04	1
Burdit	Joseph	01JUL89	2.02	1	Burks	Willis	16AUG05	3.04	1
Burdet	Joseph	19APR91	3.01	1	Burks	Willis	04AUG06	3.04	1
Burdet	Joseph	26NOV92	3.02	1	Burks	Willis	-----11	1.07	1

surname	name	date	bk.pg	TM	surname	name	date	bk.pg	TM
BURNS					Butcher	John	05JUL91	1.02	1
Burns	Arthur	30JUN97	1.03	1	Butcher	John	10JUL99	3.03	1
Burns	Benjamin	10AUG03	2.04	1	Butcher	John	31JUL01	3.04	1
Birns	Benjamin	07APR04	4.03	1	Bucher	John	28JUL02	3.03	1
Burns	Benjamin	20JUN05	2.03	1	Bucher	John	05AUG03	2.03	1
Burns	Benjamin	31JUL06	2.04	1	Butcher	John	06JUN04	4.04	1
Burns	Isabella	18JUN95	2.14	F	Butcher	John	19JUN05	2.03	1
Byrns	Peter	05JUL96	2.02	1	Butcher	Samuel	14JUN87	2.01	11
Burns	William	19MAY89	6.03		Butcher	Samuel	15NOV88	1.01	11
Listed with Elizabeth Guthrie					Butcher	Samuel	16JUN89	5.01	12
Burnes	William	17JUN09	2.03	1	Butcher	Samuel	23APR90	2.01	11
BURNSIDE					Butcher	Samuel	05JUL91	1.01	11
Burnside	Robert	21JUN87	2.01	3	Butcher	Samuel	05OCT92	2.01	12
Burnside	Walter	30JUN87	1.01	1	BUTLER				
Burnside	Walter	18APR89	6.01	1	Butler	James	01JUL89	2.02	1
Burnside	Walter	02APR90	1.01	1	Butler	Joseph	-----93	3.01	1
Burnsides	Walter	26AUG91	3.02	1	Butler	William	21JUN87	2.01	11
Burnsides	Walter	29NOV92	3.03	1	Butler	William	15NOV88	1.01	11
Burnside	Walter	21MAY94	3.03	1	BYBE				
Burnsides	Walter	25MAR95	1.01	12	Bybe	Allin	25MAR95	1.01	1
Burnside	Walter	-----96	1.03	12	Bybe	John	13MAR95	1.02	1
BURK					BYERS				
Burks	William Jr	09JUL01	3.03	1	Byers	Elizabeth	22MAY94	3.05	F
BURRIS					Byers	Elizabeth	10MAR95	1.02	F
Burris	John	-----96	1.01	1	Byers	Elizabeth	-----96	1.02	F
Burres	Walter	19JUN99	2.02	1	Byers	John	28MAR95	3.03	1
Burris	William	-----11	1.03	1	Byers	John	23MAY97	1.02	1
BURROUGHS					CADIS				
Boress	Gerrard	24AUG03	3.03	1	Cadis	Thomas	27JUN05	2.07	11
Burroughs	John	04APR95	1.02	1	CAGLE				
Bearris	Nicholas	22MAY97	1.03	1	Cagle	John	-----11	1.13	1
BURT					CAIN				
Birtt	Benjamin	03APR90	2.02	1	Cain	James	18JUL06	3.05	1
Birt	Benjamin	07AUG93	1.01	1	CALAHAN				
BURTON					Calahan	Frederick	09MAY07	1.03	1
Burton	Ambross	27JUN89	2.01	1	CALDWELL				
Burton	Ambrus	19APR91	3.01	1	Caldwell	David	27JUN87	1.01	1
Burton	Ambross	02DEC92	3.03	1	Caldwell	David	23JUN90	1.03	1
Burton	Ambrose	29MAY94	3.02	1	Caldwell	David	09AUG91	2.03	11
Burton	Ambrus	10APR95	1.03	1	Caldwell	David	13OCT92	1.03	1
Burton	Ambrose	-----96	1.02	11	Caldwell	David	13SEP93	3.03	11
Burton	Archibald	26JUL06	3.03	1	Caldwell	David	20MAY94	2.03	11
Burton	Archibald	-----07	2.02	1	Caldwell	David	20MAY94	2.03	11
Burton	Archibald	01JUL08	2.02	1	Caldwell	David	20MAY95	3.04	11
Burton	Archibald	29JUN09	1.05	1	Caldwell	David	19MAY96	?.03	21
Burton	Archabold	-----11	1.09	1	Caldwell	David	30JUN97	1.06	21
Burton	Benjamin	03JUN00	2.01	1	Caldwell	David	08JUL99	3.05	11
Barton	James	24AUG87	1.01	1	Colwell	David	04JUL00	3.08	21
Burton	James	13MAY99	1.02	1	Caldwell	David	07MAY01	3.06	11
Burton	James P.	30MAY00	2.01	1	Caldwell	David	11AUG02	3.06	11
Burton	John	23JUL06	3.03	1	Caldwell	David	29JUL03	2.06	11
Burton	John	10JUN07	2.01	1	Culwell	David	25JUN04	4.05	11
Burton	John	01JUL08	2.02	1	Caldwell	David	19JUL05	2.08	1
Burten	John	10JUL09	1.05	1	Caldwell	David	14AUG06	2.10	11
Burton	Lutton	08JUN07	2.01	1	Caldwell	David	23JUL07	2.06	12
Burton	Mary	30JUN89	5.01	F	Caldwell	David	25JUN08	2.04	11
Burton	Mary	05JUL91	1.02	F	Caldwell	David	13MAY09	1.06	11
Burton	Mary	12AUG93	1.01	F	Caldwell	Elizabeth	22JUL07	2.06	F
Burton	Mary	23MAY94	1.01	F	Caldwell	Elizabeth	25JUN08	2.04	F
Burton	Mary	08MAY95	2.01	F	Caldwell	Elizabeth	13MAY09	1.06	F
Burton	Mary	20JUN97	1.03	F	Colwell	Elizabeth	-----11	1.11	F
Barton	Mary	11JUN99	1.04	F1	Caldwell	James	14AUG06	2.10	1
Burton	Mary	26JUL00	2.03	F1	Caldwell	James	30JUN08	2.04	1
Burton	Mary	20JUL01	3.05	F2	Caldwell	James	13MAY09	1.06	1
Burton	Mary	01JUN02	2.02	F2	Caldwell	John	27JUN87	3.02	1
Burtin	Mary	21JUL03	3.03	F1	Caldwell	John	12AUG89	2.03	1
Burton	Mary	01AUG04	3.02	F1	Caldwell	John	13SEP91	3.04	1
Burton	Mary	14JUN05	3.02	F1	Caldwell	John	13OCT92	1.03	11
Burton	William	13MAY99	1.02	1	Caldwell	John	05DEC92	3.05	1
Burton	William	31MAY00	2.01	11	Caldwell	John	11NOV93	3.03	1
BUTCHER					Caldwell	John	28MAY94	2.03	1
Butcher	James	10OCT92	2.01	1	Caldwell	John	22JUN94	3.05	1

surname	name	date	bk.pg	TM	surname	name	date	bk.pg	TM
Caldwell	John	14MAY95	1.04	1	CAMP				
Caldwell	John	-----96	4.04	1	Camp	John Steel	21AUG06	3.08	1
Caldwell	John	15MAR97	2.01	1	Camp	Joseph	31JUN06	1.05	11
Caldwell	Josiah	07MAY01	3.06	1	Camp	Reuben	27JUN87	3.02	1
Caldwell	Josiah	11AUG02	3.06	1	Kemp	Reuben	12MAY95	1.08	1
Caldwell	Joseph	28JUL03	2.06	1	CAMPBELL				
Culwell	Josiah	26JUN04	4.05	1	Campbell	Alexander	03JUN95	2.04	1
Caldwell	Josiah	18JUL05	2.07	1	Campbell	Alexander	23JUN96	1.03	1
Caldwell	Josiah	05AUG06	2.09	1	Camel	Alexander	13JUN01	1.03	1
Caldwell	Josiah	18AUG07	2.08	1	Campbell	Alexander	05AUG02	2.05	1
Caldwell	Josiah	25JUL08	2.05	1	Campbell	Alexander	19JUL03	3.05	1
Caldwell	Josiah	15AUG09	1.09	1	Campbell	Alexander	21AUG04	3.05	1
Colwell	Josiah	-----11	1.11	1	Campbell	Alexander	16AUG05	3.07	1
Caldwell	Matt	13JUN96	2.04	1	Campbell	Alexander	08AUG06	3.07	1
Caldwell	Robert	27JUN87	3.02	1	Campbell	Charles	13JUN87	3.02	1
Caldwell	Robert	12AUG89	2.03	1	Campbell	Charles	27JUN89	2.03	1
Caldwell	Robert	13SEP91	3.04	1	Campbell	Charles	19SEP91	3.03	1
Caldwell	Thomas	08MAY97	3.05	1	Campbell	Charles	08DEC92	3.05	1
Caldwell	William	13MAY09	1.06	1	Campbell	Charles	02MAY94	3.06	1
CALE					Campbell	Charles	01MAY95	1.03	1
Cail	Jacob	23JUL05	2.08	1	Campbell	Charles	-----96	4.04	1
Cail	Jacob	08JUL06	2.08	1	Campbell	Daniel	08JUN96	1.03	1
Cale	Jacob	10AUG07	2.07	1	Campbell	Daniel	21APR97	3.05	1
Cale	Jacob	22JUN09	1.08	1	Campbell	Daniel	30MAY99	1.05	1
CALEKORN					Campbell	George	12MAY97	1.04	1
Calekorn	David-Heirs	07AUG04	2.05		Campbell	George	30JUL00	2.05	1
Taxes paid by DeJarnett					Campbell	George	22AUG04	3.05	1
CALFEE					Campbell	George	16AUG05	3.07	1
Calfee	John	26MAY97	1.05	1	Campbell	Henry	20AUG06	3.08	1
CALHOON					Campbell	Isaac	-----93	3.01	1
Calhoon	John	04AUG06	3.07	1	Campbell	James	08OCT91	1.02	1
CALLEMEES					Campbell	James	05OCT92	2.02	1
Callemees	Smith Wm.	10MAY94	2.03	1	Campbell	James	09AUG93	1.02	1
CALLER					Campbell	James	09AUG93	1.02	1
Caller	Anthony	03SEP89	2.04	1	Campbell	James	16MAY94	1.02	1
CALLICUT					Campble	James	19MAY94	2.03	0
Collicutt	Beverly	07JUN09	1.06	1	Campbell	James	20MAY94	1.02	1
Callicut	Beverly	-----11	1.13	1	Campbell	James	16APR95	3.03	1
CALLISON					Campbell	James	25MAY95	2.04	1
Calison	Absalom	08JUL01	3.07	1	Campbell	James-Irish	20JUN97	1.05	1
Calison	Joseph	08JUL01	3.07	1	Campbell	James	04JUN99	1.06	1
Callison	Joseph	15AUG07	2.08	1	Campbell	James	05JUN99	1.06	1
Calison	Joseph	-----08	2.06	1	Campbell	James	20JUN00	2.05	1
Callison	Joseph	21JUN09	1.07	1	Campbell	James	28JUN00	2.06	1
Calison	Robert	08MAY07	1.04	1	Campbell	James	25AUG02	2.06	1
Callison	Robert	28JUL08	2.05	1	Campbell	James	15JUN03	3.04	1
Callison	Robert	21JUN09	1.07	1	Campbell	James	07AUG04	2.03	1
Coleson	Robert	-----11	1.16	1	Campbell	James	-----05	2.36	1
Callison	William	15AUG07	2.08	1	Campbell	James	20JUN05	2.07	1
Calison	William	-----08	2.06	1	Campbell	James	29JUN05	3.06	1
Callicut	William	-----11	1.12	1	Campbell	James	28JUL06	3.06	1
CALVERT					Campbell	James	31JUL06	2.09	1
Calvert	John	18MAY90	2.02	1	Campbell	James	06JUL07	2.06	1
CAMDEN					Campbell	James	--JUN08	2.04	1
Camden	Elizabeth	02JUL07	1.05	F	Campbell	James	-----11	1.11	1
Camden	Betsey	02JUN08	1.06	F1	Campbell	John	20MAY94	1.02	1
Compoten	Elizabeth	31MAY09	2.04	F	Campbell	John	03JUN96	2.04	1
Camden	Elizabeth	-----11	1.11	F	Campbell	John	15JUN96	1.03	1
Camden	James	-----11	1.11	1	Camel	John	06JUN00	1.02	1
Cameron	Mary A.	28MAR06	2.07	F	Camel	John	12JUN00	1.02	1
Camden	Richard	02JUL07	1.05	11	Camel	John	03JUN02	1.03	1
Camden	William	25JUL89	2.03	1	Camel	John	14JUN03	1.03	1
Camdun	William	20SEP91	3.03	1	Campbell	John	24AUG03	3.06	1
Camden	William	28NOV92	3.04	1	Campbell	John	15AUG04	3.05	1
Camdem	William	05MAY94	3.06	1	Campbell	John	05AUG05	3.07	1
Camden	William	01JUN95	1.04	1	Campbell	John	20AUG06	3.08	1
Campden	William	-----96	4.04	1	Campbell	Joseph	13JUN87	2.02	1
Camlin	William	28JUN02	1.05	1	Campbell	Joseph	06SEP87	1.02	1
Camlin	William	07JUL03	1.05	1	Campbell	Joseph	14NOV88	1.03	1
Camden	William	16JUN04	2.02	11	Campbell	Joseph	12JUN89	6.08	1
Cameron	William	29JUL05	1.04	1	Campbell	Joseph	15APR90	1.02	1
Camden	William	02JUL07	1.05	1	Campbell	Joseph	23JUN91	2.02	1

surname	name	date	bk.pg	TM	surname	name	date	bk.pg	TM
Campbell	Joseph	25SEP92	1.03	1	Canifax	William	13JUN99	2.03	1
Campbell	Joseph	11OCT92	2.02	12	Cannifax	William	22JUL00	1.02	1
Campbell	Joseph	19AUG93	1.02	11	Canifax	William	23JUN01	1.03	1
Campbell	Joseph	24AUG93	3.03	11	Cannifax	William	23JUN02	1.04	1
Campbell	Joseph	09MAY94	2.04	1	Canifax	William	23JUN03	1.04	1
Campbell	Joseph	20MAY94	1.02	1	Canifax	William	01AUG04	1.04	11
Campbell	Joseph	-----95	2.26		Canifax	William	30JUL05	1.04	1
One lot in Stanford					Canifax	William	02AUG06	1.05	1
Campbell	Joseph	22APR95	3.04	2	Canifax	William	08MAY07	1.03	1
Campbell	Joseph	26MAY95	2.02	1	Canifax	William	14JUN08	1.06	1
Campbell	Joseph	02JUN96	2.04	2	Canifax	William	16JUN09	2.05	1
Campbell	Joseph	15JUN96	1.03	11	CANON				
Campbell	Joseph	07APR97	3.05	1	Cannon	John	29MAR95	3.03	1
Campbell	Joseph	02JUN97	1.04	2	Cannon	John	21APR96	2.03	1
Campbell	Joseph	04JUN99	1.06	11	Cannon	John	16MAY97	1.06	1
Campbell	Joseph	21JUN99	1.05	11	Cannon	John	02JUL99	3.04	1
Campbell	Joseph	20JUN00	2.05	11	Kanon	Thomas	26JUL03	2.18	
Campbell	Joseph	25JUN00	2.06	11	A free negro				
Campbell	Joseph	23JUL01	3.08	11	Canon	Thomas	19JUL05	2.08	
Campbell	Joseph	23JUL01	2.04	21	A free negro				
Campbell	Joseph	05AUG02	2.05	1	Canon	Thomas	19AUG06	2.10	
Campbell	Joseph	25AUG02	2.06	11	A free Negroe				
Campbell	Joseph	15JUN03	3.04	2	Cannon	Tom	10AUG07	2.07	00
Campbell	Joseph	16JUL03	3.05	1	Cannon	Tom	19JUN09	1.07	
Campbell	Joseph Jr	16JUL03	3.05	1	A free negro				
Campbell	Joseph	16JUN04	2.02	2	CARLESON				
Campbell	Joseph	07AUG04	2.03	2	Carleson	Joseph	-----11	1.15	1
Campbell	Joseph	08JUN05	2.06	1	CARMAN				
Campbell	Joseph Jr	08JUN05	2.06	1	Carman	Elijah	08AUG06	3.07	1
Campbell	Joseph	19JUN05	3.05	2	Carman	Elijah	14JUN08	1.07	1
Campbell	Joseph	07AUG06	3.07	11	Carman	John	08AUG06	3.07	1
Campbell	Joseph	21AUG06	3.08	1	CARNS				
Campbell	Joseph Jr	07AUG06	3.07	1	Carns	Joseph	23JUL00	2.06	1
Campbell	Joseph	06JUL07	2.06	21	CARPENTER				
Campbell	Joseph	--JUN08	2.04	11	Carpenter	Adam	26JUN87	1.01	1
Campbell	Joseph	28JUL08	2.05	1	Carpenter	Adam	22MAY89	6.02	1
Campbell	Joseph	08APR09	1.06	1	Carpenter	Adam	12MAY90	1.02	1
Campbell	Michael	24JUN89	5.02	1	Carpenter	Adam	04AUG91	2.03	1
Campbell	Moses	19OCT92	2.02	1	Carpenter	Adam	13SEP92	1.03	1
Campbell	Moses	09AUG93	1.02	1	Adm for John Fry				
Campbell	Moses	20MAY94	1.02	1	Carpenter	Adam	06AUG93	3.02	1
Campbell	Moses	29MAY95	2.03	1	Carpenter	Adam	10JUN94	2.03	1
Camel	Moses	19JUN99	2.03	1	Carpenter	Adam	10JUN94	2.03	1
Camel	Moscs	02JUN01	1.02	1	Paid tax for J. Fry				
Camel	Moses	04JUN02	1.03	1	Carpenter	Adam	17APR95	3.04	1
Camel	Moses	28JUN03	1.04	1	Carpenter	Adam	05JUL96	2.04	1
Camel	Moses	15JUN04	1.03	11	Carpenter	Adam	11JUL97	1.04	1
Camel	Moses	19JUN06	1.04	1	Carpenter	Adam	11JUL97	1.04	1
Cammel	Moses	02JUL07	1.05	1	Pd tax for John(heirs) Fry				
Campbell	Moses	14JUN08	1.07	1	Carpenter	Adam	25JUN99	1.07	11
Campbell	Moses	23AUG09	2.07	1	Carpenter	Adam	29JUL00	2.07	11
Cammel	Rachel	02JUL07	1.05	F	Carpenter	Adam	18JUN01	3.08	11
Campbell	Rachel	14JUN08	1.07	F	Pd tax for John Fry				
Campbell	Rachel	23AUG09	2.07	F	Carpenter	Adam	10JUN02	2.04	11
Campbell	Samuel	-----08	2.06	1	Carpenter	Adam	04AUG03	3.06	11
Campbell	Samuel	03JUL09	1.08	1	Carpenter	Adam	03AUG04	3.04	1
Campbell	Samuel	-----11	1.14	1	Carpenter	Adam	20JUN05	3.06	1
Campbell	Thomas	26NOV92	3.04	1	Carpenter	Adam (Decd)	18AUG06	3.08	D
Campbell	Thomas	05MAY94	3.06	1	Geo. Murrell & Geo.Carpenter				
Campbell	Thomas	01MAY95	1.03	1	Carpenter	Conrad	27JUN87	1.01	1
Campbell	William	13JUN87	3.02	1	Carpenter	Conrad	22MAY89	6.02	1
Campbell	William	27JUN89	2.03	1	Carpenter	Conrad	13MAY90	1.02	1
Campbell	William	25JUL89	2.03	1	Carpenter	Conrad	30APR91	2.02	1
Cambell	William	28MAY91	3.04	1	Carpenter	Conrad	13SEP92	1.03	1
Campbell	William	29NOV92	3.05	1	Carpenter	Conrad	06AUG93	3.02	1
Campbell	William	05MAY94	3.06	1	Carpenter	Conrad	10JUN94	2.03	11
Campbell	William	01MAY95	1.03	1	Carpenter	Conrad	16APR95	3.04	1
Campbell	William	-----96	4.04	1	Carpenter	Conrad	29AUG96	2.05	1
Campbell	William	12JUN97	3.06	1	Carpenter	Conrad	21JUN97	1.05	1
CAMPIS					Carpenter	Conrad	16MAY99	3.04	1
Campis	Thorton	06JUN09	2.05	1	Carpenter	Coonrod	09JUL00	3.08	1
CANIFAX					Carpenter	Conrad	18JUN01	3.07	1

surname	name	date	bk.pg	TM	surname	name	date	bk.pg	TM
Carpenter	Conrod	28JUL02	3.06	1	Carson	David	18APR08	1.04	1
Carpenter	Conrod	11AUG03	2.07	1	Carson	David	01JUL09	2.06	1
Carpenter	Conrod	05MAY04	4.04	1	Carson	James	23JUL00	2.06	1
Carpenter	Conrod	19JUN05	2.07	1	Carson	James	09JUN03	3.04	1
Carpenter	Conrod	29JUL06	2.09	1	Carson	James	05AUG05	3.06	1
Carpenter	Coonrod	22AUG07	2.08	1	Carson	James	04AUG06	3.07	1
Carpenter	Conrod	28JUL08	2.05	1	Carson	John	10JUL89	2.03	1
Carpenter	Coonrod	12JUL09	1.09	1	Carson	Joseph	03AUG04	1.04	1
Carpenter	Coonrod	-----11	1.16	1	Carson	Joseph	30JUL05	1.04	1
Carpenter	Elizabeth	06SEP87	1.02	F	Carson	Joseph	31JUN06	1.05	1
Carpenter	Elizabeth	22MAY89	6.02	F	Carson	Joseph	07MAY07	1.03	1
Carpenter	Elizabeth	13MAY90	1.02	F	Carson	Joseph	18APR08	1.04	1
Carpenter	Elizabeth	04AUG91	2.03	F	Carson	Joseph	16JUN09	2.05	1
Carpenter	George	10JUN94	2.03	0	Carson	Joseph	16JUN09	2.05	1
Carpenter	George	16APR95	3.04	0	Carson	Samuel	15AUG05	3.07	1
Carpenter	George	09JUN02	2.04	M1	Carson	Samuel	09MAY07	1.03	1
Carpenter	George	01AUG03	3.06	M1	Carson	Samuel	18APR08	1.04	1
Carpenter	George	03AUG04	3.04	11	Carson	Samuel	01JUL09	2.06	1
Carpenter	George	19JUN05	3.05	11	Carson	Thomas	11MAY96	2.03	1
Carpenter	George	21JUL06	3.06	1	Carson	Thomas	18JUL97	1.04	1
Carpenter	George	04AUG07	2.07	1	Carson	Thomas	29JUL99	3.04	1
Carpenter	George	15JUL08	2.05	1	Carson	Thomas	29JUL99	1.07	1
Carpenter	George	12JUL09	1.08	1	Carson	Thomas	23JUL00	2.06	1
Carpenter	George	-----11	1.16	1	Carson	Thomas	27MAY01	3.08	1
Carpenter	Henry	28JUL08	2.05	1	Carson	Thomas	09AUG04	3.05	1
Carpenter	Henry	11JUL09	1.08	1	Carson	Thomas	13MAY05	2.06	1
Carpenter	Henry	-----11	1.14	1	Carson	Thomas	15AUG05	3.07	1
Carpenter	Jacob	29JUL00	2.06	1	Carson	Thomas	04AUG06	3.07	1
Carpenter	Jacob	21JUL01	3.08	1	Carson	Walter	01JUN02	2.04	1
Carpenter	Jacob	21JUL01	3.08	1	Carsen	William	23JUN03	1.04	11
Carpenter	Jacob	10JUN02	2.04	1	Carson	William	03AUG04	1.04	11
Carpenter	Jacob	10JUN03	3.04	1	Carson	William	31JUL05	1.04	1
Carpenter	Jacob	03AUG04	3.04	1	Carson	William	01AUG06	1.05	1
Carpenter	Jacob	20JUN05	3.06	1	Carson	William	09MAY07	1.04	1
Carpenter	Jacob	29JUL06	3.06	1	Carson	William	02APR08	1.04	1
Pd tax for Jacob Moore					Carson	William	01JUL09	2.06	1
Carpenter	Jacob	29JUL06	3.06		CARTER				
Pd tax for John Carpenter					Carter	Charles	13JUL96	2.04	1
Carpenter	James	30MAY01	1.02	1	Carter	Charles	06JUN97	1.04	1
Carpenter	James	05JUN05	1.03	1	Carter	Charles	25JUN99	3.04	1
Carpenter	James	11JUN06	1.03	1	Carter	Charles	19JUN00	3.06	1
Carpenter	John	06JUL96	2.13	1	Carter	Charles	01MAY01	3.06	1
Tax paid by Ezra Morrison					Carter	Charles	26JUL02	3.06	1
Carpenter	John	29JUL06	3.06		Carter	Charles	10AUG04	4.06	1
Tax paid by Jacob Carpenter					Carter	Charles	10JUN05	2.06	1
Carpenter	Polly	19JUL07	2.29	F	Carter	Charles	01AUG06	1.05	M1
Tax paid by James Patton					Carter	Charles	02AUG06	2.09	1
Carpenter	Polly	-----08	2.22	F	Carter	Charles	02AUG06	2.09	1
Tax paid by James Patten					Carter	Charles	08JUN07	2.05	11
Carpenter	Polly	-----09	1.28	F	Carter	Charles	28JUL08	2.05	11
Tax paid by James Patten					Carter	Charles	17JUL09	1.09	1
Carpenter	William	19JUN05	2.07	1	Carter	Charles	-----11	1.11	21
Carpenter	William	21JUL06	3.06	1	Carter	Collin	08JUN09	1.07	11
CARRIER					Carter	Collen	-----11	1.11	0
Carrier	Jonathan	07APR97	3.04	1	Carter	Edward	07APR95	3.03	1
CARSEY					Carter	Edward	01JUN96	2.04	1
Carsey	Moses	29JUN96	1.03	1	Carter	Edward	04AUG02	2.05	1
CARSON					Carter	Edward	17JUN03	3.04	1
Carson	Elex.	29MAR90	2.02	1	Carter	Edward	06AUG04	3.05	1
Carson	Alexander	05APR91	1.02	1	Carter	Edwin	17JUN05	2.06	1
Carson	Alexander	24OCT92	2.03	1	Carter	Edward	02AUG06	2.09	1
Carson	Alexander	05AUG93	1.02	1	Carter	Edward	13JUN07	2.05	1
Carson	Alexander	12MAY94	1.03	1	Carter	Edward	31MAY08	2.04	1
Carson	Alexander	11MAY95	2.03	1	Carter	Edward	30JUN09	1.08	1
Carson	Campbell	18APR08	1.04	1	Carter	Edmond	-----11	1.16	1
Carson	Charles C.	31JUL05	1.04	M1	Carter	Henry	14SEP91	3.04	11
Carson	Charles	14JUL06	3.05	12	Carter	James	06AUG04	3.05	1
Carsen	David	23JUN03	1.04	1	Carter	Jesse	10APR95	3.04	1
Carson	David	03AUG04	1.04	1	Carter	Jesse	13JUL96	2.04	1
Carson	David	31JUL05	1.04	1	Carter	Jesse	06JUN97	1.04	1
Carson	David	01AUG06	1.05	1	Carter	Jesse	25JUN99	3.04	1
Carson	David	09MAY07	1.03	1	Carter	Jesse	17JUL00	3.08	1

surname	name	date	bk.pg	TM	surname	name	date	bk.pg	TM
Carter	Jesse	18MAY01	3.06	1	Casey	John	12JUN89	6.08	1
Carter	Jesse	26JUL02	3.06	1	Casey	John	15APR90	1.02	1
Carter	Jesse	06AUG03	2.07	1	Casey	Levy	-----11	1.14	1
Carter	Jesse	09JUN04	4.05	1	Casey	Stephen	14JUN02	3.05	1
Carter	Jesse	10JUN05	2.06	1	Casey	Stephen	20JUN03	2.05	1
Carter	Jesse	12MAY06	2.07	1	Casey	Stephen	28JUL04	4.06	1
Carter	Jesse	08JUN07	2.05	1	Casey	Stephen	15AUG07	2.08	1
Carter	Jesse	25JUL08	2.05	1	Casey	Stephen	-----11	1.15	1
Carter	Jesse	17JUL09	1.09	1	Casey	William	24AUG87	1.01	1
Carter	Jesse	-----11	1.10	1	CASH				
Carter	John	24JUN99	2.04	1	Cash	John	15APR90	1.02	1
Carter	John	26JUN01	1.03	1	CASILL				
Carter	John	23JUN02	1.05	1	Casill	John	13MAY94	1.02	1
Carter	John	23JUN03	1.04	1	CASSADY				
Carter	John	03AUG04	1.04	1	Casity	William	15NOV88	1.03	1
Carter	John	31JUL05	1.04	1	Casity	William	24JUN89	5.02	1
Carter	John	01AUG06	1.05	1	Casaday	William	02JUN90	2.02	1
Carter	John	26MAY07	1.04	1	Cassady	William	14APR91	1.02	1
Carter	John	13JUN07	2.06	1	CASWELL				
Carter	John	22APR08	1.05	1	Caswell	John	26JUN87	1.01	1
Carter	John	28JUL08	2.05	1	Caswell	John	30MAY89	6.02	1
Carter	John	17JUN09	2.05	1	Caswell	John	03APR90	1.02	1
Carter	John	16AUG09	1.09	1	Caswell	John	18MAY91	2.02	1
Carter	John	-----11	1.10	1	Caswell	John	10OCT92	1.03	1
Carter	Joseph	18MAR95	3.05	1	Caswell	John	21AUG93	3.03	1
Carter	Joseph	20MAY96	2.04	1	Caswell	John	10JUN94	2.03	1
Carter	Joseph	08AUG09	1.07	1	Caswell	John	10APR95	3.04	1
Carter	Peter	10MAY97	1.05	1	CATHEY				
Carter	Peter	09JUL99	3.05	1	Cathey	John	15JUN96	1.03	1
Carter	Peter	20JUN00	3.06	1	CATLIVE				
Carter	Peter	07MAY01	3.06	1	Catlive	Charles	20JUN87	2.02	1
Carter	Peter	31JUL02	3.06	1	CATTON				
Carter	Peter	11JUL03	2.05	1	Caten	Benjamin	26MAY02	2.04	1
Carter	Peter	10AUG04	4.06	1	Caton	George	03OCT92	1.03	1
Carter	Peter	07JUN05	2.06	1	Caton	George	13AUG93	3.03	1
Carter	Peter	02AUG06	2.09	1	Caton	George	17APR95	3.04	1
Carter	Peter	13JUN07	2.06	1	Caton	George	11MAY96	2.03	1
Carter	Peter	-----08	2.06	1	Caton	George	12JUN97	1.05	1
Carter	Peter	12JUL09	1.09	1	Cayton	George	05JUN99	1.06	1
Carter	Peter	-----11	1.10	11	Caton	George	29JUL00	2.06	1
Carter	Solomon	27JUN05	2.07	1	Katen	George	20JUN01	3.18	1
Carter	Solomon	02AUG06	2.09	1	Caten	George	01JUN02	2.04	1
Carter	Solomon	13JUN07	2.06	1	Caton	George	04JUN03	3.04	1
Carter	Solomon	25JUN08	2.04	11	Caton	George	31JUL04	3.04	1
Carter	Solomon	15AUG09	1.09	1	Caton	George	14JUN05	3.05	1
Carter	Soloman	-----11	1.10	1	Catton	George	23JUL06	3.06	1
Carter	Stephen	28JUL08	2.05	1	Caton	George	09JUN07	2.05	11
Carter	Stephen	07AUG09	1.09	1	Caton	Jesse	13AUG93	3.03	1
Carter	Stephen	-----11	1.14	1	Catton	Jessee	03OCT92	1.03	1
Carter	William	-----93	3.01	1	CAUDREY				
CARTWRIGHT					Caudrey	John	26JUN87	2.02	1
Cartright	Peter	12AUG93	3.02	1	CAUHORN				
Cartwright	William	27JUN89	2.03	1	Cauhorn	Samuel	14JUN87	2.01	1
CARVER					Cowhorn	Samuel	01JUN97	3.06	11
Carver	Reuben	30MAY03	2.05	1	CAUMLEY				
CASEY					Caumley	William	01JUL09	2.06	1
Keasy	Christopher	21APR97	3.17	1	CAVELL				
Casey	Christ.	29MAY99	1.05	11	Cavell	Joseph	26MAY01	3.08	1
Casey	Christopher	28JUN00	3.07	1	Cavill	Joseph	05AUG05	3.07	1
Casey	Christopher	14JUN02	3.05	1	Cavill	Samuel	05AUG05	3.07	1
Casey	Christopher	13JUN03	2.05	1	Capell	William	20SEP91	3.03	1
Casey	Christopher	28JUL04	4.06	1	Cavel	William	07APR95	3.03	1
Casey	Christopher	16MAY05	2.06	1	Cabbell	William	08JUN97	1.05	1
Casey	Christopher	08JUL06	2.08	1	Cavel	William	28JUL99	1.07	11
Casey	Christopher	15AUG07	2.08	1	Cabbell	William	24JUL00	2.06	11
Casey	Christipher	28JUL08	2.05	1	Cavell	William	26MAY01	3.08	11
Casey	Christopher	21JUN09	1.07	1	Cabbell	William	03AUG02	2.05	11
Casey	Christopher	-----11	1.16	12	Cabble	William Sr	15JUN03	3.04	11
Casey	James	13JUN87	2.01	1	Cabble	William Jr	23JUN03	3.05	1
Casey	James	15NOV88	1.03	1	Cavil	William	08AUG04	3.05	2
Casey	James	24JUN89	5.02	1	Cavill	William	05AUG05	3.07	11
Casey	John	24AUG87	1.02	1	Cavill	William Jr	05AUG05	3.07	1

surname	name	date	bk.pg	TM	surname	name	date	bk.pg	TM
Cabbell	William	21AUG06	3.08	11	Chapman	Daniel	18MAY90	2.02	1
Cabbell	William	04AUG06	3.07	1	Chapman	Daniel Jr	18MAY90	2.02	1
CEASER					Chapman	Daniel Sr	03NOV92	2.02	1
Ceaser	David	07AUG06	3.07	1	Chapman	Daniel	21NOV92	2.02	1
Ceaser	David	04AUG07	2.07	1	Chapman	Daniel Sr	12AUG93	1.03	1
Ceaser	David	-----08	2.06	11	Chapman	Daniel	10AUG93	1.02	1
CEMBROO					Chapman	Daniel Sr	17MAY94	1.03	1
Cembroo	James	14JUN08	1.07	11	Chapman	Daniel Jr	27MAY94	1.03	1
Limbro	James	15MAY09	2.17	1	Chapman	Daniel	02JUN95	2.03	1
CERTAIN					Chapman	Daniel	22JUN95	2.03	1
Certain	Isaac	13JUN87	3.02	1	Chapman	Daniel	20JUN96	1.03	1
Certain	Isaac	01JUL89	2.03	1	Chapman	Daniel	28JUN96	1.03	1
CHADWELL					Chapman	Daniel	24APR97	3.05	11
Chadwell	George	-----11	1.13	1	Chapman	Daniel	16JUN99	1.05	11
Chadwell	James	-----11	1.13	1	Chapman	Daniel	17JUN00	2.05	1
CHAMBERLAIN					Chapman	Daniel	21JUL01	2.04	1
ChamberlandDavid		20JUN01	3.08	1	Chapman	Daniel	11JUN02	1.03	1
ChamberlainDavis		21JUN97	1.04	1	Chapman	Daniel	30JUN03	1.04	1
ChamberlainThomas		21JUN97	1.05	1	Chapman	Daniel	01AUG04	2.03	1
CHAMBERS					Chapman	Daniel	15JUN05	1.03	1
Chambers	John	25JUL89	2.03	1	Chapman	Daniel	20JUN06	1.04	1
Chambers	John	10OCT92	1.03	1	Chapman	Daniel	24JUN07	1.05	1
Chambers	John	21AUG93	3.03	11	Chapman	Daniel	27APR08	1.05	1
Chambers	Mordica	-----11	1.12	1	Chapman	Daniel	01JUN09	2.05	1
CHANCE					Chapman	Edward	18JUN87	2.02	1
Chance	Ezekal	24JUN99	2.04	12	Chapman	Edward	16JUN96	1.03	1
Chance	Ezekiel	26JUN01	1.03	12	Chapman	Edward	09MAY97	3.06	1
Chance	Ezekiel	26JUN02	1.05	11	Chapman	Elizabeth	27APR08	1.05	F
Chance	Ezekiel	23JUN03	1.04	1	Chapman	James	01JUN09	2.05	0
Chanse	Ezekiel	03AUG04	1.04	11	Chapman	James	-----11	1.10	1
Chanc	Ezekiel	30JUL05	1.04	1	Chapman	Job	17MAY94	1.02	1
Chance	Ezekiel	02AUG06	1.05	11	Chapman	Job	17MAY94	1.02	1
Chance	Ezekiel	25MAY07	1.04	11	Chapman	Joab	12JUN95	2.03	1
Chance	Ezekiel	22APR08	1.05	11	Chapman	Job	28JUN96	1.03	1
Chance	Ezekiel	30JUN09	2.06	1	Chapman	Job	30JUN03	1.04	1
Chance	Isaiah	30JUN09	2.06	1	Chapman	Job	01AUG04	2.03	1
Chance	James	20JUN03	1.03	1	Chapman	Job	15JUN05	1.03	1
Chanse	James	01AUG04	1.04	1	Chapman	Job	20JUN06	1.04	1
Chance	James	02AUG06	1.05	1	Chapman	Job	24JUN07	1.05	1
Chance	James	25MAY07	1.04	1	Chapman	Job	23APR08	1.05	1
Chance	James	21APR08	1.05	1	Chapman	Job	01JUN09	2.05	1
Chance	James	30JUN09	2.06	1	Chapman	Jobe	-----11	1.13	11
Chanse	John	01AUG04	1.04	1	Chapman	John	03JUN00	2.05	1
Chance	John	02AUG06	1.05	1	Chapman	John	25JUL01	2.04	1
Chance	John	26MAY07	1.04	1	Chapman	John	30JUN03	1.04	1
Chance	John	21APR08	1.05	1	Chapman	John	17JUN05	1.03	1
Chance	John	30JUN09	2.06	1	Chapman	John	20JUN06	1.04	1
Chance	William	25MAY07	1.04	1	Chapman	John	14JUN09	2.05	1
Chance	William	14JUN08	1.06	1	Chapman	John	-----11	1.10	1
Chance	William	30JUN09	2.06	1	Chapman	Richard	25JUN87	2.02	1
CHANDLER					Chapman	Richard	15NOV88	1.03	1
Chandler	Isaac	10AUG97	1.04	1	Chapman	Richard	23JUN89	5.02	1
Chandler	Isaac	21MAY99	3.04	1	Chapman	Richard	18MAY90	2.02	1
Chandler	Isaac	09AUG03	2.07	1	Crumton	Richard	02OCT91	3.05	1
Chanler	John	14MAY94	1.02	1	Chapman	Richard	27OCT92	2.02	1
Chandler	John	09JUN96	1.03	11	Chapman	Richard	18AUG93	1.03	1
Chandler	Rankin	02JUL99	3.04	1	Chapman	Richard	27MAY94	1.02	1
Chanler	Ranken	27JUN00	3.07	1	Chapman	Richard	16JUN95	2.03	1
Chandler	Ranken	18MAY01	3.06	1	Chapman	Richard	08JUN96	1.03	1
Chandler	Rankin	08JUL02	3.05	1	Chapman	Richard	12JUN97	3.05	1
Chandler	Ranken	25JUL03	2.05	1	Chapman	Richard	23MAY99	1.05	1
Chandler	Ranken	25JUL04	4.06	1	Chapman	Richard	03JUN00	2.05	1
Chandler	Ranken	22JUL05	2.08	1	Chapman	Richard	04APR01	2.03	1
Chandler	Rankin	28MAR06	2.07	1	Chapman	Richard	15JUN02	1.04	1
Chanler	Ranken	23JUL07	2.06	1	Chapman	Richard	05JUL03	1.05	1
Chanler	Ranken	-----08	2.06	1	Champman	Richard	01AUG04	2.03	1
Chandler	Rankin	19JUN09	1.07	1	Chapman	Richard	17JUN05	1.03	1
Chandler	Rankin	-----11	1.15	11	Chapman	Richard	21JUN06	1.04	11
CHAPMAN					Chapman	Ritchard	23APR08	1.05	11
Chapman	Daniel	18JUN87	2.02	1	Chapman	Richard	06JUL09	2.06	1
Chapman	Daniel	28OCT88	1.02	1	Chapman	Richard	-----11	1.10	1
Chapman	Daniel	16JUN89	5.02	11	Chapman	Sarah	29OCT88	1.02	F

surname	name	date	bk.pg	TM	surname	name	date	bk.pg	TM
Chapman	Sarah	30JUN89	5.04	F	CHILTON				
Chapman	Sarah	18MAY90	2.02	F	Chelton	Chas(Heirs)	20MAR95	3.05	0
Chapman	Sarah	18OCT91	1.02	F	Chilton	Jeremiah	-----11	1.11	1
Chapman	Sarah	18OCT91	1.02	F	Chilton	Thomas	13JUN87	3.02	01
Chapman	Sarah	04OCT92	2.02	F1	Chilton	Thomas	27JUN89	2.03	1
Chapman	Sarah	15AUG93	1.02	F2	CHISM				
Chapman	Sarah	27MAY94	1.02	F1	Chism	Elisha	05JUL87	3.02	1
Chapman	Sarah	02JUN95	2.15	F	Chism	John	15JUL03	3.05	1
Chapman	Sarah	12JUN95	2.03	F	CHRISTILL				
Chapman	Sarah	16JUN96	1.02	F1	Christill	George	02AUG89	5.04	1
Chapman	Sarah	09MAY97	3.06	F	Chrystil	George	08APR91	1.02	1
Chapman	William	25JUN87	2.02	1	Chrystill	George	08APR91	1.02	1
Chapman	William	18NOV88	1.03	1	Christall	George	05MAY94	3.06	1
Chapman	William	20JUN89	5.02	1	Cristil	George	01MAY95	1.03	1
Chapman	William	18MAY90	2.02	1	CHRISTISON				
Chapman	William	13APR91	1.02	1	Christison	Christopher	23JUL05	2.08	M1
Chapman	William	21NOV92	2.02	1	Christason	Isaac	18OCT92	1.02	1
Chapman	William	12AUG93	1.03	1	Christason	Isaac	08AUG93	3.03	1
Chapman	William	17MAY94	1.02	1	Christison	Isaac	12MAY97	1.04	1
Chapman	William	16JUN96	1.02	1	Christeson	Isaac	29JUL99	3.04	1
CHAPPEL					Christeson	Isaac	25JUN00	3.06	1
Chapell	Balard	21JUL06	2.09	1	Christeson	Isaac	07MAY01	3.06	1
Chappel	Ballard	09JUN07	2.05	1	Christian	Isaac	01JUL02	3.05	1
Chappel	James	29MAY01	3.08	1	Christian	Isaac	22JUN03	2.05	1
Chapple	James	10AUG02	2.05	1	Christeson	Isaac	19JUL05	2.07	1
Chappell	James	25JUN03	3.05	1	Christison	Isaac	14AUG06	2.10	1
Chappell	James	06AUG04	3.05	1	Christeson	Jane	26JUN04	4.05	F
Chapple	James	05AUG05	3.06	1	Christeson	John	13MAY90	1.02	11
Chappell	James	04AUG06	3.07	1	Christason	John Jr	10APR90	1.02	1
Chappell	Jesse	04AUG06	3.07	1	Christison	John	17MAY91	2.02	11
Chappell	Jesse	02JUL07	1.05	1	Christison	John	05APR91	2.02	1
Chappel	Jesse	-----11	1.13	1	Christason	John	17SEP92	1.03	1
Chapple	Robert	10AUG02	2.05	M1	Christison	John Jr	17SEP92	1.03	1
Chappell	Robert	25JUN03	3.05	11	Christason	John Sr	08AUG93	3.02	1
Chappell	Robert	07AUG04	3.05	1	Christison	John Jr	08AUG93	3.02	1
Chapple	Robert	05AUG05	3.07	1	Christison	John Sr	21APR94	2.03	2
Chappell	William	10MAY97	1.05	11	Christison	John	18APR94	2.03	1
Chappell	William	26JUN99	1.07	11	Christosen	John Sr	20MAR95	3.05	1
Chapill	William	25JUL00	2.06	12	Christosen	John Jr	20MAR95	3.05	1
Chappel	William	29MAY01	3.08	1	Christison	John Sr	09MAY96	2.03	1
Chappel	William	10AUG02	2.05	1	Christison	John Jr	09MAY96	2.03	1
Chappell	William	25JUN03	3.05	11	Christison	John Sr	12MAY97	1.06	00
Chappell	William	25JUL03	3.05	11	Christison	John Jr	12MAY97	1.06	1
Chappell	William	06AUG04	3.05	11	Christeson	John	29JUL99	3.04	1
Chapple	William	05AUG05	3.06	12	Christeson	John	25JUN00	3.06	1
Chappill	William	11AUG06	3.07	11	Christeson	John	07MAY01	3.06	1
CHARTEEN					Christison	John	01JUL02	3.05	1
Charteen	Rane	22JUN94	3.05	F	Exempt from County Leavy				
CHARTER					Christison	John	10AUG02	3.06	1
Charter	Charles	03JUL99	3.05	1	Christian	John	29JUL03	2.06	1
CHEATAM					Christeson	John	26JUN04	4.05	1
Cheatam	Leonard	-----11	1.10	1	Christeson	John	19JUL05	2.07	1
CHEEK					Christison	John	14AUG06	2.10	11
Cheek	Frances	02JUN90	2.02	1	Christeson	Robert	10APR90	1.02	1
Cheek	George	02JUN90	2.02	1	Christason	Robert	05APR91	2.02	1
Cheek	George	14APR91	1.02	1	Christason	Robert	12SEP92	1.03	1
CHESNEY					Christison	Robert	13SEP93	3.03	1
Chesney	John	29JUN96	1.03	1	Christeson	Robert	28APR94	2.03	1
Chesney	John	01JUN97	3.06	1	Christosen	Robert	01MAY95	3.03	1
Chevue	John	15MAY94	1.02	1	Christison	Robert	27MAY96	2.04	1
CHILDERS					Christeson	Robert	28JUN97	1.04	1
Childers	Goldsby	23MAY89	6.02	1	Christian	Robert	27JUL99	1.07	1
Childers	Goldsby	29MAY90	1.03	1	Christison	Robert	25JUL00	2.06	1
Childers	Mary	10AUG01	2.05	F	Christison	Robert	28MAY01	3.08	1
CHILDRESS					Christeson	Thomas	13AUG90	1.03	1
Childress	Henry Sr	14MAY95	1.04	1	Christeson	Thomas	17MAY91	2.02	1
Childress	Henry Jr	14MAY95	1.04	1	Christason	Thomas	18OCT92	1.03	1
Childress	Henry Sr	-----96	4.04	1	Christason	Thomas	08AUG93	3.03	1
Childress	Henry Jr	-----96	4.04	11	Christosen	Thomas	20MAR95	3.05	1
CHILDS					Christison	Thomas	09MAY96	2.03	1
Chelse	John	15AUG09	1.09	1	Christian	Thomas	27JUL99	1.07	1
Chiels	John	-----11	1.14	1	Christison	Thomas	25JUL00	2.06	1

surname	name	date	bk.pg	TM	surname	name	date	bk.pg	TM
Christison	Thomas	28MAY01	3.08	1	Churchwell	Ephriam	20JUN89	5.02	1
Christison	Thomas	10AUG02	2.05	1	Churchwell	Ephraim	18MAY90	2.02	1
Christeson	Thomas	26JUL03	3.05	1	Churchwell	Ephram	29MAR91	1.02	1
Christian	Thomas	08AUG04	3.05	1	Churchwell	Ephraim	12OCT92	2.02	1
Christison	Thomas	05AUG05	3.07	1	Churchwell	Epheran	13AUG93	1.03	1
Christison	Thomas	20AUG06	3.08	1	Churchwell	Epheran	30MAY94	1.03	1
Christason	William	17MAY91	2.02	1	Churchwell	Ephraim	24MAY95	2.03	1
Christason	William	17SEP92	1.03	1	Churchwell	Epheram	25JUN96	1.02	1
Christason	William	08AUG93	3.03	1	Churchill	Ephram	08APR97	3.05	1
Christeson	William	21APR94	2.03	1	Churchwell	Richard	13JUN87	2.01	11
Christosen	William	19MAR95	3.05	1	Churchwell	Richard	31OCT88	1.02	11
Christison	William	09MAY96	2.03	1	Churchwell	Richard	20JUN89	5.02	11
Christison	William	12MAY97	1.04	1	Churchwell	Richard	18MAY90	2.02	1
Christeson	William	29JUL99	3.04	1	Churchwell	Richard	12OCT92	2.02	1
Christeson	William	25JUN00	3.06	1	Churchwell	Richard	12OCT92	2.02	1
Christeson	William	07MAY01	3.06	1	Churchwell	Richard	02JAN92	2.02	1
Christison	William	10AUG02	3.06	1	Churchwell	Richard Sr	14AUG93	1.02	11
Christian	William	29JUL03	2.06	1	Churchwell	Richard Jr	14AUG93	1.02	1
Christeson	William	27JUN04	4.05	1	Churchwell	Richard	30MAY94	1.03	11
Christison	William	21JUN05	2.07	1	Churchwell	Richard Jr	30MAY94	1.02	1
Christison	William	18JUL06	2.09	1	Churchwell	Richard	14JUN95	2.03	1
CHRISTMAN					Churchwell	Richard	24JUN95	2.03	1
Christman	Henry	16MAY89	6.02	1	Churchwell	Richard	23JUN96	1.03	11
CHRISTOPHER					Churchwell	Richard	30JUN96	1.03	1
ChristopherAmbros		17MAY97	1.05	1	Churchill	Richard*	01JUN97	3.06	1
ChristopherAmbros		16JUL99	3.06	1	Churchill	Richard	01JUN97	3.06	1
Admin. for Morton Christopher					Churchill	William	01JUN97	3.06	1
ChristopherAmbrose		14AUG02	3.06	1	CLAMPETT				
ChristopherAmbrose		25JUL03	2.05	1	Clampel	Jonathan	30JUN00	3.07	1
ChristopherAmbroes		28JUL04	4.06	1	Clampett	Jonathan	20MAY01	3.06	1
ChristopherAmbrose		24JUL05	2.08	1	Clampett	Jonathan	25JUL03	2.06	1
ChristipherAmbress		13AUG07	2.08	1	Clampell	Moses	01JUL00	3.07	1
ChristopherElizabeth		01JUL00	3.08	F	Clampett	Moses	20MAY01	3.06	1
ChristopherElizabeth		14AUG02	3.06	F	Clampett	Moses	14AUG02	3.06	1
ChristopherElizabeth		25JUL03	2.06	F	Clampett	Moses	25JUL03	2.06	1
ChristopherElizabeth		-----11	1.15	F	Clampet	Moses	27JUL04	4.06	1
ChristopherLewis		25JUL03	2.05	1	Clampett	Moses	23JUL05	2.08	1
ChristopherLewis		26JUL04	4.06	1	Clampett	Moses	17JUL06	2.08	1
ChristopherLewis		24JUL05	2.08	1	Clampett	Moses	04AUG07	2.07	1
ChristopherLewis		28MAR06	2.07	1	Clampett	Moses	-----08	2.06	1
ChristopherLewis		10AUG07	2.07	1	Clampett	Moses	22JUN09	1.08	1
ChristopherLewis		-----08	2.06	1	Clampet	Moses	-----11	1.15	1
ChristopherLewis		19JUN09	1.07	1	CLARK				
ChristopherMorten		23AUG96	2.05	1	Clark	Baxter	14JUN08	1.06	1
ChristopherMorton		16MAY97	1.06	1	Clark	Christopher	05AUG89	5.04	1
ChristopherMorton		16JUL99	3.06	D	Clark	Christopher	30MAY90	2.02	1
Ambros Christopher-Admin.					Clark	Christopher	28OCT92	2.02	1
CHRISTY					Clark	Christopher	05AUG93	1.02	1
Christy	James	14JUN03	3.04	1	Clark	Christopher	13MAY94	1.02	1
CHRONICK					Clark	Christopher	21MAY95	2.04	1
Chronick	Christopher	21OCT92	2.02	1	Clarke	Christopher	09JUN96	1.03	1
Cranock	Christopher	07AUG93	1.02	1	Clark	Christopher	21APR97	3.07	1
Cronock	Christopher	21MAY94	1.02	1	Clark	Chris.	30MAY99	1.06	1
Cronick	Christopher	25MAY95	2.03	1	Cleark	David	16JUL06	2.08	1
Cronock	Christopher	15JUN96	1.02	1	Clark	Henry	13JUN87	2.02	1
Cronic	Christopher	07APR97	3.04	1	Clark	Henry	30OCT88	1.02	1
Cronick	Christ.	23JUN99	1.05	1	Clark	Henry	14OCT92	2.02	1
Cronick	Chris.	24MAY00	2.05	1	Clark	Henry	13AUG93	1.03	1
Cronick	Christopher	29MAY01	2.04	1	Clark	Henry	29MAY94	1.02	1
Chronick	Christopher	17JUN02	1.04	1	Clark	Henry	12JUN95	2.03	1
Chronick	Christopher	18JUL03	1.05	1	Clarke	Henry	29JUN96	1.02	1
Chronick	Christopher	15JUN04	1.04	1	Clark	Henry	26APR97	3.05	1
Chronick	Christopher	20JUN05	1.04	1	Clark	Henry	29MAY99	2.03	11
Chronick	Christopher	23JUN06	1.04	1	Clark	Henry	19JUN00	1.02	1
Crousuch	Christopher	31MAY08	1.05	1	Clark	Henry	11JUN01	1.03	1
Cronnick	Christopher	22JUN09	2.05	1	Clark	Henry	10JUN02	1.03	1
Cronick	Christopher	-----11	1.10	1	Clark	Henry	28JUN03	1.04	1
CHUCK					Clark	Henry	03AUG04	2.03	1
Chuck	Elisha	04MAY07	1.03	1	Clark	Henry	12JUN05	1.03	1
CHURCH					Clark	Henry	18JUN06	1.03	1
Church	Aron	30JUL05	1.04	1	Clark	Henry	18JUN07	1.04	1
CHURCHWELL					Clark	Henry	04MAY08	1.05	1

surname	name	date	bk.pg	TM	surname	name	date	bk.pg	TM
Clark	Henry	07JUN09	2.05	1	Clemmens	John	-----11	1.12	1
Clark	James	15MAY95	3.04	1	CLEPOLE				
Clark	Jesse	22APR96	2.03	1	Clepole	Cornealus	06JUL07	2.06	1
Clark	Jesse	29MAY97	1.06	1	CLIFTON				
Clark	John	24JUN91	2.03	1	Clifton	Job	03AUG02	2.05	1
Clark	John	25SEP92	1.03	1	Clifton	Job	20MAY03	3.04	1
Clark	John	06OCT92	1.03	1	Clifton	Job	06AUG04	3.05	1
Clark	John	12AUG93	3.02	1	Clifton	Job	05AUG05	3.06	1
Clark	John	23MAY94	2.03	1	Clifton	Job	04AUG06	3.07	11
Clark	John	29APR95	3.03	1	CLINTON				
Clark	John	29AUG96	2.05	1	Clinton	Abraham	23MAY94	1.03	1
Clark	John	12JUN97	1.05	1	Clinton	Archibald	05JUL87	3.02	1
Clark	John	03AUG04	2.03	1	Clinton	Archiable	30JUN89	2.03	1
Cleark	John	19JUL05	2.07	1	Clinton	Archible	18SEP91	3.04	1
Clark	John	06JUL07	2.06	1	Clinton	Archibald	02MAY94	3.06	1
Clark	John	22JUL07	2.06	1	Clinton	Archabald	06MAY95	1.04	1
Clarke	John	26JUL08	2.05	1	Clinton	Archibald	-----96	4.04	1
Clark	John	-----11	1.11	1	CLONSH				
Clark	Joseph	13JUN99	2.03	1	Clonsh	William	31MAY97	3.06	1
Clark	Joseph	26JUN01	1.03	1	CLORE				
Clark	Joseph	23JUN02	1.04	1	Clore	Benjamin	04JUL99	3.05	1
Clark	Josuah	04OCT92	2.02	1	Clore	Benjamin	01JUL00	3.08	1
Clark	Margret	31AUG93	1.03	F	Clore	Benjamin	20MAY01	3.07	1
Clark	Michael	08JUL99	3.05	1	Clore	Laurance	01JUL00	3.08	11
Clark	Rawleigh	13APR97	3.05	1	Clore	Laurance	20MAY01	3.07	11
Clark	Reuben	-----11	1.11	1	Clore	Laurence	04JUL99	3.05	1
Clark	Richard	01MAY95	1.03	1	CLOYD				
Clark	Samuel	01JUN97	3.06	1	Cloyd	David	19SEP91	3.03	1
Clark	Thomas	01JUN97	3.06	11	Cloyd	David	12AUG93	1.03	1
Clark	Warner	18JUL97	1.04	1	Cloyd	David	21MAY94	1.02	1
Clark	Warner	02JUL99	1.07	1	Cloid	David	23MAY94	2.03	1
Clark	Warner	31AUG00	2.07	1	Cloid	David	30MAR95	3.04	1
Clarke	Warner	20JUL01	3.08	1	Cloyd	David	06MAY95	1.04	1
Clark	Warner	05AUG02	2.05	1	Cloyd	David	27MAY96	2.04	1
Clark	Warner	18JUL03	3.05	1	Cloid	David	11JUN00	1.02	1
Clark	Warner	07AUG04	3.05	1	Cloid	David	01JUN01	1.02	1
Clark	Warner	12JUN05	3.05	1	Cloid	Faithful	15JUN05	1.03	F
Clark	William	15MAY95	3.04	1	Cloid	Faithful	23JUN06	1.04	F
Clark	William	17MAY96	2.03	1	Cloid	Faithful	05JUN07	1.04	F
Clark	William	18JUL03	3.05	1	Cloyd	Faithful	31MAY08	1.06	F
Clark	William	24AUG04	3.05	1	Cloid	Faithful	29MAY09	2.04	F
Clark	William	17AUG05	3.07	1	Cloyd	George	19SEP91	3.03	1
Clark	William	28JUL06	3.06	1	Cloyd	James	13JUN87	2.02	1
CLARKSON					Cloyd	James	30OCT88	1.02	1
Clarkson	John	25JUL04	4.05	1	Cloyd	James	16JUN89	5.02	11
Clarkson	William	25JUL04	4.05	1	Cloyd	James	22JUN89	5.02	1
Clearkson	William	22JUL05	2.08	1	Cloyd	James	03JUN90	2.02	1
Clearkson	William	18JUL06	2.08	1	Cloyd	James	30MAR91	1.02	1
CLARY					Cloid	James	02JUN91	3.04	1
Clury	John	13AUG89	2.04	1	Cloyd	James	11OCT92	2.02	1
Clery	John	13SEP91	3.04	1	Cloyd	James	01DEC92	3.05	1
Clarry	John	08DEC92	3.05	1	Cloyd	James	14AUG93	1.02	1
Clary	John	22JUN94	3.05	1	Cloyd	James	07MAY94	3.06	1
Clary	William	22OCT92	1.03	1	Cloyd	James	18MAY94	1.02	1
CLAYBROOK					Cloyd	James	01MAY95	1.03	1
Claybrook	James	23JUL00	1.02	1	Cloyd	James	03JUN95	2.03	1
Claybrok	James	26JUN01	1.03	1	Cloyd	James	-----96	4.03	1
Claybrook	James	22JUN02	1.04	1	Cloyd	James	01JUN96	1.02	1
Claybrook	James	22JUN03	1.04	1	Cloyd	James	08APR97	3.05	1
Claybrook	James	02AUG04	1.04	1	Cloyd	James	14MAY99	1.04	1
CLEMENTS					Cloyd	James	30JUL00	2.05	1
Clements	David	22JUN07	2.06	1	Cloyd	James	22JUL01	2.04	1
Clements	David	10JUL09	1.08	1	Cloid	James	10JUN02	1.03	1
Clemmens	David	-----11	1.14	1	Cloid	James	18JUL03	1.05	1
Clemmons	Frederick	02AUG06	1.05	1	Cloyd	John	30JUN09	1.08	1
Clemens	Fredrick	14JUN08	1.06	1	Cloyd	John	-----11	1.14	11
Clement	John	01AUG04	2.03	1	Cloyd	Michael	27MAY96	2.04	1
Clements	John	10JUN05	3.05	1	Cloyd	Michael	-----11	1.14	1
Clement	John	21AUG06	3.08	1	Cloid	Patey	07AUG04	1.04	F
Clements	John	22JUN07	2.06	1	Cloid	Samuel	14JUN08	1.07	1
Clemonds	John	--JUN08	2.04	1	Cloyd	William	19APR89	6.02	1
Clemons	John	08JUN09	1.07	1	Cloyd	William	02APR90	1.02	1

surname	name	date	bk.pg	TM	surname	name	date	bk.pg	TM
Cloyd	William	19APR91	2.02	1	Tax paid by Hugh Leeper				
Cloyd	William	17SEP92	1.03	1	Cole	Micajah	13SEP92	1.03	1
Cloyd	William	17AUG93	3.03	1	Cole	Mecajah	07AUG93	3.03	1
Cloid	William	16APR94	2.03	1	Coal	McIcaga	12MAY94	2.03	1
Cloid	William	18MAR95	3.05	1	Cole	Micage	08APR95	3.03	1
CLYNE					Cole	Robert	14AUG06	2.10	11
Clyne	John	16JUN04	2.02	11	Coal	Stewart	23JUN06	1.04	1
COCKRAM					Cole	Stewart	08MAY07	1.04	1
Cockrum	James	09JUN07	2.05	1	Cole	Stawart	31MAY08	1.05	1
Cockrum	James	30JUN08	2.04	1	Cole	Stewart	20MAY09	2.04	1
Cockrum	James	27JUN09	1.08	1	COLEMAN				
Cockram	Matthew	22MAY97	3.06	1	Coleman	(heirs)	19JUN01	3.35	D
Cockram	Mathew	14JUN99	2.03	1	Tax paid by Robert Coleman				
Cockrum	Mathew	24JUL00	1.02	1	Coalman	Haley	14JUN08	1.06	1
Corkrum	Phillip	15MAR97	2.01	1	Coalman	Haley	14JUN09	2.05	1
COCKRELL					Colman	Jacob	-----11	1.12	1
Cockrel	John	08JUL99	3.05	1	Coleman	Robert	19JUN01	3.35	
Cockril	John	04JUN02	1.03	1	Paid tax for (heirs) Coleman				
Cockral	Lewis	17AUG09	2.06	1	Coleman	Samuel	06AUG04	3.04	1
Cockerl	Lewis	-----11	1.12	1	Coleman	Samuel	17AUG05	3.07	1
Cockeril	William	08JUN02	1.03	1	Coleman	Samuel	20AUG06	3.08	1
CODINGTON					COLGATE				
Cottinton	Benjamin	28NOV88	1.03	1	Colgate	Robert T.	13APR95	3.04	1
Cottinton	Benjamin	05AUG89	5.04	1	COLLET				
Coddington	Benjamin	30MAY90	2.02	1	Collet	Isaac	12MAY89	6.02	1
Codington	Benjamin	28OCT92	2.02	1	Collett	Isaac	21APR90	1.02	1
Codington	Benjamin	05AUG93	1.02	1	Collet	Isaac	28APR91	2.02	12
Codington	Benjamin	13MAY94	1.02	1	Collet	Isaac/Hepen	12SEP92	1.03	1
Codington	Benjamin	20MAY95	2.03	1	Collet	Stephen	12MAY89	6.02	1
Cotington	Benjamin	08JUN96	1.03	1	COLLIER				
Codington	Benjamin	18MAY97	1.05	1	Coyler	Aaron	14JUN95	2.03	1
COFFEY					Colyer	Aaron	14APR97	3.05	1
Coffy	Jesse	17AUG05	3.07	1	Colyer	Aaron	18JUN00	2.05	1
Coffy	Jesse	21JUL06	3.06	1	Colyer	Aaron	24JUL01	2.04	1
Coffy	John	19JUN99	2.03	1	Colyer	Aaron	03AUG04	2.03	1
Coffee	Osburn	01JUL99	1.07	1	Colyer	Aaron	25JUN07	1.05	1
Coffey	Osburn	22JUL00	2.06	1	Colyer	Aaron	30APR08	1.05	1
Coffy	Osborne	30MAY01	3.08	11	Colyer	Aaron	07JUN09	2.05	1
Coffy	Osburn	12JUL02	2.05	11	Collier	Alexander	05JUL87	3.02	13
Coffey	Osborn	30MAY03	3.04	11	Collier	Alexander	25JUL89	2.03	12
Coffee	Osborn	16AUG04	3.05	11	Colyear	Alexandria	07JUL91	3.03	1
Coffy	Orsburn	22AUG05	3.08	1	Collier	Alexander	01DEC92	3.05	1
Coffy	Osburn	21JUL06	3.06	1	Collier	Alexander	05MAY94	3.06	1
COFFMAN					Colleir	Alexander	06MAY95	1.04	1
Caufman	John	26JUN89	6.02	1	Collier	Alexander	-----96	4.04	1
Coffman	John	23JUN90	1.02	1	Coyler	Arron	18MAY94	1.02	1
Caufman	John	13SEP92	1.03	1	Colyer	Aron	12JUN99	2.03	1
Caufman	John	12SEP93	3.03	1	Colyar	Aron	10JUN02	1.03	1
COGHILL					Colyar	Aron	30JUN03	1.04	00
Coghill	James	07JUL87	3.03	1	Colyar	Aron	15JUN05	1.03	1
Coghill	James	14NOV88	1.02	1	Colyar	Aron	19JUN06	1.04	1
Coghill	James	21JUL89	5.04	11	Colyer	Aran	-----11	1.13	1
Coghill	James	03APR90	2.02	1	Colyear	James	07JUL91	3.03	1
Cogwell	James	14APR91	1.02	1	Colyear	James	26NOV92	3.04	1
Cogwell	James	14APR91	1.02	1	Colyear	James	29NOV92	3.05	1
Cogswell	James	14OCT92	2.02	1	Collier	James	01MAY94	3.05	1
Coghill	James	13AUG93	1.03	1	Collier	James	06MAY95	1.04	1
Coghill	James	29MAY94	1.02	1	Collier	James	01JUN95	1.04	1
Coghill	James	03JUN95	2.03	1	Collier	James	-----96	4.04	1
Coghill	James	29JUN96	1.02	1	Colyer	James T	14JUN08	1.06	11
Coghill	James	14APR97	3.05	1	Collier	John	25JUL89	2.03	1
COLE					Colyear	John	07JUL91	3.03	1
Cole	Barnett	-----08	2.06	1	Colyear	John	26NOV92	3.04	1
Cole	Barnett	30JUN09	1.08	1	Colyear	John	29NOV92	3.04	1
Cole	James	25JUL07	2.06	1	Collier	John	01MAY94	3.05	1
Coal	John	12JUN05	1.03	1	Collier	John	06MAY95	1.04	1
Coal	John	21JUN06	1.04	1	Collier	John	-----96	4.04	1
Cole	John	08MAY07	1.04	11	Colyar	John	24JUN01	1.03	11
Cole	John	31MAY08	1.05	11	Colyar	John	17JUN02	1.04	1
Cole	John	17AUG09	2.07	1	Colyar	John	23JUN03	1.04	1
Cole	Joseph	09JUN94	1.12	1	Colyar	John Jr	23JUN03	1.04	1
Cole	Joseph	30JUL01	2.17	0	Colyar	John Sr	03AUG04	1.04	1

surname	name	date	bk.pg	TM	surname	name	date	bk.pg	TM
Colyar	John	01AUG04	1.04	1	Collins	James	30MAY90	2.02	1
Colyar	John	29JUL05	1.04	1	Collans	Joal	18JUN96	1.13	
Colyar	John	30JUN06	1.05	1	One town lot in Stanford				
Collier	John Sr	04MAY07	1.03	1	Collins	John	18JUN96	1.03	1
free from county levy					Collins	John	16JUN99	1.05	1
Colyer	John	04MAY07	1.03	1	Collins	John	18JUN00	2.05	1
Colyer	John Sr	14JUN08	1.06	0	Collins	John	24JUL01	2.04	1
Exempt from county levy					Collins	John	30JUN03	1.04	1
Colyer	John	14JUN08	1.06	1	Collins	William	14JUN08	1.07	11
Coyer	John Jr	13JUN09	2.05	1	Collens	William	-----11	1.10	1
Colyer	Moses	04NOV88	1.02	1	COLSON				
Colyer	Moses	24JUN89	5.02	1	Colson	John	07AUG89	5.04	1
Colyear	Moses	07MAY91	3.04	1	Coleson	Robert	-----11	1.16	1
Collier	Moses	12OCT92	2.02	11	COLVIN				
Colyear	Moses	01DEC92	3.05	1	Colvin	Benjamin	24JUN00	2.06	1
Coyler	Moses	13AUG93	1.02	11	Colvin	Charles	21JUN00	2.06	1
Collier	Moses	07MAY94	3.06	1	Colvin	Charles	19APR01	2.03	1
Coyler	Moses	18MAY94	1.02	11	Colvin	Charles	26MAY02	3.05	1
Collier	Moses	01JUN95	1.04	1	Colvin	Charles	11JUN03	2.05	1
Coyler	Moses	04JUN95	2.03	1	Colvin	Charles	03AUG05	2.08	1
Collier	Moses	-----96	4.04	1	Colvin	Charles	14JUN06	2.07	1
Coyler	Moses	29JUN96	1.03	12	Colven	Charles	03AUG07	2.07	1
Colyer	Moses	08APR97	3.05	1	Colvin	Charles	23AUG09	2.07	1
Colyer	Moses	08APR97	3.04	11	Colvin	Charles	-----11	1.11	1
Colyer	Moses	29MAY99	2.03	11	Colvin	Daniel	14JUN08	1.07	1
Colyer	Moses Jr	29MAY99	2.03	1	Colvin	Daniel	23AUG09	2.07	1
Colyar	Moses	19JUN00	1.02	1	Colvin	Elijah	19MAY06	2.07	1
Colyar	Moses Sr	19JUN00	1.02	11	Colvin	Elijah	23AUG09	2.07	1
Colyer	Moses Jr	19JUN00	1.02	1	Colvin	Elijah	-----11	1.12	1
Colyar	Moses	11JUN01	1.02	1	Colvin	John	30MAY99	1.06	1
Colyar	Moses	04JUN02	1.03	1	Colvin	John	21JUN00	2.06	1
Colyar	Moses	14JUN02	1.04	1	Colvin	John	17JUL01	2.04	1
Colyar	Moses	23JUN03	1.04	1	Colvin	John	11JUN03	2.05	1
Colyar	Moses	28JUN03	1.04	11	Colvin	John	25JUL04	1.04	1
Colyar	Moses	20JUN04	1.03	1	Colvin	John	08JUN05	2.06	1
Colyar	Moses	01AUG04	2.03	1	Colven	John	03AUG07	2.07	1
Colyar	Moses Sr	12JUN05	1.03	1	Colvin	John	-----11	1.12	1
Colyar	Moses	12JUN05	1.03	1	Colvin	Joseph	02JUN90	2.02	11
Colyar	Moses	16JUN06	1.03	1	Colvin	Joseph	19OCT92	2.02	11
Colyar	Moses	18JUN06	1.04	0	Calvin	Joseph	27AUG93	1.02	12
Free (of tax)					Calvin	Joseph	15MAY94	1.02	11
Colyer	Moses	04JUN07	1.04	0	Colvin	Joseph	20APR97	3.05	12
Exempt from county levy					Colvin	Joseph	30MAY99	1.06	12
Colyer	Moses Jr	12JUN07	1.04	1	Colvin	Joseph	17JUL00	2.06	1
Colyer	Moses	22APR08	1.05	0	Colvin	Joseph	21JUN00	2.06	1
Exempt from county levy					Colvin	Joseph Sr	17JUL01	2.04	1
Clyer	Moses	31MAY08	1.05	1	Colvin	Joseph Jr	17JUL01	2.04	1
Colyer	Moses Sr	08JUN09	2.05	0	Colvin	Joseph Sr	26MAY02	3.05	11
Colyer	Moses	06JUN09	2.05	1	Colvin	Joseph Jr	26MAY02	3.05	1
Colyer	Moses Sr	-----11	1.14	0	Colvin	Joseph Sr	20JUN03	2.05	11
Colyer	Moses Jr	-----11	1.14	1	Colvin	Joseph Jr	18MAY03	2.05	1
Collier	Robert	25JUL89	2.03	1	Colvin	Joseph	26JUL04	1.04	11
Colyear	Robert	29NOV92	3.04	1	Colvin	Joseph Sr	03AUG05	2.08	1
Collier	Robert	22JUN94	3.05	1	Colvin	Joseph Jr	08JUN05	2.06	1
Collier	Robert	01JUN95	1.04	1	Colvin	Joseph Sr	06JUN06	2.07	11
Collier	Robert	-----96	4.04	1	Colvin	Joseph Jr	06JUN06	2.07	1
Colyer	Solomon	19JUN00	1.02	1	Colvin	Joseph	25JUL07	2.06	11
Colyar	Solomon	11JUN01	1.02	1	Colven	Joseph	03AUG07	2.07	1
Colyar	Solomon	04JUN02	1.03	1	Colvin	Joseph Sr	14JUN08	1.07	1
Colyar	Solomon	28JUN03	1.04	1	Colvin	Joseph	14JUN08	1.07	1
Colyar	Solomon	01AUG04	2.03	1	Colvin	Joseph Sr	23AUG09	2.07	1
Colyar	Solomon	12JUN05	1.03	1	Colvin	Joseph	23AUG09	2.07	1
Colyar	Solomon	18JUN06	1.03	1	Colvin	Joseph Sr	-----11	1.12	1
Colyar	Solaman	12JUN07	1.04	1	Colvin	Joseph Jr	-----11	1.12	1
Colyer	Solaman	06JUN09	2.05	1	Calvin	William	27AUG93	1.02	1
Colyar	Solomon	-----11	1.14	1	Calvin	William	15MAY94	1.02	1
Colyar	William	23JUN03	1.04	1	Colvin	William	25MAY95	2.03	1
Colyer	William	13JUN09	2.05	1	Colvin	William	10JUN96	1.03	1
COLLINS					Colvin	William	20APR97	3.06	1
Collins	Isal	18JUN96	1.02	1	Colvin	William	27MAY99	1.05	1
Collins	Jacob	23MAY09	2.04	1	Colvin	William	21JUN00	2.06	1
Collens	Jacob	-----11	1.14	1	Colvin	William	19APR01	2.03	1

surname	name	date	bk.pg	TM
Colvin	William	14JUN02	3.05	1
Colvin	William	04JUN03	2.05	1
Colvin	William	25JUL04	1.04	1
Colvin	William	08JUN05	2.06	1
Colvin	William	06JUN06	2.07	1
Colven	William	03AUG07	2.07	1
Colvin	William	14JUN08	1.07	1
Colvin	William	-----11	1.11	1
COMBS				
Combs	John	28JUN96	2.04	1
Combs	John	24MAY97	1.06	1
Combs	John	26JUN99	3.04	1
Combs	John	03JUN00	2.05	1
Combs	John	04JUL00	3.08	1
Combs	John	06MAY01	3.06	1
Combs	John	06AUG02	3.06	1
Comes	John	15JUN03	1.03	1
Combs	John	30JUL03	2.06	1
Combs	John	13JUN04	4.05	1
Comes	John	18JUN04	1.03	11
Comes	John	11JUN05	1.03	1
Combs	John	27JUN05	2.07	11
Comes	John	10JUN06	1.03	1
Combs	John	31JUL06	2.09	1
Combs	John Jr	31JUL06	2.09	M1
Combs	John	02JUN07	1.04	1
Combs	John	06JUL07	2.06	1
Comes	John	26JUL08	2.05	1
Combs	John Sr	12JUL09	1.09	1
Combs	John	25MAY09	2.04	1
Combs	John Jr	12JUL09	1.09	1
Combs	John Jr	-----11	1.14	1
Combs	Matthew	10JUL99	3.05	1
Cumbel	Stephen	12MAY89	6.02	1
Combs	Stephen	02JUN90	2.02	1
Comb	Stephen	25MAR91	1.02	1
Comes	Stephen	30MAY94	1.03	1
Coombs	Stephen	14JUN95	2.03	1
Combes	Stephen	14MAY99	1.04	11
Combs	Stephen	30JUL00	2.05	11
Combs	Stephen	22JUL01	2.04	11
Comes	Stephen	04JUN02	1.03	11
Comes	Stephen	15JUN03	1.03	11
Comes	Stephen	18JUN04	1.03	1
Comes	Stephen	19JUN05	1.03	1
Comes	Stephen	10JUN06	1.03	1
Combs	Stephen	02JUN07	1.04	1
Combs	Stephen	14JUN08	1.07	1
Combs	Stephen	-----11	1.14	1
Combs	William	29OCT93	3.02	1
Combs	William	18APR94	2.03	1
Combs	William	19MAR95	3.05	1
Combs	William	25JUN96	2.04	1
Combs	William	24MAY97	1.05	1
Combs	William	04JUL00	3.08	1
Combs	William	09MAY01	3.06	1
Combs	William	11AUG02	3.06	1
Combs	William	29JUL03	2.06	1
Combs	William	18AUG04	4.06	1
Comes	William	05JUN05	1.03	1
Combs	William	19JUL05	2.07	1
Comes	William	16JUN06	1.03	1
Combs	William	14AUG06	2.10	11
Combs	William	22MAY09	2.04	1
Combs	William	-----11	1.13	1
COMER				
Cromer	John	01AUG06	1.05	1
Comer	John	08MAY07	1.03	1
Comer	Richard	16MAY05	2.06	1
Comer	Richard	18JUL06	3.05	1
Comer	Richard	22JUN07	2.06	1
Commer	Richard	15JUL08	2.05	1
Comer	Richard	23MAR09	1.06	11
CONDER				
Conder	Daniel	11JUL99	3.05	M1
Conder	Daniel	10JUL00	3.08	1
Conder	Daniel	10AUG03	2.07	1
Conder	Daniel	08JUN04	4.04	1
Conder	Daniel	21JUN05	2.07	1
Conder	Daniel	30JUL06	2.09	11
Conder	John	23JUN96	2.04	1
CONDON				
Condon	James	30MAY03	3.04	1
CONLEY				
Conley	Sanford	04JUL08	2.05	1
Connally	Wilkinson	05MAY94	3.06	1
CONNOR				
Conner	George	13JUN97	3.06	1
Conner	George	04JUL99	3.05	1
Conner	Isaac	10MAY97	3.05	1
Connor	Isaac	16JUN03	3.05	
A free mulattoe above 21				
Connor	Isaac	19MAY06	2.07	
A free Mulattoe				
Connor	Thomas	19JUL03	3.05	11
Conner	Thomas Jr	19JUL03	3.05	1
Connor	Thomas	15JUN04	2.02	11
Conner	Thomas	15JUN04	2.02	11
Conner	Thomas	22AUG07	2.08	1
Conner	Wilson	14AUG05	3.07	1
CONWILL				
Conwill	John	20JUN03	1.03	1
Conwill	William	20JUN03	1.03	1
Connel	William	08MAY07	1.04	1
COOK				
Cook	Anthony	12MAY99	2.03	1
Cook	Anthony	19JUN00	1.02	1
Cook	Anthony	18JUN02	1.04	1
Cook	Anthony	11JUN03	1.03	1
Cook	Anthony	14JUN04	1.03	1
Cook	Anthony	07JUN05	1.03	1
Cook	Anthony	11JUN06	1.03	1
Cook	Anthony	18MAY07	1.04	1
Cook	Anthony	14JUN08	1.06	1
Cook	Anthony	20MAY09	2.04	1
Cook	Anthony	-----11	1.14	1
Cook	Cornealus	22AUG07	2.08	1
Cook	Cornealus	-----08	2.06	1
Cook	David	20JUN87	2.02	1
Cook	David	17NOV88	1.03	1
Cook	David	04JUL89	5.04	1
Cook	David	15JUN90	2.02	1
Cook	David	05JUL91	1.02	1
Cook	David	15OCT92	2.02	1
Cook	David	09AUG93	1.02	1
Cook	David	20MAY94	1.02	1
Cook	David	25MAY95	2.03	1
Cook	David	16JUN96	1.02	11
Cook	David	07APR97	3.05	11
Cook	David	22JUN99	1.05	12
Cook	David	24MAY00	2.05	22
Cook	David	21JUL01	2.04	1
Cook	David	18JUN02	1.04	12
Cook	David	18JUL03	1.05	11
Cook	David	14JUN04	1.03	11
Cook	David Jr	20JUN04	1.03	11
Cook	David	20JUN05	1.03	00
Cook	David Sr	20JUN05	1.04	1
Cook	David	20JUN05	1.04	1
Paid tax for Matthew Creed				
Cook	David	23JUN06	1.04	11
Cook	David Jr	23JUN06	1.04	1
Cook	David Sr	18JUN07	1.05	1
Cook	David	17JUN07	1.04	1

surname	name	date	bk.pg	TM	surname	name	date	bk.pg	TM
Cook	David Sr	31MAY08	1.05	1	Cook	Lewis	19JUN09	1.07	1
Cook	David Jr	31MAY08	1.06	11	Cook	Lewis	-----11	1.15	1
Cook	David	17AUG09	2.06	1	Cook	Lofty	03JUN02	1.03	1
Cook	David	-----11	1.13	1	Cook	Loftus	15JUL03	1.05	1
Cook	George	10AUG07	2.07	1	Cook	Loftes	01AUG04	1.04	1
Cook	George	10AUG07	2.07	1	Cook	Loftus	29JUL05	1.04	1
Cook	George	-----08	2.06	1	Cook	Loftes	30JUN06	1.05	1
Cook	George	10JUN09	1.07	1	Cook	Lofty	05MAY07	1.03	1
Cook	Henry	14JUN87	2.01	1	Cook	Loftus	14JUN08	1.06	1
Cook	Henry	18JUN87	2.02	11	Cook	Loftus	13JUN09	2.05	1
Cook	Henry Sr	05NOV88	1.02	11	Cook	Moses	25JUL05	2.08	1
Cook	Henry	28OCT88	1.02	1	Cook	Moses	16JUL06	2.08	1
Cook	Henry	16JUN89	5.02	1	Cook	Moses	10AUG07	2.07	1
Cook	Henry	30JUN89	5.02	11	Cook	Nancy	24MAY00	2.05	F
Cook	Henry	03APR90	2.02	1	Cook	Nancy	21JUL01	2.04	F
Cook	Henry	14SEP91	3.04	1	Cook	Nancy	18JUL03	1.05	F
Cook	Henry	06OCT92	2.02	1	Cook	Nancy	20JUN05	1.04	F
Cook	Henry	15AUG93	1.02	1	Cook	Nancy	23JUN06	1.04	F
Cook	Henry	02MAY94	3.06	1	Cook	Nancy	18JUN07	1.04	F
Cook	Henry	21MAY94	1.02	1	Cook	Susanna	22JUN99	1.05	F
Cook	Henry	06MAY95	1.04	2	Cook	Valentine	18JUL03	1.05	1
Cook	Henry	25MAY95	2.03	1	Cook	William	26JUN95	2.03	1
Cook	Henry	-----96	4.04	2	Cook	William	02JUN96	1.03	1
Cook	Henry	14JUN96	1.03	1	Cook	Zedekia	17JUL00	2.06	1
Cook	Henry	15MAR97	2.01	1	COOLEY				
Cook	Henry	12MAY99	2.03	1	Cooley	Charles	20MAY96	2.03	1
Cook	Henry	09JUN00	1.02	11	Cooley	Charles	24MAY97	1.05	2
Cook	Henry	01JUN01	1.02	11	Cooley	Charles	15JUL99	3.05	11
Cook	Henry	30JUN02	1.05	11	Cooley	Charles	05JUL00	3.08	1
Cook	Henry	11JUN03	1.03	11	Cooley	Charles	07MAY01	3.06	1
Cook	Henry	14JUN04	1.03	11	Cooley	Charles	10AUG02	3.06	1
Cook	Henry	05JUN05	1.03	1	Cooley	Charles	03AUG03	2.06	1
Cook	Henry	14JUN06	1.03	2	Cooly	Charles	27JUN04	4.05	1
Cook	Henry	04MAY07	1.03	2	Cooley	Charles	19JUL05	2.08	1
Cook	Henry	14JUN08	1.06	2	Cooley	Charles	19AUG06	2.10	1
Cook	Henry	23MAY09	2.04	21	Cooley	Daniel	27JUN89	2.03	1
Cook	Henry	-----11	1.13	11	Cooley	Daniel	01MAY95	1.03	1
Cook	Henry	-----11	1.14	2	Cooley	Daniel	-----96	4.04	1
Cook	Hugh	21JUL03	3.05	1	Cooley	Jabes	27JUN87	3.02	1
Cook	Hugh	03MAY04	3.04	1	Cooley	James	24MAY97	1.05	1
Cook	Hugh	13JUN05	3.05	1	Cooley	James	15JUL99	3.06	1
Cook	James	-----11	1.13	1	Cooley	James	05JUN01	3.07	1
Cook	John	26JUN87	2.02	1	Cooley	James	11AUG02	3.06	1
Cook	John	18NOV88	1.03	1	Cooley	James	28JUL03	2.06	1
Cook	John	30JUN89	5.04	1	Cooly	James	27JUN04	4.05	1
Cook	John	31MAR90	2.02	1	Cooley	James	19JUL05	2.08	1
Cook	John	23JUN90	1.02	11	Cooley	James	19AUG06	2.10	11
Cook	John	05JUL91	1.02	1	Cooley	John	01MAY95	3.04	1
Cook	John	07OCT92	2.02	1	Cooley	John	24JUN96	2.04	1
Cook	John	09AUG93	1.02	1	Cooley	John	10AUG97	1.04	1
Cook	John	07MAY94	3.06	0	Cooly	John	10JUL99	3.05	1
Cook	John	20MAY94	1.02	1	Cooley	John	09JUL00	3.08	1
Cook	John	26MAY95	2.03	1	Coley	John	30JUL01	3.07	1
Cook	John	21JUN96	1.03	1	Cooley	John	29JUL02	3.06	1
Cook	John	06APR97	3.05	1	Cooley	John	10AUG03	2.07	1
Cook	John	23MAY99	1.05	1	Cooley	John	08JUN04	4.05	1
Cook	John	30JUL00	2.05	1	Cooley	John	20JUN05	2.07	1
Cook	John	21JUL01	2.04	1	Cooley	John	30JUL06	2.09	1
Cook	John	16JUN02	1.04	1	Cooley	Joseph	24JUN96	2.04	1
Cook	John	05JUL03	1.05	1	Cooley	Joseph	15AUG07	2.08	1
Cook	John	14JUN04	1.03	1	Cooley	Reuben	30JUL06	2.09	1
Cook	John	20JUN05	1.04	1	Coley	Thadias	24JUN91	3.04	1
Cook	John	21JUN06	1.04	1	COOPER				
Cook	John	18JUN07	1.05	11	Cooper	Edward	01JUN97	3.06	1
Cook	John Sr	31MAY08	1.06	11	Cooper	Frederick	17JUL06	3.05	1
Cook	John Jr	23APR08	1.05	1	Cooper	James	03JUL02	3.05	1
Cook	John	05JUL09	2.06	1	Cooper	James	20JUN03	2.05	1
Cook	John	-----11	1.13	1	Cooper	James	19JUL05	2.08	1
Cook	John	-----11	1.13	1	Cooper	James	07AUG06	2.10	1
Cook	Lewis	23JUL05	2.08	1	Cooper	James	10AUG07	2.07	1
Cook	Lewis	24APR06	2.07	1	Cooper	James	-----08	2.06	1
Cook	Lewis	10AUG07	2.07	1	Cooper	James	10JUN09	1.07	1

surname	name	date	bk.pg	TM	surname	name	date	bk.pg	TM
Cooper	James	-----11	1.15	1	CORNETT				
Cooper	John	01MAY94	2.03	1	Cornett	Parks	23JUL07	2.06	1
Cooper	John	01APR95	3.04	1	Cornett	Park	30JUN08	2.04	1
Cooper	John	03AUG96	2.05	1	Cornett	Park	08JUN09	1.06	1
Cooper	John	22MAY97	1.06	1	Cornit	Park	-----11	1.11	1
Cooper	John	21JUN00	2.05	1	Cornett	William	23JUL07	2.06	1
Coope	John	30JUN01	2.04	1	Cornit	William	-----11	1.11	1
Cooper	John	04AUG02	2.05	1	COSBEY				
Cooper	John	13AUG02	3.06	1	Cosbey	Charles	09SEP89	2.04	1
Cooper	John	17JUN03	3.04	1	COSSY				
Cooper	John	20JUN03	2.05	1	Kosey	James	14OCT92	2.05	1
Cooper	John	27JUL04	4.06	1	Cosse	Joseph	31MAY05	2.06	1
Cooper	John	22AUG04	3.05	1	Cosse	Joseph	09AUG06	2.10	1
Cooper	John	23JUL05	2.08	11	Cosey	Joseph	25JUL07	2.06	1
Cooper	John	14AUG05	3.07	1	Cossy	Joseph	07JUN09	1.06	1
Cooper	John	24APR06	2.07	11	Cozzey	Joseph	-----11	1.14	1
Cooper	John	21AUG06	3.08	1	COTES				
Cooper	John	14AUG07	2.08	1	Cotes	George	15MAY89	6.02	1
Cooper	John	22JUN09	1.08	1	Cotes	George	03JUN91	2.02	1
Cooper	John Sr	-----11	1.15	1	COTNER				
Cooper	John Jr	-----11	1.15	1	Cotner	Frederick	03SEP89	2.04	1
Cooper	Levi	07AUG06	3.07	1	Cotner	Fredrick	19SEP91	3.03	1
Cooper	Malicki	01JUN97	3.06	1	Cotner	Featherick	03DEC92	3.05	1
Cooper	William	13JUN97	1.05	11	Cotner	Frederick	01MAY94	3.05	1
COOS					Cotner	Fredrick	14MAY95	1.04	1
Coos	Claery	16JUL06	2.08	1	Cotner	Frederick	-----96	4.04	1
COPE					Cotner	John	01MAY94	3.05	1
Cope	John Sr	22JUN97	1.05	1	COTRILL				
Cope	John Jr	22JUN97	1.05	1	Cottrele	Elizabeth	22JUN94	3.05	F
Cop	Martin	14MAY89	6.02	1	Catewill	Elizabeth	01MAY95	3.03	F1
Cop	Martin	05APR90	1.03	1	Cotrill	Thomas	01AUG04	1.04	1
Cope	Martin	18MAY91	2.02	1	Cotrill	Thomas	29JUL05	1.04	1
Cope	Martin	08OCT92	1.03	1	Cotrill	Thomas	30JUN06	1.05	1
Cope	Martin	16AUG93	3.03	1	Cotral	Thomas	13JUN09	2.05	1
Cope	Martin	23APR94	2.03	1	COUCH				
Cope	Martin	28MAR95	3.04	1	Cooch	Daniel	20JUN05	2.07	1
Cope	Martin	04AUG96	2.05	1	Cooch	Daniel	30JUL06	2.09	1
Cope	Martin	03JUL97	1.05	1	Cooch	Dedirick	30JUL01	3.07	11
Cope	Martin	21JUN00	2.05	1	Couch	Detric	29JUL02	3.06	11
Calp	Martin	08JUL01	3.07	1	Couts	Henry	09SEP89	2.04	1
Cope	Martin	15JUL06	2.08	1	Coutch	Henry	25NOV92	3.04	1
Colp	Martin	14AUG07	2.08	11	Couts	Henry	07MAY94	3.06	1
Culp	Marten	-----08	2.06	11	Couts	Henry	01MAY95	1.03	1
COPELAND					Couls	Henry	-----96	4.04	1
Copeland	Jacob	09SEP89	2.04	11	Couts	Teter	01JUN95	1.04	1
Coplin	Jacob	07SEP91	3.04	1	Kutch	Teterich	10JUL99	3.12	1
Coplen	Jacob	26NOV92	3.04	1	Keech	Teterich	10JUL00	3.16	11
Copelin	Jacob	08DEC92	3.05	1	Cooch	Tetrich	10AUG03	2.07	11
Copelin	Jacob	01MAY94	3.05	1	Cooch	Tetriarch	03JUN04	4.05	11
Caplen	Jacob	06MAY95	1.04	1	Cooch	Tetrich	20JUN05	2.07	11
Copeland	Jacob	-----96	4.03	1	Couch	Tetrich	30JUL06	2.09	11
Coplin	John	07SEP91	3.04	11	COULTER				
Coplen	John	26NOV92	3.04	01	Coulter	John	30JUL06	2.09	1
Copelin	John	02MAY94	3.06	1	Coulter	Matthew	10AUG97	1.05	1
Caplen	John	01JUN95	1.04	1	Coulter	Matthew	10JUL99	3.05	11
Copeland	John	-----96	4.04	1	Coller	Matthew	09JUL00	3.08	11
Cape	John	22APR96	2.03	1	Cotter	Matthew	30JUL01	3.07	11
Coplin	Thomas	07SEP91	3.04	11	Coulter	Mathew	29JUL02	3.06	11
Coplen	Thomas	26NOV92	3.04	01	Coulter	Mathew	09AUG03	2.07	11
Caplen	Thomas	01JUN95	1.04	1	Colter	Matthew	05MAY04	4.04	11
Copeland	Thomas	-----96	4.03	1	Coulter	Mathew	19JUN05	2.07	12
CORD					Coulter	Mathew	30JUL06	2.09	11
Cord	Chris.	25MAY89	6.02	1	Colter	Mauris	05MAY04	4.04	1
CORDER					Coulter	Morris	30JUL06	2.09	1
Corder	Balis	03MAY90	2.02	1	COUNTS				
Corder	Baylis	18MAY91	2.02	1	Counts	John	19JUN99	2.03	1
Corder	Baylis	10OCT92	1.03	1	COURTNEY				
Corder	Baylis	12AUG93	3.03	1	Courtney	Michael	20JUN87	2.02	1
Corder	Balis	30APR94	2.04	1	Couteny	Michael	05MAY94	2.03	1
Corder	Balis	02APR95	3.04	1	Catnoy	Michael	10APR95	3.04	1
CORDON					Coleney	Michael	-----08	2.06	11
Cordon	Shadrick	30APR94	2.03	1	Coatney	Michael	17AUG09	2.06	1

surname	name	date	bk.pg	TM	surname	name	date	bk.pg	TM
COVINGTON					Cocks	William	22JUN99	2.03	1
Covington	William	11AUG02	3.06	1	Cocks	William	22JUN99	2.04	1
COWAN					Cox	William	02JUL99	3.04	1
Cowan	Ann	14JUN08	1.06	F	Cox	William	01JUL00	3.07	1
Cowan	Ann	29MAY09	2.04	F	Cox	William	17AUG02	3.07	11
Coun	John	03AUG04	2.03	1	Cox	William	22JUN03	2.05	1
Cowan	Sauzanna	23JUN90	1.02	F	Cox	William	16JUL06	2.08	1
COX					Cox	William	30JUL06	3.06	11
Cox	Beverly	08JUN97	1.05	1	Cox	William	04AUG07	2.07	1
Cox	Beverley	10JUL00	3.08	1	COY				
Cox	Beaverly	30JUL01	3.07	1	Coy	Christopher	05JUL96	2.04	1
Cox	Beaverly	10JUN02	2.04	1	Coye	Chris.	08JUN97	1.05	1
Cox	Beverly	05AUG03	3.06	1	CRABILE				
Cocks	Beverly	06MAY04	4.04	1	Crabile	John	20APR91	2.02	1
Cox	Chestain	10AUG07	2.07	1	CRADDOCK				
Cocks	Christopher	22JUN99	2.04	1	Craddock	Robert	25MAY89	6.02	1
Cox	Daniel	13OCT92	1.03	1	CRAFTON				
Cox	Daniel	13SEP93	3.03	1	Crafton	Anthony	07JUN97	1.05	1
Cox	Daniel	03AUG02	2.05	1	Craftan	Anthony	-----11	1.15	1
Cox	Daniel	20MAY03	3.04	1	Crafton	James	07JUN97	1.05	1
Cox	Daniel	07AUG04	3.05	1	Crafton	Joseph	16JUN96	2.04	1
Cox	Daniel	15AUG05	3.07	1	Crafton	Joseph	07JUN97	1.04	1
Cox	Daniel	04AUG06	3.07	1	Crafton	Joseph	15JUL99	3.06	1
Cox	Edward	17JUL06	2.08	1	Craftsman	Joseph	25JUN00	3.06	1
Cocks	Frederick	21JUN99	2.03	1	Crafton	Joseph	30JUL01	3.07	1
Cox	James	09JUN89	6.02	1	Crafton	Paty	17JUN05	2.06	F
Cox	James	05APR90	1.02	11	CRAIG				
Cox	James	19APR91	2.02	11	Craig	David	-----11	1.12	1
Cox	James	08OCT92	1.03	1	Craig	Eliz./Wm.	-----08	2.06	
Cox	James	20AUG93	3.03	1	Admin for John Craig				
Cox	James	23APR94	2.03	1	Craig	Eliz./Wm.	07AUG09	1.09	
Cox	James	01MAY94	2.03	1	Executors for John Craig				
Cocks	James	18MAR95	3.04	01	Craig	Elizabeth	-----11	1.12	F
Cocks	James	02APR95	3.04	11	Exec. of J.Craig-deceased				
Cocks	Jesse	22JUN99	2.04	1	Craig	Frank	17JUN03	2.05	
Cocks	John	22JUN99	2.04	11	A free negro				
Cox	John	01JUL00	3.07	1	Craig	Frank	08MAY06	2.07	
Cox	John	20MAY01	3.07	02	A free Negroe				
Cox	John	17AUG02	3.07	11	Crage	James	14JUN87	2.01	1
Cox	John	25JUL03	2.06	1	Crage	James	28NOV88	1.03	1
Cox	John	24JUL05	2.08	1	Crage	James	04AUG89	5.04	1
Cox	John	16JUL06	2.08	1	Craig	James	30MAY90	2.02	1
Cox	John	04AUG07	2.07	1	Craig	James	05APR91	1.02	1
Cox	John	28JUL08	2.05	1	Craig	James	23OCT92	2.02	1
Cox	John	22JUN09	1.08	1	Craig	James	05AUG93	1.02	1
Cocks	Joseph	26JUL04	4.06	M1	Craig	James	12MAY94	1.02	1
Cox	Joseph	24JUL05	2.08	1	Craig	James	16JUN95	2.03	1
Cox	Joseph	16JUL06	2.08	1	Craig	James	01JUN96	1.03	11
Cox	Joseph	04AUG07	2.07	1	Craig	James	21APR97	3.07	11
Cox	Joseph	28JUL08	2.05	1	Craig	James	29MAY99	1.05	1
Cox	Joseph	22JUN09	1.08	1	Craig	James	01AUG00	2.07	1
Cox	Leroy	-----11	1.15	1	Craig	James	27APR01	2.03	1
Cocks	Margaret	23AUG96	2.04	F1	Craig	James	03JUL02	3.05	1
Cox	Margaret	17MAY97	1.05	11	Craig	James	20JUN03	2.05	1
Cox	Margaret	02JUL99	3.04	F1	Craig	James	24JUL04	1.04	1
Cox	Margaret	17AUG02	3.07	F	Craig	James	31JUL05	2.08	1
Cox	Margaret	25JUL03	2.06	F1	Craig	James	24APR06	2.07	1
Cocks	Margaret	27JUL04	4.06	F	Craig	James	03AUG07	2.07	1
Cox	Margaret	23JUL05	2.08	F	Craig	James	14JUN08	1.07	11
Cox	Margaret	16JUL06	2.08	F1	Crage	John	14JUN87	2.01	1
Cox	Margaret	04AUG07	2.07	FS	Crage	John	28NOV88	1.03	1
Cox	Margarett	28JUL08	2.05	F1	Crage	John	06AUG89	5.04	1
Cox	Margarett	22JUN09	1.08	F	Craig	John	29MAR90	2.02	1
Cox	Margaret	-----11	1.15	F2	Craig	John Sr	17OCT91	1.02	11
Cocks	Richard	18JUN06	1.03	1	Craig	John Jr	17OCT91	1.02	1
Cocks	Richard	01JUL07	1.05	1	Crag	John	14SEP91	3.04	1
Cocks	Richard	02JUN08	1.06	1	Craig	John	02OCT91	3.04	1
Cocks	Richard	29MAY09	2.04	1	Craig	John Sr	23OCT92	2.02	1
Cox	Richard	-----11	1.11	1	Craig	John Jr	23OCT92	2.02	11
Cocks	Solomon	22JUN99	2.04	1	Craig	John	29NOV92	3.05	1
Cocks	Thomas	23JUN99	2.03	1	Craig	John Jr	03AUG93	1.03	1
					Craig	John Sr	12MAY94	1.02	1

surname	name	date	bk.pg	TM	surname	name	date	bk.pg	TM
Craig	John	07MAY94	3.06	1	Craig	Samuel	-----11	1.23	
Craig	John	31MAY94	1.02	1	James Ely - Guardian				
Craig	John Sr	02MAY95	2.16	1	Craig	William	25JUL05	1.04	11
Craig	John Sr	20MAY95	2.03	1	Craig	William	23JUN06	1.05	11
Craig	John Jr	11MAY95	2.03	1	Craig	William	02JUL07	1.05	2
Craig	John Jr	11MAY95	2.15	1	Craig	William	06JUL09	2.06	1
Craig	John	01MAY95	1.03	1	Craig	William	-----11	1.12	1
Craig	John	-----96	4.04	1	Craig	William	-----11	1.12	1
Craig	John	08JUN96	1.02	1	Craig	William	-----11	1.12	1
Craig	John	30JUN96	1.03	1	Exec. of J.Craig-deceased				
Craig	John	15JUN97	3.06	1	CRAINSHAW				
Craig	John	29AUG97	3.34	1	Crainshaw	Benjamin	19MAY06	2.07	1
Craig	John Sr	01JUN99	1.06	1	CRAMER				
Craig	John Jr	03JUN99	1.06	1	Craimer	Peter	16JUL06	2.08	1
Craig	John Sr	01AUG00	2.07	1	Cramer	Peter	22JUN09	1.08	1
Craig	John Jr	01AUG00	2.07	1	Cramer	Peter	-----11	1.15	1
Craig	John Jr	01AUG00	2.07	1	CRAVENS				
Craig	John Sr	27JUN01	2.04	1	Cravens	Elijah	21NOV92	2.02	1
Craig	John Jr	20JUL01	2.05	1	Cravens	Jerry	21NOV92	2.02	1
Crabb	John	07MAY01	3.06	1	Cravens	Jeremiah	03AUG93	1.02	1
Craig	John Sr	17JUN02	3.05	1	Cravens	Jeremiah	17MAY94	1.02	1
Craig	John	21JUL02	2.05	1	Cravins	Jeremiah	28MAY95	2.03	1
Craig	John	10AUG02	3.11	0	Craven	Jeremiah	18JUN96	1.03	1
Craig	John Jr	22JUN07	2.06	1	Cravens	Jeremiah	16JUN97	3.06	1
Craig	John	10AUG02	3.11		Cravens	Jeremiah	31MAY99	1.06	11
Tax paid by John W. Gilbert					Cravens	Jeremiah	16JUN00	2.05	12
Craig	John	13JUL03	3.05	11	Cravens	Jesse	14JUN87	2.01	1
Craig	John	30JUL03	2.12	1	Cravens	Jesse	28OCT88	1.02	1
Tax pd by John W. Gilbert					Cravens	Jesse	29MAR90	2.02	11
Craig	John	30JUL04	2.03	11	Cravens	Jesse	25SEP91	1.02	1
Craig	John	30MAY05	2.13	0	Cravens	Jessey	24OCT92	2.02	1
Tax paid by John W. Gilbert					Cravens	Jesse	05AUG93	1.02	1
Craig	John	08AUG06	2.16	0	Cravens	Jesse	17MAY94	1.03	1
Tax paid by John W.Gilbert					Cravens	Jesse	18MAY03	2.05	1
Craig	John	21AUG06	3.08	1	Cravens	Michael	05JUL91	1.02	1
Craig	John	27MAY07	1.04	1	Cravens	Michael	03OCT92	2.02	1
Craig	John	25JUL07	2.06	1	Cravens	Michael	15AUG93	1.02	1
Craig	John	25JUL07	2.06	21	Cravens	Michael	31MAY94	1.02	1
Craig	John	-----08	2.06	D2	Cravins	Michael	11MAY95	2.03	1
Eliz. & Wm. Craig-Admin.					Cravens	Michael	01JUN96	1.03	1
Craig	John	19APR08	1.04	1	Cravens	Michael	13JUN97	3.06	1
Craig	John	15JUL08	2.05	1	Cravens	Michael	01JUN99	1.06	1
Craig	John	07AUG09	1.09	D	Cravins	Michael	01AUG00	2.07	1
Eliz. & Wm. Craig-Executors					Cravens	Michael	08JUN01	2.04	1
Craig	John	-----11	1.12	1	Cravens	Michael	17JUN02	3.05	1
Craig	John	-----11	1.15	12	CRAWFORD				
Craig	J.	-----11	1.12	D	Crofford	Alexander	15NOV88	1.03	1
Elizabeth Craig - Exec.					Craford	Charles	04JUL08	2.05	1
Craig	J.	-----11	1.12		Crawford	Charles	27JUN09	1.08	1
William Craig - Exec.					Crofford	James	03JUN90	2.02	1
Craig	Mary	21MAY96	2.04	F	Crawford	James	19SEP91	3.03	11
Craig	Mary	12MAY97	1.04	F	Crawford	James	25NOV92	3.04	1
Craig	S.(heirs)	18MAY01	3.12	D	Crawford	James	02MAY94	3.06	1
Tax paid by John W. Gilbert					Crawford	James	05MAY94	3.06	1
Craig	Sally	10AUG02	3.11	F	Crawford	James	01MAY95	1.03	1
Tax paid by John W. Gilbert					Crawford	James	01MAY95	1.03	1
Craig	Samuel	26JUN87	1.01	1	Crawford	James	01JUN95	1.04	1
Craig	Samuel	19MAY89	6.02	1	Crawford	James	-----96	4.04	1
Craig	Samuel	21APR90	1.03	1	Crawford	James	30MAY99	1.06	1
Craig	Samuel	19APR91	2.02	1	Crawford	James	28JUN00	3.07	1
Craig	Samuel	18OCT92	1.02	1	Crawfford	James	07JUL01	3.07	1
Craig	Samuel	18SEP93	3.03	1	Crofford	John	26JUN87	4.01	1
Craig	Samuel	21APR94	2.03	1	Crawford	John	19MAY89	6.02	1
Craig	Samuel	20MAR95	3.05	1	Crawford	John	21APR90	1.02	1
Craig	Samuel	10AUG02	3.11	0	Crawford	John	19APR91	2.02	1
Tax paid by John W. Gilbert					Crawford	John	18SEP92	1.03	1
Craig	Samuel	30JUL03	2.12	1	Crawford	John	12AUG93	3.02	1
Tax pd by John W. Gilbert					Crawford	John	19APR94	2.03	1
Craig	Samuel	30MAY05	2.13	0	Crofford	John	20APR95	3.04	1
Tax paid by John W. Gilbert					Crawford	John	26MAY96	2.04	1
Craig	Samuel	08AUG06	2.16	0	Crawfort	John	12MAY97	1.04	1
Tax paid by John W. Gilbert					Crofford	John	29JUN04	4.05	1

surname	name	date	bk.pg	TM	surname	name	date	bk.pg	TM
Crawford	Rebekah	05JUL87	3.02	F	CROUCH				
Crawford	Rebecca	10JUL89	2.03	F1	Croutch	Jonathan	24JUN89	5.02	1
Craford	Rebeckah	20SEP91	3.03	F	Crouch	Jonathan	02JUN90	2.02	1
Crawford	Robert	11JUN99	3.04	1	CROUCHER				
Crawford	Robert	28JUN00	3.07	1	Croucher	Samuel	-----11	1.11	1
Crafford	Robert	13JUL01	3.07	1	Crutcher	Sebert	27JUL99	3.04	1
Crawford	Robert	30JUN02	3.05	2	Crucher	Sebert	25JUN00	3.06	1
Crawford	Robert	01JUN03	2.05	2	Croutcher	William	14NOV88	1.02	1
Crofford	Robert	29JUN04	4.05	1	CROUT				
Crawford	Robert	08JUN05	2.06	1	Crowt	Barbary	27JUL04	4.06	F1
Crafort	William	24MAY94	1.12	1	Krout	Barbara	23JUL05	2.18	F1
Crafort	William	26JUN95	2.16	1	Crout	Barbarah	13AUG07	2.08	F1
CRAWLEY					Crout	Barbarah	-----08	2.06	F
Crawley	Abner	25JUL08	2.05	1	Crout	Barbara	22JUN09	1.08	F
CREASY					Crout	Frederick	04AUG96	2.04	1
Creasy	George	-----11	1.11	1	Crout	Frederick	23MAY97	1.05	1
CREED					Crout	Frederick	03JUL99	3.05	1
Creed	Mathew	26MAY95	2.15	1	Crout	Frederick	09JUL01	3.07	1
Creed	Mathew	21JUL01	2.04	11	Krout	Frederick	17JUN02	3.15	1
Creed	Matthew	20JUN05	1.04	0	Krout	Frederick	22JUN03	2.18	1
Tax pd by David Cook					CROW				
CREEL					Crow	Abraham	10APR90	1.03	1
Creel	Simeon	20MAY05	2.06	1	Crow	Abraham	17MAY91	2.02	1
CREWS					Crow	Abraham	02NOV92	1.02	1
Crews	William	05JUL87	3.02	1	Crow	Abraham	19AUG93	3.03	1
CRITTENDEN					Crow	Abraham	16APR94	2.03	1
Crittendon	Richard	15MAR97	2.01	2	Crow	Abraham	24MAR95	3.04	1
Crittenden	Richard	03JUN02	1.03	12	Crow	Andrew	18JUL06	2.08	1
Chrittenden	Richard	25JUN03	1.04	1	Crow	Andrew	10AUG07	2.07	1
Crittenden	Richard	15JUN04	1.03	1	Crow	Andrew	-----08	2.06	1
Crittenden	Richard	05JUN05	1.02	1	Crow	Andrew L.	22JUN09	1.08	1
Crittenden	Richard	13JUN06	1.03	1	Crow	Andrew L.	-----11	1.15	1
CROCKET					Crow	Ann	19AUG91	2.02	F
Crocket	Andrew	27MAR95	3.04	0	Crow	Ann	02JUL99	3.05	F
Crockett	John	-----96	4.04	1	Crow	Finley	03APR95	3.04	1
Crocket	Robert	-----11	1.13	1	Crow	Gillaspy	03APR95	3.04	1
CRONKRIGHT					Crow	James	24JUL05	2.08	1
Kronkright	Isaac	11JUL00	3.16	1	Crow	James	28MAR06	2.07	1
Konckright	Isaac	29JUL01	3.18	1	Crow	James	04AUG07	2.07	1
Cronkright	Isaac	10JUN02	2.04	1	Crow	James	28JUL08	2.05	1
Conkright	Isaac	05AUG03	3.06	1	Crow	James	19JUN09	1.07	1
Kronkkright	Isaac	06APR04	4.14	1	Crow	James	-----11	1.11	1
Conchright	Isaac	21JUN05	3.06	1	Crow	Joel	26MAY97	1.05	1
Conchright	Isaac	29JUL06	3.06	1	Crow	Joel	25JUN99	1.05	1
CROOK					Crow	John	10MAY90	1.03	1
Crook	Jeremiah	05JUN99	1.06	1	Crow	John	14MAY91	2.02	1
Crook	Jeremiah	22JUL00	2.06	1	Crow	John	02NOV92	1.02	1
Croock	Jeremiah	20JUL01	3.08	1	Crow	John	19AUG93	3.03	1
Crook	Jeremiah	01JUN02	2.04	1	Crow	John	16APR94	2.03	1
Crook	Jeremiah	31MAY03	3.04	1	Crow	John	24MAR95	3.04	1
Crook	Jeremiah	04AUG04	3.04	1	Crow	John	15JUN96	2.04	1
Crook	Jeremiah	13JUN05	3.05	1	Crow	John	16MAY97	1.06	1
Crook	Jeremiah	04AUG06	3.07	1	Crow	John	02JUL99	3.05	1
CROSS					Crow	John	02JUL99	3.05	1
Cross	Drury	26JUN04	4.05	1	Crow	John	26JUN00	3.06	1
Cross	Drury	27JUN05	2.07	1	Crow	John	19MAY01	3.06	1
Cross	Drury	14AUG06	2.10	1	Crow	John	28MAR06	2.07	M1
Cross	Isreal	20JUN91	2.03	1	Crow	Sarah	25JUL03	2.06	F
Cross	Isreal	12SEP92	1.03	1	Crow	Thomas	22JUL96	2.04	1
Cross	Isreal	05AUG93	3.02	1	Crow	Thomas	12MAY97	1.04	1
Cross	Isreal	13MAY94	2.03	1	Crow	Walt (Heirs	03APR95	3.04	0
Cross	Isreal	08APR95	3.03	1	Crow	Walter	23AUG96	2.04	00
Cross	Isreal	23JUN96	2.04	1	Crow	Walter	02JUL99	3.05	D
Cross	Isreal	07JUN97	1.05	1	Tax pd by William Crow				
Cross	Isreal	26JUN99	3.04	1	Crow	Walt(Heirs)	26JUN00	3.07	D
Cross	Isreal	20JUN00	3.06	11	Tax pd by William Crow				
Cross	Isreal	02MAY01	3.06	11	Crow	Walt (Heir)	19MAY01	3.07	D
Cross	Isreal	06AUG02	3.06	11	Crow	Walter	17AUG02	3.07	D
Cross	William	26JUN04	4.05	1	Crow	Walter	26JUL03	2.06	D
Cross	William	18JUL05	2.07	1	Crow	Walter	27JUL04	4.06	D
CROSSGROVE					Crow	Walter	16MAY05	2.06	1
Crossgrove	James	09JUL00	2.06	1	Crow	Walter	23JUL05	2.08	D

surname	name	date	bk.pg	TM	surname	name	date	bk.pg	TM
Crow	Walter	18JUL06	2.08	D	Critchfield	Nathaniel	16AUG09	1.09	1
Crow	Walter	13AUG07	2.08	1	Crutchfield	Nathaniel	-----11	1.75	1
Crow	Walter	-----08	2.06	1	Crutchfield	Tarry	22AUG07	2.08	1
Crow	Walter	-----08	2.06	D	Crutchfield	Tarry	25JUL08	2.05	1
Crow	Walter	19JUN09	1.07	1	Crutchfield	Terry	12JUL09	1.09	1
Crow	Walter	19JUN09	1.07	D	Crutchfield	Terry	-----11	1.75	1
William Crow-Executor					Crutchfield	William	05MAY94	3.06	1
Crow	Walter	-----11	1.15	1	Critchfield	William	06MAY95	1.04	1
Crow	William	28JUN87	1.01	1	CULBERTSON				
Crow	William	19APR89	6.02	1	Culbertson	David	24MAY00	2.05	1
Crow	William	10MAY90	1.02	1	Culbertson	David	04APR01	2.03	1
Crow	William	20APR91	2.02	1	Culbertson	David	14JUN02	3.05	1
Crow	William	10OCT92	1.03	1	Culbertson	David	11JUN03	2.05	1
Crow	William	20AUG93	3.03	1	Culbertson	David	24JUL04	1.04	1
Crow	William	01MAY94	2.03	2	Culbertson	David	08JUN05	2.06	1
Crow	William	03APR95	3.04	1	Culbertson	David	24APR06	2.07	1
Crow	William	23JUL96	2.04	1	Culbertson	David	03AUG07	2.07	1
Crow	William	16MAY97	1.04	1	Culberson	David	-----11	1.12	1
Crow	William	16MAY97	1.04	1	CULTON				
Crow	William	16MAY97	1.04	1	Culton	James	19JUN99	2.04	1
Crow	William	16MAY97	1.04	1	Culton	John	12APR97	3.05	11
Crow	William	02JUL99	3.05	11	Culton	John	02JUL99	3.04	11
Paid tax for Walter Crow					Culton	John	26JUN00	3.06	1
Crow	William	26JUN00	3.07	1	Cuttan	John	19MAY01	3.06	1
Paid tax for Walt(heirs) Crow					Culton	John	16AUG02	3.07	2
Crow	William	19MAY01	3.07	12	Culton	John	17JUN05	3.05	1
Crow	William	17AUG02	3.07	11	Culton	John	22JUL07	2.06	1
Crow	William	26JUL03	2.06	12	Culton	Robert	11JUN04	2.02	2
Crow	William	27JUL04	4.06	21	Cutton	Robert	14JUL06	3.05	2
Crow	William	23JUL05	2.08	1	CUMMINS				
Crow	William	16JUL06	2.08	1	Commins	Bengamin	06MAY95	1.04	1
Crow	William	18JUL06	2.08	1	Cummins	Benjamin	08DEC92	3.05	1
Crow	William	22AUG07	2.08	1	Commins	Benjamin	01MAY94	3.05	1
Crow	William	-----08	2.06	1	Cummons	Benjamin	11JUN03	1.03	11
Crow	William	19JUN09	1.07	1	Cummons	Benjamin	14JUN04	1.03	11
Executor for Walter Crow					Cummons	Benjamin	07JUN05	1.03	11
Crow	Wm. Capt.	-----11	1.16	1	Commins	Daniel	01MAY94	3.05	1
CROWDER					Commons	Daniel	14MAY95	1.04	1
Crowder	James	26JUN04	4.05	1	Commins	Daniel	-----96	4.04	1
CRUM					Commins	Daniel	15MAR97	2.01	1
Crum	Henry	-----11	1.15	1	Cummins	Daniel	13JUN99	2.03	1
Crum	William	25JUL04	4.06	1	Cummons	Daniel	16JUN00	1.02	1
Crumb	William	24JUL05	2.08	1	Cummons	Daniel	03JUN01	1.02	1
Crumb	William	05AUG06	2.09	1	Cumins	Daniel	27MAY07	1.04	1
Crum	William	25JUL07	2.06	12	Cummens	Daniel	19APR08	1.05	1
Crumb	William	14JUN08	1.07	12	Cummins	Daniel	01JUL09	2.06	1
Crumb	William	18AUG09	2.07	0	Commons	Gabriel	05NOV88	1.02	1
Exempt from county levy					Commons	Gabriel	24JUN89	5.02	1
CRUTCHFIELD					Cummins	Gabril	03JUN90	2.02	1
Critchfield	Arthur	05JUN04	4.04	1	Cummins	George	30NOV92	3.05	1
Critchfield	Arthur	27JUN05	2.07	11	Cummins	Hugh	22JUN99	2.04	1
Critchfield	Arthur	01AUG06	2.09	11	Cummins	John	13AUG93	3.03	1
Critchfield	Arthur	22AUG07	2.08	1	Cummins	John	22JUN99	2.04	1
Critchfield	Arthur	26JUL08	2.05	1	Cummins	Mathew	13MAY89	6.02	1
Critchfield	Arthur	08JUN09	1.06	1	Cummins	Mathew	20APR91	2.02	1
Critchfield	Arthur	-----11	1.75	1	Cummings	Moses	18SEP91	3.04	1
Critchfield	George	07JUL87	3.03	01	Commins	Moses	22JUN94	3.05	1
Critchfield	George	12SEP91	3.04	1	Commons	Moses	06MAY95	1.04	1
Critchfield	George	30NOV92	3.05	1	Cummins	Moses	-----96	4.04	1
Critchfield	George	29JUL02	3.06	1	Commins	Moses	15MAR97	2.01	1
Critchfield	George	09AUG03	2.07	1	Cummins	Moses	13JUN99	2.03	1
Critchfield	George	06JUN04	4.04	1	Cummons	Moses	16JUN00	1.02	1
Critchfield	James	12SEP91	3.04	11	Cummons	Moses	02JUN01	1.02	11
Critchfield	James	11AUG03	2.07	1	Cummons	Moses Jr	02JUN01	1.02	1
Critchfield	James	05JUN04	4.04	1	Cummins	Moses	26MAY02	3.05	11
Critchfield	James	27JUN05	2.07	1	Exempt from county leavy				
Critchfield	James	01AUG06	2.09	1	Cummins	Priestley	26MAY02	3.05	1
Critchfield	James	04AUG07	2.07	1	Cummons	Stephen	01AUG06	1.05	1
Critchfield	James	31MAY08	2.04	1	Cummings	Thomas	12SEP91	3.04	1
Critchfield	James	08JUN09	1.06	1	Cummins	William	22JUN99	2.04	1
Critchfield	James	-----11	1.75	1	Cummins	William	26MAY02	3.05	11
Critchfield	John	12SEP91	3.04	1	Cummins	William	27JUN05	2.07	1

surname	name	date	bk.pg	TM	surname	name	date	bk.pg	TM
CUNDIFF					Daily	Owen	20MAY97	3.08	1
Condiff	Lewis	04AUG06	3.07	1	Daisey	Samuel	23JUN02	1.06	1
Cundiff	Lewis	-----11	1.11	11	DAMREL				
Cundiff	Meshack	11JUN03	2.05	1	Damrel	George	13JUL97	1.07	1
Cundoff	Meshock	26JUL04	1.04	1	DAMRON				
Cundiff	Meshack	08JUN05	2.06	1	Damron	Susanna	05JUL96	2.06	F
Cundiff	Meshack	14JUN06	2.07	1	DANIEL				
Cundiff	William	06AUG04	3.05	1	Daniel	Archable	22JUL00	1.03	1
Condiff	William	16AUG05	3.07	1	Daniel	Archible	23JUN01	1.04	1
Condiff	William	21AUG06	3.08	1	Daniel	Robert	22JUL00	1.03	1
CUNNINGHAM					Daniel	Terry	19JUN99	2.04	1
Cunningham	Joseph	20JUN96	1.03	1	Daniel	William	18MAY97	3.08	1
Cunnagame	Joseph	10MAY97	3.06	1	DANNER				
Cunningham	William	05AUG03	3.06	1	Donier	Joseph	22JUN03	2.07	1
Cunningham	William	07MAY04	4.04	1	Donier	Joseph	23JUL05	2.10	1
Cunningham	William	21JUN05	3.06	1	Danier	Joseph	16JUN06	2.11	1
Cunningham	William	21JUL06	3.05	1	Danner	Joseph	22JUN09	1.11	1
CURD					Doner	Joseph	-----11	1.17	1
Curd	Dudley	15JUL87	3.03		DARLINGTON				
Listed with Walter Dewitt					Darlington	Abraham	04AUG87	1.02	1
CURREN					Darlington	Abraham	18APR89	6.02	1
Curren	James	06MAY95	1.04	1	Darlington	Abraham	17APR94	2.04	1
CURRY					DARNELL				
Curry	John	09JUN89	6.02	1	Darnel	Aaron	27JUN89	2.04	1
Curry	John	22MAY94	2.03	11	Darnel	Adam	09JUN96	1.04	1
Curry	John	13APR95	3.04	02	Darnal	Adam	23MAY97	1.06	1
Curry	John	20JUN01	3.08	1	Darnal	Adam	03JUL99	3.06	1
Curry	John	26MAY02	2.04	1	Darnell	Adam	30JUN00	3.09	1
Curry	John	04AUG04	3.04	1	Darnald	Adam	09JUL01	3.09	11
Curry	John	21JUN05	3.06	1	Darnell	Adam	18AUG02	3.07	11
Curry	John	23JUL06	3.06	1	Darnel	Jonathan	02AUG06	1.05	1
Currey	John	15AUG07	2.08	1	Darnel	Jonathan	26MAY07	1.06	1
Curry	Samuel	12JUN97	1.05	M1	Darnell	Jonathan	18APR08	1.07	1
Currey	Samuel	05JUN99	1.06	1	Darnell	Joseph	30MAY03	2.07	1
Curry	Samuel	29JUL00	2.06	1	Darnel	Joseph	28JUL04	4.07	M1
Curry	Samuel	01JUN02	2.04	1	Darnell	Joseph	17JUN06	2.11	1
Curry	Samuel	14JUN03	3.04	1	Darnell	Joseph	17AUG07	2.10	1
Curry	Samuel	31JUL04	3.04	1	Darnell	Joseph	-----08	2.08	1
Curry	Samuel	21JUN05	3.06	1	Darnell	Joseph	22JUN09	1.11	1
Curry	Samuel	21JUL06	3.05	1	Darnel	Joseph	-----11	1.17	1
Curry	Samuel	06JUL07	2.06	1	Darnel	Nelson	-----11	1.19	1
Curry	Samuel	01JUL08	2.05	1	DAUGHERTY				
Curry	Samuel	10JUL09	1.08	1	Daugherty	Alex.	18MAY99	1.07	1
Curry	Sarah	14JUN89	6.02	F	Daugherty	Charles	04MAY97	1.06	1
Curry	Sarah	02AUG90	1.02	F	Daugherty	Charles	04JUN99	1.08	1
Curry	Sarah	21JUN91	2.02	F1	Daugherty	Charles	31JUN99	1.09	1
Curry	Sarah	03OCT92	1.03	F	Daugherty	Charles	20JUN00	2.08	1
Curry	Sarah	06AUG93	3.02	F1	Daugherty	Charles	26JUN00	2.08	1
Curry	Sarah	05JUL96	2.04	F	Daugherty	Charles	25MAY01	3.10	1
CUTTING					Daugherty	Charles	01AUG01	2.06	1
Cutting	Elizabeth	08MAY97	3.05	F	Daugherty	Charles Sr	04AUG02	2.07	1
Cutting	Francis	01DEC88	1.03	1	Daugherty	Charles Jr	23AUG02	2.07	1
Cutting	Francis	29JUN89	5.02	1	Daugherty	Charles	16JUN03	3.07	1
Cuting	Francis	03APR90	2.02	1	Daugherty	Charles	11AUG03	2.08	1
Cutting	Francis	07APR91	1.02	1	Dougherty	George	10AUG93	3.04	1
Cuting	Francis	02NOV92	2.02	1	Daugherty	George Sr	06JUN97	1.07	1
Cuting	Francis	20AUG93	1.02	1	Daugherty	George Jr	06JUN97	1.07	1
Cuting	Francis	16MAY94	1.02	1	Daugherty	George	04MAY97	1.06	1
Cutting	Francis	25MAY95	2.03	1	Daugherty	George	11MAY99	2.06	1
Cuting	Francis	13JUN96	1.02	1	Daugherty	George	04JUN99	1.08	1
DADISMAN					Daugherty	George	08JUL99	3.07	1
Datisman	Matthew	05APR90	1.03	1	Daugherty	George Sr	19JUN00	3.09	1
Dadisman	Madis	19MAY94	2.04	1	Daugherty	George Jr	19JUN00	3.09	1
Dadisman	Madies	02APR95	3.06	1	Daugherty	George	02MAY01	3.09	1
Dadderman	Matthias	23MAY97	1.06	1	Daugherty	George	29JUN05	3.09	1
DAFFRON					Dougherty	George	06JUL07	2.09	1
Deffern	Rody	23AUG02	2.07	1	Dougherty	George	02JUN08	2.07	1
Dafferen	Rodham	16JUN03	3.07	1	Daugherty	George	30JUN09	1.11	1
Daffron	Rodey	01AUG04	2.04	1	Dougherty	Henry	08OCT92	1.04	11
Daffron	Rody	17JUN05	1.05	1	Dougherty	Henry	16AUG93	3.04	1
DAILEY					Daugherty	Henry	14MAY94	2.04	2
Dailey	Michael	20MAY97	3.07	1	Daugherty	Henry	18APR95	3.05	1

surname	name	date	bk.pg	TM	surname	name	date	bk.pg	TM
Daugherty	Henry	18MAY95	3.05	1	Davidson	George	03JUN95	2.04	13
Daugherty	James	08JUL00	2.08	1	Davidson	George	10JUN96	1.03	13
Daugherty	John	28JUN87	1.02	11	Davidson	George	10JUN96	1.03	1
Daugherty	John	18APR89	6.02	1	Davidson	George	13JUN97	3.08	12
Daugherty	John	01JUN90	1.03	12	Davidson	George Sr	01JUN99	1.08	3
Dougherty	John	20MAY91	2.03	12	Davidson	George Jr	24MAY99	1.08	1
Dougherty	John	20SEP92	1.04	11	Davidson	George	28JUL00	2.08	1
Dougherty	John	29AUG93	3.03	1	Davidson	George Jr	14JUN00	2.07	1
Daugherty	Michael	28JUN99	3.06	1	Davidson	George Sr	30JUL01	2.06	1
Daugherty	Robert	22JUN01	1.03	1	Davidson	George Jr	29MAY01	2.05	1
Daugherty	Thomas	22JUN99	1.09	1	Davidson	George	12JUL02	2.06	1
Daugherty	William	24AUG87	1.02	1	Davidson	George Jr	02AUG02	2.06	1
Daugherty	William	12JUN89	6.08	1	Davidson	George Sr	12JUL03	3.07	1
Daugherty	William	15APR90	1.03	11	Davidson	George Jr	18JUN03	3.07	1
Dougherty	William	23JUN91	2.03	11	Davidson	George Sr	30JUL04	2.04	1
Dougherty	William	25SEP92	1.04	12	Davidson	George	30JUL04	2.04	1
Daugherty	William	20AUG93	3.04	12	Davidson	George	16MAY05	2.09	1
Daugherty	William	08MAY94	2.04	21	Davidson	George	17JUN05	3.09	1
Daugherty	William	22APR95	3.05	11	Davidson	George Sr	18JUL06	3.09	1
Daugherty	William Jr	22APR95	3.05	1	Davidson	George	07APR06	2.10	1
Daugherty	William	27MAY95	3.06	1	Davidson	George	25JUL07	2.10	1
Daugherty	William	02JUN96	2.05	12	Davidson	George Jr	10AUG07	2.10	1
Daugherty	William Jr	02JUN96	2.05	1	Davidson	George	06JUN08	1.09	1
Daugherty	William Sr	04MAY97	1.06	1	Davidson	George	23JUN08	2.07	1
Daugherty	William Jr	02JUN97	1.07	1	Davidson	George Sr	10JUL09	1.11	1
Daugherty	William Sr	04JUN99	1.08	11	Davidson	George	06JUL09	2.08	1
Daugherty	William Jr	04JUN99	1.08	1	Davidson	George Sr	-----11	1.18	1
Daugherty	William	20JUN00	2.08	11	Davidson	George Jr	-----11	1.18	1
Daugherty	William Jr	20JUN00	2.08	1	Davidson	James	31MAR90	2.03	1
Daugherty	William Sr	01AUG01	2.06	11	Davidson	James	08JUL00	2.08	1
Daugherty	William	01AUG01	2.06	1	Davidson	James	29MAY01	2.05	1
Daugherty	William Sr	23AUG02	2.07	11	Davidson	James	23AUG02	2.07	1
Daugherty	William Jr	10AUG02	2.07	1	Davidson	James	11JUL03	3.07	1
Daugherty	William Sr	16JUN03	3.07	11	Davison	James	18JUN04	2.04	1
Daugherty	William	15JUN03	3.07	1	Davidson	James	17JUN05	3.09	1
Daugherty	William Sr	21AUG04	2.05	2	Davidson	James	23JUN06	1.07	1
Daugherty	William	29JUN05	3.09	1	Davidson	James	17AUG07	1.07	1
Daugherty	William	20AUG05	3.10	2	Davidson	James	06JUN08	1.09	1
Daugherty	William	22AUG06	3.10	2	Davidson	James	06JUL09	2.08	1
Daugherty	William Jr	22AUG06	3.10	1	Davidson	James	-----11	1.18	1
Dougherty	William Sr	06JUL07	2.09	2	Davidson	John	13JUN97	3.09	1
Dougherty	William Jr	06JUL07	2.09	1	Davidson	John	01JUN99	1.08	1
Daugherty	William	07MAY07	1.06	1	Davidson	John	14JUN00	2.08	1
Dougherty	William	-----08	2.08	1	Davidson	John	22JUN01	2.06	1
Daugherty	William	04MAY08	1.08	1	Davidson	John	12JUL02	2.06	1
Dougherty	William	02JUN08	2.07	2	One lot in the town of Stanford				
Daugherty	William Sr	30JUN09	1.11	2	Davison	John	28JUL08	2.07	1
Daugherty	William	30JUN09	1.11	1	Davidson	John	16AUG09	2.08	1
Daugherty	Wm.	-----11	1.17	2	Davidson	Mary	29OCT92	2.03	F
DAVENPORT					Davidson	Mary	10AUG93	1.03	F
Divenport	George	15AUG05	3.10	M1	Davidson	May	05JUN94	1.03	F
Davenport	George	17AUG07	2.10	1	Davidson	Michael	08JUL00	2.08	1
Davenport	George	02JUN08	2.07	1	Davidson	Michael	29MAY01	2.05	1
Davenport	George	11JUL09	1.11	1	Davidson	Michiel	12JUL02	2.06	1
Deavenport	George	-----11	1.17	1	Davidson	Michael	11JUL03	3.07	1
Divenport	Marten	22JUN05	3.09	11	Davidson	Michael	18JUN04	2.04	1
Davenport	Martin	23JUL06	3.09	11	Davidson	Michael	07APR06	2.10	1
Davenport	Marten	17AUG07	2.10	1	Davidson	Michael	15JUN07	2.08	1
Divenporty	Marten	23JUN08	2.07	1	Davidson	Michael	06JUN08	1.09	1
Davenport	William	20MAY03	3.06	1	Davidson	Michael	06JUL09	2.08	1
Davenport	William	06AUG04	3.08	1	Davidson	Samuel	23OCT92	2.03	1
Divenport	William	15AUG05	3.10	1	Davidson	Samuel	10AUG93	1.03	1
Davenport	William	22AUG06	3.10	1	Davidson	Samuel	05JUN94	1.03	1
DAVIDSON					Davidson	Samuel	13JUN95	2.04	1
Davison	George	21JUN87	2.02	11	Davidson	Samuel	10JUN96	1.03	1
Davison	George	06NOV88	1.-	11	Davidson	Samuel	13JUN97	3.08	1
Davison	George	16JUN89	5.04	12	Davidson	Samuel	26MAY99	1.08	1
Davidson	George	31MAR90	2.03	12	Davidson	Samuel	14JUN00	2.07	1
Davison	George	12APR91	1.03	13	Davidson	Samuel	29MAY01	2.05	1
Davidson	George	23OCT92	2.03	12	Davidson	Samuel	12JUL02	2.06	1
Davidson	George	10AUG93	1.03	12	Davidson	Samuel	18JUN03	3.07	1
Davidson	George	05JUN94	1.03	14	Davidson	Samuel	18JUN04	2.04	1

surname	name	date	bk.pg	TM	surname	name	date	bk.pg	TM
Davidson	Samuel	10JUN05	3.08	1	Davis	James	14APR91	1.03	11
Davidson	Samuel	18JUL06	3.09	1	Davis	James	06AUG91	2.03	11
Davidson	Samuel	22JUN07	2.09	1	Davis	James	20SEP92	1.04	11
Davidson	Samuel	-----08	2.08	1	Davis	James	27OCT92	2.03	11
Davidson	Samuel	23MAR09	1.09	1	Davis	James	20SEP92	1.04	
Davidson	Samuel	-----11	1.18	1	Abraham Miller listed with him				
Davidson	William	23OCT92	2.03	1	Davis	James	20AUG93	3.04	
Davidson	William	10AUG93	1.03	1	Paid tax for --- Miller				
Davidson	William	18JUL00	2.08	1	Davis	James	12AUG93	1.03	12
Davidson	William	15JUN01	2.05	1	Davis	James	20AUG93	3.04	11
Davidson	William	06APR09	1.10	D1	Davis	James	21APR94	2.04	12
Taxes paid by Elizabeth Dickison					Davis	James	29MAY94	1.03	11
DAVIS					Davis	James	31MAY95	3.06	1
Davis	Azel	15JUL87	3.03	1	Davis	James	16JUN95	2.04	13
Davis	Asel	09SEP89	2.04	1	Davis	James	29JUN96	1.04	13
Davis	Azariah	25MAY89	6.02	1	Davis	James	26APR97	3.07	1
Davis	Azari	10MAY90	1.03	1	Davis	James	16JUN97	3.09	11
Davis	Asael	07SEP91	3.01	1	Davis	James	25MAY99	1.08	3
Davis	Azariah	20APR91	2.03	1	Davis	James	03JUN00	2.07	4
Davis	Azariah	14SEP92	1.04	1	Davis	James	24JUL01	2.06	2
Davis	Azariah	13SEP93	3.03	1	Davice	James	11JUN02	1.05	2
Davis	Aharel	02MAY94	3.06	1	Davice	James Jr	08JUN02	1.05	0
Davis	Azriah	16APR94	2.04	1	Davise	James	04JUL03	1.07	1
Davis	Asail	04JUN95	1.05	13	Davis	James	02AUG04	2.05	2
Davis	Ahasal	-----96	1.05	1	Davise	James	15JUN05	1.05	2
Davis	Ahasel Jr	-----96	1.05	1	Davise	James	20JUN06	1.06	2
Davis	Azariah	05JUL00	3.09	1	Davise	James	24JUN07	1.07	2
Davis	Azariah	19MAY01	3.09	1	Davis	James Sr	01JUN09	2.07	1
Davis	Baxter	29JUN96	1.04	13	Davis	James	-----11	1.19	1
Davis	Baxter	26APR97	3.07	1	Davis	Jane	07JUL87	1.02	F1
Davis	Benjamin	26APR97	3.07	1	Davis	Jane	12MAY89	6.02	F
Davis	Berriman	13MAY99	1.07	1	Davis	Jane	19APR91	2.03	F1
Davis	Berriman	29MAY01	2.05	M1	Davis	Jane/Robert	21SEP92	1.04	11
Davice	Berry	11JUN02	1.06	1	Davis	Jane	10NOV93	3.03	F
Davise	Berry	04JUL03	1.07	1	Davis	Jane	29MAY94	1.03	F
Davis	Edward	29JUN04	4.07	1	Davis	Jane	29MAY94	1.03	F1
Davis	Elizabeth	05JUL87	3.03	F	Davis	Jane	03JUN95	2.04	F1
Davice	Elizabeth	30MAY99	2.05	F	Davice	Jane	30MAY99	2.05	F
Davice	Elizabeth	25JUL00	1.03	F	Davice	Jane	30MAY99	2.05	F
Tax pd by John Davice					Davice	Jane	20JUN00	1.03	F
Davice	Elizabeth	10JUN01	1.04		Tax pd by John Davice				
Tax pd by John Davice					Davice	Jane	10JUN01	1.04	F
Davice	Elizabeth	08JUN02	1.05	F	Tax pd by John Davice				
Davise	Elizabeth	20JUN03	1.06	F	Davice	Jane	23JUN01	1.03	F
Davise	Elizabeth	19JUN04	1.05	F	Davicc	Jane	08JUN02	1.05	F1
Davise	Elizabeth	16JUN06	1.06	F	Davise	Jane	20JUN03	1.06	F
Tax pd by Jane Davise					Davise	Jane	19JUN04	1.05	F1
Davis	Gabriel	27JUN05	2.09	1	Davise	Jane Jr	19JUN04	1.05	-
Davis	Goldsby	06OCT92	1.04	1	Davise	Jane	16JUN06	1.06	F
Davis	Henry	06OCT87	1.06	1	Paid tax for Elizabeth Davise				
Davis	Henry	21MAY90	1.03	1	Davise	Jane	16JUN06	1.06	
Davis	Henry	19JUL91	1.03	1	Paid tax for Joseph Davise				
Davis	Henry	29OCT92	2.03	1	Davis	Jane	11JUN07	1.06	F1
Davis	Henry	21JUN05	3.09	1	Davis	Jane	-----11	1.18	F
Davis	Henry	29JUL06	3.09	1	Davis	Jesse	13JUN87	2.02	1
Davis	Henry	23JUN08	2.07	1	Davis	Jesse	14NOV88	1.-	1
Daviss	Henry	16AUG09	1.11	1	Davis	Jesse	24JUN89	5.04	1
Davis	Isam	19JUN00	3.09		Davis	Jesse	21JUL06	3.09	1
A free black above 21					Davis	John	13JUN87	2.02	1
Davis	Isum	01MAY01	3.09		Davis	John	21JUN87	2.02	1
A black man					Davis	John	07JUL87	1.02	11
Davis	Isham	08JUN03	2.07		Davis	John	30DEC88	1.-	1
A free negro					Davis	John	31DEC88	1.-	1
Davis	Isham	02JUN08	2.07	1	Davis	John	16JUN89	5.04	1
Davis	Issarell	26NOV92	3.06	1	Davis	John	18OCT92	2.03	1
Davis	James	13JUN87	2.02	1	Davis	John	12AUG93	1.03	1
Davis	James	30DEC88	1.-	11	Davis	John	26MAY94	1.03	1
Davis	James	20JUN89	5.04	12	Davis	John	02JUN95	2.04	1
Davis	James	19MAY89	6.02	1	Davis	John	14JUN96	1.03	1
Davis	James	20APR90	1.03	11	Davis	John	28JUN96	1.04	12
Davis	James	29APR90	2.03	11	Davis	John	08APR97	3.07	1
Davis	James	02AUG90	1.03	01	Davis	John	13APR97	3.07	1

surname	name	date	bk.pg	TM	surname	name	date	bk.pg	TM
Davis	John	22MAY97	3.08	12	Davis	Joseph	30APR08	1.08	1
Davis	John	13JUN97	3.08	1	Davis	Joseph	01JUN09	2.07	1
Davice	John	30MAY99	2.05	1	Davis	Joseph	-----11	1.17	00
Davis	John	30MAY00	2.07	1	Davis	Joseph	-----11	1.19	1
Davice	John	20JUN00	1.03		Davis	Landen	26JUN00	2.08	1
Paid tax for Jane Davice					Davis	Landen	25MAY01	3.10	1
Davice	John	23JUL00	1.03	1	Davis	Landin	04AUG02	2.07	1
Davice	John	24JUL00	1.03	1	Davis	Landen	07JUN03	3.06	1
Davice	John	25JUL00	1.03		Davis	Landon	22AUG04	3.08	1
Paid tax for Elizabeth Davice					Davis	Landen	14AUG05	3.10	1
Davice	John	25JUL00	1.03		Davis	Landen	22AUG06	3.10	1
Paid tax for Joseph Davice					Davice	Mary	30MAY99	2.05	F
Davice	John	25JUL00	1.03		Davice	Mary	25JUL00	1.03	F
Paid tax for Mary Davice					Tax pd by John Davice				
Davice	John	25JUL00	1.03		Davice	Mary	10JUN01	1.04	F
Pd tax for Sam (decd) Davice					Tax pd by John Davice				
Davice	John Jr	25JUL00	1.03	1	Davice	Mary	08JUN02	1.05	F
Davice	John	10JUN01	1.04	1	Davise	Mary	20JUN03	1.06	F
Paid tax for Elizabeth Davice					Davise	Mary	19JUN04	1.05	F
Davice	John	10JUN01	1.04		Davise	Nathaniel	11JUN05	1.05	1
Paid tax for Jane Davice					Davise	Nathaniel	10JUN06	1.05	1
Davice	John	10JUN01	1.04		Davis	Nathan	17JUN07	1.06	1
Paid tax for Joseph Davice					Davis	Nathan	-----11	1.19	1
Davice	John	10JUN01	1.04		Davis	Polly	22AUG04	3.08	F
Paid tax for Mary Davice					Davise	Polley	10JUN06	1.06	F
Davice	John	10JUN01	1.04		Davis	Richard	20MAY97	3.08	1
Paid tax for Sam(heirs) Davice					Davice	Richard	20JUN99	2.04	1
Davis	John	22JUL01	2.06	1	Davis	Robert	14JUL97	1.07	1
Davice	John	08JUN02	1.05	1	Davis	Robert	29JUN99	1.09	1
Paid tax for heirs of Sam Davice					Davis	Robert	26JUL00	2.08	1
Davice	John	11JUN02	1.05	M1	Davis	Robert	29MAY01	3.10	1
Davise	John	20JUN03	1.06	11	Davis	Robert	10AUG02	2.07	1
Davice	John	20JUN03	1.06		Davis	Robert	06JUN03	3.06	1
Paid tax for Sam(heirs) Davice					Davis	Robert	16AUG04	3.08	1
Davise	John	30JUN03	1.07	1	Davis	Robert	05AUG05	3.09	1
Davise	John	20JUN04	1.05	1	Davis	Robert	19AUG06	3.10	1
Davise	John	19JUN04	1.05	1	Davis	Samuel	25JUN87	2.02	1
Davise	John	19JUN04	1.05	11	Davis	Samuel	31NOV88	1.-	1
Davice	John	19JUN04	1.05		Davis	Samuel	19JUN89	5.04	11
Paid tax for Sam(decd) Davice					Davis	Samuel	20APR91	1.03	11
Davise	John	12JUN05	1.05	1	Davis	Samuel	21OCT92	2.03	12
Davise	John	17JUN05	1.05	1	Davis	Samuel	14AUG93	1.03	11
Davise	John	20JUN06	1.07	1	Davis	Samuel	20MAY95	2.04	1
Davise	John	16JUN06	1.06	1	Davis	Samuel	26APR97	3.07	1
Davis	John	17JUN07	1.06	1	Davis	Samuel	16JUN97	3.09	1
Davis	John	11JUN07	1.06	1	Davice	Sam.	30MAY99	2.05	D
Davis	John	22APR08	1.08	1	Davis	Samuel	16MAY99	1.07	1
Davis	John	10JUN08	1.09	M1	Davice	Samuel	30MAY99	2.05	00
Daviss	John	13JUL09	1.11	1	Davice	Sam (decd)	25JUL00	1.04	D
Davis	John	25AUG09	2.08	1	Davice	Sam (decd)	25JUL00	1.03	
Davis	John	-----11	1.19	1	Tax pd by John Davice				
Davis	John	-----11	1.18	1	Davis	Samuel	18JUN00	2.08	1
Davis	Joseph	16JUN97	3.09	1	Davice	Samuel	25JUL00	1.03	1
Davice	Joseph	30MAY99	2.05	00	Davice	Sam(heirs)	10JUN01	1.04	D
Davice	Joseph	25JUL00	1.03	00	Tax pd by John Davice				
Tax pd by John Davice					Davice	Samuel	10JUN01	1.04	1
Davis	Joseph	29MAY01	2.05	1	Davis	Samuel	24JUL01	2.06	1
Davice	Joseph	10JUN01	1.04	00	Davice	Sam (decd)	08JUN02	1.05	D
Tax pd by John Davice					Tax pd for heirs by John Davice				
Davice	Joseph	08JUN02	1.05	0	Davice	Samuel	08JUN02	1.05	0
Davice	Joseph	11JUN02	1.06	1	Davice	Samuel	08JUN02	1.05	0
Davise	Joseph	20JUN03	1.06	1	Davice	Samuel	11JUN02	1.06	1
Davise	Joseph	04JUL03	1.07	1	Davise	Sam(Heirs)	20JUN03	1.06	D
Davise	Joseph	19JUN04	1.05	1	Tax pd by John Davise				
Davise	Joseph	19JUN04	1.05	1	Davise	Samuel	20JUN03	1.06	1
Davis	Joseph	07AUG04	2.05	1	Davise	Sam(Decd)	19JUN04	1.05	D
Davise	Joseph	15JUN05	1.05	1	Davice	Sam(Decd)	19JUN04	1.05	
Davise	Joseph	16JUN06	1.06	0	Tax pd for heirs by John Davise				
Tax pd by Jane Davise					Davise	Samuel	19JUN04	1.05	1
Davise	Joseph	20JUN06	1.06	1	Davis	Samuel	02AUG04	2.05	1
Davis	Joseph	08JUN07	1.06	1	Davise	Samuel	11JUN05	1.04	1
Davis	Joseph	11JUN07	1.06	1	Davise	Samuel	15JUN05	1.05	1

surname	name	date	bk.pg	TM	surname	name	date	bk.pg	TM
Davise	Sam(Heirs)	16JUN06	1.06	D	Dawson	Charity	27JUN00	3.09	F1
Davise	Samuel Sr	20JUN06	1.06	1	Dawson	Charity	21MAY01	3.09	F
Davise	Samuel	20JUN06	1.06	1	Dawson	Charity	08JUL02	3.07	F1
Davis	Sam(Decd)	11JUN07	1.06	D	Dawson	Charity	26JUL03	2.07	F1
Davis	Samuel	11JUN07	1.06	1	Dossin	Charrity	25JUL04	4.07	F1
Davis	Samuel	24JUN07	1.07	1	Dawson	Charity	24JUL05	2.10	F
Davis	Sam(Heirs)	22APR08	1.08	D	Dawson	Elijah	24JUL05	2.10	1
Davis	Samuel	04MAY08	1.08	1	Dawson	Elijah	24APR06	2.11	1
Davis	Sam(Decd)	25AUG09	2.08	D	Dawson	Elijah	25JUL07	2.10	1
Davis	Samuel	01JUN09	2.07	1	Dawson	Elijah	-----08	2.08	1
Davis	Samuel	25AUG09	2.08	1	Dawson	Elijah	-----11	1.17	1
Davis	S.	-----11	1.18	D	Dawson	James	11JUL03	2.07	1
William Davis - Exec.					Dossin	James	24JUL04	1.05	1
Davis	Samuel	-----11	1.17	1	Dawson	James	08JUN05	2.09	1
Davis	Samuel	-----11	1.19	1	Dawson	James	14JUN06	2.11	1
Davis	Samuel M.	22APR08	1.07	11	Dawson	James	25JUL07	2.10	1
Davis	Sarah	02JUN90	2.03	F	Dawson	James	-----11	1.19	1
Davis	Thomas	24AUG87	1.02	1	Dawson	John	21MAY01	3.09	1
Davis	Thomas	12MAY89	6.02	1	Dawson	Susannah	10MAY97	1.06	F
Davis	Thomas	02AUG90	1.03	1	DAY				
Davis	Thomas	19APR91	2.03	1	Day	Edward	13MAY99	1.07	11
Davis	Thomas	14SEP92	1.04	1	Day	Edward	17JUN00	2.08	11
Davis	Thomas	10NOV93	3.03	1	Day	Edward	04JUN01	2.05	1
Dives	Thomas	22MAY94	2.04	1	Day	Edward	12JUN02	1.06	11
Davis	Thomas	10APR95	3.05	1	Day	Edward	30JUN03	1.06	11
Davis	Thomas	11JUL96	2.06	1	Day	Edward	02AUG04	2.04	11
Davis	Thomas	06JUN97	1.07	1	Day	Edward	17JUN05	3.09	1
Davis	Thomas	26JUN99	3.06	1	Day	Edward	20JUN06	1.07	1
Davice	Thomas	17JUN00	1.03	1	Day	Edward	24JUN07	1.07	11
Davis	Thomas	21JUN00	3.09	1	Day	Edward	27APR08	1.08	11
Davis	Thomas	26JUN00	3.09	1	Day	Francies	17MAY94	1.03	1
Davis	Thomas	02MAY01	3.09	1	Day	Francis	01JUN95	2.04	1
Davice	Thomas	04JUN01	1.03	1	Day	Frances	10MAY97	3.08	1
Davis	Thomas	31JUL02	3.07	1	Day	Francis	21MAY99	1.07	1
Davis	Thomas	01AUG03	2.08	1	Day	Francis	17JUN00	2.08	1
Davis	Thomas	12JUN04	4.07	11	Day	Francis	04APR01	2.05	1
Davis	Thomas	18JUN05	2.09	11	Day	Francis	15JUN02	1.06	1
Davise	Thomas	16JUN06	1.06	M1	Day	Francis	11JUL03	1.07	1
Davis	Thomas	02AUG06	2.11	11	Day	Francis	23JUL04	1.05	1
Davis	Thomas	17JUN07	1.06	12	Day	Francis	13JUN05	1.05	1
Davis	Thomas	15JUL07	2.09	11	Day	Francis	15JUN05	1.06	1
Davis	Thomas	28JUL08	2.07	1	Day	Francis	05JUL09	2.08	1
Daviss	Thomas	13JUL09	1.11	1	Day	Francis	-----11	1.19	1
Davis	Thomas	-----11	1.19	11	Day	John	15MAY89	6.02	1
Davis	Thomas	-----11	1.20	2	Day	Reubin	28MAY95	3.06	01
Davis	William	-----96	1.05	11	Dey	Reubin	-----96	1.05	1
Davis	William	18MAY99	1.07	1	Day	Valentine	12JUN02	1.06	1
Davis	William	10AUG02	2.07	1	Day	Valentine	02AUG04	2.04	1
Davis	William	21JUN03	3.07	1	Day	Valentine	20JUN06	1.07	1
Davis	William	07AUG04	2.05	1	Day	Valentine	24JUN07	1.07	1
Davis	William	16MAY05	2.09	1	Day	Valentine	05JUN09	1.10	1
Davis	William	07APR06	2.10	1	Day	Valentine	-----11	1.19	1
Two lotts in Standford					Day	William	28JUN87	1.02	1
Davis	William	15JUL07	2.09	1	Day	William	17JUN05	3.09	1
Davids	William	10JUN08	1.09	1	Day	William	24JUN07	1.07	1
Davis	William	10JUN08	1.09	1	Day	William	12AUG07	2.09	D
Davis	William	06JUL09	2.08	1	Day	William	23APR08	1.08	1
Davis	William	-----11	1.18		DAYHOFF				
Exec. for S. Davis					Dayhoff	Frederick	04JUN05	1.04	1
DAWSON					Dayhoof	Frederick	13JUN06	1.05	1
Dawson	Benjamin	15APR95	3.05	1	Dayhuff	Frederick	19MAY07	1.06	1
Dawson	Benjamin	13JUL97	1.07	1	Dayhuff	Fredrick	06JUN08	1.08	1
Dawson	Benjamin	27JUN99	1.08	1	DAYNOR				
Dawson	Benjamin	24JUL00	2.08	1	Daynor	Samuel	-----08	2.08	1
Dawson	Benjamin	27MAY01	3.10	1	DEAN				
Dawson	Benjamin	03AUG02	2.06	1	Dean	John	21JUN99	2.04	11
Dawson	Benjamin	08JUN03	3.07	1	Dean	Robert	12JUN87	2.02	1
Dawson	Benjamin	06AUG04	3.08	1	Deen	William	29JUN04	4.07	1
Dawson	Benjamin	05AUG05	3.09	1	Dean	William	31MAY05	2.09	1
Dawson	Benjamin	04AUG06	3.10	1	Dean	William	07AUG06	2.11	1
Dawson	Charrity	15MAY97	1.06	F1	DEBOARD				
Dawson	Charity	28JUN99	3.06	F1	Deboard	William	30JUL05	1.05	1

surname	name	date	bk.pg	TM
Debord	William	01AUG06	1.07	1
Deboard	William	09MAY07	1.06	1
Doboard	William	12APR08	1.07	1
DEBOE				
Deboe	George	01APR91	2.03	1
DEER				
Deer	Ephram	10JUN09	1.11	1
Dear	Reuben	-----08	2.08	1
Deer	Reuben	22JUN09	1.11	1
Deir	Reuben	-----11	1.17	1
DEFOE				
Defoe	Stephen	04JUL03	1.07	1
Defoo	Stephen	07AUG04	2.05	1
Defoe	Stephen	27JUL05	1.05	1
Defow	Stephen	16JUL06	1.07	1
DeFoor	Stephen	02JUL07	1.05	1
Defoor	Stephen	06JUN08	1.09	1
Defoe	Stephen	30MAY09	2.07	1
Defore	Stephen	-----11	1.19	1
DEHART				
Dehart	John	23JUL07	2.10	1
DEJARNETT				
Dejarnett	Milly	21AUG04	2.05	F
Dejarnett	Milley	11JUN05	3.08	F
Dejarnett	Milley	12AUG06	3.10	F
Dejarne	Milly	19AUG07	2.10	F
Dejournett	Samuel	02JUL99	1.09	1
De JournettSamuel		20JUN00	2.08	1
De JournettSamuel		20JUN00	2.08	1
Dejournett	Samuel	01AUG01	2.06	1
Dezarnett	Samuel	23AUG02	2.07	1
Dezarnett	Samuel	15JUN03	3.07	1
DeJarnett	---	07AUG04	2.05	
Pd tax for David (heirs) Calekorn				
DELANY				
Delanah	Abraham	30JUL06	1.07	1
Delany	Abraham	-----11	1.19	1
Delany	James	-----11	1.19	M1
Delany	John	-----11	1.20	1
Delany	Joseph	-----11	1.19	1
DEMORY				
Demory	John	30JUN87	1.02	1
DEMOSS				
Demoss	Andrew	22JUN99	2.06	1
DENNIS				
Dennis	Elisha	27MAY94	3.07	1
Denis	Elisha	10MAR95	1.05	1
Dennis	Elisha	-----96	1.06	1
Dennis	Samuel	21APR96	2.05	1
DENNY				
Denney	Elijah	30JUL05	1.05	1
Denny	Zacheriah	02AUG04	1.05	1
Denny	Zachariah	30JUL05	1.05	1
Denny	Zaheriah	10JUN08	1.09	11
DENTON				
Denton	James	20AUG91	3.05	11
Denton	James	02MAY94	3.07	1
Denton	James	10MAR95	1.05	1
Denton	James	-----96	1.05	1
Denton	John	20AUG91	3.05	1
Denton	John	29NOV92	3.06	1
Denton	John	02MAY94	3.07	1
Denton	John	10MAR95	1.05	11
Denton	John	-----96	1.05	1
Denton	John	-----11	1.20	1
Denton	Robert	14SEP92	1.04	1
Denton	Robert	27AUG93	3.04	1
Denton	Robert	29MAY94	3.04	1
Denton	Robert	02MAY95	3.05	1
Denton	Robert	23JUN96	2.05	1
Denton	Robert	10AUG97	1.07	1
Denton	Robert	10JUL00	3.10	1
Denton	Robert	30JUL01	3.10	1
Denton	Robert	29JUL02	3.07	1
Denton	Robert	09AUG03	2.08	1
Denton	Robert	20JUN05	2.09	1
Denton	Robert	30JUN06	2.11	1
Denton	Thomas	28AUG89	2.04	1
Donton	Thomas	15JUN99	2.04	1
Denton	Thomas	12JUN00	1.02	1
Denton	Thomas	01JUN01	1.11	1
Denton	William	-----11	1.20	1
DEPAUW				
Depaugh	Charles	26JUN87	1.02	1
Depauw	Charles	16MAY89	6.02	1
Depauw	Charles	01AUG90	1.03	1
Depauw	Charles	09AUG91	2.03	1
Depauw	Charles	13OCT92	1.04	1
Depauw	Charles	14SEP93	3.03	1
Depawed	Charles	20APR95	3.05	1
Depow	Charles	29MAY96	2.05	1
Depauw	Charles	30JUN97	1.06	1
Depauw	Charles	08JUL99	3.07	1
One lot in Frankford				
Depauw	Charles	08JUL99	3.07	
Seven lots in Warwick				
Depauw	Charles	05JUL00	3.09	1
Depauw	Charles	21JUN01	3.09	1
One lot in the town of Frankfort				
Depauw	Charles	21JUN01	3.09	
Seven lots in town of Warwich				
Depau	Charles	11AUG02	3.07	11
One lott in Frankford				
Depau	Charles	11AUG02	3.07	
Seven lotts in Warrick				
Depauw	Charles	28JUL03	2.08	11
One lott in Frankford				
Depauw	Charles	28JUL03	2.08	
One lott in Warrick				
Depauw	Charles	24JUL04	4.07	1
Depeau	Charles	18JUL05	2.09	1
Dupeau	Charles	18JUL05	2.09	
One lott in Frankford				
Dupeau	Charles	18JUL05	2.09	
Two lotts in Warrick				
Depeau	Charles	13AUG06	2.11	1
Seven lotts in Warrick				
Depauw	Charles	18JUN07	2.08	1
Depauw	Charles	18JUN07	2.08	1
Depauw	Charles	23JUN08	2.07	1
Depauw	Charles	11MAY09	1.10	1
Depeau	John	19JUL05	2.09	1
Depeau	John	15AUG06	2.11	1
Depaw	John	15JUL07	2.09	1
Depaw	John	-----08	2.08	1
Depaw	John	13MAY09	1.10	2
One lott town of Liberty				
Depauw	Peter	23JUL07	2.10	1
Depauw	Peter	29JUN08	2.07	1
Depaw	Peter	16MAY09	1.10	
Seven lotts in town of Warrick				
Depow	Peter	-----11	1.20	1
Dupeau	Rachael	18JUL05	2.09	F
Depeau	Rachel	13AUG06	2.11	F1
DEVEEE				
Deveee	David	23JUN99	2.06	1
DEVER				
Dever	Edmund	-----11	1.18	1
Dever	John	11JUN89	6.02	1
Dever	John	02AUG90	1.03	1
Dever	John	19APR91	2.03	1
Dever	John	22SEP92	1.04	1
Dever	John	16AUG93	3.04	1
Dever	John	24MAY94	2.04	1

surname	name	date	bk.pg	TM	surname	name	date	bk.pg	TM
Dever	John	15APR95	3.05	1	Dierman	Jonathan	23JUN02	1.06	1
DEVINE					Diermon	Jonathan	22JUN03	1.06	1
Devine	James	24AUG87	1.02	1	Diermon	Jonathan	03AUG04	1.05	1
Devin	James	06AUG89	5.04	1	Diermon	Jonathan	31JUL05	1.06	1
Devin	James	11JUL91	1.03	1	Diermon	Jonathan	01AUG06	1.07	1
Davin	James	10AUG93	1.03	1	Dearman	Jonathan	27MAY07	1.06	1
Davin	James	29MAY94	1.03	1	Dearman	Jonathan	01JUL09	2.08	1
Diven	James	09MAY95	2.04	1	Dierman	William	18JUN99	2.04	1
Devin	James	29AUG97	3.34	1	Dierman	William	23JUL00	1.03	1
Devin	James	21MAY99	1.07	1	Diermon	William	23JUN01	1.04	1
Diven	James	08JUL00	2.08	1	Dierman	William	23JUN02	1.06	1
Diven	James	10AUG01	2.06	1	Diermon	William	22JUN03	1.06	1
Diven	James	23AUG02	2.07	1	Diermon	William	02AUG04	1.05	1
Divion	James	17JUN03	3.07	1	Dirmon	William	30JUL05	1.05	1
Diven	James	31JUL04	2.04	1	Diermon	William	01AUG06	1.07	1
Diven	James	30MAY05	3.08	1	Dearman	William	08MAY07	1.06	1
Diven	James	19JUL06	3.09	1	Dearman	William	10JUN08	1.09	1
Divin	James	19AUG07	2.10	1	Dearman	William	01JUL09	2.08	1
Diven	James	-----08	2.08	1	DILLINGHAM				
Divin	James	09MAY09	1.10	1	Dillingham	Archibald	-----96	1.05	1
Divine	James	-----11	1.18	1	Dillingham	Champl	10MAY99	2.05	1
Divine	Roger	13AUG90	1.03	1	Dillingham	Champ	09JUN00	1.02	1
Devine	Roger	21NOV93	3.03	1	Dillingham	Champ	29MAY01	1.03	1
Devin	William	06AUG89	5.04	1	Dillingham	Champ	26JUN02	1.06	1
Devion	William	26MAR90	2.03	1	Dillingham	Champness	25MAY03	3.06	1
Devin	William	28OCT91	1.03	1	Dillingham	Easther	09OCT92	2.03	F
DEWITT					Dillingham	Joshua	22NOV88	1.-	1
Dewitt	Walter	15JUL87	3.03	1	Dillingham	Joshua	-----96	1.05	1
Dudley Curd listed with him					Dillingham	Lot	-----96	1.05	1
Dewitt	Walter	25JUL89	2.04	11	Dillingham	Lott	15AUG03	3.07	1
DICKEN					Dillingham	Lot	08AUG04	3.08	1
Dicken	Benjamin	08JUL99	3.07	1	Dillingham	Lott	05AUG05	3.09	1
Dicken	Isaac	18MAY01	3.09	1	Dillingham	Lott	04AUG06	3.10	1
Dicken	John	29JUN96	2.05	1	Dillingham	Mical	20MAR97	2.01	1
Dicken	John	28JUN97	1.07	1	Dillingham	Michal	10MAY99	2.06	1
Dicken	John	08JUL99	3.07	1	Dillingham	Michael	09JUN00	1.02	1
Dicken	John	04JUL00	3.09	1	Dillingham	Michael	29MAY01	1.03	11
Dicken	John	09MAY01	3.09	1	Dillingham	Michael	28JUN02	1.06	11
Dicken	John	12AUG02	3.07	1	Dillingham	Michael	10JUN03	1.06	11
Dicken	John	28JUL03	2.08	1	Dillingham	Michael	13JUN04	1.04	12
Dicken	John	27JUN04	4.07	1	Dillingham	Michiel	05AUG05	3.09	11
Dicken	John	19JUL05	2.09	1	Dillingham	Peter	19JUN01	3.10	1
Dicken	John	15AUG06	2.11	1	Dillingham	Veach	-----96	1.06	1
Dickin	John	15JUL07	2.09	1	Dillingham	William	-----96	1.05	1
Dicking	John	29JUN08	2.07	1	DINWIDDIE				
Dicken	John	13MAY09	1.10	1	Dunwiddy	David	-----11	1.18	1
Dickin	John	-----11	1.20	1	Dinwiddie	John	01AUG04	2.04	1
Dicken	Lot	28JUN97	1.07	1	Dinwiddie	John	17JUN05	3.09	1
DICKSON					Dinwiddie	John	17JUL06	3.09	1
Dickson	Edward	-----93	3.01	1	Dinwiddie	John	15JUL07	2.09	1
Dickison	Elizabeth	06APR09	1.10		Dinwidie	John	02JUN08	2.07	1
Paid tax for William Davidson					Dinwiddie	John	05JUN09	1.10	1
Dickerson	James	-----11	1.19	1	Dunwiddy	John	-----11	1.20	1
Dickerson	James	-----11	1.20	1	Dinwiddie	William	30APR91	2.03	1
Dickson	John	25JUL04	1.05	1	Dinwidda	William	05OCT92	1.04	1
Dixon	John	03AUG05	2.10	1	Dinwiddie	William	07NOV93	3.03	1
Dixson	John	20MAY06	2.11	1	Dunwodde	William	24MAY94	2.04	1
Dickson	Nathaniel	20JUN99	2.04	1	Dinwoode	William	15APR95	3.05	1
Dickinson	William	13JUN96	2.05	1	Dinwiddie	William	12MAY96	2.05	1
Dickason	William	16MAY97	1.07	1	Dinwiddie	William	12JUN97	1.07	1
Dickison	William	28MAY05	3.08	1	Dunwiddie	William	07JUN99	1.08	1
Dickison	William	02AUG06	3.09	1	Dunwoddie	William	28JUL00	2.09	1
Dickeson	William	19AUG07	2.10	1	Dunwoodie	William	19JUN01	3.10	1
Dickison	William	28JUL08	2.07	11	Dunwoodie	William	09JUN02	2.06	1
DICKY					Dinwidy	William	25AUG03	3.08	1
Dicky	Robert	25JUL07	2.10	1	Dinwiddie	William	25AUG04	3.08	12
Dicky	Robert	-----08	2.08	1	Dinwiddie	William	19JUN05	3.09	1
DIERMON					Dinwidie	William	21JUL06	3.09	11
Dieiment	Jonathan	07DEC92	3.06	1	Dinwiddie	William	20JUN07	2.09	11
Dierman	Jonathan	13JUN99	2.04	1	Dinwiddie	William	15JUL08	2.07	1
Dierman	Jonathan	23JUL00	1.03	1	Dinwiddie	William	30JUN09	1.11	1
Diermon	Jonathan	23JUN01	1.04	1	Dunwiddy	Wm.	-----11	1.17	11

0

surname	name	date	bk.pg	TM	surname	name	date	bk.pg	TM
DISMUKES					Dodd	John	14AUG06	2.11	1
Dismukes	James	13JUN87	2.02	1	Dodd	John	15JUL07	2.09	1
Dismukes	Joseph	31JUL00	2.09	1	Dodds	John	13AUG07	2.10	2
Dismukes	Joseph	13JUL01	2.06	1	Dodds	John	08JUN09	1.10	2
Dismuke	Joseph	12JUL02	2.06	1	Dodd	John	-----11	1.20	1
Dismukes	Joseph	19JUL03	3.07	1	Dodds	John	-----11	1.17	1
Dismukes	Joseph	16JUN04	2.04	1	Dodds	Samuel	19AUG07	2.10	11
Dismukes	Joseph	30MAY05	3.08	1	Dodds	Samuel	02JUN08	2.07	1
Dismukes	Joseph	26JUL06	3.09	1	Dodds	Samuel	05JUN09	1.10	1
DOBSON					Dodds	Samuel	-----11	1.20	1
Dobson	James	04JUN99	1.08	1	Dodd	William	15JUL07	2.09	1
Dobson	James	19JUN00	2.08	1	DODSON				
Dobson	James	15JUN03	3.07	1	Dodson	Absalom	29MAY99	2.05	1
Dobson	James	-----05	3.38		Dotson	Charles	15MAR95	1.05	1
1804 tax info in 1805 tax list					Dodson	George	14APR97	3.07	1
Dobson	James	-----05	3.38	1	Dotson	James	15MAR95	1.05	1
Dobson	James	12JUN05	3.08	11	Dotson	James	-----96	1.05	1
Dobson	James	28JUN06	3.09	1	Dotson	Rebekah	15MAR95	1.05	F
Dobson	James	19AUG07	2.10	1	Dotson	Rebekah	-----96	1.05	F1
Dobson	James	02JUN08	2.07	1	DOLLINS				
Dobsen	James	10JUL09	1.11	1	Dollins	James	22APR08	1.08	1
Dobson	Joseph	11JUN89	6.02	1	Dollens	James	25AUG09	2.09	1
Dobson	Joseph	15APR90	1.03	1	Dolens	James	-----11	1.18	1
Dobson	Joseph	19APR91	2.03	1	Dolen	Michael	12AUG02	3.07	11
Dobson	Mary	09APR95	3.05	F	Dollins	Ruben	06JUL09	2.08	1
Dobson	Mary	11JUL96	2.06	F	Dollens	Reuben	-----11	1.19	1
Dobson	Robert	07JUL87	1.02	1	Dolins	William	08JUN09	2.07	1
Dobson	Robert	11JUN89	6.02	1	DOLTON				
Dobson	Robert	21APR90	1.03	11	Dolton	Jesse	13AUG07	2.10	1
Dobson	Robert	20JUN91	2.03	13	Dolton	Lewis	13AUG07	2.10	1
Dobson	Robert	14SEP92	1.04	1	DONALD				
Dobson	Robert	10NOV93	3.03	11	Donald	Thomas	05JUL87	3.03	1
Dobson	Robert	12MAY94	2.04	1	Listed with Hugh McCormack				
Dobson	Robert	07JUN97	1.07	1	DONAN				
Dobson	Robert	08JUL99	3.07	1	Donan	David	30MAY89	6.02	1
Dobson	Robert	20JUN00	3.09	1	Donnan	David	11APR90	1.03	1
Dobson	Robert	02MAY01	3.09	1	Donan	David	19MAY91	2.03	1
DODDS					Donan	David	26SEP92	1.04	11
Dodd	Allen	17JUL00	2.08	1	Donan	David	17AUG93	3.04	1
Dodd	Allen	02JUN01	1.03	1	Donner	Joseph	14AUG07	2.10	1
Dodds	Andrew	26JUN87	1.02	1	DONLEY				
Dodds	Andrew	01MAY89	6.02	1	Donnally	Charles	11JUN89	6.02	1
Dodds	Andrew	21APR90	1.03	1	Donally	Charles	21MAY90	1.03	1
Dodds	Andrew	20APR91	2.03	1	Donnally	Charles	19APR91	2.03	1
Dodd	Andrew	26SEP92	1.04	1	Donnaly	Charles	21SEP92	1.04	1
Dodd	Andrew	19AUG93	3.04	1	Donnally	Charles	09NOV93	3.03	1
Dodds	Andrew	10APR94	2.04	11	Donley	Charles	12APR94	2.04	2
Dodds	Andrew	24MAR95	3.06	1	Donley	Charles	22APR95	3.05	1
Dodds	Andrew	22APR96	2.05	1	Donley	Eupham	01JUN96	2.05	00
Dodds	Andrew	16MAY97	1.07	1	Donley	Eupham	10MAY97	1.06	F
Dodds	James	28JUN87	1.02	1	Donley	Eupham	27JUN99	3.06	F
Dodds	James	01JUN89	6.02	1	Donnelly	Euphram	19JUN00	3.09	F
Dodds	James	10APR90	1.03	1	Donley	Eupherm	21MAY01	3.09	F
Dodds	James	19APR91	2.03	1	Donnally	Uphem	31JUL02	3.07	F
Dodds	James	24MAY95	3.06	1	Donnally	Uphem	04AUG03	2.08	F
Dodds	James	21APR96	2.05	1	Donley	Eupham	13JUN04	4.07	F
Dodd	James	11JUL96	2.06	1	Donnally	Uphem	17JUN05	2.09	F
Dodds	John	22APR96	2.05	1	Donnally	Uphem	02AUG06	2.11	F
Dodd	John	01JUL96	2.05	1	Donley	Eupheam	10AUG07	2.10	0
Dodds	John	15MAY97	1.06	11	Donley	Euphram	-----08	2.08	F
Dodds	John	02JUL99	3.06	11	Donnelly	Euphema	16AUG09	1.11	F
Dodd	John	08JUL99	3.06	1	Donley	Euphram	-----11	1.20	F
Dodd	John	27JUN00	3.09	1	DONNALDSON				
Dodds	John	27JUN00	3.09	11	Donnaldson	John	04JUN01	2.22	1
Dodds	John Sr	21MAY01	3.09	11	DOOLEY				
Dodds	John Jr	21MAY01	3.09	1	Dooley	George	18APR94	2.04	1
Dodd	John Sr	08JUL02	3.07	11	Dooley	George	18APR95	3.05	1
Dodd	John Jr	08JUL02	3.07	1	Dooley	George	21APR96	2.05	1
Dodds	John	26JUL03	2.07	11	Dooley	George	15MAY97	1.07	1
Dodds	John	25JUL04	4.07	11	Dooley	George	02JUL99	3.06	1
Dodd	John	08JUL05	2.09	11	Doolen	George	20JUN00	2.08	1
Dodd	John	09JUN06	2.11	2	Dooley	George	27JUN00	3.09	1

surname	name	date	bk.pg	TM	surname	name	date	bk.pg	TM
Dooley	George	07MAY01	3.09	1	Duglas	John Sr	14JUN91	3.05	1
Dooley	George	14JUN02	3.07	1	Duglas	John	14JUN91	3.05	1
Dooley	George	01JUL03	2.07	1	Duglass	John Sr	28NOV92	3.06	1
Dooly	George	29JUN04	4.07	1	Duglass	John	10OCT92	3.05	1
Dooley	George	23AUG04	3.08	1	Douglas	John	-----93	3.02	1
Dooley	George	30MAY05	2.09	1	Douglass	John	15MAR95	1.05	1
Dooley	George	08JUL05	3.09	1	Douglass	John	-----96	1.05	1
Dooley	George	30MAY06	2.11	1	Duglas	Nathan	14JUN91	3.05	1
Dooley	George	11AUG06	3.10	1	Douglass	Nathan	02MAY94	3.07	1
Dooley	George	06JUL07	2.09	1	DOUTHIT				
Dooley	George	25JUL07	2.10	1	Douthet	Thomas	15JUL97	1.06	1
Dooley	George	-----08	2.08	00	Douthat	Thomas	23JUL00	2.08	1
Dooly	George	07JUN09	1.10	1	Douthet	Thomas	27MAY01	3.10	1
Dooley	George-Capt	-----11	1.17	1	Douthet	Thomas	10AUG02	2.07	1
Dooley	James	10JUN89	6.02	1	Douthet	Thomas	23AUG03	3.07	1
Dooley	James	21APR90	1.02	1	Douthit	Thomas J.	07AUG04	3.08	1
Dooley	James	18MAR91	2.03	11	DOVE				
Dooly	James	06OCT92	1.04	11	Dove	Francis	07JUL87	3.03	1
Dooly	James	24AUG93	3.04	1	Dove	Francis	13AUG89	2.04	1
Dooly	James	09MAY94	2.04	11	Dove	Frances	20AUG91	3.05	1
Dooley	James	28APR95	3.05	11	Dove	Francis	27MAY94	3.07	1
Dooley	James	02JUN96	2.05	12	Dove	Francis	04JUN95	1.05	1
Dooley	James	10JUL97	1.07	11	Dove	Francis	-----96	1.05	1
Dooling	James	03JUN99	1.08	1	Dove	Francis	15MAR97	2.01	1
Doolen	James	20JUN00	2.08	1	Dove	Francis	24MAY99	2.05	1
Dooley	James	31JUL01	2.06	1	Dove	Frances	17JUN00	1.03	1
Dooley	James	10MAY02	2.06	1	Dove	Francis	04JUN01	1.03	1
Dooley	James	31MAY03	3.06	11	DOWELL				
Dooley	James	03MAY04	3.08	1	Dowell	Richard	12APR97	3.07	1
Dooley	James	08JUL05	3.09	1	DOWNEY				
Dooley	James	16JUL06	3.09	1	Downey	Abraham	20JUN07	2.09	11
Dooley	James	06JUL07	2.09	1	Downey	Abraham	15JUL08	2.07	11
Dooley	James	02JUN08	2.07	1	Downing	Andrew	15JUL87	3.03	1
Dooley	Thomas	10JUL97	1.07	1	Downing	Andrew	25JUL89	2.04	1
Dooley	Thomas	02JUL99	1.09	1	Downing	Andrew	26NOV92	3.06	1
Doolen	Thomas	20JUN00	2.08	1	Downing	Ezekiel	03SEP89	2.04	1
Dulen	William	21AUG93	3.03	1	Downing	Ezekel	27MAY94	3.07	1
Dooly	William	18SEP93	3.04	1	Downing	Ezekel	15MAR95	1.05	1
Dooley	William	12MAY94	2.04	01	Downing	Ezekiel	-----96	1.05	1
Dooley	William	19MAY95	3.05	1	Downing	James	15JUL87	3.03	1
Dooley	William	03JUN96	2.05	1	Downing	James	25JUL89	2.04	1
Dooley	William	20JUN97	1.06	1	Downing	James	07MAY91	3.05	1
Dooley	William	02JUL99	1.09	1	Downing	James	26NOV92	3.06	1
Doolin	William	15JUN04	2.04	1	Downey	James	29JUN06	2.11	1
Dooley	William	29MAY05	3.08	1	Downey	James	15JUL07	2.09	1
Dooley	William	07AUG06	3.10	1	Downey	James	19AUG07	2.10	1
Doolin	William	01JUL07	1.05	1	Downey	James	15JUL08	2.07	1
Doolin	William	10JUN08	1.09	1	Downey	James	11JUL09	1.11	1
Doolin	William	30MAY09	2.07	1	Downing	James	-----11	1.17	1
DORREY					Downing	John	15JUL87	3.03	1
Dorrey	Francis	07DEC92	3.06	1	Downing	John	25JUL89	2.04	1
DORSEY					Downing	John	-----08	2.08	1
Dorsey	Amos	20JUL01	3.10	1	Downing	John	08JUN09	1.10	1
Durrsey	Ames	09JUN02	2.06	11	Downing	John	-----11	1.20	1
DOSS					Downey	William	20JUN07	2.09	1
Doss	Arron	31JUL05	2.10	1	Downey	William	15JUL08	2.07	1
DOUGLASS					Downey	William	11JUL09	1.11	1
Douglass	Alexander	25JUN87	2.02	1	Downing	William	-----11	1.17	1
Duglass	Alexander	01NOV88	1.-	1	DOYLE				
Douglass	George	05JUL87	3.03	11	Duel	Basil	20JUN96	2.05	1
Douglass	George	10JUL89	2.04	11	Dorrel	Elizabeth	15MAR95	1.05	F
Douglass	George	02MAY94	3.06	1	Dorrell	Elizabeth	13APR97	3.07	F
Douglass	George	10MAR95	1.05	11	Dorrell	James	13APR97	3.07	1
Douglass	George	-----96	1.05	2	Dorrel	James	16JUN00	1.02	1
Duglas	George	16MAY99	3.06	1	Dorrel	James	29JUL05	1.05	1
Dugles	George	19JUL00	3.10	1	Dorrel	James	04MAY07	1.05	1
Doughlas	George	23JUL01	3.10	1	Dorrel	John	15MAR95	1.05	01
Doughlas	George	04AUG02	2.07	1	Dorril	John	-----96	1.05	1
Dugless	George	19JUL03	3.07	1	Dorril	John	25JUN02	1.06	1
Douglass	George	21AUG04	3.08	1	Dorrel	John	21JUN03	1.06	1
Douglas	George	16AUG05	3.10	1	Douil	John	01AUG04	1.05	1
Doughlas	George	07AUG06	3.10	1	Dorrel	John	29JUL05	1.05	1

surname	name	date	bk.pg	TM	surname	name	date	bk.pg	TM
Dorrel	John	30JUL06	1.07	1	Dueray	Samuel	10JUN08	1.09	1
Dorrel	John	04MAY07	1.05	1	Dudarar	Samuel	23MAY09	2.07	1
Dorrel	John	10JUN08	1.09	1	DUDGEON				
Dorrel	John	13JUN09	2.07	1	Dudgeon	Alexander	20JUN06	1.07	1
Doyl	Thomas	04AUG02	2.07	1	Dudgeon	Alexander	24JUN07	1.07	1
Doyel	Thomas	06JUN03	3.06	1	Dudgeon	Alexander	27APR08	1.08	1
Doyel	Thomas	06AUG04	3.08	1	Dudgeon	Alexander	27MAY09	2.07	1
DRAKE					Dudgeon	Alexander	-----11	1.18	1
Drake	Braxton	13MAY99	3.06	1	Dugeon	John	09JUN97	3.08	1
Drake	Braxter	10AUG02	2.07	1	Dugeon	John	21MAY99	1.08	12
Drake	Braxton	25JUN03	3.07	1	Dudgin	John	04JUN00	2.07	11
Drake	Braxton	06AUG04	3.08	1	Dudgin	John	04JUN01	2.05	11
Drake	Braxter	05AUG05	3.09	1	Dudgeon	John	15JUN02	1.06	11
Drake	Braxter	04AUG06	3.09	1	Dudgons	John	05JUL03	1.07	1
Drake	Carter	05JUN97	1.07	1	Dudgons	John Jr	05JUL03	1.07	1
Drake	Carter	13MAY99	3.06	1	Dudgon	John	31JUL04	2.04	1
Drake	Carter	02AUG00	2.09	1	Dudgeon	John Jr	31JUL04	2.04	1
Drake	Carter	20JUL01	3.09	1	Dudgens	John	19JUN05	1.05	1
Drake	Carter	02AUG02	2.07	11	Dudgeon	John	20JUN06	1.07	1
Drake ·	Carter	25JUN03	3.07	1	Dudgeon	Mary	19JUN05	1.05	F
Drake	Carter	08AUG04	3.08	1	Dudgeon	Mary	20JUN06	1.07	F
Drake	Carter	05AUG05	3.09	1	Dudgeon	Mary	27APR08	1.08	F
Drake	Carter	04AUG06	3.09	1	Dudgeon	Mary	02JUN08	2.07	F1
DRESKEL					Dudgeon	Molly	05JUN09	1.10	F
Dreskel	Jesse	10JUL09	1.11	1	Dudgan	William	04JUN01	2.05	1
DREW					Dudgeon	William	15JUN02	1.06	1
Drew	John(heirs)	31MAY95	3.06	1	Dudgons	William	04JUL03	1.07	1
DRUMMOND					Dudgons	William	05JUL03	1.07	1
Drummin	James	23MAY89	6.02	1	Dugeon	William Sr	02AUG04	2.04	1
Drummin	James	03AUG91	2.03	1	Dudgon	William	31JUL04	2.04	1
Drummind	James	25SEP92	1.04	1	Dudgen	William	15JUN05	1.05	1
Drummin	James	12NOV93	3.03	1	Dudgen	William	17JUN05	1.05	1
Drummon	James	17APR95	3.05	1	Dudgeon	William	20JUN06	1.06	1
Drummond	James	10MAY96	2.05	1	Dudgeon	William	20JUN06	1.07	1
Drummond	James	13JUL97	1.07	1	Dudgeon	William	03JUN07	1.06	1
Drumming	James	06JUN99	1.08	1	Dudgeon	William	27APR08	1.08	1
Drummin	James	25JUL00	2.08	1	Dudgeon	William	02JUN08	2.07	1
Drummond	James	28MAY01	3.10	1	Dudgeon	William	27MAY09	2.07	1
Drummonds	James	10AUG02	2.07	1	Dudgeon	William	05JUN09	1.10	1
Drummond	James	25JUN03	3.07	1	Dudgeon	William	-----11	1.20	1
Drummond	James	06AUG04	3.08	1	Dudgeon	William	-----11	1.18	1
Drummond	James	05AUG05	3.09	1	DUGAN				
Drumond	James	04AUG06	3.09	1	Duggans	Alexander	23JUL06	3.09	M1
DRY					Duggin	Stephen	28JUN05	2.09	1
Dry	George	15AUG97	1.07	1	Duggins	William	02AUG90	1.03	1
Dry	George Jr	24MAY99	3.06	1	Duggin	William	01AUG91	2.03	1
Dry	George Sr	12JUL00	3.10	1	Duggin	William	25SEP92	1.04	1
Dry	George Jr	11JUL00	3.10	1	Duggin	William	28JUN05	2.09	1
Dry	George	30JUL01	3.09	1	Duggans	William	23JUL06	3.09	1
Dry	George	10JUN02	2.06	1	DUKE				
Dry	George Jr	03AUG03	3.07	1	Duke	John	21MAY99	3.06	1
Dry	George	05APR04	4.07	1	DUNAWAY				
Dry	George	20JUN05	3.09	11	Dunaway	William	-----11	1.19	1
Dry	George	30JUL06	3.09	1	DUNBAR				
DRYDEN					Dunbar	John	08APR95	3.05	1
Dryden	William	15JUL87	3.03	1	Dunbar	John	16JUN96	2.05	1
Drydon	William	01JUL89	2.04	1	Dunbar	John	08JUN97	1.06	1
Drydon	William	05MAY91	3.05	1	Dunbar	Reubin	08APR95	3.05	1
Dryden	William	01DEC92	3.06	1	Dunbar	Reubin	16JUN96	2.05	1
Dryden	William	02MAY94	3.07	1	Dunbar	Reubin	08JUN97	1.06	1
Dreyden	William	04JUN95	1.05	1	DUNCAN				
DUDDERAR					Duncan	Abraham	26JUL02	3.07	1
Duderer	Samuel	20MAR97	2.01	1	Dunkin	Benjamin	20JUN99	2.04	11
Dudderer	Samuel	10MAY99	2.06	1	Duncan	Benjamin	14JUN04	1.04	1
Dudderoo	Samuel	09JUN00	1.02	1	Duncan	Benjamin	31JUL05	1.06	1
Dudderar	Samuel	30MAY01	1.03	1	Duncan	Benjamin	20JUN06	1.07	1
Dudderar	Samuel	26JUN02	1.06	1	Duncan	Benjamin	17AUG07	1.07	1
Dudderar	Samuel	10JUN03	1.06	1	Duncan	Benjamin	10JUN08	1.09	1
Dudderrar	Samuel	13JUN04	1.04	1	Duncan	Benjamin	23MAY09	2.07	1
Dudderar	Samuel	18JUN05	1.05	1	Duncan	Benjamin	-----11	1.17	1
Dudderar	Samuel	14JUN06	1.06	1	Duncan	Charles	15SEP93	3.04	1
Dudarar	Samuel	29APR07	1.05	1	Duncin	Charles	12JUN94	2.04	1

surname	name	date	bk.pg	TM	surname	name	date	bk.pg	TM
Dunkin	Charles	16APR95	3.06	1	Duncan	Lewis	02JUN01	2.05	1
Duncan	Charles	15JUN97	1.07	1	Duncan	Lewis	12JUN02	1.06	1
Duncan	Charles	10JUL97	1.07	1	Duncan	Lewis	04JUL03	1.07	1
Duncan	Charles	24JUL00	3.10	1	Dungan	Nathan	26MAY96	2.05	1
Duncan	Charles	27JUN01	2.06	1	Duncan	Nathan	29MAY97	1.07	1
Duncan	Claburn	24AUG87	1.02	1	Duncan	Nathan	24JUL04	4.07	1
Duncan	Clayburn	23JUN91	2.03	1	Duncan	Samuel	15JUL87	3.03	11
Duncan	Clayburn	15SEP93	3.04	1	Duncan	Samuel	27JUN89	2.04	11
Duncin	Claburn	12MAY94	2.04	1	Duncan	Samuel	14MAY90	1.03	1
Dunkin	Claburn	17APR95	3.05	1	Duncan	Samuel	17MAY91	2.03	1
Dunkin	Claburn	11JUL96	2.06	1	Dunkin	Samuel	28MAY91	3.05	1
Duncan	Claburn	07JUN97	1.07	1	Duncan	Samuel	28SEP92	1.04	1
Duncan	Claburn	25MAY99	3.06	1	Dunkin	Samuel	28NOV92	3.06	1
Duncan	Claburn	24JUL00	3.10	1	Duncan	Samuel	10NOV93	3.03	1
Duncan	Cleburn	17JUN01	3.09	1	Duncan	Samuel	02MAY94	3.07	1
Duncan	Clayboarn	12AUG03	2.08	1	Dunkin	Samuel	08MAY94	2.04	1
Duncan	Clabourn	05JUN04	4.07	1	Dunkin	Samuel	30MAY95	3.06	1
Duncan	Claybourn	27JUN05	2.09	1	Duncan	Samuel	-----96	1.05	1
Duncan	Claibourn	01AUG06	2.11	1	Dunkin	Samuel	21MAY96	2.05	1
Duncan	Daniel	-----96	1.05	1	Duncan	Samuel	19JUN00	2.08	1
Duncan	George	24AUG87	1.02	1	Duncan	Samuel	14JUL01	2.06	1
Duncan	George	02AUG90	1.03	1	Duncan	Samuel	10MAY02	2.06	11
Duncan	George	21JUN91	2.03	1	Duncan	Samuel	30JUL03	2.08	11
Duncan	George	22SEP92	1.04	1	Duncan	Samuel	13JUN04	4.07	11
Duncan	George	12NOV93	3.03	1	Duncan	Samuel	04JUN05	3.08	1
Duncin	George	22MAY94	2.04	1	Duncan	Samuel	18AUG06	2.12	11
Dunkin	George	27APR95	3.05	1	Duncan	Samuel	15JUL07	2.09	1
Dunkin	George	01JUN96	2.05	1	Duncan	Samuel	28JUL08	2.07	1
Duncan	George	10JUL97	1.07	1	Duncan	Samuel	03JUL09	1.11	1
Duncan	George	02AUG00	2.09	1	Duncan	Samuel	-----11	1.17	1
Duncan	George	31JUL01	2.06	1	Duncan	Thomas	10JUN08	1.09	1
Duncan	George	21JUL02	2.06	1	Dunkin	William	28MAY91	3.05	1
Duncan	George	13JUL03	3.07	1	Duncan	William	07DEC92	3.06	1
Duncan	George	18JUN04	2.04	1	Duncan	William	-----96	1.05	1
Duncan	George	04JUN05	3.08	1	Duncan	William	15JUL07	2.09	1
Duncan	George	18JUL06	3.09	1	Duncan	William	-----08	2.08	1
Duncan	George	22JUN07	2.09	1	DUNN				
Duncan	George	22JUN07	2.09	1	Dunn	William Sr	-----96	1.05	1
Duncan	George	02JUN08	2.07	11	Dunn	William Jr	-----96	1.05	1
Duncan	George	26JUN09	1.11	1	DUNTON				
Duncan	George	-----11	1.17	12	Dunton	Thomas	05JUL87	3.03	1
Duncan	Howson	28JUL03	2.08	2	Dunton	Thomas	02MAY94	3.06	1
Duncan	Howson	27JUN04	4.07	2	Donton	Thomas	15MAR95	1.05	1
Duncan	Housan	20JUL05	2.10	1	Dunton	Thomas	-----96	1.05	1
Duncan	Housan	19AUG06	2.12	1	Dunton	Thomas	20MAR97	2.01	1
Duncan	Housen	20JUN07	2.08	1	DURHAM				
Duncan	Housen	18JUL08	2.07	1	Durham	Brint	19JUN05	3.03	
Duncan	Hawsen	08JUN09	1.10	1	Adm. for James(decd)	Hindman			
Duncan	Hawson	-----11	1.20	21	Durham	David M.	06JUN03	3.06	1
Duncan	James	24AUG87	1.02	1	Durham	David M.	22AUG04	3.08	1
Duncan	Jesse	15JUL07	2.09	1	Durham	David M.	20AUG05	3.10	1
Duncan	Jesse	29JUN08	2.07	1	Durham	David M.	04AUG06	3.10	1
Duncan	Jesse	08JUN09	1.10	1	Durham	Jacob	29JUN08	2.07	1
Dunkin	John	28MAY91	3.05	1	Durham	Michael	04MAY08	1.08	11
Dunkin	John	15OCT92	3.05	1	DWAN				
Duncan	John	10MAR95	1.05	1	Dwan	James	29OCT92	2.03	1
Duncan	John	-----96	1.05	1	DYER				
Duncan	John	21JUN97	1.07	1	Dayer	Abraham	13AUG93	1.03	1
Duncan	John	31JUN99	1.09	1	Dayer	Abraham	20MAY94	1.03	1
Duncan	John	11JUL05	2.09	1	Dyer	Abraham	02JUN95	2.04	1
Duncan	John	28JUN06	2.11	1	Dayer	Abraham	20JUN96	1.04	1
Duncan	John	18AUG06	2.12	1	Dyer	Abram	26APR97	3.08	1
Duncan	John	15JUL07	2.09	1	Dyer	Abram	16MAY99	1.07	1
Duncan	John	08JUN09	1.10	1	Dyer	Abraham	03JUN00	2.07	1
Duncan	John	-----11	1.20	1	Dyer	Abraham	22JUL01	2.06	1
Duncan	Joseph	20JUL05	2.10	1	Dyar	Abraham	11JUN02	1.05	1
Duncan	Joseph	19AUG06	2.12	11	Dyer	Abraham	30JUN03	1.07	1
Duncan	Joseph	20JUN07	2.08	11	Dyer	Abraham	02AUG04	2.05	1
Duncan	Joseph	-----08	2.08	11	Dyer	Abraham	15JUN05	1.05	1
Duncan	Joseph	08JUN09	1.10	12	Dyar	Abraham	19JUN06	1.06	1
Duncan	Joseph	-----11	1.20	11	Dyar	Abraham	01JUL07	1.05	1
Duncan	Lewis	31JUL00	2.09	1	Dyer	Abraham	27APR08	1.08	1

surname	name	date	bk.pg	TM	surname	name	date	bk.pg	TM
Dyar	Abraham	27MAY09	2.07	1	East	Joseph	15APR90	1.03	1
Dyre	Abraham	-----11	1.19	1	East	Joseph	01AUG91	2.03	1
Dyer	Betsey	26JUN00	2.08	F	East	Joseph	22SEP92	1.04	1
Dyer	Betsey	31JUL01	2.06	F	East	Joseph	14SEP93	3.04	1
Dyer	James	01JUN03	2.07	1	East	Joseph	10MAY94	2.04	1
Dyer	James	21AUG04	2.05	1	East	Joseph	14APR95	3.06	1
Dyer	James	01AUG05	2.10	1	East	Joseph	13JUL96	2.06	1
Dyer	James	07AUG06	2.11	1	East	Joseph	26MAY97	1.08	11
Dyer	James	15JUL07	2.09	1	East	Joseph	21MAY99	3.07	1
Dyer	James	-----08	2.08	1	East	Joseph	20AUG00	2.09	1
Dyer	James	10JUN09	1.11	1	East	Joseph	27JUN01	2.07	11
Dyre	James	-----11	1.17	1	East	Joseph	12JUN02	2.08	11
Dayer	Joal	20MAY94	1.03	1	East	Joseph	11JUL03	3.08	1
Dyer	Joel	02JUN95	2.04	1	East	Joseph	20JUL04	2.06	12
Dayer	Joal	20JUN96	1.04	1	East	Joseph	03JUN05	3.10	13
Dyer	William	02MAY94	3.06	1	East	Joseph	14JUL06	3.11	12
Dyre	William	-----11	1.17	1	East	Joseph	13JUN07	2.11	21
DYSERT					East	Joseph	06JUN08	2.08	11
Dysert	James	10JUN94	2.04	0	East	Joseph	03JUL09	1.12	1
Dysert	James	22JUN03	1.06	2	East	Josias	01AUG91	2.03	11
Dysert	James	03AUG04	1.05	21	East	Josiah	17SEP92	1.04	1
Dysert	James	30JUL05	1.06	11	East	Josiah	14SEP93	3.04	11
Dysert	James	01AUG06	1.07	11	East	Josiah	10MAY94	2.04	11
Dysert	James	09MAY07	1.06	11	East	Josiah	14APR95	3.06	11
Dysert	James	18APR08	1.07	11	East	Josiah	13JUL96	2.06	1
Dysert	James	16JUN09	2.08	2	East	Josiah	31MAY97	1.08	1
Dysert	John	01AUG06	1.07	1	East	Josiah	25JUN99	3.07	11
Dysert	John	09MAY07	1.06	1	East	Josiah	24JUL00	3.10	1
Dysert	John	18APR08	1.07	1	East	Josiah	17JUN01	3.11	1
Dysert	John	01JUL09	2.08	1	East	Josiah	05AUG02	2.08	1
Dysert	Samuel	22JUN03	1.06	1	East	Josiah	15JUN03	3.08	1
Dysert	Samuel	02AUG04	1.05	1	East	Josiah	03MAY04	3.07	1
Dysert	Samuel	30JUL05	1.06	1	East	Josiah	05AUG05	3.11	1
Dysert	Samuel	01AUG06	1.07	1	East	Josiah	-----11	1.21	1
Dysert	Samuel	08MAY07	1.06	1	East	Neal	11JUN89	6.03	1
Dysert	Samuel	18APR08	1.07	1	East	Neale	15APR90	1.03	1
Dysert	Samuel	01JUL09	2.08	1	East	Neal	13JUL96	2.06	1
EADES					East	Neal	20JUN97	1.08	1
Eades	Edward	15JUN07	2.11	1	East	Cornelius	07JUN99	1.09	1
Eades	Edward	07JUN09	1.12	1	East	Neal	25JUN00	2.09	1
Edes	Edward	-----11	1.23	1	East	Cornealus	29MAY01	3.11	1
Eades	Thomas Sr	15JUN07	2.11	1	East	Neal	05AUG02	2.08	1
Eades	Thomas Jr	15JUN07	2.11	1	East	Neal	10JUN03	3.08	1
Eades	Thomas	07JUN09	1.12	1	East	Neal	03MAY04	3.07	1
Edes	Thomas	-----11	1.23	1	East	Cornealus	13JUN05	3.10	1
EARLE					East	Cornealus	05JUL06	3.11	1
Urls	Joshua	04AUG00	2.28	1	East	Neal	11JUN07	2.10	1
Urls	Joshua	15JUL01	2.26	1	East	Neal	-----08	2.09	11
Urls	Joshua	01AUG02	3.27	1	East	Cornealius	27JUN09	1.12	1
Urls	Joshua	18JUN03	2.32	1	East	Neal	-----11	1.22	13
Erls	Joshua	29JUN04	4.08	1	East	North	13JUL87	1.02	1
Urls	Joshua	31MAY05	2.33	1	EASTER				
Earles	Joshua	30JUL06	3.11	1	Easter	George	27JUN03	2.09	1
Earle	Samuel	28JUL06	3.11	1	Easter	George	25JUL04	4.08	1
Urls	Thomas	01JUN03	2.32	1	ECHOLS				
EAST					Acles	Bengamin	15JUN97	3.02	1
East	Alexander	-----08	2.09	1	Achols	Benjamin	24MAY99	3.01	1
East	Isaac	17JUN01	3.11	1	Echols	Benjamin	28JUL00	3.10	1
East	Isaac	12JUN02	2.08	1	Akells	Benjamin	15JUL01	2.01	1
East	Isaac	04AUG06	3.11	1	EDENS				
East	James	15APR90	1.03	1	Edens	Andrew	31MAY97	3.10	1
East	James	02AUG04	2.06	M1	Eden	Elias	05AUG05	3.11	1
East	James	14JUL06	3.11	1	Edens	Elias	04AUG06	3.11	1
East	James	13JUN07	2.11	1	Edens	Henry	30JUN97	1.08	1
East	James	06JUN08	2.08	1	Edens	Henry	24MAY99	3.07	1
East	John	17JUN01	3.11	1	Edon	Henry	11JUL00	3.10	1
East	John	11AUG02	2.08	1	Eaden	Henry	30JUN01	3.11	1
East	John	11JUL03	3.08	1	Edens	Henry	09JUN02	2.08	1
East	John	06AUG04	3.07	1	Edens	Henry	04AUG03	3.08	1
East	John	05AUG05	3.11	1	Eaden	Henry	07APR04	4.08	1
East	John	04AUG06	3.11	1	Edens	Henry	21JUN05	3.11	1
East	Joseph	19APR89	6.03	1	Edens	Henry	30JUL06	3.11	1

surname	name	date	bk.pg	TM	surname	name	date	bk.pg	TM
Eden	John	18MAY97	3.10	1	Edwards	Lewis	30JUL06	3.11	1
Eden	John	30MAY97	3.10	1	Edwards	Mary	14AUG93	1.03	F
Edens	John	04JUN97	1.08	1	Edwards	Mary	02JUN94	3.08	F
Eden	John	26JUN99	1.10	1	Edwards	Milley	30JUN89	2.05	F
Eden	John	18JUN00	1.04	1	Edwards	Ruth	04AUG06	3.12	F1
Eden	John	25JUL00	2.09	12	Edwards	Thomas	13JUN05	3.10	1
Eadens	John	29MAY01	3.11	12	Edwards	Thomas	04AUG06	3.12	11
Edens	John	03AUG02	2.08	12	Edwards	Thomas	11JUN07	2.10	11
Edons	John	20JUN03	1.07	1	Edwards	Thomas	06JUN08	2.08	11
Edens	John	02AUG04	2.06	1	Edwards	Thomas	28JUN09	1.12	1
Eden	John	12JUN05	1.06	1	Edwards	William	28JUL06	3.11	1
Eden	John	06JUN06	1.08	1	ELDER				
Eaden	John	26MAY07	1.07	1	Elder	Andrew	-----11	1.22	1
Edens	John	31APR08	1.10	1	Elder	James	01JUN96	2.06	1
Eden	John	11MAY09	2.09	1	Alder	James	10MAY97	3.01	1
Edden	John	-----11	1.21	1	Elder	James	18MAY99	1.09	1
Edens	Phillip	04JUN97	1.08	1	Elder	James	04JUN00	2.09	1
Eden	William	13JUN97	3.10	1	Elder	James	04JUN01	2.07	1
Edens	William	03AUG02	2.08	11	Elder	James	15JUN02	1.07	1
Edens	William	18AUG03	3.08	12	Elder	James	04AUG03	2.09	1
Edens	William	06AUG04	3.07	11	Elders	Matthew	30MAY08	2.08	1
Edens	William	15AUG05	3.11	1	Elder	Mathew	16AUG09	1.12	1
Edens	William	04AUG06	3.11	11	Elder	Mathew	-----11	1.22	1
EDERINGTON					Elder	Rebeca	17JUN05	2.10	F
Ederington	James	10MAY95	1.06	1	Elder	Rebecca	18AUG06	2.13	1
EDWARDS					Elders	Rebecka	15JUN07	2.11	1
Edwards	Aaron	11AUG02	2.08	1	Elders	Rebeckah	24AUG08	2.09	F
Edwards	Aaron	05AUG05	3.11	1	Elder	Rebecca	16AUG09	1.12	F
Edwards	Aaron	04AUG06	3.11	1	Elder	Robert	01JUN96	2.06	1
Edwards	Ambross	18MAR95	3.06	01	Elder	Robert	26JUN99	3.07	1
Edwards	Ambrose	20MAY96	2.06	M1	Elder	Robert	02JUL00	3.10	1
Edwards	Ambrose	30MAY97	1.08	1	Elder	Robert	02MAY01	3.11	1
Edwards	Ambros	15JUL99	3.07	1	Elder	Robert	06AUG02	3.08	1
Edwards	Ambress	07MAY01	3.11	1	Elder	Robert	01AUG03	2.09	11
Edwards	Ambrose	12AUG02	3.08	1	Elder	Robert	12JUN04	4.08	11
Edwards	Ambrose	30MAY03	2.08	1	Elder	Robert	17JUN05	2.10	11
Edwards	Ambros	27JUN04	4.08	1	Elder	Robert	18AUG06	2.13	12
Edwards	Ambrose	29MAY05	2.10	1	Elders	Robert	15JUN07	2.11	12
Edwards	Ambrose	18JUL06	2.12	1	Elders	Robert	24AUG08	2.09	12
Edwards	Emoriah	25JUL00	2.09	1	Elder	Robert	16AUG09	1.12	1
Edwards	Ameriah	29MAY01	3.11	1	Elder	Robert	-----11	1.22	11
Edwards	Ameriah	11AUG02	2.08	1	ELINWOOD				
Edwards	Emeriah	25JUN03	3.08	1	Elinwood	Daniel	20JUN96	1.04	1
Edwards	Emery	06AUG04	3.07	1	ELLIOTT				
Edwards	Ameriah	05AUG05	3.11	1	Elliot	Alexander	25JUL89	2.05	1
Edwards	Emrey	04AUG06	3.11	1	Elliott	Alexandria	18MAY91	3.05	1
Edwards	Clabourn	10MAY09	2.09	1	Elliot	Alexander	26NOV92	3.06	1
Edwards	George	30MAY99	1.09	1	Elliot	Alexander	27MAY94	3.08	1
Edwards	George	02AUG04	2.06	1	Elliott	Alex.	04JUN95	1.05	1
Edwards	George	15JUN05	1.06	11	Elliott	Alexander	-----96	4.06	1
Edwards	George	20JUN06	1.08	11	Ellot	Barbara	04AUG06	3.12	F
Edwards	George	30JUN07	1.07	1	Ellot	Daniel	15AUG05	3.11	1
Edwards	George	27APR08	1.10	11	Ellot	Daniel	26JUL06	3.11	1
Edwards	George	31MAY09	2.09	1	Ellott	Daniel	15JUN07	2.11	1
Edwards	George	-----11	1.21	1	Ellott	Daniel	24AUG08	2.09	1
Edwards	Griffen	-----11	1.21	1	Ellott	Daniel	28JUN09	1.12	1
Edward	Henry	16APR94	2.04	1	Elliot	Daniel	-----11	1.23	1
Edwards	Henry	19MAR95	3.06	1	Elliot	George	08JUN89	6.03	1
Edward	Henry	16JUN96	2.06	1	Elliott	George	20APR90	1.04	11
Edwards	Henry	07JUN97	1.08	1	Eliott	George Sr	07MAY91	3.05	1
Edwards	Henry	10JUL09	1.12	1	Eliott	George	18MAY91	3.05	11
Edwards	James	06JUN08	2.08	1	Eliot	George Sr	27MAY94	3.07	1
Edwards	John	30JUN89	2.05	1	Elliot	George Jr	02JUN94	3.08	1
Edwards	John	-----93	2.02	1	Elliott	George Sr	10MAY95	1.06	1
Edwards	John	20APR97	3.10	1	Elliott	George Jr	04JUN95	1.05	1
Edwards	John	30MAY07	1.07	1	Elliott	George	-----96	4.06	1
Edwards	John	27APR08	1.09	11	Elliott	George Jr	-----96	4.06	1
Edwards	John	31MAY09	2.09	1	Elliot	George	26APR97	3.09	1
Edwards	John	-----11	1.21	1	Elliott	George	18MAY99	1.09	1
Edwards	Lewis	10JUN02	2.08	1	Ellott	Isaac	10AUG07	2.12	1
Edwards	Lewis	05AUG03	3.08	1	Eliott	John	05MAY91	3.05	1
Edwards	Lewis	20JUN05	3.10	1	Elliott	John	18MAY99	1.09	1

surname	name	date	bk.pg	TM	surname	name	date	bk.pg	TM
Elliott	Johnston	23JUL01	3.11	1	Elmore	Motram	23JUN01	1.05	1
Ellott	Johnston	05AUG02	2.08	1	Elmore	Matram	23JUN02	1.07	1
Ellett	Johnston	16JUL03	3.08	11	Elmore	Motrum	20JUN03	1.07	1
Ellot	Johnston	16JUN04	2.06	11	Elmore	Motrom	01AUG04	1.06	1
Elott	Johnston	05AUG05	3.11	1	Ellmore	Motram	22JUL05	1.06	1
Ellot	Johnston	04AUG06	3.11	11	Ellmore	Motram	02AUG06	1.08	1
Ellott	John	10AUG07	2.12	1	ELY				
Elliott	Joseph	04JUN01	2.07	0	Ely	James	17MAY91	2.03	1
Elliott	Joseph	10AUG01	2.07		Ely	James	17SEP92	1.04	1
Exempt from county leavy					Ely	James	10SEP93	3.04	1
Elliot	William	08JUN89	6.03	1	Eli	James	21APR94	2.04	2
ELLIS					Ely	James	20MAR95	3.06	1
Ellis	Charles	13APR96	2.06	00	Ely	James	21MAY96	2.06	11
Ellis	Isaac	29JUN01	3.11	1	Ely	James	11JUN97	1.08	11
Ellis	Isaac	10JUN02	2.08	1	Ely	James	09JUL99	3.07	11
Ellis	Isaac	05AUG03	3.08	1	Eley	James	01AUG00	3.10	12
Ellis	Isaac	06APR04	4.08	1	Ely	James	11MAY01	3.11	12
Ellis	Isaac	20JUN05	3.10	1	Ely	James	31JUL02	3.08	13
Ellis	Isaac	30JUL06	3.11	1	Ely	James	13JUN03	2.09	13
Ellis	James	05JUL96	2.06	1	Ely	James	28JUN04	4.08	12
Ellis	James	29JUN01	3.11	1	Ely	James	11MAY05	2.10	11
Ellis	James	10JUN02	2.08	1	Ely	James	16AUG06	2.13	1
Ellis	James	03AUG03	3.08	1	Ely	James	10AUG07	2.11	1
Ellis	James	06APR04	4.08	1	Ely	James	10AUG07	2.12	
Ellis	James	21AUG05	3.11	1	Partner with John King				
Ellis	James	04AUG06	3.12	1	Ely	James	-----08	2.09	1
Ellis	James	18MAY07	1.07	1	Ely	James	27JUL08	2.08	1
Ellis	James	31APR08	1.10	1	Ely	James	07JUN09	1.12	11
Ellis	John	05JUL96	2.06	12	Ely	James	-----11	1.23	11
Ellis	John Jr	05JUL96	2.06	1	Guardian for Samuel Craig				
Ellis	Jonathan	03MAY04	3.07	1	ELY/CRAIG				
Ellis	Richard	05JUL96	2.06	1	Ely/Craig	James/Sam.	-----11	1.23	0
Ellis	Richard	08AUG97	1.08	11	ELY/FORBIS				
Ellis	Richard	24MAY99	3.07	1	Ely/Forbis	-	07JUN09	1.12	0
Ellis	Richard	12JUL00	3.10	1	Ely/Forbis	-	07JUN09	1.12	0
Ellis	Richard	29JUN01	3.11	1	Ely/Forbis	-	07JUN09	1.12	0
Ellis	Richard	10JUN02	2.08	1	Ely/Forbis	-	07JUN09	1.12	0
Ellis	Richard	03AUG03	3.08	1	Ely/Forbis	-	07JUN09	1.12	0
Ellis	Richard	05APR04	4.08	1	Ely/Forbis	-	07JUN09	1.12	0
Ellis	Richard	20JUN05	3.10	1	Ely/Forbis	-	07JUN09	1.12	0
Ellis	Richard	28JUL06	3.11	1	Ely/Forbis	-	07JUN09	1.12	0
ELLISON					Ely/Forbis	-	07JUN09	1.12	0
Elliston	Amos	-----11	1.21	1	Ely/Forbis	-	07JUN09	1.12	0
Elison	Francis	09MAY07	1.07	1	Ely/Forbis	-	07JUN09	1.12	0
Ellison	James	11MAY95	2.04	1	ELY/FORBUS				
Ellison	John	07JUL87	2.03	1	Ely/Forbus	James/Jon.	-----11	1.23	0
Ellison	Lewis	11JUN95	2.04	1	Ely/Forbus	James/Jon.	-----11	1.23	0
ELMORE					Ely/Forbus	James/Jon.	-----11	1.23	0
Elmore	John	23JUN01	1.05	1	Ely/Forbus	James/Jon.	-----11	1.23	0
Elmore	John	23JUN02	1.07	1	Ely/Forbus	James/Jon.	-----11	1.23	0
Elmore	John	20JUN03	1.07	1	Ely/Forbus	James/Jon.	-----11	1.23	0
Elmore	John	01AUG04	1.06	1	Ely/Forbus	James/Jon.	-----11	1.23	0
Elmore	John	22JUL05	1.06	1	ELY/KING				
Elmore	John	30JUL06	1.08	1	Ely/King	-	07JUN09	1.12	0
Elmore	John	25MAY07	1.07	1	Ely/King	-	07JUN09	1.12	0
Elmore	John	31APR08	1.10	1	Ely/King	James/John	-----11	1.23	0
Elmore	John	12JUN09	2.09	1	Ely/King	James/John	-----11	1.23	0
Elmar	John	-----11	1.21	1	EMBREE				
Elmore	Matthew	21JUN87	2.02	1	Embree	Elijah	22MAY95	2.04	1
Elmore	Matthew	19JUN89	5.04	1	Embre	Elijah	06JUN96	1.04	1
Elmore	Mathew	13OCT92	2.03	1	Emmery	Elijah	27MAY99	1.10	1
Elmore	Mathew	14AUG93	1.03	1	Embree	Elijah	24MAY00	2.09	1
Elmore	Mathew	29MAY94	1.03	1	Embree	Elijah	25MAY01	2.07	1
Elmore	Mathew	03JUN95	2.04	1	Embree	Elijah	14JUN02	3.08	1
Elmore	Mathew	03JUN95	2.17	1	Embree	Elijah	04JUN03	2.09	1
Elmore	Mathew	30JUN96	1.04	11	Embree	Elijah	24JUL04	1.06	1
Elmore	Matthew	13APR97	3.09	11	Embree	Elijah	08JUN05	2.10	1
Elmore	Mathew	25MAY07	1.07	1	Embree	Elijah	14JUN06	2.12	1
Elmore	Mathew	22APR08	1.09	11	Emrey	Elijah	15JUN07	2.11	1
Elmore	Mathew	25AUG09	2.10	1	Embree	Elijah	02AUG08	1.10	1
Elmore	Motrum	30MAY99	2.06	11	Embry	Elijah	-----11	1.21	1
Elmore	Motram	25JUL00	1.04	11	Emmery	Elisha	02SEP93	1.03	1

surname	name	date	bk.pg	TM	surname	name	date	bk.pg	TM
Emmery	Elisha	15MAY94	1.03	1	Emmerson	Jesse	10JUN05	2.10	1
Embree	Elisha	22JUN95	2.04	1	Emmerson	Jesse	09JUN06	2.12	11
Embree	Elisha	06JUN96	1.04	1	Emmerson	Jesse	08JUN07	2.10	11
Emmery	Elisha	27MAY99	1.10	1	Emerson	Jesse	31APR08	1.10	12
Embree	Elisha	24MAY00	2.09	1	Emberson	John	22OCT92	2.03	1
Embree	Elisha	15JUN01	2.07	1	Emmerson	John	07SEP93	1.03	1
Embree	Elisha	30JUN02	3.08	1	Emmerson	John Sr	15MAY94	1.11	1
Embree	Elisha	04JUN03	2.08	1	Emmerson	John	15MAY94	1.03	1
Embree	Elisha	25JUL04	1.06	1	Emmerson	John	18MAY95	2.17	0
Embree	John	27JUN87	2.02	11	Emmerson	John	18MAY95	2.04	1
Embree	John	29OCT88	1.03	1	Emmerson	John	18MAY95	2.17	1
Embree	John	18NOV88	1.03	12	Tax paid by Joseph Glover				
Embree	John	06AUG89	5.04	13	Emberson	John	10JUN96	1.04	1
Embrey	John	01JUN90	2.03	11	Emberson	John	09JUN00	1.04	1
Embrie	John	07APR91	1.03	12	Emmerson	John	27JUL01	2.07	1
Emery	John Sr	22OCT92	2.03	13	Emmerson	John	26MAY02	3.08	1
Emery	John Jr	22OCT92	2.03	1	Emmerson	John	04JUN03	2.09	1
Emmery	John	06AUG93	1.03	12	Emmerson	John	24JUL04	1.06	1
Emmery	John	15MAY94	1.03	12	Emmerson	John	03MAY05	2.10	1
Embree	John	22MAY95	2.04	11	Amberson	John	30JUL06	3.01	1
Embree	John	06JUN96	1.04	1	Emerson	John	31APR08	1.10	1
Emmery	John	19APR97	3.09	1	Emerson	John	15AUG09	2.09	1
Emmery	John	22MAY99	1.09	1	Emmerson	John	-----11	1.22	1
Emmery	John	27MAY99	1.10	1	Emmerson	Reuben	04APR01	2.07	M1
Embree	John	07JUL00	2.09	1	Emmerson	Reuben	12AUG02	3.08	1
Embree	John	29JUN01	2.07	1	Emberson	Rheuben	15JUL03	1.08	1
Embree	John	30JUN02	3.08	1	Emmerson	Reuben	07AUG04	3.07	1
Embree	John	01JUN03	2.08	1	Emberson	Ruben	15AUG05	3.11	1
Emry	John	24JUL04	1.06	1	Amberson	Reuben	30JUL06	3.01	1
Embree	John	31JUN05	2.11	1	Emberson	Samuel	27JUN87	2.02	1
Embree	John	08JUL06	2.12	1	Emberson	Samuel	29OCT88	1.03	1
Emrey	John	15JUN07	2.11	1	Emberson	Samuel	16JUN89	5.04	1
Embree	John	02AUG08	1.10	1	Emmerson	Samuel	03APR90	2.03	1
Embree	John	23AUG09	2.10	1	Emberson	Samuel	07APR91	1.03	11
Embry	John	-----11	1.22	1	Emberson	Samuel	22OCT92	2.03	1
Embry	John	-----11	1.21	1	Emmerson	Samuel	03SEP93	1.03	1
Emrey	Joseph	18JUN87	2.02	1	Emmerson	Samuel	15MAY94	1.03	1
Emery	Josuah	22OCT92	2.03	1	Emmerson	Samuel	18MAY95	2.04	1
Emmery	Joshua	15MAY94	1.03	1	Emberson	Samuel	10JUN96	1.04	1
Embree	Joshua	18MAY95	2.04	1	Emberson	Samuel	17APR97	3.09	1
Embre	Joshus	10JUN96	1.04	1	Emberson	Samuel	22MAY99	1.09	11
Emmery	Joshua	19APR97	3.09	1	Emmerson	Samuel	19JUL00	2.09	1
Emmery	Joshua	27MAY99	1.09	1	Emmerson	Samuel	27JUL01	2.07	1
Embree	Joshua	17JUL00	2.09	1	Emmerson	Samuel	26MAY02	3.08	1
Embree	Joshus	15JUN01	2.07	1	Emmerson	Samuel	29JUN03	2.09	1
Embree	Michael	23JUL04	1.06	1	Emmerson	Samuel	25JUL04	1.06	1
Embree	Michael	17JUN05	2.10	1	Emmerson	Samuel	03MAY05	2.10	1
Emrey	Michael	14JUL06	3.11	1	Emmerson	Samuel	12MAY06	2.12	1
Emmery	Moses	26JUN99	1.10	1	Emmerson	Samuel	20MAY06	2.12	1
Embree	Moses	09JUL00	2.09	1	Emerson	Samuel	31APR08	1.10	1
Embree	Moses	19MAY01	2.07	1	Emerson	Samuel	15AUG09	2.09	1
Embree	Moses	04AUG02	3.08	1	Emmerson	Samuel	-----11	1.22	1
Embree	Moses	28MAY03	2.08	1	EMMONS				
Emry	Moses	24JUL04	1.06	1	Emmons	William	-----93	2.02	1
EMERSON					ENGLAND				
Emmerson	James	20MAY05	2.10	1	England	Abenezer	05DEC92	3.07	1
Emmerson	James	20MAY06	2.12	1	ENGLEMAN				
Emberson	Jesse	27JUN87	2.02	1	Ingleman	Jacob	05AUG93	1.05	1
Emberson	Jesse	18NOV88	1.03	1	Ingleman	Jacob	13MAY94	1.05	1
Emberson	Jesse	29JUL89	5.04	1	Ingleman	Jacob	21MAY95	2.07	1
Emmerson	Jesse	27MAR90	2.03	1	Ingleman	Jacob	21APR97	3.16	1
Emmerson	Jessey	22OCT92	2.03	1	Ingleman	Jacob	29MAY99	1.18	1
Emmerson	Jesse	03AUG93	1.03	1	Ingleman	Jacob	05JUL00	2.09	1
Emmerson	Jesse	15MAY94	1.03	1	Ingleman	Jacob	30JUN01	2.07	1
Emmerson	Jesse	08JUN96	1.04	1	Engleman	Jacob	02AUG02	3.08	1
Emberson	Jesse	19APR97	3.09	1	Engleman	Jacob	01JUN03	2.08	1
Emberson	Jesse	27MAY99	1.10	1	Engleman	Jacob	24JUL04	1.06	1
Emmerson	Jesse Sr	24MAY00	2.09	11	Engleman	Jacob	03AUG05	2.11	1
Emmerson	Jesse	04JUL01	2.07	1	Ingleman	James	26JUN87	1.03	1
Emmerson	Jesse	04AUG02	3.08	1	Ingleman	Simeon	18MAY90	2.04	1
Emmerson	Jesse	04JUN03	2.08	1	Ingleman	Simon	28OCT92	2.05	1
Emberson	Jessee	24JUL04	1.06	1	Ingleman	Simon	05AUG93	1.05	1

surname	name	date	bk.pg	TM	surname	name	date	bk.pg	TM
Ingleman	Simon	13MAY94	1.05	1	Eperson	John	-----11	1.22	1
Ingleman	Simon	21MAY95	2.07	1	Epperson	Lambert	27JUN08	2.08	1
Ingleman	Simon	08JUN96	1.07	1	Epperson	Lambert	12AUG09	1.12	1
Ingleman	Simon	21APR97	3.16	1	Epperson	Samuel	15JUN07	2.11	1
Ingleman	Simon	29MAY99	1.18	1	Eperson	Samuel	-----11	1.22	1
Engleman	Simon	17JUL00	2.09	1	ESTES				
Engleman	Simon	26MAY01	2.07	1	Eastis	Abraham	13AUG90	1.04	1
Engleman	Simon	23AUG02	3.08	1	Estice	Abraham	20APR91	2.03	1
Engleman	Simon	20JUN03	2.09	1	Estace	Abraham	17SEP92	1.04	1
Ingleman	Simon	25JUL04	1.09	1	Eastis	Abraham	18NOV93	3.04	1
Engleman	Simon	31JUN05	2.11	1	Eastis	Abraham	31MAR95	3.06	1
Engleman	Simon	14JUL06	2.12	1	Eastice	Abraham	16JUN96	2.06	1
Engleman	Samon	15JUN07	2.11	11	Estes	Abraham	10JUN97	1.07	1
Engleman	Siman	02AUG08	1.10	11	Eastes	Abram	11JUN99	3.07	1
Engleman	Simon	19AUG09	2.09	1	Estis	Abraham	12AUG00	2.09	1
Engleman	Simon	-----11	1.22	2	Estridge	Abraham	21JUL01	3.11	1
ENGLISH					Eastis	Abraham	27MAY02	2.08	1
English	Charles	12JUN87	2.02	1	Estes	Abraham	30MAY03	3.08	1
English	Charles	31OCT88	1.03	1	Estes	Abraham	16AUG04	3.07	1
English	Charles	08AUG89	5.04	1	Estridge	Abraham	15AUG05	3.11	1
English	Fanny	31OCT88	1.03	F	Estes	Abraham	14JUL06	3.11	1
English	Fanne	08AUG89	5.04	F	Estus	Abraham	06JUN08	2.08	11
English	Francis	10MAY95	1.06	F	Eastes	Abraham	28JUN09	1.12	1
English	John	12JUN87	2.02	1	Estes	Abraham	-----11	1.22	11
English	Stephen	18JUN87	2.02	1	Eastes	David	11MAY99	2.06	1
English	Stephen	31OCT88	1.03	1	Estes	David	09JUN00	1.04	1
English	Stephen	08AUG89	5.04	1	Estes	David	30MAY01	1.05	1
ENNIS					Eastes	David	13JUN04	1.06	1
Innis	John	05JUL87	3.05	1	Estes	David	05JUN05	1.06	1
Innis	John	30JUN89	2.07	1	Eastes	David	14JUN06	1.08	1
Innys	John	17JUL91	3.08	1	Eastes	David	19MAY07	1.07	1
Innis	John	21APR94	3.11	1	Eastes	David	31APR08	1.10	1
Innis	John	12MAY95	1.08	1	Eastes	Elisha	13JUN04	1.06	1
Innis	John	-----96	4.08	1	Estes	Elisha	05JUN05	1.06	1
Ennes	John	29JUN96	1.04	1	Eastes	Elisha	14JUN06	1.08	1
Innes	John	16MAR97	2.02	1	Eastes	Elisha	19MAY07	1.07	1
Ennis	John	15MAY99	2.06	11	Eastes	Elisha	31APR08	1.10	1
Enniss	John	12JUN00	1.04	11	Eastes	Elisha	23MAY09	2.09	1
Ennis	John	03JUN01	1.05	11	Estice	Isaac	13JUN07	2.10	1
Innys	William	17JUL91	3.08	1	Eastes	Obadiah	11MAY99	2.06	1
Innis	William	-----96	4.08	1	Estes	Odadiah	09JUN00	1.04	1
Innes	William	17MAR97	2.02	1	Estes	Obadiah	30MAY01	1.05	1
Ennis	William	15MAY99	2.06	1	Estes	Thomas	13MAY94	1.03	1
Enniss	William	12JUN00	1.04	11	Eastis	Thomas	26MAY95	2.04	1
Ennis	William	03JUN01	1.05	1	Estes	Thomas	13JUN96	1.04	1
EOFF					Estep	Thomas	08MAY97	3.10	1
Eoff	Isaac	12JUN87	2.02	1	Estes	Thomas	22MAY99	1.09	1
Eoff	Peter	12JUN87	2.02	21	Eastes	Thomas	29MAY00	2.09	1
EPPERSON					Estis	Thomas	25MAY01	2.07	1
Epperson	Charles	18MAY01	3.11	1	Estis	Thomas	26MAY02	3.08	1
Epperson	Charles	04AUG03	2.09	1	Eastes	Thomas	13JUN03	2.09	1
Epperson	Charles	12JUN04	4.08	1	Eastes	Thomas	25JUL04	1.06	1
Epperson	Charles	17JUN05	2.10	1	Estes	Thomas	11MAY05	2.10	1
Epperson	Charles	09AUG06	2.12	1	Eastis	Thomas	20MAY06	2.12	1
Epperson	Charles	15JUN07	2.11	12	Eastes	Thomas	28JUN07	1.07	1
Epperson	David	06AUG02	3.08	1	Eastes	Thomas	02AUG08	1.10	1
Epperson	David	04AUG03	2.09	1	Eastes	Thomas	24AUG09	2.10	1
Epperson	David	09JUN04	4.08	1	Estes	Thomas	-----11	1.21	11
Epperson	David	17JUN05	2.10	1	Eastice	William	09JUN89	6.03	1
Epperson	David	09AUG06	2.13	1	ETON				
Epperson	David	15JUN07	2.11	1	Eton	John	19JUN99	2.06	1
Epperson	David	27JUN08	2.08	1	EUBANKS				
Epperson	David	12AUG09	1.12	1	Hughbank	John	19AUG06	2.20	1
Epperson	David	-----11	1.22	1	Ubank	John	19AUG07	2.36	1
Epperson	John	18MAY01	3.11	2	Ubanks	John	28JUN08	2.28	1
Epperson	John	06AUG02	3.08	1	Eubanks	John	28JUN09	1.12	1
Epperson	John	04AUG03	2.09	11	Eubanks	John	-----11	1.23	1
Epperson	John	12JUN04	4.08	11	EVANS				
Epperson	John	17JUN05	2.11	11	Evans	Adam	18JUL00	2.09	
Epperson	John	18AUG06	2.13	11	A free negroe				
Epperson	John	27JUN08	2.08	11	Evan	Ananais	14NOV88	1.03	1
Epperson	John	09AUG09	1.12	1	Evans	Chloe	15MAY09	2.09	F

surname	name	date	bk.pg	TM	surname	name	date	bk.pg	TM
Evins	Edward	26JUN87	2.02	1	Ewings	George	19MAY94	2.04	0
Evens	Edward	04NOV88	1.03	1	Ewing	George	20JUN95	3.06	0
Evens	Edward	30JUN89	5.04	1	Ewing	John	02JUN94	3.08	1
Evens	Edward	02JUN90	2.03	1	Eweing	John	04JUN95	1.05	1
Evans	Edward	19OCT92	2.03	1	Ewing	John	-----96	4.06	1
Evens	Edward	12AUG93	1.03	1	Ewing	Urbin	10SEP93	3.04	1
Evins	Edward	27MAY94	1.03	1	Ewing	Urbin	19JUN94	2.04	1
Evans	Edward	02JUN95	2.04	1	Ewing	Urbin	20JUN95	3.06	1
Evens	Edward	28JUN96	1.04	11	Ewing	Urbin	13APR96	2.06	1
Evens	Edward	24APR97	3.09	1	Ewing	Young	26JUN87	1.02	1
Evens	Edward	10MAY99	1.09	1	FAIR				
Evans	Edward	25JUL00	1.04	1	Fair	Absolam	22JUL00	2.10	1
Evans	Edward	26JUN01	1.05	1	Fair	Absolam	07AUG04	3.07	1
Evans	Edward	23JUN02	1.07	1	Fair	Absolam	22AUG05	3.13	1
Evans	Edward	23JUN03	1.08	1	Fair	Absolam	29JUL06	3.13	1
Evans	Edward	03AUG04	1.06	1	Fair	Edmond	29MAY01	3.12	2
Evins	George Sr	02DEC92	3.07	1	Fair	Edmond	10AUG02	2.09	3
Evins	George	01DEC92	3.06	1	Fair	Edmond	02AUG03	3.09	3
Evans	George	02JUN94	3.08	1	Fair	Edmond	22AUG05	3.13	1
Evins	John	11JUN89	6.04		Fair	Edward	05AUG05	3.13	1
Listed with William Josselling					Fair	Edmond Sr	07AUG06	3.13	1
Evens	John	30JUN89	5.04	1	Fair	Edmond	19AUG06	3.13	1
Evans	John	02AUG90	1.04	1	Fair	Edmund Sr	06AUG04	3.07	1
Evins	John	05MAY91	3.05	1	Fair	Edmund Jr	08AUG04	3.07	1
Evans	John	21JUN91	2.03	1	Fair	James	05JUN99	1.11	1
Evans	John	18OCT92	2.03	1	Fair	James	02JUN02	2.09	1
Evins	John	04DEC92	3.07	1	Fair	James	11JUN03	3.08	1
Evins	John	17APR95	3.06	11	Fair	James	31JUL04	3.07	1
Evans	John	-----96	4.06	1	Fair	James	14JUN05	3.12	1
Evans	John	10JUN96	1.04	1	Fair	James	-----11	1.25	1
Evins	John	13JUL96	2.06	1	Fair	James M.	30JUL00	2.10	1
Evans	John	20MAR97	2.01	1	Fair	James M.	-----05	3.38	
Evans	John	24MAY99	2.06	1	1802 tax info in 1805 tax list				
Evans	John	18JUN00	1.04	1	Fair	James M.	-----05	3.38	1
Evans	John	03JUN01	1.05	1	Fair	James M.	21JUL06	3.12	1
Evans	John	03JUN02	1.07	1	Fair	James M.	20AUG07	2.12	1
Evans	John	15JUN03	1.07	1	Fair	James M.	01JUL08	2.09	1
Evans	John	13AUG04	1.06	1	Fair	James M.	27JUN09	1.13	1
Evans	John	29JUN05	1.06	1	Furr	Stephen	23AUG07	2.12	1
Evans	John	29JUN05	1.06	1	FALCONBERRY				
Evans	John	10JUN06	1.08	1	ForcomberryJacob		15JUN04	2.06	1
Evans	John	10JUN06	1.08	1	ForcomberryJacob		-----05	3.12	1
Evans	John	31APR08	1.10	1	FalcomberryJacob		29JUL06	3.13	1
Evans	John	15MAY09	2.09	1	FalcomberryJacob		03AUG07	2.12	1
Evans	John	-----11	1.21	1	FalcomberryJacob		28JUL08	2.10	1
Evans	Joseph	12MAY95	2.17	1	FalconberryJacob		06APR09	1.13	1
Evans	Joseph	12JUN95	2.04	1	FalconberryJacob		-----11	1.26	1
Evens	Joseph	21JUN96	1.04	1	ForcomberryWilliam		15JUN04	2.06	1
Evans	Joseph	19APR97	3.09	1	ForcomberryWilliam		-----05	3.12	1
Evans	Thomas	12JUN99	2.06	1	FalcomberryWilliam		29JUL06	3.13	1
Evans	Thomas	21JUL00	1.04	1	FalcomberryWilliam		16AUG07	2.12	1
Evans	Thomas	23JUN01	1.05	1	FalconberryWilliam		28JUL08	2.10	1
Evans	Thomas	23JUN02	1.07	1	FalconberryWilliam		06APR09	1.13	1
Evans	Thomas	13JUN03	1.07	1	FalconberryWilliam		-----11	1.26	1
Evans	Thomas	01AUG04	1.06	1	FARRELL				
Evans	Thomas	29JUL05	1.06	1	Farrell	William	03AUG04	3.07	1
Evans	Thomas	14JUL06	1.08	1	FARRIS				
Evans	Thomas	04MAY07	1.07	1	Faris	Cager	12JUN87	2.02	1
Evans	Thomas	31APR08	1.10	1	Faris	Edward	19OCT92	2.03	1
EVERHART					Faris	Edward	12AUG93	1.03	1
Everhart	David	02AUG06	1.08	1	Faris	Edward	26MAY94	1.03	1
Everhart	David	25MAY07	1.07	1	Farris	Edward	29MAY95	2.05	1
Everhart	David	22APR08	1.09	1	Faris	Edward	15JUN96	1.04	1
Everhart	David	01JUL09	2.09	1	Farris	Edward	26APR97	3.10	1
EVERY					Farris	Edward	15JUL99	1.10	1
Every	Isaac	06JUN08	2.08	1	Faris	Edward	23JUN00	2.10	1
EWING					Faris	Elisha	12JUN87	2.02	1
Ewing	Baker	13JUL87	1.02	1	Farris	Elisha	21MAY94	1.03	1
Ewing	Baker	18APR89	6.03	1	Farris	Elisha	29JUN95	2.05	1
Ewing	Baker	13AUG90	1.04	1	Farris	Elisha	15JUN96	1.04	1
Ewing	Baker	12JUL91	2.03	1	Farris	Elisha	26APR97	3.10	1
Ewing	Baker	18SEP92	1.04	1	Farris	Elisha	15JUL99	1.10	1

surname	name	date	bk.pg	TM	surname	name	date	bk.pg	TM
Faris	Elisha	12JUN02	1.07	1	Faris	James Jr	15JUN02	1.07	1
Faris	Elisha	04JUL03	1.08	1	Faris	James	15JUN02	1.07	1
Farris	George	28JUN08	2.09	1	Faris	James	30JUN03	1.08	1
Faris	Gilbart	27MAY94	1.03	1	Faris	James Jr	30JUN03	1.08	1
Faris	Gilbert	28JUN96	1.05	1	Farris	James Sr	08AUG04	2.07	1
Farris	Gilbert	26APR97	3.10	1	Farris	James Jr	14JUN04	2.06	1
Farris	Gilbert	15JUL99	1.10	1	Faris	James Jr	17AUG05	1.06	1
Farris	Gilbert	23JUN00	2.10	1	Faris	James	17AUG05	1.06	11
Farris	Gilbert	02JUN01	2.08	1	Faris	James	20JUN06	1.08	1
Fairis	Gilbert	23AUG02	2.10	1	Farris	James	24MAY07	1.08	11
Farris	Gilbert	20JUL03	3.08	1	Farris	James Sr	23APR08	1.11	11
Farris	Gilberd	14JUN04	2.06	1	Farris	James Jr	23APR08	1.11	11
Farris	Gilbert	-----05	3.12	1	Farris	James Sr	01JUN09	2.10	1
Farris	Gilbert	29JUL06	3.13	1	Farris	James	05JUL09	2.11	1
Farris	Gilbert	16AUG07	2.12	1	Faris	Jerushey	03APR90	2.03	F
Farris	Gilbert	21JUN08	2.09	1	Farris	Jerushia	25OCT91	1.03	F
Farris	Gilbert	06APR09	1.13	1	Faris	Jerusha	13OCT92	2.03	F
Faris	Gilbert	-----11	1.26	11	Faris	Jerusha	10AUG93	1.03	F
Faris	Hezekiah	15JUN02	1.07	1	Faris	Jerusha	21MAY94	1.03	F
Farris	Hezekiah	13AUG04	2.07	1	Farris	Jerusha	20MAY95	2.05	F
Faris	Hezakiah	17AUG05	1.06	1	Farris	Jerusha	29MAY95	2.17	F
Faris	Hezakiah	02AUG06	1.08	1	Faris	Jerusha	20JUN96	1.04	F
Farris	Hesekiah	24MAY07	1.08	1	Farris	Jerusha	10MAY97	3.11	F
Farris	Hesekiah	23APR08	1.11	1	Farris	Jerusha	15JUL99	1.10	F
Farris	Hesekiah	14JUN09	2.10	11	Farris	Jerushia	14JUL00	2.10	F1
Faris	Isaac	13JUN87	2.03	11	Farris	Jerushia	03JUN01	2.08	F1
Faris	Isaac	15NOV88	1.03	11	Fairis	Jerusha	09AUG02	2.09	F1
Faris	Isaac	24JUN89	5.05	1	Farris	Jerusha	20JUL03	3.09	F
Faris	Isam	14JUN87	2.03	1	Farris	Jerusha	14JUN04	2.06	F1
Faris	Isum	15NOV88	1.03	1	Faris	Jerusha	-----05	3.12	F1
Faris	Isham	24JUN89	5.05	1	Faris	John	13JUN87	2.03	11
Faris	Isham	21APR90	2.03	1	Faris	John	14NOV88	1.03	11
Farris	Isam	25MAR91	1.03	1	Faris	John	16JUN89	5.05	11
Faris	Isham	19OCT92	2.03	1	Faris	John	18MAY90	2.03	11
Faris	Isam	12AUG93	1.03	1	Farris	John	14APR91	1.03	12
Faris	Isham	26MAY94	1.03	1	Faris	John	04OCT92	2.03	11
Farris	Isham	06JUN95	2.05	1	Faris	John	10AUG93	1.04	12
Farris	Isham	28JUN96	1.05	11	Faris	John	17MAY94	1.04	1
Farris	Isham	24APR97	3.10	11	Faris	John	17MAY94	1.04	1
Farris	Isham	13MAY99	1.10	12	Farris	John	29MAY95	2.05	1
Farris	Isham	03JUN00	2.10	21	Farris	John	29MAY95	2.05	11
Farris	Isham	25JUL01	2.08	11	Faris	John	18JUN96	1.05	11
Faris	James Sr	14JUN87	2.03	1	Faris	John	20JUN96	1.04	1
Faris	James Jr	14JUN87	2.03	1	Farris	John	17MAY97	3.11	11
Faris	James Sr	15NOV88	1.03	11	Farris	John	18JUN99	2.07	11
Faris	James	28OCT88	1.03	1	Farris	John	15JUL99	1.10	1
Faris	James	16JUN89	5.05	1	Farris	John	28MAY01	2.08	1
Faris	James	30JUN89	5.05	1	Faris	John	23JUN03	1.08	1
Faris	James	03APR90	2.03	1	Farris	John	16AUG04	2.07	1
Faris	James Sr	27OCT92	2.03	1	Farris	John	-----05	3.12	1
Faris	James	18OCT92	2.03	11	Faris	John	26JUN05	1.07	1
Faris	James Sr	12AUG93	1.03	1	Faris	John	01AUG06	1.09	1
Faris	James Jr	12AUG93	1.03	11	Faris	John	16JUL06	1.09	1
Faris	James Sr	27MAY94	1.03	1	Farris	John	08MAY07	1.08	1
Faris	James	27MAY94	1.04	12	Farris	John	26MAY07	1.08	1
Farris	James Sr	29MAY95	2.05	1	Farris	John	18APR08	1.11	1
Farris	James	02JUN95	2.05	12	Farris	John	09JUN08	1.12	1
Faris	James Sr	28JUN96	1.05	11	Farris	John	28JUL08	2.10	1
Faris	James	10JUL96	1.05	11	Farris	John	13MAY09	2.10	1
Faris	James	28JUN96	1.05	1	Farris	John	01JUL09	2.11	1
Farris	James	24APR97	3.10	1	Farris	John T.	08APR09	1.13	1
Farris	James	26APR97	3.10	11	Faris	John	-----11	1.26	1
Farris	James Sr	13MAY99	1.11	11	Faris	Johnson	12JUN87	2.02	1
Farris	James Jr	13MAY99	1.10	1	Faris	Johnson	23JUN89	5.05	1
Farris	James Sr	03JUN00	2.10	1	Farris	Johnson	25MAR91	1.03	1
Farris	James Jr	03JUN00	2.10	1	Faris	Johnson	16OCT92	2.03	1
Farris	James Sr	25JUN00	2.10		Faris	Johnston	12AUG93	1.03	1
Exempt from county leavy					Faris	Johnston	21MAY94	1.03	1
Farris	James Sr	31JUL01	2.08	1	Farris	Johnson	29MAY95	2.05	1
Farris	James	03JUN01	2.08		Faris	Johnson	28JUN96	1.05	1
Exempt from county leavy					Farris	Johnson	09MAY97	3.11	1
Faris	James Sr	15JUN02	1.07	1	Farris	Johnson	15JUL99	1.10	1

surname	name	date	bk.pg	TM	surname	name	date	bk.pg	TM
Farris	Johnston	24JUN00	2.10	1	Feland	Andrew	26MAY97	1.08	1
Farris	Johnston	03JUN01	2.08	1	Feland	Andrew	05JUN99	1.11	1
Faris	Johnston	30JUN02	1.08	1	Feeland	Andrew	30JUL00	2.10	1
Faris	Johnston	07JUL03	1.08	1	Feeland	Andrew	20JUL01	3.12	1
Farris	Johnston	15JUN04	2.06	1	Feeland	Andrew	01JUN02	2.09	11
Fairis	Johnston	-----05	3.12	1	Feland	Andrew	21JUL03	3.09	1
Farris	Johnston	07AUG06	3.13	11	Fielding	Andrew	01AUG04	3.07	1
Farris	Johnston	28JUL08	2.10	11	Feeland	Andrew	13JUN05	3.12	1
Farris	Johnson	08APR09	1.13	11	Feeland	Andrew	23JUL06	3.12	1
Faris	Johnston	-----11	1.26	1	Feland	Andrew	10AUG07	2.12	1
Farris	Lewis	29MAY95	2.05	1	Feeland	Andrew	02JUN08	2.09	1
Faris	Lewis	20JUN96	1.04	1	Feeland	Andrew	27JUN09	1.13	1
Farris	Lewis	16JUN97	3.11	1	Fealand	Andrew	-----11	1.25	11
Faris	Major	18OCT92	2.03	1	Felin	Catherine	14JUN87	2.03	F
Faris	Mary	03APR90	2.03	F	Feland	Catherine	28NOV88	1.03	F
Farris	Mary	19OCT91	1.03	F	Feland	Caty	04AUG89	5.05	F1
Faris	Mary	05OCT92	2.03	F	Fawlen	Edmond	23AUG07	2.12	1
Faris	Mary	27MAY94	1.03	F	Fawling	Edward	28JUN08	2.09	1
Farris	Mary	01JUN95	2.05	F	Faulen	Edmund	13APR09	1.13	1
Faris	Mary	10MAY96	2.06	F	Freeland	Garret	30JUN89	2.05	1
Faris	Moses	23JUN02	1.08	11	Felin	James	14JUN87	2.03	1
Faris	Moses	23JUN03	1.08	1	Feland	James	18NOV88	1.03	1
Faris	Moses	03AUG04	1.07	11	Freeland	James	11JUN89	6.03	1
Farris	Moses	09MAY07	1.08	1	Feland	James	15MAY90	1.04	1
Farris	Moses	02APR08	1.11	11	Fielding	James	05APR91	1.03	1
Farris	Moses	01JUL09	2.11	1	Feeland	James	23OCT92	2.03	1
Faris	Nathan	13JUN87	2.03	1	Feland	James	20AUG93	1.03	1
Faris	Nathan	29OCT88	1.03	1	Falin	James	07AUG93	3.04	1
Faris	Nathan	07AUG89	5.05	1	Feland	James	20MAY94	1.03	1
Farris	Nathan	24MAY07	1.08	1	Fielding	James Jr	24MAY94	2.05	01
Farris	Nathan	01JUN09	2.10	0	Fielding	James	18JUN94	2.05	1
Faris	Nathan	-----11	1.26	1	Feland	James	29MAY95	2.05	1
Faris	Nimrod	18OCT92	2.03	1	Feland	James	15JUN95	3.06	M1
Faris	Nimrod	15JUN96	1.04	1	Feland	James	01JUN96	1.05	1
Farris	Nimrod	06MAY97	3.10	1	Feland	James	05JUL96	2.07	1
Farris	Nimrod	18JUN99	2.07	1	Feland	James	22APR97	3.11	1
Faris	Stephen	-----11	1.26	1	Feland	James	21JUN97	1.08	1
Farris	Thomas	15JUL99	1.10	1	Feland	James	16MAY99	3.08	1
Farris	Thomas	25JUL01	2.08	1	Felan	James	29JUL99	1.11	1
Faris	William	23MAY94	1.03	1	Feeland	James	10JUN00	2.10	1
Farris	William	24APR97	3.10	1	Feeland	James Jr	05AUG00	2.10	1
Farris	William	26APR97	3.10	1	Feland	James	15JUL01	2.08	1
Farris	William	18JUN99	2.07	1	Feland	James Jr	15JUL01	2.08	1
Farris	William	15JUL99	1.10	1	Feland	James	08JUN02	3.09	1
Farris	William	23JUN00	2.10	1	Feland	James	17JUN02	3.09	1
Farris	William	03JUN01	2.08	1	Feland	James	20JUN03	2.09	1
Fairis	William	12JUL02	2.09	1	Feland	James	07JUL03	3.08	1
Farris	William	08AUG03	3.09	1	Fielden	James	24JUL04	1.07	1
Farris	William	15JUN04	2.06	1	Feland	James	05AUG05	2.12	1
Faris	William	19JUN05	1.07	1	Feland	James Jr	22JUL05	2.12	1
Faris	William	26JUN05	1.07	1	Feland	James	09JUN06	2.14	1
Faris	William	19JUN06	1.08	1	Feland	James Jr	09JUN06	2.14	1
Farris	William	07AUG06	3.13	1	Feland	James	03AUG07	2.12	1
Farris	William	18MAY07	1.08	1	Feland	James	09JUN08	1.12	11
Farris	William	09JUN08	1.12	1	Feeland	James	24AUG09	2.11	1
Farris	William Jr	09JUN08	1.12	1	Fealand	James	-----11	1.25	1
Farris	William	20MAY09	2.10	1	Felan	John	06OCT87	1.06	1
Farris	William	30MAY09	2.10	1	Freeland	John	23MAY89	6.03	1
FARTHING					Feland	John/Andrew	14MAY90	1.04	3
Farthing	Richard	29MAY09	2.10	1	Falin	John/Thos	20JUN91	2.04	2
Farthing	William	28MAY07	1.08	1	Falin	John	14SEP92	1.05	1
FEAR					Falin	John	06AUG93	3.04	1
Fear	Jonathan	01JUN02	1.07	1	Fielding	John	20JUN94	2.05	2
FELAND					Feland	John	14APR95	3.07	2
Felan	Andrew	02JUL87	1.02	1	Feland	John	22JUN96	2.07	1
Feland	Andrew/John	14MAY90	1.04	3	Feland	John	08JUN97	1.08	1
Falin	Andrew	04AUG91	2.04	1	Feland	John	16MAY99	3.08	1
Falin	Andrew	05OCT92	1.05	1	Fealand	John	21JUN00	3.10	2
Falin	Andrew	13NOV93	3.04	1	Feeland	John	20JUL01	3.11	1
Fielding	Andrew	16MAY94	2.05	1	Feland	John	27JUN02	3.09	1
Feland	Andrew	15APR95	3.06	1	Fealen	John	06JUN04	4.09	1
Feland	Andrew	11MAY96	2.06	1	Feland	John	28JUN05	2.11	1

surname	name	date	bk.pg	TM	surname	name	date	bk.pg	TM
Feland	John	01AUG06	2.14	1	Ferrel	William	02JUN02	2.09	1
Feland	John	16AUG07	2.13	1	Ferrell	William	10JUN03	3.08	1
Feeland	John	04JUL08	2.10	1	Ferrel	William	17JUL05	3.12	1
Feeland	John	12JUL09	1.13	1	Ferral	William	29JUL06	3.12	1
Fielding	John	-----11	1.24	1	FEWELL				
Fielding	Joseph	23MAY94	2.05	1	Fewel	Charles	10AUG97	1.08	1
Feland	Joseph	16APR95	3.07	1	Fewel	Charles	10JUL99	3.08	1
Feland	Joseph	05JUL96	2.07	1	Fewel	Charles	09JUL00	3.11	1
Feland	Joseph	21JUN97	1.08	1	Fuil	Charles	29JUN02	3.09	1
Felan	Joseph	28JUN99	1.11	1	Fuill	Charles	19JUN05	2.11	1
Feeland	Joseph	27MAY01	3.11	1	Fuill	Charles	29JUL06	2.14	1
Feeland	Joseph	13AUG02	2.09	1	FIELDS				
Feland	Joseph	07JUL03	3.08	1	Fields	John	28JUN87	3.04	1
Fielding	Joseph	06AUG04	3.07	1	Fields	John	07JUL03	1.08	1
Feeland	Joseph	05AUG05	3.13	1	Field	William	28JUN87	1.02	1
Feeland	Joseph	29JUL06	3.13	1	FINLEY				
Feland	Nancy	01JUN03	2.09	F	Finley	David	19JUN99	2.07	1
Fielden	Nancy	24JUL04	1.07	F	Fendley	George	23JUN87	3.04	1
Feland	Nancy	01AUG05	2.12	F	Fenley	George	20MAR97	2.01	1
Feland	Nancy	09AUG06	2.14	F	Finley	George	21MAY99	2.06	1
Feland	Nancy	23AUG07	2.12	F	Finley	George	12JUN00	1.04	1
Feeland	Nancy	09JUN08	1.12	F	Finley	George	01JUN01	1.05	1
Fealden	Nancy	23AUG09	2.11	F	Findley	James	17MAY99	1.11	1
Fealand	Sally	-----11	1.25	F	Finley	Obediah	28MAY07	1.08	12
Falin	Samuel	04AUG91	2.04	1	Findley	Obediah	09JUN08	1.12	11
Falin	Samuel	22SEP92	1.05	1	Finly	Obadiah	06JUL09	2.11	1
Falin	Samuel	07AUG93	3.04	1	Finley	Samuel	08AUG97	1.08	1
Fielding	Samuel	24MAY94	2.05	1	Findley	Samuel	04JUN99	1.11	1
Feland	Samuel	17APR95	3.07	1	Finley	Samuel	20JUN00	2.10	1
Feland	Samuel	05JUL96	2.07	1	Finley	Samuel	10AUG01	2.08	1
Feland	Samuel	21JUN97	1.08	1	Findley	Samuel	20AUG02	2.10	1
Feland	Samuel	16MAY99	3.08	1	Finley	Samuel	09AUG03	3.09	1
Felan	Thomas	07JUL87	1.02	1	Findley	Samuel	16AUG04	2.07	1
Freeland	Thomas	11JUN89	6.03	1	Finley	Samuel	28JUL08	2.10	1
Falin	Thos/John	20JUN91	2.04	2	Findley	Samuel	03JUL09	1.13	1
Fullin	William	12JUN87	2.02	1	Finley	Samuel	-----11	1.25	11
Fullin	William	14JUN87	2.03	1	Finley	Travise	15JUN05	1.06	1
Felan	William	30JUN87	1.02	1	Findley	William	17MAY99	1.11	11
Fullen	William	30OCT88	1.03	1	Finley	William	31MAY00	2.10	11
Fullin	William	22JUN89	5.05	1	Finley	William	22JUL01	2.08	12
Feland	William	03AUG93	1.03	1	Finley	William	16JUN02	1.07	11
Fealand	William	20MAY94	1.04	1	Finley	William	14JUL03	1.09	1
Feland	William	16JUN95	2.04	1	Findley	William	18JUN04	2.06	1
Fullin	William	16JUN96	1.04	1	Finley	William	19AUG05	1.06	1
Fullen	William	17JUN97	3.11	1	Finley	William	14JUL06	1.09	1
Fullen	William	03JUN01	1.05	1	Findley	William	20MAY07	1.08	1
Fawling	William	04JUL08	2.09	1	Findley	William	02APR08	1.11	11
Faulen	William	13APR09	1.13	1	Findley	William	21JUN09	2.10	1
FEMISTER					Finley	William	-----11	1.26	11
Femaster	John	30MAY97	3.11	1	Pd tax for David(heirs) Stephenso				
Femester	John	17MAY99	1.11	1	FINN				
Femister	John	19JUL00	2.10	1	Finn	John	16AUG09	1.14	1
Femister	John	29MAY01	2.08	1	Finn	Richard	17JUN05	3.12	1
FENTON					Finn	Richard	29JUL06	3.12	1
Fenton	Zachariah	09JUN08	1.12	1	Finn	William	29JUL06	3.12	1
FERIGO					FISHER				
Ferigo	Daniel	-----11	1.25	1	Fisher	James	29JUN05	1.07	1
FERRELL					Fisher	James Sr	31JUL06	1.09	11
Ferrel	James	17MAY97	1.08	1	Fisher	James	30JUL06	1.09	1
Ferrel	John	03JUL89	2.05	1	Fisher	Lewis	20MAY99	3.08	1
Farril	John	28MAY91	3.06	1	Fisher	Mathew	23AUG02	2.09	1
Farrel	Kitty	13OCT92	2.03	F	Fisher	Mathew	30JUL03	2.10	1
Ferrill	Margaret	28JUN87	3.04		Fisher	Mathias	28JUN04	4.09	1
(widow)-Insolvent					Fisher	Mathew	30MAY05	2.11	1
Ferril	William	06AUG93	3.04	1	Fisher	Mathew	04AUG06	2.14	1
Farrel	William	24MAY94	2.05	2	Fisher	Matthew	20AUG07	2.12	2
Ferrel	William	16APR95	3.06	1	Fisher	Matthew	14JUN08	2.09	1
Farrel	William	05JUL96	2.07	1	Fisher	Mathew	26JUN09	1.13	1
Ferrel	William	22JUN97	1.08	1	Fisher	Matthew	-----11	1.25	1
Ferrell	William	24JUN99	1.11	1	Fisher	Moses	31JUN05	1.07	1
Ferrill	William	29JUL00	2.10	1	Fisher	Moses	31JUL06	1.09	1
Feiral	William	21JUL01	3.12	1	Fisher	Nathan	-----11	1.26	1

surname	name	date	bk.pg	TM	surname	name	date	bk.pg	TM
Fisher	Thadeus	17AUG02	3.09	1	Flint	Martin	25MAY09	2.10	1
Fisher	Thadeus	25JUL03	2.10	1	Flint	Martain	-----11	1.25	1
Fisher	Thadeus	24APR06	2.14	1	Flint	Samuel	-----11	1.25	1
Fisher	Thadious	14AUG07	2.12	1	FLOYD				
Fisher	Thadeus	07JUL09	1.13	1	Floyd	Benjamin	22JUN87	3.03	1
Fisher	Thadius	-----11	1.25	1	Floyd	Benjamin	10JUL89	2.05	1
Fisher	Thomas	03JUL99	3.08	1	Floyd	Benjamin	29NOV92	3.07	1
Fisher	Thomas	27JUN00	3.11	1	Floyd	Benjamin	07MAY94	3.08	1
Fisher	Thomas	20MAY01	3.11	1	Floyd	Benjamin	10MAY95	1.06	1
Fisher	Thomas	17AUG02	3.09	1	Floyd	Benjamin	-----96	4.06	1
Fisher	Thomas	20JUN03	2.09	1	Floyd	Benjamin	16JUL03	3.08	11
FITZGERALD					Floyd	Benjamin	16JUL03	3.08	11
Fitzjarrel	John	14JUN87	2.03	1	Floyd	Benjamin	16JUN04	2.06	11
Fitzgerald	John	09NOV93	3.04	1	Floyd	Benjamin	-----05	3.12	11
Fitzgerrel	John	11JUN94	2.05	1	Floyd	Benjamin	07AUG06	3.13	11
Fitzgarrel	John	15APR95	3.06	1	Floyd	Benjamin	28JUL08	2.10	11
Fitzgarrel	John	19JUL96	2.07	1	Floid	Benjamin	08APR09	1.13	2
Fitzgerald	John	26MAY97	1.08	1	Floyd	Benjamin	-----11	1.26	11
Fitzgerrel	Luis	05APR95	3.06	1	Floyd	David	22JUN87	3.03	1
Fitzgerald	Lewis	27JUN97	1.08	1	George Floyd listed with him				
FITZPATRICK					Floyd	David	10JUL89	2.05	1
FitzpatrickJohn		03AUG04	3.07	1	Floyd	David	05DEC92	3.07	1
FitzpatrickJohn		17JUN05	3.12	1	Floyd	David	23APR94	3.08	1
FitzpatrickJohn		21JUL06	3.12	1	Floyd	David	10APR95	1.06	1
FichpatrickJohn		03AUG07	2.12	1	Floyd	David	-----96	4.06	1
FLACK					Floyd	George	22JUN87	3.03	
Flack	James	28MAY07	1.08	1	Listed with David Floyd				
Flack	John A.	-----11	1.25	1	Floyd	George	10JUL89	2.05	1
Flock	William	20APR90	1.04	1	Floyd	George	05DEC92	3.07	1
Fleck	William	09JUN91	2.04	1	Floyd	George	-----93	2.02	1
Fleck	William	17NOV93	3.04	1	Floyd	George	10APR95	1.06	1
Flack	William	03JUN95	2.04	1	Floyd	George	-----96	4.06	1
Flake	William	30JUN96	1.05	1	Floid	Jacob	09MAY07	1.08	1
Flack	William	13APR97	3.10	1	Floyd	John	23JUN87	3.04	1
Flack	William	12JUN99	2.07	1	Floyd	John	10JUL89	2.05	1
Flack	William	25JUL00	1.05	1	Floyd	John	29NOV92	3.07	1
Flack	William	10JUN01	1.05	1	Floyd	John	-----93	2.02	1
Flack	William	08JUN02	1.07	1	Floyd	John	07MAY94	3.08	1
Flack	William	20JUN03	1.08	1	Floyd	John	10MAY95	1.06	1
Flack	William	03AUG04	1.07	1	Floyd	John	-----96	4.06	1
Flack	William	22JUN05	1.07	1	Floyd	John	05AUG05	3.13	1
Flack	William	02AUG06	1.09	1	Floyd	John	-----11	1.26	1
Flack	William	28MAY07	1.08	1	Floyd	Lawrence	-----11	1.25	1
Flack	William	22APR08	1.11	11	Floyd	Mathew	30JUN96	1.05	1
Flack	William	29JUN09	2.11	1	Floid	Matthew	11JUN05	1.06	1
Flack	William	-----11	1.27	1	Floyd	Sarah	28MAY91	3.06	F
FLEECE					Floyd	Sarah	29NOV92	3.07	F
Fluse	John	24JUL05	2.12	22	Floyd	Sarah	23APR94	3.08	F
Fleese	John	24APR06	2.14	22	Floyd	Sarah	10MAY95	1.06	F
Fleece	John	16AUG07	2.12	13	Floyd	Sarah	-----96	4.06	F
Fleece	John	28JUL08	2.10	13	Floyd	Singleton	15JUN04	2.06	1
Fleese	John	21JUN09	1.13	4	Floyd	Singleton	-----05	3.12	1
Fleece	John S.	-----11	1.24	3	Floyd	Singleton	01AUG06	3.12	1
FLEMING					Floyd	Singleton	28JUL08	2.10	1
Fleming	James	28MAY91	3.06	1	Floid	Singleton	08APR09	1.13	1
FLETCHER					Floyd	Singleton	-----11	1.26	1
Flasher	Elijah	20AUG07	2.12	1	Floyd	William	20JUN96	1.04	1
Flatcher	Joseph	-----05	3.12	1	Floyd	William	21MAY99	1.11	1
Flacker	Joseph	19AUG06	3.13	1	Floyd	William	04JUN00	2.10	11
Flasher	Joseph	20AUG07	2.12	1	Floyd	William	04AUG01	2.08	11
Flatcher	Joseph	13JUN08	2.09	1	Floyd	William	12JUL02	2.09	1
Fletcher	Joseph	27JUN09	1.13	1	Floyd	William	16JUN03	3.08	1
Fletcher	Joseph	-----11	1.25	1	Floyd	William	18JUN04	2.06	1
Fletcher	Thomas	30MAY90	2.03	1	Floyd	William	08JUL05	3.12	1
Fluch	Thomas	06APR91	1.03	1	Floid	William	23JUN06	1.09	1
FLINN					Floid	William	01JUL07	1.08	1
Flinn	Peter	20JUN96	1.04	1	Floid	William	02JUN08	1.11	1
FLINT					Floyd	William	06JUL09	2.11	1
Flint	John	22JUN89	5.05	1	Floyd	William	-----11	1.25	1
Flint	John	03JUN90	2.03	1	FLURRY				
Flint	John	20MAR91	1.03	1	Flurry	Godwin	-----11	1.26	1
Flint	Martin	02JUN08	1.11	11	Flory	Jacob	02JUN95	2.04	1

surname	name	date	bk.pg	TM	surname	name	date	bk.pg	TM
Flory	Jacob	16JUN96	1.04	1	Forbis	Robert	18JUN96	1.05	1
Flory	Jacob	10APR97	3.10	1	FORD				
Floro	Jacob	19APR08	1.11	1	Ford	Charles	03APR95	3.07	01
Floro	Jacob	16JUN09	2.10	1	Fort	Egburt	23JUN01	1.06	1
FOLLOWELL					Ford	Egbert	09JUN08	1.12	1
Fillwell	John	16MAY94	2.05	01	Ford	Egbert	10MAY09	2.10	1
Followell	John	14APR95	3.06	01	Ford	Frederick	31JUL01	2.08	1
Followay	Marquis	14SEP92	1.05	1	Ford	Jonathan	19JUL05	2.12	M1
Followay	Marquis	07AUG93	3.04	1	Ford	John	06APR06	2.14	1
Followell	Marquis	10MAY94	2.05	1	Ford	John	16AUG07	2.12	1
FORBIS					Ford	John	02JUN08	1.11	1
Forbis	George	18JUN96	1.04	1	Ford	John	24MAY09	2.10	1
Forbis	George	09MAY97	3.11	1	Ford	John	-----11	1.25	1
Forbus	George	21MAY99	1.11	1	Ford	Jonathan	-----11	1.27	1
Forbush	James	14JUN87	2.03	2	Ford	Peter	23JUN87	3.04	
Forbis	James	28OCT88	1.03	11	Insolvent				
Forbis	James	05NOV88	1.03	1	Ford	Sary	27JUN04	4.09	F
Forbis	James	23JUN89	5.05	11	Ford	Sarah	18JUL05	2.12	F
Forbis	James	17JUN89	5.05	1	Ford	William	25MAY89	6.03	1
Forbus	James	31MAR90	2.03	1	Ford	William	21APR90	1.04	1
Forbus	James Jr	31MAR90	2.03	11	Ford	William	10AUG91	2.04	11
Forbush	James	08OCT91	1.03	1	Ford	William	13OCT92	1.05	12
Forbus	James	29OCT91	1.03	1	Ford	William Sr	20AUG93	3.04	1
Forbush	James Sr	04OCT92	2.03	11	Ford	William Jr	20AUG93	3.04	1
Forbush	James	06OCT92	2.03	1	Ford	William Sr	18JUN94	2.05	11
Forbis	James Sr	07AUG93	1.04	1	Ford	William	18JUN94	2.05	
Forbis	James Jr	07AUG93	1.04	1	Paid tax for J. Gillmore				
Forbis	James Sr	27MAY94	1.03	1	Ford	William Sr	18JUN94	2.05	
Forbis	James	20MAY94	1.03	1	Paid tax for S. Larriman				
Forbis	James	06JUN95	2.05	1	Ford	William Jr	22JUN94	2.05	1
Forbis	James	25MAY95	2.05	1	Ford	William Sr	02MAY95	3.06	1
Forbis	James	18JUN96	1.05	1	Ford	William Jr	01MAY95	3.06	1
Forbis	James	13JUN96	1.04	1	Ford	William Sr	28JUN96	2.07	1
Forbis	James	10MAY97	3.11	1	Ford	William	28JUN96	2.07	1
Forbis	James Jr	24JUL01	2.08	1	Ford	William Jr	28JUN96	2.07	1
Forbis	James	02AUG06	1.08	1	Ford	William Sr	28JUN97	1.08	2
Forbis	James	14JUL07	1.09	1	Ford	William	29MAY99	3.08	1
Forbis	James Jr	15JUL07	1.09	1	Ford	William Sr	05JUL00	3.11	1
Forbis	James(heirs	21JUN09	2.11	D	Ford	Williamsin	19MAY01	3.11	2
Forbes	John	06OCT87	1.06	1	Ford	William	11AUG02	3.09	1
Forbis	John	01JUN95	2.04	1	Ford	William	11AUG02	3.09	1
Forbis	John	18JUN96	1.04	1	Ford	William	28JUL03	2.10	1
Forbis	Jonathan	28OCT88	1.03	1	Two lotts in Danville				
Forbis	Jonathan	23JUN89	5.05	1	Ford	William Jr	28JUL03	2.10	1
Forbus	Jonathan	24MAR90	2.03	1	Ford	William	27JUN04	4.09	1
Forbus	Jonathan	18OCT91	1.03	1	Ford	William	18JUL05	2.12	1
Forbush	Jonathan	04OCT92	2.03	1	Ford	Worrinor	12JUN87	2.02	1
Forbis	Jonathan	04SEP93	1.03	1	FOREMAN				
Forbis	Jonathan	29MAY95	2.05	1	Foreman	David	30MAY89	6.08	1
Forbis	Jonathan	09AUG97	3.11	1	Foreman	David	05APR90	1.04	1
Forbus	Jonathan	20MAY99	1.11	1	Foreman	David	17MAY91	2.04	1
Forbis	Jonathan	04JUN00	2.10	1	Foreman	David	26SEP92	1.05	11
Forbis	Jonathan	24JUL01	2.08	1	Foreman	David	20NOV93	3.04	11
Forbush	Jonathan	17JUN02	1.07	1	FORGUSON				
Forbush	Jonathan	11JUL03	1.08	1	Forguson	Nathaniel	28JUL08	2.10	11
Forbis	Jonathen	18JUN04	2.07	1	FORKER				
Forbush	Jonathan	19JUN05	1.07	1	Forkner	James	23AUG02	2.09	1
Forbis	Jonathan	02AUG06	1.08	1	Forker	James	31MAY03	3.08	1
Forbis	Jonathan	16AUG06	2.13	1	FORREST				
Forbis	Jonathan	14JUL07	1.08	1	Forrest	Samuel	13JUN96	2.06	1
Forbis	Jonathan	09JUN08	1.12	11	Forest	Samuel	30MAY99	1.11	1
Forbis	Jonathan	21JUN09	2.11	1	FORSYTHE				
Forbus	Jonathan	-----11	1.26	1	Fosith	James	16MAY94	1.04	1
Forbis	Morgan	10AUG93	1.03	1	Forsithe	James	20MAY95	2.05	1
Forbis	Margan	24MAY94	1.04	1	Forsithe	James	13JUN96	1.04	1
Forbis	Morgan	25MAY95	2.05	1	Forsythe	James	17APR97	3.10	1
Forbis	Nathaniel	18JUN96	1.04	1	Forsythe	James	24MAY99	1.11	11
Forbis	Nathaniel	09MAY97	3.11	1	Forsythe	James	28JUN00	2.10	11
Forbus	Nathaniel	21MAY99	1.11	1	Forsythe	James	04JUN01	2.08	11
Forbis	Nathan	04JUN00	2.10	2	Forsythe	James	14JUN02	3.09	1
Forbis	Robert	27JUN89	2.05	1	Forseythe	James	18JUL03	1.09	1
Forbis	Robert	01JUN95	2.04	1	Forsythe	James	23JUL04	1.07	11

surname	name	date	bk.pg	TM	surname	name	date	bk.pg	TM
Forscythe	James	20JUN05	1.07	11	French	James	16MAY89	6.03	1
Forseythe	James	23JUN06	1.09	1	French	James	28MAR91	1.03	1
Forsythe	James	20MAY07	1.08	11	French	James	07DEC92	3.07	1
Forsythe	James	02JUN08	1.11	12	French	James	20MAR97	2.01	1
Forsythe	James Sr	25MAY09	2.10	1	French	James	12MAY99	2.07	1
Forsythe	James Jr	25MAY09	2.10	1	French	James	18JUN00	1.04	11
Forsythe	James Sr	-----11	1.26	11	French	James	30MAY01	1.05	1
Forsythe	James	-----11	1.25	1	French	James	03JUN02	1.07	1
Forsaythe	John	18JUN00	1.04	1	French	James	11JUN03	1.08	1
Forsythe	John	05JUN01	1.05	1	Frances	James	06JUN04	4.09	1
Forsaythe	John	03JUN02	1.07	1	French	James	15JUN04	1.07	1
Forsythe	John	14JUN02	3.09	M1	French	James	05JUN05	1.06	1
Forsythe	John	14JUN03	1.08	1	Frentch	James	11JUN06	1.08	1
Forsythe	John	18JUN04	1.07	1	French	John	26JUN87	1.02	1
Forsythe	Joseph	28APR95	3.06	1	French	John	30MAY89	6.08	1
Forsyth	Joseph	02JUN96	2.06	1	French	John	03APR90	1.04	1
Forsythe	Thomas	25MAY99	2.06	1	French	John	-----96	4.06	1
Forsaythe	Thomas	17JUN00	1.04	1	French	John	20JUN00	1.04	1
Forsythe	Thomas	04JUN01	1.05	1	Frances	John	31JUL01	3.11	1
FOSTER					French	Katy	19MAY91	2.04	F
Foster	William	03JUN08	2.09	1	French	Richard	02AUG04	2.07	1
Foster	William	11JUL09	1.13	1	Frentch	Richard	15JUN05	1.06	1
FOURNEY					FRESH				
Flourney	John	-----93	2.02	1	Fresh	Benjamin	23MAY97	1.08	1
Fourney	Nicholas	30MAY89	6.03	1	Fresh	Benjamin	03JUL99	3.08	1
Finney	Nicholas	03APR90	1.04	1	Fresh	Benjamin	22JUN03	2.10	11
Frame	Nicholas	06APR91	1.03	1	Fresh	Benjamin	28JUL04	4.09	1
Furway	Nicholas	08OCT92	1.05	1	Fresh	Benjamin	25JUL05	2.12	11
Furnay	Nicholas	21AUG93	3.04	1	Fresh	Benjamin	16JUL06	2.14	1
FOWLER					Fresh	Benjamin	14AUG07	2.12	1
Fowler	William	10MAY95	1.06	1	Fresh	Benjamin	28JUL08	2.10	1
Fowler	William	12JUN97	1.08	1	Fresh	Benjamin	22JUN09	1.13	1
FOX					Fresh	Benjamin	-----11	1.24	1
Fox	Abram	29MAY99	1.11	1	Fresh	Francis	10JUL89	2.05	1
Fox	Abraham	07JUL00	2.10	1	Fresh	Francis	02JUN94	3.08	1
Fox	Gatehis	19AUG06	3.13	1	Fresh	Francis	02APR95	3.07	1
Fox	John(Heirs)	17APR95	3.07	0	Fresh	Francis	21JUN96	2.07	1
Fox	John(Heirs)	17APR95	3.07	0	Fresh	Francis	23MAY97	1.08	1
FRANCIS					Fresh	Francis	03JUL99	3.08	1
Francis	Henry	02JUN97	3.11	1	Fresh	Francis	30JUN00	3.11	1
Francis	John	13JUN97	1.08	1	Fresh	Gasper	08JUN89	6.03	1
Francis	John	28JUN02	3.09	1	Frush	Gasper	10AUG91	2.04	1
Francis	John	09AUG03	2.10	1	Fresh	Nicholas	01JUL00	3.11	M1
FRANKLIN					FRIEND				
Franklin	Elijah	03JUN97	3.11	1	Friend	Thomas	25MAY95	2.05	1
Franklin	Robert	21APR90	1.04	1	FRILEY				
Franklin	Thomas	-----11	1.25	1	Friley	John	07MAY94	3.08	1
FRAZIER					FRISTO				
Frazer	John	22JUL05	2.12	1	Fristo	William	24MAR95	3.07	0
FREEMAN					Froggit	William	10JUN02	1.07	1
Freeman	Elijah	29NOV92	3.07	1	FRIZZLE				
Freeman	Elisha	23JUN87	3.04	1	Frizzle	John	26APR97	3.10	1
Freeman	Elisha	30MAY89	6.08	1	FRY				
Freeman	Elisha	09SEP89	2.05	1	Fry	John	13SEP92	1.03	
Freeman	Elisha	10APR90	1.04	1	Adam Carpenter - Adm.				
Freeman	Elisha	-----93	2.02	1	Fry	J.	10JUN94	2.03	0
Freeman	Elisha Sr	07MAY94	3.08	1	Paid by Adam Carpenter				
Freeman	Elisha Jr	07MAY94	3.08	1	Fry	John(heirs)	11JUL97	1.04	D
Freeman	Elisha Sr	10APR95	1.06	1	Tax paid by Adam Carpenter				
Freeman	Elisha Jr	10MAR95	1.06		Fry	John(Heirs)	11JUL97	1.04	1
"Gone to Harden County"					Fry	John	18JUN01	3.08	1
Freeman	Elisha	-----96	4.06	1	Fry	John	18JUN01	3.08	D
Freeman	Nancy	13JUN05	1.06	F1	Tax paid by Adam Carpenter				
Freeman	William	04AUG04	3.07	1	Fry	John	02JUN02	2.09	M1
Freeman	William	22AUG05	3.13	1	Fry	John	06AUG03	3.09	M1
Freeman	William	21JUL06	3.12	1	Fry	John	04AUG04	3.07	1
Freeman	William	20AUG07	2.12	1	Fry	John	21JUL06	3.12	1
Freeman	William	14JUN08	2.09	1	FUKEWAY				
Freeman	William	11JUL09	1.13	1	Fukeway	Aaron	06JUN97	1.08	1
FRENCH					FUNK				
French	Frances	19APR91	3.06	1	Funk	Gabriel	-----11	1.26	1
French	Francis	16NOV92	3.07	1	Funck	John	30MAY99	2.06	1

surname	name	date	bk.pg	TM	surname	name	date	bk.pg	TM
Funk	John	11JUN01	1.06	1	Gaines	William	-----11	1.29	1
FREEMAN					GALLAGHER				
FUNK					Goliher	Charles	09AUG91	2.04	1
Funk	Josesh	06OCT87	1.06	1	GALLAN				
Funk	Joseph	13SEP93	3.04	1	Gallan	Betsy	26JUN09	1.15	F
GABBERT					GALLOWAY				
Gabbert	George	19JUL05	2.14	1	Galloway	John	10APR95	1.07	1
Gabbert	George Jr	19JUL05	2.14	1	GARDINER				
Gabert	George	13AUG06	2.16	1	Gardiner	Nancy	14OCT92	2.04	F
Gabbert	George	15JUN07	2.13	1	GARLAND				
Gabbert	George Jr	15JUN07	2.13	1	Garland	Anderson	17JUN05	2.13	1
Gabbert	George	27JUN08	2.11	11	Garland	Anderson	01AUG06	2.16	1
Gabbert	George Jr	27JUN08	2.11	1	Garland	Anderson	20JUN07	2.13	1
Gabbert	George	08JUN09	1.15	1	Garland	Anderson	04JUN08	2.11	1
Gabbert	George	-----11	1.27	12	Garland	Anderson	13JUL09	1.16	1
Gabbert	Jacob	18JUN04	2.07	1	Garland	Anderson	-----11	1.30	1
Gabbert	Jacob	19JUL05	2.14	1	Garland	James	01JUL09	2.12	1
Gabert	Jacob	13AUG06	2.16	1	Garland	John	26JUL02	3.10	1
Gabbert	Jacob	15JUN07	2.13	1	Garland	John	04AUG03	2.12	1
Gabbert	Jacob	-----08	2.12	11	Garland	John	09JUN04	4.10	1
Gabbert	Jacob	27JUN08	2.11	1	Garland	John	24MAY05	2.12	1
Gabbert	Jacob	08JUN09	1.15	1	Garland	John	18AUG06	2.17	1
Gabbert	Jacob Jr	08JUN09	1.15	1	Garland	John	16JUL07	2.14	1
Gabbert	Jacob	-----11	1.27	1	Garland	John	27JUN08	2.11	1
Gabbert	John	08AUG03	3.10	1	Garland	John	07JUL09	1.16	1
Gabbert	John	18JUN04	2.07	1	GARNER				
Gabbert	John	05AUG05	3.15	1	Garner	Henry	06JUN97	1.09	1
Gabbert	John	21AUG06	3.15	1	GARRANT				
Gabbert	John	-----11	1.27	1	Garrant	John	-----93	2.02	1
Gabbert	Thomas	19JUL05	2.14	M1	Garrant	Obediah	-----93	2.01	1
Gabbert	Thomas	25JUL07	2.14	1	Tax paid by John Bryant				
Gabbert	Thomas	30JUN08	2.11	1	GARRARD				
Gabert	Thomas	16MAY09	1.14	1	Garad	Francis	-----11	1.29	1
GABRIEL					Garrard	John	02JUN01	1.06	1
Gabriel	Morecan	13SEP91	3.06	1	GARRETT				
GADBERRY					Garret	Bartlet	01AUG06	1.10	1
Gadberry	John	03AUG04	1.07	1	Garrat	Bartholomew	09MAY07	1.09	1
Gadberry	John	07MAY07	1.09	1	Garrat	Benjamin	11MAY99	2.07	1
GADD					Garrat	Beth(heirs)	01JUL09	2.32	D
Gadd	Thomas	05MAY07	1.09	1	Garrat	Bethlaham(D	01JUL09	2.32	
Gadd	Thomas	09JUN08	1.13	1	Tax paid by Charles Stewart				
Gad	Thomas	14JUN09	2.12	1	Garrat	John	09MAY07	1.09	1
GADDIS					Garrat	Mary	18APR08	1.12	F
Gaddes	George W.	25JUL07	2.14	1	GARRISON				
Gadus	George W.	30MAY08	2.10	1	Garrison	Abraham	18JUL87	3.04	1
Gaudes	Thomas	24JUN07	2.13	1	Garrison	Abraham	07AUG89	2.05	1
Gadus	Thomas	30MAY08	2.10	1	Garrison	Bailey	10AUG02	3.11	1
GAINES					Garrison	Bailey	20JUL05	2.14	1
Gaines	Edward	-----11	1.31	1	Garrison	Bailey	18JUL06	2.15	1
Gaines	Frances	25JUL07	2.14	11	Garrison	Bailey	16JUL07	2.14	1
Gaines	Frances	-----08	2.12	11	GARTEN				
Gaines	Francis	21JUN09	1.15	1	Garton	Uriah	05JUL96	2.08	1
Gaines	Francis Sr	-----11	1.31	1	Garten	Uriah	22JUN97	1.09	1
Gaines	Francis Jr	-----11	1.31	1	GARVEY				
Gains	Richard	11JUL97	3.13	1	Garvey	David	26AUG93	1.04	1
Gains	Richard	21MAY99	1.13	11	Garvey	David	30MAY94	1.04	1
Gains	Richard	19JUN00	2.11	12	GARVIN				
Gains	Richard	10AUG01	2.10	12	Garvin	Isaac	29JUN87	1.02	1
Gains	Richard	13AUG02	2.12	1	Garvin	Isaac	22MAY89	6.03	1
Gains	Richard	17JUN03	3.09	11	Garvin	Isaac	13AUG90	1.05	1
Gaines	Richard	09JUL04	2.07	11	Garvine	Isaac	04AUG91	2.04	1
Wolf Rn = Barnett Fk of Ruff Ck					Garvine	Isaac	04DEC92	1.05	1
Gaines	Richard	03JUN05	3.14	11	Garvine	Isaac	07AUG93	3.05	1
Gaines	Richard	17JUL06	3.14	11	Garven	Isaac	24MAY94	2.05	1
Gaines	Richard	21AUG07	2.15	11	Garvin	Isaac	16APR95	3.08	1
Gaines	Richard Jr	21AUG07	2.15	1	Gaven	Isaac	05JUL96	2.08	1
Gaines	Richard	04JUN08	2.11	11	Garvan	Isaac	21JUN97	1.09	1
Gaines	Richard	09MAY09	1.14	1	Garvan	Isaac	13MAY99	3.08	1
Gaines	Richard	-----11	1.29	1	Garvin	Isaac	18JUN00	3.11	1
Gaines	Thomas L.	-----11	1.29	1	Garvin	Isaac	18JUN01	3.13	1
Gaines	William	25JUL07	2.14	1	Garven	Isaac	28JUL02	3.10	1
Gaines	William	21JUN09	1.15	1	Garven	Isaac	11AUG03	2.13	1

surname	name	date	bk.pg	TM	surname	name	date	bk.pg	TM
Garven	Isaac	05JUN04	4.10	1	Gay	John	25MAY97	1.09	1
Garven	Isaac	28JUN05	2.13	1	Gay	John	30JUL00	2.12	1
Gawin	Isaac	01AUG06	2.16	1	Gay	John	03AUG01	2.10	1
Garven	Isaac	21AUG07	2.15	1	Gay	John	02AUG02	2.11	1
Garven	Isaac	-----08	2.12	1	Gay	John	18JUN03	3.10	1
Garven	Isaac	12JUL09	1.16	1	Gay	John	07AUG04	1.07	1
Garvin	Isaac	-----11	1.30	11	Gay	John Jr	04AUG04	3.09	1
Garvin	John	21APR08	1.12	1	Gay	John	07JUN05	2.13	1
GASS						One lott in Standford			
Gass	John	24JUN01	1.06	0	Gay	John	06APR06	2.15	1
Tax pd by John Davice					Gay	John	07APR06	2.15	
GASTON						One lott in Standford			
Gaston	Alexander	21JUN87	2.03	1	Gay	John	15JUN07	2.13	1
Gaster	Alexander	22NOV88	1.03	1	Gay	John	04JUN08	2.11	1
Gaston	Alexander	29MAR90	2.03	1	Gay	John	16AUG09	1.16	1
Gaston	Alexander	05APR91	1.03	1		One lott in town of Standford			
Gastion	Alexander	26SEP92	1.05	1	Gay	John	-----11	1.30	1
Gasten	Hugh	21JUN99	2.08	1	Gay	Patsey	06AUG03	3.10	F
GATELY					Gay	Samuel	02AUG02	2.11	M1
Galeley	Isom	15MAY99	2.07	1	Gay	Samuel	11AUG03	3.10	1
Gatley	Isom	17JUN00	1.05	1	Gay	Samuel	04AUG04	3.09	1
Gately	Isom	10JUN01	1.06	1	Gay	Samuel	03JUN05	3.14	1
GATHWRIGHT					Gay	Samuel	-----11	1.30	1
Gathwright	Samuel	14AUG06	2.17	1	Gay	Thomas	23MAY89	6.03	1
GATLIFF					Gay	Thos/Alex	14MAY90	1.04	21
Gatliff	Charles	06NOV88	1.03	1	Gay	Thos/Alex	30APR91	2.04	11
Gatliff	Charles	16JUN89	5.05	1	Gay	Ths/Alx/Jn	03OCT92	1.05	3
Gatliff	Charles	31MAR90	2.03	1	Gay	Thomas	13AUG93	3.05	11
Gatliff	Charles	22JUN99	2.08	1	Gay	Thomas	13MAY94	2.05	1
Gatliff	James	22JUN99	2.08	1	Gay	Thomas	16APR95	3.07	11
Gatliff	Neel	19JUN99	2.07	1	Gay	Thomas	10MAY96	2.07	11
Gatliff	Reece	22MAY97	3.12	1	Gay	Thomas Jr	10MAY96	2.07	1
Gatliff	Reas	22JUN99	2.08	1	Gay	Thomas Sr	23JUN97	1.09	1
GAULDON					Gay	Thomas Jr	23JUN97	1.09	1
Gauldon	Andrew	20AUG06	3.15	1	Gay	Thomas Sr	25JUN99	1.12	11
GAULT					Gay	Thomas Jr	25JUN99	1.12	1
Gault	William	29APR95	3.07	0	Gay	Thomas Sr	29JUL00	2.12	11
GAY					Gay	Thomas	28JUN00	2.11	1
Gay	Alexander	13AUG93	3.05	1	Gay	Thomas Sr	21JUL01	3.14	11
Gay	Alexander	10JUN94	2.05	1	Gay	Thomas Sr	21JUL01	3.14	1
Gay	Alexander	28APR95	3.07	1	Gay	Thomas Sr	11JUN02	2.10	1
Gay	Alex	03JUN96	2.07	1	Gay	Thomas Jr	11JUN02	2.10	1
Gay	Alexander	25MAY97	1.09	1	Gay	Thomas	06AUG03	3.10	1
Gay	Alexander	24JUN99	1.12	1	Gay	Thomas	03AUG04	3.09	1
Gay	Alex.	28JUN00	2.11	1	Gay	Thomas	03JUN05	3.14	1
Gay	Alexander	13JUL01	2.09	1	Gay	Thomas	22JUL06	3.14	1
Gay	Alexander	27MAY02	2.10	1	Gay	Thomas	16AUG07	2.15	1
Gay	Alexander	06AUG03	3.10	1	Gay	Thomas	31MAY08	2.10	1
Gay	Alexander	04AUG04	3.09	1	Gay	Thomas	11JUL09	1.16	1
Gay	Alexander	03JUN05	3.14	1	Gay	Thomas	-----11	1.30	1
Gay	Alexander	14JUL06	3.13	1	GEARY				
Gay	Alexander	25JUL07	2.14	1	Geary	William	29MAY97	1.09	1
Gay	Alexander	31MAY08	2.10	1	Geery	William	15JUL99	3.09	1
Gay	Alexander	11JUL09	1.16	1	Gaary	William	25JUN00	3.12	11
Gay	Alexander	-----11	1.30	1	GEE				
Gay	Allin	28APR95	3.07	1	Gee	John	26JUN89	6.08	1
Gay	James	05JUN99	1.12	1	Gee	John	18JUN90	1.04	1
Gay	James	29JUL00	2.12	1	Gee	John	03NOV92	1.05	1
Gay	James	25JUL01	2.10	1	Gee	John	28AUG93	3.05	1
Gay	James	02AUG02	2.11	1	Gee	John	29MAY94	2.05	1
Gay	James	09AUG03	2.13	1	Gee	John	23JUN96	2.08	1
Gay	James	05JUN04	4.10	1	Gee	John	10AUG97	1.10	1
Gay	James	03JUN05	3.14	1	Gee	John	10JUL99	3.09	1
Gay	James	05AUG06	3.14	1	Gee	John	09JUL00	3.12	1
Gay	James	14JUL07	2.13	1	Gee	John	31JUL01	3.14	11
Gay	James	-----08	2.12	1	Gee	John	29JUL02	3.10	11
Gay	James	11JUL09	1.16	1	Gee	John	09AUG03	2.13	1
Gay	John	13AUG93	3.05	1	Jee	John	06JUN04	4.13	11
Gay	John	11JUN94	2.05	1	Gee	John	20JUN05	2.13	11
Gay	John	16APR95	3.07	1	Gee	John	30JUL06	2.16	11
Gay	John	02MAY95	3.07	1	Gee	Mark	10AUG03	2.13	1
Gay	John	12MAY96	2.07	1	Jee	Mark	08JUN04	4.13	1

surname	name	date	bk.pg	TM	surname	name	date	bk.pg	TM
Gee	Mark	20JUN05	2.13	1	Gipson	Hugh	11JUN05	1.07	1
Gee	Mark	30JUL06	2.16	1	Gibson	Jacob	10APR95	3.08	1
Gee	Robert	10AUG97	1.10	1	Gibson	Jacob	13JUL96	2.08	1
Gee	Robert	10JUL99	3.09	1	Gibson	Jacob	31MAY97	1.09	1
Gee	Robert	09JUL00	3.12	1	Gibson	Jacob	18MAY99	3.08	1
Gee	Robert	31JUL01	3.14	11	Gibson	Jacob	17JUN01	3.12	1
Gee	Robert	09AUG03	2.13	1	Gibson	Jacob	06AUG02	3.10	1
Jee	Robert	06JUN04	4.13	1	Gibson	Jacob	05AUG03	2.13	1
Gee	Robert	19JUN05	2.13	1	Gibson	Jacob	05JUN04	4.10	1
Gee	Robert	30JUL06	2.16	1	Gibson	Jacob	29JUN05	2.13	1
GENTRY					Gibson	Jacob	29JUL06	2.16	1
Gentrey	Henry	06SEP93	1.04	1	Gibson	Jacob	25JUL07	2.14	1
Gentry	Henry	17MAY94	1.04	1	Gibson	James	16MAY94	1.04	1
Gentry	Isom	22JUL05	1.07	1	Gibson	James	25JUL07	2.14	1
Gentry	Isoom	11AUG06	1.10	1	Gibson	James	-----08	2.12	1
Gentry	Isham	25MAY07	1.09	1	Gibsen	James	06APR09	1.14	1
Gentry	Isham	09JUN08	1.13	1	Gibsen	Joel	16AUG09	1.16	1
Jentry	Isham	10MAY09	2.16	1	Gibson	John	15AUG93	1.04	1
Gentry	Isom	-----11	1.28	1	Gibson	John	16MAY94	1.04	11
Gentry	John	09JUN08	1.13	M1	Gibson	John	25JUN04	1.07	12
Jentry	John	10MAY09	2.16	1	Gibson	John	19AUG05	3.15	11
Jentry	Nicholess	31MAR90	2.04	11	Gibson	John	05AUG06	3.15	11
Gentry	Nicholas	13APR91	1.04	1	Gibson	John	25JUL07	2.14	11
Gentry	Nicholas	04OCT92	2.03	11	Gibson	John	25JUL08	2.11	11
Gentry	Nicholas	12AUG93	1.04	11	Gibsen	John	06APR09	1.14	11
Gentry	Nicholas	17MAY94	1.04	11	Gibson	Richard	05AUG06	3.15	1
Gentry	Nicholas	09MAY95	2.06	11	Gibson	Richard	-----08	2.12	1
Gentry	Nicholas	18JUL96	1.05	1	Gibsen	Richard	06APR09	1.14	1
Gentry	Nicholas	12JUN97	3.12	1	Gibson	Richard	-----11	1.28	1
Gentry	Zechariah	12JUN97	3.12	1	Gibson	Samuel	15AUG93	1.04	1
GERRY					Gibson	Samuel	28MAY94	1.04	1
Geary	William	29MAY97	1.09	1	Gibson	Samuel	06AUG04	2.07	1
Gaary	William	25JUN00	3.12	11	Gibson	Samuel	03JUN05	3.14	1
GESFORD					Gibson	William	21JUN99	2.08	1
Gilford	Joel	07AUG04	3.09	M1	Gibson	William	15JUL99	3.09	1
Gesford	Joal	05AUG05	3.15	1	Gibson	William	25JUN00	3.12	1
Gasford	Joal	04AUG06	3.14	M1	Gibson	William	21MAY01	3.12	1
GETWOOD					GIDCOM				
Getwood	David	04JUN99	1.13	1	Gidcom	Joseph	18JUL87	3.04	1
GIBBS					GILBERT				
Gibbs	Ezekiel	27JUN89	2.05	1	Gilbert	Isam	28JUN00	3.12	1
Gibs	Ezekiel	14AUG05	3.15	1	Gilbert	Isum	08JUN01	3.12	1
Gibs	Ezekiel	08AUG06	3.15	1	Gilbert	Isham	01JUL02	3.10	1
Gibbs	George	09AUG04	3.09	1	Gilbert	Isham	01JUL03	2.11	1
Gibbs	Hugh	15AUG93	3.05	1	Gilbert	Isham	28JUN04	4.10	1
Gibbs	Jeremiah	27JUN89	2.05	1	Gilbert	Isham	24MAY05	2.12	1
Gibs	John	01JUL99	1.12	1	Gilbert	Isham	18AUG06	2.17	1
Gibbs	John Sr	27JUN00	2.11	1	Gilbert	Isham	25JUL07	2.14	1
Gibs	John	18JUN01	3.13	1	Gilbert	Isham	-----08	2.12	1
Gibs	John	22JUL01	3.14	1	Gilbert	Isiam	07JUN09	1.15	1
Gibbs	John	13AUG02	2.11	11	Gilbert	Isom	-----11	1.31	1
Gibbs	John Jr	13AUG02	2.12	1	Gilbert	James	29MAY97	1.09	1
Gibbs	John Sr	03JUN03	3.09	11	Gilbert	John	27JUN99	3.08	1
Gibbs	John	09AUG03	2.13	1	Gilbert	John	28JUN00	3.12	1
Gibbs	John	09AUG04	3.09	1	Gilbert	John	18MAY01	3.11	1
Gibbs	John	05AUG05	3.15	1	Gilbert	John	10AUG02	3.11	1
Gibbs	John	22JUL06	3.14	1	Gilbert	John	01AUG03	2.12	1
Gibs	John	22AUG06	3.15	11	Gilbert	John	28JUN04	4.10	1
Gibs	Richard	01JUL99	1.12	1	Gilbert	John	24MAY05	2.12	1
Gibbs	Richard	27JUN00	2.11	1	Gilbert	John	18AUG06	2.17	1
Gibs	Richard	30MAY01	3.14	1	Gilbert	John	25JUL07	2.14	1
Gibbs	Richard	03AUG02	2.11	11	Gilbert	John	04JUL08	2.11	11
Gibbs	Richard	07JUN03	3.09	11	Gilbert	John	25JUL08	2.11	1
Gibbs	Richard	06AUG04	3.09	11	Gilbert	John	08JUN09	1.15	1
Gibs	Richard	16AUG05	3.15	11	Gilbert	John	-----11	1.30	1
Gibbs	Samuel	09OCT92	1.05	1	Gilbert	John	-----11	1.31	1
Gibbs	Samuel	15AUG93	3.05	1	Gilbert	John W.	12MAY96	2.07	31
GIBSON					Gilbert	John W.	11MAY97	1.09	31
Gibsen	Bailey	16AUG09	1.16	1	Gilbert	John W.	27JUN99	3.08	2
Gibson	Bailey	-----11	1.29	1	Gilbert	John W.	20JUN00	3.11	1
Gibson	Catherine	-----11	1.28	F1	Gilbert	John W.	18MAY01	3.12	1
Gibson	Edward	19JUN00	2.11	1	Paid tax for S. (heirs) Craig				

surname	name	date	bk.pg	TM	surname	name	date	bk.pg	TM
Gilbert	John W.	10AUG02	3.11		Gill	Richard	08AUG89	5.05	11
Paid tax for John Craig					Gell	Richard	29MAY97	3.12	11
Gilbert	John W.	10AUG02	3.11		Gill	Samuel	18JUL87	3.04	1
Paid tax for Sally Craig					Joshua VanMeter listed with him				
Gilbert	John W.	10AUG02	3.11		Gill	Samuel	27JUN89	2.05	1
Paid tax for Samuel Craig					Gill	Samuel	27APR91	3.06	1
Gilbert	John W.	10AUG02	3.11		Gill	Samuel	14OCT92	3.08	1
Paid tax for Zacheriah Tucker					Gill	Samuel	23APR94	3.09	1
Gilbert	John W.	30JUL03	2.12	1	Gill	Samuel	10APR95	1.06	11
Paid tax for John Craig					Gill	Samuel	-----96	4.07	1
Gilbert	John W.	30JUL03	2.12		GILLANWATER				
Paid tax for Samuel Craig					Gillanwater	John	17APR95	3.07	1
Gilbert	John W.	30JUL03	2.12		GILLESPIE				
Paid tax for Zacheriah Tucker					Gellaspie	John	20JUL05	2.14	1
Gilbert	John W.	28JUN04	4.10	1	Gillaspie	John	18JUL06	2.15	1
Gilbert	John W.	30MAY05	2.13	1	Gelespie	William	19JUN89	5.05	1
Paid tax for John Craig					Gillespe	William	25MAR90	2.03	1
Gilbert	John W.	30MAY05	2.13		GILLETT				
Paid tax for Samuel Craig					Gillot	Jonathan	23MAY94	2.05	1
Gilbert	John W.	08AUG06	2.16	1	Jillot	Jonathan	19MAY95	3.09	1
Paid tax for John Craig					Gillet	Jonathan	12MAY96	2.07	1
Gilbert	John W.	08AUG06	2.16		Gillet	Jonathan	13JUN97	1.09	1
Paid tax for Samuel Craig					Gellet	Jonathan	07JUN99	1.12	1
Gilbert	John W.	16AUG07	2.15	1	Jillett	Jonathan	28JUL00	2.15	1
Gilbert	John W.	12AUG09	1.16	1	Gillet	Jonathen	20JUN01	3.14	1
Gilbert	Mary(widow)	-----11	1.31	1	Gillet	Jonathan	09JUN02	2.10	1
GILBREATH					Gillet	Jonathan	31MAY03	3.09	1
Galbrath	Alexander	26MAY95	2.05	1	Gillet	Jonathan	31JUL04	3.09	1
Gilbrath	Alexander	21JUN96	1.05	1	Gillett	Jonathan	03JUN05	3.14	1
Galbreath	Alex.	07APR97	3.12	1	Gillett	Jonathan	28JUL06	2.16	1
Gilbreath	Alexander	12MAY99	2.07	1	Gillet	Jonathan	15JUL07	2.13	1
Gilbreath	Alexander	13JUN00	1.05	1	Gillitt	Jonathen	30MAY08	2.10	1
Galbreath	Alexander	04AUG01	1.06	1	Gillett	Jonathan	30JUN09	1.16	1
Galbreath	Alexander	03JUN02	1.08	1	Gillett	Jonathan	-----11	1.30	11
Galbreath	Alexander	15JUN03	1.09	1	GILMORE				
Galbreath	Alexander	14JUN04	1.07	1	Gilmore	Alexander	20APR91	2.04	1
Galbreath	Alexander	30JUL05	1.08	1	Gilmore	Alex.	09OCT92	1.05	1
Galbreath	Alexander	11JUN06	1.09	1	Gilmore	Alexander	17AUG93	3.05	1
Galbreath	Alexander	29APR07	1.09	11	Gilmore	George	-----11	1.31	1
Gilbreath	Alexander	06JUN08	1.13	11	Gillmore	Ginney	27JUL03	2.11	F
Gilbreath	Alexander	10MAY09	2.11	1	Gilmore	Hugh	20JUN96	1.05	1
Gilbreath	Alexander	-----11	1.28	1	Gilmore	James Forks	23APR94	2.06	1
Kilbreath	Evan	06OCT87	1.06	1	Gilmore	Jas.Forks	21MAR95	3.08	1
Kilbreath	Evan	18APR89	6.04	1	Gilmore	J L.Forks	20JUN96	2.08	1
Killbraith	Evan	20APR90	1.05	1	Gilmore	James	29JUN87	1.02	1
Kilbraith	Evan	20APR91	2.05	1	Gilmore	James	19MAY89	6.03	1
Kilbreth	Hugh	13JUN87	2.04	1	Gilmore	James	11MAY90	1.04	1
Galbreath	Hugh	06NOV88	1.03	1	Gilmore	James/Alex	06APR90	1.04	2
Galbreth	Hugh	20JUN89	5.05	1	Gilmore	James	14MAY91	2.04	1
Galbreath	Hugh	15JUN90	2.03	1	Gilmore	James	17AUG93	3.05	1
Gilbreath	Hugh	05JUL91	1.04	11	Gilmore	James	19APR94	2.05	1
Galbreath	Hugh	16OCT92	2.04	11	Gilmore	J.	18JUN94	2.05	0
Galbreath	Hugh	17SEP93	1.04	11	Tax paid by William Ford Sr				
Galbreath	Hugh	20MAY94	1.04	11	Gilmore	James	20MAR95	3.08	1
GILELAND					Gilmore	James	08JUL96	2.08	1
Gileland	Robert	31MAY97	3.12	1	Gilmore	James	30APR97	3.12	1
GILES					Gilmore	James	17MAY97	1.09	1
Giles	John	19AUG05	3.15	11	Gilmore	James Sr	03JUL99	3.09	1
Giles	Lucindah	01AUG05	3.15	F	Gilmore	James Jr	13MAY99	3.08	1
Giles	Lucinda	17JUL06	3.14	F	Gilmore	James Sr	28JUN00	3.12	1
Giles	Lucinda	13JUL07	2.13	F	Gilmore	James Jr	28JUN00	3.12	1
Giles	Lucenda	-----08	2.12	F	Gilmore	James Sr	08JUL01	3.13	11
Giles	Lucinda	04JUN09	1.14	F	Gilmore	James Jr	08JUN01	3.12	1
Giles	Lucy	-----11	1.29	F	Gilmore	James	21JUL02	2.11	1
Giles	Thomas	09JUN08	1.13	1	Gillmore	James	13AUG02	3.11	12
Jeles	Thomas	06JUL09	2.16	1	Gillmore	James	22JUN03	2.11	11
Giles	Thomas	-----11	1.29	1	Gilmore	James	28JUL04	4.11	12
GILL					Gillmore	James	23JUL05	2.14	12
Gill	James	26JUN05	2.13	1	Gilmore	James	16AUG07	2.15	21
Gill	John	24JUN89	5.05	1	Gilmore	James	-----08	2.12	21
Gell	Moses	03JUN97	3.12	1	Gilmore	James	21JUN09	1.15	3
Gill	Richard	01DEC88	1.04	1	Gilmore	James Sr	-----11	1.31	21

surname	name	date	bk.pg	TM	surname	name	date	bk.pg	TM
Gilmore	James Capt.	14MAY91	2.04	1	Givens	George	07MAY01	3.12	11
Gilmore	James Capt.	20SEP92	1.05	1	Givens	George	10AUG02	3.11	11
Gilmore	James Capt	17AUG93	3.05	1	Givens	George Jr	10AUG02	3.11	1
Gilmore	James T.	14MAY89	6.03	1	Givens	George Sr	30JUL03	2.12	11
Gilmore	James Tay.	26SEP92	1.05	1	Givens	George Jr	11JUL03	2.11	1
Gilmore	Samuel	06SEP87	1.42	1	Givens	George	29JUN04	4.10	11
Gilmore	Samuel	19MAY89	6.03	1	Givens	George Jr	29JUN04	4.11	1
Gilmore	Samuel	20APR90	1.04	11	Givens	George Sr	29MAY05	2.13	11
Gilmer	Samuel	28MAR91	1.03	1	Givens	George Jr	29MAY05	2.13	1
Gilmore	Samuel	19OCT92	2.04	12	Givens	George Sr	15AUG06	2.17	11
Gilmore	Samuel	27AUG93	1.04	1	Givens	George Jr	08AUG06	2.16	1
Gilmore	Samuel	23MAY94	1.04	1	Givens	George Sr	25JUL07	2.14	11
Gilmore	Samuel	16JUN95	2.05	1	Givens	George Jr	25JUL07	2.14	1
Gilmore	Samuel	16JUN96	1.05	1	Givens	George	30JUN08	2.11	11
Gilmore	Samuel	30MAY97	3.12	1	Givens	George Jr	30JUN08	2.11	1
GIVENS					Givens	George Sr	08JUN09	1.15	1
Givens	Alexander	01JUN97	1.09	1	Givens	George Jr	07JUN09	1.15	1
Givens	Alexander	28JUN99	3.09	1	Givens	George	-----11	1.31	2
Givins	Alexander	27JUN00	3.12	1	Givens	George Jr	-----11	1.30	1
Givens	Alexander	21MAY01	3.12	1	Givins	James/Benj	20JUN91	2.04	2
Givens	Alexander	01JUL02	3.10	1	Givens	James	06SEP87	1.02	1
Givens	Alexander	01JUL03	2.11	1	Givens	James	02OCT87	1.02	1
Givens	Alexander	29JUN04	4.10	1	Givens	James Sr	12MAY89	6.03	1
Givens	Alexander	31MAY05	2.13	1	Givens	James Jr	05MAY89	6.03	1
Givens	Alexander	07AUG06	2.16	1	Givens	James	12MAY89	6.08	1
Givens	Alexander	25JUL07	2.14	1	Givens	James/Benj	13MAY90	1.04	2
Givens	Alexander	-----08	2.12	1	Givens	James	13AUG90	1.05	1
Givens	Alexander	10JUN09	1.15	1	Givens	James Jr	13MAY90	1.04	1
Givens	Alexander	-----11	1.30	1	Givins	James	23JUN91	2.04	1
Givens	Allen	02JUN96	2.07	1	Givins	James Jr	20JUN91	2.04	1
Givens	Allen	10JUL97	1.09	1	Givens	James Caro	06OCT92	1.05	1
Givens	Benj.	12MAY94	2.05	1	Givens	James Jr	12SEP92	1.05	1
Givens	Benj.	09APR95	3.07	2	Givens	James	12SEP92	1.05	2
Givens	Benj.	16JUN96	2.07	2	Givens	Jas Carolin	08AUG92	3.05	1
Givens	Benj.	07JUN97	1.09	2	Givens	James Jr	14AUG93	3.05	1
Givens	Benjamin	26JUN99	3.08	2	Givens	James	05AUG93	3.05	2
Givens	Benjamin	24JUN00	3.11	2	Givens	James Sr	10JUN94	2.05	1
Givens	Benjamin	01MAY01	3.12	2	Givens	James Jr	05MAY94	2.05	1
Givens	Benjamin	06AUG02	3.10	1	Givens	James Cl	09MAY94	2.06	1
Givens	Benjamin	30JUL03	2.12	1	Givens	James Cl	28APR95	3.07	1
Givens	Benjamin	13JUN04	4.10	1	Givens	James	17APR95	3.07	1
Givens	Benjamin	29JUN05	2.14	1	Givens	James C	03JUN96	2.07	1
Givens	Benjamin	18AUG06	2.17	1	Givens	James	12MAY96	2.07	1
Givens	Benjamin	25JUL07	2.14	1	Givens	James;Car	10JUL97	1.10	1
Givens	Benjamin	25JUL08	2.11	1	Givens	James Jr	01JUN97	1.09	
Givens	Benjamin	16AUG09	1.16	1	Paid tax for William Robertson				
Givens	Benjamin	-----11	1.29	1	Givens	James Jr	01JUN97	1.09	1
Givens	Eleazor	24AUG93	3.05	1	Givens	James	04JUN99	1.12	1
Givens	Eleazer	09MAY94	2.06	1	Givens	James	04JUN99	1.13	1
Givens	Eliazer	29APR95	3.07	1	Givens	James	07JUN99	1.12	1
Givens	Eleazer	02JUN96	2.07	1	Givens	James	20JUN00	2.11	1
Givens	Eliezer	10JUL97	1.10	1	Givens	James C.	28JUN00	2.11	1
Givens	Eleazer	04JUN99	1.12	1	Givens	James C.	31JUL01	2.10	1
Givens	Eleazor	20JUN00	2.11	1	Givens	James	19JUN01	3.14	1
Givens	Eliezar	31JUL01	2.10	1	Givens	James	26MAY02	2.10	1
Givens	Eliezer	26MAY02	2.10	1	Givens	James	09JUN02	2.10	1
Givens	Elizara	15JUN03	3.09	1	Givens	James	15JUN03	3.09	1
Givens	Eliezer	07AUG04	2.08	1	Givins	James	13JUL03	3.10	1
Givens	Elizer	03JUN05	3.13	1	Givens	James	07AUG04	2.08	1
Givens	Eliezer	26JUL06	3.14	1	Givens	James	31JUL04	3.09	1
Givens	George	02OCT87	1.02	1	Givens	James C.	03JUN05	3.14	1
Givens	George	22MAY89	6.03	1	Givens	James	19JUL06	3.14	1
Givens	George	21MAY90	1.04	13	Givens	James	16JUL06	3.13	1
Givins	Geo/Sam	17MAY91	2.04	2	Givens	James C.	20JUN07	2.13	1
Givens	George	21SEP92	1.05	12	Givens	James Jr	25JUL07	2.14	1
Givens	George	05AUG93	3.05	12	Givens	James A.	04JUN08	2.11	1
Givens	George	06MAY94	2.05	21	Givens	James C.	04JUN08	2.11	1
Givens	George	19MAR95	3.08	21	Givens	James	-----08	2.12	1
Givens	George	08JUN96	2.07	22	Givens	James	26JUN09	1.15	1
Givens	George	30MAY97	1.08	12	Givens	James	30JUN09	1.16	1
Givens	George	16JUL99	3.09	11	Givens	James	-----11	1.30	1
Givens	George	25JUN00	3.11	12	Givens	James	-----11	1.30	11

surname	name	date	bk.pg	TM	surname	name	date	bk.pg	TM
Givens	John	05JUN89	6.03	1	Givens	Robert	07JUN99	1.12	1
Givens	John	13MAY90	1.04	1	Givens	Robert Jr	20JUN00	2.11	11
Givins	John	14MAY91	2.04	1	Givens	Robert	31JUL01	2.10	11
Givens	John	18OCT92	1.05	1	Givens	Robert	10MAY02	2.10	12
Givens	Jn Carolina	21AUG93	3.05	1	Givins	Robert	21JUL03	3.10	11
Givens	John	10JUN94	2.05	1	Givens	Robert	03MAY04	3.09	11
Givens	John	09APR95	3.07	1	Givens	Robert C.	03JUN05	3.13	11
Givens	John	02JUN96	2.07	1	Givens	Robert C.	26JUL06	3.14	11
Givens	John	16JUN96	2.08	1	Givens	Robert C.	20JUN07	2.13	2
Givens	John;Car	21JUN97	1.09	1	Givens	Robert	20JUN07	2.13	1
Givens	John	07JUN97	1.09	1	Givens	Robert C.	31MAY08	2.10	1
Givens	John	26JUN99	3.08	1	Givens	Robert C.	26JUN09	1.15	1
Givens	John	02JUL99	1.14	1	Givens	Robert	-----11	1.30	11
Givens	John	31JUL00	2.12	1	Givens	Samuel	12JUN89	6.03	1
Givens	John	02MAY01	3.12	1	Givens	Samuel	12JUN89	6.08	1
Givens	John	22JUL01	3.14	1	Givens	Samuel	13MAY90	1.04	1
Givens	John	26MAY02	2.10	1	Givins	Samuel	20JUN91	2.04	1
Givens	John	11JUN02	2.10	1	Givens	Samuel Sr	12SEP92	1.05	1
Givins	John	13JUL03	3.10	1	Givens	Samuel	12SEP92	1.05	11
Givins	John	18JUL03	3.10	11	Givins	Samuel	05AUG93	3.05	12
Givens	John	22AUG04	2.08	1	Givens	Samuel	09AUG93	3.05	1
Givens	John	24AUG04	3.09	12	Givens	Samuel	06APR94	2.06	1
Givens	John Sr	03JUN05	3.14	11	Givens	Samuel	12MAY94	2.05	1
Givens	John	29MAY05	2.13	1	Givens	Samuel	08APR95	3.07	1
Givens	John	03JUN05	3.14	1	Givens	Samuel Jr	19MAR95	3.08	13
Givens	John	03JUN05	3.14	1	Givens	Samuel	08JUN96	2.07	12
Givens	John	16JUL06	3.13	1	Givens	Samuel Sr	07JUN97	1.09	1
Givens	John	28JUL06	3.14	11	Givens	Samuel Jr	08AUG97	1.10	1
Givens	John	15AUG06	2.17	1	Givens	Samuel	21MAY99	3.08	1
Givens	John C.	11JUN07	2.13	12	Givens	Samuel	31MAY99	1.12	11
Givens	John	25JUL07	2.14	1	Givens	Samuel	31MAY99	1.40	
Givens	John	25JUL07	2.14	1	One lott in Stanford				
Givens	John	04JUN08	2.11	1	Givens	Samuel	20JUN00	3.11	1
Givens	John	30JUN08	2.11	1	Givens	Samuel	01MAY01	3.12	1
Givens	John	07JUN09	1.15	1	Givens	Samuel	27JUL02	3.10	1
Givens	John	26JUN09	1.15	1	Givens	Samuel	05AUG03	2.13	1
Givens	John	-----11	1.31	1	Givens	Samuel	06AUG04	4.11	1
Givens	John	-----11	1.30	1	Givens	Samuel	29JUN05	2.14	1
Givens	Mary	28APR95	3.07	F	Givens	Samuel	14JUL06	2.15	1
Givens	Mary	02JUN96	2.07	F	Givens	Samuel	15JUL07	2.13	1
Givens	Mary	20JUN97	1.09	F	Givens	Samuel	25JUL08	2.11	1
Givens	Robert	29JUN87	1.02	1	Givens	Samuel	16MAY09	1.14	1
Givens	Robert Sr	12MAY89	6.03	1	Givens	Samuel	-----11	1.29	11
Givens	Robert	12MAY89	6.08	1	Givens	William	16JUL99	3.09	1
Givens	Robert	13MAY90	1.04	1	Givins	William	12AUG00	3.13	1
Givens	Robert	13AUG90	1.05	1	Givens	William	09MAY01	3.12	1
Givins	Robert	23JUN91	2.04	1	Givens	William	29JUL01	3.13	1
Givens	Robert Capt	12SEP92	1.05	1	Givens	William	14JUN02	3.10	1
Givens	Robert Capt	08AUG93	3.05	1	Givens	William	01JUL03	2.11	1
Givens	Robert	13MAY94	2.05	1	Givens	William	29JUN04	4.10	1
Givens	Robert	08APR95	3.07	1	Givens	William	31MAY05	2.13	1
Givens	Robert	16JUN96	2.07	1	Givens	William	09APR06	2.15	1
Givens	Robert	07JUN97	1.09	1	Givens	William	25JUL07	2.14	1
Givens	Robert	01JUN99	1.13	1	Givens	William	-----08	2.12	1
Givens	Robert	20JUN00	2.11	1	Givens	William	10JUN09	1.15	1
Givens	Robert Sr	31JUL01	2.10	1	Givens	William	-----11	1.30	1
Givens	Robert	26MAY02	2.10	11	Gladon	Littleton	29MAY05	3.13	1
Givins	Robert	08AUG03	3.10	11	Gladon	Littleton	05AUG06	3.15	1
Givens	Robert Sr	07AUG04	2.08	11	GLAZEBROOK				
Givens	Robert	03JUN05	3.14	11	Glazebrook James		08JUN04	4.10	1
Givens	Robert	22AUG06	3.15	11	GlazebrooksJames		29MAY05	2.13	1
Givens	Robert	16AUG07	2.15	2	Glazebrook James		18JUL06	2.16	1
Givens	Robert	04JUN08	2.11	1	GlazebrooksJames		30JUL06	2.16	1
Givens	Robert	30JUN09	1.16	1	Glazebrook James		16JUL07	2.14	1
Givens	Robert	-----11	1.30	11	GlazebrooksJohn		13AUG06	2.16	1
Givins	Robert car.	23JUN91	2.04	1	Glazebrook John		16JUL07	2.14	1
Givens	Robert Caro	25SEP92	1.05	1	Glazebrook John		27JUN08	2.11	1
Givens	Rbt Carolin	24AUG93	3.05	1	GlazebrooksJordan		29MAY05	2.13	M1
Givens	Robert Jr	09MAY94	2.06	1	Glazebrook Jordan		18JUL06	2.16	1
Givens	Robert Cl	28APR95	3.07	1	Glazebrook Jordon		16JUL07	2.14	1
Givens	Robert C	03JUN96	2.07	1	Glazebrook Julias		11JUL99	3.09	12
Givens	Robert;Car	10JUN97	1.09	1	Glazebrook Julis		10JUL00	3.12	12

surname	name	date	bk.pg	TM	surname	name	date	bk.pg	TM
Glaisbrook	Julius	31JUL01	3.13	11	Glover	Joseph Jr	14JUN02	3.10	11
GlazebrooksJulius		29JUL02	3.10	11	Glover	Joseph Sr	14JUN03	2.11	1
GlazebrooksJulias		09AUG03	2.13	1	Glover	Joseph Jr	18MAY03	2.10	12
Glazebrook	Julus	08JUN04	4.10	11	Glover	Joseph Sr	06AUG04	2.07	1
Glazerooks	Julius	21JUN05	2.13	11	Glover	Joseph Jr	06AUG04	2.08	11
GlazebrooksJulias		30JUL06	2.16	1	Glover	William	26JUN87	2.03	1
GlazebrooksWilliam		10AUG03	2.13	1	Glover	William	22NOV88	1.04	1
Glazebrook	Richard	20JUL05	2.14	1	Glover	William	04AUG89	5.05	1
GlazebrooksRichard		14AUG06	2.17	1	Glover	William	27MAR90	2.03	11
GLEESON					Glover	William	08APR91	1.03	1
Gleeson	Thomas	17JUN00	2.11	1	Glover	William	06OCT92	2.04	1
GLENN					Glover	William	03AUG93	1.04	1
Glenn	Nehemiah	18JUN06	1.09	1	Glover	William	14MAY94	1.04	1
Glenn	Nehemiah	30JUN07	1.10	1	Glover	William	16JUN95	2.05	1
Glen	Nehemiah	09JUN08	1.13	1	Glover	William	06JUN96	1.05	1
Glen	Nehemiah	29MAY09	2.11	1	Glover	William	15JUN97	3.12	11
Glenn	Nehemiah	-----11	1.28	1	Glover	William	31MAY99	1.12	11
Glens	Thomas	25MAY99	3.08	1	Glover	William	05JUL00	2.12	1
GLORE					Glover	William Jr	05JUL00	2.12	11
Glore	Lawrence	08JUL02	3.10	11	Glover	William Sr	15JUL01	2.09	1
GLOVER					Glover	William Jr	04APR01	2.09	1
Glover	Abner	11MAY95	2.06	1	Glover	William	07JUN02	3.09	1
Glover	Abner	06JUN96	1.05	1	Glover	William Jr	07JUN02	3.09	1
Glover	Abner	01JUN99	1.13	1	Glover	William Sr	14JUN03	2.11	1
Glover	Abner	01JUN99	1.40		Glover	William Jr	14JUN03	2.11	1
One lott in Stanford					Glover	William	13AUG04	2.08	1
Glover	Abner	04APR01	2.09	1	GOFF				
Glover	Abner	08JUN02	3.10		Goff	Andrew	05JUL00	3.12	1
One lott in Standford					Gough	Jesse	01DEC92	3.08	1
Glover	Abner	18MAY03	2.11		Goff	John	14MAY90	1.04	01
One lott in Standford					Gough	John	05APR91	2.04	1
Glover	Abner	06AUG04	2.08	1	Goff	John	27JUN08	2.11	1
Glover	Abner	21MAY05	2.12	1	Goff	John	10MAY09	2.11	1
Glover	Elizabeth	01JUN09	2.12	F	Goff	John	-----11	1.28	1
Glover	Elizabeth	-----11	1.28	F	Gau	William	23MAY89	6.03	1
Glover	Joab	08APR91	1.03	1	Gough	William	14MAY90	1.04	1
Glover	John	26JUN87	2.03	1	Goph	William	24JUN91	2.04	1
Glover	John	22NOV88	1.04	1	Goff	William	25SEP92	1.05	1
Glover	John	01JUN99	1.13	M1	GOGGIN				
Glover	John	29MAY01	2.09	1	Goggins	John	26JUN87	2.03	1
Glover	John	24AUG02	3.10	1	Goggins	William	26JUN87	2.03	1
Glover	John Jr	07JUN02	3.10	1	Goggins	William	29NOV88	1.04	1
Glover	John	18MAY03	2.11	1	Goggins	William	08AUG89	5.05	1
Glover	John Jr	18MAY03	2.11	1	Gogin	William	18MAY90	2.03	1
Glover	John	18JUN04	2.07	1	Goggins	William	05APR91	1.04	1
Glover	John	13AUG04	2.08	1	Goggon	William	23OCT92	2.04	1
Glover	Joseph	26JUN87	2.03	1	Gogins	William	05AUG93	1.04	1
Glover	Joseph	22NOV88	1.04	1	Gogin	William	13MAY94	1.04	1
Glover	Joseph	04AUG89	5.05	1	Goggins	William	30MAY95	2.05	1
Glover	Joseph	27MAR90	2.03	1	Gogin	William	08JUN96	1.05	1
Glover	Joseph	08APR91	1.03	11	Goggin	William	21APR97	3.13	1
Glover	Joseph	06OCT92	2.04	11	Goggin	William	28MAY99	1.12	1
Glover	Joseph	03AUG93	1.04	11	Goggin	William	20JUN00	2.11	1
Glover	Joseph	12MAY94	1.04	11	Goggin	William	30JUN01	2.09	11
Glover	Joseph	11MAY95	2.05	1	GOLDSBY				
Glover	Joseph	18MAY95	2.17		Goldsby	James	12JUN89	6.08	1
Paid tax for John Emmerson					Goldsby	James	14MAY90	1.04	1
Glover	Joseph	20JUN96	1.05	11	Goldsby	James	24JUN91	2.04	1
Glover	Joseph	15JUN97	3.12	11	Goldsby	James	06OCT92	1.05	1
Glover	Joseph	01JUN99	1.13	1	Goldsby	James	12AUG93	3.05	11
Glover	Joseph	01JUN99	1.13	11	GOLDSMITH				
Glover	Joseph	01JUN99	1.40		Goldsmith	Vincent	29JUN04	4.10	1
One lott in Stanford					Goldsmith	John	19JUL05	2.14	1
Glover	Joseph	16JUN00	2.11	11	Goldsmith	John	19AUG06	3.15	1
One lott in Standford					Goldsmith	Samuel	19JUL05	2.14	1
Glover	Joseph Jr	17JUN00	2.11	1	Goldsmith	Samuel	04AUG06	3.14	1
Glover	Joseph Jr	05JUL00	2.12	1	GOLSON				
Glover	Joseph Sr	15JUL01	2.09	1	Golson	Samuel	03MAY04	3.09	1
Glover	Joseph	04APR01	2.09	1	GOOCH				
Glover	Joseph	25JUL01	2.09	13	Gooch	Charles	25MAY99	3.08	1
One lott in Standford					Gooch	Charles	04JUL00	3.12	1
Glover	Joseph Sr	07JUN02	3.10	1	Gooch	Debner	26JUL05	1.07	1

surname	name	date	bk.pg	TM	surname	name	date	bk.pg	TM
Gooch	Dabner	16JUL06	1.09	1	Goard	Gabriel	11AUG03	3.10	1
Gooch	Dabny	08JUN07	1.10	1	Goard	Gabriel	06APR04	4.10	1
Gooch	Dabney	27APR08	1.13	1	Good	Gabriel	03JUN05	3.14	1
Gooch	Dabney	29MAY09	2.12	1	Good	Gabriel	29JUL06	3.14	1
Gooch	Dabney	-----11	1.28	1	Goode	Jenny	10JUL00	3.12	F1
Gooch	Jessey	07MAY94	3.09	12	Good	Jeney	30JUL01	3.13	F1
Gooch	Jesse	10APR95	1.06	11	Good	Ginney	29JUL02	3.10	F1
Gooch	Jessee	-----96	4.06	1	Good	Ginney	10AUG03	2.13	F
Gooch	Liner	26JUL05	1.07	11	Goode	Jinny	08JUN04	4.10	F
Gooch	Liner	16JUL06	1.09	11	Goode	John	24JUN96	2.08	1
Gooch	Lener	08JUN07	1.10	11	Good	John	06JUN97	1.09	1
Gooch	Liner	09JUN08	1.13	11	Good	John	10AUG97	1.10	1
Gooch	Linen	29MAY09	2.12	1	Good	John	28JUN99	1.13	1
Gooch	Liner	-----11	1.28	11	Good	John	10JUL99	3.09	1
Gooch	Nicholas	07JUN09	1.15	1	Good	John	22JUL00	2.12	1
Gooch	Rowland	-----11	1.28	4	Good	John	26MAY01	3.14	1
Gooch	Thomas	09JUN08	1.13	M1	Good	John	03AUG02	2.11	1
Gooch	Thomas	29MAY09	2.12	1	Good	John C.	19JUL05	2.14	1
Gooch	Thomas	-----11	1.29	1	Good	John	14AUG06	2.17	1
Gooch	Thomas W.	27JUL03	2.11	1	Good	Joseph	30JUN08	2.11	1
Goosh	William	01DEC92	3.08	1	Good	Robert	26MAY01	3.14	1
Gooch	William	13JUL96	2.08	1	Good	Robert	10AUG02	2.11	1
Gooch	William	28JUN99	3.09	1	Good	Timothy	30JUL06	2.16	1
Gooch	William	04JUL00	3.12	M1	Good	William	04APR01	2.09	1
Gooch	William	08JUL00	3.12	1	Good	William	07JUN02	3.10	1
Gooch	William	22JUL01	3.14	1	Good	William	12AUG03	2.13	1
Gooch	William	17JUN02	3.10	1	Good	William	06AUG04	3.09	1
Gooch	William	28JUL02	3.10	1	Good	William	05AUG05	3.15	1
Gooch	William	18MAY03	2.11	1	Good	William	04AUG06	3.14	1
Gooch	William	11AUG03	2.13	1	GOODNIGHT				
Gooch	William	29JUN04	4.10	1	Goodnight	Isaac	28MAY99	1.14	M1
Gooch	William	31MAY05	2.13	1	Goodknight	Isaac	21JUL02	2.11	1
Gooch	William	14JUL06	2.15	1	Goodnight	Isaac	08AUG03	3.10	1
Gooch	William	16JUL06	1.10	1	Goodnight	Isaac	09JUL04	2.07	1
Gooch	William	08JUN07	1.10	1	Goodnight	Isaac	03JUN05	3.13	1
Gooch	William	25JUL07	2.14	1	Goodnight	Isaac	22AUG06	3.15	1
Gooch	William	-----08	2.12	1	Goodnight	Isaac	16JUL07	2.14	1
Gooch	William	-----08	2.25		Goodnight	Jacob	30MAY89	6.03	1
Paid tax for Joel Atkenson					Goodnight	Jacob	05APR90	1.04	1
Gooch	William D.	09JUN08	1.13	1	Goodnight	Jacob	09JUN91	2.04	1
Gooch	William	29MAY09	2.12	1	Goodnight	Jacob	08OCT92	1.05	1
Gooch	William	07JUN09	1.15	1	Goodnight	Jacob	16AUG93	3.05	1
Gooch	William	-----11	1.31	1	Goodnight	Jacob	23APR94	2.05	1
Gooch	William	-----11	1.28	1	Goodnight	Jacob	16JUN95	2.05	1
GOOD					Goodnite	Jacob	30JUN96	1.05	1
Good	Benjamin	04AUG03	2.12	1	Goodnight	Jacob	12JUN97	3.12	1
Good	Benjamin Sr	13JUN04	4.10	1	Goodnight	Jacob	01JUN99	1.12	1
Good	Benjamin	12JUN04	4.10	1	Goodnight	Jacob	01AUG00	2.12	1
Good	Benjamin	17JUN05	2.13	1	Goodnight	Jacob	30JUL01	2.10	1
Good	Benjamin	25JUL08	2.11	11	Goodknight	Jacob	14JUN02	2.11	1
Good	Benjamin	16AUG09	1.16	1	Goodnight	Jacob	12JUL03	3.10	1
Goode	Benjamin	-----11	1.29	1	Goodnight	Jacob	18JUN04	2.07	1
Good	Campbell	28MAY99	1.14	11	Goodnight	Jacob	03JUN05	3.13	1
Good	Camill	24MAY00	2.10	2	Goodnight	Jacob	17JUL06	3.14	1
Good	Campbell	27JUN01	2.09	1	Goodnight	Jacob	16JUL07	2.13	1
Good	Campbell	07JUN02	3.10	1	Goodnight	Jacob	04JUN08	2.11	1
Good	Campbell	12AUG03	2.13	1	Goodnight	Jacob	-----11	1.29	1
Good	Campbell	06AUG04	3.09	1	GOODWIN				
Good	Campbell	05AUG05	3.15	1	Gooding	Alexander	18MAY97	3.12	1
Good	Campbell	04AUG06	3.14	1	Gooden	Alexander	21JUN99	2.08	1
Goode	Fleming	12JUL96	2.08	1	Goodwin	John	10APR95	1.06	M1
Good	Flemin	06JUN97	1.09	1	Gooding	Thomas	18MAY97	3.12	11
Good	Flemmin	25JUN99	3.08	1	Gooden	Thomas	19JUN99	2.07	11
Good	Fleming	24JUL00	2.12	1	GORDON				
Good	Flammen	27MAY01	3.14	1	Gorden	John	19JUN99	2.08	1
Good	Fleming	03AUG02	2.11	1	Gordon	Rachel	10OCT92	2.04	F
Good	Fleming	06AUG03	2.13	1	GOSS				
Goode	Flemin	23MAY04	4.10	1	Goss	Kinshon	03JUN05	3.13	1
Goard	Gabriel	28MAY99	1.12	1	Goss	Kinchen	22AUG06	3.15	1
Goard	Gabriel	24MAY00	2.10	1	Goss	Kinchen	25JUL07	2.14	1
Good	Gabriel	30JUN01	2.09	11	GOSSETT				
Goard	Gabriel	07JUN02	3.10	1	Gossett	Reuben	-----11	1.28	1

surname	name	date	bk.pg	TM	surname	name	date	bk.pg	TM
Gosset	Stanley	06JUN09	2.12	1	Greeves	James	19MAY97	3.12	1
Gossett	Stanley	-----11	1.28	1	Graves	James	12JUN99	2.07	11
GOTNER					Graves	James	23JUL00	1.05	11
Gotner	Frederick	18JUL87	3.04	1	Graves	James	13JUN01	1.06	11
GOWEN					Graves	James	22JUN02	1.08	11
Gowin	Allin	10APR95	1.07	1	Graves	James	13JUN03	1.09	11
Goan	Charles	11MAR97	2.02	1	Graves	James	03AUG04	1.07	1
Goan	Charles	18MAY99	2.07	1	Graves	James	30JUL05	1.08	1
Goan	Charles	16JUN00	1.05	1	Graves	James	31JUL06	1.10	1
Goan	Claben	21JUN99	2.08	1	Graves	James	07MAY07	1.09	1
Gowen	David	01JUL03	2.11	1	Graves	James	09JUN08	1.13	1
Gowen	Gilbert	01JUL03	2.11	1	Graves	James	15JUN09	2.12	1
Goan	Isach	21JUN99	2.08	1	Graves	Joseph	31JUL06	1.10	1
Gowen	Martin	01JUL03	2.11	1	Graves	Joseph	08MAY07	1.09	1
Goin	William	14JUN96	1.05	1	Graves	Joseph	18APR08	1.12	1
Goin	William	31MAY99	1.14	1	Graves	Lewis	21APR08	1.12	11
Goan	William	29JUL01	3.13		Graves	Martin	21APR08	1.12	1
A black freeman					Graves	Robert	17JUL09	2.12	1
Goan	William	10JUN02	2.10		Graves	Robert	24AUG09	2.12	1
A free black man					Graves	William	17SEP91	3.06	1
Goin	William	06APR04	4.10	1	Graves	William	07DEC92	3.08	1
GRAHAM					Graves	William	23APR94	3.09	1
Greham	Andrew	13AUG02	2.11	1	Graves	William	10APR95	1.07	1
Graham	Andrew	21JUN03	3.10	1	Graves	William	-----96	4.06	1
Graham	Andrew	06AUG04	3.09	1	Graves	William	11MAR97	2.02	1
Graham	Andrew	14AUG05	3.15	1	Graves	William	24MAY99	2.07	1
Greham	Andrew	22AUG06	3.15	1	Graves	William	17JUN00	1.05	1
Grayham	James	29JUN87	1.02	1	Graves	William	03JUN01	1.06	1
Graham	James	16MAY89	6.03	1	Graves	William	02AUG04	1.07	1
Grayham	James	02APR90	1.04	1	Graves	William	30JUL05	1.08	1
Graham	James	14MAY91	2.04	1	Graves	William	31JUL06	1.10	1
Graham	James	10APR95	1.06	1	Graves	William	07MAY07	1.09	1
Graham	James	29JUN99	1.12	11	Graves	William O.	07MAY94	3.09	1
Graham	James	26JUN00	2.11	1	Graves	Williamson	09JUN08	1.13	1
Graham	James	27MAY01	3.14	2	GRAY				
Greham	James	13AUG02	2.11	1	Gray	Hugh	23OCT92	2.04	1
Graham	James	09JUN03	3.09	11	Gray	Hugh	30AUG93	1.04	1
Graham	James	06AUG04	3.09	11	Gray	Hugh	31MAY94	1.04	1
Graham	James	14AUG05	3.15	11	Gray	Hugh	-----95	2.18	
Greham	James	22AUG06	3.15	11	one lot in Stanford				
Graham	John	18JUL87	3.04	1	Gray	Hugh	09MAY95	2.05	1
Graham	John	27JUN89	2.05	1	Gray	Hugh	07JUN96	1.05	1
Graham	John	13SEP91	3.06	1	Grey	Hugh	24MAY99	1.13	1
Graham	John	23APR94	3.09	1	Gray	Hugh	14JUN00	2.11	11
Graham	John	10APR95	1.07	1	Gray	Hugh	04JUN01	2.09	11
Graham	John	-----96	4.07	1	Gray	Hugh	03JUN02	3.09	
Grayham	John	-----08	2.12	1	Half-lott in Standford				
Graham	Luke	-----96	4.07	1	Gray	Hugh	18MAY03	2.10	1
Graham	Thomas	23APR94	3.09	1	Gray	Hugh	13MAY05	2.12	1
Graham	Thomas	10APR95	1.07	1	Gray	Hugh	07APR06	2.15	
Graham	Thomas	-----96	4.07	1	1/2 Lott in Standford				
Graham	William	23APR94	3.09	1	Gray	Hugh	30JUN07	1.10	1
Graham	William	-----08	2.12	1	Gray	Hugh	06JUN08	1.13	1
Grayham	William	21JUN09	1.15		Gray	Hugh	01JUL09	2.15	1
One riding carriage four wheels					Gray	Hugh	-----11	1.30	1
Graham	William	-----11	1.31	1	Gray	James	10APR95	1.06	1
GRAVEL					Gray	Robert	19MAY89	6.03	1
Gravell	John	13JUL97	1.10	1	Gray	Robert	09AUG91	2.04	1
Greyville	John	06JUN99	1.12	1	Gray	Robert	13JUN99	2.07	1
Gravel	John	25JUN00	3.12	1	Gray	Thomas	19JUN01	3.13	1
Grayville	John	07MAY01	3.12	1	Gray	Thomas	26JUL02	3.10	1
GRAVES					Gray	Thomas	08AUG03	2.13	1
Graves	Benjamin	08AUG89	5.05	1	Gray	Thomas	25AUG04	3.09	1
Graves	Benjamin	14APR91	1.03	1	Gray	Thomas	17JUN05	2.13	1
Graves	Benjamin	11OCT92	2.04	1	GREEN				
Graves	James	30MAR91	1.03	1	Green	Robert	06AUG89	2.05	1
Graves	James	30MAR91	1.03	1	Green	Willis	27SEP87	1.02	11
Graves	James	12OCT92	2.04	1	Green	Willis	-----89	6.03	1
Graves	James	14AUG93	1.04	1	Green	Willis	12JUN89	6.09	1
Graves	James	26MAY94	1.04	1	Green	Willis	14AUG90	1.05	1
Graves	James	29MAY95	2.06	1	Green	Willis	23JUN91	2.04	1
Graves	James	01JUL96	1.05	1	Green	Willis	23JUN91	2.06	

surname	name	date	bk.pg	TM	surname	name	date	bk.pg	TM
Matthew McCay listed with him					Grisom	Joab	02JUN95	2.05	11
Green	Willis	14SEP92	1.05	1	Grisom	Job	16JUN96	1.05	11
Green	Willis	14AUG93	1.04	1	Grerham	Job	11APR97	3.12	11
Green	Willis	-----94	1.12	1	Gresham	Job	14MAY99	1.13	12
Green	Willis	13MAY94	1.04	2	Grisham	Job	03JUN00	2.11	12
Green	Willis	03APR95	3.07	11	Grisham	Joab	22JUL01	2.09	11
Green	Willis	13JUL96	2.08	1	Grissham	Joabe	16JUN02	1.08	1
Green	Willis	23MAY97	1.28	1	Grissham	Job	16JUN02	1.08	
Green	Willis	08AUG97	1.10	0	Paid tax for Thomas Griham				
Green	Willis	-----99	3.23	1	Grisham	Job	05JUL03	1.09	11
Green	Willis	08JUL00	3.34	1	Gresham	Job	05JUL03	1.09	
Green	Willis	13JUL01	3.13	21	Paid tax for Thomas Gresham				
Green	Willis	21AUG02	3.11	21	Grisham	Job Jr	05JUL03	1.09	1
Green	Willis	27JUL03	2.12	22	Gresham	Job	20JUN04	1.07	11
Green	Willis	07AUG04	4.11	11	Gresham	Job	19JUN05	1.07	11
Green	Willis	20JUL05	2.14	1	Gresham	Job	21JUN06	1.09	12
Green	Willis	18JUL06	2.15	11	Paid tax for Thomas Gresham				
Green	Willis	25JUL07	2.15	11	Gresham	Job	20JUN07	1.09	11
Green	Willis	-----08	2.12	2	Gresham	Job	06JUN08	1.13	11
Green	Willis	21AUG09	1.16	2	Paid tax for Moses Gresham				
Green	Willis	-----11	1.27	2	Grisham	Job	15AUG09	2.12	1
GREENLEE					Grisham	John	30JUL00	2.12	1
Greenlee	James	24MAY00	2.10	1	Gresham	John	20JUN07	1.09	1
Greenlee	John	09MAY95	2.17	1	Greshom	John	-----08	2.12	1
Greenlee	John	14JUN00	2.11	1	Gresham	John	23APR08	1.13	1
Greenlee	John	26MAY01	2.09	1	Gresham	John	21JUN09	1.15	1
One lott in South Frankfort					Grisham	John	15AUG09	2.12	1
Greenlee	John	01JUL05	3.14	1	Gresham	John	-----11	1.29	1
Greenlee	John	07APR06	2.15		Gresham	John	-----11	1.31	1
One lott in Frankford					Gresham	Joseph	-----11	1.29	3
Greenlee	John	07APR06	2.15		Graceham	Laurance	21JUN87	2.03	1
One lott in Standford					Grissum	Laurence	22NOV88	1.03	1
Greenlee	Mary	09MAY95	2.17	F	Grissum	Laurence	06AUG89	5.05	1
Greenlee	Mary	26MAY01	2.09	F	Grisson	Lawrence	29MAR90	2.03	1
Greenlee	Samuel	03AUG93	1.04	1	Gresham	Lawrence	05APR91	1.04	1
GREENUP					Grissom	Laranie	03OCT92	2.03	1
Greenup	Christopher	14AUG93	1.04	0	Grison	Larrance	26AUG93	1.04	1
GREENWOOD					Grissom	Larrance	17MAY94	1.12	1
Greenwood	Abraham	-----11	1.29	1	Grisom	Larrance	17MAY94	1.04	11
Greenwood	Bartley	11JUN02	1.08	1	Grisom	Laurance	11MAY95	2.05	11
Greenwood	Bartley	05JUL03	1.09	1	Gresham	Moses	06JUN08	1.13	1
Greenwood	Bartlett	02AUG04	2.07	1	Tax pd by Job Gresham				
Greenwood	Bartley	15JUN05	1.07	1	Grisham	Phillip	05JUL03	1.09	1
Greenwood	Bartley	19JUN06	1.09	11	Gresham	Philip	20JUN04	1.07	1
Greenwood	Bartlett	08JUN07	1.10	11	Gresham	Philip	19JUN05	1.07	1
Greenwood	Bartlet	09JUN08	1.14	1	Gresham	Philip	20JUN06	1.09	1
Greenwood	Bartlett	07JUN09	1.14	1	Gresham	Phillip	20JUN07	1.09	1
Greenwood	Bartlee	-----11	1.31	1	Gresham	Phillip	06JUN08	1.13	1
Greenwood	Joseph	01JUL99	1.12	1	Grisham	Philip	05JUL09	2.12	1
Greenwood	Joseph	27JUN00	2.11	1	Gresham	Phillip	-----11	1.29	1
Greenwood	Joseph	13JUL01	3.14	11	Grisham	Thomas	22JUL01	2.09	1
Greenwood	Joseph	13AUG02	2.12	1	Griham	Thomas	16JUN02	1.08	0
Greenwood	Joseph	11JUN03	3.09	1	Tax pd by Jaobe Grissham				
Greenwoode	William	15JUN03	3.09	M1	Grisham	Thomas	05JUL03	1.09	0
Greenwoode	William	17JUL06	2.15	M1	Gresham	Thomas	05JUL03	1.09	
Greenwood	William	25JUL07	2.14	1	Tax pd by Job Gresham				
Greenwood	William	-----08	2.12	1	Gresham	Thomas	21JUN06	1.09	1
GREER					Tax pd by Job Gresham				
Gicor	Solomon	01JUN96	1.05	1	Gresham	Thomas	20JUN07	1.09	1
Greeham	Solamon	22APR97	3.13	1	Grisham	Thomas	15AUG09	2.12	1
Greer	Solomon	15JUL99	3.09	1	Gresham	T.(heirs)	-----11	1.29	D
GREGORY					Grisom	Uriah	02JUN95	2.05	1
Gregory	Jonathan	16AUG93	3.05	1	Grissom	Airiah	-----96	4.07	1
Gregory	Smith	31MAY00	2.11	1	Grisom	Uriah	11MAR97	2.02	1
Gregory	Smith	22JUL01	2.09	1	Grissom	Uriah	18JUN99	2.07	1
GRESHAM					GRIFFIN				
Grissom	Jobe	15NOV88	1.03	1	Griffin	James	10MAY97	3.11	1
Grissum	Jobe	07AUG89	5.05	1	Griffin	James	14MAY99	1.13	1
Grissom	Job	05OCT92	2.03	11	Griffin	James	18JUN00	2.11	1
Grisom	Job	15AUG93	1.04	1	Griffin	John	04JUN95	2.05	1
Grissom	Job	26MAY94	1.11	1	Griffin	John	30JUN96	1.05	1
Grisom	Job	26MAY94	1.04	11	Griffin	John	10MAY97	3.11	1

surname	name	date	bk.pg	TM	surname	name	date	bk.pg	TM
Griffon	John	21JUN99	2.07	1	Hackney	Samuel	08MAY97	3.14	1
Griffin	Solaman	06MAY07	1.09	1	HADDON				
Griffin	Solaman	09JUN08	1.13	1	Haddon	Samuel	05JUL87	3.05	1
Griffin	Solomon	14JUN09	2.12	1	Haddon	William	05JUL87	3.05	1
Griffin	William	08JUL99	3.09	1	HAGEN				
Griffin	William	04JUL00	3.12	1	Hagen	Arthur	19JUN05	3.17	21
Griffen	William	07MAY01	3.12	1	HAGGARD				
GRIGGS					Haggard	Benjamin	12JUN87	2.03	1
Grigg	Wright	16JUL07	2.14	1	Haggard	Benjamin	12AUG89	2.06	1
Griggs	Right	13MAY09	1.14	1	Haggart	Benjamin	13OCT92	2.04	1
GRIMES					Hagard	Benjamin	30JUN96	1.06	1
Grimes	Daniel	27APR08	1.13	1	Hagart	Bengamin	13APR97	3.13	1
Grimes	Daniel	-----11	1.28	1	Haggard	Benjamin	14MAY99	2.09	1
Grimes	Enock	15JUN05	1.07	1	Haggard	Benjamin	25JUL00	1.06	1
Grimes	Enoch	19JUN06	1.09	1	Haggard	Benjamin	26JUN01	1.08	1
Graham	Enoch	08JUN07	1.10	1	Haggard	Benjamin	23JUN02	1.11	1
Grimes	George	27APR08	1.13	M1	Haggard	Benjamin	23JUN03	1.10	11
Grimes	John	05DEC92	3.08	1	Haggard	Benjamin	03AUG04	1.09	11
Grimes	Margot	25MAY07	1.09	F	Haggard	Benjamin	22JUL05	1.09	11
Grimes	Margaret	27APR08	1.13	F	Haggard	Benjamin	02AUG06	1.12	11
Grimes	Peggy	13MAY09	2.11	F	Haggard	Benjamin	27MAY07	1.11	1
GRINDSTAFF					Haggard	Benjamin	01JUL09	2.14	1
Grindstaff	Jacob	21JUN99	2.08	1	Hagard	Henry	30JUN96	1.06	1
GROVE					Hagart	Henry	13APR97	3.13	1
Grove	Henson	05JUN05	1.07	1	Haggard	Henry	14MAY99	2.09	1
GROVER					Haggard	Henry	25JUL00	1.06	1
Glover	Benjamin	29MAY05	2.13	1	Haggard	Henry	26JUN01	1.08	1
GRUBB					Haggard	Henry	23JUN02	1.11	1
Grubb	Dabney	-----11	1.29	1	Haggard	Henry	23JUN03	1.10	1
GRUNTER					Haggard	Henry	03AUG04	1.09	1
Grunter	Samuel	23OCT92	2.04	1	Haggard	Henry	31JUL05	1.09	1
GUINN					Haggard	Henry	02AUG06	1.12	1
Guin	Mathew	01DEC88	1.04	1	Haggard	Henry	25MAY07	1.11	1
Guinn	Ruthey	27JUN08	2.11	F	Haggard	Henry	22APR08	1.14	1
Guinn	Ruthy	13MAY09	1.14	F	Haggard	Henry	01JUL09	2.15	1
GUMM					Haggard	John	27MAY07	1.11	1
Gum	Isaac	10JUL09	1.16		Haggard	John	01JUL09	2.14	1
A free negro					Haggard	William	05JUL87	3.05	11
Gum	Norten	13AUG02	2.12	1	HAGWOOD				
Gumm	Norton	15JUL03	3.10	1	Hagwood	Josiah	15JUN03	1.10	1
GUNN					HALE				
Gunn	John	30JUN03	1.09	1	Hales	James	18MAY97	3.15	1
GUTHRIE					Hail	James	18MAY99	2.09	1
Guthrie	Daniel	31JUL01	2.10	1	Haild	James	24MAY99	1.15	1
Guthrey	Daniel	21JUL02	2.11	1	HALEY				
Guthrie	Daniel	11JUL03	3.10	1	Haley	Barnaba	05MAY07	1.10	11
Guttery	Daniel	05JUN04	4.10	1	Haley	Bartlett	07JUN09	1.17	1
Guthrie	Daniel	03JUN05	3.14	1	Hailey	Bartlett	-----11	1.35	1
Guthrie	Daniel	16JUL06	3.13	1	Haly	Francis	14MAY90	1.05	1
Guthrie	Daniel	13JUL07	2.13	1	Haley	Silas	07JUN09	1.17	1
Guthrie	Daniel	30MAY08	2.10	1	Hailey	Silas	-----11	1.35	1
Gutherie	Daniel	30JUN09	1.16	1	HALL				
Guthrie	Daniel	21AUG09	1.16		Hall	Andrew	04JUN00	2.12	1
Executor for Isaac Blain					Hall	Andrew	04JUN01	2.11	1
Guthrie	Daniel	-----11	1.30		Hall	Andrew	12JUL02	2.13	1
Exec for Isaac Blaine deceased					Hall	Andrew	17JUN03	3.11	1
Guthrey	Elizabeth	19MAY89	6.03	F	Hall	Andrew	01AUG04	2.09	1
William Burns listed with her					Hall	Andrew	08JUL05	3.18	1
Guthrey	Robert	13MAY89	6.03	1	Hall	Andrew	13JUL07	2.14	1
Guthrey	Robert	07AUG90	1.11	1	Hall	Andrew	22APR08	1.14	1
Gutrey	William	--JUN90	2.03	1	Hall	Andrew	01JUN09	2.13	1
Guthrie	William	10JUN02	2.10	1	Hall	Andrew	-----11	1.37	1
Guthrie	William	05AUG03	3.10	1	Hall	George	08JUL05	3.17	M1
Gutry	William	06APR04	4.10	1	Hall	George	05JUN09	1.17	1
Guthrie	William	03JUN05	3.14	1	Hall	Henry	21MAY95	2.06	1
Guthrie	William	29JUL06	3.14	1	Hall	Henry	15MAY97	1.12	1
HACKLEY					Hall	James	14NOV88	1.04	1
Hackley	Joseph	18AUG09	2.15	1	Hall	James	-----96	4.08	1
Hackley	Joseph	-----11	1.36	2	Hall	James	18MAY99	1.15	1
Hackley	Richard	-----11	1.36	1	Hall	James	04JUN01	2.11	1
HACKNEY					Hall	James	27MAY02	2.12	1
Hackney	Samuel	13JUN96	1.07	1	Hall	James	11JUL03	2.15	1

surname	name	date	bk.pg	TM	surname	name	date	bk.pg	TM
Hall	James	23JUL04	1.08	1	Executor for John Barnett				
Hall	James	03MAY05	2.15	1	Hall	Joseph	-----11	1.37	12
Hall	James	28JUL06	2.19	1	Pd tax for John Barnett (Deceased				
Hall	James	15JUL07	2.17	1	Hall	Leonard	21JUL87	3.05	1
Hall	James	02JUN08	1.15	1	Hall	Leonard	25JUL89	2.06	1
Hall	James	15AUG09	2.15	1	Hall	Leonard	14SEP91	3.08	1
Hall	James	-----11	1.34	1	Hall	Leanord	29NOV92	3.09	1
Hall	John	20JUN87	2.04	11	Hall	Leonard Sr	23APR94	3.09	1
Hall	John	06NOV88	1.04	11	Hall	Leonard Jr	24APR94	3.10	1
Hall	John	16JUN89	5.06	11	Hall	Leonard Sr	12MAY95	1.07	1
Hall	John	19MAY90	2.04	11	Hall	Leonard Jr	25MAR95	1.07	1
Hall	John/Wm	29OCT91	1.04	21	Hall	Levi	19JUL05	2.16	1
Hall	John Sr	16OCT92	2.04	1	Hall	Mahlon	12MAY95	1.07	1
Hall	John	04DEC92	3.08	1	Hall	Michael	16JUL03	1.12	1
Hall	John	12AUG93	1.04	1	Hall	Miles	02JUN02	1.08	1
Hall	John	21MAR94	1.04	1	Hall	Nathaniel	30JUN03	1.12	1
Hall	John	20MAY94	3.11	1	Hall	Nathaniel	01AUG04	2.09	1
Hall	John	25MAR95	1.07	1	Hall	Nathaniel	16AUG05	3.19	1
Hall	John	01JUN95	2.07	1	Hall	Nathaniel	28MAY06	3.15	1
Hall	John	-----96	4.07	11	Hall	Nathaniel	13JUL07	2.16	1
Hall	John	20JUN96	1.06	1	Hall	Nathaniel	18JUL08	2.14	1
Hall	John	20JUN96	1.06	1	Hall	Nathaniel	05JUN09	1.17	1
Hall	John	10MAY97	3.14	1	Hall	Nathaniel	-----11	1.37	1
Hall	John	10MAY97	3.14	1	Hall	Randolph	-----96	4.07	1
Hall	John	18MAY99	1.15	1	Hall	Robert	11JUN99	1.14	1
Hall	John	23JUN00	2.13	1	Hall	Thomas	21APR96	2.08	1
Hall	John	28MAY01	2.11	1	Hall	Thomas	16MAY97	1.11	1
Hall	John	27MAY02	2.12	1	Hall	William	14JUN87	2.04	1
Hall	John	23AUG02	2.15	11	Hall	William	05NOV88	1.04	1
Hall	John Sr	11JUL03	3.11	1	Hall	William	29OCT91	1.04	1
Hall	John	28MAY03	2.14	1	Hall	William	02NOV92	2.04	1
Hall	John	23JUL04	1.08	1	Hall	William	12AUG93	1.04	1
Hall	John Jr	01AUG04	2.09	1	Hall	William	01MAY95	2.06	1
Hall	John	01AUG04	2.09	1	Hall	William	18JUN96	1.06	1
Hall	John	03MAY05	2.15	1	Hall	William	10MAY97	3.14	1
Hall	John	08JUL05	3.18	1	Hall	William	16AUG05	3.19	1
Hall	John	28JUL06	2.18	1	HAM				
Hall	John	15JUL07	2.17	1	Ham	Drury	24JUN00	2.13	1
Hall	John	02JUN08	1.15	1	Ham	Drury	03JUN01	2.11	1
Hall	John	23MAY09	2.13	1	Ham	Drury	30JUN03	1.11	1
Hall	John	15AUG09	2.15	1	Ham	Drury	07JUL03	1.11	1
Hall	John	-----11	1.40	1	Ham	Drurey	09JUL04	2.08	11
Hall	John	-----11	1.34	1	Ham	Drury	26JUL05	1.09	1
Hall	Joseph	26JUN87	2.04	1	Ham	Drury	10JUL06	1.11	1
Hall	Joseph	23JUN89	5.06	1	Ham	Drury	01JUL07	1.12	1
Hall	Joseph	19MAY90	2.03	1	Ham	Drury	02JUN08	1.16	1
Hall	Joseph	13APR91	1.04	1	Ham	Drury	13MAY09	2.12	1
Hall	Joseph	16OCT92	2.04	1	Ham	Drury	-----11	1.38	1
Hall	Joseph	10AUG93	1.04	1	HAMILTON				
Hall	Joseph	21MAY94	1.04	1	Hamilton	Alexander	08APR91	1.04	1
Hall	Joseph	06JUN95	2.07	1	Hammelton	Charles	25JUN03	3.11	1
Hall	Joseph	27JUN96	1.06	1	Hamilton	Charles	05AUG05	3.18	1
Hall	Joseph	10MAY97	3.14	1	Hamelton	Charles	19AUG06	3.17	1
Hall	Joseph	18MAY99	1.15	1	Hamilton	James	12JUN87	2.03	1
Hall	Joseph	04JUN00	2.12	1	Hambleton	James	26JUN89	6.04	1
Hall	Joseph	04JUN01	2.11	1	Hambleton	James	23JUN90	1.05	1
Hall	Joseph	14JUN02	2.13	1	Hambleton	James	01NOV92	2.04	1
Hall	Joseph	11JUL03	3.12	1	Hamilton	James	14AUG93	1.05	1
Hall	Joseph	13AUG04	2.10	1	Hamilton	James	27AUG93	3.06	1
Hall	Joseph	17JUN05	3.17	11	Hamilton	James	30MAY94	1.05	1
Paid tax for John(heirs)Barnett					Hamilton	James	03JUN95	2.07	1
Hall	Joseph	23AUG06	3.18	11	Hamelton	James	30JUN96	1.06	1
Hall	Joseph	26AUG06	3.18		Hamilton	James	13APR97	3.13	1
Paid tax for John(heirs)Barnett					Hamilton	James	13JUN06	1.10	1
Hall	Joseph	22JUN07	2.16	12	Hamilton	James	10AUG08	1.17	1
Paid Tax for John Barnett					Hamilton	John	12JUN87	2.03	1
Hall	Joseph	18JUL08	2.14	12	Hambleton	John	26JUN87	3.04	1
Paid tax for John Barnett					Hamilton	John	01NOV88	1.04	1
Hall	Joseph	05JUN09	1.17	11	Hambleton	John	01JUL89	2.06	1
Hall	Joseph	23MAY09	2.13		Hamilton	John	18MAY90	2.03	1
Exempt					Hamelton	John	19APR91	3.06	1
Hall	Joseph	05JUN09	1.17		Hamhilton	John	05DEC92	3.09	1

surname	name	date	bk.pg	TM	surname	name	date	bk.pg	TM
Hambleton	John	05MAY94	3.10	1	Hammond	John	23MAY99	1.15	11
Hambleton	John	25MAR95	1.07	1	Hammet	John	29MAY00	2.12	11
Hambleton	John	-----96	4.07	1	Hammond	John	29MAY01	2.11	11
Hamilton	John	24MAY99	3.10	1	Hammon	John	10JUN02	1.09	1
Hamilton	John	11JUL00	3.15	11	Hammon	John	18JUL03	1.12	11
Hambleton	John	30JUL01	3.15	1	Hammond	John	25JUN04	1.08	11
Hamelton	John	09JUN02	2.13	11	Hammond	John	20JUN05	1.09	11
Hammelton	John	05AUG03	3.13	11	Hammond	John	23JUN06	1.11	11
Hammilton	John	06APR04	4.11	11	Hammond	John	09JUN07	1.11	11
Hambleton	John	19JUN05	3.17	1	Hammons	John	02JUN08	1.15	1
Hamilton	John	29JUL06	3.17	1	Hammonds	John	28JUN09	2.14	1
Hamilton	Thomas	26JUN87	2.04	11	Hammon	John	-----11	1.37	11
Hamelton	Thomas	18NOV88	1.04	11	Hammons	Thomas	02JUN08	1.15	1
Hamilton	Thomas	04AUG89	5.06	12	Hammonds	Thomas	28JUN09	2.14	1
Hamilton	Thomas	18MAY90	2.03	11	Hammons	Thomas	-----11	1.38	1
Hambleton	Thomas	03NOV92	2.04	1	HAMPTON				
Hamilton	Thomas	06AUG93	1.05	11	Hampton	George	09JUL01	3.15	1
Hamilton	Thomas	15MAY94	1.04	11	Hampton	George	31JUL05	2.17	1
Hammilton	Thomas	22MAY95	2.06	11	Hampton	George	15JUL06	2.18	1
Hamilton	Thomas	22MAY95	2.18	1	Hampton	George	15JUL07	2.18	1
Hamilton	Thomas	10JUN96	1.06	11	Hampton	George	10AUG08	1.17	1
Hamilton	Thomas	20APR97	3.14	11	Hampton	George	09JUN09	1.18	1
Hambleton	Thomas	19JUN05	3.17	1	Hampton	George	-----11	1.32	1
Hambleton	William	26JUN87	3.04	1	Hampton	James	22AUG06	3.17	1
Hambleton	William	27JUN89	2.06	11	Hampton	Joal	22AUG06	3.17	11
Hamelton	William	13SEP91	3.07	1	Hampton	Lebarn	23AUG06	3.18	1
Hamhilton	William	05DEC92	3.09	1	Hampton	Ruben	05AUG05	3.18	0
Hambleton	William	05MAY94	3.09	1	HANCOCK				
Hambleton	William	12MAY95	1.08	1	Hancock	Sarah	26JUL03	2.15	F
Hambleton	William	-----96	4.08	2	HANDSMORE				
Hambleton	William	16MAR97	2.02	1	Handsmore	William	07APR95	3.08	1
Hamilton	William	10MAY99	2.09	1	HANLEN				
Hamilton	William	28JUL00	1.06	1	Handlin	Thomas	16AUG02	3.14	1
Paid tax for Mary Baughman					Handlin	Thomas	26JUL03	2.16	1
Hamilton	William	16JUN01	1.08	1	Hanlen	Thomas	25JUL04	4.12	1
Paid Tax for Mary Baughman					Handlin	Thomas	22JUL05	2.16	1
Hamilton	William	16JUL02	1.11	1	Handlin	Thomas	13AUG06	2.19	1
Paid tax for Mary Baughman					HANLEY				
Hamilton	William	11JUN03	1.09	1	Hanley	Joel	09MAY95	2.07	11
Hamilton	William	14JUN04	1.07	1	HANNA				
Hamilton	William	05JUN05	1.08	12	Hannah	Alexander	26JUN87	2.04	1
Hamilton	William	13JUN06	1.10	12	Hannah	Alexander	30OCT88	1.04	1
Hamilton	William	06JUL07	1.12	11	Hannah	Alexander	22JUN89	5.06	11
Hamilton	William	02JUN08	1.15	12	Hanah	Elex.	18MAY90	2.03	12
Hamelton	William	24MAY09	2.13	1	Hanor	Christopher	28NOV88	1.05	11
Hamilton	William Sr	-----11	1.39	1	Haner	Christopher	05AUG89	5.06	11
Hamilton	William Jr	-----11	1.39	1	Heynor	Christopher	30MAY90	2.03	1
HAMMER					Heanor	Christopher	05APR91	1.04	1
Hammer	Frederick	05AUG05	2.17	M1	Henor	Christopher	25OCT92	2.04	1
Hamer	George	15JUN96	1.06	1	Henner	Christopher	05AUG93	1.05	1
Hammar	George	17MAY99	1.15	1	Hener	Christopher	13MAY94	1.05	1
Hammer	George	30MAY00	2.12	1	Henor	Christopher	20MAY95	2.06	1
Hammer	George	22JUL01	2.12	1	Henor	Christopher	08JUN96	1.06	1
Hammer	George	16JUN02	1.09	1	Haner	Christopher	21APR97	3.16	1
Hammer	George	05JUL03	1.12	11	Haner	Christopher	29MAY99	1.14	1
Hammer	George	19JUN05	1.09	11	Haynor	Christopher	17JUL00	2.14	1
HAMMOND					Haynor	Christopher	25MAY01	2.10	1
Hammond	Airs	14SEP93	3.05	1	Haynor	Christopher	18AUG02	3.14	1
Hammons	Christopher	11JUN07	2.16	1	Haynor	Christopher	21JUN03	2.14	1
Hammons	Christopher	-----08	2.13	1	Haner	Christopher	25JUL04	1.08	1
Hammon	George	07APR97	3.13	1	Haynor	Christopher	25JUL05	2.17	1
Hammon	George	17JUN02	1.09	1	Haynor	Christopher	08JUL06	2.18	1
Hammon	George	18JUL03	1.12	1	Hener	Christopher	15JUL07	2.18	1
Hammond	George	25JUN04	1.08	1	Haner	Christopher	04MAY08	1.17	1
Hamond	George	26JUN04	1.08	11	Hannah	Ichabad	24MAY96	2.08	1
Hammond	George	20JUN05	1.09	1	Hannah	Isabella	30MAR91	1.04	F
Hammond	George	23JUN06	1.11	1	Hannah	John	24JUN00	3.13	1
Hammond	George	16AUG07	2.19	1	Hannah	John	01MAY01	3.14	1
Hammons	George	02JUN08	1.15	1	Hanna	William	03JUN00	2.12	1
Hammons	George	05JUN09	1.17	1	Hanna	William	07JUN02	3.12	1
Hammon	George	-----11	1.36	1	Hanna	William	01JUN03	2.14	11
Hammond	Huston	14SEP93	3.05	1	Hannah	William	16AUG04	2.10	11

surname	name	date	bk.pg	TM	surname	name	date	bk.pg	TM
Hanna	William	03AUG05	2.17	1	Hardwick	Carey	19JUL06	3.16	11
Hanna	William	09AUG06	2.19	1	Hardedge	Will	02OCT87	1.03	1
Hannah	William	15JUL07	2.17	2	Hardwick	William	26JUN89	6.04	1
Hannah	William	-----08	2.13	11	Hardwick	William	23JUN90	1.05	1
Henen	William	02JUN08	1.15	1	Hardwich	William	03NOV92	1.06	1
Hannah	William	11MAY09	1.17	1	Hardwich	William	27AUG93	3.06	1
Hanner	William	-----11	1.35	2	Harding	William	02MAY95	3.08	1
HANSBROUGH					Hardry	William	24JUN96	2.08	2
Hansbrough	John	18MAY91	2.04	1	Hardridge	William	10MAY97	1.11	1
HansboroughJohn		10OCT92	1.06	1	Hardridge	William	10JUL99	3.11	2
Hansbrough	John	19AUG93	3.05	1	Hardridge	William	09JUL00	3.14	1
Hansbrough	Morris	26JUN87	1.02	11	Hardwick	William	30JUL01	3.16	11
HansboroughMoriah		09JUN89	6.04	1	Hardwick	William	29JUL02	3.13	11
Hansberry	Morias/Geo	10MAY90	1.05	22	Hardwitch	William	09AUG03	2.16	11
Hansbrough	Morias/Geo	12MAY91	2.05	2	HARDY				
HansboroughMorias		10OCT92	1.06	1	Hardy	George	15JUL07	2.18	1
Hansbrough	Morias	19AUG93	3.05	1	Hardy	Judether	15JUL07	2.18	1
Hansberry	Moriss	18APR94	2.06	11	Hardy	Thomas	04AUG00	2.15	1
Hansberry	Morris	27MAR95	3.09	11	Hardy	Thomas	04JUN01	2.11	1
Hamsberry	Morris	16JUL96	2.09	11	Hardy	Thomas	10JUN02	1.09	1
HANSFORD					Hardy	Thomas	29JUN03	1.11	1
Hansford	Bengamin	13APR97	3.13	1	Hardy	Thomas	13JUN04	2.08	1
Hansford	Thomas	13APR97	3.13	1	Hardey	Thomas	18JUN06	1.11	1
Hanceford	William	-----93	2.02	1	Hardy	Thomas	15JUL07	2.17	1
HAR					HARGHFIELD				
Har	Coonrod	27JUL04	4.13	1	Harghfield	Fredrick	14MAY94	1.04	1
Hon	Conrod	25JUL05	2.17	1	Harghfield	Frederick	21MAY95	2.06	1
HARBERT					Harghfield	John	13MAY94	1.11	1
Harbart	Amos	21JUL87	3.05	11	Harghfield	John	14MAY94	1.04	1
Harber	Amos	25JUL89	2.06	1	Harghfield	John	21MAY95	2.06	1
Harber	Amus	12SEP91	3.07	1	Harghfield	Martin M.	03JUN95	2.06	1
Harbert	Amos	20MAY94	3.11	1	HARGNOD				
Harberd	Amos	12MAY95	1.08	1	Hargnod	Cathrine	19AUG09	2.15	F
Harbour	Amos	-----96	4.08	1	HARGROVE				
Harbart	Elisha Sr	21JUL87	3.05	11	Hartgrave	Francis	13JUN96	1.06	1
Harbart	Elisha Jr	05JUL87	3.05	1	Hardgrove	Francis	20APR97	3.14	1
Harber	Elijah	07AUG89	2.06	1	Handgrave	Francis	27MAY99	1.15	1
Harber	Elisha	17SEP91	3.06	1	Hartgrove	James	03JUN95	2.07	1
Harber	Elijah	12SEP91	3.07	1	Hardgrove	James	20MAY96	2.08	1
Harber	Elisha	04DEC92	3.08	1	Hartgrove	James	22JUN96	1.06	1
Harber	Elijah Jr	05DEC92	3.09	1	Hardgrove	James	15APR97	3.13	1
Harbert	Elisha Sr	22MAY94	3.11	1	Hardgrave	James	29MAY97	1.12	1
Harbert	Elisha Jr	07MAY94	3.10	1	Hartgrove	John	27JUN87	2.04	1
Hurberd	Elisha Sr	25MAR95	1.07	11	Hartgrove	John	14NOV88	1.04	1
Harber	Elisha	12MAY95	1.08	1	Hartgrove	John	24JUN89	5.06	1
Harbour	Elisha Sr	-----96	4.07	2	Hartgrove	John	14APR91	1.04	11
Harbour	Elisha Jr	-----96	4.07	1	Hartgrove	John Sr	13AUG93	1.04	11
Harber	Joseph	14SEP91	3.08	1	Hartgrove	John Jr	13AUG93	1.04	1
Harber	Joseph	27NOV92	3.09	1	Hartgrove	John	18MAY94	1.04	13
Herbert	Joseph	23APR94	3.09	1	Hartgrove	John	03JUN95	2.07	1
Harbour	Joseph	-----96	4.07	1	Hartgrove	John	03JUN95	2.07	12
Harbert	William	12MAY95	2.06	1	Hartgrove	John	22JUN96	1.06	12
Harbert	William	10JUN96	1.06	1	Hartgrove	John Jr	22JUN96	1.07	1
HARBISON					Hardgrove	John	15APR97	3.14	1
Harbeson	John	10MAY97	1.11	1	Hardgrove	John	15APR97	3.13	12
Harbison	John	11JUL99	3.11	1	Hardgrove	John	12JUN99	1.17	11
Harbeson	John	10JUL00	3.15	1	Hargrove	Valentine	14MAY99	1.15	1
Harbison	John	30JUL01	3.16	1	Hartgrove	Valentine	18JUN00	2.13	1
Harbison	John	29JUL02	3.13	1	Hartgrove	Vallentine	24JUL01	2.12	1
Harbison	John	10AUG03	2.16	1	Hartgrove	Valentine	10JUN02	1.09	1
Harberson	John	30JUN04	4.12	1	Hartgrove	Valentine	29JUN03	1.11	1
HARDIN					Hartgrove	Vallentine	07AUG04	2.10	1
Harder	James	29JUN05	3.17	1	Hartgrove	Valentine	13JUN05	1.09	1
Hardin	James	18AUG06	2.20	1	Hartgrove	Valentine	19JUN06	1.11	1
Harden	James	18AUG07	2.19	1	Hargrove	Valentine	12JUN07	1.12	1
Harden	James	-----08	2.13	1	Hargrove	Valentine	22APR08	1.14	1
Hardin	James	07JUL09	1.19	1	Hargrove	Valentine	06JUN09	2.14	1
Hardin	James	-----11	1.34	1	Hartgrove	William	22JUN96	1.07	1
Harden	Joseph	-----93	2.03	1	Hardgrove	William	15APR97	3.14	1
Harden	Thomas	25MAR90	2.04	1	HARKLEY				
Harden	William	23AUG06	3.17	1	Harkley	Hugh	06JUN09	2.14	1
HARDRIDGE					HARLAN				

surname	name	date	bk.pg	TM	surname	name	date	bk.pg	TM
Harlan	Bonam	04JUL99	3.10	1	HARMON				
Harlan	Boneham	01JUL00	3.14	1	Harmon	Callenbine	11OCT92	2.04	1
Harland	Bonum	14AUG02	3.14	1	Harmon	Israel	13JUN87	2.03	1
Harland	Bonum	30MAY03	2.14	1	Harmon	Jacob	27JUN87	2.04	11
Harland	Bonam	28JUL04	4.13	1	Harmon	Jacob	05JUL87	3.05	1
Harlin	Bonum	24JUL05	2.17	1	Harmon	Jacob	30OCT88	1.04	1
Harland	Bonum	24APR06	2.17	1	Harmon	Jacob	19JUN89	5.06	1
Harland	Elijah	16AUG07	2.19	1	Harmon	Jacob Jr	12AUG89	2.06	11
Harlin	George	02OCT87	1.03	1	Harmer	Jacob	12SEP91	3.07	1
Harlin	George	26JUN89	6.04	1	Harmer	Jacob	13SEP91	3.07	1
Harlan	George	23JUN90	1.05	1	Harmer	Jacob	05DEC92	3.09	1
Harlan	George	09JUN91	2.05	1	Harmon	Jacob	22MAY94	3.11	1
Harlan	George	09OCT92	1.06	1	Harmon	Jacob Jr	05MAY94	3.09	1
Harland	George	16AUG93	3.06	1	Harmon	Jacob Sr	12MAY95	1.08	1
Harlen	George	30APR94	2.06	1	Harmon	Jacob Jr	12MAY95	1.08	1
Harland	George	27MAR95	3.08	1	Harmon	Jacob Sr	11MAR97	2.02	1
Harland	George	27MAR95	3.08	1	Harmon	Jacob Jr	11MAR97	2.02	1
Harlin	George	03AUG96	2.09	1	Harmon	Jacob	12MAY99	2.09	1
Harlin	George	03AUG96	2.09	1	Harmon	Jacob	11JUN00	1.05	1
Harlan	George	17MAY97	1.12	1	Harmon	Jacob Sr	08JUN01	1.07	1
Harlan	George	04JUL99	3.10	1	Harmon	Jacob Jr	08JUN01	1.07	1
Harlan	George	30JUN00	3.13	1	Harmon	Philip	20JUN87	2.04	1
Harland	George	08JUL01	3.15	1	Harmon	Stephen	16MAY99	2.09	1
Harland	George	14AUG02	3.14	1	Harmon	Stephen	12JUN00	1.05	1
Harland	George	22JUN03	2.15	1	Harmon	Stephen	01JUN01	1.07	1
Harland	George Jr	25JUL03	2.15	1	Harmon	Valentine	27JUN87	2.04	1
Harlan	George	27JUL04	4.13	11	Harmon	Valentine	30OCT88	1.04	11
Harland	George	28JUL04	4.13	1	Harmon	Valentine	19JUN89	5.06	11
Harlin	George	23JUL05	2.16	11	Harmin	Valentine	03JUN90	2.03	1
Harlin	George J-	24JUL05	2.17	1	Harmon	Valentine	30MAR91	1.04	1
Harland	George	24APR06	2.17	1	Harmer	Valentine	13SEP91	3.07	11
Harlin	George	17JUL06	2.18	11	Harman	Valentine	15AUG93	1.05	1
Harland	George	15JUL07	2.18	1	Harman	Valintine	28MAY94	1.04	1
Harland	George	16AUG07	2.19	1	Herman	Valentine	03JUN95	2.06	1
Harling	George	02AUG08	2.15	11	Harmon	Valentine	22MAY97	3.15	1
Harland	George	22JUN09	1.18	1	Harmon	Valuntine	13MAY99	2.09	1
Harlan	George Sr	-----11	1.32	21	Harmon	Valentine	22JUL00	1.06	1
Harlan	George Jr	-----11	1.32	1	Harmon	Valentine	23JUN01	1.07	1
Harlin	Jacob	12APR97	3.13	1	Harmon	Valentine	22JUN02	1.10	1
Harlan	Jacob	28JUN00	3.13	1	Harmon	Valentine	23JUN03	1.10	1
Harland	Jacob	22JUN09	1.18	1	Harmon	Valentine	01AUG04	1.09	1
Harlan	Jacob	-----11	1.32	1	Harmon	Valentine	30JUL05	1.09	1
Harland	James	14AUG02	3.14	1	Harmon	Valentine	02AUG06	1.12	1
Harland	James	25JUL03	2.15	1	Harmon	Valentine	08MAY07	1.10	1
Harland	James	28JUL04	4.13	1	HARNESS				
Harlin	James	24JUL05	2.17	1	Harnish	Richard	11AUG02	3.13	1
Harland	James	24APR06	2.17	1	Harness	Richard	28JUL03	2.16	1
Harland	James	31JUL07	2.18	1	Harness	Richard	27JUN04	4.12	1
Harling	James	02AUG08	2.15	1	Harness	Richard	19AUG06	2.20	1
Harland	Joel	22JUN03	2.14	1	HARPER				
Harland	Joel	28JUL04	4.13	1	Harper	Henry	11AUG03	2.16	M1
Harlin	Joel	23JUL05	2.16	1	Harper	Henry	05JUN04	4.11	1
Harland	Joel	24APR06	2.17	1	Harper	Harry	18JUN05	2.15	1
Harland	Joal	16AUG07	2.19	1	Harper	Henry	02AUG06	2.19	1
Harling	Joel	02AUG08	2.15	1	Harper	Henry	20JUN07	2.16	1
Harland	Joel	21JUN09	1.18	1	Harper	Henry	-----08	2.13	1
Harlan	Joel	-----11	1.32	1	Harper	Henry	13JUL09	1.20	1
Harlen	Reubin	12MAY94	2.06	1	Harper	Joseph	17JUL06	3.16	12
Harlon	Walter	05JUL96	2.09	1	Harper	William	28JUL03	2.16	1
Harlon	Walter	26MAY97	1.12	1	Harper	William	27JUN04	4.12	1
HARLEY					Harper	William	19JUL05	2.16	1
Harley	Daniel	18MAY06	2.17	1	HARRIS				
Harley	Daniel	15JUL07	2.18	1	Harris	Claburn	02MAY09	1.17	1
Harly	Daniel	09JUN09	1.18	1	Harris	Edwin L.	23MAY99	1.15	1
Harly	John	13OCT92	1.06	1	Harris	Edwin L.	14JUN00	2.12	1
HARLOW					Harris	Edwin L.	14JUN00	2.12	1
Harlow	John	26JUN09	1.18	1	Harris	George F.	02MAY05	2.15	1
Harlow	Michall	29NOV92	3.09	1	Harris	George	12AUG07	2.18	13
Harlow	Michael	24APR94	3.10	1	Harris	Gillam	25JUN00	2.13	11
Harlow	Reuben	25MAY95	2.06	1	Harris	Gillam	23JUL01	3.16	1
Harlow	Walter	25MAY95	2.06	1	Hairis	Gilliam	04AUG02	2.14	11
Harlow	Walter	26JUN00	3.13	1	Harris	Gilliam	15JUL03	3.12	11

surname	name	date	bk.pg	TM	surname	name	date	bk.pg	TM
Harris	Gillum	21AUG04	3.10	11	Harveu	John	10JUN03	1.09	1
Harris	Gilliam	14AUG05	3.18	11	Harvey	John	05JUL03	1.12	1
Harris	Graves	12AUG07	2.18	1	Harvey	John	25JUN04	1.08	1
Harris	Isaac	23JUL01	3.16	1	Harvey	John	25MAY07	1.11	1
Hairis	Isaac	04AUG02	2.14	1	Harvey	John	16AUG09	2.15	1
Harris	Isaac	15JUL03	3.12	1	Harvey	John	-----11	1.38	1
Harris	Isaac	21AUG04	3.10	1	Harvey	William	25MAY95	2.06	11
Harris	Isaac	14AUG05	3.18	1	Harvey	William	15JUN96	1.06	11
Harris	Isaac	05JUL06	3.16	1	Harvey	William	29AUG97	3.16	11
Harris	John	19MAY99	2.09	1	Harvey	William	23MAY99	1.15	1
Harris	John	19APR08	1.31	1	Harvey	William	30MAY00	2.12	1
Harris	Joseph	02OCT87	1.03	1	Harvey	William	21JUL01	2.12	1
Harris	Mary	02OCT87	1.03	F	Harvy	William	16JUN02	1.09	1
Harris	Samuel	10JUN02	1.09	1	Harvey	William	05JUL03	1.11	1
Harris	Samuel	29JUN03	1.11	1	Harvey	William	15JUN04	1.07	1
Harris	Samuel	02AUG04	2.09	1	Harvey	William	20JUN05	1.09	1
Harris	Samuel	13JUN05	1.09	1	Harvey	William	21JUN06	1.11	1
Harris	Samuel	18JUN06	1.11	1	Harvey	William	09JUN07	1.11	1
Harris	Samuel	04MAY08	1.15	1	Harvey	William	22APR08	1.14	1
Harris	Thomas/Thos	23JUN90	1.05	21	Harvey	William	16AUG09	2.15	1
Harris	Thomas G.	03NOV92	1.06	1	Harvey	William	-----11	1.37	11
Harris	Thomas G.	19AUG93	3.05	1	HARWOOD				
Harris	Wm Woods	31MAY94	1.12	1	Harwood	William	12JUN87	2.03	1
Harris	William	20JUN06	1.06	1	HASHER				
Harris	William	13JUN00	1.05	1	Hasher	John	17JUL06	3.16	1
Harris	William	05JUL06	3.16	1	Hasher	John	20JUN07	2.16	1
Harris	William	02AUG06	2.19	1	Hasher	John	-----08	2.13	1
Harris	William	18JUN07	2.16	1	HASHFIELD				
Harris	William	01JUL07	1.12	1	Hashfield	John	30MAY89	6.03	1
HARRISON					HASHWOOD				
Harrison	Milly	-----11	1.40	F	Hashwood	Look	24JUN07	1.12	1
Harrison	Thomas	26JUN89	6.04	1	HASLEWOOD				
Harrisson	Thomas	19AUG91	2.04	1	Haslewood	Benjamin	06JUL09	2.15	1
Harison	William	18MAY90	2.04	1	HATCHITT				
Harrison	William	28MAR91	1.04	1	Hatchitt	John	23APR96	2.08	1
Harrison	William	28JUN03	1.10	1	HATFIELD				
HARROD					Hatfield	John	10AUG93	3.05	1
Herrod	James	22JUN02	1.09	1	HATTER				
Herrod	James	02AUG04	1.09	1	Hatter	James	30MAY03	3.10	1
Harrod	James	31JUL06	1.12	1	Hatter	Samuel	05AUG03	3.13	M1
Harrad	James	06MAY07	1.10	1	HATWOOD				
HART					Hatwood	John	20JUN05	2.15	1
Hart	Abraham	17MAY99	2.09	1	HAVORD				
Hart	Abraham	23JUL00	1.06	11	Havord	George	12JUN89	6.08	1
Hart	Isreal	20JUN87	2.04	1	HAWKINS				
Hart	Isreal	09JUL89	2.06	1	Hockings	Elijah	19APR91	3.06	1
Heart	Isaral	13SEP91	3.07	1	Hawkins	Elisha	08NOV92	3.08	1
Hart	Issarel	04DEC92	3.08	1	Hawkins	Elijah	05MAY94	3.10	1
Hart	Isreal	22MAY94	3.11	1	Hawkins	Elijah	12MAY95	1.07	1
Hart	Israel	12MAY95	1.08	1	Hauskins	James	12MAY95	1.07	1
Hart	Isreal	-----96	4.07	11	Hawkins	James	-----96	4.07	1
Hart	Israel	24APR97	3.14	11	Hawkins	John	12AUG89	2.06	11
Hart	Jack	04JUN03	2.14		Hockings	John	19APR91	3.06	1
A free negro					Hawkins	John	29OCT92	3.08	1
Hart	Jack	13AUG04	2.10		Hawkins	John	05MAY94	3.10	1
A free black man					Hawkins	John	12MAY95	1.07	1
Hart	Jack	13MAY05	2.15		Hawkins	John	12MAY95	1.08	1
A free negro					Hawkins	John	-----96	4.07	1
Hart	Jack	08MAY06	2.17		Hawkins	John	11JUN02	1.09	1
A free negroe					Hawkins	John	18JUN04	1.07	1
Hart	Jack	31JUL07	2.18	0	Hawkins	John	06JUN05	1.08	1
Hart	Jack	18JUL08	2.14		Hawkins	John B.	28MAY07	1.11	1
(black)					Hawkins	John B.	10MAY09	2.12	1
Hart	Thomas	20JUN87	2.04	11	Hawkins	Robert	26SEP92	2.04	0
HARVEY					Hockings	Wedin	19APR91	3.06	11
Harvey	John	16MAY89	6.03	1	Hawkins	Weaden	08NOV92	3.08	1
Harvey	John	15APR90	1.05	1	Hawkins	Weedon	05MAY94	3.09	1
Harvey	John	18MAR91	2.04	1	Hawkins	Weedon	-----96	4.07	1
Harvey	John	21MAY99	1.15	1	HAYNES				
Harvey	John	23MAY99	1.15	1	Hains	Andrew	21MAY99	2.09	1
Harvey	John	21JUL01	2.12	1	Haynes	Andrew	25JUL01	2.12	1
Harvy	John	16JUN02	1.09	1	Haynes	Andrew	15JUN02	1.09	1

surname	name	date	bk.pg	TM	surname	name	date	bk.pg	TM
Hanes	James	-----11	1.36	1	Tax pd by Hugh Hays				
Aines	Reuben	16AUG09	1.01	1	Hays	James	30JUL04	2.09	
Haines	William	07MAY91	2.04	1	Paid tax for James(heirs) Hays				
HAYS					Hays	James(heirs	30JUL04	2.09	0
Hays	David	28MAY03	2.14	1	Hays	James(heirs	30JUL04	2.09	0
Hayse	David	25JUL05	1.09	1	Tax paid by James Hays				
Hays	Elizabeth	16JUN03	3.11	F	Hays	James(Decd)	10JUN05	3.16	0
Hays	Elizabeth	16JUN03	3.11	F	Hays	James(Decd)	10JUN05	3.16	0
Hays	Hugh	26JUN87	2.04	1	Hays	Jas.(heirs)	23AUG06	3.18	
Hays	Hugh	05NOV88	1.04	1	Tax paid by Hugh Hays				
Hays	Hugh	07AUG89	5.06	11	Hays	James(Decd)	18AUG07	2.19	D
Hays	Hugh	30MAR90	2.03	11	Hays	James(Decd)	18AUG07	2.19	d
Hays	Hugh	25MAR91	1.04	11	Taxes pd by Hugh Hays				
Hays	Hugh	26OCT92	2.04	11	Hays	James	26JUN09	1.18	D
Hays	Hays	30AUG93	1.05	11	Hays	James	26JUN09	1.18	d
Hays	Hugh	31MAY94	1.11	1	Hays	James	-----11	1.35	D
Hays	Hugh	31MAY94	1.05	1	Taxes paid by Hugh Hays Sr.				
Hays	Hugh	11JUN95	2.07	1	Hay	John	03JUL89	2.06	1
Hays	Hugh	30MAY96	1.07	1	Hays	John	03AUG93	1.05	1
Hays	Hugh	12JUN97	3.15	1	Hays	John	17MAY94	1.04	1
Hays	Hugh	31MAY99	1.17	1	Hays	John	09MAY95	2.06	1
Hays	Hugh	19JUN00	2.13	1	Hays	John	30JUN96	1.06	1
Hays	Hugh	13JUL01	2.12	1	Hays	John	31MAY97	3.15	11
Hays	Hugh	12JUL02	2.14		Hays	John	31MAY99	1.17	1
Paid tax for Jas.(heirs) Hays					Hays	John	14JUN00	2.12	1
Hays	Hugh	16JUN03	3.11	1	One lott in Standford				
Hays	Hugh	30JUL04	2.09	1	Hays	John	28MAY01	2.11	
Hays	Hugh	10JUN05	3.16	1	One lott in Standford				
Hays	Hugh	23AUG06	3.18	1	Hays	John	14JUN02	2.13	1
For the heirs of Jas. Hays					Hays	John	16JUN03	3.11	1
Hays	Hugh	18AUG07	2.19	11	Hays	John	27JUL04	4.13	1
Paid taxes for James(decd) Hays					Hays	John	30JUL04	2.09	1
Hays	Hugh	02AUG08	2.15	11	Hays	John	10JUN05	3.16	1
Paid tax for Sam.(heirs) Hays					Hays	John	18JUL06	2.18	1
Hays	Hugh	26JUN09	1.18	1	Hays	John	23AUG06	3.18	1
Hays	Hugh Sr	-----11	1.35	1	Hays	John	13JUL07	2.16	1
Paid tax for James Hays					Hays	John	02AUG08	2.15	1
Hays	Hugh Jr	-----11	1.35	1	Hays	John	26JUN09	1.18	1
Hays	James	26JUN87	2.04	1	Hays	John	-----11	1.35	1
Hays	James	06NOV88	1.04	1	Hay	Kinnard	-----08	2.13	1
Hays	James	07AUG89	5.06	1	Hays	Kennard	07JUN09	1.17	1
Hays	James	30MAR90	2.03	1	Hays	Samuel	02AUG08	2.15	D
Hays	James	25MAR91	1.04	1	Taxes paid for heirs by Hugh Hays				
Hays	James	26OCT92	2.04	1	Hay	William	26JUN87	3.04	1
Hays	James	20AUG93	3.06	1	Hay	William	27JUN89	2.06	1
Hays	James	26AUG93	1.04	1	Hays	William	28APR91	3.06	1
Hays	James	24MAY94	1.05	1	Hays	William	17MAY94	1.04	1
Hays	James	19JUN94	1.12	1	Hays	William	09MAY95	2.06	1
Hays	James	-----95	2.26		Hays	William	13JUN97	3.16	11
Four lots in Standford					Hays	William	13JUN97	3.33	
Hays	James	10JUN95	2.07	1	One town lot in Stanford				
Hays	James	27JUN96	1.05	1	Hays	William	29JUL00	2.14	1
Hays	James	27JUN96	1.13		Hais	William	21JUL01	3.16	1
Four town lots in Standford					Hays	William	01JUN02	2.13	1
Hays	James	13JUN97	3.33		Hays	William	16JUN03	3.11	1
Four town lots in Stanford					Hays	William	30JUL04	2.09	1
Hays	James	16JUN97	3.16	1	Hays	William	23AUG06	3.18	1
Hays	James	24MAY99	1.16	1	Hays	William	13JUL07	2.17	1
Hays	James	24MAY99	1.40		Hays	William	-----08	2.13	1
Five lotts in Stanford					Hays	William	26JUN09	1.18	1
Hays	James	24MAY99	1.40		Hays	William	-----11	1.35	1
One lott in Stanford					HAZELWOOD				
Hays	James	19JUN00	2.13	1	Hazelwood	Benjamin	18JUL08	2.14	1
Two lotts in Standford					Hazelwood	Benjamin Jr	-----11	1.37	1
Hays	James	21JUL01	2.12	1	Hazelwood	Luke	17JUN05	3.17	11
Three lotts in Standford					Hazelwood	Luke	17JUL06	3.16	1
Hays	Jas.(heirs)	12JUL02	2.14	0	Hazelwood	Luke	23AUG06	3.18	1
Hays	Jas.(heirs)	12JUL02	2.14	0	Hazelwood	Luke	18AUG07	2.19	11
Hays	Jas.(heirs)	12JUL02	2.14	0	Hazelwood	Luke	-----08	2.13	12
Hays	Jas.(heirs)	12JUL02	2.14	0	Hazelwood	Luke	07AUG09	1.20	1
Four lots in the town of Stanford					Hazlewood	Luke	-----11	1.38	1
Hays	Jas.(heirs)	12JUL02	2.14		Hazlewood	Luke	-----11	1.37	12

surname	name	date	bk.pg	TM	surname	name	date	bk.pg	TM
HEADRICK					Helms	George	08JUN97	1.12	11
Hederick	George	11JUN05	1.08	1	Helms	George	25JUN99	3.10	1
Hederick	George	16JUN06	1.10	11	Helm	George	24JUN00	3.13	1
Hedreck	George	28MAY07	1.11	1	Hellemns	George	01MAY01	3.14	1
Headrick	George	22APR08	1.14	11	Helms	George	30JUL02	3.13	11
Hedrick	George	07JUN09	2.14	1	Helms	George	09JUN04	4.12	12
Hedrick	George	-----11	1.38	1	Helms	George	27JUN05	2.16	12
Headrick	Jacob	29MAY94	1.04	1	Helms	George	02AUG06	2.19	12
Headrick	Jacob	03JUN95	2.07	11	Helms	George Jr	02AUG06	2.19	1
Hadrick	Jacob	18JUL96	1.07	11	Helm	George	16AUG07	2.19	1
Hederick	Jacob	29MAY99	2.08	1	Helm	George Jr	09JUN07	2.15	1
Hederick	Jacob	20JUN00	1.05	1	Helm	George	18JUL08	2.14	1
Hederick	Jacob	23JUN01	1.07	1	Helm	George Jr	18JUL08	2.14	1
Hedreck	Michael	11JUN07	1.11	1	Hellams	Joseph	15AUG93	1.04	1
Headrick	Michael	05JUN09	2.14	1	Hellem	Joseph	13MAY94	1.04	1
HEADSPATH					Helms	Joseph	21MAY95	2.06	1
Hedgepeth	David	13MAY94	2.06	1	Helm	Joseph	20JUN96	1.05	11
Hudspeth	David	27MAR95	3.09	1	Helms	Joseph	29AUG97	3.34	1
Headspeath	Ralph	31MAY94	1.05	1	Helms	Joseph	29MAY99	1.16	1
Hudspeth	Ralph	08MAY95	2.06	1	Helm	Joseph	17JUL00	2.14	1
Hudspeth	Ralph	13JUN97	3.16	1	Helm	Joseph	28JUL01	2.12	1
Headspath	Ralph	30JUL02	3.13	1	Helms	Joseph	30JUN02	3.12	1
Headspath	Ralph	15JUN03	2.14	1	Helm	Joseph	21JUN03	2.14	1
Headspath	Ralph	03MAY05	2.15	1	Helms	Joseph	06AUG03	2.16	12
Headspath	Ralph	12MAY06	2.17	1	Helms	Joseph	26JUL04	1.08	1
Hadspeath	Rolfe	13JUL07	2.17	1	Helms	Joseph	26JUL04	1.09	11
Hedgepeth	Relph	18JUL08	2.14	1	Helm	Joseph	31JUL05	2.17	11
HEASLY					Helm	Joseph	14JUL06	2.18	11
Heesley	Adam	26JUL03	2.16	1	Helm	Joseph	15JUL07	2.18	11
Heasly	Adam	25JUL04	4.12	1	Helm	Joseph Sr	10AUG08	1.17	1
Heisley	Adam	20JUL05	2.16	1	Helm	Joseph Jr	10AUG08	1.17	M1
Heesley	Daniel	26JUL03	2.15	1	Helm	Joseph	19AUG09	2.16	1
Heesley	Henry	26JUL03	2.15	1	Helm	Joseph Jr	19AUG09	2.16	1
Heasly	Henry	25JUL04	4.12	1	Helm	Joseph Sr	-----11	1.36	1
HEATON					Helm	Joseph Jr	-----11	1.35	1
Heaton	Benjamin	15AUG91	3.07	1	Helms	Leonard	20SEP87	1.02	1
Heaton	Hailey	-----11	1.37	1	Helms	Leonard	23MAY89	6.04	1
Hetin	John	16JUL06	2.18	1	Helms	Leonard	14MAY90	1.05	1
Heatton	John	16AUG07	2.19	1	Helms	Leonard	20APR91	2.05	1
Heaten	John	05JUN09	1.17	1	Helms	Leonard	14SEP92	1.06	1
Heaten	John	09JUN09	1.18	1	Helms	Leonard	07AUG93	3.05	1
Heaton	John	-----11	1.40	1	Helms	Leonard	22APR94	2.06	1
HELLACOST					Helms	Lenard	19APR95	3.08	1
Hellicosh	George	09JUN89	6.03	1	Helms	Leonard	05JUL96	2.09	1
Hillicost	George	10MAY90	1.05	11	Helms	Leonard	31MAY97	1.11	11
Hellacost	George	08MAY91	2.05	1	Helms	Marquis	20SEP87	1.02	1
Hellacost	Jacob	18MAY91	2.05	1	Helms	Marquis	12MAY89	6.03	1
HELLET					Helms	Marquis	14MAY90	1.05	1
Hollet	Richard	30JUL05	1.09	1	Helms	Marquis	20JUN91	2.04	1
Hellett	Richard	02AUG06	1.12	1	Helms	Marquis	14SEP92	1.06	1
Hellet	Richard	06MAY07	1.10	1	Helms	Marquis	20MAY94	2.06	1
HELMS					Helms	Marquis	13APR95	3.08	1
Helms	George	20SEP87	1.02	1	Helms	Marquis	05JUL96	2.09	1
Helms	George	23MAY89	6.04	1	Helms	Marquis	08JUN97	1.12	1
Helms	George	14MAY90	1.05	1	Helms	Marquis	25JUN99	3.10	1
Helms	George	19APR91	2.05	1	Helm	Marquis	21JUN00	3.13	1
Helms	George	13SEP92	1.06	1	Hellemns	Markam	02MAY01	3.14	1
Helms	George	20AUG93	3.06	11	Helms	Marquis	30JUL02	3.13	1
Helms	George	22MAY94	2.06	11	Helms	Marquis	06AUG03	2.16	1
Helms	George	14APR95	3.08	11	Helms	Marquis	05APR04	4.11	1
Helms	George	14JUN96	2.08	11	Helms	Marquis	27JUN05	2.15	1

surname	name	date	bk.pg	TM	surname	name	date	bk.pg	TM
Helms	Marquis	02AUG06	2.19	1	One lott in Lancaster				
Helm	Marquis	13JUL07	2.17	11	Henderson	William	01AUG00	2.14	
Helm	Marquis	18JUL08	2.14	11	One lott in Standford				
Helms	Marquis	09AUG09	1.20	1	Henderson	William	28MAY01	2.11	
Helm	Marquis	-----11	1.34	2	One lott in Standford				
Helm	Meredeth	11JUN07	2.16	11	Henderson	William	24JUN01	1.07	1
Helm	Meridith	-----08	2.13	11	Henderson	William	17JUN02	1.09	1
Hellem	Thomas	13MAY94	1.11	1	Henderson	William	22JUN02	1.10	1
Helms	Thomas	28JUL06	2.19	M1	Henderson	William	11JUL03	1.12	1
Helm	Thomas	18AUG07	2.19	1	Henderson	William	11JUL03	1.11	1
Helm	Thomas	02JUN08	1.15	1	Henderson	William	13JUN04	2.08	1
Helm	Thomas	06JUL09	2.15	1	Henderson	William	15AUG05	1.25	11
Helm	Thomas	-----11	1.34	1	Name not taken in previous year				
HENDERSON					Henderson	William	12AUG06	1.12	1
Henderson	Alexander	02AUG04	1.09	1	Henderson	William	07MAY07	1.10	1
Henderson	Alexander	31JUL05	1.09	1	Henderson	William	04MAY08	1.16	11
Henderson	Alexander	31JUL06	1.12	1	Henderson	William	15JUN09	2.14	1
Henderson	Alexander	26MAY07	1.11	1	HENRY				
Henderson	Alexander	19APR08	1.14	1	Henry	David	31MAY99	1.16	1
Henderson	Alexander	16JUN09	2.14	1	Henry	David	24MAY00	2.12	1
Henderson	Christopher	16JUL06	2.18	1	Henry	David	22JUN01	2.11	11
Henderson	James	21MAY89	6.03	1	Henry	David	01JUL02	3.12	12
Henderson	James	12AUG90	1.05	1	Henry	David	11JUL03	1.12	11
Henderson	James	20APR91	2.05	1	Henry	Samuel	29MAY94	2.06	1
Henderson	James	02NOV92	1.06	1	Henry	Samuel	02MAY95	2.08	1
Henderson	James	20AUG93	3.06	1	Henry	Samuel	25JUN96	2.08	1
Henderson	James	01MAY94	2.07	1	Henry	Samuel	09AUG97	1.11	1
Henderson	James	24MAR95	3.09	1	Henry	Thomas	03APR90	2.03	1
Henderson	James	13MAY99	2.09	1	Henry	Watson	14JUN87	2.04	1
Henderson	James	23JUL00	1.06	1	Henry	Watson	28NOV88	1.05	1
Henderson	James	24JUN01	1.07	1	Henry	Watson	16JUN89	5.06	1
Henderson	James	22JUN02	1.11	1	Henry	Watson	03APR90	2.03	1
Henderson	James	22JUN03	1.10	1	Henry	Watson	05APR91	1.04	1
Henderson	James	02AUG04	1.09	1	Henery	Watson	03NOV92	2.04	1
Henderson	James	20JUN05	1.09	1	Henry	Watson	03AUG93	1.04	1
Henderson	James	31JUL06	1.12	1	Henry	Watson	15MAY94	1.04	11
Henderson	James	07MAY07	1.10	1	Henry	Watson	12MAY95	2.06	11
Henderson	James	15JUN09	2.14	1	Henry	Watson	06JUN96	1.06	1
Henderson	John	02JUL99	3.10	1	Henry	Watson	22APR97	3.16	1
Henderson	John	26JUN00	3.13	1	Henry	Watson	31MAY99	1.16	1
Henderson	John	19MAY01	3.15	1	Henry	Watson	26JUL00	2.14	11
Henderson	John	16AUG02	3.14	1	Henry	Watson	04APR01	2.10	1
Henderson	John	26JUL03	2.15	11	Henry	Watson	07JUN02	3.12	1
Henderson	John	25JUL04	4.12	1	Henry	Watson	14JUN03	2.14	11
Henderson	John	22JUL05	2.16	1	Henry	Watson	23JUL04	1.08	1
Henderson	John	19APR08	1.14	1	Henry	Watson	09AUG05	2.17	1
Henderson	John	16JUN09	2.14	1	Henry	William	21JUL87	3.05	1
Henderson	Joseph	08MAY07	1.10	1	Henry	William	-----11	1.39	1
Henderson	Joseph	19APR08	1.14	1	HENSLEY				
Henderson	Joseph	01JUL09	2.15	1	Hunsley	Charles	18NOV88	1.04	1
Henderson	Richard	31MAY97	3.15	11	Hounsly	Charles	04AUG89	5.06	1
Henderson	Rowland	-----11	1.32	1	Hounsellor	Charles	22OCT92	2.04	1
Henderson	Susanah	02AUG08	2.15	F	Hounsler	Charles	17AUG93	1.04	1
Henderson	William	29MAY90	1.05	1	Hounsler	Charles	15MAY94	1.04	1
Henderson	William	30MAR91	1.04	1	Hounsler	Charles	18MAY95	2.06	1
Henderson	William	10OCT92	2.04	1	Hounslee	Charles	10JUN96	1.06	1
Henderson	William	07MAY94	3.10	1	Hounsler	Charles	09JUL00	2.14	1
Henderson	William	31MAY94	1.05	1	Hensley	Davidson	17AUG02	3.14	1
Henderson	William	08MAY95	2.06	1	Hansley	John	12AUG07	2.18	1
Henderson	William	27JUN96	1.13		Hansley	John	02AUG08	2.15	1
One town lot in Standford					Hensley	John	10JUN09	1.18	1
Henderson	William	22MAY97	3.15	1	Hensley	John	-----11	1.32	1
Henderson	William	12JUN97	3.15	1	Hants	Laurence	20JUN03	1.10	1
Henderson	William	13JUN97	3.33		Hensel	Laurence	19JUN04	1.08	1
One town lot in Stanford					Hansel	Laurance	11JUN05	1.08	1
Henderson	William	13MAY99	2.09	1	Hanceley	Laurance	16JUN06	1.11	11
Henderson	William	03JUN99	1.14	1	Hansel	Laurence	07MAY07	1.10	1
Henderson	William	03JUN99	1.40		Hansel	Laurence	04MAY08	1.16	1
One lott in Lancaster					Hansley	Lawrence	05JUN09	2.14	1
Henderson	William	15JUL99	3.11	1	Hansel	Laurence	-----11	1.39	1
Henderson	William	23JUL00	1.06	1	Hensley	Willes	17AUG02	3.14	M1
Henderson	William	01AUG00	2.14	1	Hensly	Willis	26JUL04	4.13	1

surname	name	date	bk.pg	TM	surname	name	date	bk.pg	TM
HERRICK					Hickman	Jacob	29JUN09	1.18	1
Herrick	William	27JUN96	1.13		Hickman	Jacob	-----11	1.33	1
One town lot in Standford					Hickman	James	11JUN99	3.10	1
HERRIN					Hickman	James	28JUN00	3.13	1
Harran	Dinnis	01JUN96	1.06	1	Hickman	James	07JUL01	3.15	1
Herring	Dennis	19APR97	3.14	1	Hickman	James	03JUL02	3.12	1
Herring	Dinnis	28MAY99	1.16	11	Hickman	James	31MAY03	3.10	1
Hern	Dennis	24MAY00	2.12	11	Hickman	James	22JUN03	2.15	1
Hern	Dennis	15JUL01	2.12	11	Hickman	James	01AUG04	3.10	1
Hern	Dinnes	08JUN02	3.12	11	Hickman	James	06AUG04	4.13	1
Herrin	Dennis	20JUN03	2.14	11	Hickman	James	10JUN05	3.16	1
Herns	Dennis	26JUL04	4.12	1	Hickman	James	24JUL05	2.16	1
Hern	Dennis	06AUG05	3.18	1	Hickman	James	08JUL06	2.18	1
Hern	Dinnis	21AUG06	3.17	1	Hickmond	James	31JUL07	2.18	1
Hern	Dinnes	-----08	2.12	11	Hickman	James	02AUG08	2.15	1
Herns	Levy	26JUL04	4.13	1	Hickman	James	02AUG08	2.15	1
Hearn	Levi	06AUG05	3.18	1	Hickman	James	21JUN09	1.18	1
Hern	Levi	21AUG06	3.17	1	Hickman	James	-----11	1.32	1
Herrin	Polly	-----11	1.45	F	Hickman	John	03JUN99	1.14	11
Tax paid by Hugh Logan					Hickman	John	22JUL00	2.14	11
Herrin	Washington	19AUG06	2.20	1	Hickman	John Sr	20JUL01	3.16	12
Herron	Washington	16AUG07	2.19	1	Hickman	John Jr	20JUL01	3.16	1
Herren	Washington	02JUN08	1.15	1	Hickman	John Sr	01JUN02	2.13	21
Herrin	Washington	22AUG09	2.15	1	Hickman	John Jr	01JUN02	2.13	1
Herren	William	24MAY09	2.13	1	Hickman	John Sr	31MAY03	3.11	11
Herrin	William	-----11	1.36	1	Hickman	John Jr	31MAY03	3.11	1
HERRINGTON					Hickman	John	21JUL03	3.13	1
Herrington	Charles	25MAR95	3.09	2	Hickman	John Sr	01AUG04	3.10	11
Harrington	John	25SEP93	3.06	1	Hickman	John Jr	01AUG04	3.10	1
Harrington	John	16APR94	2.07	1	Hickman	John	01AUG04	3.10	1
Herrington	John	18MAR95	3.09	1	Hickman	John Jr	10JUN05	3.16	1
Harrington	Jonathan	23JUL05	2.16	M1	Hickman	John	10JUN05	3.16	2
Herrington	Jonathan	17JUL06	2.18	M1	Hickman	John	16JUL06	3.16	1
Aaronton	John	13JUL07	2.01	1	Hickman	John	20JUN07	2.16	1
Herington	Jonathen	02AUG08	2.15	1	Hickman	John	-----08	2.13	1
Herrington	Jonathan	22JUN09	1.18	1	Hickman	John	29JUN09	1.18	1
Aarenton	John	10JUL09	1.01	11	Hickman	John	-----11	1.32	1
Arrington	John	-----11	1.01	1	Hickman	Nicodemus	20JUL01	3.16	1
Harington	Joseph	26JUL03	2.15	M1	Hickman	Nichodemus	14JUN02	2.13	1
Harrington	Joseph	23JUL05	2.16	M1	Hickman	Nichodemus	13JUL03	3.12	1
Herrington	Joseph	17JUL06	2.18	1	Hickman	Nicodemus	04AUG04	3.10	1
Herrington	Joseph	09JUN09	1.18	1	Hickmond	Nichomus	16AUG05	3.19	1
Herrington	Lot	-----11	1.32	1	Hickman	Nichodemus	31JUL06	3.16	1
Herington	Nathaniel	19JUN05	3.17	1	Hickman	Nichodemus	11JUN07	2.16	1
Herrington	Samuel	11MAY99	1.14	1	Hickmond	Nichodemus	18JUL08	2.14	1
HESS					Hickman	Nichademus	26JUN09	1.18	1
Hess	Michael	04AUG91	2.05	1	HICKS				
HICKISON					Hicks	Agnes	20JUN87	2.03	F
Hickison	Ezekiel	27JUN99	1.17	1	Hicks	Anthony	-----11	1.36	1
Hickison	Ezekiel	24JUL00	2.14	1	Hicks	Henery	03NOV92	2.04	1
Hickison	Ezekiel	28MAY01	3.16	1	Hixt	Joseph	-----96	4.07	1
Hickison	Ezekiel	04AUG02	2.14	1	Hicks	William	24MAY99	2.08	1
Hickerson	Ezekiel	07JUL03	3.11	1	Hicks	William	18JUN00	1.05	1
Hickason	Ezekiel	08AUG04	3.10	1	HIGDON				
Hickison	Ezekiel	06AUG05	3.18	1	Higdon	James	14APR91	1.04	1
Hickerson	Thomas	05NOV88	1.04	1	Higdon	James	16OCT92	2.04	1
Hickeson	Thomas	13MAY90	1.05	1	HIGGINS				
Hickason	Thomas	20JUN91	2.05	1	Highens	John	01MAY94	2.07	1
Hickerson	Thomas	14SEP92	1.06	1	Higgins	John	02APR95	3.08	1
HICKMAN					Higgins	John	24JUN96	2.08	1
Hickman	Andrew	31MAY03	3.10	1	Higgins	John	28JUN99	3.10	1
Hickman	Andrew	01AUG04	3.10	1	Higins	Peter	27JUN87	2.04	1
Hickman	Andrew	10JUN05	3.16	1	Higgens	Peter	14NOV88	1.04	1
Hickman	Andrew	-----08	2.12	1	Higgens	Peter	30JUN89	5.06	1
Hickman	Andrew	-----11	1.33	1	Hegans	Peter	02JUN90	2.04	1
Hickman	Jacob	27JUL02	3.12	1	Higgins	Peter	13APR91	1.04	1
Hickman	Jacob	31MAY03	3.10	1	Higgens	Peter	02OCT92	2.04	1
Hickman	Jacob	01AUG04	3.10	1	Higans	Peter	12AUG93	1.04	1
Hickman	Jacob	10JUN05	3.16	11	Hugans	Peter	21MAY94	1.04	1
Hickman	Jacob	16JUL06	3.16	1	Higgans	Peter	01JUN95	2.07	1
Hickman	Jacob	14JUL07	2.17	1	Higans	Peter	28JUN96	1.06	1
Hickman	Jacob	-----08	2.12	1	Higgins	Peter	10MAY97	3.14	1

surname	name	date	bk.pg	TM	surname	name	date	bk.pg	TM
Higgens	Peter	18MAY99	1.15	1	HINDS				
Higgens	Peter	04JUN00	2.12	1	Hinds	James	26JUN87	3.04	11
Higgins	Peter	04JUN01	2.11	1	Listed with Samuel Hinds				
Higgins	Samuel	21JUL03	3.13	1	Hind	James	01JUL89	2.06	1
HIGINBOTHAM					Hines	James	-----93	2.02	1
Higinbotham	James	12MAY95	1.07	1	Hynes	John	28APR91	3.06	1
Higginbotom	James	28JUL96	2.09	1	Hines	John	27JUL97	1.12	1
HILL					Hinds	Samuel	26JUN87	3.04	
Hill	Clemual	21JUL87	3.05	1	Listed with James Hinds				
Hilk	David	15APR95	3.08	1	Hines	Samuel	28NOV88	1.05	1
Hill	David	18AUG09	2.15	1	Hines	Samuel	06AUG89	5.06	1
Hill	James	23MAY94	2.06	11	Hynes	Samuel	28APR91	3.06	1
Hill	James	10APR95	3.08	11	Hinds	Samuel	24APR94	3.10	1
Hill	James	04JUN96	2.08	11	Hinds	Samuel	25MAR95	1.07	1
Hill	James	06JUN97	1.11	11	Hinds	Samuel	-----96	4.07	1
Hill	John	12MAY95	2.06	11	HINTON				
Hill	John	01JUN96	1.06	11	Henton	George	26JUN87	2.04	1
Hill	John	21APR97	3.16	1	Hinton	William	28APR94	2.06	1
Hill	John	13AUG04	2.10	1	Hinton	William	13AUG02	3.13	
Hill	John	13JUN06	1.10	1	A free negro				
Hill	John	18JUN07	1.12	1	HISE				
Hill	John	04MAY08	1.16	1	Hise	George	31JUL01	2.13	M1
Hill	John	23MAY09	2.13	1	HITCH				
Hill	John	-----11	1.39	1	Hitch	John	10JUN03	1.09	1
Hill	Rubin	11JUL03	3.12	1	HITE				
Hill	Ruben	29JUN05	3.17	1	Hite	Henry	29JUL03	2.16	1
Hill	Thomas	07JUN00	1.05	1	Hite	Henry	19JUL05	2.16	1
Hill	Thomas	15JUL01	2.12	1	Hight	Pattrick	22JUL01	3.16	1
Hill	Thomas	08JUL02	3.12	1	Hite	Patrick	04AUG02	2.14	1
Hill	Thomas	01JUN03	2.14	1	Hite	Patrick	30MAY03	3.10	1
Hill	Thomas	08JUL05	2.16	1	Hight	Patrick	05AUG05	3.18	1
Hill	William	19AUG91	2.05	1	Hite	Patrick	23AUG06	3.17	1
Hill	William	12SEP91	3.07	1	Hite	Thomas	26JUN89	6.04	1
Hill	William	29NOV92	3.09	1	Hite	Thomas	23JUN90	1.05	1
Hill	William	20MAY94	3.11	1	Hite	Thomas	19AUG91	2.04	1
Hill	William	25MAR95	1.07	1	Hite	Thomas	18OCT92	1.06	1
Hill	William	-----96	4.07	1	Hite	Thomas	25AUG93	3.06	1
Hill	William	20JUN97	1.11	1	Hight	Thomas	29MAY94	2.06	1
Hill	William	21JUL00	2.14	1	Hight	Thomas	02MAY95	3.08	1
Hill	William	19JUN01	3.16	1	Hight	Thomas	02MAY95	3.08	1
Hill	William	12JUL02	2.14	1	Hite	Thomas	09MAY96	2.08	1
Hill	William	11JUL03	3.12	1	Hight	Thomas	29JUN97	1.12	1
Hill	William	06AUG04	2.10	1	Hite	Thomas	12JUL99	3.11	1
Hill	William	17JUN05	3.17	1	Hete	Thomas	04JUL00	3.14	11
Hill	William	19JUL05	2.16	M1	Hight	Thomas	08MAY01	3.15	12
Hill	William	18JUL06	3.17	1	Hite	Thomas	11AUG02	3.13	12
Hill	William	20JUN07	2.16	1	Hite	Thomas	29JUL03	2.16	11
Hill	William	-----08	2.13	1	Hite	Thomas	26JUN04	4.12	1
Hill	William	10JUL09	1.19	1	Hite	Thomas	19JUL05	2.16	1
Hill	William	-----11	1.36	1	Hite	Thomas	14AUG06	2.19	11
Hill	William	-----11	1.32	1	Hite	Thomas	18JUN07	2.16	11
Hill	Zacheriah	30MAY09	2.13	1	Hite	Thomas	-----08	2.13	1
Hill	Zacheriah	-----11	1.38	1	Hite	Thomas	12MAY09	1.17	1
HILLEY					HOBBS				
Hilly	Francis	12JUN89	6.08	1	Hobbs	James	12MAY95	1.08	1
Hilla	Francis	24JUN91	2.05	1	Hobs	James	16MAY97	3.15	1
Hilly	Francis	19MAR95	3.09	1	Hobs	James	10MAY99	2.09	1
Hilley	Francis	25MAY97	1.12	1	HOCKER				
HILTON					Hocker	Alfred	-----11	1.35	1
Hilton	Jessey	26JUN87	3.04	1	Hacker	George	06AUG04	2.10	11
Hilton	Jessey	05MAY94	3.09	1	Hocker	George	06AUG05	3.18	M1
Helton	Jesse	12MAY95	1.07	1	Hocker	George	23AUG06	3.18	1
Helton	Jessee	-----96	4.07	2	Hocker	George	16AUG07	2.19	1
Helton	Jesse	11MAR97	2.02	11	Hocker	George	-----08	2.13	1
Helton	John	13SEP91	3.07	1	Hocker	George	03JUL09	1.19	1
Helton	John	20SEP92	3.08	1	Hocker	George	-----11	1.34	1
HINDMAN					Hocker	John	31JUL01	2.13	1
Hineman	James	15AUG97	1.11	1	Hocker	John	12JUL02	2.14	1
Hineman	James	24MAY99	3.10	1	Hocker	John	18MAY03	2.13	1
Hendeman	Mary	11JUL00	3.15	F	Hocker	John	07AUG04	2.10	1
Hindman	James(decd)	19JUN05	3.03	0	Hocker	John	29JUN05	3.17	1
Brint Durham - Adm.					Hocker	John	18JUL06	3.17	1

surname	name	date	bk.pg	TM	surname	name	date	bk.pg	TM
Hocker	John	20JUN07	2.16	1	Hocker	Samuel Jr	-----11	1.32	2
Hocker	John	20JUN07	2.16	1	Hocker	Weaver R.	09JUL04	2.08	1
Hocker	John	-----08	2.13	1	Hocker	Weaver	08JUL05	3.18	1
Hocker	John	10JUL09	1.19	1	Hocker	Weaver	18JUL06	3.17	1
Hocker	John	-----11	1.33	1	Hocker	Weaver	07JUL09	1.19	1
Hocker	Joseph	-----11	1.33	1	Hackor	William	07JUN96	1.05	1
Hacker	Nicholas	07JUN96	1.06	11	Hawker	William	31MAY97	3.15	11
Hawker	Nicholas	12JUN97	3.15	11	Hocker	William	10JUL97	1.12	1
Hawker	Nicholas	03JUN99	1.16	21	Hawker	William	03JUN99	1.15	1
Hocker	Nicholas	19JUN00	2.13	2	Hawker	William Jr	03JUN99	1.14	1
Hocker	Nicholas	01AUG01	2.13	1	Hocker	William	19JUN00	2.13	1
Hocker	Nicholas	03JUN02	2.13	1	Hocker	William	01AUG00	2.14	1
Hocker	Nicholas	12JUL02	2.14	02	Hocker	William Sr	01AUG01	2.13	11
Hocker	Nicholas Sr	16JUN03	3.11	1	Hocker	William	31JUL01	2.13	1
Hocker	Nicholas Jr	11JUL03	3.12	12	Hocker	William Sr	23AUG02	2.15	1
Hocker	Nicholas	09JUL04	2.08	1	Hocker	William	14JUN02	2.13	1
Hocker	Nicholas	30JUL04	2.09	1	Hocker	William Sr	13JUL03	3.12	1
Hocker	Nicholas	10JUN05	3.16	1	Hocker	William	11JUL03	3.12	1
Hocker	Nicholas	28MAY06	3.15	1	Hawker	William	30JUN04	4.12	1
Hocker	Nicholas	22JUN07	2.16	1	Hocker	William	04JUN05	3.16	1
Hocker	Nicholas	-----08	2.13	11	Hocker	William	28JUL06	2.19	1
Hocker	Nicholas	22JUN09	1.18	1	Hocker	William	15JUL07	2.17	1
Hocker	Nicholas	-----11	1.35	1	Hocker	William	02AUG08	2.14	1
Hocker	Phillip	10JUL97	1.12	1	Hocker	William	11JUL09	1.19	1
Hocker	Philip	01AUG00	2.14	1	Hocker	William	-----11	1.33	1
Hocker	Phillip	31JUL01	2.13	1	HODGES				
Hocker	Phillip Sr	03JUN02	2.13	1	Hodges	Abner	30JUN96	1.06	1
Hocker	Phillip	03JUN02	2.13	1	Hodges	Abner	24APR97	3.14	1
Hocker	Phillip	16JUN03	3.11	1	Hodge	Abner	04JUN99	1.17	1
Hocker	Phillip	09AUG03	3.13	1	Hodges	Abner	26JUL00	2.14	1
Hocker	Phillip	30JUL04	2.08	1	Hodges	Abner	01AUG01	2.13	11
Hocker	Phillip Jr	30JUL04	2.09	1	Hodge	Abner	04AUG02	2.15	11
Hocker	Philip	29JUN05	3.17	1	Hodges	Abner	06JUN03	3.11	11
Hocker	Phillip	31MAY05	3.16	1	Hodge	Abner	16AUG04	3.10	11
Hocker	Phillip	19JUL06	3.16	12	Hodge	Abner	10JUN07	2.15	1
Hocker	Philip	28MAY06	3.16	1	Hodge	Abner	-----08	2.13	11
Hocker	Phillip	13JUL07	2.16	1	Hodge	Abner	29JUN09	1.19	1
Hocker	Phillip	15JUL07	2.18	1	Hodges	Amos	26MAY97	1.11	1
Hocker	Philip	-----08	2.13	1	Hodge	Amos	24JUN99	1.17	1
Hocker	Philip	02AUG08	2.14	1	Hodges	Amos	29JUL00	2.14	11
Hocker	Phillip	03JUL09	1.19	1	Hodge	Amos	28MAY01	3.16	12
Hocker	Phillip Jr	03JUL09	1.19	1	Hodge	Ames	03AUG02	2.14	12
Hocker	Phillip	-----11	1.32	1	Hodges	Amos	08JUN03	3.11	11
Hocker	Phillip	-----11	1.34	1	Hodges	Amasa	08JUN03	3.11	1
Hocker	Richard W.	-----08	2.13	1	Hodge	Amos	06AUG04	3.10	11
Hocker	Richard W.	-----11	1.35	1	Hodge	Amasa	07AUG04	3.10	1
Hocker	Samuel	10JUL97	1.12	12	Hodge	Amos	05AUG05	3.18	1
Hawker	Samuel Sr	03JUN99	1.14	12	Hodge	Amos	05AUG05	3.18	1
Hawker	Samuel	03JUN99	1.17	1	Hodge	Ames	04AUG06	3.17	1
Hocker	Samuel	20JUN00	2.13	1	Hodge	Amas Jr	04AUG06	3.17	1
Hocker	Samuel	01AUG00	2.14	21	Hodges	James	23JUN97	1.11	1
Hocker	Samuel	28MAY01	2.11	1	Hodge	Moses	10JUN07	2.15	1
Hocker	Samuel	31JUL01	2.13	12	Hodge	Mose	01JUL08	2.14	1
Hocker	Samuel Sr	03JUN02	2.13	11	Hodge	Moses	29JUN09	1.19	1
Hocker	Samuel	24MAY02	2.12	1	Hodge	Moses	-----11	1.32	1
Hocker	Samuel	12JUL02	2.14	11	Hodges	Moses	-----11	1.34	1
Hocker	Samuel Sr	13JUL03	3.12	11	Hodges	William	26MAY97	1.12	1
Hocker	Samuel Jr	10JUN03	3.11	12	Hodge	William	03AUG04	2.09	1
Hocker	Samuel Sr	18JUN04	2.08	11	Hodge	William	28JUN05	2.16	1
Hocker	Samuel	09JUL04	2.08	1	Hodge	William	05AUG05	3.18	1
Hocker	Samuel	06AUG04	2.10	2	Hodge	William	29JUL06	3.17	1
Hocker	Samuel	04JUN05	3.16	11	Hodge	William	31JUL06	3.16	1
Hocker	Samuel	17JUN05	3.17	1	Hodge	William	26JUL08	2.14	1
Hocker	Samuel	29JUN05	3.17	2	Hodge	William	-----11	1.36	1
Hocker	Samuel Sr	18JUL06	3.17	11	HOEBACK				
Hocker	Samuel	19JUL06	3.16	2	Hoeback	Peter	19JUL05	2.16	1
Hocker	Samuel Sr	20JUN07	2.16	1	HOGAN				
Hocker	Samuel Jr	20JUN07	2.16	2	Hogan	James Sr	30JUN96	1.06	1
Hocker	Samuel	-----08	2.13	2	Hogan	James	20JUN96	1.06	11
Hocker	Samuel	02AUG08	2.15	2	Hogan	James	06MAY97	3.14	11
Hocker	Samuel Sr	26JUN09	1.18	2	Hogan	James	18MAY99	1.15	1
Hocker	Samuel Jr	29JUN09	1.18	2	Hogan	James Sr	17JUN00	2.13	1

surname	name	date	bk.pg	TM	surname	name	date	bk.pg	TM
Hogan	James	17JUN00	2.12	1	Holte	Elijah	27MAR95	3.09	1
Hogan	James Sr	04JUN01	2.11	1	Holt	Francis	02JUN09	2.13	1
Hogan	James	04JUN01	2.11	11	Holt	Francis	-----11	1.39	1
Hogan	James Sr	12JUN02	1.09	1	Holts	Joseph	06APR97	3.14	1
Hogan	James Jr	12JUN02	1.09	11	Holt	Tanley	-----11	1.40	1
Hogan	John	08JUN02	1.08	1	HOLTON				
Hogan	John	14JUN03	1.10	1	Holton	Alexander	06JUN96	1.06	11
Hogan	John	07JUN06	2.17	1	Holton	William	10JUN96	1.06	1
Hogan	Joseph	20JUN87	2.04	1	HOLTZCLAW				
Hogan	Joseph	17NOV88	1.04	1	Holtzclaw	Abner	05JUN05	1.08	1
Hogan	Joseph	03AUG89	5.06	1	Holtzclaw	Abner	13JUN06	1.10	1
Hogan	Joseph	23JUN91	2.05	1	Holtzclaw	Abner	18MAY07	1.11	1
Hogan	Joseph	10OCT92	1.06	1	Holtzclaw	Amos	05JUN05	1.08	1
Hogan	Macaijah	15JUN96	1.06	1	Holtzclaw	Amos	11JUN06	1.10	1
Hogan	Micagah	26APR97	3.14	1	Holtzclaw	Amos	18MAY07	1.11	1
Hogan	Micajah	04MAY08	1.15	1	Holtzclaw	Amos	04MAY08	1.16	1
Hogan	Micajah	07JUN09	2.14	1	Holtzclaw	Amos	20MAY09	2.13	1
HOGG					Holtzclaw	Amos	-----11	1.40	1
Hogg	Aron	09JUN89	6.04	1	Holtzclaw	Benjamin	13JUN06	1.10	11
Hog	Anderson	13JUN04	4.12	1	Holtzclaw	Benjamin	18MAY07	1.10	12
Hogg	Anderson	28JUN05	2.16	1	Holtzclaw	Benjamin	02JUN08	1.16	12
Hogg	Anderson	18AUG06	2.20	1	Holtzclaw	Benjamin	24MAY09	2.13	1
Hogg	Anderson	18AUG07	2.19	1	Holtzclaw	Benjamin Jr	24MAY09	2.13	1
Hogg	Anderson	18JUL08	2.14	1	Holtzclaw	Benjamin	-----11	1.39	1
Hogg	Anderson	12JUL09	1.19	1	Holtzclaw	Benjamin	-----11	1.40	1
Hogg	Anderson	-----11	1.34	1	Holtzclaw	Jeziah	05JUN05	1.08	1
Hogg	Andrew	23AUG05	3.19	11	Holtzclaw	Jeziah	13JUN06	1.10	1
Hogg	Andrew	31JUL06	3.17	11	Holtzclaw	Jeziah	18MAY07	1.11	1
HOLDERMAN					Holtzclaw	Jesiah	02JUN08	1.16	1
Holderman	Jacob	10JUL99	3.10	1	Holtzclaw	Jeziah	24MAY09	2.13	1
Holderman	Jacob	10JUL00	3.15	2	Holtzclaw	Josiah	-----11	1.39	1
Holderman	Jacob	30JUN01	3.16	1	Holtzclaw	Martin	-----11	1.39	1
Holdiman	Jacob	29JUL02	3.13	1	HOOD				
Holdiman	Jacob	10AUG03	2.16	1	Hood	John	30JUN09	1.19	1
Holderman	Jacob	08JUN04	4.12	1	HOPKINS				
Holdiman	Jacob	20JUN05	2.15	1	Hopkins	Eldridge	01SEP91	3.07	11
Holdiman	Jacob	28JUL06	2.19	1	Hopkins	Francis	21JUL87	3.05	1
HOLLAND					Hopkins	Francis	06AUG89	2.06	1
Holland	Hezekiah	18JUN07	2.16	1	Hopkins	Frances	22MAY91	3.06	1
Holland	John	26MAY89	6.08	1	Hopkins	Francis	27NOV92	3.08	1
Holland	John	10APR90	1.05	1	Hopkins	Francis	24APR94	3.10	1
Holand	John	20APR91	2.05	1	Hopkins	Francis	25MAR95	1.07	1
Holland	John	27NOV92	3.09	1	Hopkins	Stephen	24MAY99	2.08	1
Holland	John	05MAY94	3.10	1	Hopkins	Stephen	12JUN00	1.05	1
Holland	John	10MAR95	1.15		Hopkins	Stephen	03JUN01	1.07	1
"Removed I know not where"					Hopkins	Stephen	14JUN03	1.10	1
Holland	Major	12AUG07	2.18	1	Hopkins	Stephen	18JUN04	1.08	1
HOLLEY					Hopkins	Stephen	29JUN05	1.09	1
Holley	Daniel	27NOV92	3.09	1	Hopkins	William	21JUL87	3.05	1
HOLLIDAY					Hopkins	William	25JUL89	2.06	11
Holliday	Anthony	12MAY95	1.08	1	Hopkins	William	15AUG91	3.07	1
HOLLOWAY					Hopkins	William	30NOV92	3.09	1
Holloway	James	25JUN03	3.11	M1	HOPPER				
Holaway	James	05AUG05	3.18	11	Happer	John	03JUN95	2.07	1
Holaway	James	04AUG06	3.17	1	Hopper	John	25JUL96	1.07	1
HOLMES					Hopper	John	30MAY97	3.15	1
Homes	Edward	11MAR97	2.02	1	Hopper	Thomas	28JUN03	1.10	1
Homes	Edward	24MAY99	2.08	1	Hopper	Thomas	20JUN04	1.08	1
Homes	Edward	04JUN01	1.07	11	Hopper	Thomas	13JUN05	1.09	1
Homes	John	14JUN87	2.04	1	HOPWOOD				
Homes	John	21JUL87	3.05	1	Hopwood	Christopher	20MAY09	2.13	1
Homes	John	04JUN01	1.07	1	HORD				
Homes	John	30JUL06	1.12	1	Hord	Charles	27JUN87	1.02	1
Homes	John	04MAY08	1.16	1	HORINE				
Holmes	John	17APR09	2.12	1	Horrin	Cleaver	-----96	4.07	1
Holms	Joseph	-----93	2.03	1	Horrel	Cleves	23JUN97	1.11	1
HOLSY					Horine	George	30MAY89	6.03	1
Holsy	Thomas	12JUN02	1.09	1	Horine	George	05APR90	1.05	12
HOLT					Horine	George	18MAY91	2.05	1
Holte	Ambroes	27MAR95	3.09	11	Horine	George	18OCT92	1.06	1
Holt	Ambrose	03AUG96	2.09	1	Horoine	Jacob	06SEP87	1.03	1
Holts	Berriman	06APR97	3.14	1	Horine	Jacob	11MAY89	6.09	1

surname	name	date	bk.pg	TM	surname	name	date	bk.pg	TM
Horine	Jacob	05APR90	1.05	1	Howdeshalt	Jacob	05AUG93	1.05	11
Horine	Jacob	20APR91	2.05	1	Howdeshell	Jacob	13MAY94	1.05	11
Horine	Jacob	16AUG93	3.06	1	Howdashall	Jacob	20MAY95	2.06	11
Horine	Jacob	23APR94	2.06	1	Howdeshall	Jacob	08JUN96	1.06	1
Horine	Jacob	28MAR95	3.08	1	Howdeshell	Jacob	21APR97	3.14	1
Horine	Jacob	03AUG96	2.09	1	Howdeshell	John	21APR97	3.16	1
Horien	Jacob	23MAY97	1.12	1	HowdershellJohn		29MAY99	1.14	1
Horine	Jacob	30JUN00	3.14	1	HowdershellJoseph		27OCT92	2.04	1
Horenes	Jacob	-----11	1.33	1	Howdeshalt	Joseph	05AUG93	1.05	1
Horrel	James	21JUN97	1.11	1	Howdeshell	Joseph	31MAY94	1.05	1
Horine	John	30JUN00	3.14	1	Howdashall	Joseph	20MAY95	2.06	1
Horine	John	22JUN03	2.14	1	Howdeshall	Joseph	08JUN96	1.06	1
Horine	John	27JUL04	4.13	1	HorodeshellJoseph		21APR97	3.16	1
Horoine	Michael	06SEP87	1.03	1	HOWELL				
Horine	Michael	30MAY89	6.03	1	Howell	Andrew	30JUN96	1.06	1
Horine	Michael	05APR90	1.05	1	Howel	David	18MAY99	2.09	1
Horine	Michael	14MAY91	2.04	1	Howell	Emmos	14APR97	3.13	1
Horine	Michael	18OCT92	1.06	1	Howell	Joseph	29JUN96	1.06	11
Horine	Michael	20AUG93	3.06	11	Howell	Joseph	15APR97	3.14	11
Horine	Michael	30APR94	2.06	11	HOXSEY				
Horine	Michael	28MAR95	3.09	11	Hoxsey	William	28MAY05	3.16	1
Horine	Michael	03AUG96	2.09	12	HUCKEBY				
Horine	Michael	22MAY97	1.11	21	Huckeby	John	20JUN07	1.12	1
Horine	Michael	03JUL99	3.10	4	Huckeby	Joshua	20JUN07	1.12	1
Paid tax for --- Beamer					Hukebee	Joshua	23MAY09	2.13	1
Horine	Michael	30JUN00	3.14	11	Huckeby	Thomas	20JUN07	1.12	11
Horerine	Michael	08JUN01	3.15	21	Hukebee	Thomas	23MAY09	2.13	1
Horine	Michael	13AUG02	3.13	12	Hukebee	William	23MAY09	2.13	1
Horine	Michael	22JUN03	2.15	11	HUDGENS				
Paid tax for Henry Beamer					Hudgens	Amos	29JUL96	2.09	1
HOSKINS					Hudgens	Anny	28NOV88	1.05	F
Haskins	Basel	18AUG09	2.15	1	Hudgens	Anne	04AUG89	5.06	F
Hoskins	Bazle	-----11	1.36	1	Hudgen	Daniel	14JUN87	2.04	1
Haskins	Samuel	02JUN08	1.15	1	Hudgens	Daniel	28OCT88	1.04	1
Hoskins	William	04MAY08	1.17	1	Hudgens	Daniel	16JUN89	5.06	1
HOUCHINS					Hudgens	Daniel	03APR90	2.03	1
Houchangs	Francis	25MAR95	1.07	1	Huggens	Daniel	15OCT92	2.04	1
Houchins	Joseph	13JUN87	2.03	1	Hudgans	Daniel	10AUG93	1.04	1
HOUK					Hudgans	Daniel	17MAY94	1.05	1
Houk	Jacob	23MAY99	1.16	1	Hudgans	Daniel	09MAY95	2.06	1
Howkes	Nicholas	16APR94	2.06	1	Hudgans	Daniel	18JUN96	1.06	1
Houk	Nicholess	28MAR95	3.09	1	Hudgeons	Daniel	12JUN97	3.15	1
Houk	Nicholas	03AUG96	2.09	1	Hugeon	Daniel	21MAY99	1.15	1
Houck	Nicholas	22MAY97	1.11	1	Hudgins	Daniel	19JUN00	2.13	1
Hauk	Sampson	31MAY97	3.15	1	Hudgins	Daniel	14JUL01	2.12	1
HOUSE					Hudgeance	Daniel	12JUL02	2.13	1
House	George	-----11	1.34	1	Hudgens	Daniel	17JUN03	3.11	1
House	Moses	-----11	1.32	1	Hudgance	Daniel	07AUG04	2.10	1
House	William	30OCT88	1.04	1	Hudgiance	Daniel	08JUL05	3.18	1
HOWARD					Hudgeance	Daniel	17JUL06	3.16	1
Howard	Allen	18JUL05	2.16	1	Hudgans	Daniel	08JUN07	2.15	1
Howard	Allen	19AUG06	2.20	1	Hudgeanes	Daniel	18JUL08	2.14	1
Howard	Allen	15JUL07	2.17	1	Hudgeons	Daniel	07AUG09	1.20	1
Howard	Allen	18JUL08	2.14	1	Hudgens	Daniel	-----11	1.34	1
Howard	Allen	09AUG09	1.20	1	Hudgins	John	30MAR91	1.04	1
Howard	Ephraim	01JUL09	2.15	1	Hudgeance	John	04AUG02	2.14	1
Howard	Julius	29JUN96	2.08	1	Hudgins	Medley	-----11	1.36	1
Howard	Julius	14AUG00	3.15	1	Hudgens	Thomas	01JUN90	2.04	1
Howert	Jules	26JUN01	1.08	1	Hudgins	Thomas	19JUL91	1.04	1
Howert	Jules	23JUN02	1.11	1	Hugans	William	18JUN96	1.06	1
Howert	Jules	22JUN03	1.10	1	Hudgeons	William	23JUN02	1.11	1
Howerton	Obediah	13JUN04	4.12	1	Hudgins	William	23JUN03	1.10	1
Howard	Obadiah	27JUN05	2.15	1	HUDSON				
Howerton	Obadiah	02AUG06	2.19	1	Hutson	Bengamin	25MAR95	1.07	1
Howerton	Obediah	18AUG07	2.19	1	Hudson	Benjamin	19APR91	3.06	1
HOWDESHELL					Hudson	Benjamin	24APR94	3.10	1
Howdeshell	Jacob	26JUN87	2.04	1	Hudson	Benjamin	-----96	4.07	1
Howdeshel	Jacob	28NOV88	1.05	12	Hudson	John	08APR97	3.13	1
Howdeshel	Jacob	05AUG89	5.06	12	HUFF				
Howdyshell	Jacob	03MAY90	2.03	13	Huff	Jonathen	-----08	2.13	1
HowdershellJacob Sr		27OCT92	2.04	1	Huff	Jonathan	29JUN09	1.18	1
HowdershellJacob		27OCT92	2.04	1	Huff	Susanna	05MAY07	1.10	F1

surname	name	date	bk.pg	TM
HUFFMAN				
Hufmond	Daniel	28MAR95	3.09	1
Huffman	Daniel	12MAY95	1.07	
Invalid				
Hoffman	Daniel	23MAY97	1.12	1
Huffman	Frederick	06AUG89	5.06	1
Huffman	Frederick	07AUG89	2.06	11
Huffman	Frederick	26MAR90	2.04	1
Huffman	Fredrick	01SEP91	3.07	1
Huffman	Fredrick	14SEP91	3.07	1
Huffman	Featherick	29NOV92	3.09	1
Huffman	Featherick	01DEC92	3.09	1
Houghman	Fred Jr	23APR94	3.09	1
Hufman	Fred Jr	12MAY95	1.08	1
Hufman	Fred Sr	12MAY95	1.08	1
Hufman	Fred. Jr	-----96	4.08	1
Hufman	Fred. Sr	-----96	4.07	1
Huffman	Henry	14SEP91	3.07	1
Huffman	Henry	29NOV92	3.09	1
Houghman	Henry	07MAY94	3.10	1
Hufman	Henry	25MAR95	1.07	1
Hufman	Henry	-----96	4.08	1
Hoffman	Jacob	18APR89	6.03	1
Hoffman	Jacob	10APR90	1.05	1
Hoffman	Jacob	31MAR91	2.05	1
Hoffman	Jacob	20SEP92	1.06	1
Hoffman	Jacob	08AUG93	3.05	1
Huffman	Jacob	21APR94	2.06	1
Hufmond	Jacob	20MAR95	3.09	0
Huffmans	Jacob	23MAY96	2.08	1
Huffman	Jacob	30MAY97	1.12	1
Huffman	John	12SEP91	3.07	1
Huffman	John	27NOV92	3.09	1
Houghfman	John	05MAY94	3.10	1
Huffman	Michael	24APR94	2.06	21
Hufmond	Michael	28MAR95	3.09	1
Huffman	Michael	03AUG96	2.09	1
Hoffman	Michael	23MAY97	1.12	1
Huffman	William	27NOV92	3.09	01
Houghman	William	05MAY94	3.09	1
Hufman	William	12MAY95	1.08	1
Hufman	William	-----96	4.07	1
HUFNER				
Hufner	Michael	15JUL99	3.11	1
HUGHES				
Huse	Burk	04AUG96	2.10	1
Hughes	Burkett	14JUN06	2.18	1
Hughes	Burkett	10AUG07	2.18	1
Hughes	Burket	02JUN08	1.15	1
Hughes	Edward	20MAY01	3.15	1
Hughes	Edward	08JUL02	3.12	1
Hughes	Edward	11JUL03	2.15	1
Hughes	Edward	25JUL04	4.12	1
Hughes	Ephraim	02JUN90	2.03	1
Hughes	Francis	28MAY99	1.14	1
Hughes	Francis	21JUN00	2.13	1
Hughes	Francis	24JUN01	2.11	1
Hughes	Francis	03AUG02	3.13	1
Hughes	Francis	28MAY03	2.13	1
Hughes	Francis	25JUL04	1.08	1
Hughes	Francis	21MAY05	2.15	1
Hughes	Frances	12MAY06	2.17	1
Hughes	Frances	10AUG07	2.18	1
Hughes	Frances	-----08	2.13	1
Hughes	Francis	07JUN09	1.17	1
Hughes	Francis	-----11	1.34	1
Hughs	Gabriel	20APR97	3.14	1
Hughes	Gabriel	22MAY99	1.15	1
Hughes	Gabriel	21JUN00	2.13	1
Hughes	Gabriel	19MAY01	2.10	1
Hughes	Gabriel	14JUN02	3.12	1
Hughes	Gabriel	13JUN03	2.14	1
Hughes	Gabriel	13MAY05	2.15	1
Hughes	Gabriel	30MAY06	2.17	1
Hughes	Gabriel	15JUL07	2.18	1
Hughes	Gabrell	04MAY08	1.16	1
Hughs	Gabriel	21AUG09	2.15	1
Hughes	Gabriel	-----11	1.38	1
Hughs	George	18OCT92	1.06	1
Hughs	George	15MAY97	1.12	1
Hughes	George	28MAY99	1.16	1
Hughes	George	06JUN06	2.17	1
Hughes	James	-----08	2.13	1
Hughes	James	08JUN09	1.17	1
Hughs	John	26JUN87	1.02	1
Hughs	John	16MAY89	6.03	1
Hughs	John	05APR90	1.05	1
Hughs	John	18MAY91	2.05	1
Hughs	John	18SEP92	1.06	12
Hughs	John	16AUG93	3.06	12
Hughs	John	23APR94	2.06	12
Hughs	John	27MAR95	3.09	21
Hughs	John	03AUG96	2.09	21
Hughs	John	23MAY97	1.12	2
Hughes	John	28MAY99	1.14	1
Hughes	John	21JUN00	2.13	11
Hughes	John	08JUN01	2.11	11
Hughes	John	07JUN02	3.12	12
Hughes	John	11JUN03	2.14	1
Hughes	John Sr	25JUL04	1.08	11
Hughes	John	25JUL04	1.08	1
Hughes	John	21MAY05	2.15	2
Hughes	John Jr	13MAY05	2.15	1
Hughes	John Sr	14JUN06	2.18	1
Hughes	John	15JUL07	2.18	1
Hughes	John	07JUN09	1.17	1
Hughes	John	-----11	1.35	1
Hughs	Reuben	05APR90	1.05	1
Hughes	Reuben	16JUN00	2.12	1
Hughes	Reuben	04APR01	2.10	1
Hughes	Reuben	08JUN02	3.12	1
Hughes	Reuben	18MAY03	2.13	1
Hughes	Ruben	18JUN04	2.08	1
Hughes	Reuben	16MAY05	2.15	1
Hughes	Reuben	12MAY06	2.17	1
Hughes	Reuben	15JUL07	2.17	1
Hughes	Reuben	-----08	2.13	1
Hughes	Reuben	07JUN09	1.17	1
Hughes	Reuben	-----11	1.35	1
Hughes	Thomas	10JUN94	1.11	1
Hughes	Thomas	11JUN03	2.14	M1
Hughes	Thomas	15JUL07	2.17	1
Hughes	Thomas	04JUL08	2.14	1
Hughes	Thomas	02JUN09	1.17	1
Hughs	William	19APR91	2.05	11
Hughs	William	26SEP92	1.06	11
Hughs	William	16AUG93	3.06	12
Hughs	William	23APR94	2.06	12
Hughs	William	28MAR95	3.09	21
Hughs	William	03AUG96	2.09	2
Hughs	William	15MAY97	1.12	11
Hughes	William	28MAY99	1.16	2
Hughes	William	16JUN00	2.12	11
Hughes	William	01JUL02	3.12	11
Hughes	William	28MAY03	2.13	11
Hughes	William	07AUG04	2.10	2
Hughes	William Sr	05AUG05	2.17	1
Hughes	William Jr	10JUN05	2.15	M1
Hughes	William Sr	12MAY06	2.17	1
Hughes	William Jr	12MAY06	2.17	1
Hughes	William Sr	10AUG07	2.18	11
Hughes	William	15JUL07	2.17	1
Hughes	William	-----08	2.13	1
Hughs	William Sr	07JUL09	1.19	1

surname	name	date	bk.pg	TM	surname	name	date	bk.pg	TM
Hughs	William Jr	07JUL09	1.19	1	Hunt	Richard	29MAY94	1.05	1
Hughes	William Sr	-----11	1.34	1	Hunt	Richard	03JUN95	2.07	1
Hughes	William Jr	-----11	1.34	1	Hunt	Richard	29JUN96	1.06	11
HULTS					Hunt	Richard	26APR97	3.14	11
Hults	James	28JUL03	2.16	11	Hunt	Richard	14MAY99	1.14	11
HUMBER					Hunt	Richard	18JUN00	2.13	11
Humber	Charles	04MAY08	1.15	1	Hunt	Richard	24JUL01	2.12	11
HUMBLE					Hunt	Richard	04JUN02	1.08	11
Humble	Michael	19JUN00	2.13	1	Hunt	Richard	29JUN03	1.11	12
HUMPHREYS					Hunt	Richard	03AUG04	2.09	11
Humphrey	David	28JUN99	1.17	1	Hunt	Richard	13JUN05	1.08	11
Humphrey	David	25JUN00	2.13	1	Hunt	Richard	18JUN06	1.11	11
Humphrey	David	23JUL01	3.16	1	Hunt	Richard	04JUN07	1.11	1
Humphreys	David	04AUG02	2.14	1	Hunt	Richard	04MAY08	1.14	1
Humphrey	David	15JUL03	3.12	1	Hunt	Richard	06JUN09	2.14	1
Humphrey	David	21AUG04	3.10	1	Hunt	Richard	-----11	1.38	1
Humphreys	David	12AUG05	3.19	1	Hunt	Robert	04JUN07	1.11	1
Humphreys	David	08AUG06	3.17	1	Hunt	Robert	04MAY08	1.15	1
Humphreys	Isaiah	04AUG02	2.14	1	Hunt	Robert	-----11	1.38	1
Humphrey	John	28JUN99	1.17	1	HUNTER				
Hunphrey	John	27JUN00	2.13	1	Hunter	Daniel	21JUN03	1.10	1
Humphreys	John	19JUN01	3.16	1	Hunter	Daniel	01AUG04	1.09	1
Humphreys	John	04AUG02	2.14	1	Hunter	Daniel	07JUN05	1.08	1
Humphrey	John	11JUL03	3.12	1	Hunter	Daniel	30JUL06	1.12	1
Humphrey	John	06AUG04	3.10	11	Hunter	Daniel	25MAY07	1.11	1
Humphreys	John	12AUG05	3.19	1	Hunter	Daniel	14JUN08	1.16	1
Humphreys	John	23AUG06	3.17	11	Hunter	Daniel	14JUN08	1.16	1
Humphras	William	14JUN96	1.06	1	Hunter	Daniel	05JUN09	2.14	1
Humphrey	William	28JUN99	1.17	1	Hunter	Daniel	-----11	1.38	1
Humphrey	William	23JUL00	2.14	1	Hunter	George	10AUG07	2.18	1
HUNDLEY					Hunter	George	01AUG08	2.14	1
Hunley	James	11JUN02	2.13	1	Hunter	George	15AUG09	1.20	1
Hunley	James	05AUG03	2.16	1	Hunter	John	14MAY89	6.03	1
Hundley	James	05APR04	4.11	11	Hunter	Samuel	28OCT92	2.04	1
Humley	James	28JUN05	2.16	11	Hunter	Titus	19JUN05	3.17	11
Hunley	James	31JUL06	2.19	1	Hunter	Titus	29JUL06	3.17	11
Hunley	James	18AUG07	2.19	1	HUNTSMAN				
Hunley	James	26JUL08	2.14	1	Huntsman	Benjamin	-----11	1.33	1
Hundley	James	-----11	1.34	1	Huntsman	George	-----11	1.34	1
Humley	Samuel	28JUN05	2.16	1	Huntsman	Jean	28JUL01	2.13	F1
HUNN					Huntsman	Jean	28JUL01	2.13	FS
Hunn	Anthony	23JUL05	2.16	1	Hunsman	Jenny	23JUL06	3.16	F2
Hunn	Anthony	14JUL06	2.18	1	Hunsman	Jeney	11JUN07	2.16	F2
Hunn	Anthoni	15JUL07	2.18	1	Hunsman	Jenney	-----08	2.13	F1
Hunn	Anthony	04MAY08	1.17	1	Huntsman	Jenny	26JUN09	1.18	F
Hunn	Anthony	18AUG09	2.15	1	With two white males above 21				
HUNT					Huntsman	Joseph	24AUG87	1.03	1
Hunt	Hackley	14MAY99	1.14	1	Huntsman	Josiah	26MAR90	2.04	1
Hunt	Hackley	18JUN00	2.13	1	Huntsman	Joseph	26SEP92	2.04	1
Hunt	Hackley	24JUL01	2.12	1	Huntsman	Josiah	17SEP93	1.04	1
Hunt	Hackley	04JUN02	1.08	1	Huntsman	Josiah	03MAY94	1.04	1
Hunt	Heckley	29JUN03	1.12	1	Huntsman	Josiah	08MAY95	2.06	1
Hunt	Hackley	03AUG04	2.09	1	Huntsman	Josiah	30MAY96	1.07	1
Hunt	Heckley	13JUN05	1.08	1	Huntsman	Josiah	12JUN97	3.15	1
Hunt	Heckley	18JUN06	1.11	1	Huntsman	Josiah	01JUN99	1.16	11
Hunt	Hackney	04JUN07	1.11	1	Huntsman	Josiah	01AUG00	2.15	11
Hunt	Hackney	22APR08	1.14	1	Hunsman	William	27MAY02	2.12	11
Hunt	Hackney	06JUN09	2.14	1	Huneman	William	21JUL03	3.12	1
Hunt	Hackley	-----11	1.38	1	Huntsman	William	01AUG04	3.10	11
Hunt	James	03AUG04	2.09	1	Hunsman	William	10JUN05	3.16	11
Hunt	James	13JUN05	1.08	1	Hunsman	William	23JUL06	3.16	1
Hunt	James	04JUN07	1.11	1	Hunsman	William	11JUN07	2.15	1
Hunt	James	04MAY08	1.15	1	Hunsman	William	-----08	2.13	1
Hunt	James	06JUN09	2.14	1	Huntsman	William	26JUN09	1.18	1
Hunt	James Sr	-----11	1.38	1	Huntsman	William	-----11	1.33	1
Hunt	James Jr	-----11	1.38	1	HURLEY				
Hunt	Richard	13JUN87	2.03	1	Hurly	John	13AUG93	3.05	1
Hunt	Richard	14NOV88	1.04	1	Hurley	John	10JUN94	2.06	1
Hunt	Richard	24JUN89	5.06	1	Hurley	John	17APR95	3.08	1
Hunt	Richard	03APR90	2.03	1	Hurly	John	05JUL96	2.09	1
Hunt	Richard	14OCT92	2.04	1	Hurley	John	23JUN97	1.11	1
Hunt	Richard	13AUG93	1.04	1					

surname	name	date	bk.pg	TM	surname	name	date	bk.pg	TM
Hurley	John	06JUN99	1.14	1	Huston	Mary	05JUL96	2.09	F
Hurley	John	29JUL00	2.14	1	Huston	Nathan	26JUN87	2.04	1
Hurley	John	20JUN01	3.16	1	Huston	Nathan	28OCT88	1.04	1
Hurley	John	09JUN02	2.13	1	Huston	Nathan	15APR90	1.05	1
Hurley	John	14JUN03	3.11	1	Huston	Nathan	19APR91	2.05	1
Hurley	John	31JUL04	3.10	1	Huston	Nathan	02OCT92	1.06	1
Hurley	John	22JUN05	3.17	1	Huston	Nathan	06AUG93	3.05	1
Hurley	John	23JUL06	3.16	1	Huston	Nathan	24APR94	2.06	1
HURST					Huston	Nathan	24APR94	2.06	1
Hurst	John	26MAY97	1.12	1	Huston	Nathan	22APR95	3.08	1
Hurst	William	26MAY97	1.12	11	Huston	Nathan	22APR95	3.08	1
HUSBAND					Huston	Nathan	29JUL96	2.09	1
Husband	Vezy	27JUN04	4.12	1	Paid tax for George Huston				
Husbands	Valzy	15AUG06	2.20	1	Huston	Nathan	03JUL97	1.12	1
Husband	Vezy	15JUL07	2.17	1	Paid tax for George Huston				
Husband	Uzy	02AUG08	2.15	1	Huston	Nathan	12JUN99	1.17	1
HUSK					Huston	Nathan	12JUN99	1.40	
Husk	John	28JUN94	2.06	1	One lott in Stanford				
Husk	John	14JUL95	3.08	0	Huston	Nathan	28JUN00	2.14	1
HUSTON					One lott in Standford				
Huston	Anne	31JUL06	3.16	F	Huston	Nathan	01AUG01	2.13	1
Huston	Anne	11JUN07	2.16	F	One lott in Standford				
Huston	Anne	-----08	2.12	F	Huston	Nathan	01AUG01	2.13	
Huston	Anne	02AUG08	2.15		Partner of Joseph F. Lewis				
Adm. estate of Nathan Huston					Huston	Nathan	23AUG02	2.15	1
Huston	Anne	30JUN09	1.19	F	Partner of Joseph F.Lewis				
Huston	Archable	19JUN89	5.06	1	Huston	Nathan	21JUL03	3.12	1
Huston	Archibald	25MAR91	1.04	1	Huston	Nathen	16AUG04	2.10	1
Huston	Archy	18OCT92	1.06	1	Huston	Nathan	16AUG04	2.10	
Huston	Archibald	07AUG93	3.05	1	Paid taxes for George Huston				
Huston	Archible	23MAY94	2.06	1	Huston/LewiNathen/Jos		16AUG04	2.10	0
Huston	Archable	14APR95	3.08	1	Huston/LewiNathen/Jos		16AUG04	2.10	0
Huston	Arch	02JUN96	2.08	1	Huston/LewiNathen/Jos		16AUG04	2.10	0
Huston	Archibald	02JUN97	1.12	1	Huston/LewiNathen/Jos		16AUG04	2.10	0
Huston	Archibald	16MAY99	3.10	1	Huston/LewiNathen/Jos		16AUG04	2.10	0
Huston	Archabald	08JUL00	3.14	1	Huston	Nathan	12AUG05	3.19	1
Huston	Archibald	18JUN01	3.15	1	Huston	Nathan	15JUL07	2.17	0
Huston	Archibald	28JUL02	3.12	1	Huston	Nathen	02AUG08	2.15	D
Huston	Archibald	29JUN03	2.15	1	Estate adm by Anne Huston				
Huston	Archy	05JUN04	4.12	1	Huston	Nathen	02AUG08	2.15	
Huston	Archibald	16MAY05	2.15	1	Estate adm by George Murrell				
Huston	Archibald	14JUL06	2.18	1	Huston	Nathen	02AUG08	2.15	
Huston	Archibald	20JUN07	2.16	1	Estate adm by Stephenson Huston				
Huston	Archibald	-----08	2.13	1	Huston	Nathan	13JUL09	1.19	D
Huston	Archibald	12JUL09	1.19	1	Huston	Nathan	-----11	1.50	D
Huston	Archibald	-----11	1.33	11	Taxes paid by William Montgomery				
Huston	George	26MAY94	1.11	1	Huston	Stephen	02SEP87	1.02	1
Huston	George	29JUL96	2.09	0	Huston	Stephen	23MAY89	6.04	1
Tax pd by Nathan Huston					Huston	Stephenson	21APR90	1.05	1
Huston	George	29JUL96	2.09	0	Huston	Stephenson	19APR91	2.05	1
Tax pd by Stephenson Huston					Huston	Stephenson	02OCT92	1.06	1
Huston	George	03JUL97	1.12	1	Huston	Stephenson	07AUG93	3.05	1
Tax pd by Nathan Huston					Huston	Stephenson	23APR94	2.06	1
Huston	George	08AUG97	1.11	1	Huston	Stephenson	29JUL96	2.09	1
Tax pd by Stephen Huston					Paid tax for George Huston				
Huston	George	16AUG04	2.10	0	Huston	Stephen	08AUG97	1.11	1
Taxes paid by Nathen Huston					Paid tax for George Huston				
Huston	George	12AUG05	3.19	1	Huston	Stephen	08AUG97	1.11	
Huston	George	15JUL07	2.17	1	Paid tax for Robert Sconce				
Huston	George	02AUG08	2.14	1	Huston	Stephenson	24MAY99	3.10	1
Taxes paid by Stephenson Huston					Huston	Stephenson	21JUN00	3.13	1
Huston	George	13JUL09	1.19	1	Huston	Stephenson	18JUN01	3.15	1
Huston	George	-----11	1.33	1	Huston	Stephen	28JUL02	3.13	1
Huston	George	-----11	1.33	1	Huston	Stephen	29JUN03	2.15	1
Huston	Landy	-----11	1.36	F	Huston	Stephen	05JUN04	4.11	1
Huston	Mary	23MAY89	6.04	F	Huston	Stephen	19JUN05	2.15	1
Huston	Mary	13AUG90	1.05	F1	Huston	Stephen	29JUL06	2.19	1
Huston	Mary	17MAY91	2.05	F1	Huston	Stephenson	15JUL07	2.17	1
Huston	Mary	18OCT92	1.06	F	Huston	Stephenson	02AUG08	2.14	1
Huston	Mary	07AUG93	3.05	F	Huston	Stephenson	02AUG08	2.15	
Huston	Mary	24APR94	2.06	F	Adm. estate of Nathan Huston				
Huston	Mary	16APR95	3.08	F	Huston	Stephenson	02AUG08	2.14	

surname	name	date	bk.pg	TM	surname	name	date	bk.pg	TM
Paid taxes for George Huston					Hutchason	Thomas	10JUN01	1.07	1
Huston	Stephen	13JUL09	1.19	1	Hutchason	Thomas	08JUN02	1.09	11
Huston	Stephen	-----11	1.33	1	Hutchason	Thomas	20JUN03	1.10	12
HUSTON/LEWI					Hutchason	Thomas	19JUN04	1.08	11
Huston/LewiNathan/Jos	12AUG00	2.24	0		Hutchason	Thomas	11JUN05	1.08	12
Huston/LewiNathan/Jos	12AUG00	2.24	0		Hutchason	Thomas	16JUN06	1.11	11
Huston/LewiNathan/Jos	12AUG00	2.24	0		Hutchison	Thomas S./L	18AUG06	2.20	1
Huston/LewiNathan/Jos	12AUG00	2.24	0		Hutcheson	Thomas	11JUN07	1.12	1
Huston/LewiNathan/Jos	12AUG00	2.24	0		Hutcheson	Thomas	11JUN07	1.11	12
HUTCHINS					Hutcheson	Thomas	02JUN08	1.16	11
Hutchins	Aaron	21MAY90	1.05	1	Hutcheson	Thomas	04JUL08	2.14	11
Hutchings	Elizabeth	30JUL06	2.19	F	Hutcheson	Thomas	25AUG09	2.16	1
Hutchings	Gabriel	10JUL00	3.14	1	Hutchison	Thomas S.	08JUN09	1.17	1
Hutchings	Gabriel	03AUG02	3.13	1	Hutcheson	Thomas	-----11	1.39	1
Hutchings	Gabriel	10AUG03	2.16	1	Hutchison	Thomas	-----11	1.40	21
Hutchins	Gabriel	08JUN04	4.12	1	HYATT				
Huchens	James	10AUG07	2.18	12	Hiatt	Abner	23APR94	3.09	1
Hutchens	James	04MAY08	1.17	12	Hyat	Benjamin	04JUN01	2.11	1
Hutchings	James	22AUG09	2.15	1	Hiatt	Benjamin	12JUN02	1.09	1
Hutchings	James	-----11	1.36	1	Hiatt	Benjamin	04JUL03	1.11	1
Hutchons	John	10AUG97	1.11	1	Hiatt	Benjamin	01AUG04	2.09	1
Hutchings	John	10JUL99	3.10	1	Hiatt	Benjamin	17JUN05	1.09	1
Hutchings	John	10JUL00	3.15	1	Hiatt	Benjamin	20JUN06	1.11	1
Hutchings	John	30JUL01	3.16	1	Hiatt	Benjamin	03JUN07	1.11	1
Hutchings	John	29JUL02	3.13	1	Hyatt	Benjamin	22APR08	1.14	1
Hutchings	John	10AUG03	2.16	1	Hyatt	Benjamin	22APR08	1.14	1
Huchins	John	08JUN04	4.12	1	Hyatt	Benjamin	31MAY09	2.13	1
Hutchings	John	21JUN05	2.15	1	Hiatt	Benjamin	-----11	1.37	1
Hutchings	John	30JUL06	2.19	1	Hiat	Frederick	08JUL00	2.14	1
Hutchings	Lemuel	-----11	1.36	1	Hyat	Frederick	02JUN01	2.11	1
Hutchens	Thomas	07JUL90	2.03	1	Hiatt	Frederick	17JUN03	3.11	1
Hutchens	Thomas	29OCT92	2.04	1	Hiatt	Frederick	01AUG04	2.09	1
Hutchings	Thomas	06AUG93	1.05	1	Highatt	Fredrick	17JUN05	3.17	1
Hutchings	Thomas	14MAY94	1.04	1	Highatt	Fredrick	14JUL06	3.16	1
Hutchings	Thomas	22MAY95	2.06	1	Hyatt	Frederick	30JUN07	1.12	1
Hutchings	Thomas	09JUN96	1.06	1	Hyatt	Fredrick	22APR08	1.14	1
Hutchons	Thomas	10MAY97	1.11	1	Hyatt	Fredrick	07AUG09	2.15	1
Hutchings	Thomas	10JUL99	3.10	1	Heatt	Frederick	-----11	1.37	1
Hutchings	Thomas	10JUL00	3.14	1	Hiatt	John	26JUN87	3.04	12
Hutchings	Thomas	30JUL01	3.16	1	Hyatt	John	13SEP91	3.07	1
Hutchings	Thomas	29JUL02	3.13	1	Hiatt	John	07MAY94	3.10	1
Hutchings	Thomas	10AUG03	2.16	1	Hiatt	John	12MAY95	1.07	1
Hutchins	Thomas	08JUN04	4.12	1	Hiatt	John	-----96	4.08	1
Hutchings	Thomas	20JUN05	2.15	1	Hiat	John	23JUN00	2.13	1
Hutchings	Thomas	30JUL06	2.19	1	Hyat	John	02JUN01	2.11	1
Huchings	Thomas	18AUG07	2.19	1	Highat	John	23AUG02	2.15	1
HUTCHISON					Hiatt	John	17JUN03	3.11	1
Hutcheson	Elijah	-----11	1.39	1	Hiatt	John	01AUG04	2.09	1
Hutchison	James	04APR01	2.10	1	Highatt	John	17JUN05	3.17	1
Hutchason	Joseph	16JUN06	1.11	1	Highatt	John	17JUL06	3.16	1
Hutcheson	Joseph	25MAY07	1.11	1	Highatt	John	31JUL07	2.18	1
Hutcheson	Joseph	02JUN08	1.16	1	Hyatt	John	-----08	2.13	1
Hutcheson	Joseph	05JUN09	2.14	1	Hyatt	John	06APR09	1.17	1
Hutcheson	Joseph	-----11	1.39	1	Hiatt	John	-----11	1.38	1
Hutcheson	Lewis	06JUN09	2.13	1	Hyette	Joseph	27JUN89	2.06	1
Hutcheson	Lewis	-----11	1.39	1	Hyatt	Joseph	13SEP91	3.07	1
Hutcherson	Philip	25MAR95	1.07	1	Hyette	William	30JUN89	2.06	1
Hutchinson	Phillip	28AUG93	3.05	1	Hiat	William	23JUN00	2.13	1
Hutcherson	Phillip	05MAY94	3.10	1	Hyat	William	02JUN01	2.11	1
Hutchenson	Phillip	-----96	4.07	1	Hiatt	William	11JUL03	1.12	1
Hutchison	Thomas	12JUN87	2.03	11	Hiatt	William	02AUG04	2.09	1
Hutcherson	Thomas	01NOV88	1.04	1	Hiatt	William	17JUN05	1.09	11
Hutcherson	Thomas	19JUN89	5.06	1	Hiatt	William	20JUN06	1.11	1
Hutchison	Thomas	29MAR91	1.04	1	Hyatt	William	30JUN07	1.12	1
Hutcheson	Thomas	13OCT92	2.04	1	Hyatt	William	22APR08	1.14	1
Hutchison	Thomas	14AUG93	1.04	1	Hyatt	William	31MAY09	2.13	1
Hutchison	Thomas	29MAY94	1.05	1	Hyatt	William	-----11	1.37	1
Hutchinson	Thomas	03JUN95	2.06	1	Hyatt	Wilson	-----11	1.37	1
Hutchison	Thomas	09JUN96	1.06	1	ILKINS				
Hutchison	Thomas	13APR97	3.13	1	Ilkins	Joshua	16APR94	2.07	1
Hutchason	Thomas	30MAY99	2.08	1	INGHAM				
Hutchason	Thomas	20JUN00	1.05	1	Ingham	Ebenezer	20MAY94	3.11	1

surname	name	date	bk.pg	TM	surname	name	date	bk.pg	TM
INGRAM					Jackman	Jane	03JUN02	3.14	F1
Ingram	John	08JUN08	1.18	1	Jackman	Jean	04AUG03	2.17	F1
INMAN					Jackmond	Jean	22AUG04	2.11	F1
Innman	William	13JUN05	1.10	1	Jackman	Jean	18JUL05	2.18	F1
Innman	William	18JUN06	1.12	1	Jackman	Jean	12AUG06	2.20	F1
Juman	William	12MAY07	1.13	1	Jackmond	Jean	01AUG07	2.20	F
Inman	William	10AUG08	1.17	11	Jackmon	Jane	10MAY09	1.20	F
Inman	William	06JUL09	2.16	1	Jackman	Jane	-----11	1.41	F
Inman	William	-----11	1.41	1	Jackman	John	15JUL87	3.05	1
IRVIN					Jackman	John	27JUN89	2.07	1
Urven	Annanias	20JUN87	2.07	1	Jackman	John	28MAY91	3.08	1
Erven	Benjamin	02AUG04	2.06	1	Jackman	John	18NOV92	3.10	1
Irvin	Benjamin	18JUN05	2.17	1	Jackman	John	20MAY94	3.11	1
Irvine	Benjamin	26JUL06	3.19	1	Jackman	John	12MAY95	1.08	1
Ervin	Francis	02AUG04	1.06	1	Jackman	John	-----96	4.08	13
Erven	Francis	30JUL05	1.06	1	Jackman	Joseph	12MAY95	1.08	0
Ervin	Francis	01AUG06	1.08	1	Jackman	Mary	29JUL01	2.14	F
Ervin	Francis	26JUN07	1.07	1	Jackman	Mary	30JUL01	2.14	F
Ervin	Francis	18APR08	1.09	1	Jackman	Mary	27MAY02	3.14	F
Erwin	Jamison	24MAY99	1.09	1	Jackman	Mary	27MAY02	3.14	F
Erwin	Jamison	08JUL00	2.09	1	Jackman	Mary	27MAY02	3.14	F
Ervin	Jamison	13JUL01	2.07	1	Jackman	Mary	20JUN03	2.17	F1
Arvin	John	-----11	1.01	1	Jackman	Mary	20JUN03	2.17	FS
Arvin	Starling	18MAY07	1.01	1	Jackman	Mary	20JUN03	2.17	FS
Erwin	Starling	02AUG08	1.10	1	Jackman	Mary	26JUL04	1.10	F1
Arven	William	25JUN08	2.01	12	Jackman	Mary	26JUL04	1.10	FS
Ervin	William	13MAY09	2.09	0	Jackman	Mary	26JUL04	1.10	FS
Exempt	(from county levy)				Jackman	Richard	13JUN87	2.04	1
Arvin	William	-----11	1.01	1	Jackman	Richard	18NOV88	1.05	1
ISAACS					Jackman	Richard	22APR90	2.04	1
Isaacs	John	26JUN87	1.03	1	Jackman	Richard	06APR91	1.04	1
Isaacs	John	16MAY89	6.04	1	Jackman	Richard	20AUG93	1.05	11
Isaac	John	21APR90	1.06	1	Jackman	Richard	14MAY94	1.05	1
Isaacs	John	09MAY91	2.05	1	Jackman	Richard	11MAY95	2.07	11
Isaacs	John	13OCT92	1.06	1	Jackman	Richard	21MAY95	2.19	1
Isaacs	John	13SEP93	3.06	1	Jackman	Richard	09AUG96	1.07	1
Isaac	John	28MAY94	2.07	1	Jackman	Richard	11JUL97	3.17	1
Isaacs	John	08JUN95	3.09	1	Jackman	Richard	26JUN99	1.19	2
Isaacs	John	27MAY96	2.10	1	Jackman	Richard	17JUL00	2.15	2
Isaacs	John	28JUN97	1.13	11	Jackman	Thomas	10AUG91	2.05	11
Isaacs	John	12JUL99	3.11	11	Jackman	Thos/Elijah	08OCT92	1.06	2
Isaacs	John	14AUG00	3.16	11	Jackman	Thomas	21AUG93	3.06	2
Isaacs	William	13OCT92	1.06	1	Jackman	Thomas	01MAY94	2.07	1
ISBELL					Jackman	Thomas	01MAY94	2.07	2
Isbels	Godfrey	31MAY97	3.16	1	Jackman	Thomas	01APR95	3.10	2
Isable	Thomas	22JUL01	3.18	1	Jackman	William	29NOV92	3.10	1
Isable	Thomas	05AUG02	2.16	1	Jackman	William	21APR94	3.11	1
Isbell	Thomas D.	11JUN03	3.13	1	Jackman	William	12MAY95	1.08	1
Isbell	Thomas D.	06AUG04	3.11	1	Jackman	William	-----96	4.08	11
Isbell	Thomas D.	12JUN05	3.20	1	JACKSON				
Isbell	Thomas D.	01AUG06	3.19	1	Jackson	Christopher	25MAY89	6.04	11
JACK					Jackson	Ephraim	17NOV88	1.05	1
Jack	---	07JUN09	1.20		Jackson	Ephraim	25MAR91	1.04	1
A free negroe					Jackson	Ephraim	23OCT92	2.05	1
JACKMAN					Jackson	Ephraram	07AUG93	1.05	1
Jackman	(heirs)	17JUN08	1.04	0	Jackson	Epheram	14MAY94	1.05	1
Taxes paid by Elijah Baley					Jackson	Ephraim	18MAY95	2.07	1
Jackman	Falix	09JUN96	1.07	1	Jackson	Epheram	06JUN96	1.07	1
Jackman	Jane	27JUN87	2.04	F	Jackson	Ephraim	17APR97	3.16	12
Jackmon	Jane	27NOV88	1.05	F1	Jackson	Ephraim C.	27MAY99	1.18	1
Jackmon	Jane	17MAR90	2.04	F1	Jackson	Ephraim	09JUL00	2.15	1
Jackman	Jane	07APR91	1.04	F	Jackson	Ephraim	17JUL01	2.14	1
Jackman	Jane	06OCT92	2.04	F	Jackson	Ephraim	14JUN02	3.14	1
Jackman	Jane	03AUG93	1.05	F	Jackson	Ephraim	18JUN03	2.17	1
Jackman	Jane	12MAY94	1.05	F	Jackson	Ephrem	24JUL04	1.10	1
Jackman	Jane	12MAY95	2.07	F	Jackson	Ephraim	02MAY05	2.17	1
Jackman	Jane	12MAY95	2.19	F	Jackson	Ephraim	20MAY06	2.20	1
Jackman	Jane	06JUN96	1.07	F	Jackson	Ephrem	01AUG07	2.20	1
Jackman	Jean	15JUN97	3.17	F	Jackson	Ephraigm	07JUN08	1.18	1
Jackman	Jean	31MAY99	1.18	F	Jackson	Ephraim	24AUG09	2.16	1
Jackman	Jane	07AUG00	2.16	F	Jackson	Ephraim	-----11	1.41	1
Jackman	Jean	15JUL01	2.14	F					

surname	name	date	bk.pg	TM	surname	name	date	bk.pg	TM
Jackson	James	27MAY99	1.18	1	A free negro				
Jackson	James	21JUN00	2.15	1	Jackson	Michael	17JUL01	2.14	
Jackson	James	08JUN01	2.14	1	A free negro				
Jackson	James	31JUL02	3.15	1	Jackson	Michael	17JUN02	3.14	
Jackson	James	04JUN03	2.16	1	A free negro				
Jackson	James	23JUL04	1.09	1	Jackson	Michael	18JUN03	2.17	
Jackson	James	13MAY05	2.17	2	A free negro				
Jackson	James	30JUL06	3.19	1	Jackson	Michael	22AUG04	2.11	
Jackson	James	-----11	1.41	1	A free black man				
Jackson	Joel	30MAY90	2.04	1	Jackson	Michael	05AUG05	2.18	
Jackson	Joel	23OCT92	2.05	1	A free negro				
Jackson	Joal	03AUG93	1.05	1	Jackson	Michael	08MAY06	2.20	
Jackson	Joal	12MAY94	1.05	1	A free negroe				
Jackson	Joel	19MAY95	2.07	1	Jackson	Michael	-----08	2.16	
Jackson	Joel	19MAY95	2.19	1	(black)				
Jackson	Joal	01JUN96	1.07	1	Jackson	Michall	07JUN09	1.20	
Jackson	Joel	19APR97	3.16	1	A free negroe				
Jackson	John	13JUN87	2.04	11	Jackson	Patsy	11JUL00	3.16	F
Jackson	John	18NOV88	1.05	11	Jackson	Samuel	20SEP92	1.06	1
Jackson	John	16JUN89	5.06	11	Jackson	Samuel	21APR94	3.11	1
Jackson	John	03APR90	2.04	2	Jackson	Samuel	12MAY95	1.08	1
Jackson	John	25MAR91	1.04	11	Jackson	Samuel	-----96	4.08	1
Jackson	John	28OCT92	2.05	11	Jackson	Thomas	20MAY89	6.04	1
Jackson	John	03AUG93	1.05	11	Jackson	William	08JUN97	1.13	11
Jackson	John	12MAY94	1.05	11	Jackson	William	15AUG97	1.13	1
Jackson	John	19MAY95	2.07	1	Jackson	William	02AUG04	1.10	1
Jackson	John	19MAY95	2.07	12	Jackson	William	05MAY07	1.13	1
Jackson	John	08JUN96	1.07	12	Jackson	William	07JUN08	1.18	1
Jackson	John	19APR97	3.16	1	Jackson	William	05JUN09	1.20	1
Jackson	John	19APR97	3.16	11	Jackson	William	-----11	1.41	1
Jackson	John Sr	27MAY99	1.18	1	Jacob	Jeremiah	10OCT92	1.06	1
Jackson	John	27MAY99	1.18	1	Jacobs	Jeremiah	19AUG93	3.06	1
Jackson	John Sr	09JUL00	2.15	1	JAMES				
Jackson	John Jr	21JUL00	2.15	1	James	George	31OCT88	1.05	1
Jackson	John Sr	15JUN01	2.14	1	James	George	29JUL89	5.07	1
Jackson	John Jr	04JUL01	2.14	1	James	George	14AUG93	1.05	1
Jackson	John Sr	04JUN03	2.16	1	James	Henry	14JUN97	3.17	1
Jackson	John Jr	04JUN03	2.16	1	James	John	13JUN87	2.04	1
Jackson	John	23JUL04	1.09	1	James	John	01NOV88	1.05	1
Jackson	John Jr	23JUL04	1.09	1	James	John	20JUN89	5.07	1
Jackson	John Jr	10MAY05	2.18	1	James	John	03JUN90	2.04	1
Jackson	John Jr	18MAY06	2.20	2	James	John	30MAR91	1.04	1
Jackson	John	29JUN07	1.13	1	James	John	21OCT92	2.04	1
Jackson	John	05AUG07	2.20	1	James	John	14AUG93	1.05	11
Jackson	John	05JUN09	1.20	11	James	John	30MAY94	1.05	11
Jackson	John	-----11	1.40	11	James	John	03JUN95	2.20	1
Jackson	Joseph	27JUN87	2.04	2	James	John	03JUN95	2.07	12
Jackson	Joseph	17NOV88	1.05	1	James	John	01JUL96	1.07	12
Jackson	Joseph	16JUN89	5.06	11	James	John	14JUN97	3.17	11
Jackson	Joseph	08APR90	2.04	2	James	Thomas	26JUN99	3.11	1
Jackson	Joseph	20SEP91	1.04	1	JAMISON				
Jackson	Joseph	22OCT92	2.04	1	Jameson	James	01JUN99	1.18	1
Jackson	Joseph	05AUG93	1.05	1	Jamison	James	01AUG00	2.16	1
Jackson	Joseph	14MAY94	1.05	1	Jamison	James	30JUL01	2.14	1
Jackson	Joseph Sr	18MAY95	2.19	1	Jameson	James	21JUL02	2.16	1
Jackson	Joseph Jr	03JUN95	2.20	1	Jameson	James	12JUL03	3.13	1
Jackson	Joseph	18MAY95	2.07	1	Jimmerson	James	09JUN04	4.13	1
Jackson	Joseph	06JUN96	1.07	1	Jamison	James	17JUN05	2.18	1
Jackson	Joseph	17APR97	3.16	1	Jamison	James	18AUG06	2.20	1
Jackson	Joseph	30MAY99	2.15	0	Jamison	James	22JUN07	2.19	1
Taxes given in by William Pearl					Jamison	James	-----08	2.16	1
Jackson	Joseph	20AUG00	1.12	0	Jamison	James	16JUL09	1.21	1
Tax paid by William Pearrel					Jamesson	James	-----11	1.41	1
Jackson	Joseph	23JUN01	1.14	0	Jamison	William	15MAY99	2.09	1
Tax paid by William Pearrel					JANUARY				
Jackson	Joseph	08JUN02	1.17	0	January	John	23JUN00	2.15	1
Tax paid by William Pearrel					January	John	02JUN01	2.14	1
Jackson	Joseph	11JUL03	1.19	0	JEFFRIES				
Tax paid by William Pearrel					Jeffries	Swep	29JUL03	2.17	1
Jackson	Joseph	03AUG04	1.16	1	Jeffries	Swepson	26JUN04	4.14	1
Tax paid by William Perrel					JEKES				
Jackson	Michael	09JUL00	2.15		Jekes	Frederick	06MAY07	1.13	1

surname	name	date	bk.pg	TM	surname	name	date	bk.pg	TM
Jekes	Peter	06MAY07	1.13	1	Johnston	Andrew	18JUL05	2.18	1
JENKINS					Johnston	Andrew	31JUN06	2.20	11
Jenkins	Samuel	19JUN89	5.06	1	Johnston	Andrew	13AUG06	2.20	1
Jenkins	William	16JUL03	3.13	1	Johnston	Andrew	07JUN08	1.17	1
Jinkens	William	16JUN04	2.11	11	Johnson	Anthony	08JUN09	1.20	1
Jinkens	William	06AUG05	3.20	11	Jonson	Benjamin	10APR94	2.07	1
Jenkings	William	08AUG06	3.19	11	Johnson	Benjamin	10MAY95	3.09	1
Genkens	William	08JUN07	1.10	1	Johnson	Benjamin	06JUN97	1.13	1
JENNINGS					Johnson	Benjamin	07JUN99	1.18	1
Ginnings	Alexander	13AUG02	3.11	1	Johnson	Benjamin	28JUN00	2.15	1
Ginnings	Alexander	12AUG03	2.13	1	Johnson	Benjamin	01JUN03	3.13	1
Genings	John	20JUL05	2.14	1	Johnson	Benjamin	31JUL04	3.11	1
Ginnings	John	30JUL06	2.16	1	Johnston	Benjamin	20JUN01	3.17	1
Genings	Josiah	14JUN02	2.11	M1	Johnston	Benjamin	01JUN02	2.16	1
Ginnings	Josiah	29JUL02	3.10	M1	Johnston	Benjamin	08JUL05	3.20	1
Ginnings	Josiah	10AUG03	2.13	1	Johnston	Benjamin	26JUL06	3.19	1
Jinnens	Josiah	07APR04	4.13	1	Johnston	Benjamin	13JUL07	2.19	1
Jinings	Josiah	20JUN05	2.18	1	Johnston	Benjamin	31MAY08	2.15	1
Ginings	Josiah	31JUL06	2.16	1	Johnson	Benjamin	30JUN09	1.21	1
Jennings	William	04JUL91	3.08	1	Johnson	Benjamin	-----11	1.41	1
Jinnings	William Sr	05DEC92	3.10	1	Johnson	Charles	13AUG90	1.06	1
Jinings	William	18NOV92	3.10	1	Johnston	Daniel	23JUN99	2.10	1
Jennings	William Sr	20MAY94	3.11	1	Johnston	David	15APR90	1.06	1
Jennings	William Jr	21MAY94	3.12	1	Johnston	David	21JUN91	2.05	1
Jennings	William Sr	12MAY95	1.08	1	Johnston	David	04DEC92	1.06	1
Jennings	William Jr	12MAY95	1.08	1	Johnston	David	14SEP93	3.06	1
Jinnings	William Sr	-----96	4.08	1	Johnston	David	05JUL96	2.10	1
Jinnings	William Jr	-----96	4.08	11	Johnson	David	02JUN97	3.17	1
Jennings	William	10JUL99	3.11	1	Johnston	David.	-----11	1.40	1
Gennings	William	10JUL00	3.12	1	Johnston	Edward	12JUN00	1.06	1
Gennings	William	14JUN02	2.11	1	Johnston	Edward	03JUN01	1.09	1
Jennings	William	05AUG03	3.14	1	Johnston	Elias	20AUG06	3.19	1
Jinnings	William	06APR04	4.13	1	Johnson	Elias	-----11	1.41	1
Ginnings	William	03JUN05	3.14	1	Johnson	Isaac	24AUG04	3.11	M1
Genings	William	12MAY06	3.13	1	Johnston	Jacob	10JUL00	3.15	1
JERVES					Johnston	Jacob	29JUL01	3.17	1
Jerves	William	02JUN97	3.17	1	Johnston	Jacob	29JUL03	3.15	1
JESTES					Johnston	Jacob	10AUG03	2.17	1
Jestes	John	18MAY03	2.16	1	Johnston	Jacob	07APR04	4.13	1
Jestes	Thomas	25JUL03	2.17	1	Johnston	Jacob	20JUN05	2.18	1
JINKENSON					Johnston	Jacob	31JUN06	2.20	1
Jinkenson	John	10JUN96	1.07	1	Johnston	James	16AUG96	2.10	1
JNYARD					Johnson	James	20MAY97	3.17	1
Jnyard	John	31MAY08	2.15	1	Johnston	James	19JUN99	2.10	1
Jnyart	John	28JUN09	1.20	1	Johnson	James	16MAY99	1.18	1
JOB					Johnston	James	15JUN02	1.11	1
Job	Thomas	24AUG04	3.11	1	Johnston	James	05JUL03	1.12	1
JOHNS					Johnson	James	26JUN04	1.09	1
John	William	02APR90	1.06	1	Johnston	James	20JUN05	1.10	1
Johns	William	19APR91	2.05	1	Johnston	James	23JUN06	1.12	1
Johns	William	09OCT92	1.07	1	Johnston	James	04MAY07	1.13	1
Johns	William	10AUG93	3.06	1	Johnston	James	08MAY07	1.13	1
Johns	William	18MAR95	3.10	1	Johnston	James	06JUN08	1.17	1
John	William	23APR96	2.10	1	Johnston	James	07JUN08	1.18	1
JOHNSTON					Johnston	James	23JUN09	2.16	1
Johnson	Alexander	22MAY95	2.07	1	Johnson	James	10MAY09	1.20	1
Johnson	Alexander	10JUN96	1.07	1	Johnston	James	-----11	1.41	11
Johnson	Alexander	20APR97	3.17	1	Johnson	Jobe	16MAR97	2.02	11
Johnson	Andrew	16MAY89	6.04	1	One fourwheel carriage				
Johnson	Andrew	03AUG90	1.05	1	Johnston	Jobe	12MAY99	2.10	1
Johnston	Andrew	09AUG91	2.05	1	Johnston	Job	12JUN00	1.06	1
Johnston	Andrew	03NOV92	1.06	1	Johnston	Jobe	02JUN01	1.08	1
Johnston	Andrew	14SEP93	3.06	1	Johnson	John	13JUN87	2.04	1
Johnson	Andrew	28JUN94	2.07	1	Johnson	John	05JUL87	3.05	1
Jonson	Andrew	01MAY95	3.09	1	Johnson	John	04NOV88	1.05	11
Johnston	Andrew	29JUN96	2.10	1	Johnson	John	19JUN89	5.06	11
Johnston	Andrew	10JUL00	3.15	1	Johnson	John	25JUL89	2.07	1
Johnston	Andrew	29JUL01	3.17	1	Johnson	John	03JUN90	2.04	11
Johnston	Andrew	29JUL02	3.15	1	Johnston	John Sr	05JUL96	2.10	1
Johnston	Andrew	10AUG03	2.17	1	Johnston	John Sr	26JUL02	3.14	1
Johnson	Andrew	07APR04	4.13	1	Johnson	John	15JUN96	1.07	1
Johnston	Andrew	20JUN05	2.18	1	Johnson	John	17MAR97	2.02	11

surname	name	date	bk.pg	TM	surname	name	date	bk.pg	TM
Johnston	John	05JUL96	2.10	1	Johnston	Samuel	-----08	2.16	11
Johnston	John Jr	12JUL02	3.14	1	Johnston	Samuel	-----08	2.16	2
Johnson	Joseph	19MAY97	3.17	1	Johnson	Samuel	08JUN09	1.20	1
Johnston	Joseph	23JUN99	2.10	1	Johnson	Samuel	09JUN09	1.20	2
Johnson	Joseph	21MAY04	4.13	1	Johnson	Samuel	-----11	1.40	21
Johnston	Joseph	27JUN05	2.18	1	(Taylor)				
Johnston	Joseph	13AUG06	2.20	1	Johnston	Tabitha	06AUG03	2.17	F
Johnston	Joseph	04AUG07	2.20	1	Johnston	Tabitha	18JUN05	2.18	F
Johnston	Joseph	-----08	2.16	11	Johnston	Tobitha	02AUG06	2.20	F
Jonson	Luke	20APR95	3.09	1	Johnston	Tobitha	12AUG07	2.20	F
Johnston	Luke	08JUN96	2.10	1	Johnston	Tabitha	-----08	2.16	F
Johnson	Luke	02JUL99	3.11	1	Johnson	Tabitha	13JUL09	1.21	F
Johnston	Luke	21JUN00	3.15	1	Johnson	Tabitha	-----11	1.40	F
Johnston	Luke	20MAY01	3.17	1	Johnson	Tandy	10MAY95	3.09	1
Johnston	Luke	08JUL02	3.14	1	Johnston	Tandy	01JUN96	2.10	1
Johnston	Luke	25JUL03	2.17	1	Johnson	Tandy	10MAY97	1.13	1
Johnson	Luke	25JUL04	4.14	1	Johnson	Tandy	26JUN99	3.11	1
Johnston	Luke	22JUL05	2.18	1	Johnson	Tandey	21JUN00	3.15	1
Johnston	Luke	22MAR06	2.20	1	Johnston	Tandy	01MAY01	3.17	1
Johnston	Luke	13JUL07	2.19	1	Johnston	Tandy	31JUL02	3.15	1
Johnston	Luke	-----08	2.16	1	Johnston	Tandy	11JUL03	2.17	1
Johnson	Luke	09JUN09	1.20	1	Johnson	Tandy	29JUN04	4.14	1
Johnson	Luke	-----11	1.41	1	Johnston	Tandy	18JUN05	2.18	1
Johnston	Matilda	18JUN05	2.18	F	Johnston	Tandy	09JUN06	2.20	11
Johnston	Michael	15JUN02	1.11	1	Johnston	Tandy	13JUL07	2.19	1
Johnston	Michael	05JUL03	1.12	1	Johnston	Tandy	-----08	2.16	1
Johnston	Michael	19JUN05	1.10	1	Johnson	Tandy	13JUL09	1.21	1
Johnston	Michael	19JUN05	1.25		Johnston	Thomas	28MAY91	3.08	1
Name not taken in previous year					Jonson	Thomas	28JUN94	2.07	1
Johnston	Michael	21JUN06	1.12	1	Johnson	Thomas	25MAY95	2.07	1
Johnston	Michael	06JUN08	1.17	1	Johnson	Thomas	25MAY95	2.19	1
Johnston	Michael	15AUG09	2.16	1	Johnston	Thomas	13JUN97	3.17	1
Johnson	Moses	10MAY09	1.20	1	Johnston	Thomas	19JUN99	2.10	1
Johnson	Moses	-----11	1.41	1	Johnston	Thomas	10MAY09	1.20	1
Johnson	Noel	13JUL87	1.03	1	Johnston	William	27JUN89	2.07	1
Johnson	Noel	12MAY89	6.04	1	Johnston	William	28MAY91	3.08	1
Johnson	Noel	15APR90	1.05	11	Johnston	William	16JUL91	3.08	1
Johnson	Noel	23JUN91	2.05	11	Johnson	William	18MAY95	2.07	12
Johnston	Noel	24OCT92	1.07	11	Johnson	William	28MAY95	2.19	1
Johnston	Noel	10AUG93	3.06	11	Johnson	William	19JUN96	1.07	12
Johnson	Noel	10APR94	2.07	1	Johnson	William	11APR97	3.16	12
Johnson	Noil	10MAY95	3.09	1	Johnson	William	15APR97	3.16	12
Johnston	Noel	01JUN96	2.10	1	Johnson	William	16MAY99	1.18	21
Johnson	Noal	03JUN97	1.13	1	Johnston	William	03JUN00	2.15	3
Johnson	Noal	09JUL99	3.11	1	Johnson	William	16MAY99	1.18	11
Johnson	Noell	19JUN00	3.15	1	Johnson	William	10JUN00	2.15	11
Johnston	Noal	01MAY01	3.17	1	Johnston	William	28MAY01	2.14	1
Johnston	Noel	26JUL02	3.14	1	Johnston	William	24JUL01	2.14	3
Johnston	Polly	23MAY07	1.13	F	Johnston	William	15JUN02	1.11	1
Johnston	Polly	07JUN08	1.18	F	Johnston	William	15JUN02	1.11	1
Johnson	Presley	22MAY95	2.07	1	Johnston	William	05JUL03	1.12	1
Johnston	Robert	05JUL96	2.10	1	Johnston	William	18JUL03	1.12	1
Johnston	Samuel	26JUN87	1.03	1	Johnston	William	26JUN04	1.09	1
Johnston	Samuel	21MAY89	6.04	1	Johnston	William	07AUG04	2.11	1
Johnson	Samuel	10APR90	1.06	1	Johnston	William	06AUG05	3.20	1
Johnson	Samuel	19MAY91	2.05	1	Johnston	William	17JUL06	3.18	1
Johnson	Samuel	26OCT92	1.07	1	Johnston	William	11JUN07	2.19	1
Johnston	Samuel	15AUG93	3.06	1	Johnston	William	22JUN07	2.19	1
Johnson	Samuel	18APR94	2.07	1	Johnston	William	-----08	2.16	1
Johnson	Samuel	18MAR95	3.10	1	Johnston	William	31MAY08	2.15	1
Johnston	Samuel	22APR96	2.10	1	Johnston	William	22AUG09	2.16	1
Johnson	Samuel	25MAY97	1.13	1	Johnston	William	-----11	1.41	1
Johnson	Samuel	02JUL99	3.11	1	JONES				
Johnston	Samuel	27JUN00	3.15	11	Jones	Abraham	22JUL01	3.18	1
Johnston	Samuel	20MAY01	3.17	11	Jones	Abramham	05AUG02	2.16	1
Johnston	Samuel	08JUL02	3.14	11	Jones	Abraham	06JUN03	3.13	1
Johnston	Samuel	26JUL03	2.17	11	Jones	Abraham	07AUG04	3.11	1
Johnston	Samuel	25JUL04	4.14	11	Jones	Abraham	12JUN05	3.20	1
Johnston	Samuel	20JUL05	2.18	11	Jones	Abraham	18JUL06	3.18	1
Johnston	Samuel	07AUG06	2.20	2	Jones	Allen	31JUL01	3.17	1
Johnston	Samuel	12AUG07	2.20	11	Jones	Ambries	20JUN06	1.12	1
Johnston	Samuel	12AUG07	2.20	2	Jones	Anbrose	23MAY07	1.13	1

surname	name	date	bk.pg	TM	surname	name	date	bk.pg	TM
Jones	Abrose	07JUN08	1.18	1	Jones	John	20MAY94	3.11	1
Jones	Ambrose	05JUN09	1.20	1	Jones	John	21MAY94	3.12	1
Jones	Ambrose	-----11	1.41	1	Jones	John (Capt)	12MAY95	1.08	1
Jones	Arthur	16MAY89	6.04	1	Jones	John Sr	15APR95	3.10	11
Jones	Arthur	20APR91	2.05	1	Jones	John Jr	15MAY95	3.10	1
Jones	Arthur	24OCT92	1.07	1	Jones	John	12MAY95	1.08	1
Jones	Arthur	10AUG93	3.06	1	Jones	John Sr	25MAY97	1.13	1
Jones	Arthur	18APR94	2.07	1	Jones	John Jr	25MAY97	1.13	1
Jones	Arthur	28JUN97	1.13	1	Jones	John Sr	24JUN99	1.19	1
Jones	Arthur	13AUG06	2.20	1	Jones	John Jr	24JUN99	1.19	1
Jones	Balaam	29NOV92	3.10	1	Jones	John Sr	30JUL00	2.16	1
Jones	David	11JUN94	2.07	1	Jones	John	08JUL00	2.15	1
Jones	David	15MAY95	3.09	1	Jones	John Sr	22JUL01	3.17	1
Jones	David	25MAY97	1.13	1	Jones	John Jr	13JUL01	3.17	1
Jones	David	24JUN99	1.19	1	Jones	John Sr	27MAY02	2.16	1
Jones	David	09JUN09	1.20	1	Jones	John Jr	01JUN02	2.16	1
Jones	David	-----11	1.40	1	Jones	John Sr	06AUG03	3.14	1
Jones	Evens	28JUL96	2.10	1	Jones	John Jr	20MAY03	3.13	1
Jones	Evan	20JUN97	1.13	1	Jones	John	21JUN03	1.12	1
Jones	Even	24JUN99	1.19	1	Jones	John Jr	07AUG04	3.11	1
Jones	Even	22JUL00	2.15	11	Jones	John	18JUN04	1.09	1
Jones	Even	20JUL01	3.17	11	Jones	John Sr	12JUN05	3.20	1
Jones	Even	27MAY02	2.16	1	Jones	John	31MAY05	2.17	1
Jones	Evan	21JUL03	3.13	1	Jones	John	06AUG05	3.20	1
Jones	Evan	01AUG04	3.11	1	Jones	John Sr	31JUL06	3.19	1
Jones	Even	12JUN05	3.20	1	Jones	John	13JUN06	1.12	1
Jones	Even	31JUL06	3.19	1	Jones	John	21AUG06	3.19	1
Jones	Even	10JUN07	2.19	1	Jones	John Sr	10JUN07	2.19	1
Jones	Even	-----08	2.16	1	Jones	John	31MAY08	2.15	11
Jones	Evan	29JUN09	1.20	1	Jones	John	07JUN08	1.18	1
Jones	Evan	-----11	1.40	1	Jones	John	29JUN09	1.20	1
Jones	George	21APR94	3.11	0	Jones	John	-----11	1.40	11
Jones	George	12MAY95	1.08		Jones	Jonathen	05AUG02	2.16	1
Invalid					Jones	Jonathan	06JUN03	3.13	1
Jones	George	18JUL06	3.18	1	Jones	Jonathen	-----05	3.38	
Jones	Jabez	11MAY96	2.10	11	1804 tax info in 1805 tax list				
Jones	Jabez	18JUL97	1.13	12	Jones	Jonathen	-----05	3.38	11
Jones	Jabas	02JUL99	1.19	12	Jones	Jonathen	06AUG05	3.20	1
Jones	Jabez	27JUN00	2.15	12	Jones	Jonathen	18JUL06	3.18	1
Jones	Jabez	22JUL01	3.18	1	Jones	Joseph	13JUL91	3.08	1
Jones	Jabus	05AUG02	2.16	11	Jones	Joseph	01DEC92	3.10	1
Jones	Jabez	18JUL03	3.13	1	Jones	Michael	02JUL99	1.19	1
Jones	Jabez	06AUG04	3.11	1	Jones	Michael	22JUL00	2.15	1
Jones	Jabus	12JUN05	3.20	1	Jones	Michael	22JUL01	3.18	1
Jones	Jabus	16JUL06	3.18	1	Jones	Michael	20MAY02	2.16	1
Joanes	James	16JUN00	1.06	1	Jones	Michael	18JUL03	3.13	1
Jones	James	23JUL00	2.15	1	Jones	Michael Sr	24AUG04	3.11	1
Jones	James	09JUN01	1.09	1	Jones	Michael Jr	24AUG04	3.11	M1
Jones	James	18JUN01	3.17	1	Jones	Michiel	12JUN05	3.20	1
Jones	James	28JUL02	3.14	1	Jones	Michiel	06AUG05	3.20	1
Jones	James	25JUN03	3.13	M1	Jones	Michael	05JUL06	3.18	11
Jones	James	11AUG03	2.17	1	Jones	Robert	25MAY97	1.13	1
Jones	James	05JUN04	4.13	1	Jones	Robert	24JUN99	1.19	1
Jones	James	12JUN05	3.20	1	Jones	Robert	30JUL00	2.15	1
Jones	James	28JUN05	2.18	1	Jones	Robert	13JUL01	3.17	1
Jones	James	01AUG06	3.19	1	Jones	Robert	01JUN02	2.16	1
Jones	James	12AUG07	2.20	1	Jones	Robert	06AUG03	3.14	1
Jones	Joshua	21JUL03	3.13	M1	Jones	Robert	04AUG04	3.11	1
Jones	Jeshua	03MAY04	3.11	1	Jones	Robert	12JUN05	3.20	1
Jones	John	26JUN87	2.04	1	Jones	Robert	31JUL06	3.19	1
Jones	John	27JUN87	2.04	1	Jones	Robert	14AUG06	2.20	1
Jones	John	27NOV88	1.05	1	Jones	Robert	03AUG07	2.20	1
Jones	John	16JUN89	5.06	1	Jones	Robert	31MAY08	2.15	1
Jones	John	25JUL89	2.07	1	Jones	Robert	29JUN09	1.20	1
Jones	John	15JUN90	2.04	1	Jones	Robert	-----11	1.40	1
Jones	John	07MAY91	3.08	1	Jones	Samuel	24MAY97	1.13	1
Jones	John	29MAY91	3.08	1	Jones	Samuel	18JUL97	1.13	1
Jones	John	29NOV92	3.10	1	Jones	Samuel	01JUL99	1.19	1
Jones	John	04DEC92	3.10	1	Jones	Samuel	22JUL00	2.15	1
Jones	John	13AUG93	3.06	12	Jones	Samuel Sr	22JUL01	3.17	1
Jones	John Sr	11JUN94	2.07	11	Jones	Samuel Jr	22JUL01	3.17	1
Jones	John Jr	11JUN94	2.07	1	Jones	Samuel	20MAY02	2.16	11

surname	name	date	bk.pg	TM	surname	name	date	bk.pg	TM
Jones	Samuel	05AUG02	2.16	1	Josselling	John	24OCT92	1.07	1
Jones	Samuel	06JUN03	3.13	1	Josselling	John Sr	12AUG93	3.06	1
Jones	Samuel Jr	06JUN03	3.13	1	Josselling	John	14AUG93	3.06	1
Jones	Samuel Jr	07AUG04	3.11	1	Jossling	John Sr	09APR94	2.07	1
Jones	Samuel	12JUN05	3.20	1	Jossling	John	10APR94	2.07	1
Jones	Samuel	06AUG05	3.20	1	Josling	John	10MAY95	3.09	1
Jones	Samuel	01AUG06	3.19	1	Josling	John	04JUN96	2.10	1
Jones	Taverner	-----93	2.03	1	Josling	John	25JUN97	1.13	1
Jones	Thomas	12JUN89	6.08	1	Joslin	John	26JUN99	1.19	1
Jones	Thomas	21APR90	1.06	1	Joslin	John	25JUL00	2.15	1
Jones	Thomas	28MAY95	3.07	1	Josling	John	29MAY01	3.17	1
Joanes	Thomas	16JUN00	1.06	1	Josling	John	05AUG02	2.16	1
Jones	Thomas	09JUN01	1.09	11	Joslin	John	26JUL03	3.13	11
Jones	Thomas	05AUG02	2.16	1	Josling	John	07AUG04	3.11	11
Jones	Thomas	06JUN03	3.13	1	Josling	John	06AUG05	3.20	11
Jones	Thomas	22JUN03	1.12	1	Josling	John	04AUG06	3.19	11
Jones	Thomas	06AUG03	3.14	1	Josselling	William	11JUN89	6.04	1
Jones	Thomas	03MAY04	3.11	1	Josselling	William	11JUN89	6.04	1
Jones	Thomas	02AUG04	1.10	1	John Evins listed with him				
Jones	Thomas	07AUG04	3.11	1	Josselling	William	02AUG90	1.05	1
Jones	Thomas	30JUL05	1.10	1	Josselling	William	21JUN91	2.05	1
Jones	Thomas	31JUL05	1.10	1	Josselling	William	24OCT92	1.07	1
Jones	Thomas	23AUG06	3.19	1	Josselling	William	14AUG93	3.06	1
Jones	Thomas	06MAY07.	1.13	1	Jossling	William	09MAY94	2.07	1
Jones	Thomas	07JUN08	1.18	1	Josling	William	16JUN95	3.09	1
Jones	Thomas	14JUN09	2.16	1	Josling	William	13JUL96	2.10	1
Jones	Thomas E.	12JUN05	3.20	1	Josling	William	25JUN97	1.13	1
Jones	Thomas E.	28JUL06	3.19	1	Josling	William	13MAY99	3.11	1
Jones	Thomas E.	20JUN07	2.19	1	Joslin	William	19JUN00	3.15	1
Jones	William	02AUG87	1.03	1	Josling	William	20MAY01	3.17	1
Jones	William	23JUL89	2.07	1	Joslin	William	26JUL02	3.14	1
Jones	William	16APR94	2.07	1	Joslin	William	03AUG03	2.17	1
Jones	William C.	06JUN95	2.20	1	Josling	William	05JUN04	4.13	1
Jones	William	28JUL96	2.10	1	Joslin	William	31MAY05	2.17	1
Jones	William	10MAY97	1.13	1	JOURNEY				
Jones	William	14JUL97	1.13	1	Journey	John	01JUN97	3.17	1
Jones	William	26JUN99	1.18	11	Journey	Nathaniel	01JUN97	3.17	1
Jones	William	18JUN00	3.15	1	JUMP				
Jones	William	04JUL00	3.16	1	Jump	Peter	22MAY90	2.04	1
Jones	William	12JUL00	3.16	M1	Jump	Peter	02AUG90	1.05	1
Jones	William	22JUL00	2.15	11	JUPITER				
Jones	William	09MAY01	3.17	1	Jupiter	---	01JUN02	1.11	
Jones	William	30MAY01	3.17	12	A free negro				
Jones	William	05AUG02	2.16	11	KAVANAGH				
Jones	William	11AUG02	3.15	1	Cavender	William	13JUN87	2.01	1
Jones	William	06JUN03	3.13	11	Cavanaugh	William	05NOV88	1.02	1
Jones	William	29JUL03	2.17	1	Cavanaugh	William	22MAY89	5.02	11
Jones	William	06AUG04	3.11	12	Kavonaugh	William	31MAR90	2.04	1
Jones	William	06AUG05	3.20	12	Cavenar	William	25MAR91	1.02	1
Jones	William	20JUN06	1.12	1	Kavaughna	William	04OCT92	2.05	11
Jones	William	20JUN06	1.12	1	Kavaughna	Charles	26SEP92	2.05	1
Jones	William	18JUL06	3.19	11	KEAN				
Jones	William	23MAY07	1.13	1	Keen	Charles	10MAY90	1.05	1
Jones	William Sr	07JUN08	1.18	1	Kean	Charles	14MAY91	2.06	1
Jones	William	-----08	2.16	1	Keen	Fleming	10MAY09	1.21	1
Jones	William	07JUN08	1.18	1	Kean	Fleming	-----11	1.42	1
Jones	William	07APR09	1.20	1	Kean	Francis	-----11	1.42	1
Jones	William	24MAY09	2.16	1	Keen	John	10MAY09	1.21	1
Jones	William	-----11	1.40	1	Kean	John	-----11	1.42	1
Jones	Wilson	29JUN09	1.20	1	Kean	Samuel	14MAY89	6.04	1
Jones	Wilson	-----11	1.40	1	Keene	Thomas B.	10MAY90	1.05	1
JOSLIN					Kean	Thomas B.	14MAR91	2.05	1
Joslen	James	12JUN00	1.06	M1	Kean	William	14MAY89	6.04	1
Joslen	James	01JUN01	1.08	M1	KEANY				
Jossling	John	26AUG87	1.03	1	Keany	William	01JUL99	1.20	1
Josselling	John Jr	16MAY89	6.04	1	KEENOR				
Josslen	John Jr	11JUN89	6.08	1	Kenor	Abraham	28APR96	2.10	1
Josselling	John	21APR90	1.05	1	Keenor	Abraham	16MAY97	1.13	1
Josselling	John Jr	02AUG90	1.05	1	KELLAM				
Josselling	John Sr	21JUN91	2.05	1	Kellam	John	21JUN00	2.16	1
Josselling	John Jr	20JUN91	2.05	1	Kellam	John	10AUG01	2.15	1
Josselling	John Sr	24OCT92	1.07	1	Kellam	John	14JUN02	3.15	1

surname	name	date	bk.pg	TM	surname	name	date	bk.pg	TM
Kellam	John	11JUN03	2.17	1	Kemper	John	16NOV92	3.11	1
Kellam	John	25JUL04	1.10	1	Kamper	John	21MAY94	3.12	1
Killum	John	05AUG05	3.21	1	Kamper	John	12MAY95	1.08	1
Killum	John	04AUG06	3.20	1	Kamper	John	-----96	4.08	1
KELLAND					KENDRICK				
Kelland	John	10JUL01	3.18	1	Kendrick	Alexander	01JUL99	1.20	1
KELLER					Kindrick	Alexander	30JUL00	2.16	1
Keller	Antoney	07MAY91	3.08	1	Kendrick	Alexander	13JUL01	3.18	1
Kellow	Anthorney	26NOV92	3.11	1	Kendricks	Alexander	26MAY02	3.17	1
Kiler	George	06JUL09	2.17	1	Kendrick	Alexander	03MAY04	3.12	1
KELLISON					Kindrick	Alexander	05AUG05	3.21	1
Kellison	Absalom	12JUN99	2.10	1	Kindricks	Alexander	22AUG06	3.20	1
Kellison	Absalom	25JUL00	1.07	1	Kindrick	Austing	07AUG04	3.12	1
Kellason	Absolam	13AUG02	3.15	1	Kindrick	Austin	05AUG05	3.21	1
Kellason	Absalom	20JUN03	2.17	1	Kindrick	Turner	07AUG04	3.12	1
Kellason	Joseph	13AUG02	3.15	1	Kindrick	Turner	05AUG05	3.21	1
Kellason	Joseph	22JUN03	2.18	1	Kindricks	Turner	22AUG06	3.20	1
Kellyson	Joseph	28JUL04	4.14	1	Keenly	James	20JUN87	2.04	1
Kellason	Joseph	23JUL05	2.18	1	Kinley	James	17NOV88	1.05	1
Kellason	Joseph	17JUL06	2.21	1	Kinley	James	03AUG89	5.07	1
Kellason	William	25JUL05	2.19	1	Kenly	James	27MAR90	2.04	1
Kellason	William	17JUL06	2.21	1	Kennerly	James	18OCT92	2.05	1
KELLY					Kennely	James	19AUG93	1.05	1
Kelly	Bachum	06AUG06	2.21	1	KENNEDY				
Kelly	Beachem	15AUG07	2.20	1	Kennady	James	20APR90	1.05	1
Kelly	Baucamp	25JUN08	2.16	1	Kennady	James	19AUG91	2.06	1
Kelly	Bechham	13JUL09	1.21	1	Kennady	James	13SEP92	1.06	1
Kelly	Bickham	-----11	1.42	1	Kennady	James	27AUG93	3.06	1
Kelly	Benjamin	21JUN05	3.21	M1	Keneday	James	16APR94	2.07	1
Kelly	Benjamin	22JUN06	3.20	1	Kennady	James	18MAR95	3.10	1
Kelly	Hugh	14JUN05	3.21	1	Kannady	James	05AUG05	3.21	M1
Kelly	Hugh	21JUL06	3.20	1	Keneday	James	04AUG06	3.20	1
Kelly	Hugh	10JUN07	2.20	1	Kenaday	John	03AUG02	2.17	1
Kelley	Isaac	09JUN04	4.14	1	Kennedy	John	20MAY03	3.14	1
Kelly	Isaac	17JUN05	2.18	1	Kennedy	John	09AUG04	3.12	11
Kelly	Isaac	30JUL06	2.21	1	Kannady	John	05AUG05	3.21	1
Kelly	Isaac	18JUN07	2.20	1	Keneday	John	04AUG06	3.20	11
Kelly	Isaac	25JUN08	2.16	1	Kennedy	Joseph	08APR09	1.21	1
Kelly	Isaac	13JUL09	1.21	1	Kennady	Michael	12JUN89	6.08	1
Kelly	Isaac	-----11	1.42	1	Kennady	Michael	13AUG90	1.05	1
Kelly	Joel	01JUL99	1.20	1	Kennady	Michael	24JUN91	2.05	1
Kelley	Joel	26JUN00	2.16	1	Kennady	Michael	05OCT92	1.06	1
Kelly	Joel	22JUL01	3.18	1	Kennady	Michael	23AUG93	3.06	1
Kelly	Joel	11AUG03	2.18	1	Keneday	Michael	12JUN94	2.07	1
Kelly	John	-----96	4.08	1	Kennady	Michael	28APR95	3.10	1
Kelley	Jonathan	27JUN00	2.16	11	Kennady	Michael	11MAY96	2.10	1
Kelly	Jonathen	22JUL01	3.18	1	Kannada	Michael	23JUN97	1.13	1
Kelly	Jonathen	13AUG02	2.17	1	Kennady	Michael	07JUN99	1.20	1
Kelley	Jonathan	06APR04	4.14	1	Kennady	Michael	27JUN00	2.16	1
Kelly	Jonathen	22JUN05	3.21	1	Kennady	Michael	01AUG01	2.15	1
Kelly	Jonathen	22JUL06	3.20	1	Kenady	Michael	01JUN02	2.17	11
Kelly	Reuben	06AUG06	2.21	1	Kennedy	Michael	21JUN03	3.14	1
Kelly	Reuben	15AUG07	2.20	1	Kennedy	Michael	03MAY04	3.12	1
Kelly	Reuben	25JUN08	2.16	1	Kenneday	Michiel	13JUN05	3.21	11
Kelly	Reuben	08JUN09	1.21	1	Keneday	Michael	16JUL06	3.20	11
Kelly	Richard	19JUN99	1.20	11	Kennady	Michael	20JUN07	2.20	11
Kelley	Richard Sr	27JUN00	2.16	1	Kenaday	Michael	31MAY08	2.16	12
Kelley	Richard	25JUN00	2.16	1	KEREY				
Kelly	Richard Sr	22JUL01	3.18	1	Kerey	Christopher	01JUN96	1.07	1
Kelly	Richard Jr	22JUL01	3.18	1	Kerey	Isaac	08JUN96	1.07	1
Kelly	Richard Sr	13AUG02	2.18	11	Kerey	James	26MAY94	1.05	1
Kelly	Richard	03AUG02	2.17	1	KERKENDALL				
Kelley	Richard	06APR04	4.14	1	Kerkendall	Richard	17MAR97	2.02	1
Kelly	Richard	03AUG04	3.12	1	KERLEY				
Kelly	Richard Sr	22JUN05	3.21	1	Carley	James	31JUL00	2.06	1
Kelly	Richard	20JUN05	3.21	1	Kearly	James	03AUG01	3.18	1
Kelly	Richard	22JUL06	3.20	1	Kerly	William	11MAY96	2.10	11
Kelly	Richard	26JUL06	3.20	1	Kerley	William	18JUL97	1.13	11
KEMPER					Kerley	William	08JUL99	1.21	11
Camper	John	07JUL87	3.03	1	Carley	William	31JUL00	2.06	11
Kemper	John	25JUL89	2.07	1	Kearly	William	13JUL01	3.18	11
Kemper	John	19APR91	3.08	1	KERR				

surname	name	date	bk.pg	TM	surname	name	date	bk.pg	TM
Kerr	Andrew	15JUL99	1.19	M1	Ketchem	Jesse	04AUG00	2.16	1
Car	Andrew	04JUL03	1.05	1	Ketchem	Jesse	27JUN01	2.14	1
Karr	Andrew	09JUL04	2.11	1	Ketchem	Mark W.	29JUL02	3.15	1
Carr	Andrew	17JUN05	1.03	1	Ketchem	Tabitha	29JUL02	3.15	F
Kar	Andrew	09JUN07	1.13	1	Ketchem	Tenipe	27JUL03	2.18	F
Kar	Andrew	27APR08	1.18	1	KEY				
Carr	Andrew	31MAY09	2.04	1	Key	Abner	26JUN01	1.09	1
Karr	Armstrong	21OCT92	2.05	1	Keys	George	15JUL87	3.05	1
Karr	Armstrong	12AUG93	1.05	1	Caise	George	25JUL89	2.03	1
Kerr	Armstrong	21MAY94	1.05	1	Keys	George	07MAY91	3.08	1
Kass	Armstrong	01JUN95	2.07	1	Keys	George	01DEC92	3.11	1
Carr	Armstrong	20JUN96	1.03	1	Keys	George	10APR94	3.12	1
Kerr	Armstrong	10MAY97	3.17	1	Keys	George	12MAY95	1.08	1
Kerr	Armstrong	11MAY99	1.20	1	Keys	George	-----96	4.08	1
Carr	Armstrong	08JUL00	2.05	1	Key	James	13JUL01	2.15	1
Carr	Armstrong	29APR01	2.03	1	Key	James	26JUL02	3.15	1
Car	Armstrong	12JUN02	1.04	1	Caise	John	06AUG89	2.03	11
Car	Armstrong	04JUL03	1.05	1	Keys	John	16NOV92	3.11	1
Karr	Armstrong	01AUG04	2.11	1	Keys	John	21MAY94	3.12	1
Carr	Armstrong	17JUN05	1.03	1	Keys	John	-----96	4.08	1
Kerr	Armstrong	20JUN06	1.12	1	Key	Thomas	02AUG90	1.05	1
Kar	Armstrong	09JUN07	1.13	1	Keys	Thomas	30MAR91	1.05	1
Kar	Armstrong	07JUN08	1.18	1	Key	Thomas	10AUG93	3.06	1
Carr	Armstrong	31MAY09	2.04	1	Kee	William	27JUN89	2.07	1
Kerr	Armstrong	-----11	1.41	1	Kee	William	06MAY91	3.08	1
Carr	James	14JUN87	2.01	1	KIDD				
Carr	James	15NOV88	1.02	1	Kidd	James	25JUL89	2.07	1
Karr	James	19MAY90	2.04	1	KILBURN				
Karr	James	12JUN90	2.04	1	Kilburn	Henry	20JUN87	2.04	1
Kerr	James	13APR91	1.05	1	Kilburn	Henry	14NOV88	1.05	1
Karr	James	16OCT92	2.05	1	Kilburn	Henry	03AUG89	5.07	1
Karr	James	13AUG93	1.05	1	Kilbourn	Henry	05JUL91	1.05	1
Kerr	James	21MAY94	1.05	1	Kellum	Henery	08OCT92	2.05	1
Kerr	James	15JUL99	1.19	1	Kilbourn	Henry	10APR94	3.12	1
Carr	John	13JUN87	2.01	11	Kilbern	Henry	12MAY95	1.08	1
Carr	John	14NOV88	1.02	11	Kelbern	Henry	17MAR97	2.02	1
Karr	John	23JUN89	5.07	12	Killburn	Henry	18JUN99	2.10	1
Karr	John	19MAY90	2.04	11	Kilburn	Henry	16JUN00	1.07	1
Kerr	John	13APR91	1.05	11	Kilburn	Henry	02JUN01	1.09	1
Karr	John	21OCT92	2.05	1	Kilburn	John	05JUN99	1.20	1
Karr	John	13AUG93	1.05	1	KILLIN				
Kerr	John	21MAY94	1.05	1	Killin	John	09JUL99	3.12	1
Kass	John	01JUN95	2.07	1	Killen	John	01JUL00	3.16	1
Karr	John	01JUN95	2.20	1	KIMBERLAND				
Carr	John	20JUN96	1.03	11	Kimberlin	Abraim	23MAR90	2.04	2
Kerr	John	10MAY97	3.17	1	Kimberland	Abraham	25OCT91	1.05	1
Kerr	John	11MAY99	1.20	1	Kimberland	Abraham	14OCT92	2.05	1
Carr	John	17JUN00	2.05	1	Kimberlin	Henry	23MAR90	2.04	1
Car	John	12JUN02	1.03	1	Kimberlin	Jacob	16JUN89	5.07	11
Car	John	04JUL03	1.05	1	Kimberlin	Jacob	23MAR90	2.04	2
Kerr	Matthew	01JUN97	3.17	1	Kimberland	John	14OCT92	2.05	1
Carr	Petter	13SEP91	3.04	1	KIMBLE				
Ker	Thomas	13OCT92	2.05	1	Kimple	Henry	31JUL01	2.15	1
Kerr	Thomas	-----11	1.41	1	Kimble	Henry	27JUL03	2.18	1
Carr	William	06NOV88	1.02	1	Cimble	Henry	18JUL06	2.08	1
Karr	William	19MAY90	2.04	1	Cimble	S.	06MAY90	1.01	
Carr	William	25MAR91	1.02	1	Listed with Robert Anderson				
Karr	William	22NOV92	2.05	1	KINCAID				
Karr	William	12AUG93	1.05	1	Kincaid	Andrew	15JUL87	3.05	1
Kerr	William	31MAY94	1.05	1	Kincaid	John	21JUN06	1.12	1
Kerr	William	15JUL99	1.19	1	Kincaid	Robert	15JUL87	3.05	1
KERTLEY					KING				
Kertley	Elijah	02AUG06	1.13	1	King	Benjamin	03JUN96	2.10	1
Kertley	Elijah	08MAY07	1.13	1	King	Benjamin	20JUN97	1.13	1
Kirtley	Elijah	27APR08	1.18	1	King	Benjamin	12JUN99	1.20	1
Kertley	Elijah	16JUN09	2.17	1	King	David	15AUG07	2.20	1
Kertley	Willis	20JUN07	2.20	1	King	Englis	29JUN99	1.20	1
Kertly	Willis	31MAY08	2.16	1	King	Engles	23JUL01	3.18	1
Kertly	Willis	30JUN09	1.21	1	King	Englis	04AUG02	2.17	1
Kirktley	Willis	-----11	1.42	1	King	Englis	21AUG04	3.12	1
KETCHEM					King	Engles	05AUG05	3.21	1
Ketcham	Jesse	28JUL99	3.11	1	King	Harbert	23JUL04	1.10	1

surname	name	date	bk.pg	TM	surname	name	date	bk.pg	TM
King	Harbert	10JUN05	2.18	1	Kinney	Thomas	21JUN05	3.21	1
King	Harbert	06APR06	2.21	1	Kinney	Thomas	26JUL06	3.20	11
One lott in Standford					Kinney	William	26JUL06	3.20	M1
King	Harbert	15JUN07	2.20	1	KIRBY				
King	Harbert	27APR08	1.18	1	Kirby	Jesse	01JUN96	1.07	11
King	Harbert	16AUG09	2.17	1	KIRKLAND				
King	Harbert	-----11	1.42	1	Kirkland	Charles	10AUG97	1.13	1
King	Henry	18JUN99	2.10	1	Kirkland	Charles	10JUL99	3.12	1
King	Henry Jr	18JUN99	2.10	1	Kerkland	Charles	10JUL00	3.18	1
King	Henry	20JUN00	3.16	1	Kirkland	Charles	30JUL01	3.18	1
King	Henry	02MAY01	3.18	1	Kirkland	Charles	29JUL02	3.15	1
King	Henry	27JUN01	2.14	1	Kirkland	Charles	10AUG03	2.18	1
King	Henry	29JUL02	3.15	1	Kirkland	Charles	08JUN04	4.14	1
King	Ingles	04AUG06	3.20	1	Kirkland	Charles	20JUN05	2.18	1
King	Jacob	04AUG04	3.12	1	Kirkland	Charles	30JUL06	2.21	1
King	John	14JUN87	2.04	1	KIRKPATRICK				
King	John	05NOV88	1.05	1	Kirkpatrick	Agness	25JUN08	2.16	F
King	John	16JUN89	5.07	1	Kirkpatrick	James	30JUN87	1.03	1
King	John	31MAR90	2.04	1	Kirkpatrick	James	14MAY89	6.04	1
King	John	28MAR91	1.05	1	Kirkpatrick	James	20APR90	1.05	1
King	John	23NOV92	2.05	1	Kirkpatrick	James	14MAY91	2.06	1
King	John	17SEP93	1.05	1	Kirkpatrick	James	18OCT92	1.06	1
King	John	31MAY94	1.05	1	Kirkpatrick	James	18SEP93	3.06	1
King	John	08MAY95	2.20	1	Kirkpatrick	James	23APR94	2.07	1
King	John	18JUN95	2.07	1	Kirkpatrick	James	27MAR95	3.10	1
King	John	19JUN96	1.07	1	Kilpatrick	James	20JUN96	2.10	1
King	John	12JUN97	3.17	1	Kirkpatrick	James	17MAY97	1.13	1
King	John	03JUN99	1.20	1	Kirkpatrick	James	18MAY99	3.11	1
King	John	10JUN00	2.16	1	Kilpatrick	James	28JUN00	3.16	1
King	John	05AUG01	2.15	1	Cirkpatrick	James	08JUL01	3.07	1
King	John	12JUL02	2.17	12	Kilpatrick	James	13AUG02	3.15	1
King	John	25AUG03	3.15	12	Kilpatrick	James	20JUN03	2.17	1
King	John	30JUL04	2.11	12	Kirkpatrick	James	28JUL04	4.14	1
King	John	09AUG04	3.12	1	Kilpatrick	James	23JUL05	2.19	1
King	John	03JUN05	3.21	12	Kilpatrick	James	08JUL06	2.21	1
King	John	15JUL06	3.20	12	Kirkpatrick	James	15AUG07	2.20	1
King	John	16AUG06	2.13	1	Kirkpatrick	Nancy	-----11	1.42	F
King	John	10AUG07	2.20	21	KISLER				
King	John	10AUG07	2.12		Kisler	Henry	10APR94	3.12	1
Partner with James Ely					KISSAH				
King	John	31MAY08	2.16	11	Kissah	Richard	31JUL05	1.10	1
King	John Jr	25JUN08	2.16	1	KISSINGER				
King	John Sr	10JUL09	1.21	1	Kislinger	Henry	30MAR91	1.05	1
King	John Jr	10JUL09	1.21	1	Kissinger	John	14JUN87	2.04	1
King	John Sr	-----11	1.42	1	Kissinger	John	30OCT88	1.05	1
King	John Jr	-----11	1.42	1	Kissinger	John	19JUN89	5.07	1
King	Philip	08JUL99	3.12	1	Kisinger	John	03JUN90	2.04	1
King	Ransdale	-----11	1.42	3	Kisinger	John	30MAR91	1.05	1
King	Robert	10JUN03	3.14	1	Kisinger	John	10OCT92	2.05	1
King	Robert	16JUN04	2.11	1	Kisinger	John	14AUG93	1.05	1
King	Robert	30MAY05	3.21	1	Kishinger	John	28MAY94	1.05	1
King	Robert	14JUL06	3.20	1	Kisinger	John	03JUN95	2.07	1
King	Robert	08JUN07	2.20	1	Kisinger	John	03JUN95	2.07	1
King	Robert	25JUN08	2.16	1	Kisinger	John	01JUL96	1.07	1
King	Robert	28JUN09	1.21	1	Kesoner	John	06APR97	3.17	1
King	Robert	-----11	1.42	11	Kesoner	John	11MAY99	1.20	1
King	William	20JUN00	3.16	11	Kishner	John	30MAY00	2.16	1
King	William	02MAY01	3.18	1	Kishner	John	22JUL01	2.15	1
King	William	27JUL02	3.15	1	Kisinger	John	03JUN02	1.11	1
King	William	04AUG03	2.18	1	Kissinger	John	03JUN03	1.12	1
King	William	06JUN04	4.14	1	Kissinger	John	20JUN04	1.10	1
King	William	20JUN05	2.18	1	Kissinger	John	15JUL05	1.10	1
King	William	30JUL06	2.21	1	Kissinger	John	19JUN06	1.12	1
KINNEY					Kisinger	John	05JUN07	1.13	1
Kenny	Daniel	16JUL89	6.08	1	Kisinger	John	27APR08	1.18	1
Kenney	Michel	07MAY91	3.08	1	Kisinger	John	01JUN09	2.17	1
Kenny	Thomas	14SEP92	1.06	1	Kishner	John	-----11	1.41	1
Kenney	Thomas	13MAY94	2.07	1	KISTER				
Kinny	Thomas	10APR95	3.10	1	Kester	Lewis	30JUN00	3.16	1
Kenny	Thomas	10MAY96	2.10	1	Kaster	Lewis	09JUL01	3.18	1
Kinney	Thomas	26MAY97	1.13	1	Kister	Lewis	17AUG02	3.15	1
Kinney	Thomas	28JUL00	2.16	1	Kister	Lewis	30MAY03	2.17	1

surname	name	date	bk.pg	TM	surname	name	date	bk.pg	TM
Kister	Lewis	27JUL04	4.14	1	Knox	James	11JUN99	1.20	1
Kister	Lewis	25JUL05	2.19	1	Knox	James	28JUL00	2.16	1
Kister	Lewis	15JUL06	3.20	1	Knox	James	27JUN01	2.14	1
KNARY					Knox	James	26MAY02	2.17	1
Kenary	Christian	26JUN87	1.03	1	Knox	James	08AUG03	3.14	1
Knary	Chris	25MAY89	6.04	1	Knox	James	06AUG04	2.11	1
Knary	Christian	10MAY90	1.05	1	Nokes	John	12JUN99	2.13	M1
KNIGHT					Noaks	John	23JUN02	1.15	1
Knight	Absalom	31JUL05	1.10	1	Noaks	John	20JUN03	1.16	1
Knight	Absolom	25MAY07	1.13	1	Noaks	John	03AUG04	1.14	1
Knight	George B.	-----11	1.41	1	Noaks	John	22JUL05	1.14	1
Night	James	17JUN00	1.08	1	Noaks	John	02AUG06	1.16	1
Night	James	04JUN01	1.11	1	Noaks	John	30JUN07	1.18	1
Night	James	16JUL03	1.16	1	Noax	John	17JUN08	1.25	1
Night	John	16AUG09	2.23	1	Nokes	John	30JUN09	2.23	1
Nutt	Robert	13MAY97	1.18	1	Noakes	Thomas	31OCT88	1.07	1
Night	Robert	24MAY99	2.13	1	Nocks	Thomas	19MAY90	2.06	1
Night	Robert	17JUN00	1.08	1	Nocks	Thomas	12OCT92	2.06	1
Night	Robert	26JUN01	1.12	1	Nokes	Thomas	14AUG93	1.07	1
Night	Robert	06JUL03	1.16	1	Nokes	Thomas	28MAY94	1.07	1
Night	Robert	15AUG04	1.14	1	Nikes	Thomas	04JUN95	2.10	1
Knight	Robert	30JUL06	1.12	1	Nokes	Thomas	13APR97	3.22	1
Knight	Robert	04MAY07	1.13	1	Nokes	Thomas	12JUN99	2.13	1
Night	Robert	17JUN08	1.25	1	Nokes	Thomas	25JUL00	1.08	1
Night	Robert	30JUN09	2.23	1	Noaks	Thomas	26JUL01	1.12	1
KNOX					Noaks	Thomas	--JUN02	1.15	1
Nokes	Benjamin	12JUN87	2.06	1	Noaks	Thomas	20JUN03	1.16	1
Noakes	Benjamin	31OCT88	1.07	1	Noaks	Thomas	19JUN04	1.13	1
Nokes	George Sr	12JUN87	2.06	11	Noaks	Thomas	22JUL05	1.13	1
Noakes	George Sr	31OCT88	1.07	1	Noaks	Thomas	02AUG06	1.16	1
Noakes	George Jr	31OCT88	1.07	1	Noaks	Thomas	30JUN07	1.18	1
Noakes	George Sr	19JUN89	5.09	1	Noaks	Thomas	07JUN08	1.18	1
Noakes	George Jr	19JUN89	5.09	1	Nokes	Thomas	12MAY09	2.23	1
Nocks	George	19MAY90	2.06	1	KOONS				
Nocks	George Jr	19MAY90	2.06	1	Kunce	John	16NOV92	3.11	1
Nocks	George	28MAR91	1.06	1	Koons	John	10APR94	3.12	1
Nocks	George	13OCT92	2.06	1	Coons	Samuel	-----11	1.12	1
Nokes	George	14AUG93	1.07	1	LACKEY				
Nokes	George	29MAY94	1.07	1	Lackey	Gabriel	12JUL03	3.15	1
Nokes	George	03JUN95	2.10	1	Lacky	Gabriel	03AUG04	2.12	1
Nokes	George	30JUN96	1.09	1	Lackey	Gabriel	17JUN05	3.22	1
Nokes	George	13APR97	3.22	1	Lacky	Gabriel	06AUG06	3.22	1
Nokes	George Sr	14JUN99	2.13	1	Lackey	Gabriel	19AUG07	2.22	1
Nokes	George	12JUN99	2.13	1	Lackey	Gabriel	-----08	2.17	1
Nokes	George	25JUL00	1.08	11	Lacky	Gabriel	07AUG09	1.22	1
Nokes	George Jr	25JUL00	1.08	1	Lackey	Gabriel	-----11	1.43	1
Noaks	George	10JUN01	1.11	11	Luckey	James	23AUG89	2.08	
Noaks	George Jr	10JUN01	1.11	11	A white servant				
Noaks	George	23JUN02	1.15	1	Luckey	Robert	12AUG89	2.08	1
Noaks	George Jr	23JUN02	1.15	1	Lackey	Samuel	29APR95	3.10	0
Noaks	George	20JUN03	1.16	1	Lucky	William A.	07JUN08	1.19	1
Noaks	George Jr	20JUN03	1.16	1	Lucky	William	06JUL09	2.18	1
Noaks	George Sr	03AUG04	1.14	1	Luckie	William A.	-----11	1.44	1
Noaks	George	01AUG04	1.14	1	LAIN				
Noaks	George	22JUL05	1.13	1	Lain	Nathaniel	30JUL06	3.21	1
Noaks	George Jr	22JUL05	1.13	1	LAIR				
Noaks	George Sr	02AUG06	1.16	1	Lare	Andrew	26JUN87	2.05	11
Noaks	George	02AUG06	1.16	1	Lare	Andrew	18NOV88	1.06	1
Noaks	George	30JUN07	1.18	1	Lare	Andrew	05AUG89	5.08	1
Noaks	George Jr	30JUN07	1.18	1	Lear	Andrew	01JUN90	2.04	1
Knoax	George	27APR08	1.18	1	Lair	Andrew	07APR91	1.05	1
Nokes	George Sr	30JUN09	2.23	1	Lair	Andrew	29OCT92	2.05	1
Nokes	George	12MAY09	2.23	1	Lair	Andrew	22MAY95	2.20	1
Noaker	George	-----11	1.57	1	Lair	Andrew	30JUN96	1.08	11
Knox	James	29JUN89	5.07	1	Lair	Andrew	20APR97	3.19	11
Knox	James	24MAR90	2.04	1	Lair	Andrew	18JUL00	2.17	1
Knox	James	04JAN91	1.05	1	Lair	Andrew	15JUN01	2.16	1
Knox	James	26OCT92	2.05	1	Lair	Andrew	27MAY02	3.16	1
Knox	James	17SEP93	1.05	1	Lair	Andrew	28MAY03	2.18	1
Knox	James	31MAY94	1.05	1	Lare	Andrew	25JUL04	1.11	1
Knox	James	10JUN94	1.11	1	Lare	Andrew	25JUL04	1.11	1
Knox	James	08MAY95	2.08	1	Lair	Andrew	05AUG05	2.20	1

surname	name	date	bk.pg	TM	surname	name	date	bk.pg	TM
Lair	Andrew	06JUN06	2.21	1	Laney	Joseph Sr	10JUN08	1.20	1
Lear	Andrew	25JUL07	2.21	1	Laney	Joseph	13MAY09	2.17	1
Lear	Andrew	10JUN08	1.21	1	Laney	Joseph Sr	13MAY09	2.17	1
Lare	Andrew	23AUG09	2.19	1	LANGDON				
Law	Andrew	-----11	1.43	1	Langdon	Duncan	26AUG93	1.05	1
Lare	George	27JUN87	2.05	1	Langdon	Duncan	30MAY94	1.05	1
Lare	John	18NOV88	1.06	1	Langdon	Joseph	22JUN03	1.12	1
Lair	John	13AUG90	1.06	1	Langdon	Joseph	01JUL09	2.18	1
Lear	John	30APR91	2.06	1	Langden	Samuel	30JUL05	1.11	1
Lair	John	22SEP92	1.06	1	Langden	Samuel	01AUG06	1.13	1
Lear	John	06AUG93	3.06	1	Langdan	Samuel	08MAY07	1.14	1
Laird	John	10MAY94	2.08	1	Langdon	Samuel	18APR08	1.19	1
Lare	Matthias	01DEC88	1.06	1	Langdon	Samuel	16JUN09	2.17	1
Lare	Matthias	05AUG89	5.08	1	LANGFORD				
LAMBERT					Langford	Benjamin	12JUN87	2.05	1
Lambert	Cotland	23JUN06	1.13	1	Langford	Benjamin	15NOV88	1.06	1
Lambert	Meredith	29MAY05	2.19	1	Langford	Benjamin	23JUN89	5.07	1
Lambert	Meredith	07AUG06	2.22	1	Lankford	Benjamin	02JUN90	2.04	1
Lambert	Merideth	-----11	1.43	1	Langford	Benjamin	25MAR91	1.05	1
LAMME					Langford	Benjamin	16MAY97	3.18	1
Lamb	Fredrick	25MAY89	6.04	1	Langford	Benjamin	25JUN99	2.10	1
Lamb	James	-----11	1.42	1	Langford	Benjamin	23JUL00	1.07	11
Lamme	Nathan	07JUL87	3.06	1	Langford	Benjamin	24JUN01	1.09	1
Lamm	Nathan	07AUG89	2.07	1	Langford	Benjamin	22JUN02	1.12	1
Lamb	Nathan	12SEP91	3.09	1	Langford	Benjamin	13JUN03	1.12	1
Lamme	Nathan	29NOV92	3.11	1	Langford	Benjamin	02AUG04	1.11	1
Lamme	Nathan	23APR94	3.13	1	Langford	Benjamin	01AUG05	1.11	1
Lamme	Nathan	-----95	1.09	1	Langford	Levinah	23JUL00	1.07	F
Lamone	Nathan	-----96	4.09	1	Langford	Mary	12JUN87	2.05	F
Lampton	John	25JUL89	2.07	1	Langford	Mary	14NOV88	1.06	F
Lampton	William	27JUN87	3.06	11	Langford	Mary	23JUN89	5.07	F
Lampton	William	12JUL89	2.07	1	Lankford	Mary	13APR90	2.04	F
Lampton	William	25JUL89	2.07	11	Langford	Mary	14APR91	1.05	F
LANCASTER					Langford	Mary	16OCT92	2.05	F
Lancaster	Aron	14JUN04	1.10	11	Langford	Mary	12AUG93	1.05	F
Lancaster	Thomas	24AUG09	2.18	1	Langford	Mary	21MAY94	1.05	F
Lancaster	Thomas	-----11	1.43	1	Langford	Mary	01JUN95	2.08	F
Lancaster	William	10JUN08	1.21	1	Langford	Mary	01JUN95	2.20	F
Lancaster	William	24AUG09	2.18	1	Langford	Mary	20JUN96	1.08	F
Lancaster	William	-----11	1.43	1	Lankford	Mary	26APR97	3.18	F
LANDIS					Langford	Mary	18MAY99	1.22	F
Landess	Felix	24MAY99	3.12	1	Lankford	Mary	17JUN00	2.17	F
Landess	Felex	11JUL00	3.17	1	Lankford	Mary	04JUN01	2.15	F
Landis	Felex	29JUL01	3.20	1	Langford	Milly	29OCT92	2.05	F
Lendis	Felix	10JUN02	2.18	1	Langford	Stephen	12JUN87	2.05	1
Landes	Felix	03AUG03	3.15	1	Langford	Stephen	31OCT88	1.05	1
Landess	Felix	06APR04	4.14	1	Langford	Stephen	30JUN89	5.07	1
Landes	Felex	21JUN05	3.22	1	Lankford	Stephen	13JUN90	2.04	1
Landis	Felix	19JUL06	3.21	11	Langford	Stephen	28MAR91	1.05	1
Landess	Henry	24MAY99	3.12	1	Langford	Stephen	12AUG93	1.05	1
Landess	Henry	11JUL00	3.17	1	Langford	Stephen	16MAY97	3.19	1
LANDSDOWN					Langford	Stephen	10JUL99	2.10	1
Lansdon	John	06JUN96	1.08	1	Langford	Stephen	24JUL00	1.07	1
Lansdown	John	19APR97	3.18	1	Langford	Stephen	16JUN01	1.09	1
Landsdown	John	28MAY99	1.22	1	Langford	Stephen	--AUG02	1.13	1
Landsdown	John	05JUL00	2.17	1	Langford	Stephen	11JUL03	1.13	1
Landsdown	John	30JUN01	2.16	1	Langford	Stephen	02AUG04	1.11	1
Landsdown	John	01JUL02	3.16	1	Langford	Stephen	22JUL05	1.10	1
Landsdown	John	01JUN03	2.18	1	Langford	Stephen	01AUG06	1.14	11
Landsdown	John	13AUG04	2.12	1	Langford	Stephen	04MAY07	1.14	11
Landsdown	John	01AUG05	2.20	1	Langford	Stephen	10JUN08	1.20	12
Landsdown	Mary	07AUG06	2.22	F	Langdon	Stephen	16JUN09	2.18	1
LANEY					Lankdon	Walker	18MAY90	2.04	1
Laney	Abraham	01JUL07	1.15	1	Langford	Walker	29MAY94	1.05	1
Laney	Abraham	10JUN08	1.20	1	Langford	Walker	04JUN95	2.08	1
Laney	Abraham	13MAY09	2.17	1	Lankford	Walker	18AUG97	3.19	1
Laney	John	10JUN08	1.20	1	Langford	Walter	23JUN01	1.09	1
Lany	John	12MAY09	2.17	1	Langford	Walker	04JUN02	1.12	1
Lang	John	08JUN09	2.17	1	Langford	Walker	23JUN03	1.13	1
Laney	Joseph Sr	01JUL07	1.15	1	Langford	Walker	20JUN04	1.10	1
Laney	Joseph	01JUL07	1.15	1	Langford	Walter	29JUN96	1.08	1
Laney	Joseph Jr	10JUN08	1.20	1	LANGLEY				

surname	name	date	bk.pg	TM	surname	name	date	bk.pg	TM
Langley	Elisha	18MAR95	3.10	1	Lawrence	Hugh	28MAY03	2.18	1
Langla	Elisha	22APR96	2.11	1	Laurence	Hugh	25JUL04	1.11	1
LARGER					Lawrence	Hugh	27JUN05	2.20	1
Lorger	John	08MAY89	6.04	1	Lawrence	Hugh	31MAY06	2.21	1
Lorger	John	03APR90	1.08		Laurance	Hugh	25JUL07	2.21	2
Listed with Gasper Pope					Laurence	Hugh	02JUN08	1.19	1
Lorger	John	20APR91	2.06	1	Laurence	Hugh	25MAY09	2.17	21
Lorger	John	10OCT92	1.06	1	Laurence	Hugh	-----11	1.44	2
Lorger	John	21AUG93	3.07	1	Lawrence	Hugh	-----11	1.44	
Larger	John	23APR94	2.08	1	Paid tax for J.(heirs) Shacklefor				
Larker	John	28MAR95	3.10	1	Laurance	Isaac	20JUN05	3.22	1
Lorger	John	29JUL96	2.11	1	Lawrence	Jacob	27JUN87	3.06	1
Larker	John	03JUL97	1.14	1	Lorance	Jacob	19APR91	3.09	1
Larger	John	20JUN00	2.17	1	Lawrence	James	13APR90	2.04	1
Larger	John	09JUL01	3.20	1	Laurence	James	24OCT92	2.05	1
Larger	John	18MAY06	2.21	1	Larrance	James	07AUG93	1.06	1
LARRIMAN					Larrance	James	17MAY94	1.05	1
Larriman	S.	18JUN94	2.05	0	Larrance	James	-----95	2.26	
Tax paid by William Sr. Ford					One lot in Standford				
LASEFIELD					Laurance	James	12MAY95	2.08	1
Larfield	Benjamin	20JUN96	2.11	1	Larrance	James	13JUN96	1.08	1
Larfield	Benjamin	18MAY97	1.14	1	Lawrence	James	08MAY97	3.18	1
Lasefield	Benjamin	03JUL99	3.12	1	Lawrence	James	09JUL99	1.23	1
Lacefield	Benjamin	30JUN00	3.17	1	Larrence	James	08JUN01	2.16	1
Lasefield	Ezekiel	12JUL89	2.07	1	Lawrence	James	26MAY02	3.16	1
Lacefield	Ezekiel	19APR91	3.09	1	Lawrence	James	28MAY03	2.18	1
Lasefield	Ezekiel	31JUL05	1.11	1	Laurence	James	25JUL04	1.11	1
Lacefield	Ezekiel	01AUG06	1.13	1	Laurence	James	21MAY05	2.19	1
Lasswell	Jesse	08MAY07	1.14	1	Laurence	James	21AUG06	3.22	1
Lasswell	Jesse	02JUN08	1.18	1	Laurence	James	17JUN08	1.19	1
Lasswell	Jesse	06JUN09	2.18	1	Laurence	James	-----11	1.44	1
Lasefield	John	23JUN03	1.12	1	Lawrance	John	16JUN03	3.15	M1
Lasefield	John	23JUN03	1.13	1	Laurance	John	13AUG04	2.12	1
Lasefield	John	03AUG04	1.11	1	Laurence	John	20JUL05	2.20	1
Lasefield	John Jr	03AUG04	1.11	1	Laurence	John	23JUN06	1.13	1
Lasefield	John Sr	31JUL05	1.11	1	Laurence	John	09JUN07	1.15	1
Lasewell	John	29JUL05	1.11	1	Laurence	John	10JUN08	1.21	1
Lasefield	John	01AUG06	1.14	1	Laurence	John	15AUG09	2.19	1
Lasswell	John	25MAY07	1.14	1	Laurence	John	-----11	1.44	1
Lasswell	John	18APR08	1.19	1	Laurence	Mary	29JUN89	5.07	F1
Lasswell	John	01JUL09	2.18	1	Lawrence	Mary	07APR91	1.05	F
Leecewell	Joseph	25JUN96	1.08	1	Larrance	Mary	07AUG93	1.05	F
Lasswell	Joseph	10APR97	3.18	1	Larrance	Mary	16MAY94	1.05	F1
Lacefield	Joseph	14JUN99	2.11	11	Laurance	Mary	18MAY95	2.20	F
Lacefield	Joseph	22JUL00	1.07	11	Laurance	Mary	18MAY95	2.08	F1
Lacefield	Joseph	23JUN01	1.09	11	Larrance	Mary	20JUN96	1.07	F1
Lacefield	Joseph	23JUN02	1.13	11	Lawrence	Mary	08MAY97	3.18	F2
Lasefield	Joseph	23JUN03	1.13	11	Lawrence	Mary	22MAY99	1.22	F1
Lasefield	Joseph	03AUG04	1.11	11	Larance	Nancy	24OCT92	2.05	F
Lasefield	Joseph	31JUL05	1.11	11	Lawrence	Samuel	22MAY99	1.22	1
Lasefield	Joseph	01AUG06	1.14	1	Lawrence	Samuel	24JUN99	1.23	1
Laswell	Joseph	08MAY07	1.14	1	Lawrence	Samuel	29JUL00	2.18	1
Lasswell	Joseph	02JUN08	1.18	1	Larrence	Samuel	08JUN01	2.16	M1
Lasswell	Joseph	06JUN09	2.18	1	Laurance	Samuel	19JUN01	3.20	1
LAUGHLIN					Lawrence	Samuel	01JUL02	3.16	1
Laughlin	John	23JUN99	2.10	1	Lawrence	Samuel	14AUG02	3.16	1
Laughlin	John	24JUN99	2.10	1	Lawrence	Samuel	28MAY03	2.18	1
LAWLESS					Laurance	Samuel	18JUN04	2.12	1
Lawles	Augustus	13JUN06	1.13	12	Laurence	Samuel	25JUL04	1.11	1
Lawless	Augustin	02JUN08	1.19	12	Laurence	Samuel	13MAY05	2.19	1
LAWRENCE					Lawrence	Samuel	20JUL05	2.20	1
Lawrence	David	25JUL03	2.19	1	Lawrence	Samuel	28MAR06	2.21	1
Larrance	David	12JUN04	4.14	1	Lawrence	Samuel	31MAY06	2.21	1
Lawrence	David	20JUL05	2.20	1	Laurance	Samuel	01AUG07	2.22	1
Laurance	David	01AUG07	2.21	1	Laurance	Samuel	-----08	2.17	1
Laurence	David	10JUN08	1.21	1	Laurence	Samuel	02JUN08	1.19	1
Lawrence	George	20JUL05	2.20	M1	Laurence	Samuel	07AUG09	1.22	1
Laurence	George	-----11	1.45	1	Larrance	Solomon	20JUN96	1.08	1
Lawrence	Hugh	22MAY99	1.22	1	Lawrence	Solomon	13MAY97	3.18	1
Lawrence	Hugh	19JUL00	2.17	11	Lawrence	Solomon	21MAY99	1.22	1
Larrence	Hugh	08JUN01	2.16	1	Larrence	Solomon	04JUN00	2.17	1
Lawrence	Hugh	14JUN02	3.16	1	Larrence	Solomon	28MAY01	2.15	1

surname	name	date	bk.pg	TM	surname	name	date	bk.pg	TM
Lawrance	Solomon	16JUN03	3.15	1	Lee	George	19JUN01	3.20	2
Laurance	Solomon	30JUL04	2.12	11	Lee	George	11JUN02	2.18	2
Lawrance	Solomon	-----08	2.17	1	Lee	George	03AUG03	3.15	1
Laurence	Soloman	15AUG09	2.19	1	Lee	George	24AUG04	3.12	1
Larrance	William	18JUN96	1.08	12	Lee	George	01AUG05	3.22	1
Laurence	William	10MAY97	3.18	12	Lee	George	31JUL06	3.21	11
Laurence	William	04JUL99	3.12	11	Lee	George	18AUG07	2.22	11
Laurance	William Sr	01JUL00	3.17	12	Lee	George	-----08	2.17	11
Laurance	William Jr	01JUL00	3.17	1	Lee	George	11JUL09	1.22	2
Laurance	William Sr	10MAY01	3.20	11	Lee	George	-----11	1.42	21
Laurance	William Jr	07JUL01	3.20	1	Lee	James	20JUL05	2.20	1
Lawrence	William	01JUL02	3.16	1	Lae	John	01JUL02	3.16	1
Lawrence	William	14AUG02	3.16	11	One lott in New Glasco				
Lawrence	William	17JUN03	2.18	11	Lay	John	12JUL03	3.15	1
Lawrence	William	25JUL03	2.19	1	Lea	John	25JUL04	1.11	1
Laurance	William	18JUN04	2.12	11	Lay	John	01AUG07	2.22	1
Larrance	William	26JUL04	4.14	11	Leigh	Nicholas	10APR90	1.06	1
Larrance	William	13MAY05	2.19	11	Lee	Richard	01JUN97	3.19	1
Lawrence	William	20JUL05	2.20	1	Lee	Richard	24JUN99	1.23	1
Lawrence	William	28MAY06	2.21	1	Lee	Richard	03AUG03	3.15	1
Laurence	William	15JUN07	2.21	1	Lee	Richard	17JUN05	3.22	1
Laurence	William	17JUN08	1.19	1	Lee	Richard	14AUG06	3.22	1
Laurence	William	15AUG09	2.19	1	Lee	Richard	21AUG06	3.22	1
Laurence	William	-----11	1.44	1	Lee	Richard	13JUL07	2.21	1
LAWSON					Lee	Richard	31MAY08	2.16	1
Lawson	Aron	25AUG96	1.08	1	Lee	Richard H.	07JUL09	1.22	1
Lawson	Aaron	01JUN97	3.19	1	Lee	Richard	-----11	1.44	1
Lawson	David	25JUL89	2.07	1	Lee	Thomas	01JUN97	3.19	1
Lawson	David	07DEC92	3.12	1	LEECH				
Lawson	David	23APR94	3.12	1	Leech	Edward	09JUN08	1.19	1
Lawson	David	-----95	1.09	1	Leech	Edward	30MAY09	2.17	1
Lawson	David	-----96	4.09	1	Leech	Edward	-----11	1.45	1
Lawson	James	23APR94	3.13	1	Leech	Humphres	19JUN06	1.13	1
Lawson	James	-----95	1.09	1	Leech	Humphrey	12JUN07	1.15	1
Lawsen	Thomas	08JUN09	1.21	1	Leech	Humphrey	18APR08	1.19	1
LEASURE					Leech	Mathew	28JUN06	3.21	1
Leasure	John	24AUG07	2.22	1	Leach	Matthew	13JUN07	2.21	1
Leasure	John	31MAY08	2.16	1	Leech	Mathew	-----08	2.17	1
Leasure	Joseph	06JUN07	1.14	1	Leech	Mathew	06APR09	1.21	1
Leasun	Joseph	12JUN07	1.15	1	Leech	Matthew	-----11	1.45	1
Leasure	William	06JUN07	1.14	1	Leech	Reuben	19AUG07	2.22	1
LEATHAN					Leech	Reuben	19AUG07	2.22	1
Leathan	John	28AUG97	3.34	1	Leech	Reuben	-----08	2.17	1
LEAVILL					Leach	Reuben	08APR09	1.21	1
Levil	Stephen	19MAY07	1.14	1	Leech	Reuben	-----11	1.45	1
Leavill	Stephen	02JUN08	1.19	1	LEEPER				
Levelle	Stephen	-----11	1.45	1	Leeper	Andrew	06NOV88	1.06	1
LEE					Leeper	Andrew	16JUN89	5.07	1
Lee	Ambrose	12AUG00	2.18	1	Leeper	Andrew	26MAR90	2.07	1
Lee	Ambress	27MAY02	2.18	1	Leeper	Andrew	20APR91	3.09	1
Lee	Ambros	03AUG03	3.15	1	Leeper	Andrew	16NOV92	3.11	1
Lee	Ambrose	24AUG04	3.12	1	Leeper	Andrew	23APR94	3.12	1
Lee	Ambress	06AUG05	3.22	1	Leeper	George	28OCT91	1.05	1
Lee	Ambress	31JUL06	3.21	1	Leeper	George	23NOV92	2.05	1
Lee	Ambress	01AUG07	2.22	1	Leeper	George	13JUN95	2.20	1
Lee	Ambress	31MAY08	2.16	1	Leaper	Hugh	21JUN87	2.05	1
Lee	Ambrose	29JUN09	1.21	1	Leeper	Hugh	29OCT88	1.05	1
Lee	Ambrose	-----11	1.43	1	Leeper	Hugh	16JUN89	5.07	1
Lay	Burell	18JUL06	3.21	1	Leeper	Hugh	26MAR90	2.07	1
Lay	Burrell	31MAY08	2.16	1	Leeper	Hugh	28OCT91	1.05	1
Lee	Fleming	31JUL06	3.21	1	Leeper	Hugh	23NOV92	2.05	1
Lee	Fleming W.	18AUG07	2.22	1	Leeper	Hugh	17SEP93	1.05	1
Lee	William F.	-----08	2.17	1	Leeper	Hugh	20MAY94	1.05	1
Lee	Wm. Fleming	11JUL09	1.22	1	Leeper	Hugh	13JUN95	2.20	1
Leas	George	09JUN91	2.06	1	Leeper	Hugh	13JUN95	2.08	11
Lee	George	11JUN94	2.07	21	Leeper	Hugh	15JUN96	1.07	1
Lee	George	14APR95	3.10	21	Leeper	Hugh	09AUG97	3.19	1
Lee	George	11MAY96	2.11	21	Leeper	Hugh	01JUN99	1.21	1
Lee	George	26MAY97	1.14	21	Leeper	Hugh	01AUG00	2.18	1
Lee	George	01JUN97	3.19	1	Leeper	Hugh	30JUL01	2.17	1
Lee	George	24JUN99	1.21	1	Paid tax for Joseph Cole				
Lee	George	30JUL00	2.18	2	Leeper	Hugh	30JUL01	2.17	

surname	name	date	bk.pg	TM	surname	name	date	bk.pg	TM
Paid tax for Joseph Linn					Lewis	John	03AUG91	2.06	1
Leeper	Hugh	26JUL02	3.16	11	Lever	John	26NOV92	3.11	1
Leeper	Hugh	18JUL03	2.19	12	Lewis	John	-----93	2.03	1
Leeper	Hugh	06AUG05	3.22	13	Lewis	John F.P.	31MAY97	1.14	1
Leiper	Hugh	16AUG06	2.22	0	Lewis	John F.P.	13MAY99	3.12	1
Tax paid by William Logan					Lewis	John F.P.	18JUN00	3.17	11
Leeper	Hugh	13JUL07	2.21	0	Lewis	John T.F.	17JUN01	3.20	11
Tax paid by William Logan					Lewis	John P.F.	26JUL02	3.16	11
Leeper	Hugh	-----09	1.26	0	Lewis	John P.F.	12AUG03	2.19	12
Tax paid by William Logan					Lewis	John	05JUN04	4.14	12
Leeper	Hugh	-----09	1.26		Lewis	John P.F.	18JUN05	2.19	12
This entry was for 1808 taxes					Lewis	John F.P.	29JUL06	2.22	1
Leeper	Hugh	26AUG09	1.26	0	Lewis	John F.P.	29JUL06	2.22	12
Tax paid by William Logan					Lewis	John P.F.	24AUG07	2.22	21
Leeper	Hugh	-----11	1.44	0	Lewis	John P.F.	-----08	2.17	3
Tax paid by William Logan					Lewis	John P.F.	13JUL09	1.22	3
LEESE					Lewis	John F.P.	-----11	1.43	2
Leice	Ichaball	17APR97	3.18	1	Lewis	Joseph	14JUN87	2.04	1
Leecefield	John	09JUN96	1.08	1	Lewis	Joseph	04NOV88	1.06	1
Leice	John	17APR97	3.18	1	Lewis	Joseph	30JUN89	5.07	1
Leice	John	22MAY99	1.22	1	Lewis	Joseph	03JUN90	2.04	1
Lease	John	25MAY00	2.16	1	Lewis	Joseph	28MAR91	1.05	1
Leese	John	04APR01	2.15	1	Lewis	Joseph	26OCT92	2.05	12
Leese	John	26MAY02	3.16	1	Lewis	Joseph	15AUG93	1.06	11
Leese	John	04JUN03	2.18	1	Lewis	Joseph	28MAY94	1.05	12
Lease	John	23JUL04	1.11	1	Lewis	Joseph	-----95	2.26	
Leese	John	02AUG05	2.20	1	One lot in Standford				
Leese	John	04AUG06	2.22	1	Lewis	Joseph	02JUN95	2.20	1
Leese	John	01AUG07	2.21	1	Lewis	Joseph	02JUN95	2.08	14
Leese	John	07JUN08	1.19	1	Lewis	Joseph	13JUN96	1.07	13
Legg	John	07JUN09	1.21	11	Lewis	Joseph	26APR97	3.18	13
Leese	John	18AUG09	2.19	1	Lewis	Joseph	13MAY99	1.21	1
Legg	John	-----11	1.43	1	Lewis	Joseph	16MAY99	1.21	12
Leese	John	-----11	1.44	1	Lewis	Joseph F.	03JUN00	2.17	13
Leece	Jonathan	10JUN96	1.08	1	Lewis	Joseph	03JUN00	2.17	1
Leice	Jonathan	17APR97	3.18	1	Lewis	Joseph F.	01AUG01	2.13	1
Lease	Jonathan	24MAY00	2.16	1	Partner of Nathan Huston				
Leese	Jonathan	27MAY01	2.15	21	Lewis	Joseph	22JUL01	2.16	2
Leese	Jonathan	26MAY02	3.16	21	Lewis	Joseph	25JUL01	2.16	12
Leese	Jonathan	29JUN03	2.19	2	Lewis	Joseph	11JUN02	1.12	1
Lease	Jonathan	23JUL04	1.11	11	Lewis	Joseph	15JUN02	1.12	11
Leese	Jonathan	02AUG05	2.20	11	Lewis	Joseph F.	23AUG02	2.15	
Leece	Michael	10JUN96	1.08	1	Partner of Nathan Huston				
Leice	Michael	22MAY99	1.22	2	Lewis	Joseph	17JUN03	2.18	1
Lease	Michael	14JUN00	2.17	11	Lewis	Joseph	04JUL03	1.13	11
Lease	Michael	23JUL04	1.11	1	Lewis	Joseph	09JUL04	1.10	11
Leese	Michael	02AUG05	2.20	1	Lewis	Joseph	13AUG04	2.12	1
Leese	Michael	28JUL06	2.22	21	Lewis	Joseph	13MAY05	2.19	1
Leece	Michael	13JUL07	2.21	21	Lewis	Joseph	15JUN05	1.10	12
One town lott					Lewis	Joseph	14JUN06	2.21	1
Leese	Michael	17JUN08	1.19	21	Lewis	Joseph	19JUN06	1.13	12
Leese	Michael	15AUG09	2.19	21	Lewis	Joseph F.	06JUN07	1.14	11
Leese	Michael	-----11	1.44	2	Lewis	Joseph	13JUN07	2.20	1
LEFOE					Lewis	Joseph F.	01JUN08	1.19	12
Lefoe	Stephen	30JUN02	1.13	1	Lewis	Joseph F.	07JUN09	2.17	21
LEOPERD					Lewis	Messenger	15JUN02	1.12	1
Leoperd	Robert	20JUN00	1.07	1	Lewis	Messenger	03AUG04	2.12	1
LESTER					Lewis	Messemger	17JUN05	1.10	1
Lester	William	25JUN96	1.08	1	Lewis	Messenger	17JUL06	1.13	1
LEVI					Lewis	Messenger	20JUN07	1.15	11
Levy	Solomon	18NOV88	1.06	1	Lewis	Mesinger	18APR08	1.19	11
Levi	Solomon	16JUN89	5.07	1	Lewis	Samuel	10JUN02	1.12	1
LEWIS					Lewis	Samuel	09JUL04	1.10	1
Lewis	Cutlipp	18MAY90	2.04	1	Lewis	Samuel	15JUN05	1.10	1
Lewis	Ezekiah	-----96	4.09	1	Lewis	Samuel	08JUL05	1.10	1
Lewis	James	23JUN02	1.13	1	Lewis	Samuel	19JUN06	1.13	1
Lewis	James	22JUN03	1.12	1	Lewis	Samuel	06JUN07	1.14	1
Lewis	James	02AUG04	1.11	1	Lewis	Samuel	17JUN07	2.21	1
Lewis	James	30JUL05	1.11	1	Lewis	Samuel	07JUN08	1.19	1
Lewis	James	01AUG06	1.13	1	Lewis	Samuel	07JUN09	2.17	1
Lewis	James	08MAY07	1.14	1	Lewis	Thadius B.	10JUN08	1.21	1
Lewis	John	12JUN87	2.05	11	Lewis	Thadious	18AUG09	2.19	1

surname	name	date	bk.pg	TM	surname	name	date	bk.pg	TM
Lewis	Thadeus	-----11	1.43	1	Litten	Burton	01AUG07	2.21	M1
Lewis	Thomas	27JUN87	3.06	1	LITTLE				
Lewis	William	12JUN87	2.05	1	Little	Benjamin	01AUG91	2.06	1
Lewis	William	10JUN94	1.11	1	Little	Benjamin	14SEP92	1.06	1
LIGGET					Little	Benjamin	13AUG93	3.07	1
Ligget	John	20JUN87	2.05	1	Little	Benjamin	23APR94	3.13	1
LIKENS					Little	Bengamin	-----95	1.09	1
Likens	Mark	03AUG04	1.11	1	LITTLEJOHN				
Likings	William	15AUG93	1.05	1	Littlejohn	Charles	03JUN99	1.23	1
LINDSEY					Littlejohn	Charles	27JUN00	2.17	1
Linsey	Isaac	-----08	2.17	1	Littlejohn	Charles	19JUN01	3.20	11
LINEBERRY					Littlejohn	Charles	04AUG02	2.19	1
Lineberry	Frederick	15MAY99	3.12	1	Littlejohn	Charles	07JUN03	3.15	11
Lineberere	Frederick	18JUN00	3.17	1	Littlejohn	Charles	06AUG04	3.12	11
Limeberry	Frederick	01AUG01	2.17	1	Littlejohn	Charles	16AUG05	3.22	11
Limeberry	Frederick	28JUL02	3.16	1	Littlejohn	Charles	06AUG06	3.22	1
Limeberry	Frederick	29JUN03	2.19	1	Littlejohn	Henry	03JUN99	1.21	1
Lineberry	Frederick	05JUN04	4.14	1	Littlejohn	Henry	26JUL00	2.18	1
Limeberry	Frederick	27JUN05	2.19	1	Littlejohn	Henry	01AUG01	2.17	1
Limeberry	Frederick	28JUL06	2.22	1	Littlejohn	Henry	01JUN02	2.18	2
Linebarger	Frederick	09JUN07	2.20	1	Littlejohn	Henry	07JUN03	3.15	M1
Linesbarger	Frederick	-----08	2.17	1	Littlejohn	Henry	30JUL03	2.19	1
Limeberry	Frederick	12JUL09	1.22	1	Littlejohn	Henry	21AUG04	3.12	1
Lineberry	Frederick	-----11	1.43	1	Littlejohn	Henry	30MAY05	2.19	1
LINK					Littlejohn	Henry Jr	06AUG06	3.22	1
Link	Absolam	08MAY94	2.08	M1	Littlejohn	Henry	11JUN07	2.20	1
Link	Absolam	27APR95	3.10	M1	Littlejohn	Samuel	03JUN99	1.21	1
Link	Henry	23MAR90	2.04	1	Littlejohn	Samuel	26JUL00	2.18	1
Link	Henry	13APR91	1.05	1	Littlejohn	Samuel	01AUG01	2.17	1
Link	Henry	23NOV92	2.05	1	Littlejohn	Samuel	30JUL03	2.19	1
Linch	Henry	13AUG93	3.07	1	Littlejohn	Samuel	22AUG04	2.12	2
Link	Henry	08MAY94	2.08	1	Littlejohn	Samuel	30MAY05	2.19	1
Link	Henry	27APR95	3.10	1	Littlejohn	Samuel	02AUG06	2.22	2
Linch	Joseph	13AUG93	3.07	1	Littlejohn	Samuel	04AUG06	3.21	1
Link	Joseph	12JUN94	2.08	1	Littlejohn	Samuel	11JUN07	2.20	1
Link	Joseph	12JUN94	2.08	1	Littlejohn	Samuel	31MAY08	2.16	1
Link	Joseph	15APR95	3.10	1	Littlejohn	Samuel	26JUN09	1.21	1
LINTHICUM					Littlejohn	Silas	03JUN99	1.21	1
Linthecomb	John	27JUN05	2.19	1	Littlejohn	Silas	26JUL00	2.18	1
Linthecomb	Thomas	27JUN05	2.19	1	Littlejohn	Silas	01AUG01	2.17	1
Linticome	Thomas	01AUG06	3.21	11	Littlejohn	Silas	01JUN02	2.18	1
Linticome	William	01AUG06	3.21	1	Littlejohn	Siless	12JUL03	3.15	1
LIPSEY					Littlejohn	Silas	03MAY04	3.12	1
Lapley	James	10APR94	3.12	1	Littlejohn	Silas	19AUG05	3.22	1
Lapsley	James	-----95	1.09	1	Littlejohn	Silas	16JUL06	3.21	1
Lapsley	James	-----96	4.09	1	Littlejohn	Silas	11JUN07	2.20	1
Lapsley	John	27JUN87	3.06	1	Littlejohn	Siles	31MAY08	2.16	1
Lapesley	John	06JUL89	2.08	1	LOCK				
Lapsley	John	02JUN91	3.09	1	Lock	Benjamin	19MAY90	2.04	1
Lapsley	John	02DEC92	3.11	1	Lock	Benjamin	03JUN95	2.08	1
Lapsley	John	23APR94	3.12	1	Lock	James	13JUL07	1.13	1
Lapsley	John	-----95	1.09	1	Lock	Jonas	19JUN05	2.19	M1
Lapsley	John	-----96	4.09	1	Lock	Samuel	19MAY90	2.04	1
Lepsey	John	30MAY97	3.19	1	Lock	Samuel	08DEC92	3.12	1
Lipsey	John	20JUN04	1.10	1	Lock	Samuel	14AUG93	1.05	1
Lipsey	John	11JUN05	1.10	1	Lock	Samuel	02JUN95	2.08	1
Lipsey	John	20JUN06	1.13	1	Lock	Samuel	03JUN95	2.20	1
Lipsy	John	18MAY07	1.14	1	Lock	Samuel	12JUN99	2.11	1
Lepsey	John	10JUN08	1.21	1	LOGAN				
Lipsey	John	06JUN09	2.17	1	Logan	Agness	16JUN96	1.08	F1
Lepsey	John	-----11	1.45	1	Logan	Anne	18JUL03	1.14	F
LITLER					Logan	Ann	09JUL04	1.10	F
Littler	John	13JUL87	1.03	1	Logan	Ann	23JUN06	1.13	F
Litler	John	22MAY89	6.04	1	Logan	Benj(heirs)	13AUG04	2.12	O
Litler	John	13MAY90	1.06	1	Tax pd by David Logan				
Litler	John Jr	30APR91	2.06	1	Logan	Benj(heirs)	13JUL07	2.21	D
Litler	John	13SEP92	1.06	1	Tax paid by William Logan				
Litler	John	23MAY94	2.08	1	Logan	Benj(heirs)	26AUG09	1.26	D
Litler	John	28JUL96	1.11	1	Tax paid by William Logan				
Litter	John	22JUN97	1.14	1	Logan	Benjamin	26JUN87	2.05	1
Literal	John	30MAY99	2.11	1	Logan	Benjamin	18NOV88	1.06	1
LITTEN					Logan	Benjamin	07AUG89	5.08	1

surname	name	date	bk.pg	TM	surname	name	date	bk.pg	TM
Logan	Benjamin	26MAR90	2.07	1	Logan	Hugh	31MAY99	1.22	1
Logan	Benjamin	19OCT91	1.05	1	Logan	Hugh	09JUL99	1.23	1
Logan	Benjamin	21OCT92	2.05	11	Logan	Hugh Sr	26JUL00	2.18	1
Logan	Benjamin	17SEP93	1.05	11	Logan	Hugh Jr	03JUN00	2.17	1
Logan	Benjamin	21MAY94	1.05	12	Logan	Hugh	19JUL00	2.17	1
Logan	Charles	24OCT92	2.05	1	Logan	Hugh Sr	13JUL01	2.16	1
Logan	Charles	15AUG93	3.07	1	Logan	Hugh	02JUN01	2.15	1
Logan	David	20JUN87	2.05	11	Logan	Hugh	08JUN01	2.16	1
Logan	David	28OCT88	1.05	1	Logan	Hugh	16JUN02	1.12	1
Logan	David	13MAY89	6.04		Logan	Hugh	31JUL02	2.19	1
Shown with Mathew Logan					Logan	Hugh	17JUN02	1.12	1
Logan	David	16JUN89	5.07	1	Logan	Hugh	13JUL03	3.15	1
Logan	David	03APR90	2.04	1	Logan	Hugh	18JUL03	1.14	1
Logan	David	10APR90	1.06	2	Logan	Hugh	09JUL04	1.10	1
Shown with Jonathan Logan					Logan	Hugh	31JUL04	2.12	1
Logan	David	07MAY91	2.06	1	Logan	Hugh	22AUG04	2.13	1
Logan	David	05JUL91	1.05	1	Logan	Hugh	17JUN05	3.22	1
Logan	David	26SEP92	1.06	1	Logan	Hugh	25JUL05	1.11	1
Logan	David	21OCT92	2.05	1	Logan	Hugh	23JUN06	1.13	1
Logan	David	07AUG93	1.06	1	Logan	Hugh	19JUL06	3.21	11
Logan	David	15AUG93	3.07	1	Logan	Hugh	09JUN07	1.15	1
Logan	David	17APR94	2.08	1	Logan	Hugh	25AUG07	2.22	11
Logan	David	20MAY94	1.05	1	Logan	Hugh	-----08	2.17	12
Logan	David	30MAY95	2.08	1	Logan	Hugh	02JUN08	1.19	1
Logan	David	30MAY95	2.20	1	Logan	Hugh	03JUL09	1.22	1
Logan	David	13JUN96	1.08	1	Logan	Hugh	15AUG09	2.19	1
Logan	David	08MAY97	3.18	1	Logan	Hugh Jr	15AUG09	2.19	1
Logan	David Sr	23MAY99	1.22	11	Logan	Hugh Sr	-----11	1.44	1
Logan	David Sr	29MAY00	2.17	2	Logan	Hugh	-----11	1.42	1
Logan	David Jr	17JUN00	2.17	1	Logan	Hugh	-----11	1.45	1
One lott in Standford					Logan	Hugh	-----11	1.44	11
Logan	David Jr	17JUN00	2.17		Logan	Hugh	-----11	1.43	21
Two lotts in Shelbyville					Logan	Hugh	-----11	1.45	
Logan	David	29MAY01	2.15	2	Paid tax for Polly Herrin				
Logan	David	08JUN01	2.16	1	Logan	James	30JUN87	1.03	13
Logan	David	30JUL01	2.17	1	Logan	James Jr	30JUN87	1.03	1
One lott in Standford					Logan	James	14MAY89	6.04	1
Logan	David	30JUL01	2.17		Logan	James	20APR90	1.06	1
Paid tax for David Shaver					Logan	James	08OCT92	1.06	11
Logan	David	14JUN02	2.18	1	Logan	James	07AUG93	1.06	1
Logan	David	17JUN02	1.12	1	Logan	James	15AUG93	3.07	11
Logan	David	17JUN02	1.12	1	Logan	James	19APR94	2.08	1
Logan	David	16JUN03	3.15	1	Logan	James	19APR94	2.08	11
Logan	David	15JUL03	1.13	11	Logan	James	13MAY94	1.06	1
Logan	David Jr	18JUL03	1.13	1	Logan	James	14APR95	3.10	2
Logan	David	25JUN04	1.10	1	Logan	James	11JUN95	2.08	1
Logan	David	13AUG04	2.12	00	Logan	James	27JUN96	2.11	2
Paid tax for Benj(heirs) Logan					Logan	James	12MAY97	1.14	2
Logan	David	20JUN05	1.10	11	Logan	James	18MAY99	3.12	11
Logan	David	25JUL05	1.11	1	Logan	James	28JUN00	3.17	12
Logan	David Sr	23JUN06	1.13	11	Logan	James	08JUN01	3.20	12
Logan	David	23JUN06	1.13	1	Logan	James	16JUN02	1.12	1
Logan	David	18JUL06	3.21	1	Logan	James	01JUL02	3.16	12
Logan	David	15JUN07	2.21	1	Logan	James	20JUN03	2.19	21
Logan	David	20JUN07	1.15	12	Logan	James	14JUL03	1.13	1
Logan	David	25AUG07	2.22	1	Logan	James	31JUL04	2.12	1
Logan	David	-----08	2.17	1	Logan	James	06AUG04	4.14	21
Logan	David	29JUN09	1.21	1	Logan	James	20JUN05	2.19	32
Logan	David	06JUL09	2.18	1	Logan	James Jr	20JUL05	2.20	1
Logan	David	-----11	1.44	1	Logan	James	21JUN06	1.13	1
Logan	David	-----11	1.45	1	Logan	James	07AUG06	2.22	22
Logan	George	28MAY03	2.18	1	Logan	James	04JUN07	1.14	1
Logan	Hugh	11JUN89	6.08	1	Logan	James	01AUG07	2.22	22
Logan	Hugh	15APR90	1.06	1	Logan	James	-----08	2.17	21
Logan	Hugh	19APR91	2.06	1	Logan	James	10JUN08	1.20	1
Logan	Hugh	06OCT92	1.06	1	Logan	James	10JUN09	1.21	3
Logan	Hugh	25AUG93	3.07	1	Logan	James	-----11	1.45	1
Logan	Hugh	09MAY94	2.08	1	Logan	James	-----11	1.43	2
Logan	Hugh	09MAY94	2.08	1	Logan	Jane	28OCT91	1.05	F
Logan	Hugh	23APR95	3.10	1	Logan	Janie	24OCT92	2.05	F
Logan	Hugh	02JUN96	2.11	1	LOGAN				
Logan	Hugh	02JUN97	1.14	1	Logan	John	21JUN87	2.05	1

surname	name	date	bk.pg	TM
Logan	John	28OCT88	1.05	1
Logan	John	17JUN89	5.07	1
Logan	John	24MAR90	2.04	1
Logan	John	13APR90	2.04	1
Logan	John Jr	03APR90	2.04	1
Logan	John	20SEP91	1.05	1
Logan	John Jr	17MAY91	2.06	1
Logan	John	21OCT92	2.05	1
Logan	John Jr	26OCT92	2.05	1
Logan	John Sr	07AUG93	1.06	11
Logan	John Jr	13AUG93	1.05	1
Logan	John Sr	20MAY94	1.05	11
Logan	John	21MAY94	1.05	11
Logan	John	10JUN94	2.07	1
Logan	John	24JUN94	1.12	1
Logan	John	15MAY95	2.08	11
Logan	John	25MAY95	2.20	1
Logan	John	13JUN96	1.07	11
Logan	John	14JUN96	1.08	1
Logan	John	07APR97	3.18	11
Logans	John	16MAY97	3.18	1
Logan	John	31MAY99	1.22	1
Logan	John	19JUN99	2.11	1
Logan	John	19JUL00	2.17	1
Logan	John	29MAY01	2.15	1
Logan	John	17JUN02	1.12	1
Logan	John	23JUL04	1.10	1
Logan	John	12AUG05	1.11	1
Logan	John	25MAY06	2.21	1
Logan	John	07AUG06	2.22	1
Logan	John	25JUL07	2.21	1
Logan	John Jr	13JUL07	2.21	M1
Tax paid by William Logan				
Logan	John	-----08	2.17	1
Logan	Jonathan	13MAY89	6.04	
Shown with Mathew Logan				
Logan	Jonathan	10APR90	1.06	
Shown with David Logan				
Logan	Jonathan	07MAY91	2.06	1
Logan	Jonathan	08OCT92	1.06	1
Logan	Jonathan	18SEP93	3.07	1
Logan	Jonathan	17APR94	2.08	11
Logan	Marget	26JUN87	2.05	F
Logan	Margaret	26AUG93	1.05	F
Logan	Margrat	21MAY94	1.05	F
Logan	Margaret	10JUN95	2.08	F
Logan	Margrat	24JUN96	1.08	F
Logan	Margaret	13JUN97	3.19	F
Logan	Margaret	25JUL01	2.16	F1
Logan	Margrett	14JUN02	2.18	F
Logan	Margaret	16JUN03	3.15	F
Logan	Margaret	19AUG05	3.22	F
Logan	Margrett	30JUL04	2.12	F
Logan	Margaret	21AUG06	3.22	F
Logan	Margaret	25AUG07	2.22	F
Logan	Martha	15AUG93	3.07	F
Logan	Mathew	13MAY89	6.04	3
Shown with David Logan				
Logan	Mathew	13MAY89	6.04	
Shown with Jonathan Logan				
Logan	Matthew	10APR90	1.06	1
Logan	Matthew	14MAY91	2.06	1
Logan	Matthew	09OCT92	1.06	1
Logan	Matthew	15AUG93	3.07	1
Logan	Matthew	01MAY94	2.08	1
Logan	Mathew	24MAR95	3.10	1
Logan	Matthew	21APR96	2.11	1
Logan	Nancy	11APR97	3.18	F1
Logan	Nathaniel	26JUN87	2.05	1
Logan	Nathaniel	29OCT88	1.05	1
Logan	Nathaniel	14MAY89	6.04	1
Logan	Nathaniel	11JUN89	6.08	1
Logan	Nathaniel	21MAY90	1.06	1
Logan	Nathaniel	07JUL91	1.05	1
Logan	Nathaniel	01NOV92	2.05	1
Logan	Nathaniel	24JUN01	2.16	1
Logan	Nathaniel	12JUL02	1.13	1
Logan	Nathaniel	17JUN03	3.15	1
Logan	Nathaniel	15JUN04	2.12	1
Logan	Nathaniel	30MAY05	3.22	1
Logan	Peggy	14JUN00	2.17	F
Logan	Peggy	05JUN09	1.21	F
Logan	Robert	-----08	2.17	1
Logan	Thomas	28OCT88	1.05	1
Logan	Thomas	29JUN89	5.07	1
Logan	Thomas	03APR90	2.04	1
Logan	Thomas	07APR91	1.05	1
Logan	Thomas	24OCT92	2.05	1
Logan	William	21JUN87	2.05	1
Logan	William	03NOV88	1.06	1
Logan	William	21JUL89	5.07	1
Logan	William	03APR90	2.04	1
Logan	William	07OCT91	1.05	1
Logan	William	05OCT92	2.05	11
Logan	William	07AUG93	1.06	1
Logan	William Jr	15AUG93	1.05	1
Logan	William	23MAY94	1.06	1
Logan	William	18JUN94	2.05	0
Logan	William	12JUN95	2.08	1
Logan	William	21JUN95	2.20	1
Logan	William	25JUN95	2.08	1
Logan	William	19JUL00	2.17	1
Logan	William	23JUL01	2.16	1
Logan	William	17JUN02	1.12	1
Logan	William	04AUG02	2.19	1
Logan	William	26JUN03	2.19	1
Logan	William	04JUL03	1.13	1
Logan	William	15JUL03	1.13	1
Logan	William	25JUN04	1.10	1
Logan	William	31JUL04	2.12	1
Logan	William	22AUG04	2.13	1
Logan	William	15JUN05	1.10	1
Logan	William	05AUG05	2.20	1
Logan	William	20JUN06	1.13	1
Logan	William	16AUG06	2.22	1
Paid tax for Hugh Leiper				
Logan	William	08JUN07	1.15	1
Logan	William	13JUL07	2.21	1
Paid tax for Benj(heirs) Logan				
Logan	William	13JUL07	2.21	
Paid tax for Hugh Leeper				
Logan	William	13JUL07	2.21	
Paid tax for John Jr Logan				
Logan	William	-----08	2.17	1
Logan	William	18APR08	1.19	1
Logan	William	-----09	1.26	
1808 tax info in 1809 tax list				
Logan	William	07AUG09	2.18	1
Logan	William	26AUG09	1.26	1
Paid Tax for Benj(heirs) Logan				
Logan	William	26AUG09	1.26	
Paid tax for Hugh Leeper				
Logan	William	-----11	1.44	1
Logan	William	-----11	1.44	1
Paid tax for Hugh Leeper				
LOGWOOD				
Logwood	William	-----93	2.03	1
LONG				
Long	Benjamin	14MAY94	1.05	1
Long	Benjamin	20APR97	3.19	1
Long	Benjamin	12MAY99	2.11	1
Long	Benjamin	30MAY00	2.17	1
Long	Benjamin	25JUL01	2.16	1
Long	Benjamin	04JUN02	1.12	1

surname	name	date	bk.pg	TM	surname	name	date	bk.pg	TM
Long	Benjamin	14JUN03	1.12	1	Lowe	Joseph	17JUN07	2.21	1
Long	David	10JUN08	1.20	1	Low	Samuel	07JUL87	1.03	1
Long	John	07MAY91	3.09	1	Low	Samuel	11JUN89	6.04	1
Long	William	26JUN87	2.05	1	Lowe	Samuel	23APR94	3.12	1
Long	William	18NOV88	1.06	1	Low	Samuel	-----95	1.09	1
Long	William	01JUL89	2.07	11	Lowe	Thomas	10MAY94	2.07	M1
Long	William	13JUL91	3.09	1	Low	Thomas	14APR95	3.10	M1
Long	William	02DEC92	3.11	1	Lowe	Thomas	05JUL96	2.11	1
Long	William	14MAY94	1.05	11	Low	Thomas	05JUN97	1.14	1
Long	William	21MAY95	2.08	1	Lowe	Thomas	15MAY99	3.12	1
Long	William	09JUN96	1.08	1	Lowe	Thomas	12AUG00	3.17	1
Long	William	20APR97	3.18	1	Low	Thomas	17JUN01	3.20	1
Long	William	12MAY99	2.11	1	Lowe	Thomas	02JUN02	2.18	1
Long	William	11JUN00	1.07	1	Lowe	Thomas	14JUN03	3.15	1
Long	William	01JUN01	1.09	11	Lowe	Thomas	07AUG04	3.12	1
Long	William	03JUN02	1.11	11	Lowe	Thomas	27JUN05	2.19	1
Long	William	11JUN03	1.12	12	Lowe	Thomas	01AUG06	2.22	1
Long	William	14JUN04	1.10	12	Law	Thomas	17JUN07	2.21	1
LONGDON					LOWER				
Longden	John B.	25JUN04	4.14	11	Lower	John	13JUL07	2.21	1
Longden	John	18JUL05	2.20	2	LOWRY				
Longdon	John B.	04AUG06	2.22	2	Lowrey	Edde	20JUN03	2.19	F
Longdon	John B.	17JUN07	2.21	2	Lowery	Robert	28JUN00	3.17	1
Longden	Patrick	25JUN04	4.14	1	Lowry	Robert	07JUL01	3.20	1
LOVE					Lowery	Robert	13AUG02	3.16	1
Love	John	06APR91	1.05	1	LUCAS				
Love	Robert	07JUL87	3.06	1	Lucas	Charles	01AUG07	2.21	1
Love	Robert	27JUL89	2.08	1	Lucus	Charles	10JUN08	1.21	1
LOVIN					Lucas	Charles	18AUG09	2.19	1
Lovin	John	07JUL87	3.06	11	Ludin	Charles	-----11	1.43	1
LOWE					Lucas	John	28MAY99	1.22	1
Low	Edward	13JUL87	1.03	1	Lucas	John	24MAY00	2.16	1
Low	Edward	11JUN89	6.04	1	Lucas	John	04APR01	2.15	1
Lowe	Edward	15APR90	1.06	1	Lucas	John	01JUN03	2.18	1
Loe	Edward	18MAR91	2.06	1	Lukis	John	24JUL04	1.11	1
Loe	Edward	04SEP92	1.06	1	Lucas	John	08JUN05	2.19	1
Loe	Ned	14AUG93	3.07	1	Lukus	John	01AUG06	3.21	1
Lowe	Edward	11JUN94	2.07	1	Lucus	Seth	15JUN04	2.12	1
Low	Edward	11MAY97	1.14	1	Lucas	William	28MAY99	1.22	1
Lowe	Edward	24JUN99	1.23	1	Lucas	William	16JUN00	2.17	1
Lowe	Edward	19JUL00	3.17	1	Lucas	William	04APR01	2.15	1
Low	Edward	17JUN01	3.20	1	Lucas	William	07JUN02	3.16	1
Lowe	Edward	27JUL02	3.16	1	Lucas	William	01JUN03	2.18	11
Lowe	Edward	06AUG03	2.19	1	Lukis	William	23JUL04	1.11	11
Low	Edmond	05JUN04	4.14	1	Lucas	William	02AUG05	2.20	11
Lowe	Edward	18JUN05	2.19	1	Lucas	William	18MAY06	2.21	11
Low	Elizabeth	13JUL87	1.03	F	Lucas	William	01AUG07	2.21	1
Loe	Elizabeth	14SEP92	1.06	F	Lucus	William	10JUN08	1.21	1
Loe	Elizabeth	14AUG93	3.07	F	Lucas	William	18AUG09	2.19	1
Lowe	Elizabeth	10MAY94	2.04	F	LUMPKINS				
Lowe	Elizabeth	05JUL96	2.11	F	Lumpkins	John	15NOV88	1.06	11
Low	George	06JUN96	1.08	1	Lumpkins	John	22JUN89	5.07	11
Low	George	15JUN97	3.19	1	Lumpkins	Philip	20JUN87	2.05	1
Loe	George	30JUL04	2.12	M1	Lumpkins	Phillip	15NOV88	1.06	1
Low	George	08JUL05	3.22	11	Lumpkins	Phillip	16JUN89	5.07	1
Loe	George	21AUG06	3.22	12	Lumpkins	Philip	30MAR91	1.05	1
Low	George	01JUL07	1.15	1	Lumpkin	Phillip	05OCT92	2.05	1
Lowe	George	01JUN09	2.17	1	Lumpkin	Phillip	26AUG93	1.06	1
Lowe	Isaac	20MAY96	2.11	1	Lumkin	Phillip	23MAY94	1.06	1
Low	Isaac	29MAY97	1.14	1	Lumkin	Phillip	23MAY94	1.11	1
Lowe	Jesse	13MAY99	1.21	11	Lumpkins	Philip	02JUN95	2.20	1
Lowe	Jesse	03JUN00	2.17	11	Lumkins	Phillip	12JUN95	2.08	1
Lowe	Jesse	22JUL01	2.16	1	Lumpkin	Phillip	18JUL96	1.08	1
Low	Jesse	15JUN02	1.12	11	Lumpkins	Phillip	07APR97	3.18	1
Lowe	Jessee	04JUL03	1.13	11	Lumpkins	Phillip	20MAY99	1.22	1
Loe	Jesse	03AUG04	2.12	11	LUNSFORD				
Low	Jesse	17JUN05	1.10	1	Lunsford	Rhodum	10JUN08	1.21	1
Low	Jessee	20JUN06	1.13	1	Lunsford	Rwrodum	24MAY09	2.17	1
Lowe	Jesse	20JUN07	1.15	1	Lanceford	Rhodunt	-----11	1.43	1
Low	Jesse	18APR08	1.19	1	LUSK				
Lowe	Jesse	01JUN09	2.17	1	Lusk	William	-----95	1.09	1
Loe	Jesse	-----11	1.45	1	Lusk	William	-----96	4.09	1

surname	name	date	bk.pg	TM
LUTTRELL				
Luttrell	Abner	-----95	1.09	1
Luttrell	Abner	-----96	4.09	1
Lotterell	Abner	17MAR97	2.02	1
Lutral	Abner	11MAY99	2.11	1
Luttrel	Abner	09JUN00	1.07	1
Lutteral	Abner	30MAY01	1.09	1
Lutteral	Abner	28JUN02	1.13	1
Luteral	Jesse	27MAY01	3.20	1
Luthrell	Jesse	06AUG05	3.22	1
Lutterol	John	-----95	1.09	1
Luthrell	John	06AUG05	3.22	1
Lotthell	Lot	12JUL97	1.14	1
Luttrell	Lott	28JUN99	1.23	1
Littrell	Lott	24JUL00	2.17	1
Lutteral	Lott	27MAY01	3.20	1
Lutterell	Lott	31JUL02	2.19	1
Luttrell	Lott	21JUN03	3.15	1
Luttrel	Lot	08AUG04	3.12	1
Luthrell	Lott	06AUG05	3.22	1
Luttrell	Lott	21AUG06	3.22	1
Lottrell	Michael	13JUL97	1.14	1
Lutrell	Nathan	29JUL96	2.11	1
Lottrell	Nathan	12JUL97	1.14	1
Luttrell	Nathan	28JUN99	1.23	1
Littrell	Nathan	24JUL00	2.18	1
Luteral	Nathen	27MAY01	3.20	1
Lutterell	Nathen	31JUL02	2.19	1
Luttrell	Nathan	21JUN03	3.15	11
Luttrel	Nathan	08AUG04	3.12	11
Luthrell	Nathen	06AUG05	3.22	1
Luttrell	Nathen	21AUG06	3.22	12
Lutrell	Robert	17MAR97	2.02	1
Lutrell	Rodum	29JUL96	2.11	1
Lottrell	Rodham	12JUL97	1.14	1
Luttrell	Rodham	28JUN99	1.23	1
Littrell	Rodham	24JUL00	2.18	1
Luteral	Rodeham	27MAY01	3.20	1
Lutterell	Rodeham	10MAY02	2.18	1
LYON				
Linn	Alexander	06AUG06	3.21	1
Linn	Alexander	19AUG07	2.22	1
Linn	Alexander	19AUG07	2.22	1
Linn	Alexander	19AUG07	2.22	1
Linn	Alexander	-----08	2.17	1
Linn	Alexander	06APR09	1.21	11
Lynn	Alexander	-----11	1.45	11
Lynim	Andrew	07AUG89	2.08	1
Linum	Andrew	24JUN91	3.09	1
Linum	Andrew	27NOV92	3.11	1
Lynn	Charles	-----11	1.45	1
Lyon	Charles P.	04MAY07	1.13	1
Lyon	Charles P.	10JUN08	1.20	1
Lyon	Charles P.	13JUN09	2.17	1
Lyon	David	07JUL87	3.06	1
Linn	Fanney	08MAY05	2.19	F
Linn	Fanny	21AUG06	3.22	F1
Lion	James	23JUN03	1.12	1
Lyon	James	31JUL05	1.11	1
Lyon	James	13JUN09	2.17	1
Linn	John	24JUN91	3.09	1
Lin	Joseph	14JUN87	2.04	1
Lyn	Joseph	05NOV88	1.06	1
Lyn	Joseph	16JUN89	5.07	1
Linn	Joseph	26MAR90	2.07	1
Linn	Joseph	13APR91	1.05	1
Lynn	Joseph	23NOV92	2.05	1
Lenn	Joseph	30AUG93	1.06	1
Line	Joseph	23APR94	3.12	1
Linn	Joseph	31MAY94	1.05	1
Linn	Joseph	-----95	1.09	1
Linn	Joseph	16MAY95	2.08	1

surname	name	date	bk.pg	TM
Line	Joseph	-----96	4.09	1
Linn	Joseph	17JUN96	1.07	1
Linn	Joseph	12JUN97	3.19	1
Linn	Joseph	01JUN99	1.21	1
Linn	Joseph	01AUG00	2.18	11
Linn	Joseph	30JUL01	2.17	M1
Tax paid by Hugh Leeper				
Linn	Joseph	30JUL01	2.17	
Tax pd by Hugh Leeper				
Lenn	Joseph	14JUN02	2.18	11
Linn	Joseph	12JUL03	3.15	11
Linn	Joseph	18JUN04	2.12	11
Lyon	Peter	14MAY90	1.06	1
Lyon	Stephen	31JUL05	1.11	11
Lyon	Stephen	04MAY07	1.13	1
Lyon	Stephen	10JUN08	1.20	1
Lyon	Stephen	13JUN09	2.17	1
Lyne	Thomas	-----08	2.17	1
Linn	William	18JUN04	2.12	1
Lenn	William	06AUG05	3.22	1
Lenn	William	21AUG06	3.22	1
MACKEY				
McKay	James	13JUL87	1.04	1
Mackey	James	13MAY89	6.04	1
Macky	James	29MAY90	1.06	1
Mackey	James	20APR91	2.07	1
Mackey	James	11APR95	3.12	21
Mackey	James	15JUN96	2.12	1
Mackey	James	10MAY97	1.15	1
Mackey	James	05JUL00	3.20	1
Macky	James	19MAY01	3.21	1
Mackey	James	30JUL03	2.21	1
McKey	James	28JUN04	4.16	1
Mackey	James	27JUN05	2.22	1
Mackey	James	02AUG06	2.25	1
Mackey	James	24AUG08	2.20	11
Mackey	James	07JUN09	1.22	11
McKay	John	16SEP91	3.11	1
Mackey	John	27MAY94	1.06	1
McKee	John	01JUN95	2.09	1
McKee	John	28JUN96	1.09	1
Macky	John	15JUL99	1.28	1
Mackey	John	25JUN00	2.20	1
Mackey	John	03JUN01	2.18	1
Mackey	John	11JUN02	2.21	1
McKey	John	30JUN03	1.15	1
Mackey	John	02AUG04	2.14	1
McKey	John	17JUN05	1.13	1
McKey	John	20JUN06	1.15	1
McCay	Matthew	23JUN91	2.04	
Listed with Willis Green				
McKee	Samuel	14MAY99	2.12	1
McKay	Samuel	06MAY07	1.16	1
McKee	William	06MAY94	1.11	1
McKey	William	-----96	4.09	2
McKee	William Sr	17MAR97	2.02	3
McKee	William	14MAY99	2.11	1
McKee	William	11JUN00	1.08	1
McKee	William Jr	11JUN00	1.08	1
McKee	William	01JUN01	1.10	1
McKee	William Jr	01JUN01	1.10	1
McKee	William	24AUG08	2.20	1
Macky	William	07JUL09	1.24	1
MACKSBERRY				
Macksbury	Isaac	28MAY94	3.14	1
Macksbury	Isaac	-----95	1.09	M1
Marksberry	Isaac	-----96	4.10	1
Maxberry	John	07AUG89	2.09	1
Maxbury	John	20AUG91	3.10	1
Macksbury	John	-----95	1.09	1
Marksberry	John	-----96	4.10	1
Macksbury	Samuel	21JUL87	3.06	11

surname	name	date	bk.pg	TM	surname	name	date	bk.pg	TM
Maxberry	Samuel	25JUL89	2.09	1	Magill	James	17APR94	2.09	1
Maxberry	Samuel	07AUG89	2.09	1	McGill	James	23MAY96	2.11	1
Maxbury	Samuel Sr	20AUG91	3.10	1	McGill	James	24JUN00	2.19	11
Maxbury	Samuel	20AUG91	3.10	1	Magill	James	03JUN01	2.18	11
Maxbury	Samuel Sr	27NOV92	3.12	1	Magill	James	20JUL03	3.18	1
Maxbury	Samuel	27NOV92	3.12	1	Magill	James	15JUN04	2.13	1
Macksbury	Samuel Sr	24MAY94	3.15	1	Magill	James	19MAY05	3.23	11
Macksbury	Samuel Jr	28MAY94	3.15	1	Magill	James	31MAY05	2.21	1
Macksbury	Samuel Sr	-----95	1.09	1	Magill	James	31JUL06	3.24	12
Macksbury	Samuel Jr	-----95	1.09	1	Magill	James	21AUG07	2.26	12
Marksberry	Samuel Sr	-----96	4.10	1	Magill	James	-----08	2.19	12
Marksberry	Samuel Jr	-----96	4.09	1	Magill	James	20MAR09	1.22	1
MADDOX					Magil	James	-----11	1.47	1
Maddox	Edward	13AUG07	2.25	1	McGill	John	24AUG87	1.04	1
Mattocks	Edward	17JUN08	1.25	1	McGill	John	11JUN89	6.08	1
Mattox	Edward	-----11	1.46	1	Hugh McGill listed also				
Mattocks	Ralph	10JUL89	2.08	1	McGill	John	15APR90	1.07	2
Maddux	Ralph	-----93	2.03	1	Hugh McGill listed also				
Maddox	Ralph	-----96	4.11	1	McGill	John	23JUN91	2.06	2
Matocks	Smallwood	27JUL03	2.21	1	Hugh McGill listed also				
Maddox	Smallwood	27JUN04	4.16	1	McGill	John	18OCT92	1.09	2
Maddox	William	13JUN06	1.14	1	Hugh McGill listed also				
Maddox	William	13AUG07	2.25	1	McGill	John	24AUG93	3.08	2
Mattocks	William	17JUN08	1.25	1	Hugh McGill listed also				
Mattox	William	-----11	1.51	1	Magill	John	08MAY94	2.09	1
MADLOCK					Magill	John	08MAY94	2.09	1
Medlock	John	16MAY94	2.10	1	Magill	John	22APR95	3.11	2
Medlock	John	10JUL99	3.14	1	Magill	John	04MAY97	1.15	1
Medlock	John	09JUL00	3.21	1	McGill	John	04JUN99	1.26	1
Madlock	John	30JUL01	3.23	1	McGill	John	20JUN00	2.19	1
Madlock	John	09JUN02	2.21	1	Magill	John	03JUN01	2.18	1
Medlock	John	04AUG03	3.18	1	Magill	John	13JUL01	2.19	1
Medlock	John	06APR04	4.15	1	Magill	John	24AUG02	2.23	1
Medlock	Sarah	09APR95	3.12	F	Magill	John	01AUG03	2.21	1
Medlock	Sarah	08JUN97	1.16	F	Magill	John	08JUN04	4.15	1
Medlock	Salley	11JUL00	3.21	F	Magill	John	30MAY05	2.21	1
MAGGERT					Magill	John	15AUG06	2.26	1
Maggard	Jacob	23JUN06	1.15	1	Magill	John	17AUG07	2.26	1
Maggert	Jacob	30JUN07	1.18	1	Magill	John Sr	17JUN08	1.24	11
Maggert	Jacob	10JUN08	1.23	1	Magill	John	-----08	2.19	1
MAGILL					Magill	John	17JUN08	1.24	1
McGill	David	24AUG93	3.08	1	Magill	John	19JUN09	1.23	1
Magill	David	09MAY94	2.09	1	Magill	John	-----11	1.56	1
Magill	David	22APR95	3.11	1	Magill	John	-----11	1.55	1
McGill	David	02JUN96	2.12	1	Magill	Robert	21APR94	2.10	1
Magill	David	02JUN97	1.15	1	Magill	Samuel	15JUN04	2.13	M1
McGill	David	04JUN99	1.26	1	Magill	Samuel	22AUG05	1.13	1
McGill	Hugh	11JUN89	6.08		Magill	Samuel	08AUG06	3.24	1
Listed with John McGill					Magill	Samuel	21AUG07	2.26	1
McGill	Hugh	15APR90	1.07		Magill	Samuel Sr	-----08	2.21	1
Listed with John McGill					Magill	Samuel	-----08	2.21	1
McGill	Hugh	23JUN91	2.06		McGill	Will	24AUG87	1.04	11
Listed with John McGill					McGill	William	12JUN89	6.08	1
McGill	Hugh	18OCT92	1.09		McGill	William	15APR90	1.07	11
Listed with John McGill					McGill	William	19APR91	2.06	11
McGill	Hugh	24AUG93	3.08		McGill	William	25SEP92	1.08	11
Listed with John McGill					McGill	William	19AUG93	3.09	12
McGill	Hugh	02JUN96	2.12	2	Magill	William	09MAY94	2.09	11
Magill	Hugh	02JUN97	1.17	2	Magill	William	28APR95	3.11	21
McGill	Hugh	04JUN99	1.26	1	McGill	William	02JUN96	2.12	21
McGill	Hugh	19JUN00	2.19	2	Magill	William	04MAY97	1.17	11
Magill	Hugh	03AUG01	2.20	2	McGill	William Sr	04JUN99	1.26	1
Magill	Hugh	24AUG02	2.23	2	McGill	William Jr	04JUN99	1.26	1
Magill	Hugh	15JUN03	3.16	2	McGill	William Sr	20JUN00	2.19	1
Magill	Hugh	13AUG04	2.15	2	McGill	William Jr	19JUN00	2.19	1
Magill	Hugh	24AUG05	3.27	21	Magill	William	01AUG01	2.20	11
Magill	Hugh	26AUG06	3.26	2	Magill	William Sr	24AUG02	2.23	11
Magill	Hugh	24AUG07	2.27	2	Magill	William Jr	24AUG02	2.23	1
Magill	Hugh	-----08	2.21	2	Magill	William	15JUN03	1.14	1
Magill	Hugh	03JUL09	1.24	2	Magill	William	16JUN03	3.16	12
Magill	Hugh	-----11	1.52	1	Magill	William	13AUG04	1.13	1
McGill	James	08AUG93	3.08	1	Magill	William	13AUG04	2.15	12

surname	name	date	bk.pg	TM	surname	name	date	bk.pg	TM
Magill	William	05JUN05	1.11	1	Mann	John	01DEC92	3.13	M1
Magill	William	24AUG05	3.27	12	Mann	John	14MAY94	1.06	1
Magill	William	11JUN06	1.14	1	Mann	John	22MAY95	2.09	1
Magill	William	26AUG06	3.26	11	Mann	John	09JUN96	1.09	1
Magill	William	18MAY07	1.16	1	Mann	John	20APR97	3.20	1
Magill	William	24AUG07	2.27	11	Mann	John	30MAY99	1.25	1
Magill	William	-----08	2.21	2	Mann	John	18JUL00	2.20	1
Magill	William	17JUN08	1.24	1	Mann	John	17JUL01	2.19	1
Magill	William	20MAR09	1.22	1	Mann	John	27MAY02	3.17	1
Magill	William	10MAY09	2.19	1	Mann	John	20JUN03	2.20	1
Magill	William	03JUL09	1.24	2	Mann	Robert	22JUN97	1.16	1
Magil	William	-----11	1.47	1	Mann	Robert	29JUL00	2.21	1
Magill	William	-----11	1.46	1	Mann	Robert	21JUL01	3.24	1
Magill	William	-----11	1.53	2	Man	William	18JUN87	3.06	1
MAHONY					Mann	William	27JUN89	2.08	1
Mahonney	James	30JUN97	1.16	1	Man	William	27APR91	3.09	1
MAIN					Mann	William	01DEC92	3.13	1
Main	William	30JUN87	1.03	1	Man	William	20APR94	3.13	11
Main	W.	14MAY89	6.01		Mann	William	-----95	1.09	1
Paid tax for Jane Aikman					MANNERS				
MAIOURITY					Manners	Alexander	28MAY96	2.12	1
Maiourity	Joseph	03JUL99	3.14	1	Manner	Alexander	28JUN97	1.15	1
MAJORS					Manners	Alexander	12JUL99	3.14	1
Majors	Grenaugh	30MAY99	1.32	0	Manners	Alexander	05JUL00	3.20	1
Majors	Grenaugh	30MAY99	1.32	0	Mannah	Alexander	19MAY01	3.21	1
Majors	Grenaugh	30MAY99	1.32	0	Manners	Alexander	12AUG02	3.19	1
Tax pd by Jacob Swope					Manners	Alexander	28JUL03	2.21	1
Majures	Isaac	10MAY09	2.19		Manners	Alexader	27JUN04	4.16	1
A free negroe					Manners	Alexander	20JUN05	2.22	1
Majors	William	26JUN87	1.03	1	Manners	Alexander	15AUG06	2.26	1
MALONE					MANSFIELD				
Melone	Jeremiah	18JUN00	1.09	1	Mankspile	Elijah	05AUG93	3.07	1
Melon	Jeremiah	05JUN01	1.11	1	Mansfield	Elijah	18APR94	2.08	11
Melone	Jeremiah Sr	03JUN02	1.13	1	Manspile	Elijah	27APR95	3.11	1
Mlone	Jeremiah	01JUN02	1.13	1	Manspile	Jesse	16JUN96	2.12	11
Melone	Jeremiah	14JUN03	1.14	1	Mansfield	Jesse	07JUN97	1.17	M1
Melone	John	03JUN01	1.10	1	Mansfield	John	01JUN89	6.05	1
Melone	Thomas	24MAY99	2.12	1	Manspile	John	13MAY90	1.07	1
Melone	Thomas	18JUN00	1.09	1	Manspile	John	20JUN91	2.07	1
Melon	Thomas	05JUN01	1.11	1	Mansfile	John	12SEP92	1.09	1
Melone	Thomas	04JUN02	1.14	1	Mankspile	John	05AUG93	3.07	1
Melon	Thomas	07JUN05	1.12	1	Mansfield	John	12MAY94	2.10	1
Melone	Thomas	16JUN06	1.14	1	Manspile	John	09APR95	3.11	1
MALONEY					Mansfield	Molly	04AUG02	3.19	F
Malone	Banister	30JUN09	1.24	1	Manspile	William	08MAY94	2.09	M1
Maloney	Robert	27JUN96	1.09	1	Manspile	William	10APR95	3.12	1
Maloney	Robert	16MAY97	1.15	1	Manspile	William	02JUN96	2.12	1
Meloney	Robert	26JUN00	3.20	1	Mansfield	William	04MAY97	1.15	1
MANN					MANSON				
Mann	Andrew	05SEP93	1.07	1	Manson	Peter	06MAY94	1.11	1
Man	Charles	25JUN87	2.05	12	MARK				
Mann	Charles	28NOV88	1.07	13	Mark	Andrew	13AUG07	2.25	1
Mann	Charles	05AUG89	5.09	13	MARKS				
Man	Charles	22MAY90	2.05	13	Marks	William	24MAY09	2.20	1
Man	Charles	06APR91	1.06	13	MARSHALL				
Man	Charles	29OCT92	2.06	1	Marshal	Baley	21JUN00	3.18	1
Mann	Charles	06AUG93	1.06	1	Marshall	Bailey	21MAY99	3.13	1
Mann	Charles	14MAY94	1.06	1	Marshall	Bealey	18JUN01	3.23	1
Mann	Charles	22MAR95	2.09	1	Marshall	Bailey	27JUL02	3.18	11
Mann	Charles	22MAY95	2.21	1	Marshall	Bailey	06AUG03	2.22	1
Mann	Charles	10JUN96	1.09	1	Paid tax for Markham Marshall				
Mann	Charles	20APR97	3.20	1	Marshall	John	13JUL87	1.04	1
Mann	Charles	30MAY99	1.25	1	Marshall	John	13SEP92	1.09	
Mann	Charles	18JUL00	2.20	1	Listed with Marcham Marshall				
Mann	Francis	27JUN87	1.03	1	Marshall	John	06AUG93	3.07	1
Man	George	29OCT92	2.06	1	Marshall	John	23MAY94	2.09	1
Mann	George	06AUG93	1.06	1	Marshall	John	22APR95	3.11	1
Mann	George	10JUN96	1.09	1	Marshal	John	-----96	4.10	1
Mann	Jacob	28NOV88	1.07	1	Marshall	John	15JUN96	2.12	1
Mann	Jacob	05AUG89	5.09	1	Marshell	John	25MAY97	1.17	1
Man	Jacob	28MAY91	3.10	1	Marshall	John	14AUG00	3.21	1
Mann	Jacob	16JUN95	2.09	1	Marshall	John	18JUN01	3.22	1

surname	name	date	bk.pg	TM	surname	name	date	bk.pg	TM
Marshall	John	27JUL02	3.18	1	Martin	Isaac	01JUN96	2.12	1
Marshall	John	28JUL02	3.18	1	Martin	James	-----11	1.48	1
Marshall	John T.	22MAY89	6.05	1	Martin	John	13JUL87	1.04	1
Marshall	John T.	18OCT92	1.09	1	Martain	John	01DEC88	1.07	1
Marshall	J.Taylor	10JUN94	2.09	1	Martin	John	14MAY89	6.05	1
Marshall	John(talor)	10APR95	3.12	1	Martin	John	13JUN89	6.04	1
Marshall	John T.	21JUN96	2.12	1	Martin	John	16JUN89	5.08	1
Marshell	John T.	05JUN97	1.17	1	Martin	John(Capt)	20APR90	1.07	1
Marshall	John T.	20MAY99	3.13	1	Martin	John	10APR90	1.07	1
Marshal	John T.	21JUN00	3.18	1	Martin	John	25APR91	2.07	1
Marshall	John T.	17JUN01	3.22	11	Martin	John	21JUN91	2.07	1
Marshall	John T.	11AUG03	2.22	1	Martin	John(Capt)	24SEP92	1.08	1
Marshall	John T.	09JUN07	2.22	1	Martin	John	18OCT92	1.09	1
Marshall	John T.	05JUN04	4.15	1	Martin	John(Capt)	14AUG93	3.08	1
Marshall	John T.	28JUN05	2.22	1	Martin	John	15AUG93	3.07	1
Marshall	John T.	01AUG06	2.24	1	Martin	John	16APR94	2.09	1
Marshall	John T.	-----08	2.19	1	Martin	John	12JUN94	2.10	1
Marshall	John T./F.	10JUL09	1.25	1	Martin	John	22JUN95	3.10	1
Marshall	John T.	-----11	1.53	1	Martin	John	13AUG96	2.14	1
Marshall	Mark	03JUL87	1.03	1	Martin	John	10MAY97	1.18	1
Marshall	Marcham	12MAY89	6.04	1	Martin	John	22JUN99	2.11	1
Marshall	Mark	21APR90	1.07	11	Martin	John	26JUL99	3.14	1
Marshall	Marcham	20JUN91	2.07	12	Martin	John	21JUN00	3.19	1
Marshall	Marcham	13SEP92	1.09	2	Martin	John	04AUG01	3.25	1
John Marshall listed also					Martin	John	04AUG02	3.18	1
Marshall	Marcham	06AUG93	3.07	12	Martin	John	04AUG03	2.22	1
Marshall	Markham	13MAY94	2.10	11	Martin	John	09JUN04	4.15	11
Marshall	Markham	08APR95	3.11	1	Martin	John	17JUN05	2.21	1
Marshall	Markham	15JUN96	2.12	11	Martin	John	02AUG06	2.25	1
Marshell	Markham	08JUN97	1.16	1	Martin	John	18JUN07	2.23	1
Marshall	Markham	21MAY99	3.13	1	Marten	John	22JUL07	2.24	1
Marshal	Markum	21JUN00	3.18	1	Martin	John	24AUG08	2.20	1
Marshall	Markham	17JUN01	3.22	11	Martin	John	15AUG09	1.26	1
Marshall	Markham	27JUL02	3.18	1	Martin	John	18AUG09	2.22	1
Marshall	Markham	06AUG03	2.22	D1	Martin	John	-----11	1.53	1
Tax pd by Bailey Marshall					Martin	Laodicea	07JUL01	3.23	F
Marshall	Sarah	02JUL89	2.08	F	Martin	Littleton	07JUL01	3.23	1
Marshall	Sarah	20APR94	3.13	F1	Martin	Nicholas	-----11	1.48	1
Marshall	William	27JUN87	2.05	1	Martin	Obediah	13JUL07	2.24	1
Martial	William	19NOV88	1.07	11	Marten	Obediah	-----08	2.19	1
Martial	William	05AUG89	5.09	11	Martin	Obediah	02JUN09	1.22	1
Marshall	William	30MAY90	2.05	12	Martin	Obediah	-----11	1.48	1
Marshall	William	05APR91	1.06	11	Martin	Rebecca	-----11	1.48	F
Marshall	William	27OCT92	2.06	1	Martin	Silvester	-----11	1.48	1
Marshall	William	05AUG93	3.07	1	Martin	Solomon	02AUG05	2.23	
Marshall	William	23MAY94	2.09	M1	A free negroe				
Marshall	William	08APR95	3.11	1	Martin	Solomon	06JUN06	2.23	
Marshall	William	15JUN96	2.12	1	A free negro				
Marshall	William	21MAY99	3.13	1	Martin	Stephen	-----11	1.48	1
Marshal	William	21JUN00	3.18	1	Martin	Thomas	15APR95	3.12	0
Marshall	William	08JUN01	3.22	1	Martin	Thomas	26MAY97	1.01	1
Marshall	William	27JUL02	3.18	1	Martain	William	22JUN99	2.11	1
Marshall	William	11JUL03	2.21	1	Martin	William	-----11	1.48	1
Marshall	William	06JUN04	4.15	1	Martin	William	-----11	1.75	
Marshall	William	29JUN05	2.22	1	Tax paid by James Spears				
Marshall	William	01AUG06	2.24	1	MASON				
Marshall	William	20JUN07	2.23	1	Mason	Edward	04JUN01	1.10	1
Marshall	William	-----08	2.19	1	Mason	Elijah	24MAY99	2.12	11
Marshall	William	10JUN09	1.23	1	Mason	Elijah	04JUN01	1.11	1
Marshall	William	-----11	1.55	1	Mason	Hugh	11JUN03	3.16	1
MARTIN					Mason	Hugh	-----11	1.55	1
Martin	Adam	27MAY02	3.17		Mason	James	03JUL87	1.03	1
A free negro					Mason	James	23MAY89	6.05	1
Martin	Adam	28MAY03	2.19		Mason	James	21APR90	1.07	1
(a free negro) one tithe					Mason	James	30MAR91	2.07	1
Martin	Adam	02AUG05	2.23		Mason	James	13OCT92	1.08	1
A free negroe					Mason	James	23MAY94	2.09	1
Martin	Anne B.	09JUN09	1.22	F	Mason	James	30MAY94	1.06	1
Martin	Benjamin	-----11	1.48	0	Mason	James	22JUN95	3.11	1
Martin	Henry	14AUG05	3.26	11	Mason	James	05JUL96	2.13	1
Marten	Henry	22AUG06	3.25	1	Mason	James	28JUN97	1.16	1
Martin	Isaac	22JUN95	3.12	1	Mason	James	25MAY99	2.12	1

surname	name	date	bk.pg	TM	surname	name	date	bk.pg	TM
Mason	James	26JUN99	1.27	1	Masterson	William	30JUL04	2.13	12
Mason	James	25JUL00	2.21	1	Masterson	William	14JUN05	3.24	11
Mayson	James	29JUL01	3.23	1	Masterson	William	31JUL06	3.24	13
Mason	James	10AUG02	2.23	1	Masterson	William	13JUL07	2.24	12
Mason	James	01AUG03	3.18	1	Masterson	William	-----08	2.19	13
Mason	James	06AUG04	3.14	1	Masterson	William	10JUL09	1.24	1
Mayson	James	05AUG05	3.25	11	Masterson	William	-----11	1.49	2
Mayson	James	04AUG06	3.24	11	MATHERLY				
Masen	Mary	17JUN00	1.08	F	Matherly	Isreal	15AUG09	1.26	1
Mason	Richard	14AUG93	3.08	1	Matheney	Richard	30JUL04	2.14	1
Mason	Richard	12APR94	2.08	1	MATTHEWS				
Mason	Richard	14APR95	3.12	1	Mathis	Brister	08AUG89	5.09	1
Mason	Richard	05JUL96	2.13	1	Mathews	Bristol	14MAY91	2.07	1
Mason	Richard	23JUN97	1.16	1	Matthews	Bristo	26SEP92	1.08	1
Mason	Richard	14JUN99	1.27	1	Matthew	Bristo	13AUG93	3.08	1
Mason	Richard	26JUL00	2.21	1	Mathias	Brister	24MAY94	2.09	1
Mason	Richard	29MAY01	3.25	1	Matthias	Bristorel	16APR95	3.12	1
Mason	Richard	29JUL01	3.23	1	Matthews	Brister	26MAY97	1.15	1
Mason	Richard	03AUG02	2.22	1	Mathews	Bristoe	29JUL00	2.21	0
Mason	Richard	06JUN03	3.16	1	A free negroe and tithe				
Mason	Richard	06AUG04	3.13	1	Mathis	Brister	21JUL01	3.24	0
Mayson	Richard	05AUG05	3.25	1	A free negro				
Mayson	Richard	04AUG06	3.24	1	Mathews	Brister	01JUN02	2.20	0
Mason	Thompson	03AUG02	2.22	M1	A black man free				
Mason	Thomas	25JUN03	3.17	M1	Mathes	Bristo	06AUG03	3.18	1
Mason	Thompson	06AUG04	3.13	M1	A free black above 21				
Mayson	Thompson	05AUG05	3.25	1	Mathews	Bristoe	15AUG04	3.14	1
Mayson	Thompson	22JUL06	3.23	1	Mathews	Edward	29JUL00	2.21	
Mayson	Thompson	10JUN07	2.23	1	A free negroe and tithe				
Mayson	Thompson	-----08	2.18	1	Mathias	Edward	21JUL01	3.24	
Maysen	Thompson	26JUN09	1.23	1	A free negro				
Mason	William	29JUN87	1.03	1	Mathews	Edward	01JUN02	2.20	
Mason	William	03JUL87	1.03	1	A free black man				
Mason	William Jr	23MAY89	6.05	11	Mathes	Edward	06AUG03	3.18	
Mason	William Sr	11JUN89	6.05	1	A free black above 21				
Mason	William	20APR90	1.07	11	Matthews	John	21JUL87	3.06	1
Mason	William Jr	15APR90	1.07	1	Mathews	John	24JUN91	2.06	1
Mason	William	30MAR91	2.07	11	Mathas	John	01AUG91	2.06	1
Mason	William Jr	27MAR91	2.07	1	Mathews	Ned	15AUG04	3.14	1
Mason	William	03OCT92	1.09	1	Mathews	Ned(negro)	08AUG05	3.25	0
Mason	William Jr	18OCT92	1.09	11	Mathews	Ned	18JUL06	3.23	e
Mason	William Sr	13AUG93	3.08	1	Mathew	William	12JUN89	6.08	1
Mason	William Sr	24MAY94	2.09	1	Matthews	William	14MAY90	1.06	12
Mason	William Sr	16APR95	3.12	1	Mathews	William	24JUN91	2.07	11
Mason	William Sr	10APR96	2.11	1	MAUK				
Mason	William	15JUN97	1.16	1	Mauk	Randolph	20MAY01	3.21	1
Mason	William	06JUN99	1.26	11	MAUM				
Mason	William	29JUL00	2.21	11	Maum	Dennis	18AUG09	2.22	1
Mason	William	19JUL01	3.24	11	MAXEY				
Mason	William	02JUN02	2.20	1	Maxey	William	20APR94	3.13	M
Mayson	William	17JUL06	3.22	1	MAXWELL				
Mayson	William	08JUN07	2.22	1	Maxill	John Jr	24AUG87	1.04	11
Maysen	William	30MAY09	1.22	1	Maxel	John	26JUL04	1.13	1
Mason	William	-----11	1.48	1	Maxwell	John	08JUL05	2.23	1
MASSEY					Maxwell	John	15AUG06	2.26	1
Masey	James	14JUN06	2.23	1	Maxwell	John	18JUN07	2.23	1
Massie	James	22JUL07	2.24	1	Maxwell	Robert	01DEC92	3.13	1
Massey	James	17JUN08	1.24	1	Maxwell	Robert	-----96	4.11	1
Mesur	John	19JUN99	2.13	1	MAY				
Maugey	John	13JUN06	1.14	1	May	Andrew	28JUL00	2.21	1
Manzy	John	19MAY07	1.16	1	May	Andrew	09JUN02	2.21	1
Mazee	John	10JUN08	1.23	2	May	Andrew	14JUN03	3.16	1
Mawzy	John	24MAY09	2.20	1	May	Andrew	31JUL04	3.13	1
Manzy	John	-----11	1.46	1	May	Andrew	14JUN05	3.23	1
MASTERSON					May	Andrew	21JUL06	3.23	1
Masterson	Lazirous	30JUL04	2.13	1	May	Andrew	22AUG07	2.26	1
Masterson	Lazerus	22JUL06	3.23	1	May	Andrew	-----08	2.20	1
Masterson	Lazarus	-----08	2.23	1	May	Andrew	30JUN09	1.23	1
Masterson	William	28JUN00	3.20	1	May	Andrew	-----11	1.52	1
Masterson	William	09MAY01	3.21	1	May	Benjamin	28JUL00	2.21	1
Mastison	William	31JUL02	3.18	11	May	Benjamin	02JUN02	2.20	1
Mastison	William	13JUN03	2.20	12	May	Benjamin	14JUN03	3.16	1

surname	name	date	bk.pg	TM	surname	name	date	bk.pg	TM
May	Benjamin	31JUL04	3.13	1	May	James	10JUL00	3.21	1
May	Benjamin	14JUN05	3.23	1	May	James	29JUL02	3.18	1
May	Benjamin	21JUL06	3.23	1	May	James	09AUG03	2.22	1
May	Benjamin	10JUN07	2.22	1	May	Jessey	28MAY94	3.14	1
May	Benjamin	30JUN09	1.23	1	May	Jesse	-----95	1.10	1
May	Benjamin	-----11	1.56	1	May	Jessee	-----96	4.09	1
May	David	10JUN07	2.22	1	May	John	28NOV88	1.07	1
May	David	-----08	2.18	1	May	John	30MAY90	2.05	1
May	David	30JUN09	1.23	1	May	John	24JUN91	2.07	1
May	David	-----11	1.52	1	May	John	05OCT92	1.08	
May	George	10JUN07	2.22	1	Listed with Jacob May				
May	George	-----08	2.18	1	May	John	13AUG93	3.07	1
May	George	-----11	1.56	1	May	John	11APR94	2.10	1
May	Henry	22MAY90	1.07	1	May	John	14APR95	3.12	1
May	Humphrey	26JUN89	6.05	1	May	John	05JUL96	2.13	1
May	Humphrey	22MAY90	1.07	1	May	John	12JUN97	1.16	1
May	Humphrey	19SEP91	2.07	1	May	John	07JUN99	1.26	1
May	Humphrey	03NOV92	1.09	1	May	John	28JUL00	2.21	1
May	Humphrey	28AUG93	3.08	1	May	John	20JUN01	3.24	1
May	Humphrey	29MAY94	2.10	1	May	John	02JUN02	2.20	1
May	Humphrey	02MAY95	3.11	1	May	John	14JUN03	3.16	1
May	Humphrey	25JUL96	2.13	1	May	John	31JUL04	3.13	1
May	Humphrey	29JUN97	1.17	1	May	John	14JUN05	3.24	1
May	Humphrey	08JUL99	3.14	1	May	John	21JUL06	3.23	1
May	Humphrey	05JUL00	3.21	1	May	John	10JUN07	2.23	1
May	Humphrey	08MAY01	3.21	1	May	John	-----08	2.18	1
May	Humphrey	11AUG02	3.19	1	May	Rowlin	30MAY90	2.05	1
May	Humphrey	29JUL03	2.21	1	May	Roland	05APR91	1.06	1
May	Humphrey	26JUN04	4.16	1	May	Rolin	09OCT92	1.08	1
May	Humphrey	19JUL05	2.23	1	May	Rolin	08OCT93	3.08	1
May	Humphrey	14AUG06	2.26	1	May	Rolen	-----95	1.09	1
May	Humphrey	18JUN07	2.23	1	May	Rooling	-----96	4.09	11
May	Humphrey	-----08	2.19	1	May	Roland	-----97	2.03	11
May	Humphrey	12MAY09	1.22	11	May	Rolen	10MAY99	2.13	1
May	Jacob	28NOV88	1.07	1	May	Rolen	07JUN00	1.07	1
May	Jacob	05AUG89	5.09	11	May	Roland	01MAY01	3.21	1
May	Jacob	30MAY90	2.05	1	May	Rowland	31JUL02	3.18	1
May	Jacob	24JUN91	2.07	1	May	Rowland	06AUG03	2.22	1
May	Jacob	05OCT92	1.08	2	May	Roland	09AUG04	4.17	11
John May listed also					May	Rowland	18JUN05	2.22	11
May	Jacob	13AUG93	3.07	11	May	Roland	02AUG06	2.24	11
May	Jacob	11JUN94	2.09	1	May	Roland	01AUG07	2.25	11
May	Jacob Jr	11JUN94	2.10	1	May	Roland	-----08	2.19	2
May	Jacob Sr	14APR95	3.12	1	May	Roland	15AUG09	1.26	1
May	Jacob Jr	14APR95	3.12	1	May	Rowland	-----11	1.56	1
May	Jacob	12MAY96	2.11	1	May	Stephen	07JUN94	2.10	1
May	Jacob	29JUL96	2.13	12	MAYBERRY				
May	Jacob Sr	12JUN97	1.16	12	Mayberry	Abraham	09JUN00	1.07	1
May	Jacob Jr	12JUN97	1.16	1	Mayberry	Abraham	29MAY01	1.09	1
May	Jacob	15MAY99	3.13	1	Mayberry	Abraham	24MAY02	3.17	1
May	Jacob	07JUN99	1.26	13	Mayberry	Abraham	28MAY03	2.19	1
May	Jacob	28JUL00	2.21	11	Mayberry	David	15JUN01	2.18	1
May	Jacob Jr	18JUN00	3.18	1	Mayberry	David	10JUN03	1.14	1
May	Jacob Sr	20JUN01	3.24	11	Mayberry	David	-----05	2.36	1
May	Jacob	20JUN01	3.23	1	Mayberry	David	19JUN05	2.22	1
May	Jacob Sr	09JUN02	2.20	12	Mayberry	David	29JUL06	2.24	1
May	Jacob Sr	14JUN03	3.16	12	Maybury	John	20APR94	3.13	1
May	Jacob	11JUL03	3.17	1	Mayberry	William	18APR94	2.08	1
May	Jacob Sr	31JUL04	3.13	21	Mayberry	William	24MAR95	3.12	1
May	Jacob Jr	31JUL04	3.13	1	Mayberry	William	22APR96	2.11	11
May	Jacob Sr	14JUN05	3.24	11	MAYFIELD				
May	Jacob	14JUN05	3.23	1	Mayfield	George	30JUN87	3.07	1
May	Jacob	21JUL06	3.23	11	Mayfield	George	25JUL89	2.09	11
May	Jacob Jr	21JUL06	3.23	1	Mayfield	Isaac	30JUN87	3.07	1
May	Jacob Sr	10JUN07	2.22	1	Mayfield	Isaac	06AUG89	2.09	1
May	Jacob	22AUG07	2.26	1	Mayfield	Isaac	20APR91	3.09	1
May	Jacob	-----08	2.20	1	Mayfield	Isaak Sr	27NOV92	3.13	1
May	Jacob	-----08	2.18	1	Mayfield	Isaak Jr	27NOV92	3.13	1
May	Jacob	30JUN09	1.23	1	Mayfield	Isaac Sr	24MAY94	3.14	1
May	Jacob	12JUL09	1.25	1	Mayfield	Isaac Jr	24MAY94	3.14	1
May	Jacob Sr	-----11	1.52	1	Mayfield	Isaac	-----95	1.10	1
May	Jacob Jr	-----11	1.52	1	Mayfield	Isaac	-----96	4.09	1

surname	name	date	bk.pg	TM	surname	name	date	bk.pg	TM
Mayfield	James	-----95	1.09	1	McBride	David	20JUN05	3.24	1
Mayfield	Randle	14JUL97	1.17	1	McBride	David	21JUL06	3.23	1
Mayfield	Randle	01JUL99	1.27	1	McBride	David	17AUG07	2.26	1
Mayfield	Randolph	26JUL00	2.21	1	McBride	David	-----08	2.20	1
Mayfield	Randolph	30JUL01	3.24	1	McBride	David	11JUL09	1.25	1
Mayfield	Randel	10AUG02	2.23	1	McBride	David	-----11	1.52	1
Mayfield	Randolph	11JUN03	3.16	1	McBride	Robert	13SEP91	3.11	1
Mayfield	Randolph	17AUG05	3.26	11	McBride	Robert	-----92	3.14	1
Mayfield	Randolph	19AUG06	3.24	11	McBride	Wachman	14JUN05	3.24	1
MC ALEXANDER					MC CABE				
McAlexander	Alexander	13JUN95	2.21	1	McKabe	John	04JUN00	2.19	1
McAlexander	David	14JUN05	3.24	1	McKabe	John	05AUG01	2.20	1
MC ALLISTER					McCabe	John	10MAY02	2.19	1
McOlister	George	15NOV88	1.07	1	MC CAFFERTY				
McColester	George	30JUN89	5.08	1	McCafferty	Owen	24JUN91	2.07	1
McCollester	John	02JUN96	2.12	1	McAfferty	Owen	23AUG93	3.08	1
McAlester	John	02JUN97	1.16	1	McCaferty	Owen	28JUN00	2.20	1
McCollister	John	24JUN00	2.20	1	McKaffordy	Simon	12JUN89	6.08	1
McCollister	John	26JUN09	1.23	1	McAfferty	Simon	06OCT92	1.08	1
McColliston	John	-----11	1.55	1	McAfferty	Simon	23AUG93	3.08	1
McCollister	Joseph	-----92	3.14	1	McCaffary	Simon	23JUN97	1.16	1
McCollistr	Joseph	28MAY94	3.14	1	McCafferty	Simon	28JUN00	2.20	1
McColister	Joseph	-----95	1.10	1	McCaffrey	Simon	19JUN01	3.24	1
McAllester	Joseph	31MAY97	3.21	1	MC CAGEE				
McCollistr	Robert	-----93	2.03	1	McCagee	Procter	16SEP91	3.11	1
McColastor	Sarah	02JUN90	2.05	F	MC CAIN				
McColastor	Sarah	02JUN90	2.05	F	McCain	James	26JUN99	3.13	1
MC ANELLY					McKain	James	02MAY01	3.21	1
McHenally	John	08APR90	2.05	1	McCain	James	31JUL02	3.18	1
McAnelly	John	01AUG91	2.06	1	McCain	James	04AUG03	2.22	1
McAnelly	John	06OCT92	1.08	1	McKane	Robert	13JUL87	1.03	1
McAnelly	John	20AUG93	3.09	1	McCain	Robert	12JUN89	6.09	1
McInnely	John	31JUN96	1.08	1	McKean	Robert	06AUG91	2.06	1
McAnelly	John	15JUL97	1.17	1	McKean	Robert	20SEP92	1.08	1
McEnelley	John	04JUN99	1.26	1	McKean	Robert	10AUG93	3.07	1
McAnelly	John	28JUL00	3.21	1	McCain	Robert	22JUN94	2.08	11
McAnelly	John	20MAY01	3.22	1	McCain	Robert	07APR95	3.11	11
McAnelly	John	14JUL02	3.17	1	McCain	Robert	11JUL96	2.13	11
McAnelly	John	13JUN03	2.20	1	McAin	Robert	06JUN97	1.16	11
McNally	John	28JUL04	4.17	1	McCain	Robert	26JUN99	3.13	1
McAnelly	John	08JUL05	2.23	1	McCain	Robert	19JUN00	3.18	1
McAnelly	John	08JUL05	2.23	1	McKain	Robert	02MAY01	3.21	1
McAnelly	John	01AUG06	2.24	1	McCain	Robert	31JUL02	3.18	1
McAnelly	John	01AUG06	2.24	1	McCain	Robert	06AUG03	2.22	1
McAnelly	John	20JUN07	2.23	1	McCain	Robert	12JUN04	4.15	1
McAnelly	John	-----08	2.20	1	McCain	Robert	20JUN05	2.22	1
MC ANINCH					McCain	Wiliam	27JUN05	2.22	11
McNinch	Daniel	16MAY99	3.13	11	McCain	William	15AUG06	2.26	11
McAninch	Daniel	21JUN00	3.18	11	MC CALF				
McAninch	Daniel	13JUL01	3.24	1	McCalf	Noris	18JUL96	1.09	1
McAninch	Daniel	05AUG02	2.22	1	McCalf	Norris	22MAY97	3.21	1
McAninch	Daniel	02AUG03	3.18	11	MC CAMPBELL				
McAninch	Daniel	06AUG04	3.13	11	McCampbell	Robert	20JUN05	2.22	1
McAninch	Daniel	14AUG05	3.26	11	MC CANDLESS				
McAninch	Daniel	08AUG06	3.24	11	McKenlas	John	11JUN89	6.04	1
McAninch	James	08AUG06	3.24	M1	McAndless	John	15APR90	1.07	1
McAninch	John	13JUL01	3.24	1	McCandless	John	14SEP92	1.09	1
McAninch	John	04AUG02	2.22	1	McKanlas	John	14AUG93	3.08	1
McAninch	John	07JUN03	3.16	1	McCanliss	John	17APR94	2.09	1
McAninch	John	06AUG04	3.14	1	McCanless	John	19MAR95	3.13	1
McAninch	John	14AUG05	3.26	1	McCanlass	John	23MAY96	2.11	1
McAninch	John	22AUG06	3.25	1	McAndlass	William	14NOV88	1.06	1
McNinih	William	12JUN97	1.16	1	MC CANN				
McAninch	William	05AUG02	2.22	1	McAnne	Thomas	04AUG04	3.13	1
McAninch	William	15JUL03	3.18	1	McCann	Thomas	13JUN05	3.23	1
McAninch	William	06AUG04	3.14	1	McCan	Thomas	22JUL06	3.23	1
McAninch	William	14AUG05	3.26	1	MC CARLAND				
McAninch	William	08AUG06	3.24	1	McCarland	Andrew	02JUN97	3.21	1
MC ATHER					MC CARLEY				
McAther	George	-----93	1.03	1	McCarley	James	16JUN89	5.08	12
MC BRIDE					McCarley	James	23MAR90	2.05	11
McBride	David	29JUN04	4.16	M1	McCarley	James	24MAY94	3.14	1

surname	name	date	bk.pg	TM	surname	name	date	bk.pg	TM
McCarley	James	-----95	1.10	1	McLure	John	22MAY95	2.09	1
McCarley	James	-----96	4.10	1	McLure	John	21JUN96	1.08	1
McCarley	James	17MAR97	2.02	1	McClure	John	17APR97	3.20	1
McCarley	Moses	-----92	3.14	1	McClure	John	08JUL00	2.20	1
McCarley	Moses	24MAY94	3.14	1	McClure	John	13APR01	2.18	1
McCarley	Moses	-----95	1.10	1	McClure	John	15JUL03	1.16	1
McCarley	Moses	-----96	4.10	1	McClure	John	25JUN04	1.12	1
MC CARROLL					McClure	Moses	13JUN05	1.12	1
McCairell	Charles	02JUN02	2.20	1	McClure	Moses	12JUN07	1.17	1
McCarrel	John	16MAY94	2.10	1	McClure	Moses	04MAY08	1.22	1
McCarrel	John	10APR95	3.10	1	McLure	Nathan	27JUN87	2.05	1
McCarrel	John	13JUL96	2.13	1	McClure	Nathan	18NOV88	1.07	1
McArel	John	06JUN97	1.16	11	McClure	Nathan	03JUL89	5.08	1
McKarell	John	07JUN99	1.26	11	McLure	Nathan	22MAY90	2.05	1
McCarrill	John	21JUL00	2.20	12	McClure	Nathan	25MAR91	1.06	1
McCarrell	John	31JUL01	2.20	21	McLure	Robert	25JUN87	2.05	1
McCairell	John	02JUN02	2.20	11	McClure	Robert	01NOV88	1.06	1
McCarrell	John	16JUN03	3.17	11	McClure	Robert	29JUN89	5.08	1
MC CARTER					McClurr	Robert	15OCT92	2.06	1
McCarter	Robert	22JUN91	2.07	1	McClure	Robert	13AUG93	1.06	1
McCarter	Robert	05OCT92	1.08	1	McLure	Robert	29MAY94	1.06	1
McCarter	Robert	07AUG93	3.07	1	McLure	R-----	03JUN95	2.22	1
MC CARTY					McClure	Robert	14APR97	3.20	1
McCarty	Timothy	28JUN05	2.22	1	McClure	Robert	14MAY99	1.23	1
McCarty	Timothy	31JUL06	2.24	1	McClure	Robert	18JUN00	2.19	1
McCarty	Timothy	24AUG07	2.26	1	McClure	Robert	24JUL01	2.20	1
McCarty	Timothy	-----Q8	2.19	1	McClure	Robert	10JUN02	1.14	1
MC CLANAHAN					McClure	Robert	29JUN03	1.15	1
McClanahan	Robert	10JUN94	1.11	1	McClure	Robert	02AUG04	2.14	1
MC CLURE					McClure	Robert	13JUN05	1.12	1
McLure	Andrew	25JUN87	2.05	11	McClure	Robert	19JUN06	1.15	1
McLure	Arther	13AUG93	1.06	1	McClure	Robert	12JUN07	1.17	1
McClure	Arthur	14APR91	1.06	1	McClure	Robert	27APR08	1.22	1
McClurr	Arthur	15OCT92	2.06	1	McClure	Robert	06JUN09	2.21	1
McLure	Arthur	29MAY94	1.06	1	McClure	Thomas	05NOV88	1.06	1
McLure	Arthur	03JUN95	2.09	1	McClure	Thomas	29JUN89	5.08	1
McClure	Benoni	03JUL09	1.24	1	McLure	Thomas	03APR90	2.05	1
McClure	Daniel	23JUN02	1.15	1	McClure	Thomas	09AUG93	1.06	1
McClure	Daniel	23JUN03	1.14	1	McClure	Thomas	30MAY97	3.21	1
McClure	Daniel	02AUG04	1.13	1	McClure	Thomas	23JUN00	2.19	1
McLure	Francis	29JUN96	1.09	F	McClure	Thomas	26APR01	2.18	1
McClure	Francess	15APR97	3.20	F	McClure	Thomas	25JUN04	1.12	1
McClure	Frances	14MAY99	1.23	F	McLure	William	27JUN87	2.05	1
McClure	Frances	18JUN00	2.19	F	McClure	William	29OCT88	1.06	1
McClure	Frances	24JUL01	2.20	F	McLure	William	16JUN89	5.08	1
McClure	Francis	10JUN02	1.14	F	McLure	William	23MAR90	2.05	1
McClure	Francis	29JUN03	1.15	F	McClure	William	25MAR91	1.06	1
McClure	Frances	02AUG04	2.14	F	McClure	William	23NOV92	2.06	1
McClure	Francis	13JUN05	1.12	1	McLure	William	15JUN95	2.09	1
McClure	George	22APR95	3.11	0	McClure	William	11JUL00	3.21	1
McClure	Halbert	06MAY07	1.16	1	McClure	William	30JUL01	3.23	1
McClure	Halbert	10JUN08	1.23	1	McLure	William	09JUN02	2.21	1
McClure	Halbert	15JUN09	2.21	1	McClure	William	04AUG03	3.18	1
McLure	James	20JUN87	2.05	1	McCluer	William	06APR04	4.15	1
McClure	James	28OCT88	1.06	1	McClure	William	21JUN05	3.24	1
McClure	James	29JUN89	5.08	1	McClure	William	29JUL06	3.23	11
McLure	James	24MAR90	2.05	1	MC COLLOM				
McClure	James	20SEP91	1.06	11	McCollom	Archibald	28MAY94	3.15	1
McClure	James	05OCT92	2.06	11	MC COMBE				
McClure	James	07AUG93	1.06	11	McCombe	John	26JUN96	1.09	1
McLure	James	22MAY94	1.06	11	Macomb	John	07APR97	3.19	1
McClure	Jane	05JUL91	1.06	F	McKonally	John	26MAR90	2.06	1
McLure	John	20JUN87	2.05	1	McConnall	John	20JUN05	1.13	1
McLure	John	25JUN87	2.05	1	McConnell	Jonathan	19JUL03	3.18	1
McClure	John	05NOV88	1.06	1	McConnal	Jonathen	15JUN04	2.13	1
McClure	John	29JUN89	5.08	1	McConnal	Jonathen	14JUN05	3.24	1
McLure	John	16MAY90	2.05	1	MC CORKLE				
McClure	John	28OCT91	1.06	1	McCorkle	Samuel	21MAY99	3.13	1
McClurr	John	21OCT92	2.06	1	MC CORMACK				
McClure	John	09AUG93	1.06	1	McCormack	Adam	06AUG91	2.06	1
McLure	John	22MAY94	1.06	1	McCormack	Adam	21SEP92	1.08	1
McClure	John	12MAY95	2.21	1	McCormack	Adam	10AUG93	3.07	1

surname	name	date	bk.pg	TM	surname	name	date	bk.pg	TM
McCormack	Adam	22MAY94	2.10	1	McCormack	Joseph	13AUG93	3.08	1
McCormack	Adam	30MAR95	3.12	0	McCormack	Joseph	22MAY94	2.10	1
McCormick	Daniel	13JUL87	1.04	11	McCormack	Joseph	15APR95	3.12	1
McCormick	Daniel	13MAY89	6.05	1	McCormack	Joseph	11MAY96	2.11	1
McCormac	Daniel	21APR90	1.07	11	McCormack	Joseph	26MAY97	1.15	1
McCormack	Daniel	21JUN91	2.07	1	McCormack	Joseph	14JUN99	1.27	1
McCormack	Daniel	25SEP92	1.08	1	McCormack	Joseph	29JUL00	2.21	1
McCormack	Daniel Jr	21SEP92	1.08	1	McCormack	Joseph	21JUL01	3.24	1
McCormack	Daniel	10AUG93	3.07	1	McCormack	Joseph	27MAY02	2.20	1
McCormack	Daniel	14AUG93	3.08	1	McCormick	Joseph	06AUG03	3.19	1
McCormack	Daniel	22MAY94	2.10	2	McCormack	Joseph	06AUG04	2.15	M1
McCormack	Daniel Jr	07APR95	3.11	2	McCormick	Joseph	16AUG04	3.14	1
McCormick	Daniel	01JUN96	2.12	2	McCormack	Joseph	12NOV05	3.26	1
McCormack	Daniel	10MAY97	1.15	2	McCormack	Joseph	18JUL06	3.22	1
McCormack	Daniel	16JUL99	3.14	2	McCormack	Joseph	22JUL06	3.23	11
McCormick	Daniel Jr	20JUN00	3.18	2	McCormack	Joseph	17AUG07	2.26	11
McCormack	Daniel	21MAY01	3.21	2	McCormack	Joseph	-----08	2.19	1
McCormack	Daniel	31JUL02	3.18	2	McCormack	Joseph	-----08	2.19	11
McCormack	Daniel	06AUG03	2.22	2	McCormack	Joseph	07JUL09	1.24	1
McCormack	Daniel Jr	29JUN04	4.16	2	McCormack	Joseph	-----11	1.53	1
McCormick	Daniel	17JUN05	2.21	2	McCormack	Joseph	-----11	1.52	2
McCormack	Daniel	02AUG06	2.24	2	McCormack	Samuel	07AUG04	2.15	1
McCormack	Daniel	20JUN07	2.23	2	McCormack	Samuel	19MAY05	3.23	1
McCormack	Daniel	-----08	2.19	2	McCormack	Samuel	-----11	1.47	1
McCormack	Daniel	07JUL09	1.24	1	McCormick	William	13JUL87	1.04	1
McCormack	Daniel	07JUL09	1.24	2	McCormick	William	13MAY89	6.05	1
McCormack	Daniel	-----11	1.56	1	McCormac	William	21APR90	1.07	1
McCormack	Hugh	05JUL87	3.03		McCormack	William	20APR91	2.07	1
Listed with Thomas Donald					McCormack	William	24SEP92	1.08	1
McCormack	Hugh	01JUL89	2.08	1	McCormack	William	10AUG93	3.07	1
McCormick	Hugh	13SEP91	3.11	1	McCormack	William	23MAY94	2.09	1
McCormack	Hugh	23MAY94	3.14	1	McCormack	William	07APR95	3.11	1
McCormack	Hugh	-----95	1.10	1	McCormack	William	15APR95	3.12	1
McCormack	Hugh	-----96	4.10	1	McCormick	William	11JUL96	2.13	1
McCormack	Hough	-----97	2.03	1	McCormack	William	30MAY97	1.17	1
McCormac	Hugh	19JUN99	2.13	11	McCormack	William	26JUN99	3.13	1
McCormac	Hugh	11JUN00	1.07	1	McCormick	William	19JUN00	3.18	11
McCormac	Hugh	01JUN01	1.10	1	McCormack	William	02MAY01	3.21	11
McCormack	James	26JUL06	3.23	1	McCormack	William	31JUL02	3.18	12
McCormick	John	13JUL87	1.03	1	McCormack	William	06AUG03	2.22	12
McCormac	John	13MAY89	6.04	1	McCormack	William	12JUN04	4.15	13
McCormac	John	21APR90	1.06	1	McCormack	William	17JUN05	2.22	22
McCormack	John	18MAR91	2.07	1	McCormack	William	14JUL06	2.23	12
McCormack	John	28SEP92	1.09	1	McCormack	William	20JUN07	2.23	1
McCormack	John	10AUG93	3.07	1	McCormack	William	20JUN07	2.23	11
McCormack	John	08APR94	2.08	1	McCormack	William	20JUN07	2.23	11
McCormack	John	27APR95	3.11	1	McCormack	William	-----08	2.18	1
McCormick	John	04AUG96	2.14	1	McCormack	William	-----08	2.18	11
McCormack	John	04MAY97	1.17	1	McCormack	William	07JUL09	1.24	1
McCormack	John	04MAY97	1.17	1	McCormack	William	07JUL09	1.24	1
McCormac	John	11JUN99	1.27	1	McCormack	William	-----11	1.56	3
McCormack	John	01AUG00	2.22	1	MC COWN				
McCormack	John	30JUL01	2.20	11	McCown	Edward	14AUG05	3.26	M1
McCormack	John	14JUN02	2.21	12	McCown	Francis	10MAY97	3.21	1
McCormick	John	12JUL03	3.17	12	McCown	George	04JUN04	4.15	1
McCormick	John	07AUG04	2.15	11	McCoun	George	28JUN05	2.22	1
McCormack	John	19MAY05	3.23	1	McCown	George	22AUG06	3.25	1
McCormack	John Jr	19MAY05	3.23	M1	McCown	George	04MAY08	1.22	1
McCormack	John Sr	18JUL06	3.23	1	McCoun	George	26JUN09	1.23	1
McCormack	John	14JUL06	2.23	1	McConn	James	24APR97	3.20	1
McCormack	John	20JUN07	2.23	1	McCown	James	24APR97	3.20	11
McCormack	John	20JUN07	2.23	1	McCown	James	14AUG05	3.26	M1
McCormack	John	-----08	2.18	1	McCown	James	22AUG06	3.25	M1
McCormack	John	-----08	2.18	11	McConn	John	24APR97	3.20	1
McCormack	John	07JUL09	1.24	1	McCown	John	10AUG03	2.22	1
McCormack	John	07JUL09	1.24	1	McCown	John	07APR04	4.15	1
McCormack	John	-----11	1.55	1	McCoun	John	20JUN05	2.22	1
McCormack	John	-----11	1.54	11	McCoun	John	31JUL06	2.24	1
McCormick	Joseph	13JUL87	1.04	1	McCoun	Melcom	17JUN05	2.22	1
McCormick	Joseph	13MAY89	6.05	1	McCown	Malcom	22AUG06	3.25	1
McCormac	Joseph	15APR90	1.07	1	MC COY				
McCormack	Joseph	24SEP92	1.08	1	McCoy	Edward	18JUN87	3.06	1

surname	name	date	bk.pg	TM	surname	name	date	bk.pg	TM
McCoy	John	28MAY94	3.14	1	McDowell	James	03JUN95	2.09	1
McCoy	Samuel	02AUG04	1.13	1	McDowell	James	13JUN95	2.21	1
McCoy	Samuel	17JUN08	1.23	1	McDowel	James	29JUN96	1.09	1
McCoy	Samuel	14JUN09	2.21	1	McDowel	James	13APR97	3.20	1
MC CULLOCH					McDowell	James	25MAY99	1.24	1
McCulla	Benjamin	-----11	1.55	02	McDowell	James	12JUN07	1.17	1
McColley	Daniel	29JUN99	3.14	1	McDowell	James	22APR08	1.21	1
McCulla	James	17JUN08	1.25	12	MC ELHANEY				
McCuller	James	18AUG09	2.22	1	McElheny	John	09AUG02	3.19	M1
McCulla	James	-----11	1.47	1	McElheny	Patrick	26APR01	2.18	1
McCulloch	John	05APR91	2.07	1	McElhaney	Patrick	14JUN02	2.21	1
McCulloch	John	12SEP92	1.09	1	McElheny	Patrick	17JUN03	3.17	11
McCulloch	John	04AUG02	3.18	1	McElheney	Patrick	06AUG04	2.15	1
McCullock	John	05AUG03	2.22	1	McElheney	Patrick	14JUN05	3.24	1
McCulley	John	21MAY04	4.15	11	McElheney	Patrick	11AUG06	3.24	1
McCulloch	John	29JUN05	2.22	11	McElheney	Patrick	21AUG07	2.26	1
McCulla	Robert	-----11	1.46	1	McElheney	Patrick	-----08	2.18	1
McCulloch	Sarah	15AUG06	2.26	F	McElheny	Patrick	02JUN09	1.22	1
McCully	Sally	18AUG07	2.26	F	McElheny	Patrick	-----11	1.51	1
McCully	Sally	-----08	2.19	F	MC ELMORE				
McCully	Sally	15AUG09	1.26	F	McElmore	John	19APR08	1.21	1
MC CUTCHEN					McClemore	Wright	09MAY07	1.16	1
McCutchen	John	10JUN01	1.11	1	McElmore	Wright	20APR08	1.21	1
McCutcheon	John	04JUN02	1.14	1	McElmore	Wright	01JUL09	2.21	1
McCutchen	John	23JUN03	1.15	1	MC ELWAIN				
McCutchen	John	19JUN04	1.12	1	McElwain	James	02JUN02	2.20	1
McCutcheon	John	11JUN05	1.12	11	MC ELWEE				
McCutchen	John	16JUN06	1.15	11	McElwee	David	19APR94	2.08	1
McCutchen	John	28MAY07	1.16	11	McElwee	David	20MAR95	3.13	1
McCutchen	John	22APR08	1.21	11	McElwee	David	27JUL96	2.13	1
McCruchin	John	09JUN09	2.21	1	McElewee	Jane	15NOV88	1.07	F
McCutheon	John	-----11	1.46	1	McElwee	Jane	22JUN89	5.08	F
McCutchin	William	09JUN09	2.21	1	McElwee	Jane	03JUN90	2.05	F
MC DALE					McElwee	Jane	23NOV92	2.06	F
McDale	Charles	16APR94	2.09	1	McElwee	William	27JUN87	2.05	1
MC DONALD					McElwee	William	03JUN90	2.06	1
McDonnell	Cornelius	28MAY91	3.10	1	McElwee	William	01NOV92	2.06	1
McDonold	Daniel	05DEC92	3.13	1	McIlwee	William	14AUG93	1.06	1
McDonnell	Donnell	13SEP91	3.11	1	McElwee	William	23MAY94	1.06	1
McDaniel	Jeremiah	-----05	2.20	1	McElwee	William	14JUN95	2.21	1
McDonnell	John	13SEP91	3.11	1	McIlwee	William	16JUN96	1.08	1
McDonold	John	05DEC92	3.13	1	McElwee	William	10APR97	3.19	1
McDaniel	John	-----96	4.09	1	McElwee	William	13MAY99	1.23	1
McDaniel	Spencer	26APR97	3.20	1	McElwee	William	31MAY00	2.19	1
McDaniel	Thomas	03AUG02	2.22	1	McElwee	William	24JUL01	2.20	1
McDaneld	Thomas	07JUN03	3.16	1	McElewee	William	11JUN02	1.14	1
McDaniel	Thomas	-----11	1.46	1	McElwee	William	04JUL03	1.15	1
McDonnell	William Sr	04JUN91	3.10	1	McElwee	William	03AUG04	2.14	1
McDonnell	William	04JUN91	3.10	1	McElwee	William	19JUN05	1.13	1
McDaniel	William	27JUN00	2.20	11	McElwee	William	20JUN06	1.15	1
McDaniel	William	22JUL01	3.24	2	McElwee	William	22JUN07	1.17	1
McDaniel	William	09AUG02	2.23	1	McElwee	William	04MAY08	1.22	1
McDaneld	William	06JUN03	3.16	1	McClewee	William	01JUN09	2.21	1
McDonald	William	06AUG04	3.13	1	MC EVOY				
McDaniel	William	05AUG05	3.25	1	McEvoy	Daniel	23NOV92	2.06	1
McDaniel	William	04AUG06	3.24	1	MC EWEN				
MC DOUGAL					McEwen	David	27JUN89	2.08	11
McDoogle	William	08JUL99	3.14	1	McEwen	William	27JUN89	2.08	1
McDoogle	William	04JUL00	3.20	1	MC FADDEN				
MC DOWELL					McFadden	John	20APR94	3.13	1
McDowell	Alexander	27AUG89	2.09	1	MC FAGGIN				
McDowell	Alexander	19OCT92	2.06	11	McFaggin	Hugh	21JUL87	3.06	11
McDowell	Alexander	13AUG93	1.06	1	McFaggin	James	05JUL87	3.07	1
McDowel	Alexander	15AUG93	1.06	1	McFadgen	James	-----92	3.14	1
McDowel	Alexander	21MAY94	1.06	1	McFadgen	John	05DEC92	3.13	1
McDowell	Benjamin	01AUG01	2.20	1	MC FALL				
McDowell	Charles	15OCT92	2.06	1	McFall	Daniel	19SEP91	2.07	1
McDowell	Charles	13AUG93	1.06	1	MC FARLAND				
McDowell	Daniel	18JUN87	3.06	1	McPharlin	James	13MAY90	1.07	1
McDowell	James	16OCT92	2.06	1	McFarling	James	14MAY91	2.06	1
McDowell	James	13AUG93	1.06	1	McFarland	James	17SEP92	1.09	1
McDowel	James	29MAY94	1.06	1	McFarland	J.	06JUN95	3.15	0

surname	name	date	bk.pg	TM	surname	name	date	bk.pg	TM
McFarland	J.	06JUN95	3.15		McIntosh	Joseph	08MAY97	3.21	1
Tax paid by Isaac Shelby					McIntosh	Joseph	29MAY00	2.18	1
McFarland	John	29JUL03	2.29	0	McIntosh	Joseph	08JUN01	2.18	1
Tax paid by Isaac Shelby					McIntosh	Joseph	18JUN02	1.14	1
McFarland	John	28JUN04	4.22	0	McIntosh	Joseph	18JUL03	1.16	1
Tax paid by Isaac Shelby					McIntosh	Joseph	25JUL04	1.13	1
McFarland	John	18JUL05	2.30	0	McIntosh	Joseph	20JUN05	1.13	1
Tax paid by Isaac Shelby					McIntosh	Joseph	23JUN06	1.15	1
McFarland	John	16AUG06	2.35	0	McIntouch	Joseph	20JUN07	1.17	1
Tax paid by Isaac Shelby					McIntouch	Joseph	02JUN08	1.22	1
McFarland	John	-----08	2.25	0	McIntouch	Joseph	15AUG09	2.22	1
Tax paid by Isaac Shelby					McIntosh	William	24JUN00	2.20	1
McFarland	John	21AUG09	1.32	0	McIntosh	William	03JUN01	2.18	1
Tax paid by Evan Shelby					MC KINLEY				
McFarland	John	21AUG09	1.32		McKenly	Hanah	23MAR90	2.05	F
Tax paid by Isaac Shelby					McKinly	Hannah	01AUG91	2.06	F
McPharlin	Thomas	13MAY90	1.07	1	McKinly	Hannah	24SEP92	1.08	F
McFarling	Thomas	19APR91	2.06	1	McKinley	Hannah	06JUL96	2.13	F
McFarland	Thomas	13SEP92	1.09	1	McKinley	Hannah	22JUN97	1.16	F
MC FERRIN					McKinney	Hanna	05JUN99	1.26	F
McFerrin	James	07MAY91	3.09	1	McKinley	Hannah	29JUL00	2.21	F
McFarren	James	24SEP92	1.08	1	McKenley	Hannah	23AUG02	2.23	F
McFarran	James	13SEP93	3.08	1	McKinley	Hannah	30JUL04	2.14	F
McFarren	James	26APR94	2.09	1	McKinley	Hanner	02JUN08	1.22	F
McPherren	James	01MAY95	3.11	1	McKinley	Hannah	-----11	1.49	F
McFerrin	James	29JUN96	2.13	1	MC KINNEY				
McFarren	James	28JUN97	1.16	1	McKinney	Abram	09MAY97	3.21	1
McFarrin	James	12JUL99	3.14	1	McKinney	Abraham	29MAY99	2.12	1
McFerren	James	26JUN00	3.20	1	McKinney	Abraham	25JUL00	1.09	1
McFerron	James	18MAY01	3.21	1	McKinney	Abraham	17JUN01	2.19	1
McFerrin	James	12AUG02	3.19	1	McKinney	Abraham	21JUL02	2.21	1
McFerrin	James	28JUL03	2.21	1	McKinney	Abraham	12JUL03	3.17	1
McFerrin	James	27JUN04	4.16	1	McKenney	Abraham	18JUN04	2.13	1
McFerrin	James	09JUL05	2.23	1	McKenney	Abraham	12NOV05	3.26	1
McFerrin	James	15AUG06	2.26	1	McKinney	Abraham	17JUL06	3.22	1
McFerron	James	20JUN07	2.23	1	McKenney	Abraham	22JUL07	2.24	1
McFerron	James	24AUG08	2.20	1	McKenney	Abraham	-----08	2.18	1
McFerrin	James	08JUN09	1.22	1	McKinny	Abraham	07JUL09	1.24	1
McFerrin	James	-----11	1.46	1	McKinney	Abraham	-----11	1.49	1
McFarran	John	12OCT92	1.09	1	McKinzey	Alexander	26JUN96	1.08	1
McFarran	John	15AUG93	3.08	1	McKinney	Alexander	26JUL03	2.21	1
McFarran	John	27MAY94	1.06	1	McKinney	Alexander	26JUL04	1.13	1
McFarran	John	01JUN95	2.09	1	McKinney	Alexander	27JUL05	1.13	11
McFarran	John	28JUN96	1.09	1	McKinney	Alexander	13JUN06	1.14	1
McFarren	John	10MAY97	3.21	1	McKinney	Alexander	16JUL06	1.16	11
McFarran	Samuel	02NOV92	1.09	1	McKenny	Alexander	20MAY07	1.16	1
McFerren	Samuel	20APR94	3.13	1	McKenzy	Alexander	02JUL07	1.15	11
McFarren	Samuel	-----95	1.10	1	McKenny	Alexander	17JUN08	1.25	1
MC GEEHE					McKenzy	Alexander	02JUN08	1.22	11
McGeehe	Samuel	09JUN96	1.09	1	McKenny	Alexander	24MAY09	2.20	1
MC GINNIS					McKenzy	Alexander	31MAY09	2.20	1
Meginnis	John	05JUL00	3.20	1	McKinney	Alexander	-----11	1.51	1
McGinnis	John	09MAY01	3.21	1	McKinney	Alexander	-----11	1.47	11
MC GRAW					McKinley	Andrew	27JUN87	2.05	1
McGraw	John	26JUN87	1.03	1	McKinley	Andrew	22NOV88	1.07	1
Magraw	John	30MAY89	6.05	1	McKinley	Andrew	04AUG89	5.09	1
McGraw	John	19JUN05	2.22	1	McKenny	Arch	24AUG87	1.04	1
McGraw	John	29JUL06	2.24	1	McKinney	Archable	05NOV88	1.06	1
MC HATTON					McKenny	Archable	07AUG89	5.09	1
McHaddin	Archibald	05APR91	1.06	1	McKinney	Archey	03APR90	2.05	1
McHatton	Archibald	23NOV92	2.06	1	McKenny	Archibald	05JUL91	1.06	1
MC HENRY					McKinney	Archibald	24AUG93	3.08	1
McHenry	Isaac	08AUG04	3.14	1	McKinney	Archable	12JUN94	2.09	1
McHenry	John	24JUN89	5.08	1	McKinney	Archable	22APR95	3.11	1
McHenry	John	21JUL89	5.08	1	McKenny	Arch	03JUN96	2.12	1
McHenry	Joseph	24JUN89	5.08	1	McKinney	Archibald	20JUN97	1.16	1
MC INTOSH					McKinney	Archibald	11JUN99	1.27	1
McIntosh	John	27JUN87	2.05	1	McKinney	Archibald	08JUL00	2.20	1
McIntosh	Joseph	02NOV92	2.06	1	McKinney	Archibald	01AUG01	2.20	1
McIntosh	Joseph	02SEP93	1.07	1	McKenny	Archibald	27MAY02	2.20	1
McIntosh	Joseph	16MAY94	1.06	1	McKinney	Archibald	11JUL03	3.17	1
McIntosh	Joseph	25MAY95	2.08	1	McKenney	Archibald	03MAY04	3.13	1

surname	name	date	bk.pg	TM	surname	name	date	bk.pg	TM
McKenney	Archibald	13JUN05	3.23	1	McKenney	Daniel	14JUN05	3.24	1
McKinney	Archibald	28JUN06	3.22	1	McKinney	Daniel	01AUG05	2.23	1
McKenny	Archibald	11JUN07	2.23	1	McKinney	Daniel	14JUL06	3.22	2
McKenney	Archibald	-----08	2.19	11	McKinney	Daniel	26JUL06	3.23	1
McKinny	Archibald	26JUN09	1.23	1	McKenney	Daniel	14JUL07	2.24	1
McKinney	Archibald	-----11	1.55	12	McKenny	Daniel	01AUG07	2.25	2
McKinney	Catherine	30JUN01	2.19	F	McKenney	Daniel	-----08	2.19	1
McKenny	Charles	16AUG09	2.22	M1	McKenney	Daniel	-----08	2.18	2
McKenny	Colin	03APR90	2.05	1	McKinny	Daniel	29JUN09	1.23	1
McKinney	Collin	05JUL91	1.06	1	McKinney	Daniel Sr	-----11	1.55	1
McCinney	Collin	10AUG93	1.06	1	McKinney	Daniel Jr	-----11	1.55	1
McKinney	Collin	17MAY94	1.06	1	McKinney	Denny	22NOV88	1.07	1
McKinney	Collin	29MAY95	2.09	1	McKinney	Denes	07AUG89	5.09	1
McKinney	Collon	14AUG96	2.14	1	McKenny	Dennis	31MAR90	2.06	1
McKinney	Collin	12JUN97	1.16	1	McKinny	Dennis	23JUN91	2.06	1
McKinney	Collin	14JUN99	1.27	1	McKinney	Dennis	20SEP92	1.08	1
McKinney	Collin	21JUL00	2.20	1	McKenny	Dennis	08AUG93	3.08	1
McKenny	Collen	20JUL01	3.24	1	McKinney	Dennes	16MAY94	1.07	1
McKenney	Collen	27MAY02	2.20	1	McKinny	Denis	10APR95	3.10	1
McKinney	Collen	11JUN03	3.16	1	McKinney	Dennis	16JUN96	2.12	1
McKenney	Collen	01AUG04	3.13	1	McKinney	Dinnis	10MAY97	1.15	1
McKenney	Collon	14JUN05	3.24	1	McKinney	Dennis	14JUN00	2.19	1
McKinney	Collen	26JUL06	3.23	1	McKinney	Dennis	13JUL01	2.19	1
McKenny	Collen	10JUN07	2.23	1	McKenney	Dennis	24JUN02	2.21	1
McKenney	Collen	-----08	2.19	1	McKinney	Dennis	16JUN03	3.16	1
McKinny	Collin	29JUN09	1.23	1	McKenney	Dinnis	18JUN04	2.13	1
McKinney	Collin	-----11	1.55	1	McKenney	Dennis	21JUN05	3.24	1
McKenny	Daniel	24AUG87	1.04	1	McKinney	Dinnis	18JUL06	3.23	1
McKinney	Daniel	28OCT88	1.06	13	McKenney	Dinnis	20JUN07	2.23	1
McKinney	Daniel	30JUN89	5.08	13	McKenney	Dinnes	-----08	2.18	1
McKenny	Daniel	16JUL89	6.08	1	McKinny	Dennis	20MAR09	1.22	1
McKenny	Daniel	03APR90	2.05	1	McKenny	Abenezer	03APR90	2.05	1
McKinzy	Daniel	20MAY90	1.07	1	McKenney	Ebinezor	22NOV92	2.06	1
McKinney	Daniel	05APR91	1.06	2	McCinney	Ebenazor	21AUG93	1.06	1
McKinney	Daniel	05JUL91	1.06	1	McKinney	Ebenezar	01JUN95	2.08	1
McKenny	Daniel Sr	26OCT92	2.06	1	McKinney	Abenezer	29JUN09	1.23	1
McKenny	Daniel Jr	27OCT92	2.06	1	McKinney	Ebinezar	-----11	1.55	1
McKenny	Daniel	06OCT92	1.08		McKenny	Enoch	23JUN89	6.05	1
Listed with James McKenny					McKenny	Enoch	03APR90	2.05	1
McCinney	Daniel	12AUG93	1.06	1	McKinney	George	08MAY95	2.09	1
McCinney	Daniel Jr	12AUG93	1.06	1	McKinney	George	14AUG96	2.13	1
McKenny	Daniel	24AUG93	3.08	1	McKinney	George	12JUN97	1.16	1
McKinney	Daniel Sr	22MAY94	1.06	1	McKinney	George	02JUL99	1.27	1
McKinney	Daniel Jr	22MAY94	1.06	1	McKinney	George	29JUL00	2.21	1
McKinney	Daniel	28MAY95	2.08	1	McKenny	George	13JUL01	3.24	1
McKinney	Daniel	28MAY95	2.21	1	McKenny	George	26MAY02	2.19	1
McKinney	Daniel	29MAY95	2.09	1	McKinney	George	18JUL03	3.18	1
McKinney	Daniel	30MAY96	2.12	1	McKiney	George	08JUN04	4.15	1
McKinney	Daniel	03JUN96	2.12	2	McKinney	George	20JUN05	2.22	1
McKinney	Daniel	14AUG96	2.14	1	McKinney	George	30JUL06	2.24	1
McKinney	Daniel Sr	20JUN97	1.16	2	McKenny	James	20AUG87	1.04	1
McKinney	Daniel Jr	12JUN97	1.16	1	McKinney	James	11JUN89	6.05	1
McKinney	Daniel	11MAY97	1.17	1	McKinzy	James	15APR90	1.07	1
McKinsey	Daniel	31MAY97	3.21	1	McKinney	James	02AUG90	1.06	11
McKinney	Daniel	05JUN99	1.26	2	McKenny	James	19APR91	2.06	11
McKinney	Daniel Jr	05JUN99	1.26	1	McKenny	James	06OCT92	1.08	2
McKinney	Daniel Sr	28JUN00	2.20	1	Daniel McKenny listed also				
McKinney	Daniel Jr	26JUL00	2.21	1	McKenny	James	24AUG93	3.08	1
McKinney	Daniel	20JUN00	2.19	1	McKinney	James	09MAY94	2.08	1
McKiney	Daniel	04APR01	2.18	1	McKinney	James	27APR95	3.11	11
McKenny	Daniel	20JUL01	3.24	1	McKinsey	James	-----96	4.09	1
McKinney	Daniel	01AUG01	2.20	2	McKinney	James	01JUN96	2.12	11
McKenney	Daniel Sr	27MAY02	2.20	2	McKinney	James	19JUN00	1.09	1
McKenney	Daniel	27MAY02	2.20	1	McKinney	James	11JUN01	1.11	1
McKenney	Daniel	08JUL02	3.17	1	McKinney	James	04JUN02	1.14	1
McKinney	Danniel Sr	21JUL03	3.18	2	McKinney	James	28JUN03	1.15	1
McKinney	Danniel Jr	11JUN03	3.16	1	McKenney	James	02AUG04	2.14	1
McKinney	Daniel	01JUN03	2.20	1	McKiney	James	13JUL05	1.13	1
McKenney	Daniel Sr	01AUG04	3.13	2	McKinney	James	18JUN06	1.15	1
McKenney	Daniel Jr	01AUG04	3.13	1	McKinney	James	31JUL06	2.24	M1
McKenney	Daniel	13AUG04	2.15	1	McKenny	James	29MAY07	1.17	1
McKenney	Daniel Sr	13JUN05	3.23	2	McKenney	James	13AUG07	2.25	1

surname	name	date	bk.pg	TM	surname	name	date	bk.pg	TM
McKinny	James	31MAY08	1.22	1	McKnite	Robert	23MAY94	2.09	1
McKenny	James	09JUN09	2.21	1	McNight	Robert Sr	14APR95	3.12	1
McKinney	James	-----11	1.46	1	McNight	Robert Jr	14APR95	3.12	1
McKinney	James	-----11	1.51	1	McKnight	Robert	05JUL96	2.13	1
McKenzie	John	30JUN87	1.04	12	McKnight	Robert	05JUN97	1.16	1
McKenny	John	24AUG87	1.04	1	McNight	Robert	13MAY99	3.13	1
McKensey	John	11JUN89	6.08	1	McKnight	Robert	08JUL00	3.21	1
McKinney	John	26MAR90	2.06	1	MC LARDY				
McKinzy	John Jr	13AUG90	1.07	1	McLardy	Alexander	-----93	2.03	1
McKinzy	John	15APR90	1.06	1	MC LARNING				
McKensey	John	28MAY91	3.10	1	McLaning	John	22AUG04	2.15	1
McKinney	John	20SEP91	1.06	1	McLearning	John	19MAY05	3.23	1
McKinney	John	26SEP92	2.06	1	Mclarning	John	14JUL06	3.22	11
McCinney	John	15AUG93	1.06	1	McLarning	John	15JUL07	2.24	11
McKenzie	John	20APR94	3.13	1	MC LAUGHLIN				
McKinney	John	31MAY94	1.06	1	McGluchlin	Daniel	10JUN96	1.09	1
McKinney	John	08MAY95	2.09	1	McLaughlin	Daniel	20APR97	3.22	1
McKinney	John	08MAY95	2.21	1	McLaughlin	Daniel	09JUN00	1.07	1
McKinney	John	-----96	4.09	1	McLaughlen	Daniel	29MAY01	1.09	1
McKinley	John	14JUN96	1.09	11	McLaughlin	Daniel	28JUN02	1.15	1
McKiney	John	30JUN96	1.09	1	McLaughlen	Daniel	10JUN03	1.14	1
McKinley	John	07JUN99	1.26	1	McLaughlin	Daniel	04JUN05	1.11	1
McKinley	John	14JUN00	2.19	1	McLaughlin	Daniel	20MAY07	1.16	1
McKinley	John	08JUN01	2.18	1	McLaughlin	Daniel	17JUN08	1.25	1
McKinney	John	16JUN03	3.17	1	McGlachlan	John	13MAY94	1.06	1
McKinney	John	26JUL03	2.21	1	McLaughlin	Thomas	-----96	4.10	1
McKinley	John	22AUG04	2.15	1	McGloughlin	Thomas	-----92	3.14	1
McKinney	John	04JUN05	1.11	1	McGlocklin	Thomas	23MAY94	3.14	1
McKinney	John	23JUL05	2.23	1	McLaughlin	Thomas	-----95	1.10	1
McKinney	John	13JUN06	1.14	1	McLaughlin	Thomas	24JUN96	2.12	1
McKinley	John	30JUL06	2.24	1	McLaughlin	Thomas	-----97	2.03	1
McKinley	John	02AUG06	2.25	1	McLaughlin	Thomas	13MAY99	2.13	1
McKenny	John	24MAY09	2.20	1	McLaughlen	Thomas	13JUN00	1.08	1
McKinney	Peter	04JUN02	1.14	1	McLaughlen	Thomas	30MAY01	1.10	1
McKinney	Polly	26JUL03	2.21	F	McLaughlin	Thomas	26JUN02	1.15	1
McKinney	Rayney	28JUN03	1.15	1	McLaughlin	Thomas	11JUN03	1.14	1
McKenney	Rane	02AUG04	2.14	1	McLaughlin	Thomas	15JUN04	1.12	1
McKinney	Rane	12JUN05	1.12	1	McLaughlin	Thomas	04JUN05	1.11	11
McKinney	Rane	18JUN06	1.15	11	McLaughlen	Thomas	14JUN06	1.14	11
McKenny	Raney	13JUN07	1.17	11	McLaughlin	Thomas	02JUL07	1.15	11
McKenny	Raney	31MAY08	1.22	11	MC MAHAN				
McKenny	Raney	06JUN09	2.21	1	McMahan	Joseph	26SEP92	1.08	1
McKinney	Rane	-----11	1.46	1	MC MANNIS				
McKintee	Robert	06OCT87	1.04	1	McMamis	William	15MAY99	2.12	1
McKinsey	Rolly	25JUN87	2.05	1	McMannes	William	12JUN00	1.08	1
McKinsey	Rawleigh	19APR97	3.20	1	McMannes	William	04JUN01	1.10	1
McKenny	Stephen	30JUN87	1.03	11	McMannes	William	20JUN02	1.15	1
McKenny	William	02OCT92	1.09	1	McMannis	William	04MAY07	1.16	1
McKenny	William	14AUG93	3.08	1	McMannes	William	15JUN08	1.23	1
McKinney	William	23MAY94	2.10	1	McManus	William	13JUN09	2.21	1
McKinney	William	05JUL96	2.13	1	MC MICHAEL				
McKinney	William	12JUN97	1.16	1	McMichael	James	30JUN89	5.08	1
McKinney	William	27JUN00	2.20	1	McMicheal	James	31MAR90	2.05	1
McKinney	William	30JUL01	3.24	1	McMical	James	05JUL91	1.06	1
McKinney	William	28JUL02	3.18	1	McMichel	James	21OCT92	2.06	1
McKinney	William	08AUG03	3.19	11	Michael	James	09AUG93	1.06	1
McCinney	William	05JUN04	4.15	1	MC MORNE				
McKinney	William	28JUN05	2.22	11	McMorne	William	22JUN99	2.11	1
McKinney	William	31JUL06	2.24	1	MC MULLEN				
McKeney	William	05AUG07	2.25	1	McMullen	James	01JUL07	1.15	1
McKenney	William	-----08	2.19	1	McMillen	James	02JUN08	1.22	1
McKinny	William	12JUL09	1.25	1	McMullen	James	30MAY09	2.20	1
McCinnsey	William	-----11	1.49	1	McMullen	John	06AUG89	2.09	1
MC KNIGHT					McMullen	John	-----08	2.20	1
McNight	John	07AUG93	3.07	1	MC MURRAY				
McNight	John	10APR95	3.12	1	McMerry	John	12AUG89	5.09	1
McNight	Robert	19MAY89	6.05	1	McMurry	Thomas	13JUL87	1.04	1
McKnight	Robert	15APR90	1.07	1	McMurray	Thomas	19MAY89	6.05	1
McNight	Robert	20APR91	2.06	1	McMurry	Thomas	15APR90	1.07	1
McNight	Robert	25SEP92	1.08	1	McMurray	Thomas	18MAR91	2.07	1
McNight	Robert	07AUG93	3.07	1	McMurray	Thomas	24SEP92	1.08	1
McNight	Robert	12AUG93	3.07	1	McMurray	Thomas	08AUG93	3.08	1

surname	name	date	bk.pg	TM	surname	name	date	bk.pg	TM
McMurry	Thomas	08MAY94	2.08	1	McQuary	John	19NOV92	3.12	1
McMurry	Thomas	30MAR95	3.12	1	McQuerry	John	23MAY94	3.14	1
McMurray	Thomas	01JUN96	2.12	1	McQuary	John	-----95	1.10	1
McMurry	Thomas	10MAY97	1.15	1	McQuary	John	-----97	2.03	1
McMurry	Thomas	21MAY99	3.13	1	McQuerrey	John	13JUN00	1.08	1
McMurrey	Thomas	19JUN00	3.18	1	McQuerrey	John	02JUN01	1.10	1
McMurrey	Thomas	21MAY01	3.21	11	McQuerrey	John	03JUN02	1.13	1
McMurry	Thomas	04AUG02	3.18	11	McQuerrey	John	11JUN03	1.14	1
McMurray	Thomas	04AUG03	2.21	11	McQuary	Joseph	-----97	2.03	1
McMurry	Thomas	12JUN04	4.15	11	McQuerry	Joseph	13MAY99	2.13	1
McMurray	Thomas	17JUN05	2.21	11	McQuerrey	Joseph	13JUN00	1.08	1
McMurray	Thomas	02AUG06	2.25	11	McQuerrey	Joseph	02JUN01	1.10	1
McMurry	Thomas	05AUG07	2.25	1	McQuerrey	Joseph	03JUN02	1.13	1
McMurry	Thomas	-----08	2.19	1	McQuirrey	Samuel	02JUL89	2.08	1
McMurry	Thomas	15AUG09	1.26	1	McQuerry	Samuel	13SEP91	3.11	1
McMurry	Thomas	-----11	1.56	1	McQuary	Samuel	-----92	3.14	1
McMurray	William	02AUG06	2.25	1	McQuary	Samuel	24MAY94	3.14	1
McMurry	William	05AUG07	2.25	1	McQuerry	William	18JUN87	3.06	11
MC NEAL					McQuirrey	William	02JUL89	2.08	1
McNeal	Peggy	19MAR95	3.13	F	McQuerry	William	13SEP91	3.11	1
MC NEELY					McQuerry	William	13SEP91	3.11	11
McNeally	David	21JUL87	3.06	13	McQuerry	William	24MAY94	3.14	1
McNeeley	David	16JUN00	2.19	M1	McQuary	William	-----95	1.10	1
McNeeley	David	24JUN01	2.19	1	McQuerry	William	-----96	4.10	11
McNeally	David	12JUL02	2.21	1	MC QUEEN				
McNealy	David	17JUN03	3.17	1	McQuene	John	12JUN05	1.12	1
McNeeley	David	06AUG04	2.15	1	MC QUIRE				
McNeeley	David	08JUL05	3.25	1	McQuire	Joseph	30JUN89	5.08	1
McNeally	George	21JUL87	3.06	1	McQuire	Laurence	30JUN89	5.08	11
McNeely	James	10AUG93	1.06	1	MC REA				
McNeely	James	17MAY94	1.06	1	McCray	Alexander	22APR08	1.21	1
McNeally	John	21JUL87	3.06	1	McRae	Alexander	07JUN09	1.22	1
McNella	John	06OCT87	1.04	1	MC ROBERTS				
McNeely	John	27JUN89	2.08	1	McRoberts	Andrew	24JUL01	2.20	1
McNeely	John	10APR90	1.07	1	McRoberts	Andrew	21AUG02	3.19	1
McNely	John	09MAY94	2.08	1	McRoberts	Andrew	17JUN03	2.20	1
McNealey	John	-----96	4.11	1	McRoberts	Andrew	23JUL04	1.12	1
McFarson	Mark	20MAY94	1.06	1	McRoberts	Andrew	02AUG05	2.23	1
McFarson	Mark	16JUN95	2.09	1	McRoberts	Andrew	07AUG06	2.25	1
McFarson	Mark	26JUN96	1.09	1	McRoberts	Andrew	03AUG07	2.25	1
McPherson	Mark	17MAY99	1.24	1	McRoberts	Andrew	17JUN08	1.23	1
McPherson	Mark	30MAY00	2.18	1	McRoberts	Andrew	17JUL09	2.21	1
McPhersin	Mark	22JUL01	2.20	1	McRoberts	Andrew	-----11	1.47	1
McFerson	Mark	12JUN02	1.15	1	McRoberts	Andrew	-----11	1.46	1
McFerson	Mark	15JUL03	1.16	1	McRoberts	Charles	23AUG09	2.22	1
McPherson	Mark	15JUN04	1.12	1	McRoberts	Charles	-----11	1.51	2
McPherson	Mark	25JUL05	1.13	1	McRoberts	George	17MAY94	1.06	1
McPherson	Mark	21JUN06	1.15	1	McRoberts	George	12MAY95	2.09	1
McFearson	Mark	18JUN07	1.17	1	McRoberts	George	13JUN95	2.21	1
McFearson	Mark	22APR08	1.21	1	McRoberds	George	27JUN96	1.08	1
McFearson	Mark	17JUL09	2.21	1	McRoberds	George	27JUN96	1.13	
McPherson	Mark	-----11	1.47	1	Two town lots in Stanford				
MC QUARY					McRoberts	George	11JUL97	3.21	1
McQuary	Daniel	-----97	2.03	1	McRoberts	George	27MAY99	1.24	1
McQuerry	Daniel	13MAY99	2.13	1	McRoberts	George	12AUG00	2.22	1
McQuerrey	Daniel	13JUN00	1.08	1	McRoberts	George	08AUG01	2.21	1
McQuerrey	Daniel	02JUN01	1.10	1	Two lotts in Stanford				
McQuerrey	Daniel	03JUN02	1.13	1	McRoberts	George	21AUG02	3.19	1
McQuerrey	Daniel	11JUN03	1.14	1	McRoberts	George	16AUG03	2.23	1
McQuerrey	Daniel	14JUN04	1.12	1	One lott in Standford				
McQuerrey	Daniel	29JUN05	1.13	1	McRoberts	George	24JUL04	1.13	1
McQuerry	Daniel	11JUN06	1.14	1	McRoberts	George	09AUG05	2.24	1
McQuerry	Daniel	04MAY07	1.16	1	McRoberts	George	21AUG06	2.27	1
McQuerry	Daniel	17JUN08	1.23	1	McRoberts	George	22JUL07	2.24	1
McQuerry	Daniel	20MAY09	2.20	1	McRoberts	George	17JUN08	1.25	2
McQuerry	Daniel	20MAY09	2.19	1	McRoberts	George	23AUG09	2.22	21
McQuerry	Daniel	-----11	1.46	1	McRoberts	George	-----11	1.52	2
McQuerry	Elizabeth	12JUL04	1.12	F	McRoberts	Isaac	21AUG06	2.27	1
McQuerry	Elizabeth	07JUN05	1.12	F	McRoberts	Isaac	03AUG07	2.25	1
McQuerry	John	18JUN87	3.06	1	McRoberts	Isaac	23AUG09	2.22	1
McQuirrey	John	02JUL89	2.08	1	McRoberts	Isaac	-----11	1.51	1
McQuerry	John	13SEP91	3.11	1	McRoberts	John	12MAY95	2.09	1

surname	name	date	bk.pg	TM	surname	name	date	bk.pg	TM
McRoberts	John	12MAY95	2.09	11	McWhorter	James	14JUL07	2.24	1
McRoberds	John	27JUN96	1.08	1	McWhorter	James	-----08	2.18	1
McRoberds	John	27JUN96	1.08	11	McWhertor	John	11MAY96	2.11	12
McRobards	John	13JUN97	3.22	1	McWhertor	John Jr	11MAY96	2.11	1
McRobards	John	13JUN97	3.33		McWhortor	John	15JUL97	1.17	12
Two town lots in Stanford					McQuerter	John	12MAY99	2.13	1
McRobards	John Sr	28MAY99	1.25	11	McWherter	John	01JUL99	1.27	12
McRoberts	John	29MAY99	1.40		McWhorter	John	22JUL00	2.20	1
One lott in Stanford					McWhorter	John	30JUL01	3.23	1
McRoberts	John Sr	01AUG00	2.21	11	McWhoter	John	10AUG02	2.23	1
McRoberts	John Jr	05AUG00	2.22	1	McWhorter	John	25AUG03	3.19	1
Two lotts in Standford					McWhorter	John	16AUG04	3.14	1
McRoberts	John Sr	18JUL01	2.19	11	McWhorter	John	23AUG05	3.27	11
McRoberts	John Jr	06AUG01	2.21	1	McWhorter	John	19AUG06	3.24	11
McRoberts	John Sr	07AUG02	3.19	11	McQuerter	Robert	19JUN99	2.11	1
McRoberts	John Jr	17JUL02	3.17	1	MC YULY				
One lott in Standford					McYuly	James	15OCT92	2.06	1
McRoberts	John Sr	17JUN03	2.20	11	MEADE				
McRoberts	John Jr	08AUG03	2.22	1	Mead	Maztin	-----11	1.54	1
McRoberts	John Sr	25JUL04	1.13	21	Made	Thomas	01JUN02	2.20	11
McRoberts	John	23JUL04	1.12	1	Made	Thomas	11JUN03	3.16	11
McRoberts	John Sr	-----05	2.20	21	Made	Thomas	27JUN04	4.16	1
McRoberts	John Jr	02AUG05	2.23	1	Meade	Thomas	19JUL05	2.23	1
McRoberts	John Sr	19AUG06	2.27	11	Mead	Thomas	19AUG06	2.26	1
McRoberts	John Jr	20AUG06	2.27	1	Mades	Thomas	22JUL07	2.24	1
McRoberts	John	15JUL07	2.24	11	MEANS				
McRoberts	John	22JUL07	2.24	1	Meens	James	29MAY94	1.06	1
McRoberts	John Sr	23AUG09	2.22	1	MEEK				
McRoberts	John	23AUG09	2.22	1	Meek	Jeremiah	-----11	1.53	1
McRoberts	John Jr	-----11	1.51	1	Meek	William	01JUN97	3.21	11
McRobards	Thomas	11JUL97	3.21	1	MENEFEE				
McRoberts	Thomas	27MAY99	1.24	1	Manefee	James	29JUN96	1.09	1
McRoberts	Thomas	29MAY99	1.40		Manifee	James	14APR97	3.20	1
One lott in Port William					Menefee	James	29MAY99	2.12	1
McRoberts	Thomas	07JUL00	2.20	1	Menefee	James	19JUN00	1.09	1
McRoberts	Thomas	06AUG01	2.21	1	Menefee	James	11JUN01	1.11	1
One lott in Port William					Menefee	James	04JUN02	1.13	1
McRoberts	Thomas	17JUL02	3.17		Menefee	James	28JUN03	1.15	1
Half lott in Port William					Menefee	James	02AUG04	2.14	1
McRoberts	Thomas	18JUN03	2.20		Menefee	James	12JUN05	1.12	1
One lott in Port William					Menefee	James	18JUN06	1.15	1
McRoberts	Thomas	24JUL04	1.13	1	Menfee	James	12JUN07	1.17	1
McRoberts	Thomas	23JUL05	2.23	1	Menefee	James	31MAY08	1.22	1
One lott in Port William					Menefee	James	06JUN09	2.21	1
McRoberts	Thomas Sr	19AUG06	2.27	1	Menifee	James	-----11	1.46	1
McRoberts	Thomas	06JUN06	2.23	1	Menefee	Jerot	20MAY94	1.11	1
One lott in Port William					Manefee	Garrat	29JUN96	1.09	1
McRoberts	Thomas	22JUL07	2.24	1	Manifee	Gerrot	14APR97	3.20	1
McRoberts	Thomas	03AUG07	2.25	1	Menefee	Jerrot	29MAY99	2.12	1
McRoberts	Thomas Sr	17JUN08	1.25	1	Menefee	Jarrot	19JUN00	1.09	1
McRoberts	Thomas	23AUG09	2.22	1	Menefee	Jarrot	11JUN01	1.11	1
MC SWAIN					Menefee	Jarrot	04JUN02	1.13	1
McSwain	Thomas	-----96	4.10	11	Menefee	Jarrot	28JUN03	1.15	1
MC VAY					Menefee	Jarrot	11JUN05	1.12	1
McVay	Hugh	06JUN06	2.23	1	Menefee	John	12MAY99	2.13	1
McVay	Hugh	06MAY07	1.16	1	Menefee	John	18JUN00	1.09	1
McVay	Langston	16MAY05	2.21	1	Menefee	John	30MAY01	1.09	1
McVay	Langston	03AUG07	2.25	1	Menefee	John	04JUN02	1.14	1
MC WHORTER					Menefee	John	23JUN03	1.15	1
McWaters	Aaron	-----95	1.10	1	Manefee	John	02AUG04	2.14	1
McWhertor	George	11MAY96	2.11	11	Menefee	John	11JUN05	1.12	1
McWhorter	George	14JUL97	1.17	11	Menefee	John	04JUN07	1.17	1
McWhorter	George	26JUL00	2.21	1	Menefee	John	22APR08	1.21	1
McWhorter	George	30JUL01	3.23	1	Manifee	Nimrod	12AUG89	2.09	1
McWhorter	George	04JUN03	3.16	1	Manife	Reuben	-----95	1.09	1
McQuerter	James	19JUN99	2.12	1	Menefee	Rubin	29JUN96	1.09	1
McWhorter	James	26JUL00	2.21	1	Manife	Reuben	14APR97	3.20	1
McWhorter	James	30JUL01	3.23	1	Menefee	Reuben	29MAY99	2.12	1
McWhorter	James	25AUG03	3.19	1	Menefee	Rheuben	19JUN00	1.09	1
McWhorter	James	26AUG04	3.14	1	Menefee	Rheuben	11JUN01	1.11	1
McWhorter	James	21JUN05	3.24	1	Menefee	Rheuben	04JUN02	1.13	1
McWhorter	James	21JUL06	3.23	1	Menefee	Rheuben	28JUN03	1.15	1

surname	name	date	bk.pg	TM	surname	name	date	bk.pg	TM
Menefee	Ruben	02AUG04	2.14	2	Midleton	Henry	20MAY94	1.06	1
Menefee	Rheuben	12JUN05	1.12	2	Middleton	Henry	26MAY95	2.09	1
Menefee	Rheuben	18JUN06	1.15	1	Midleton	Henry	30JUN96	1.09	1
Menfee	Ruben	12JUN07	1.17	1	Middleton	Henry	14APR97	3.20	1
Menefee	Ruben	31MAY08	1.22	1	Middleton	Henry	30MAY99	2.12	1
Menefee	Ruben	06JUN09	2.21	1	Middleton	Henry	20JUN00	1.09	1
Menifee	Reuben	-----11	1.56	1	Middleton	Henry	11JUN01	1.11	11
Manifee	William	21JUL87	3.06	1	Middleton	Henry	08JUN02	1.14	1
Manifee	William	12AUG89	2.09	1	Middleton	Henry	11JUL03	1.16	1
Manefee	William	20APR91	3.09	1	Middleton	Henry	03AUG04	2.14	1
Manifee	William	-----92	3.14	1	Middleton	Henry	12JUN05	1.12	1
Manifee	William	28MAY94	3.14	1	Middleton	Henry	16JUN06	1.15	1
Manifee	William	-----95	1.09	1	Middleton	Henry	28MAY07	1.16	1
Menefee	William	-----96	4.10	11	Middleton	Henry	10JUN08	1.23	1
Menefee	William	-----97	2.03	11	Middleton	Henry	12MAY09	2.19	1
Menefee	William	25MAY99	2.12	11	Middleton	Henry	-----11	1.46	1
Menefee	William	18JUN00	1.09	11	Middleton	Jacob	03OCT92	2.06	1
Menefee	William	05JUN01	1.11	12	Mideleton	Jacob	20AUG93	1.06	1
Menefee	William	03JUN02	1.13	12	Middleton	John	-----92	3.14	M1
Menefee	William	13JUN03	1.14	11	Middleton	Thomas	-----92	3.14	1
Menefee	William	19JUN04	1.12	1	Midleton	Thomas	09AUG93	1.06	1
Menefee	William	11JUN05	1.12	1	Midleton	Thomas	20MAY94	1.06	1
Menefee	William Jr	11JUN05	1.12	1	Midleton	Thomas	26MAY94	1.11	1
Menefee	William	10JUN06	1.14	1	Middleton	Thomas	29MAY09	2.20	1
Menefee	William Jr	10JUN06	1.14	1	Midleton	Thomas Sr	26MAY94	1.06	1
Menefee	William	04JUN07	1.17	1	Middleton	Walter	03JUN90	2.05	12
Menefee	William Jr	04JUN07	1.17	1	Middleton	Walter	05JUL91	1.06	11
Menefee	William	02JUN08	1.23	1	Middleton	Walter	-----92	3.14	1
MERRITT					Middleton	Walter	08SEP92	2.06	1
Merritt	Richard	17JUL00	2.20	1	Midleton	Walter	09AUG93	1.06	1
Merritt	Richard	20JUN03	2.20	1	Midleton	Walter	20MAY94	1.06	1
Merrit	Richard	28JUL04	4.16	1	Midleton	Walter	26MAY94	1.06	1
Merritt	Richard	23JUL05	2.23	11	Middleton	Walter	26MAY95	2.08	1
Merritt	Richard	17JUL06	2.23	11	Middleton	Walter	26JUN95	2.22	1
Merret	Richard	05AUG07	2.25	12	Midleton	Walter	15JUN96	1.09	1
Merrit	Richard	17JUN08	1.25	1	Middleton	Walter	07APR97	3.21	1
Merrit	Richard	19AUG09	2.22	1	Middleton	Walter	22MAY99	1.24	1
MERSHON					Middleton	Walter	10JUN00	2.19	1
Mershon	Andrew	10JUN03	1.14	1	Middleton	Walter	08JUN01	2.18	1
Mershon	Andrew	13JUN04	1.12	11	Middleton	Walter	12JUN02	1.15	1
Mershon	Andrew	05JUN05	1.11	11	Middleton	Walter	15JUL03	1.16	1
METLE					Middleton	Walter	25JUN04	1.12	1
Metle	Elizabeth	09JUN00	1.07	F	Middleton	Walter	15JUN05	1.12	1
MICHAEL					Middleton	Walter	23JUN06	1.15	1
Michael	Michael	-----11	1.51		Middleton	Walter	18JUN07	1.17	1
(negro)					Middleton	Walter	02JUN08	1.22	1
MICKELBORO					Middleton	Walter	22JUN09	2.21	1
MickeleboroRobert		24MAY94	3.15	1	MIKESEL				
MIDDLETON					Mikesel	Peter	23JUN01	1.11	1
Middleton	Charles	31JUL06	1.16	1	Mikesel	Peter	20JUN02	1.15	1
Middleton	Charles	04MAY07	1.16	1	MILAM				
Middleton	Charles	17JUN08	1.24	1	Mileham	George	07JUN97	1.17	1
Middleton	Charles	27AUG09	2.19	1	Mailom	Stephen	01JUN96	1.08	1
Middleton	Elijah	29MAY09	2.20	1	Milam	Stephen	04JUN01	2.18	1
Middleton	Hawkins	24MAY94	3.15	1	MILES				
Middleton	Hawkins	-----95	1.09	1	Miles	Isaac	08AUG05	3.25	1
Middleton	Hawkins	-----96	4.09	1	Miles	Isaac	04AUG06	3.24	1
Middleton	Hanley	26MAY95	2.08	1	Miles	Wilford	24AUG03	3.19	1
Midleton	Handly	25JUN96	1.09	1	Miles	Wilfred	15AUG04	3.14	1
Midleton	Hanley	11APR97	3.19	1	Miles	Wilford	08AUG05	3.25	1
Middleton	Handley	29MAY00	2.18	1	Miles	Wilford	20AUG06	3.25	1
Middleton	Handley	21JUL01	2.19	1	Miles	William	02JUL07	1.15	1
Middleton	Henley	10JUN02	1.14	1	MILLER				
Middleton	Henly	25JUN04	1.12	1	Miller	Abraham	05JUL87	3.07	1
Middleton	Henley	25JUL05	1.13	1	Miller	Abraham	27JUN89	2.08	1
Middleton	Henley	23JUN06	1.15	1	Miller	Abraham	28MAY91	3.10	1
Middleton	Henly	20JUN07	1.17	1	Miller	Abraham	20SEP92	1.04	1
Middleton	Henley	02JUN08	1.22	1	Shown with James Davis				
Middleton	Henley	22JUN09	2.21	1	Miller	Abraham	01DEC92	3.13	1
Middleton	Hendley	-----11	1.48	1	Miller	---	20AUG93	3.04	1
Middleton	Henry	08OCT92	2.06	1	Tax pd by James Davis				
Midleton	Henry	09AUG93	1.06	1	Miller	Abraham	27MAR95	3.12	M1

surname	name	date	bk.pg	TM	surname	name	date	bk.pg	TM
Miller	Abraham	31MAR95	3.12	1	Miller	John	13JUN95	2.09	1
Miller	Abraham	01JUN96	2.12	1	Miller	John	12MAY96	2.11	1
Miller	Abraham	22JUL96	2.13	1	Miller	John	23MAY96	2.11	1
Miller	Abraham Sr	10MAY97	1.15	1	Miller	John	11MAY97	1.17	1
Miller	Abraham Jr	17MAY97	1.15	1	Miller	John	17MAY97	1.15	1
Miller	Abram	29JUN99	3.14	1	Miller	John	31MAY97	3.21	1
Miller	Abraham	20JUN00	3.18	1	Miller	John	24JUN00	3.20	1
Miller	Abraham	08JUN01	3.22	1	Miller	John	22AUG06	3.25	1
Miller	Abraham	07AUG02	3.19	1	Miller	John	31MAY08	1.22	1
Miller	Abraham	01AUG03	2.21	1	Miller	John	10JUN09	1.23	1
Miller	Abraham	12JUN04	4.15	1	Miller	Jonathan	25JUL96	2.13	0
Miller	Abraham	29JUN05	2.22	1	Miller	Jonathan	19MAY01	3.21	1
Miller	Abraham	15AUG06	2.26	1	Miller	Joseph	17JUL09	1.25	1
Miller	Abraham	17AUG07	2.26	1	Miller	Joseph	-----11	1.53	1
Miller	Abraham	-----08	2.18	2	Miller	Marth	13JUN95	2.22	1
Miller	Abraham	24AUG08	2.20	1	Miller	Martha	-----11	1.52	F
Miller	Abraham	15AUG09	1.26	1	Miller	Matthias	26JUN99	1.27	1
Miller	Abraham	-----11	1.56	1	Miller	Mathias	25JUL00	2.20	1
Miller	Abram	-----11	1.46	0	Miller	Mathias	29JUL01	3.23	1
Miller	Alexander	17AUG07	2.26	2	Miller	Mathias	10AUG02	2.23	1
Miller	Alexander	30JUN09	1.23	1	Miller	Matthias	25JUN03	3.17	1
Miller	Alexander	30JUN09	1.24	2	Miller	Mathias	07AUG04	3.14	1
Miller	Allen	17JUL09	1.25	1	Miller	Mathias	05AUG05	3.25	1
Miller	Allen	-----11	1.53	1	Miller	Mathias	04AUG06	3.24	1
Millar	Andrew	07JUL87	1.03	1	Millor	Matty	01OCT92	1.09	F
Miller	Charles	22AUG06	3.25	1	Miller	Nathan	-----11	1.52	1
Miller	Daniel	20JUN99	2.11	1	Miller	Peter	04AUG06	3.24	1
Miller	David	-----11	1.54	1	Millor	Polly	18SEP92	1.09	F
Millar	Eleoner	06OCT87	1.04	F	Miller	Samuel	23JUN01	1.11	1
Millar	George	13JUL87	1.04	11	Miller	Samuel	23JUN02	1.15	1
Miller	George	26MAY89	6.05	1	Miller	Samuel	22JUN03	1.14	1
Miller	George	06AUG89	2.09	12	Miller	Samuel	01JUL03	2.20	1
Miller	George	14MAY90	1.07	1	Miller	Samuel	28JUN04	4.16	11
Millor	George	24JUN91	2.07	1	Miller	Samuel	02AUG04	1.13	1
Miller	George	01AUG91	2.06	1	Miller	Samuel	31MAY05	2.21	11
Miller	George Sr	12SEP91	3.10	1	Miller	Samuel	15AUG06	2.26	12
Miller	George	12SEP91	3.10	11	Miller	Samuel	10AUG07	2.25	12
Millor	George	05OCT92	1.09	1	Miller	Samuel	24AUG08	2.20	12
Miller	George	30NOV92	3.13	1	Miller	Sarah	09JUN89	6.05	F
Miller	George	13AUG93	3.08	1	Miller	Sarah	10MAY90	1.07	F
Miller	George	14MAY94	1.06	1	Millor	Sarah	18MAY91	2.07	F
Miller	Henry	06JUN03	3.16	1	Miller	Thomas	13JUN96	2.13	2
Miller	Henry	06AUG04	3.13	1	Miller	Thomas	05JUN97	1.16	2
Miller	Henry	23AUG05	3.26	1	Miller	Thomas	13MAY99	3.13	1
Miller	Henry	19AUG06	3.24	1	Miller	Thomas	19JUN00	3.18	1
Miller	Jacob	03JUL99	3.14	1	Miller	Thomas	17JUN01	3.22	1
Miller	Jacob	17JUL00	2.20	1	Miller	Thomas	26JUL02	3.17	1
Miller	Jacob	19APR01	2.18	1	Miller	Thomas	11JUL03	2.21	1
Miller	Jacob	24MAY02	3.17	1	Miller	Thomas	23JUL04	4.16	1
Miller	Jacob	04JUN03	2.20	1	Miller	Thomas	10JUN05	2.21	1
Miller	Jacob	23JUL04	1.12	1	Miller	Thomas	09JUN06	2.23	1
Miller	Jacob	31JUL05	2.23	1	Miller	Thomas	20JUN07	2.23	11
Miller	Jacob	19MAY06	2.22	1	Miller	Thomas	-----08	2.18	11
Miller	Jacob	22JUL07	2.24	1	Millar	Will	06OCT87	1.04	1
Miller	Jacob	24AUG08	2.20	11	Miller	William	16MAY89	6.05	1
Miller	Jacob	22JUN09	1.23	1	Miller	William	01JUL90	1.07	1
Miller	Jacob	-----11	1.54	1	Millor	William	17MAY91	2.06	1
Miller	James	05JUN97	1.17	1	Millor	William	24JUN91	2.07	1
Miller	James	13MAY99	3.13	1	Millor	William	02OCT92	1.09	1
Miller	James	19JUN00	3.18	1	Millor	William	06OCT92	1.08	1
Miller	James	17JUN01	3.22	1	Miller	William	07SEP93	3.08	1
Miller	James	26JUL02	3.17	1	Miller	William	28APR94	2.09	1
Miller	James	04JUL03	1.15	1	Miller	William	17JUN94	2.08	1
Miller	James	01AUG04	2.14	1	Miller	William	01MAY95	3.10	1
Miller	James	19JUN05	1.13	1	Miller	William	11MAY96	2.11	1
Miller	James	02AUG06	2.24	1	Miller	William	17MAY96	2.11	1
Millar	John	02OCT87	1.06	1	Miller	William	27MAY96	2.12	1
Miller	John	26JUN89	6.05	1	Miller	William	13JUN97	3.22	1
Miller	John	23JUN90	1.07	1	Miller	William	20JUN97	1.16	1
Miller	John	12SEP91	3.10	1	Miller	William	21MAY99	1.24	1
Miller	John	30NOV92	3.13	1	Miller	William	19JUN00	2.19	1
Miller	John	14MAY94	1.06	1	Miller	William	02MAY01	3.21	1

surname	name	date	bk.pg	TM	surname	name	date	bk.pg	TM
Miller	William	31JUL02	3.18	1	Mitchel	Daniel	29MAY94	2.10	1
Miller	William	01AUG03	2.21	1	Michal	James	24MAY99	2.12	1
Miller	William	01AUG03	2.21	1	Michel	James	16JUN00	1.08	1
Miller	William	05JUN04	4.15	1	Mitchel	James	03JUN01	1.10	1
Miller	William	14JUN05	3.24	1	Mitchel	John	05NOV88	1.06	1
Miller	William	26AUG06	3.25	1	Mitchel	John	13AUG89	2.09	1
Miller	William	20JUN07	2.23	1	Michel	John	16SEP91	3.11	1
Miller	William	30JUN07	1.18	1	Mitchell	Samuel	03JUN01	2.18	1
Miller	William	02JUN08	1.22	1	Mitchel	William	27JUN87	2.05	1
Miller	William	07AUG09	1.26	2	MITCHELTREE				
Miller	William	-----11	1.46	1	MichelltreeGeorge		22JUL01	3.24	1
Miller	William	-----11	1.52	3	Micheltree	George	26MAY02	2.19	1
MILLS					MitcheltreeGeorge		06JUN03	3.16	1
Mills	Archable	13MAY99	2.13	1	MitcheltreeGeorge		09AUG04	3.14	1
Mills	William	08APR06	2.22	1	MitcheltreeGeorge		05AUG05	3.25	1
MILNER					Micheltree	George	23AUG06	3.25	1
Milner	Armsted	11MAY95	2.08	1	MIZENER				
Milner	Armsted	01JUN96	1.09	1	Misener	Jacob	05AUG02	2.23	1
Milner	Amsted	28JUN99	3.13	1	Misener	Jacob	19JUL03	3.18	1
Milner	Armsted	28JUN99	3.13	1	Mizener	Jacob	06AUG04	3.13	1
Miller	Armited	28JUN00	3.20	1	Mizener	Jacob	12JUN05	3.23	1
Millner	Armstead	11AUG01	2.21	1	MOBERLY				
Millner	Armstead	08JUL02	3.17	1	Mobley	Benjamin	30JUN89	2.08	1
Millner	Armstead	25JUL03	2.21	1	Mobley	Benjamin	16SEP91	3.11	1
Miller	Amsted	24JUL04	1.13	1	Mobley	Edward	02JUL89	2.08	1
Millner	Armstead	16MAY05	2.21	1	Mobley	Edward	-----92	3.14	1
Millner	Armstead	08APR06	2.22	1	Mobley	Edward	23MAY94	3.14	1
Miller	Armstead	22JUL07	2.24	1	Mobley	Edward	-----95	1.09	1
Miller	Armstead	17JUN08	1.24	1	Mobley	Edward	-----96	4.10	11
Miller	Armstead	17JUN08	1.24	11	Mobley	Edward	-----97	2.03	1
Milner	Armstead	18AUG09	2.22	1	Mobley	Edward	11MAY99	2.13	11
Milner	Armstead	-----11	1.51	1	Moberly	Edward	09JUN00	1.07	11
Milner	John	03AUG89	5.08	11	Moberley	Edward	01JUN01	1.10	1
Millnor	John	03APR90	2.05	11	Moberly	Edward	04MAY07	1.16	1
Milner	John	05APR91	1.06	11	Mobley	James	18JUN87	3.06	1
Millinear	John	08OCT92	2.06	1	Mobley	James	13AUG89	2.09	1
Milner	John	15AUG93	1.06	1	Mobley	James	23MAY94	3.14	1
Milner	John	15MAY94	1.06	11	Mobley	James	-----95	1.10	1
Milner	John	18MAY95	2.21	1	Mobley	James	-----96	4.09	1
Milner	John	02JUN95	2.09	11	Mobley	James	-----97	2.03	1
Milnor	John	09JUN96	1.09	11	Mobley	James	15MAY99	2.12	1
Melner	John	21APR97	3.22	1	Moberly	James	16JUN00	1.08	1
Millner	John	28JUL00	2.21	1	Moberley	James	23JUN01	1.11	1
Milner	John	-----08	2.20	1	Mobley	James	20JUN02	1.15	1
Milner	John	-----11	1.50	1	Moberley	James	22JUN03	1.14	1
Melner	John M.	22APR97	3.22	1	Moberley	James	01AUG04	1.13	1
Milner	John M.	01JUN99	1.24	1	Moberley	James	29JUL05	1.13	1
Milner	Luke	02NOV92	2.06	1	Moberley	James	30JUL06	1.16	1
Milner	Sarah	31MAY99	1.25	F	Moberley	James	04MAY07	1.16	11
Millner	Sally	28JUL00	2.21	F	Moberly	James	15JUN08	1.23	11
Millner	Salley	14JUL01	2.19	F1	Moberley	Jobe	11JUN00	1.08	1
MINOR					Mobley	Josiah	13SEP91	3.11	1
Minor	Coleman	01AUG06	2.24	1	Moberly	Mary	13JUN09	2.21	F
Miner	Coleman	24AUG07	2.26	1	MODREL				
Miner	Colman	-----08	2.19	1	Moderel	Robert	19OCT92	2.06	1
Miner	Coleman	08AUG09	1.26	1	Modral	Robert	18JUN95	2.08	1
Minor	Coleman	-----11	1.56	1	Modral	Robert	26JUN96	1.09	1
Minor	Cyras	01AUG06	2.24	11	Modreal	Robert	14APR97	3.20	1
Miner	Cyrus	24AUG07	2.26	11	MOFFETT				
Miner	Cyrus	-----08	2.19	11	Moffet	John	28SEP92	1.09	1
Minor	Cyrus	08AUG09	1.26	1	Moffit	John	10AUG93	3.07	1
Minor	Cyrus	-----11	1.56	11	Moffet	John	19MAR95	3.13	1
Minor	Henry	30JUL06	2.24	M1	Moffett	John	28JUL96	2.13	1
Miner	Henry	24AUG07	2.26	1	Moffet	John	30MAY97	1.15	1
Minor	James	-----11	1.56	1	Moffet	John	26JUN99	3.13	1
Minor	Thomas	11MAY90	1.07	1	Moppen	John	24JUN00	3.20	1
MINTER					Moffett	John	31JUL01	2.20	1
Minter	William	21JUL87	3.06	1	Maffett	John	03JUN02	2.20	1
MITCHAM					Moffet	John	12JUL03	3.18	1
Mitcham	John	29MAY05	2.21	11	Moffet	John	06AUG04	2.15	1
Mitcham	Spencer	29MAY05	2.21	1	Mophet	John	30MAY05	2.21	1
MITCHELL					Mophett	John	02AUG06	2.24	1

surname	name	date	bk.pg	TM	surname	name	date	bk.pg	TM
Maffett	John	15JUL07	2.24	1	Montgomery	Jean	30JUL04	2.14	F
Maffett	John	24AUG08	2.20	1	Montgomery	Jean	19MAY05	3.23	F
MOHON					Montgomery	Jenny	14JUL06	3.22	F
Mohon	James	19JUN99	2.12	11	Montgomery	John	23MAY89	6.05	1
Mohon	Thomas	22JUN99	2.11	1	Montgomery	John	14MAY90	1.06	1
MONDAY					Montgomery	John	30MAR91	2.07	1
Monday	James	-----05	3.38		Montgomery	John	05OCT92	1.08	1
1804 tax info in 1805 tax list					Montgomery	John	13AUG93	3.07	1
Monday	James	-----05	3.38	1	Montgomery	John	11JUN94	2.10	1
Monday	James	23JUL04	1.12	1	Montgomery	John	30JUN09	1.23	1
Monday	James	19MAY05	3.23	1	Montgomery	John	-----11	1.50	1
Monday	John	28JUL03	2.21	1	Montgomery	John	-----11	1.48	1
Monday	William	23JUL04	1.12	1	Montgomery	Joseph	13JUN95	2.21	1
MONFORT					Montgomery	Mathew	24JUN91	2.07	21
Monfort	Francis	02NOV92	1.09	1	Simpson Montgomery listed also				
Monfort	Francis	19AUG93	3.08	1	Montgomery	Matthew	25SEP92	1.08	1
MONTGOMERY					Montgomery	Nathan	29OCT92	2.06	1
Montgomery	Alexander	08JUL00	2.20	M1	Montgomery	Nathan	03SEP93	1.07	1
Montgomery	Alexander	26APR01	2.18	1	Montgomery	Polly	21MAY99	1.24	F
Montgomery	Alexander	30JUL04	2.14	1	Montgomery	Polly	04JUN00	2.19	F
Montgomery	Alexander	-----11	1.51	1	Montgomery	Polley	10AUG01	2.21	F
Montgomery	Benjamin	22JUN09	1.23	1	Montgomery	Polley	31MAY05	2.21	F
Montgomery	Cleton	08JUL05	3.25	1	Montgomery	Polley	20AUG06	2.27	F
Montgomery	Cleton	18JUL06	3.23	1	Montgomery	Robert Sr	30JUN87	3.07	1
Montgomery	Esther	28MAY94	3.15	F	Montgomery	Robert	30JUN87	3.07	1
Montgomery	Ester	-----95	1.10	F	Montgomery	Robert	25JUL89	2.09	1
Montgomery	Esther	-----96	4.09	F1	Montgomery	Robert	31MAR90	2.06	1
Montgomery	Ezekial	07AUG93	1.06	1	Montgomery	Robert	07SEP91	3.10	1
Montgomery	Ezekial	15MAY94	1.07	1	Montgomery	Robert	18OCT91	1.06	21
Montgomery	Ezekiel	30MAY99	1.25	1	Montgomery	Robert	20APR94	3.13	1
Montgomery	Ezekiel	20JUN00	2.19	1	Montgomery	Robert	-----95	1.10	1
Montgomery	Ezekiel	15JUN01	2.18	1	Montgomery	Robert	-----96	4.09	1
Montgomery	Ezekiel	10JUN03	1.14	1	Montgomery	Samuel	25JUL89	2.09	1
Montgomery	Ezekiel	25JUL04	1.13	1	Montgomery	Samuel	19APR91	3.09	1
Montgomery	Ezekiel	17JUN08	1.25	1	Montgomery	Samuel	18NOV92	3.12	11
Montgomery	Ezekiel	24MAY09	2.20	1	Montgomery	Samuel	19NOV92	3.12	1
Montgomery	Ezekiel	-----11	1.51	1	Montgomery	Samuel	28MAY94	3.15	1
Montgomery	James	05OCT92	2.06	1	Montgomery	Samuel	-----95	1.10	1
Montgomery	James	10AUG93	1.06	1	Montgomery	Samuel	-----96	4.09	1
Montgomery	James	27MAY94	1.06	1	Montgomery	Simpson	24JUN91	2.07	
Montgomery	James	09MAY95	2.21	1	Listed with Mathew Montgomery				
Montgomery	James	29MAY95	2.08	1	Montgomery	Thomas	27JUN87	2.05	1
Montgomery	James	18JUN96	1.08	1	Montgomery	Thomas	30JUN87	3.07	1
Montgomery	James	12JUN97	3.21	1	Montgomery	Thomas	05NOV88	1.06	1
Montgomery	James	24MAY99	1.24	1	Montgomery	Thomas	16JUN89	5.08	1
Montgomery	James	14JUN00	2.19	1	Montgomery	Thomas	25JUL89	2.09	1
Montgomery	James	20JUN00	2.19	M1	Montgomery	Thomas	03SEP93	1.07	1
Montgomery	James	19JUL00	2.20	1	Montgomery	Thomas	17MAY94	1.06	1
Montgomery	James	17JUL01	2.19	1	Montgomery	Thomas	01JUN95	2.09	1
Montgomery	James	21JUL01	3.24	1	Montgomery	Thomas	16JUN95	2.08	1
Montgomery	James	27MAY02	3.17	1	Montgomery	Thomas	18JUN95	2.22	1
Montgomery	James	28MAY03	2.19	1	Montgomery	Thomas	16JUN96	1.08	1
Montgomery	James	04JUN03	2.20	1	Montgomery	Thomas	04AUG96	2.14	1
Montgomery	James	25JUL04	1.13	1	Montgomery	Thomas	08AUG97	1.17	1
Montgomery	James	07AUG04	2.15	1	Montgomery	Thomas	08AUG97	1.17	1
Montgomery	James	08JUN05	2.21	1	Montgomery	Thomas	08AUG97	1.17	s
Montgomery	James	19MAY06	2.23	1	Pd tax for Wm(heirs) Montgomery				
Montgomery	James	19MAY07	1.16	1	Montgomery	Thomas	09AUG97	3.22	1
Montgomery	James	22JUL07	2.24	1	Montgomery	Thomas	04AUG00	2.22	1
Montgomery	James	17JUN08	1.25	1	One lott in Standford				
Montgomery	James	18AUG09	2.22	1	Montgomery	Thomas	04AUG01	2.20	11
Montgomery	James	-----11	1.51	1	Montgomery	Thomas	01JUL02	3.17	1
Montgomery	Jane	22NOV88	1.07	F2	Montgomery	Thomas	25JUN03	2.20	1
Montgomery	Jane	23JUN89	5.08	F2	Montgomery	Thomas	23JUL04	1.12	11
Montgomery	Jane	09MAY95	2.08	F	Montgomery	Thomas	31MAY05	2.21	12
Montgomery	Jane	28JUN96	1.09	F	One lot in Standford				
Montgomery	Jenny	10MAY97	3.21	F	Montgomery	Thomas	07AUG06	2.26	12
Montgomery	Jean	21MAY99	1.24	F	One lott in Standford				
Montgomery	Ginney	19JUN00	2.19	F	Montgomery	Thomas	15JUN07	2.31	1
Montgomery	Ginny	10AUG01	2.21	F	Montgomery	Thomas	17JUN08	1.24	1
Montgomery	Jenny	23AUG02	2.23	F	Montgomery	Thomas	24AUG09	2.22	21
Montgomery	Jenny	16JUN03	3.17	F	Montgomery	Thomas	-----11	1.49	1

surname	name	date	bk.pg	TM	surname	name	date	bk.pg	TM
MONTGOMERY					Moor	Alexander	02JUN97	3.21	1
Montgomery	Wm. Colonel	27JUN87	2.05	1	Moore	Alexander	18JUL05	2.23	1
Montgomery	William Sqr	27JUN87	2.05	1	Moore	Amy	22AUG93	3.09	F
Montgomery	William	27JUN87	2.05	1	Moore	Anna	09MAY94	2.08	F
Montgomery	William	30JUN87	3.07	1	Moore	Amy	28APR95	3.11	F
Montgomery	William	28OCT88	1.06	1	More	Ann	19JUN06	1.15	F1
Montgomery	William	22NOV88	1.07	1	More	Anne	06JUN07	1.17	F1
Montgomery	William	16JUN89	5.08	1	Moor	Austin	23JUN00	2.19	1
Montgomery	William	29JUN89	5.08	1	Moore	Austin	03JUN01	2.18	1
Montgomery	William	25JUL89	2.09	1	Moore	Austin	05AUG02	2.22	1
Montgomery	William	03APR90	2.05	11	Moore	Austin	16JUL03	3.18	1
Montgomery	William Jr	30MAR90	2.05	1	Moor	Daniel	21JUL00	2.20	1
Montgomery	William	25MAR91	1.06	1	Moore	David	03JUN95	2.09	1
Montgomery	William	07SEP91	3.10	1	More	David	16JUN96	1.09	1
Montgomery	William	20SEP91	1.06	12	Moor	David	08APR97	3.19	1
Montgomery	William Sr	21OCT92	2.06	11	More	David	12JUN99	2.13	1
Montgomery	William Jr	21OCT92	2.06	1	More	David	21JUL00	1.09	1
Montgomery	William	19NOV92	3.12	1	More	David	23JUN01	1.11	1
Montgomery	William Sr	07AUG93	1.07	11	More	David	20JUN02	1.15	1
Montgomery	William	13AUG93	1.06	1	More	David	13JUN03	1.14	1
Montgomery	William	20APR94	3.13	1	More	David	01AUG04	1.13	1
Montgomery	William	23MAY94	1.06	11	More	David	29JUL05	1.13	1
Montgomery	William	09JUN94	1.12	1	More	David	30JUL06	1.16	11
Montgomery	William	09JUN94	1.06	1	More	David	04MAY07	1.16	11
Montgomery	William	-----95	1.09	1	More	David	10JUN08	1.23	11
Montgomery	William	13MAY95	2.09	1	Moore	David	13JUN09	2.21	1
Montgomery	William	13JUN95	2.20	1	Moore	Edward	13JUL87	1.04	1
Montgomery	William	13JUN95	2.21	1	Moore	Edward	11JUN89	6.08	1
Montgomery	Wm(heirs)	19MAR95	3.13	0	Moore	Edward	23JUN91	2.06	11
Montgomery	William	-----96	4.09	1	Moore	Edward	26MAY02	2.19	M1
Montgomery	William	15AUG96	1.08	1	Moore	Edward	11JUN03	3.16	M1
Montgomery	William	11JUN97	3.22	1	Moore	Edward	06AUG04	3.13	1
Montgomery	Wm(heirs)	08AUG97	1.17	0	Moore	Edward	17AUG05	3.26	1
Tax pd by Thomas Montgomery					Moore	Edward	11JUN07	2.23	1
Montgomery	William	01JUN99	1.25	11	Moore	Edward	-----08	2.18	1
Montgomery	William	04AUG00	2.22	11	More	Elener	21JUN09	2.21	F
Montgomery	William	30JUN01	2.19	1	Moore	Elener	-----11	1.48	F1
Montgomery	William	02AUG02	2.22	1	Moore	Elisha	11JUN94	2.10	1
Montgomery	William	30JUL04	2.14	1	Moore	Elisha	15APR95	3.12	1
Montgomery	William	12NOV05	3.26	1	Moore	Elisha	11MAY96	2.11	1
Montgomery	William	26AUG06	3.25	1	Moore	Elisha	26MAY97	1.15	1
Montgomery	William	13JUN07	2.23	M1	Moore	Elisha	10AUG02	3.19	1
Montgomery	William	01AUG07	2.25	1	Moore	Elisha	06AUG03	3.19	1
Montgomery	William	17JUN08	1.23	1	Moore	Elisha	15AUG04	3.14	1
Montgomery	William	23AUG08	2.20	1	Moore	Elisha	21JUN05	3.24	1
Montgomery	William	07AUG09	1.25	1	Moore	Elisha	31JUL06	3.24	1
Montgomery	William	-----11	1.50	1	More	George	24AUG87	1.04	1
Paid tax for Nathan Huston					Moore	George	11JUN89	6.08	1
MOODY					Moore	George	13MAY90	1.07	1
Moody	Alexander	13AUG02	3.19	1	Moore	George	17APR94	2.08	1
Moody	Alexander	25JUL03	2.21	1	Moore	George	02JUN96	2.12	1
Moody	Alexader	25JUL04	4.16	1	Moore	George	20JUN97	1.16	1
Moody	Alexander	16MAY05	2.21	1	Moor	George	02JUL99	1.27	1
Moody	Alexander	16JUL06	2.23	1	Moore	George	04JUL00	3.20	1
Moody	Alexander	13AUG07	2.25	1	Moor	George	31JUL00	2.21	1
Moody	Alexander	24AUG08	2.20	1	Moore	George	06MAY01	3.21	1
Moody	Alexander	09JUN09	1.22	1	Moore	George	24JUL01	3.24	1
Moody	Alexander	-----11	1.54	1	Moore	George	14JUN02	2.21	1
Moody	Andrew	09AUG04	3.14	1	Moore	George	07AUG02	3.19	1
Moody	Blanks	-----96	4.10	11	Moore	George	28JUL03	3.17	1
Moody	Judith	18JUN95	2.09	F	Moore	George	29JUL03	2.21	1
Moody	Judith	10JUN96	1.08	F	Moore	George	03MAY04	3.13	1
Moody	William	21APR90	2.05	1	Moore	George	27JUN04	4.16	1
Mudy	William	27APR91	3.09	1	Moore	George	19JUN05	3.24	1
Moody	William	02OCT92	3.12	1	Moore	George	24AUG05	3.27	11
Moody	William	06AUG93	1.06	1	Moore	George	05JUL06	3.22	1
Moody	William	17MAR94	1.06	1	Moore	George	11JUN07	2.23	1
MOONEY					Moore	George	-----08	2.18	1
Moony	William	19AUG93	3.08	1	Moore	George	27JUN09	1.23	1
Mooney	William	18MAR95	3.13	1	Moore	George	-----11	1.55	1
MOORE					Moore	Henry	03JUN95	2.09	1
Moore	Abel	24AUG05	3.27	1	More	Henry	26JUN96	1.09	1

surname	name	date	bk.pg	TM	surname	name	date	bk.pg	TM
Moor	Henry	08APR97	3.19	1	Moore	Obediah	05JUN97	1.16	1
More	Henry	30JUN03	1.15	1	Moore	Obediah	19JUN00	3.18	1
More	Henry	20JUN04	1.12	1	Moore	Obediah	17JUN01	3.22	1
Moore	Isaac	27MAY02	2.20	M1	Moore	Obediah	02AUG02	2.22	1
Moore	Isaac	21JUL03	3.18	M1	Moore	Obediah H.	25JUL03	3.18	1
Moore	Isaac	19MAY05	3.23	M2	Moore	Obediah	06AUG04	3.14	1
Moore	Jacob	05AUG02	2.22	1	Moore	Obediah	06AUG05	3.25	1
Moore	Jacob	16JUL03	3.18	1	Moore	Obediah	20AUG06	3.25	1
Moore	Jacob	29JUL06	3.06		Moore	Obediah	15AUG09	1.26	1
	Tax paid by Jacob Carpenter				Moore	Robert	25JUN87	2.05	1
Moore	James	15JUL07	2.24	1	Moore	Robert	05NOV88	1.06	1
Moore	James	-----08	2.19	1	Moore	Robert	30JUN89	5.08	1
Moore	John	15JUN97	1.15	1	Moor	Robert	16MAY90	2.05	1
Moore	John	20MAY99	3.13	1	Moore	Robert	25MAR91	1.06	1
More	John	04MAY07	1.16	1	Moore	Robert	19OCT92	2.06	1
Moore	John	-----11	1.48	1	More	Robert	27AUG93	1.06	1
Moore	Jonathan	18OCT92	1.09	1	More	Robert	18MAY94	1.06	1
Moore	Jonathan	24AUG93	3.09	1	Moore	Robert	03JUN95	2.21	1
Moore	Jonathan	13APR94	2.08	1	Moor	Robert	01JUL96	1.09	1
Moore	Jonathan	22APR95	3.11	1	Moor	Robert	12APR97	3.20	1
Moore	Jonathan	02JUN96	2.12	1	Moor	Robert	14MAY99	1.23	1
Moore	Jonathan	10JUL97	1.17	1	Moor	Robert	31MAY00	2.18	1
Moor	Jonathan	03JUN99	1.26	1	Moore	Robert	22JUL01	2.19	1
Moor	Jonathan	21JUL00	2.20	1	More	Robert	10JUN02	1.14	1
Moore	Jonathan	31JUL01	2.20	1	More	Robert	30JUN03	1.15	1
Moore	Jonathen	02AUG02	2.22	1	More	Robert	06AUG04	1.13	1
Moore	Jonathan	12JUL03	3.18	1	More	Robert	15JUN05	1.12	11
Moore	Jonithan	11JUN04	4.15	1	Moore	Samuel	23MAY89	6.05	1
Moore	Jonathen	19MAY05	3.23	1	Moore	Samuel	14MAY90	1.07	1
Moore	Jonathan	18JUL06	3.22	1	Moore	Samuel	30MAR91	2.07	1
Moore	Jonathan	20JUN07	2.23	1	Moore	Samuel	25SEP92	1.08	1
Moore	Jonathen	-----08	2.19	1	Moore	Samuel	06OCT92	1.08	1
Moore	Jonathan	10JUL09	1.25	1	Moore	Samuel	13AUG93	3.07	1
Moore	Joseph	27JUN87	2.05	1	Moore	Samuel	24AUG93	3.08	1
Moore	Joseph Jr	27JUN87	2.05	1	Moore	Samuel	09MAY94	2.08	1
Moor	Joseph	04AUG99	1.28	1	Moore	Samuel	23MAY94	2.09	1
Moor	Joseph	10JUN00	2.19	12	Moore	Samuel	14APR95	3.12	1
Moore	Joseph	24JUL01	2.20	11	Moore	Samuel	26APR95	3.11	1
More	Joseph	16JUN02	1.14	11	Moore	Samuel	02JUN96	2.12	1
More	Joseph	04JUL03	1.15	12	Moore	Samuel	05JUL96	2.13	1
Moore	Joseph	30JUL04	2.14	1	Moore	Samuel	05JUN97	1.16	1
More	Joseph	19JUN05	1.13	1	Moore	Samuel	10JUL97	1.17	1
More	Joseph	14JUL06	1.15	11	Moore	Samuel	25MAY99	3.13	1
More	Joseph	29JUN07	1.18	1	Moor	Samuel	03JUN99	1.25	1
More	Joseph	27APR08	1.21	11	Moore	Samuel	18JUN00	3.18	1
Moore	Joshua	22AUG93	3.09	1	Moore	Samuel	30JUN00	3.20	1
Moore	Joshua	02JUN96	2.12	1	Moore	Samuel	18MAY01	3.21	1
Moore	Joshua	10JUL97	1.17	1	Moore	Samuel	29MAY01	3.25	1
Moor	Joshua	02JUL99	1.27	1	Moore	Samuel	31JUL01	2.20	1
Moor	Joshua	21JUL00	2.20	1	Moore	Samuel	14JUN02	2.21	1
Moore	Joshua	13JUL01	3.24	1	Moore	Samuel	28JUL02	3.18	1
Moore	Joshua	26MAY02	2.19	1	Moore	Samuel	10AUG02	3.19	1
Moore	Joshua	30MAY03	3.16	1	Moore	Samuel	12JUL03	3.18	1
Moore	Joshua	22AUG04	3.14	1	Moore	Samuel	25JUL03	2.21	1
Moore	Joshua	08JUL05	3.25	1	Moore	Samuel	29JUL03	2.21	1
Moore	Josha	04AUG06	3.24	1	Moore	Samuel	09AUG03	2.22	1
Moore	Mordicai	31JUL01	2.20	1	Moore	Samuel	03MAY04	3.13	1
Moore	Mordicai	21JUL02	2.21	1	Moore	Samuel	25JUN04	4.16	1
Moore	Mordeca	12JUN04	4.15	1	Moore	Samuel	23JUL04	4.16	1
Moore	Mordecai	27JUN05	2.22	1	Moore	Samuel	19MAY05	3.23	1
Moore	Mordecai	15AUG06	2.26	1	Moore	Samuel	28JUN05	2.22	1
Moore	Mordicai	17AUG07	2.26	1	Moore	Samuel	18JUL05	2.23	1
Moore	Mordicai	-----08	2.20	1	Moore	Samuel	20MAY06	2.23	1
Moore	Mordicai	-----11	1.56	1	Moore	Samuel	18JUL06	2.23	1
Moore	Obediah H.	12JUN89	6.05	1	Moore	Samuel	28JUL06	2.24	1
Moor	Obadiah	26JUN99	1.27	1	Moore	Samuel	09JUN07	2.22	1
Moore	Obediah	15APR90	1.06	1	Moore	Samuel	15JUL07	2.24	1
Moore	Obediah	14AUG93	3.08	1	Moore	Samuel	22JUL07	2.24	1
Moore	Obediah	23MAY94	2.09	1	Moore	Samuel	-----08	2.19	1
Moore	Obediah	14APR95	3.12	1	Moore	Samuel	-----08	2.19	1
Moore	Obediah	13JUL96	2.13	1	More	Samuel	17JUN08	1.23	1
					Moore	Samuel	13MAY09	1.22	1

surname	name	date	bk.pg	TM	surname	name	date	bk.pg	TM
Moore	Samuel	29MAY09	2.20	1	Morris	Edward	22AUG06	3.25	1
Moore	Samuel	10JUL09	1.25	1	Moriss	Isaac	28MAY94	2.09	1
Moore	Samuel	-----11	1.47	1	Morris	Jesse	27JUN87	2.05	1
Moore	Samuel	-----11	1.46	1	Morris	Jesse	13AUG89	2.09	1
Moor	Thomas	31MAY00	2.19	1	Morris	Jesse	13SEP91	3.11	1
Moore	William Sr	27JUN87	2.05	1	Morris	John	27APR91	3.09	1
More	Will	24AUG87	1.04	1	Morris	John	17AUG93	3.08	1
Moore	William	11JUN89	6.08	1	Morris	John	-----95	1.10	1
Moore	William	23JUN91	2.06	1	Morres	John	12JUN00	1.08	1
Moore	William	18OCT92	1.08	1	Morrice	John	01JUN01	1.10	1
Moore	William	19AUG93	3.08	1	Morris	John	22AUG06	3.25	1
Moore	William	24AUG93	3.09	1	Morris	John	-----11	1.53	
Moore	William	17APR94	2.09	1	Failed to give in his list last y				
Moore	William	09MAY94	2.08	1	MORRISON				
Moore	William	27APR95	3.11	1	Morrison	David	11JUN89	6.05	1
Moore	William	02JUN96	2.12	1	Morison	David	30APR90	2.06	1
Moore	William	30JUN97	1.16	1	Morrison	David	25MAR91	1.06	1
Moor	William	24MAY99	1.24	1	Morrison	David	08OCT92	2.06	1
Moor	William	03JUN99	1.25	1	Morison	David	19AUG93	1.06	11
Moor	William	20JUN00	2.19	11	Morison	David	29MAY94	1.06	11
Moore	William	31JUL01	2.20	11	Morrison	David	26MAY95	2.09	11
Moore	William	14JUN02	2.21	1	Morrison	David	26JUN95	2.21	1
Moore	William	12JUL03	3.18	11	Morison	David	15JUN96	1.09	11
Moore	William	18JUN04	2.13	11	Morrison	David	06APR97	3.21	11
Moore	William	19MAY05	3.23	12	Morrison	Eleazar	04JUN04	4.15	1
Moore	William	14JUL06	3.22	12	Morrison	Ezra	14MAY90	1.07	1
Moore	William	29JUL06	3.23	1	Morrison	Ezra	01AUG91	2.06	1
Moore	William	13JUN07	2.23	1	Morrison	Ezra	13SEP92	1.08	1
Moore	William	-----08	2.18	1	Morrisson	Ezra	22AUG93	3.08	1
Moore	William	26JUN09	1.23	1	Morrison	Ezra	10MAY94	2.08	1
Moore	William	-----11	1.53	12	Morrison	Ezra	22JUN95	3.12	1
MORDOCK					Morrison	Ezra	06JUL96	2.13	1
Mordock	David	03OCT92	2.06	1	Paid tax for John Carpenter				
MOREHEAD					Morrison	Ezra	31MAY97	1.14	1
Morehead	Abner	19JUN04	1.12	1	Morrison	Ezra	13MAY99	3.12	1
Morehead	Abner	12JUN05	1.12	1	Morrison	Ezra	21JUN00	3.19	1
Morehead	Abner	12JUN07	1.17	1	Morrison	Ezra	17JUN01	3.22	11
Morehead	Abner	04MAY08	1.22	1	Morrison	Ezra	27JUL02	3.18	1
Morehead	Abner	30MAY09	2.20	1	Morrison	Ezra	11AUG03	2.22	1
Muirhead	Abner	-----11	1.47	1	Morrison	Ezra	28JUN05	2.22	1
Moorhead	Daniel	30JUN96	1.08	1	Morrison	Ezra	01AUG06	2.24	1
Muirhead	Daniel	14APR97	3.20	1	Morrison	Ezra	22AUG07	2.26	1
Morehead	Daniel	30MAY99	2.12	1	Morison	Ezra	-----08	2.18	1
Morehead	Daniel	19JUN00	1.09	1	Morrison	Ezra	13JUL09	1.25	1
Morehead	Daniel	23JUN03	1.15	11	Morrison	Ezra	-----11	1.53	12
Morehead	Daniel	19JUN04	1.12	1	Morrison	James	29APR95	3.11	0
Morehead	Daniel	12JUN05	1.12	1	Morrison	John	06NOV88	1.06	1
Morehead	Daniel	12JUN07	1.17	1	Morrison	John	07AUG89	5.09	1
Morehead	Daniel	04MAY08	1.22	1	Morison	John	31MAR90	2.06	1
Morehead	Daniel	30MAY09	2.20	1	Morrison	John	13APR91	1.06	1
Muerhead	Daniel	-----11	1.47	1	Morrison	John	28MAY91	3.10	1
MORGAN					Morrison	John	09OCT92	2.06	11
Morgan	Elizabeth	09JUL99	3.14	F	Morison	John	30AUG93	1.06	11
Morgain	Elizabeth	27JUN00	3.20	F	Morison	John	31MAY94	1.06	11
Morgan	John	01DEC88	1.07	1	Morrison	John	09MAY95	2.08	12
Morgan	Joseph	16MAY97	1.15	1	Morrison	Michael	04DEC92	3.13	1
Morgan	Joseph	09JUL99	3.14	1	Morrison	Thomas	29APR95	3.11	0
Morgan	Joseph	17JUL00	2.20	1	MORROW				
Morgan	Joseph	19APR01	2.18	1	Morrow	Thomas	14AUG00	3.21	1
Morgan	Joseph	14JUL02	3.17	1	MOSELY				
Morgan	William	16MAY97	1.15	1	Mosely	Micajah	-----11	1.46	1
MORRICK					Mosley	Robert	-----93	2.03	1
Moirick	Andrew	23JUL05	2.23	1	Mosley	Thomas	-----93	2.03	1
Morrick	Andrew	15JUL06	2.23	1	MOSS				
MORRIS					Moss	Samuel	11AUG02	3.19	1
Moris	Andrew	28JUN96	1.08	1	Moss	Sheldon	-----11	1.46	1
Morris	Andrew	22JUN97	1.17	1	MOTESED				
Morris	Benjamin	27MAY07	1.16	1	Motesed	Nathaniel	03AUG89	5.08	1
Morris	Benjamin	22APR08	1.21	1	MOUNTS				
Morris	Benjamin	30JUN09	2.21	1	Mounce	Mary	05JUL87	3.07	F2
Morris	Benjamin	-----11	1.46	1	Mounce	Mary	28MAY94	3.15	F
Morris	Cleburn	14JUN05	3.24	1	Mounce	Mathias	07MAY91	3.09	1

surname	name	date	bk.pg	TM	surname	name	date	bk.pg	TM
Mounce	Matthias	19NOV92	3.12	1	Murphy	Catherine	25JUL03	3.18	F
Mounce	Matthias	20APR94	3.13	1	Murphy	Kitty	06AUG04	3.13	F
Mounce	Matthias	-----95	1.09	1	Murphy	Catty	06AUG05	3.25	F1
Mounce	Matthias	-----96	4.09	1	Murphy	Catty	04AUG06	3.24	F1
Mounts	Mathias	08JUN05	2.21	1	Murphy	Peter	05JUL96	2.13	1
Mounts	Mathias	19MAY06	2.23	1	Murphy	Peter	13JUL97	1.17	1
Mounts	Mathias	22JUL07	2.24	1	Murphey	Peter	29JUL00	2.21	1
Mounce	Smith	19APR91	3.09	1	Murphy	Peter	29JUL01	3.23	1
Mounce	Smith	19NOV92	3.12	1	Murphey	Peter	28JUL02	3.18	1
Mounce	Smith	28MAY94	3.15	1	Murphy	Richard	28MAY96	2.12	1
Mounce	Smith	-----95	1.09	11	Murphy	Richard	21JUN97	1.15	1
Mounce	Smith	-----96	4.09	1	Murphy	Richard	16MAY99	3.13	11
MOURTON					Murphey	Richard	29JUL00	2.21	1
Mourton	William	29MAY09	2.20	1	Murphy	Richard	18JUN01	3.22	1
MOUSER					Murphey	Richard	28JUL02	3.18	1
Mouser	Frederick	28JUN99	3.14	1	Murphey	Richard	11AUG03	2.22	1
MULHY					Murphey	Richard	05APR04	4.15	1
Mulhy	John	07APR97	3.21	1	Murphy	Richard	21JUN05	3.24	1
MULLICAN					Murphey	Richard	29JUL06	3.23	1
Mullican	William	14AUG05	3.26	1	Murphy	Richard	22AUG07	2.26	1
Mullican	William	22AUG06	3.25	1	Murphy	Richard	12JUL09	1.25	1
MULLINS					Murphy	Richard	-----11	1.55	1
Mullin	Samuel	-----96	4.10	1	Murphy	Rody	02JUN08	1.23	0
MULVANEY					Murphy	Stephen	27JUN99	1.27	1
Mulvaney	John	29JUN04	4.16	1	Murphey	Stephen	24JUL00	2.20	1
Mulveny	John	07AUG06	2.25	1	Murphy	Stephen	28JUL01	3.23	1
MUMFORD					Murphey	Stephen	10AUG02	2.23	1
Mumford	William	-----11	1.54	1	Murfey	Thomas	12SEP91	3.10	1
MUNRONY					Murphy	Thomas	26JUL96	1.09	1
Munrony	Selvestor	26JUN87	1.03	1	Murphy	Thomas	29MAY97	3.21	1
MURPHY					Murphy	Thomas	27JUN99	1.27	1
Murphy	Daniel	20MAY96	2.11	1	Murphey	Thomas	24JUL00	2.20	1
Murphy	Daniel	21APR97	3.22	1	Murphy	Thomas	28JUL01	3.23	1
Murphy	Daniel	28MAY99	1.24	1	Murphey	Thomas	10AUG02	2.23	1
Murphy	Edward	13JUN97	3.22	1	Murphy	Thomas	25JUL03	3.18	1
Murphey	Gabriel	14JUL07	2.24	1	Murphy	Thomas	06AUG04	3.13	1
Murphy	Gabriel	-----08	2.19	1	Murphy	Thomas	06AUG05	3.25	1
Murphey	Gabriel	29JUN09	1.23	1	Murphy	Thomas	21AUG06	3.25	1
Murphy	Gabriel	-----11	1.55	1	Murphy	Thomas	-----11	1.47	1
Murphy	John	05JUL87	3.07	1	Murphy	William	26JUL05	1.13	1
Murphey	John	06AUG89	2.09	1	Murphy	William	16JUL06	1.16	1
Murfey	John	24JUN91	3.10	1	Murphy	William	02JUL07	1.15	1
Murphy	John	27NOV92	3.12	1	Murphy	William	02JUN08	1.23	1
Murphy	John	20APR94	3.13	1	Murphy	William	30MAY09	2.20	1
Murphy	John(inval)	-----95	1.09	1	Murphy	William	-----11	1.47	1
Murphey	John	-----96	4.10	1	Murphey	Zephaniah	27JUN89	2.08	1
Murphy	John	05JUL96	2.13	1	MURRELL				
Murphy	John	27JUN99	1.27	1	Murell	George	02OCT87	1.06	1
Murphy	John	15JUL99	1.28	11	Murral	George	23MAY89	6.05	1
Murphey	John	24JUN00	2.19	1	Murrel	George	14MAY90	1.07	1
Exempt from County leavy					Murrel	George	30MAR91	2.07	1
Murphy	John	03JUN01	2.18	01	Murril	George	06AUG93	3.08	1
Exempt from leavy					Murrel	George	24MAY94	2.10	1
Murfy	John	30JUN02	1.15	11	Murrel	George	19MAY95	3.11	1
Murphy	John	07JUL03	1.16	1	Murrel	George	05JUL96	2.13	1
Murphy	John	09JUL04	2.13	00	Murrel	George	22JUN97	1.16	1
Murphy	John	26JUL05	1.13	00	Murrell	George	06JUN99	1.26	1
Murphy	John	14JUL06	1.16	0	Murrell	George	29JUL00	2.21	1
Free of taxes					Murrel	George	19JUL01	3.24	1
Murphy	John	02JUL07	1.15	11	Murell	George	09JUN02	2.21	11
Murphy	John	02JUN08	1.23	00	Murrell	George	15JUN03	3.16	11
Murphy	John	30MAY09	2.20	0	Murrel	George	31JUL04	3.13	11
Exempt from county levy					Murrel	George	21JUN05	3.24	11
Murphy	John	-----11	1.47	M1	Murrel	George	21JUL06	3.23	11
Murphy	Joseph	21JUN97	1.15	1	Murrell	George	18AUG06	3.08	
Murphey	Joseph	29JUL00	2.21	1	Adm. for Adam (decd) Carpenter				
Murphy	Joseph	19JUL01	3.24	1	Murrel	George	15JUL07	2.24	11
Murphy	Joseph	22AUG07	2.26	1	Murell	George	-----08	2.18	11
Murphy	Kitty	27JUN99	1.27	F	Murrell	George	02AUG08	2.15	
Murphey	Catherine	24JUL00	2.20	F	Adm. estate of Nathan Huston				
Murphy	Katty	28JUL01	3.23	F	Murrell	George	11JUL09	1.25	1
Murphey	Katty	10AUG02	2.23	F	Murrell	George	-----11	1.52	21

surname	name	date	bk.pg	TM	surname	name	date	bk.pg	TM
Murrel	James	15JUL07	2.24	1	Moyers	Jacob	28JUL04	4.16	1
Murell	James	-----08	2.18	1	Moyers	Jacob	28JUL04	4.16	1
Murrell	James	11JUL09	1.25	1	Mires	Jacob	09AUG05	2.24	1
Murrell	James	-----11	1.52	1	Mires	Jacob	12AUG06	2.26	11
Modral	Robert	20AUG93	1.06	1	Myres	Jacob	13AUG07	2.25	2
MURREN					Myres	Jacob	24AUG08	2.20	11
Murren	Michael	27NOV88	1.07	1	Myers	Jacob	22JUN09	1.23	2
Murren	Michael	02JUL89	2.08	1	Myers	Jacob	-----11	1.54	2
Murrin	Michael	23MAY94	3.14	1	Myers	John	16AUG93	3.08	11
Murren	Michael	-----95	1.10	1	Myers	John	23APR94	2.09	1
Murren	Mical	-----97	2.03	1	Myers	John	27MAR95	3.12	1
Murren	Michael	30MAY99	2.12	1	Myers	Lewis	13JUL87	1.03	1
Murren	Michael	06JUN00	1.07	1	Myers	Lewis	18APR89	6.05	1
Murren	Michael	29MAY01	1.09	1	Myers	Lewis	03APR90	1.06	1
Murren	Michael	18JUN02	1.14	1	Myers	Lewis	14MAY91	2.06	1
Murren	Michael	16JUN03	1.14	1	Myers	Lewis	06OCT92	1.08	1
Murron	Michael	13JUN04	1.12	1	Myors	Lewis	-----93	2.03	1
MURRY					Myres	Lewis	16AUG93	3.08	1
Murry	Capel	26NOV92	3.12	1	Myors	Lewis	23APR94	3.13	1
Murry	James	25MAY07	1.16	1	Myers	Lewis	-----95	1.09	1
MUSICK					Myers	Lewis	-----96	4.10	1
Musick	Thomas	20MAY95	2.09	1	Myers	Mary	20JUN96	2.12	F
MYERS					Myres	Mary	13MAY97	1.15	F
Mires	Benjamin	17JUL02	3.17	1	Myres	Mecheal	08JUL01	3.23	1
Mi-ers	Benjamin	30MAY03	2.20	1	Mires	Michael	17JUL02	3.17	1
Moyers	Benjamin	27JUL04	4.16	1	Mires	Michael	22JUN03	2.20	1
Mires	Benjamin	23JUL05	2.23	1	Moyers	Michael	28JUL04	4.16	1
Mires	Benjamin	17JUL06	2.24	1	Myers	Michiel	23JUL05	2.23	1
Mtres	Benjamin	13AUG07	2.25	1	Mires	Michael	17JUL06	2.23	1
Myres	Benjamin	-----08	2.20	1	Guardian for Henry Pope				
Myers	Benjamin	22JUN09	1.23	1	Myres	Michael	13AUG07	2.26	1
Myers	Benjamin	-----11	1.55	1	Myers	Michael	24AUG08	2.20	1
Myers	Christopher	22MAY97	3.21	1	Myers	Michael	22JUN09	1.23	1
Moyers	Christopher	29MAY99	2.12	1	Myers	Michael	-----11	1.54	1
Mires	Christopher	31MAY00	2.18	1	Myers	Michael	-----11	1.54	1
Moyers	Christopher	04JUN02	1.13	1	Myers	Michael	-----11	1.54	1
Myers	David	27MAR95	3.13	1	Myres	Nicholas	28JUN97	1.15	1
Myers	David	20JUN96	2.12	1	One lot in Danville				
Myers	David	19APR97	3.20	1	NANSTEEL				
Myers	David	29JUN99	3.14	1	Nansteel	Andrew	17JUL00	2.23	1
Myers	David	28JUN00	3.20	1	Nansteel	Andrew	12JUL02	3.20	1
Myres	David	08JUL01	3.23	1	Nansteel	Andrew	22JUN03	2.23	1
Mires	David	17JUL02	3.17	1	Nansteel	Andrew	23JUL05	2.24	1
Mires	David	17JUN03	2.20	1	Nansteel	Andrew	16JUL06	2.27	1
Moyers	David	28JUL04	4.16	1	NASH				
Mires	David	23JUL05	2.23	1	Nash	Arthur	12JUN95	2.10	1
Mires	David	30MAY06	2.23	1	Nash	Arthur	06JUN96	1.09	1
Myres	David	01AUG07	2.25	1	Nash	Arthur	02MAY97	3.23	1
Myres	David	-----08	2.21	1	Nash	Arthur	28MAY99	1.28	1
Myers	David	10JUN09	1.22	1	Nash	Arthur	08JUL00	2.23	1
Myers	David	-----11	1.54	1	Nash	Arthur	24JUN01	2.21	1
Myers	Jacob	21AUG87	1.04	1	Nash	Arthur	07JUN02	3.20	1
Myers	Jacob	08JUN89	6.05	1	Nash	Arthur	20JUN03	2.23	1
Myers	Jacob	08JUN89	6.05	1	Nash	Arthur	26JUN04	1.13	1
Thomas Buckner listed also					Nash	Arthur	06AUG05	2.24	1
Myers	Jacob	03APR90	1.06	1	Nash	Arthur	19AUG06	2.27	1
Myers	Jacob Jr	03APR90	1.06	1	Nash	Arthur	30JUL07	2.02	1
Myers	Jacob Jr	14MAY91	2.06	1	Nash	Arthur	17JUN08	1.25	1
Myers	Jacob	18OCT92	1.08	1	Nash	Arthur	23AUG09	2.23	1
Myers	Jacob	16AUG93	3.08	1	Nash	Arthur	-----11	1.57	0
Myers	Jacob Jr	23APR94	2.09	11	Nash	Arthur B.	04JUN00	2.22	M1
Myers	Jacob	27MAR95	3.13	2	Nash	Arthur B.	04JUN01	2.21	1
Myers	Jacob	03AUG96	2.13	1	Nash	Arthur B.	17JUN03	3.19	1
Myers	Jacob	02MAY97	1.14	1	Nash	Arthur B.	30JUL04	2.15	1
Moyers	Jacob	29MAY99	2.12	1	Nash	Arthur B.	19AUG05	3.27	1
Myres	Jacob	03JUL99	3.14	1	Nash	John	12JUL87	3.07	1
Mires	Jacob	31MAY00	2.18	1	Nash	John	17MAY94	1.07	1
Myers	Jacob	30JUN00	3.20	1	Nash	John	12JUN95	2.09	1
Moyers	Jacob	11JUN01	1.11	1	Nash	John	20JUN96	1.09	1
Myres	Jacob	08JUL01	3.23	1	Nash	John	09AUG97	3.23	1
Mires	Jacob	13AUG02	3.19	1	Nash	John	24MAY99	3.15	1
Mires	Jacob	22JUN03	2.20	1	Nash	John	04JUL00	3.22	1

surname	name	date	bk.pg	TM	surname	name	date	bk.pg	TM
Nash	Marvel	14JUN87	2.06	1	Neal	John	01AUG04	2.15	1
Nash	Marvill	18NOV88	1.07	1	Neel	John	01AUG04	1.14	1
Nash	Marvill	16JUN89	5.09	1	Neel	Pallace	20JUN96	1.09	1
Nash	Marvel	27MAY90	2.06	11	Neel	Paleres	10MAY97	3.23	1
Nash	Marvel	25MAR91	1.06	12	Neel	Pallas	29JUN99	1.28	1
Nash	Marvel	23OCT92	2.06	12	Neel	Palles	25JUN00	2.22	1
Nash	Marvel	03AUG93	1.07	11	Neele	Rudolph	18JUN03	3.19	11
Nash	Marvel	12MAY94	1.07	11	Neal	Randolph	01AUG04	2.15	11
Nash	Marvel	12MAY95	2.10	1	Neal	Thomas	-----93	2.04	1
Nash	Marvel	21JUN96	1.09	1	Neal	William	14JUN87	2.06	1
Nash	Marvel	13JUN97	3.23	1	Neal	William	14NOV88	1.07	1
Nash	Marvel	14JUN97	3.23	1	Neel	William	23JUN89	5.09	1
Nash	Marvel	21MAY99	1.28	11	Neall	William	31MAY90	2.06	1
Nash	Marvel	24MAY99	3.15	1	Niel	William	13APR91	1.06	1
Nash	Marvle Sr	04JUN00	2.22	1	Neale	William	25SEP92	1.09	1
Nash	Marvle Jr	04JUN00	2.22	1	Neel	William	22NOV92	2.07	11
Nash	Marvle Sr	24JUN01	2.21	1	Neel	William	10AUG93	1.07	11
Nash	Marvle Jr	22JUN01	2.21	1	Neale	William	13AUG93	3.09	1
Nash	Marvle	08JUL02	3.20	1	Neel	William	21MAY94	1.07	1
Nash	Marvill	23AUG02	2.24	1	Neel	William	12JUN94	2.10	1
Nash	Marvel Sr	17JUN03	3.19	1	Neel	William	03JUN95	2.10	11
Nash	Marvell Jr	04JUN03	3.19	1	Neel	William	20JUN96	1.09	11
Nash	Marvel	14JUN04	2.15	1	Neel	William	10MAY97	3.23	11
Nash	Marble	28JUN04	4.17	1	Neal	William	21MAY99	1.28	11
Nash	Marvel	09JUN05	1.13	1	Niele	William	10JUN00	2.22	11
Nash	Marvle Jr	02MAY05	2.24	1	NEALY				
Nash	Marvelle	24MAY06	2.27	1	Nealy	Isaac	23MAY89	6.05	1
Nash	Webb	19APR91	3.11	1	Neely	Isaac	13MAY90	1.07	1
Nash	William	26JUN87	2.06	1	Nealy	Isaac	03AUG91	2.07	1
Nash	William	19MAR90	2.06	1	Neely	Thomas	23MAR09	1.27	1
Nash	William	25MAR91	1.06	1	NEFF				
Nash	William	26SEP92	2.06	1	Neff	Adam	24JUN00	3.21	1
Nash	William	30AUG93	1.07	1	Naff	Adam	18MAY01	3.25	1
Mash	William	21MAY94	1.07	11	Niff	Adam	07AUG02	3.20	1
Nash	William	08JUN95	2.09	1	Niff	Adam	30JUL03	2.23	1
Nash	William	27JUN96	1.09	1	Neff	Adam	13JUN04	4.17	1
Nash	William	30JUN96	1.09	1	Niff	Adam	18JUN05	2.24	1
Nash	William	14JUN97	3.23	1	Niff	Adam	02AUG06	2.27	1
Nash	William	24MAY99	3.15	1	Neff	Adam	15JUL07	2.02	1
Nash	William	11JUL00	3.22	1	Neff	Adam	-----08	2.21	1
Nash	William	24JUL01	2.21	1	Neff	Adam	10JUL09	1.27	1
One lott in George Town					Neff	Francis	15JUN96	2.14	1
Nash	William	29JUL01	3.25	1	Neff	Francis	13MAY97	1.18	1
Nash	William	10JUN02	2.24	1	Neff	Francis	06JUL99	3.15	1
Nash	William	17JUN02	1.15	11	Neff	Francis	25JUN00	3.21	1
Nash	William	04JUN03	3.19	1	Naff	Francis	09MAY01	3.25	1
Nash	William	07APR04	4.17	11	Niff	Francis	11AUG02	3.20	1
Nash	William	14JUN05	3.27	11	Niff	Francis	30JUL03	2.23	1
Nash	William	24JUL06	3.26	11	Neff	George	08AUG93	3.09	1
NAUL					Neff	George	02JUL00	3.22	1
Nall	Martin	04JUN96	2.14	1	Neff	Henry	06SEP87	1.04	1
Naul	Martin	17MAY97	1.18	1	Neff	Henry	11MAY89	6.09	1
Naul	Martin	02JUL99	3.15	1	Naff	Henry	05APR90	1.07	1
NAYLOR					Neff	Henry	18MAR91	2.07	1
Naylor	George	08JUN89	6.05	1	Neff	Henry	24SEP92	1.09	1
NEAL					Neff	Henry	08AUG93	3.09	1
Neal	Barnard	18APR89	6.08	1	Neff	Henry	05MAY94	2.10	1
Neale	Bernard	16APR90	1.07	1	Neff	Henry	09APR95	3.13	1
Neel	Bryant	06AUG89	5.09	1	Neff	Henry	23JUN96	2.14	1
Neal	George	06OCT87	1.04	1	Neff	Henry	10MAY97	1.18	1
Neal	George	12JUN89	6.08	1	Neff	Henry	29MAY99	3.15	1
Neall	George	26MAR90	2.06	1	Neff	Henry	24JUN00	3.21	1
Neale	George	20APR91	2.07	1	Naff	Henry	06MAY01	3.25	1
Neale	George	05OCT92	1.09	1	Neff	John	25JUN00	3.21	1
Neel	George	12JUN94	2.10	1	Naff	John	07MAY01	3.25	1
Neel	George	28APR95	3.13	1	Niff	John	07AUG02	3.20	1
Neal	George	12MAY96	2.14	1	NELSON				
Neel	George	20JUN97	1.18	1	Nelson	Abraham Sr	16SEP91	3.12	1
Neel	George	05JUN99	1.28	1	Nelson	Abraham	16SEP91	3.12	1
Neel	George	27JUN00	2.23	1	Nelson	Abraham	-----96	4.11	1
Neal	George	22JUL01	3.25	1	Nelson	Abraham	-----97	2.03	1
Neele	John	17JUN03	3.19	1	Nelson	James	24MAY99	2.13	1

surname	name	date	bk.pg	TM	surname	name	date	bk.pg	TM
Nelson	James	-----08	2.21	1	NIFONG				
Nelson	Joal	-----08	2.21	1	Nifeong	Daniel	16MAY97	1.18	1
Nelson	Joel	13AUG04	2.15	1	Nifong	Daniel	03JUL99	3.15	1
Nelson	Joel	20MAY05	2.24	1	Nifong	Daniel	17JUN02	3.20	1
Nelson	Joel	16AUG09	2.23	1	NINO				
Nelson	Samuel	27JUN89	2.10	1	Nimo	David	16AUG05	3.27	1
Nelson	Samuel	02JUN91	3.12	1	Nino	David	23AUG06	3.26	1
Nelson	William	12JUL87	3.07	11	NOBLE				
Nelson	William	11JUL89	2.10	1	Noble	Darrell	25JUL89	2.10	1
Nelson	William	19APR91	3.11	1	Noble	Darrill	12SEP91	3.12	1
Nilson	William	04JUN95	1.10	1	Noble	Dirrel	16NOV92	3.13	1
NEVILL					Noble	Dorrell	16NOV92	3.15	1
Nevil	James	26JUN87	2.06	11	Noble	Dorrill	24MAY94	3.15	1
Nevil	James	18NOV88	1.07	11	Noble	Dorrell	-----95	1.10	1
Nevill	James	10AUG89	5.09	11	Noble	Dorril	-----96	4.11	1
Neavell	James	21APR90	2.06	11	Noble	James	02MAY95	3.13	1
Nevel	James	24OCT92	2.07	1	Noble	James	23JUN96	2.14	1
Navel	James	06AUG93	1.07	1	Noble	James	10AUG97	1.18	1
Navel	James	17MAY94	1.11	1	Noble	James	10JUL99	3.15	11
Navel	James	17MAY94	1.07	1	Knoble	James	09JUL00	3.16	11
Navel	James	22MAY95	2.10	1	Nobill	James	31JUL01	3.25	12
Navel	James	22MAY95	2.22	1	Noble	James	12JUL02	3.20	12
Navel	James	08JUN96	1.09	1	Noble	James	09AUG03	2.23	11
Navel	James	20APR97	3.23	1	Noble	James	06JUN04	4.17	1
Nevel	John	24OCT92	2.07	1	Noble	James	19JUN05	2.24	1
Navel	John	06AUG93	1.07	1	Noble	James	29JUL06	2.27	1
Navel	John	14MAY94	1.07	1	Noble	John	07AUG89	2.10	1
Navel	John	22MAY95	2.10	1	Noble	John	12SEP91	3.12	1
Navel	John	08JUN96	1.09	1	Noble	John	16NOV92	3.13	1
NEW					Noble	John	16NOV92	3.15	1
New	David	-----96	4.11	1	Noble	John	24MAY94	3.15	1
New	David	22APR97	3.23	1	Noble	John	-----95	1.10	1
New	John	19APR97	3.22	1	Noble	John	-----96	4.11	1
New	Pleasant	08JUN97	1.18	1	Noble	Mark	07AUG89	2.10	1
NEWAL					Noble	Mark	12SEP91	3.12	1
Newal	John	24JUL06	3.26	1	Noble	Mark	06JUN04	4.17	1
Newal	John	-----08	2.21	1	Noble	Mark	19JUN05	2.24	1
NEWCOMB					Noble	Mark	29JUL06	2.27	1
Newcom	Nelson	25MAY07	1.18	1	Noble	Thomas	09AUG03	2.23	1
Newcomb	William	-----11	1.57	1	Noble	Thomas	06JUN04	4.17	1
NEWLAND					Noble	Thomas	19JUN05	2.24	1
Newlin	Ezekel	24MAY94	3.15	1	Noble	Thomas	29JUL06	2.27	1
NEWMAN					Noble	William	25JUL89	2.10	1
Newman	Peter	29JUN99	1.28	1	Noble	William	12SEP91	3.12	1
NEWTON					Noble	William	16NOV92	3.13	1
Newton	James	-----96	4.11	2	Noble	William	16NOV92	3.15	1
Newton	Peter	07AUG89	2.10	1	Noble	William	24MAY94	3.15	1
NEZBIT					Noble	William	-----95	1.10	1
Nezbit	James	05AUG89	5.09	1	Noble	William	-----96	4.11	1
NICE					NOE				
Nice	Cornelius	07AUG06	2.27	11	Noc	James	26MAY99	3.15	1
NICHOLS					Knowe	James	20JUN00	3.16	1
Nickolds	Edmond	07JUL01	3.25	1	Noe	James	18MAY01	3.25	1
NICHOLSON					NOEL				
Nicholson	James	13AUG89	2.10	1	Noell	Archibald	24MAY94	3.15	1
Nicholson	James	16SEP91	3.12	1	Nowell	Archibald	-----95	1.10	1
Nicholson	James	16SEP91	3.12	1	Nowel	Archibald	-----96	4.11	1
Nicholison	James	24MAY94	3.15	1	Nowel	Berry	-----96	4.11	1
Nicholson	James	04JUN95	1.10	4	Nowell	Drusilla	13AUG89	2.10	F1
Nicleson	James	-----96	4.11	1	Nowel	Jusila	19APR91	3.11	F
Nicleson	James Jr	24MAY99	2.13	1	Nowel	Drusiler	16NOV92	3.15	F
Nickleson	James	13JUN00	1.08	1	Noell	Lucellar	24MAY94	3.15	F
Niceleson	James	30MAY01	1.11	1	Nowell	Lucilla	-----95	1.10	F
Nicoleson	Joseph	20JUN05	1.13	1	Nowell	Garret	25JUL89	2.10	1
Niceleson	Richard	19JUN99	2.13	1	Nowel	Garnet	19APR91	3.11	1
Niceleson	Sarah	03JUN01	1.11	F	Novel	Joel	-----96	4.11	1
NICKEN					Nowel	Joel	14JUN97	3.23	1
Niccun	John	21MAY99	1.28	1	Nowel	Joel	30MAY99	1.28	1
Nickum	Michael	19MAY91	2.07	1	Noel	Joel	08JUL00	2.23	1
Nicken	Peter	02AUG06	2.27	1	Noel	Joel	17JUL01	2.21	1
NICKLE					Noel	Joel	30JUN02	3.20	2
Nickle	Thomas	13MAY09	1.27	1	Noel	Joel	20JUN03	2.23	1

surname	name	date	bk.pg	TM	surname	name	date	bk.pg	TM
Noel	Joel	26JUL04	1.14	1	Norwell	Hugh	14JUL06	2.27	1
Noel	Joel	25JUL05	2.24	1	Nowvell	Hugh	14AUG07	2.02	1
Noel	Joel	16MAY06	2.27	1	Norvell	Hugh	-----08	2.21	1
Nowell	Joel	30JUL07	2.02	1	Norvell	Hugh	23MAY09	1.27	1
Noel	Joel	17JUN08	1.25	1	Norvell	Hugh	-----11	1.57	1
Noel	Joel	19AUG09	2.23	1	Narvill	Lipscomb	02JUN91	3.12	1
Noel	Joel	-----11	1.57	1	Norrel	Libscomb	16NOV92	3.13	1
Noell	John	24MAY94	3.15	1	Norrell	Lipscomb	16NOV92	3.15	1
Nowell	John	-----95	1.10	11	Norvell	Lipscomb	24MAY94	3.15	1
Knoel	John	29JUL05	1.10	1	Norvill	Lipscomb	-----95	1.10	1
Noel	Littleberry	14JUL06	2.27	1	Norvell	Lipscomb	-----96	4.11	1
Noel	Lott	20JUN03	2.23	1	Norvil	Thomas	24MAY99	3.15	1
Noel	Lot	26JUL04	1.14	1	NUGENT				
Noel	Lott	31JUL05	2.24	1	Newgent	Charles	28JUN00	3.22	M1
Noel	Lott	19MAY06	2.27	1	Nugen	Charles	22JUN03	2.23	1
Nowell	Lott	30JUL07	2.02	11	Nugent	Charles	28JUN04	4.17	1
Noel	Lott	17JUN08	1.25	11	Nugen	Edward	24APR06	2.27	1
Nowel	Lot	19AUG09	2.23	1	Newgan	Edward	16MAY97	1.18	1
Noel	Lott	-----11	1.57	1	Nugen	Edward	16JUL99	3.15	1
Nowell	Musker	27JUN89	2.10	1	Newgent	Edward	28JUN00	3.22	1
Nowel	Muscoes	16NOV92	3.15	1	Newgart	Edward	08JUL01	3.25	1
Noele	Musher	24MAY94	3.15	1	Nugen	Edward	14AUG02	3.20	1
Nowell	Musker	-----95	1.10	1	Nugen	Edward	20JUN03	2.23	1
Nowel	Musco	-----96	4.11	1	Nugent	Edward	28JUN04	4.17	1
NOLAND					Nugin	Edward	24JUL05	2.24	1
Noelin	Danel	25JUN00	2.22	1	Nugen	Edward	14AUG07	2.02	1
Noland	Daniel	25MAY01	3.25	1	Neugen	Edward	-----08	2.21	1
Nowlin	James	28MAR91	1.06	1	Nudgen	Edward	21MAY09	1.27	1
Nowlin	James	09MAY94	2.10	11	Neugent	Thomas	24MAY97	1.18	1
Nowlen	William	30MAY99	2.13	1	O'BANNON				
NORTHCUTT					Obannon	James	23MAY89	6.05	1
Northcut	Archibald	26JUN99	1.28	1	Obannon	James	14MAY90	1.08	1
Northcut	Archibald	25JUL00	2.23	1	Obannon	James	14SEP92	1.09	1
Northcut	Archilus	03AUG02	2.24	1	O'HARA				
Norcutt	Archibald	25JUN03	3.19	1	O'Hara	Patrick	11AUG01	2.21	1
Northcut	Archibald	06AUG04	3.15	1	Pd tax for Patrick Boyle				
Northcutt	Archillas	05AUG05	3.27	1	O'NEAL				
Northcut	Archillus	19AUG06	3.26	1	O'Neal	Barnett	04JUN01	2.21	1
Norcut	Arthur	-----11	1.57	1	O'Neal	Bryan	21JUN87	2.06	1
Norcut	Edward	-----11	1.57	1	O'Neal	Briant	22NOV88	1.07	1
Northcutt	John	14JUN05	3.27	11	O'Neall	Briant	27MAR90	2.06	1
Northcut	John	16JUL06	3.26	11	O'Neel	Bryant	06OCT92	2.07	1
Northcut	John	15JUL07	2.02	12	O'Neal	Bryant	03AUG93	1.07	1
Northcutt	John	-----08	2.21	12	O'Neel	Briant	12MAY94	1.07	1
Northcutt	John	10JUL09	1.27	1	O'Neal	Bryant	05APR91	1.06	1
Norcut	John	-----11	1.57	11	O'Neel	John	02AUG06	1.17	1
Northcut	Lewis	28JUN99	1.28	1	O'Neel	John	05MAY07	1.18	1
Northcut	Norvill	04AUG03	2.23	1	O'Neel	John	30APR08	1.27	1
Northcut	Ri--	31JUL02	3.20	1	O'Neel	John	14JUN09	2.24	1
Norcut	Bial	12JUN04	4.17	1	O'Neal	Thomas	19APR91	3.12	1
Northcutt	Urial	02AUG06	2.27	1	O'Neal	Thomas	07DEC92	3.15	1
Northcutt	Royall	-----08	2.21	1	OAKS				
Northcutt	Urial	10JUL09	1.27	1	Oakes	David	09JUN09	1.27	1
Norcut	Rial	-----11	1.57	1	OATMAN				
Northcut	Richard	26JUN99	1.28	1	Oateman	Joseph	14OCT92	3.15	1
Northcut	Richard	25JUL00	2.23	1	Oteman	Joseph	23MAY94	3.16	1
Northcut	Richard	27MAY01	3.25	2	Oatman	Joseph	-----95	1.11	1
Northcut	Richard	03AUG02	2.24	1	Oatman	Joseph	-----96	4.12	1
Norcutt	Richard	25JUN03	3.19	1	Oateman	Peter	14OCT92	3.15	1
Northcut	Richard	06AUG04	3.15	1	Oteman	Peter	23MAY94	3.16	1
Northcutt	Richard	05AUG05	3.27	1	Oatman	Peter	-----95	1.11	1
Northcut	Richard	04AUG06	3.26	1	OCAH				
Northcut	William	13MAY94	2.10	1	Ocah	Samuel	20JUN99	2.14	1
Northcut	William	13JUN96	2.14	11	ODAM				
Northcut	William	28JUN99	1.28	1	Odam	Willis	13AUG89	2.10	11
Northcut	William	24JUL00	2.23	1	OGLESBY				
Northcut	William	27MAY01	3.25	1	Oglesby	Samuel	31JUL07	2.27	1
Northcut	William	12AUG02	2.24	1	Oglesby	Samuel	30APR08	1.27	1
Norcut	William	-----11	1.57	1	Oglesby	Samuel	-----11	1.59	1
NORTON					OHLAR				
Norton	James	27MAR90	2.06	1	Ohlan	Reuben	-----11	1.59	1
NORVELL					OLEAHY				

surname	name	date	bk.pg	TM	surname	name	date	bk.pg	TM
Oleahy	Michael	14OCT92	3.15	1	Oshwall	Michael	30JUN87	1.04	1
OLIVER					Ozwell	Michael	18MAY91	2.07	1
Oliver	Drury	18MAY03	2.23	1	Ozwell	Michael	13SEP93	3.09	1
Oliver	Drury	27JUN04	4.17	1	Ozwald	Michael	28APR94	2.11	1
Ollever	William	-----97	2.03	1	OTT				
Oliver	William	30MAY99	2.14	1	Ott	Frederick	22JUL00	1.10	1
Oliver	William	19JUN00	1.10	1	Ott	Frederick	23JUN01	1.13	1
Oliver	William	10JUN01	1.12	1	Ott	Frederick	07JUN02	1.16	1
Oliver	William	08JUN02	1.16	1	Ott	Frederick	23JUN03	1.17	11
Oliver	William	20JUN03	1.17	1	Ott	Frederick	02AUG04	1.14	11
Oliver	William	26JUN04	4.17	11	Ott	Frederick	30JUL05	1.14	11
Oliver	William	03AUG04	2.16	1	Ott	Frederick	01AUG06	1.17	1
Oliver	William	28MAY07	1.18	1	Ott	Frederick	05MAY07	1.18	1
Oliver	William	10MAY09	2.24	1	Ott	Frederick	02APR08	1.25	1
Oliver	William	-----11	1.59	1	Ott	Henry	23JUN01	1.13	1
ONSTOTT					Ott	Henry	29JUN03	1.17	1
Onstot	Nicholas	23MAY94	3.16	1	Ott	Henry	02AUG04	1.14	1
Onstot	Nicholas	-----95	1.11	1	Ott	Henry	30JUL05	1.14	1
Onstat	Nicholass	-----96	4.11	1	Ott	Henry	01AUG06	1.17	1
ORIENT					OVERLEESE				
Orient	Frederick	14MAY91	2.07	1	Overlees	Coonrod	02AUG06	1.17	1
ORKEES					Overlees	Coonrod	25MAY07	1.18	1
Artgas	Henry	26AUG87	1.01	1	Overleese	Conrod	18APR08	1.26	1
Ortgiss	Henry	25MAY89	6.08	1	Overlees	Conrod	30JUN09	2.24	1
Ortgiss	Henry	10APR90	1.08	1	OWENS				
Ortgiss	Henry	18MAY91	2.07	11	Owens	Arthur	-----93	2.04	1
Ortgiz	Henry	09NOV92	1.09	11	Oins	David	03AUG04	1.14	1
Ortgiss	Henry	19AUG93	3.09	11	Owen	David	31JUL05	1.14	11
Oathis	Henry	16APR94	2.10	21	Owin	David	01AUG06	1.17	1
Orthis	Henry	28MAY95	3.13	21	Owen	David	26MAY07	1.18	1
Orkees	Henry	13JUN96	2.14	11	Owen	David	02APR08	1.25	11
Orthis	Henry	16MAY97	1.18	21	Owens	David	01JUL09	2.24	1
Ortkis	Henry	02JUL99	3.15	11	Owen	Elisha	30JUL05	1.14	1
Ortkies	Henry	26JUN00	3.22	2	Owin	Elisha	01AUG06	1.17	1
Orkies	Henry	19MAY01	3.26	2	Owen	Elisha	26MAY07	1.18	1
Orkees	Henry	16AUG02	3.20	2	Owen	Elisha	02APR08	1.25	1
Orkees	Henry	26JUL03	2.23	2	Owens	Elisha	01JUL09	2.24	1
Ortkies	Henry	25JUL04	4.17	11	Owens	James	31JUL07	2.27	1
Orkees	Henry	22JUL05	2.24	11	Owings	John	19JUN05	2.24	1
Orkees	Henry	16JUL06	2.28	1	Owings	John	29JUL06	2.28	1
Ortkus	Henry	14AUG07	2.27	1	Owin	Martin	01AUG06	1.17	1
Orkees	Henry	-----08	2.21	1	Owen	Martin	26MAY07	1.18	1
Paid taxes for Jacob Orkees(D)					Owen	Martin	18APR08	1.26	1
Orkees	Henry	09JUN09	1.27	1	Owens	Marton	16JUN09	2.24	1
Adm. for Jacob Orkees					Owin	Morton	01AUG06	1.17	1
Orkees	Henry	09JUN09	1.27		Owen	Mourton	26MAY07	1.18	1
Pd taxes for Jacob Orkees(D)					Owen	Mourton	18APR08	1.26	1
Orkeese	Henry	-----11	1.57	1	Owings	Robert	29JUL06	2.28	1
Ortkis	Jacob	02JUL99	3.15	1	Owings	William	21JUN87	2.06	1
Ortkis	Jacob	02JUL99	3.15	1	Owens	William	14APR91	1.06	1
Ortkies	Jacob	26JUN00	3.22	1	OWSLEY				
Orkies	Jacob	19MAY01	3.26	1	Owsley	Anthony	28JUN87	3.07	1
Orkees	Jacob	16AUG02	3.20	1	Owsley	Anthony	13AUG89	2.10	1
Orkees	Jacob	26JUL03	2.24	1	Owsley	Antoney	19APR91	3.12	1
Ortkies	Jacob	25JUL04	4.17	1	Owsley	Anthoney	08DEC92	3.15	1
Orkees	Jacob	22JUL05	2.24	1	Owsley	Anthony	23MAY94	3.16	1
Orkees	Jacob	16JUL06	2.28	1	Owsley	Anthony	-----95	1.11	1
Ortkus	Jacob	14AUG07	2.27	1	Owsley	Anthony	-----96	4.12	11
Orkees	Jacob	-----08	2.21	D	Owsley	Anthony	-----97	2.03	1
Taxes pd by He-ry Orkees					Owsley	Anthony	25MAY99	2.14	1
Orkees	Jacoo	09JUN09	1.27	D	Owsley	Anthony	18JUN00	1.10	1
Pd by Henry Orkees - Adm.					Owsley	Anthony	18JUN00	1.09	1
Ortkies	John	25JUL04	4.17	1	Owsley	Anthony	03JUN01	1.12	1
Orkees	John	22JUL05	2.24	1	Owsley	Anthony	02JUN02	1.15	1
ORMSBY					Owsley	Anthony	20JUN03	1.17	1
Ownsbey	John	28JUN87	3.07	1	Owsley	Anthony	06AUG04	1.15	1
Ormsby	John W.	16MAY94	1.07	1	Owsley	Anthony	06JUN05	1.14	1
OSBURN					Owsley	Anthony	10JUN06	1.16	1
Osburn	Elijah	19JUN05	2.24	1	Owsley	Anthony	17JUN07	1.19	1
Osburn	Elijah	07AUG06	2.28	1	Owsley	Anthony	30APR08	1.26	1
Osburn	Elijah	--JUL07	2.27	1	Owsley	Anthony	19MAY09	2.23	1
OSWALD					Owsley	Anthony	-----11	1.59	1

surname	name	date	bk.pg	TM
Owsley	Anthony	-----11	1.58	11
Ownsler	Charles	17APR97	3.23	1
Owsley	Daniel	12AUG89	2.10	1
Owsley	Daniel	19APR91	3.12	1
Owsley	Daniel	08DEC92	3.15	1
Owsley	Daniel	23APR94	3.16	1
Owsley	Daniel	-----95	1.11	1
Owsley	Daniel	-----96	4.11	1
Owsley	Daniel	-----97	2.03	1
Owsley	Daniel	11JUN99	2.14	1
Owsley	Daniel	18JUN00	1.10	1
Exec. for Thomas Owsley				
Owsley	Daniel	04JUN01	1.12	1
Exec. for Thomas Owsley				
Owsley	Daniel	25JUN02	1.16	1
Pd tax for Thomas Owsley				
Owsley	Daniel	16JUL03	1.17	1
Exec. for Thomas Owsley				
Owsley	Daniel	18JUN04	1.14	1
Exec. for Thomas Owsley				
Owsley	Daniel	16AUG05	1.15	1
Owsley	Daniel	02AUG06	1.18	1
Owsley	Daniel	02AUG06	1.17	1
Owsley	Daniel	17JUN07	1.19	1
Owsley	Daniel	30APR08	1.26	1
Owsley	Daniel	26AUG09	2.28	1
Owsley	Daniel	---*-11	1.58	11
Owsley	Henry	12AUG89	2.10	1
Owsley	Henry	19APR91	3.12	1
Owsley	Henry	08DEC92	3.15	1
Owsley	Henry	23APR94	3.16	1
Owsley	Henry	-----95	1.10	11
Owsley	Henry	-----96	4.11	11
Owsley	Henry	-----97	2.03	1
Owsley	Henry	11JUN99	2.14	1
Owsley	Henry	18JUN00	1.10	1
Owsley	Henry	04JUN01	1.12	11
Owsley	Henry	03JUN02	1.16	11
Owsley	Henry	22JUN02	1.16	1
Owsley	Henry	14JUN03	1.16	11
Owsley	Henry	18JUN04	1.14	11
Owsley	Henry	16AUG05	1.14	12
Owsley	Henry	11JUN06	1.17	11
Owsley	Henry	17JUN07	1.19	11
Owsley	Henry	30APR08	1.26	2
Owsley	Henry Jr	17AUG09	2.24	1
Owsley	Henry Sr	19MAY09	2.23	1
Owsley	Henry	-----11	1.58	11
Owsley	Jonathan	28JUN87	3.07	1
Ousley	Jonathan	-----11	1.59	1
Ousley	Levi	-----11	1.59	M1
Owsley	Martha	-----11	1.58	F
Owsley	Martha	-----11	1.58	F
Owsley	Nudigate	04JUN01	1.12	1
Owsley	Nadiget	25JUN02	1.16	1
Owsley	Nudiget	15JUN03	1.16	1
Owsley	Nauget	18JUN04	1.14	1
Owsley	Judiget	07JUN05	1.14	1
Owsley	Nudiget	18JUN06	1.17	1
Owsley	Nudget	04JUN07	1.19	1
Owsley	Nudeget	07APR08	1.25	1
Owsley	Nudget	10MAY09	2.24	1
Owsley	Samuel	25JUN02	1.16	1
Owsley	Samuel	14JUN03	1.16	1
Owsley	Samuel	18JUN04	1.14	1
Owsley	Samuel	07JUN05	1.14	1
Owsley	Samuel	16AUG06	1.18	1
Owsley	Samuel	17JUN07	1.19	1
Owsley	Samuel	30APR08	1.26	1
Owsley	Samuel	02JUN09	2.24	1
Owsley	Samuel	-----11	1.58	1
Owsley	Thomas Sr	28JUN87	3.07	11

surname	name	date	bk.pg	TM
Owsley	Thomas Jr	28JUN87	3.07	1
Owsley	Thomas Sr	01JUL89	2.10	1
Owsley	Thomas Jr	12AUG89	2.10	1
Owsley	Thomas	-----97	2.03	D
Owsley	Thomas	11JUN99	2.14	1
Owsley	Thomas	18JUN00	1.10	D
Daniel Owsley - Exec.				
Owsley	Thomas	04JUN01	1.12	1
Owsley	Thomas	04JUN01	1.12	D
Daniel Owsley - Exec.				
Owsley	Thomas	01JUN02	1.15	1
Owsley	Thomas	25JUN02	1.16	D
Owsley	Thomas	25JUN02	1.16	D
Tax paid by Daniel Owsley				
Owsley	Thomas	16JUL03	1.17	11
Owsley	Thomas	16JUL03	1.17	D
Daniel Owsley - Exec.				
Owsley	Thomas	18JUN04	1.14	D
Daniel Owsley - Exec.				
Owsley	Thomas	15AUG04	1.15	11
Owsley	Thomas	29JUL05	1.14	1
Owsley	Thomas	16AUG05	1.15	D
Owsley	Thomas	30JUL06	1.17	1
Owsley	Thomas	17JUN07	1.19	1
Owsley	Thos(heirs)	17JUN07	1.19	D
Owsley	Thos(heirs)	17JUN07	1.19	D
Owsley	Thomas	30APR08	1.26	1
Owsley	Thos(heirs)	30APR08	1.27	D
Owsley	Thomas Sr	11JUN09	2.24	1
Owsley	Thomas	10MAY09	2.24	1
Owsley	Thomas	19MAY09	2.23	1
Owsley	Thomas	-----11	1.60	1
Owsley	Thomas	-----11	1.58	11
Owsley	William	28JUN87	3.07	1
Owsley	William	13AUG89	2.10	1
Owsley	William	19APR91	3.12	1
Owsley	William	08DEC92	3.15	1
Owsley	William	23MAY94	3.16	1
Owsley	William	-----95	1.11	11
Owsley	William	-----96	4.11	1
Owsley	William	-----97	2.03	11
Owsley	William	16MAY99	1.29	1
Owsley	William	25MAY99	2.14	12
Ousley	William	18JUN00	2.23	1
Ousley	William	25JUL00	1.10	11
Owsley	William	04JUN01	1.12	12
Owsley	William	24JUL01	2.21	1
Owsley	William	10JUN02	1.16	1
Owsley	William	25JUN02	1.16	1
Owsley	William	06JUL03	1.17	1
Owsley	William	18JUN04	1.14	1
Owsley	William	02AUG04	2.16	1
Owsley	William Sr	07JUN05	1.14	11
Owsley	William	06JUN05	1.14	1
Owsley	William	18JUN06	1.17	11
Owsley	William Jr	19JUN06	1.17	1
Owsley	William	04JUN07	1.18	1
Owsley	William	04JUN07	1.19	12
Owsley	William	30APR08	1.26	1
Owsley	William	30APR08	1.26	12
Owsley	William	02JUN09	2.24	1
Owsley	William Jr	06JUN09	2.24	1
Owsley	William	-----11	1.59	1
Owsley	William	-----11	1.58	11
Owsley	Zachariah	-----11	1.59	1
OXFORD				
Oxford	Samuel	27JUN00	2.23	1
Oxford	Samuel	19MAY01	3.26	1
Oxford	Samuel	13AUG02	2.24	1
PADGET				
Pagin	David	26NOV92	3.16	1
Pagget	Fanny	-----11	1.65	F

surname	name	date	bk.pg	TM		surname	name	date	bk.pg	TM
PAGE						Painter	Joshua	02JUN08	1.28	11
Page	Dellard	-----11	1.61	1		Pantor	Joshua	23MAY09	2.25	1
Page	Nicholas	27MAY02	2.24	1		Painter	Joshua	-----11	1.61	1
PAINE						Painter	William	30JUN89	5.09	1
Pain	Ambrose	26JUL08	1.29	11		Pinter	William	23MAY94	1.07	1
Payne	Edmund	09MAY91	3.13	1		Pinter	William	16JUN96	1.10	1
Paine	Edmond	28APR94	3.18	1		PANKEY				
Payne	Edmund	29MAY95	2.10	1		Panky	Philip	27JUN05	2.25	1
Pain	Edmond	01JUN96	1.10	1		Pankey	Philip	15AUG06	2.29	1
Paine	Edmond	15JUN03	3.24	1		Panky	Phillip	22JUN07	2.28	1
Paine	Edmond	28MAY99	1.30	1		Pankey	Phillip	-----08	2.22	1
Paine	Edmund	01AUG00	2.24	1		Panky	Philip	16AUG09	1.29	1
Paine	Edmund	04APR01	2.22	11		Pankey	Phillip	-----11	1.60	1
Paine	Edmond	08JUN02	3.20	1		PANNEL				
Payne	Edmond	28MAY03	2.24	1		Pannel	John	17JUN05	3.28	1
Pain	Edmond	16AUG04	2.16	1		PARKER				
Paine	Edmond	20JUL05	2.26	1		Parker	Eli	28JUN87	3.08	1
Paine	Edmond	08MAY06	2.28	1		Parker	Ichabod	-----96	4.13	1
Paine	Edmond	18MAY06	2.28	1		Parker	Isaiah	15APR90	1.08	1
Pain	John	18OCT92	2.07	1		Parker	Isaiah	14MAY91	2.08	1
Pain	John	12AUG93	1.07	1		Parker	Isiah	26SEP92	1.10	1
Pain	John	26MAY94	1.07	1		Parker	Jeremiah	13JUN87	2.06	1
Payne	John	25MAY95	2.10	1		Parker	Orrange	20SEP92	1.10	1
Pain	John	18JUN96	1.10	1		Parker	Orrange	15AUG93	3.09	1
Paine	John	24APR97	3.24	1		Parker	Orrang	16APR94	2.11	1
Pain	John	-----11	1.62	1		Parker	Orange	28JUN96	2.15	1
Pain	John	-----11	1.65	1		Parker	Orange	05JUL00	3.24	1
Paine	Laban	28APR94	3.18	1		Parker	Orange	16AUG02	3.22	1
Pain	Laban	-----96	4.12	1		Parker	Orange	26JUL03	2.24	1
Pain	Laban	-----97	2.04	1		Parker	Orrange	25JUL04	4.18	1
Payne	Laban	10MAY99	2.15	1		Parker	Orange	18JUL06	2.29	1
Payne	Obediah	19JUN99	2.14	12		Park	Orange	22JUN07	2.28	1
Pain	Ruben	05APR91	1.07	1		Parker	Orange	-----09	1.28	1
Payne	Rubin	09MAY91	3.13	1		Parker	Thomas	12AUG89	2.11	1
Pain	Reubin	04DEC92	3.16	1		Parker	Thomas	-----93	2.04	1
Pain	Ruben	26OCT92	2.07	1		Parker	Warren	19MAY91	2.08	1
Pain	Rubin	23AUG93	1.07	1		PARKS				
Paine	Reuben	28APR94	3.18	1		Parks	John	19MAY07	1.20	1
Pain	Rubin	12MAY94	1.07	1		Parks	John	26JUL08	1.29	1
Payne	Reuben	-----95	1.11	1		Parks	John	23MAY09	2.25	1
Payne	Reuben	12MAY95	2.10	1		Parks	John	-----11	1.61	1
Pain	Reubin	-----96	4.12	1		Parks	Moses	22JUL00	2.24	1
Pain	Rubin	01JUN96	1.10	1		Parks	Moses	30MAY01	3.28	1
Pain	Rubin	-----97	2.04	1		Parks	Moses	05AUG02	2.25	1
Paine	Reubin	02MAY97	3.24	1		Parks	Paten	11JUN03	1.18	1
Payne	Rheuben	10MAY99	2.15	1		Parks	Ruben	23MAY09	2.25	1
Payne	Rheuben	07JUN00	1.10	1		Parks	Reuben	-----11	1.61	1
Payne	Rheuben	29MAY01	1.13	1		Parks	Samuel	08NOV92	3.15	1
Pain	Reuben	28JUN02	1.18	1		Parks	Samuel	03AUG93	1.07	1
Pain	Reuben Jr	28JUN02	1.18	1		Parks	Samuel	12MAY94	1.07	1
Payne	Rheuben	10JUN03	1.18	1		Parks	Samuel	20MAY95	2.10	1
Payne	Rheuben Jr	10JUN03	1.18	1		Parks	Samuel	01JUN96	1.10	1
Payne	Rheuben Sr	13JUN04	1.15	1		Parks	Samuel	19APR97	3.24	1
Payne	Rheuben	13JUN04	1.15	1		Parks	Samuel	28MAY99	1.30	1
Payne	Rheuben Sr	05JUN05	1.15	1		Parks	Samuel	21JUN00	2.23	1
Payne	Rheuben	05JUN05	1.15	1		Parks	Samuel	21JUN00	2.23	1
Payne	Rheuben Sr	13JUN06	1.19	1		Parks	Samuel	04APR01	2.22	1
Payne	Rheuben	13JUN06	1.18	1		Parks	Samuel	14JUN02	3.20	1
Pain	Ruben Sr	19MAY07	1.20	1		Parks	Samuel	28MAY03	2.24	1
Pain	Ruben	19MAY07	1.20	1		Parks	Samuel	06JUN04	4.18	1
Pain	Ruben	23MAY09	2.25	1		Parks	Samuel	08JUL05	2.26	1
Pain	Ruben	24MAY09	2.25	1		Parks	Samuel	18MAY06	2.28	1
Payne	Reuben Sr	-----11	1.64	1		Parks	Samuel	01AUG07	2.28	1
Payne	Reuben	-----11	1.62	1		Parks	Samuel	26JUL08	1.29	1
Payne	Sabun	09MAY91	3.13	11		Parks	Samuel	24AUG09	2.27	1
Payne	William	12JUN99	2.16	1		Parks	Samuel	-----11	1.61	1
Payne	Zadok	06AUG04	3.15	1		Parks	Solomon	17MAY99	1.29	1
PAINTER						Parks	William	28JUN87	3.08	1
Painter	David	-----11	1.61	1		Parks	William	17JUL91	3.13	1
Painter	Joshua	04JUN05	1.15	1		Parks	William	04AUG91	2.08	1
Paynter	Joshua	13JUN06	1.18	1		Parks	William	26NOV92	3.16	1
Painter	Joseph	20MAY07	1.20	1		Parks	William(DR)	28APR94	3.18	1

surname	name	date	bk.pg	TM	surname	name	date	bk.pg	TM
Parks	William(SC)	28APR94	3.17	1	Patton	Alex.Jr	18JUN00	3.22	1
Parks	William	-----95	1.11	1	Patton	Alexander	19JUN01	3.26	1
Parks	William	-----95	1.11	1	Patton	David	13JUL91	3.13	1
Parks	William	-----96	4.12	1	Pattern	David	27NOV92	3.16	1
Parks	William	-----96	4.12	1	Patton	David	27APR94	3.17	1
Parks	William	24JUN96	2.15	1	Patton	Jacob	13JUL87	1.04	1
Parks	William	-----97	2.04	1	Paton	Jacob	11JUN89	6.05	1
Parks	William	10AUG97	1.20	1	Pattin	Jacob	29MAY90	1.08	1
Parks	William	10MAY99	2.15	11	Patton	Jacob	18MAR91	2.08	1
Parks	William	10JUL99	3.16	1	Patten	James	13JUN97	1.19	1
Parks	William	07JUN00	1.10	11	Patton	James	18JUN00	3.22	1
Parks	William	10JUL00	3.24	1	Pattan	James	17JUN01	3.26	1
Parks	William	28MAY01	3.28	1	Patton	James	27MAY02	2.24	1
Parks	William	29MAY01	1.13	11	Patton	James	14JUN03	3.20	1
Parks	William	28JUN02	1.18	11	Patton	James	03AUG04	3.15	1
Parks	William	29JUL02	3.21	1	Pattin	James	19JUN05	3.28	1
Parks	William	10JUN03	1.17	12	Patton	James	22JUL06	3.27	1
Parks	William	10AUG03	2.25	1	Pd tax for Thomas Patton (decd)				
Parks	William	08JUN04	4.18	1	Patten	James	19JUL07	2.29	1
Parks	William	25JUL04	1.16	21	Pd tax for Polly Carpenter				
Parks	William	04JUN05	1.15	22	Patten	James	19JUL07	2.29	
Parks	William	20JUN05	2.25	1	Pd tax for Thomas Patten (decd)				
Parks	William	13JUN06	1.18	12	Patten	James	-----08	2.22	1
Parks	William	30JUL06	2.29	11	Pd tax for Thomas Patten heirs				
Parks	William	20MAY07	1.20	12	Patten	James	-----08	2.22	
Parks	William	26JUL08	1.29	21	Pd tax for Polly Carpenter				
Parks	William	24MAY09	2.25	1	Patten	James	-----09	1.28	1
Parks	William	-----11	1.61	2	Paid tax for Polly Carpenter				
PARMELEE					Patten	James	-----09	1.28	
Parneblee	Joseph	19JUN05	3.28	1	Pd tax for Thomas Patten (decd)				
Parmelee	Joseph	22JUL06	3.27	1	Patton	James	-----11	1.61	1
PARR					Patton	Philip	24MAY94	2.11	11
Pair	John	27JUL03	2.24	1	Patton	Philip	16APR95	3.13	11
Parr	John	24JUL04	4.18	1	Pattern	Robert	-----97	2.04	1
Pair	John	29MAY05	2.25	1	Patton	Robert	-----11	1.60	1
Pair	John	07AUG06	2.29	1	Patton	Thomas	22JUL06	3.27	D
Parr	John	01AUG07	2.28	1	Patton	Thomas(D)	22JUL06	3.27	
Parr	John	-----08	2.22	1	Tax paid by James Patton				
Parr	John	-----09	1.28	1	Patten	Thomas	19JUL07	2.29	D
Parr	Thomas	22JUN07	2.28	1	Patten	Thomas(D)	19JUL07	2.29	
PARRETT					Tax paid by James Patten				
Parrett	Joseph	22JUN07	2.28	1	Patten	Thomas	-----08	2.22	D
PARSONS					Patten	Thomas(H)	-----08	2.22	
Parsons	Benjamin	15JUN96	1.10	1	Tax paid by James Patten				
Parsons	James	16OCT92	2.07	1	Patten	Thomas	-----09	1.28	D
Parsons	James	18MAY94	1.07	1	Patten	Thomas(D)	-----09	1.28	
Person	James	26MAY95	2.10	1	Tax paid by James Patten				
Parsons	James	15JUN96	1.10	11	Patton	Will	13JUL87	1.04	1
Parsons	Joseph	05JUN05	1.15	1	Patten	William	14APR89	6.05	1
Parsons	Joseph	11JUN06	1.18	1	Patten	William	15APR90	1.08	11
Parsons	Joseph	18MAY07	1.20	1	Patten	William	19APR91	2.08	11
Parsons	Joseph	26JUL08	1.29	1	Patton	William	05AUG93	1.07	1
Parsons	Joseph	20MAY09	2.24	1	Patton	William	18SEP93	3.09	12
Parsons	Naomi	18OCT92	2.07	F	Patton	William	12JUN94	2.11	21
PASSWATERS					Patton	William	29APR95	3.13	11
Passwater	Zale	29JUN99	1.30	1	Patton	William	05JUL96	2.15	21
Passwaters	Zeal	23JUL00	2.24	1	Patton	William	31MAY97	1.19	21
PATTERSON					Pd tax for Sam Bell heirs				
Patterson	George	11JUN06	1.18	11	Patton	William	22JUL99	3.16	11
Paterson	George	18MAY07	1.20	11	Patton	William	22JUL99	3.17	
Patterson	Hamlet	11JUN05	1.15	1	Paid tax for Samuel Bell				
Patterson	James	23JUN99	2.16	1	Patton	William	08JUL00	3.24	11
Paterson	William	24MAY90	1.08	1	Patton	William	19JUN01	3.27	12
Patterson	William	13APR97	3.23	1	Paid tax for Samuel Bell (heirs)				
Patterson	William	19JUN99	2.16	11	Patton	William	27JUL02	3.21	21
PATTON					Patton	William	12AUG02	2.25	1
Patton	Alex.	02AUG87	1.04	1	Patton	William	21JUN03	3.20	1
Paton	Alexander	12MAY96	2.14	1	Patton	William	08AUG03	2.25	21
Patton	Alexander	10MAY97	1.19	1	Patton	William	09AUG04	3.15	1
Patton	Alexander	20MAY99	3.15	11	Patton	William	10AUG04	4.19	21
Patton	Alex. Jr	22JUL99	3.17	1	Patton	William	18JUN05	2.25	21
Patton	Alex. Sr	26JUN00	3.25	1					

surname	name	date	bk.pg	TM		surname	name	date	bk.pg	TM
Patten	William	08JUL05	3.29	1		Payton	Augustis	26MAY99	3.16	1
Patten	William	28JUL06	2.29	3		Paton	Augusta	20JUN00	3.23	1
Patten	William	20AUG06	3.28	1		Payton	Augusta	02MAY01	3.26	1
Patten	William	10AUG07	2.28	3		Payton	Augusta	06AUG02	3.21	1
Paid tax for Rachel Bell						Payton	Augusta	01AUG03	2.25	1
Patten	William	-----08	2.22	3		Peyton	Augusty	21MAY04	4.18	1
Paid Tax for Rachel Bell						Payton	Augusta	27JUN05	2.26	1
Patten	William	-----09	1.28	2		Payton	Augusta	15AUG06	2.30	1
Paid tax for Rachell Bell						Payton	Buford	24JUN02	2.25	1
Patten	William Jr	-----09	1.28	1		Payton	Buford	11JUL03	3.20	1
Patton	William	-----11	1.60	1		Peyton	Buford	14AUG04	4.19	1
PAUL						Payton	Buford	08JUL05	3.28	1
Paul	Samuel	-----08	2.22	1		Payton	Buford	22JUL06	3.27	1
Paul	Samuel	09AUG09	1.29	1		Peyton	Charles	15MAY89	6.05	1
Paul	Samuel	-----11	1.60	1		Payton	Charles	02AUG90	1.08	1
PAWLING						Peyton	Charles	01AUG91	2.08	1
Pawling	Henry	28JUN87	3.08	1		Peyton	Charles	28SEP92	1.10	1
Pawling	Henry	27JUN89	2.11	1		Peyton	Charles	10AUG93	3.09	1
Pawling	Henry	09MAY91	3.13	1		Payton	Charles	08MAY94	2.11	1
Pawling	Henry	17NOV92	3.16	1		Payton	Charles	07APR95	3.13	1
Pawling	Henry	23MAY94	3.16	1		Payton	Charles	03JUN96	2.15	1
Pawling	Henry(Esq)	-----95	1.12	1		Payton	Charles	04MAY97	1.19	1
Pawling	Henry	-----96	4.12	1		Peyton	Charles	07JUN99	1.29	1
Pawling	William	09MAY91	3.13	1		Payton	Charles	01AUG00	2.24	1
Pawling	William	17NOV92	3.16	1		Payton	Charles	31JUL01	2.22	1
Pawling	William	28APR94	3.17	1		Payton	Charles	24JUN02	2.25	1
Pawling	William	-----95	1.11	1		Payton	Charles	11JUL03	3.20	1
Pawling	William	-----96	4.12	1		Payton	Charles	16AUG04	2.16	1
PAXTON						Payton	Charles	07JUN05	2.25	1
Paxton	John	07AUG93	1.07	1		Payton	Charles	02AUG06	2.29	1
Paxton	John	11MAY94	1.07	1		Payton	Charles	22JUN07	2.28	1
Paxton	John	25MAY95	2.10	1		Payton	Charles	-----08	2.22	1
Paxton	John	13JUN96	1.10	1		Peyton	Daniel	13JUL87	1.04	1
Paxton	John	08MAY97	3.24	1		Peyton	Daniel	11JUN89	6.06	1
Paxton	John	23MAY99	1.29	1		Peyton	Daniel	15APR90	1.08	1
Paxton	John	19JUL00	2.24	1		Peyton	Daniel	19APR91	2.08	1
Paxton	John	28MAY01	2.22	1		Peyton	Daniel	04DEC92	1.10	1
Paxton	John	28MAY01	2.22	1		Peyton	Daniel	04NOV93	3.10	1
Paxton	John	18JUN02	1.18	1		Payton	Daniel	24MAY94	2.11	1
Packston	John	15JUL03	1.19	1		Payton	Daniel	22APR95	3.13	1
Paid tax for William Packston						Payton	Henry	10MAY94	2.11	1
Packston	John	25JUN04	1.15	1		Payton	Henry	01JUN96	2.15	1
Paid tax for William Packston						Payton	Henry	26MAY99	3.16	1
Paxton	John	25JUL05	1.16	1		Paton	Henry	20JUN00	3.23	1
Paxton	John	25JUL05	1.17			Pohon	Henry	02MAY01	3.26	1
Paid tax for William Packston						Payton	Henry	07AUG02	3.21	1
Paxton	John	23JUN06	1.19	1		Payton	Henry	01AUG03	2.25	1
Paid tax for William Paxton						Peyton	Henry	21MAY04	4.18	1
Paxton	John	08JUN07	1.21	1		Payton	Henry	17JUN05	2.25	1
Paxton	John	02JUN08	1.27	1		Payton	Harry	15AUG06	2.29	1
Paid tax for William Paxton						Payton	James	14OCT88	1.08	1
Paxton	John	15AUG09	2.27	1		Peyton	James	02AUG90	1.08	1
Paxton	John	-----11	1.62	11		Peyton	James	10AUG93	3.09	1
Paxton	Joseph	-----11	1.62	1		Payton	James	12MAY94	2.11	1
Paxton	William	08JUL00	2.23	1		Payton	James	29APR95	3.13	1
Packston	William	15JUL03	1.19	0		Payton	James	14JUN96	2.15	1
Tax pd by John Packston						Payton	James	07JUN97	1.19	1
Packston	William	25JUN04	1.15	0		Payton	James	26MAY99	3.16	1
Tax paid by John Packston						Paton	James	20JUN00	3.23	1
Packston	William	25JUL05	1.17	1		Payton	James	02MAY01	3.26	1
Tax paid by John Packston						Payton	James	06AUG02	3.21	1
Paxton	William	23JUN06	1.19	1		Payton	James	04AUG03	2.25	11
Paxton	William	08JUN07	1.21	1		Peyton	James	05APR04	4.17	11
Paxton	William	02JUN08	1.27	0		Peyton	James	27JUN05	2.26	11
Tax paid by John Paxton						Payton	James	15AUG06	2.30	11
Paxton	William	15AUG09	2.27	1		Peyton	John	10AUG93	3.09	12
Paxton	William	-----11	1.63	1		Payton	John	13MAY94	2.11	12
PAYTON						Payton	Lewis	24AUG87	1.05	1
Peyton	Augustus	10AUG93	3.09	1		Peyton	Lewis	22SEP92	1.10	1
Payton	Augustus	13MAY94	2.11	1		Peyton	Lewis	07AUG93	3.09	1
Payton	Augustin	13APR95	3.13	1		Peyton	Luis	13APR95	3.13	1
Payton	Augustine	14JUN96	2.15	1		Peyton	Loucy	13MAY89	6.06	F1

surname	name	date	bk.pg	TM	surname	name	date	bk.pg	TM
Peyton	Loucy	02AUG90	1.08	F1	Payton	William	21MAY01	3.26	1
Peyton	Martin	01AUG91	2.08	1	Payton	William	24JUN02	2.25	1
Peyton	Martin	28SEP92	1.10	1	Payton	William	01AUG03	2.25	1
Peyton	Martin	10AUG93	3.09	1	Payton	William	11AUG04	2.16	1
Payton	Martin	08MAY94	2.11	1	Payton	William	08MAY05	2.25	1
Payton	Martin	27APR95	3.13	1	Payton	William	08JUL05	3.28	1
Payton	Martin	01JUN96	2.15	1	Payton	William	15AUG06	2.29	1
Payton	Martin	04MAY97	1.19	1	Peyton	Yelverton	26JUN87	2.06	1
Payton	Martin	07JUN99	1.29	1	PEAK				
Payton	Martin	12AUG00	2.24	1	Peake	Jesse	07JUN09	1.27	1
Payton	Martin	31JUL01	2.22	1	Peak	Jesse	-----11	1.62	1
Payton	Martin	24JUN02	2.25	1	Peke	John	08MAY06	2.28	1
Payton	Martin	11JUL03	3.20	1	Peake	Spencer	-----09	1.28	M1
Payton	Martin	16AUG04	2.16	1	Peake	Spencer	-----11	1.60	11
Payton	Martin	28MAY05	3.27	1	Peake	William	-----11	1.60	1
Payton	Marten	18JUL06	3.27	1	PEARL				
Payton	Marten	20JUN07	2.28	1	Pearl	Henry	24JUL01	2.22	1
Payton	Marten	-----08	2.22	1	Perral	Henry	12AUG04	2.16	1
Peyten	Martin	-----09	1.28	1	Perrel	Henry	15JUN05	1.16	1
Payton	Martin	-----11	1.60	11	Perril	Henry	19JUN06	1.19	1
Peyton	Philip	24AUG87	1.05	1	Pearl	Henry	04JUN07	1.20	1
Peyton	Phillip	11JUN89	6.05	1	Pearl	Henry	04MAY08	1.27	1
Peyton	Phillip	23JUN91	2.08	1	Pearl	Henry	13MAY09	2.24	1
Peyton	Phillip Jr	28SEP92	1.10	1	Perl	John	11JUN02	1.17	1
Payton	Philip	10MAY94	2.11	1	Perril	John	20JUN03	1.18	1
Payton	Philip	10APR95	3.14	1	Perril	John	31JUL05	1.17	1
Payton	Randle	25MAY97	1.19	1	Pearrel	Ann	12AUG00	1.12	F
Peyton	Randolph	03JUN99	1.30	1	Pearrel	Nancy	23JUN01	1.14	F
Payton	Randolph	03AUG03	2.25	1	Perl	Nancy	08JUN02	1.17	F
Payton	Randolph	14AUG04	4.19	1	Pearrel	Nancy	11JUL03	1.19	F
Payton	Randolph	18JUN05	2.25	1	Perril	Nancy	05AUG04	1.16	F
Payton	Randolph	11AUG06	2.29	1	Perril	Nancy	11JUN05	1.16	F
Payton	Randolph	20JUN07	2.27	1	Perril	Nancy	02AUG06	1.20	F
Payton	Randolph	-----08	2.22	1	Pearl	Nancy	23JUN07	1.21	F
Payton	Randolph	13JUL09	1.28	1	Pearl	Samuel	30MAY99	2.15	0
Peyton	Randolph	-----11	1.61	2	Given in by William Pearl				
Paton	Robert	05DEC92	3.16	1	Pearrel	Samuel	20AUG00	1.12	0
Peyton	Valentine	24AUG87	1.05	1	Tax paid by William Pearrel				
Peyton	Valentine	11JUN89	6.05	1	Pearrel	Samuel	23JUN01	1.14	0
Peyton	Valentine	02AUG90	1.08	1	Tax paid by William Pearrel				
Payton	Valentine	21JUN91	2.08	1	Pearrel	Samuel	08JUN02	1.17	
Payton	Valentine	20AUG93	3.10	11	Tax paid by William Pearrel				
Payton	Valentine	22MAY94	2.11	1	Pearrel	Samuel	11JUL03	1.19	0
Payton	Vaullintine	18APR95	3.14	11	Tax paid by William Pearrel				
Payton	Vallentine	03JUN96	2.15	11	Perrel	William	10OCT88	1.08	11
Payton	Valentine	25MAY97	1.19	1	Perrel	William	04JUL89	5.10	11
Payton	Valentine	03JUN99	1.30	11	Perrel	William	02NOV92	2.07	1
Payton	Valentine	12AUG00	2.24	21	Perral	William	20AUG93	1.07	11
Payton	Vallentine	31JUL01	2.22	21	Perral	William	29MAY94	1.07	12
Payton	Valentine	24JUN02	2.25	2	Perral	William Jr	29MAY94	1.07	1
Payton	Valentine	13JUL03	3.20	11	Parral	William	04JUN95	2.10	12
Payton	Valuntine	14AUG04	4.19	11	Perral	William	30JUN96	1.10	11
Payton	Valentine	28MAY05	3.27	11	Parral	William Jr	30JUN96	1.10	1
Payton	Valentine	18JUL06	3.26	11	Pearl	William	14APR97	3.23	1
Payton	Valentine	20JUN07	2.28	11	Pearl	William	14APR97	3.25	12
Payton	Valentine	-----08	2.22	1	Pearl	William	30MAY99	2.15	1
Payten	Valentine	13JUL09	1.28	1	Taxes given in for Joseph Jackson				
Peyton	Valentine	-----11	1.60	1	Pearl	William	30MAY99	2.15	
Payton	Vincent	14AUG04	4.19	1	Taxes given in for Samuel Pearl				
Payton	Vincent	25JUN08	2.22	1	Pearrel	William	20AUG00	1.11	1
Payton	Will	13JUL87	1.04	1	Pearrel	William	20AUG00	1.12	
Peyton	William	02AUG90	1.08	1	Paid tax for Joseph Jackson				
Peyton	William	25OCT91	1.07	1	Pearrel	William	20AUG00	1.12	
Peyton	William	28SEP92	1.10	1	Paid tax for Samuel Pearrel				
Payton	William	10AUG93	3.09	1	Pearrel	William	23JUN01	1.13	1
Payton	William	08MAY94	2.11	1	Pearrel	William	23JUN01	1.14	
Payton	William	30MAY95	3.14	1	Paid tax for Joseph Jackson				
Payton	William	01JUN96	2.15	1	Pearrel	William	23JUN01	1.14	
Payton	William	10MAY97	1.19	1	Paid tax for Samuel Pearrel				
Payton	William	27MAY99	3.16	1	Pearrel	William	08JUN02	1.17	1
Pohon	William	18JUN99	2.16	1	Paid tax for Joseph Jackson				
Paton	William	19JUN00	3.23	1	Pearrel	William	08JUN02	1.17	

surname	name	date	bk.pg	TM	surname	name	date	bk.pg	TM
Paid tax for Samuel Pearrel					Pence	Amanuel	02JUN08	1.28	1
Pearrel	William	11JUL03	1.19	1	Pence	Amanuel	22JUN09	2.26	1
Paid tax for Joseph Jackson					Pence	Emanuel	-----11	1.63	1
Pearrel	William	11JUL03	1.19		Pence	Jacob	25JUL05	1.17	1
Paid tax for Samuel Pearrel					Pence	Jacob	13JUN06	1.18	1
Perrel	William	03AUG04	1.16	1	Pence	Judith	07JUN08	1.28	F
Paid tax for Joseph Jackson					Piner	Judith	01JUN09	2.25	F
Perril	William	11JUN05	1.16	1	Pinor	Judith	-----11	1.64	F
Perril	William	02AUG06	1.20	1	PENDERGRASS				
Pearl	William	23JUN07	1.21	1	Pendleton	John	-----11	1.65	1
Pearl	William	07JUN08	1.28	11	Pendleton	John *	-----11	1.65	1
Pearl	William	05JUN09	2.26	1	PendergrassThomas		10JUL99	3.16	1
Pearl	William	-----11	1.63	1	PendergrassThomas		09JUL00	3.24	1
PEARSON					PendergrassThomas		30JUL01	3.28	1
Pierson	Abraham	05JUL03	1.18	1	PendergrassThomas		28JUL02	3.21	1
Pierson	Abraham	15JUN04	1.15	1	PendergrassThomas		08AUG03	2.25	1
Pierson	Abraham	20JUN05	1.16	1	PendergrassThomas		05APR04	4.17	1
Pierson	Abraham	21JUN06	1.19	1	PendergrassThomas		19JUN05	2.25	1
Pearson	Abraham	20JUN07	1.21	1	PendergrassThomas		29JUL06	2.29	1
Pearson	Abraham	23APR08	1.27	1	Pendexter	Thomas	01AUG07	2.28	1
Pearson	Abraham	14JUN09	2.26	1	Pendleton	Timothy	14OCT92	2.07	1
Percen	Bengamin	07APR97	3.25	1	PENECK				
Pierson	Jacob	21JUN06	1.19	1	Penicks	Charles	11JUL00	3.25	1
Pearson	Jacob	20JUN07	1.21	1	Penix	Edward	15AUG97	1.20	1
Pearson	Jacob	10MAY09	2.24	1	Penick	Edward	24MAY99	3.16	1
Person	Jacob	-----11	1.64	1	Penicks	Edward	11JUL00	3.25	1
Persons	James	09AUG93	1.07	1	Penex	Edward	29JUL01	3.27	1
Percen	James	07APR97	3.25	11	Penex	Edward	10JUN02	2.25	1
Pierson	James	17MAY99	1.29	13	Penicks	Edward	05AUG03	3.20	1
Pierson	James	30MAY00	2.23	13	Penick	Edward	06APR04	4.17	1
Pierson	James	21JUL01	2.22	21	Penex	Edward	22JUN05	3.28	1
Pearson	James	16JUN02	1.18	12	Penex	Edward	30JUL06	3.27	1
Pierson	James	05JUL03	1.18	11	Pennex	James	13JUN87	2.06	1
Pierson	James	15JUN04	1.15	12	Penix	James	15OCT88	1.08	1
Pierson	James	20JUN05	1.16	12	Penicks	James	30JUN89	5.09	1
Pierson	James	21JUN06	1.19	11	Penix	James	23APR90	2.06	1
Pierson	James Jr	21JUN06	1.19	1	Penicks	James	04OCT92	2.07	1
Pearson	James	20JUN07	1.21	11	Penix	James	10AUG93	1.07	1
Pearson	James	16AUG09	2.26	1	Penix	James	16MAY94	1.07	1
Pearson	James Jr	16AUG09	2.27	1	Penix	James	01JUN95	2.10	1
Pearson	James Sr	-----11	1.64	1	Penix	James	20JUN96	1.10	1
Pearson	James Jr	-----11	1.64	1	Penix	James	26APR97	3.24	1
Parson	Joseph	-----11	1.64	1	Penix	James	15JUL99	1.30	1
Parson	Messiah	06APR91	1.07	1	Penix	James	23JUN00	2.23	1
Pierson	Meshek	05DEC92	3.16	1	Penix	James	03JUN01	2.22	1
Pearson	Reuben	16JUN02	1.18	1	Penex	James	14JUN02	2.25	11
Pierson	Rheuben	05JUL03	1.18	1	Penicks	James	20JUL03	3.20	11
Pierson	Rheuben	15JUN04	1.15	1	Pinex	James	14JUN04	2.16	11
Pearson	Ruben	16AUG09	2.26	1	Penix	James	28MAY05	3.27	11
Pearson	Reuben	-----11	1.64	1	Peneck	James	02AUG06	3.27	1
Pearson	Rigs	23JUN02	1.18	1	Pennex	James	19JUL07	2.29	1
Pierson	Silas	23JUN03	1.18	1	Penex	James	-----08	2.22	11
PELHAM					Pennix	James	09APR09	1.27	11
Pelham	Abraham	13JUL87	1.04	1	Penick	James	-----11	1.63	13
Pelham	Francis	18AUG91	2.08	1	Penex	Jeremiah	29JUL01	3.27	1
PELS					Penex	Jeremiah	10JUN02	2.25	1
Pels	Joseph	20JUN97	1.20	1	Penicks	Jeremiah	05AUG03	3.20	1
PEMBERTON					Penick	Jerry	07APR04	4.17	1
Pemberton	John	-----11	1.60	1	Penex	Jeremiah	22JUN05	3.28	1
Pemberton	Thomas	31JUL04	3.15	1	Penick	Jeremiah	28MAY06	3.26	1
Pemberton	Thomas	19JUN05	3.28	1	Penyx	John	04JUN05	1.15	1
Pemberton	Thomas	14JUL06	3.26	1	Penyx	John	13JUN06	1.18	1
Pemberton	Thomas	19JUL07	2.29	1	Peneck	John	01AUG06	3.27	M1
Pemberton	Thomas	31MAY08	2.21	1	Peneck	John	20MAY07	1.20	1
Pemberton	Thomas	-----11	1.61	1	Pennek	John	19JUL07	2.29	1
Pemberton	William	23JUN99	2.14	1	Penex	John	-----08	2.22	1
PENCE					Penix	John	02JUN08	1.27	1
Pence	Emmanuel	17JUN02	1.18	1	Pennix	John	08APR09	1.27	1
Pence	Emanuel	15JUL03	1.19	1	Penix	John	23MAY09	2.25	1
Pence	Emanuel	25JUN04	1.15	1	Penick	John	-----11	1.62	1
Pence	Emanuel	25JUL05	1.17	1	Penick	John	-----11	1.63	1
Pence	Emanuel	23JUN06	1.19	1	Penix	William	14OCT88	1.08	1

surname	name	date	bk.pg	TM	surname	name	date	bk.pg	TM
Penicks	William	22MAY89	5.09	1	Pennington	Timothy	30OCT88	1.07	1
Penix	William	09MAY91	3.13	1	Penington	Timothy	24JUN89	5.09	1
Penick	William	04DEC92	3.16	1	Penelton	Timothy	14AUG93	1.07	1
Penix	William	27APR94	3.17	1	Penalton	Timothy	29MAY94	1.07	11
Penix	William	-----95	1.11	1	Penalton	Timothy	04JUN95	2.10	11
Pennix	William	-----96	4.12	1	Penleton	Timothy	29JUN96	1.10	11
Penix	William	-----97	2.04	1	Pennington	Timothy	12APR97	3.23	1
Penyx	William	30MAY99	2.15	1	Pennington	Timothy	29MAY99	2.15	1
Penyx	William	06JUN00	1.10	11	Pennington	Timothy	20JUN00	1.11	1
Penyx	William	29MAY01	1.13	11	Pennington	Timothy	20JUN00	1.11	1
Penix	William	28JUN02	1.18	11	Peniton	Timothy	08JUL05	3.29	11
Penyx	William	10JUN03	1.17	11	Peniston	Timothy	20AUG06	3.28	11
Penyx	William	13JUN04	1.15	11	Pennington	William	04AUG03	3.20	M1
Penyx	William	04JUN05	1.15	1	Peniston	William	20AUG06	3.28	1
Penyx	William	13JUN06	1.18	1	Pennington	William	09JUN09	2.25	1
Peneck	William	20MAY07	1.20	1	Pennington	William	-----11	1.63	1
Paid tax for James Baley					Pendleton	Sac	29JUL02	3.21	1
Penix	William	02JUN08	1.27	1	Pennington	Zacheriah	04AUG03	3.20	1
Penx	William	02JUN08	1.28		Pennington	Sack	08JUN04	4.18	1
Guardian for James Baley					PERKINS				
Penix	William	07JUN08	1.28	11	Perkins	Christian	01JUL89	2.11	1
Penix	William Sr	23MAY09	2.25	1	Pirkins	Christopher	05DEC92	3.16	1
Piner	William	01JUN09	2.25	1	Perkins	Christopher	28APR94	3.18	1
Piner	William	-----11	1.64	1	Perkins	Christian	-----95	1.11	1
Penick	William	-----11	1.64	1	Perkins	Christian	15MAY99	2.16	1
PENMAN					Perkins	Christian	12JUN00	1.11	1
Penman	Darby	26JUN00	3.25	1	Perkins	Christian	02JUN01	1.13	11
Penman	Dorby	19MAY01	3.26	1	Perkins	David	26JUL96	1.10	1
Penman	Darby	16AUG02	3.22		Perkens	David	-----97	2.04	1
A free negro					Perkins	David	09JUL02	1.19	1
Penman	Dorby	01AUG07	2.28		Perkins	David	22JUL05	1.16	1
Black					Perkins	David	31JUL06	1.19	1
Peniman	Samuel	25MAY07	1.20	1	Purkins	John	25JUN03	3.20	M1
Periman	Samuel	01JUL09	2.26	1	Perkins	Reubin	10OCT92	1.10	1
PENNAL					Perkins	Reubin	02JUL99	1.30	1
Pennell	John	04AUG04	3.15	1	Perkins	Ruben	18JUL03	3.20	1
Pennal	John	21AUG06	3.28	1	Perkins	Reuben	24AUG04	3.16	1
Pennel	Pierce	06APR04	4.17	1	Pirkins	Reuben	02AUG06	3.28	1
Pennal	Price	08JUL05	3.28	11	Pirkens	Reuben	-----08	2.22	1
Pennal	Price	20AUG06	3.28	11	Perkins	Reuben	-----11	1.63	11
PENNINGTON					Perkins	Stephen	22APR08	1.27	1
Penninton	Asa	21JUN03	3.20	1	Perkins	Stephen	08APR09	1.27	1
Penneton	Asa	09AUG04	3.15	1	Perkins	Stephen	14JUN09	2.26	1
Peniton	Asa	08JUL05	3.29	1	Perkins	Thomas	28APR94	3.18	1
Peniston	Asa	20AUG06	3.28	1	Perkins	Thomas	-----95	1.11	1
Pennington	Dennis	12JUL00	3.25	1	Perkens	Thomas	-----97	2.04	1
Pennington	Dennis	30JUL01	3.28	1	Perkins	Thomas	15MAY99	2.16	1
Penington	Denis	10JUN02	2.25	1	Perkins	Thomas	12JUN00	1.11	1
Pennington	Dannis	08JUN04	4.18	1	Perkins	Thomas	03JUN01	1.13	11
Pennington	Edward	24MAY99	3.15	1	PERRIGOE				
Pennington	Edward	12JUL00	3.24	1	Perrigoe	Daniel	18JUL07	2.29	1
Pennington	Edward	29JUL01	3.27	1	Perrigo	Daniel	-----08	2.22	1
Pennington	Elizabeth	29JUL01	3.27	F	Perrigo	Daniel	08AUG09	1.29	1
Penington	Jacob	08JUN96	1.10	1	Peringer	Leonard	14MAY91	2.08	1
Peniton	Joal	08JUL05	3.29	1	PERRIN				
Peniston	Joal	02AUG06	3.28	1	Perrin	Archilles	14MAY99	1.29	1
Pennington	Mary	23JUN01	1.13	F	Perrin	Archilas	30MAY00	2.23	1
Pennington	Mary	04JUN02	1.17	F	Perrin	Archilas	22JUL01	2.22	1
Pennington	Mary	23JUN03	1.18	F	Perren	Archillus	11JUN02	1.17	1
Penneton	Moses	09AUG04	3.15	1	Perren	Achales	30JUN03	1.18	1
Peniton	Moses	08JUL05	3.28	1	Perren	Archales	15JUN05	1.16	1
Penuton	Moses	02AUG06	3.27	1	Perren	Achales	19JUN06	1.19	1
Pennington	Patrick L.	12JUL00	3.25	1	Perren	Archillis	04JUN07	1.20	1
Penington	Patrick	10JUN02	2.25	1	Perren	Accillus	16AUG09	2.27	1
Pennington	Patrick	03AUG03	3.20	1	Perrin	Achillis	-----11	1.64	1
Pennington	Patrick	06APR04	4.17	1	Perran	Clapton	16JUN96	1.10	1
Penington	Patrick	22JUN05	3.28	1	Perrin	Clapton Wm.	10APR97	3.23	1
Pennington	Patrick	30JUL06	3.27	1	Perin	Josephus	26JUN87	2.06	1
Pennington	Polly	13AUG04	2.16	F1	Perren	Josephus	30OCT88	1.07	11
Pennenton	Simon	07JUN03	3.19	1	Perren	Josephus	16JUN89	5.09	11
Peniton	Simon	08JUL05	3.29	1	Perrin	Josephus	--MAY90	2.06	12
Penington	Simon	02AUG06	3.27	1	Perrin	Josephus	30MAR91	1.07	1

surname	name	date	bk.pg TM	surname	name	date	bk.pg TM
Perran	Josephus	23MAY94	1.07 1	Pettit	Benj. Sr	01JUN99	1.30 11
Parran	Josephes	06JUN95	2.10 1	Pettitt	Benj. Jr	29JUN99	1.30 1
Perin	Cassandra	10OCT92	2.07 F1	Pettit	Benj. Jr	05JUL00	2.23 11
Perran	Kissander	15AUG93	1.07 F1	Pettit	Benj. Jr	26JUL00	2.24 1
Perran	Kisander	23MAY94	1.07 F1	Pettit	Benjamin	28MAY01	3.28 1
Parron	Casander	03MAY95	2.10 F1	Pettit	Benjamin	03AUG02	2.25 1
Parran	Casander	03JUN95	2.22 F	Pettit	Benjamin	03JUN03	3.19 1
Perran	Kisandre	16JUN96	1.10 F	Poteet	Benjamin	17JUN09	2.26 1
Perrin	Casander	08APR97	3.23 F1	Pettit	James	24JUN00	2.23 1
Perrin	Cisandor	11JUN02	1.17 F	Pettit	Jeremiah	24JUN00	2.23 1
Perren	Kissandrah	20JUN04	1.15 F	Peteate	Tobiores	11MAY96	2.18 1
Perren	Kissandrah	15JUN05	1.16 F	Puttett	Tobias	14JUL97	1.20 1
Perren	Kisander	08JUN07	1.21 F	PETTUS			
PERRY				Pettus	Thomas	17JUL06	3.26 1
Perry	James	15APR90	1.08 1	Pettes	Thomas	24JUN07	1.21 1
Perry	Jeremiah	12MAY99	2.16 1	Pettes	Thomas	23APR08	1.27 1
Perry	Jeremiah	13JUN00	1.11 1	PETTY			
Perry	Jeremiah	30MAY01	1.13 1	Petty	Abner	-----11	1.65 1
Perry	Jeremiah	14JUN02	1.18 1	Petty	John P.	26JUN99	1.29 1
Perry	Jeremiah	14JUN04	1.15 1	Petty	John	-----11	1.65 1
Perry	Jerremiah	11JUN03	1.18 1	PETTYJOHN			
Parie	John	-----08	2.23 1	Pettyjohn	Peter	14JUL97	1.20 1
Perry	Richard	30JUN87	1.04 11	PEW			
Perry	Richard	26JUN89	6.06 1	Pew	Rheuben	03AUG04	1.16 1
Perry	Richard	20APR90	1.08 11	Pew	Rheuben	31JUL05	1.17 1
PERSISE				Pew	Rheuben	01AUG06	1.19 11
Percize	Daniel	26JUN87	2.06 1	Peaw	Ruben	09JUN07	1.20 11
Prosythe	Daniel	07AUG93	1.07 1	Pew	Ruben	30APR08	1.27 11
Prosithe	Daniel	15MAY94	1.07 1	Pew	Ruben	01JUL09	2.26 1
Prosithe	Daniel	18MAY95	2.10 1	PHILLIPS			
Prosythe	Daniel	-----96	4.12 1	Phillips	Aron	09JUN96	1.10 1
Prosythe	Daniel	07JUN00	1.10 1	Philips	Aron	02AUG06	1.20 1
Procise	Daniel	29MAY01	1.13 1	Philips	Aron *	02AUG06	1.20 1
Procise	Daniel	28JUN02	1.18 1	Phillips	Aaron	06JUN07	1.20 1
Procise	Daniel	10JUN03	1.17 1	Phillips	Charles	24AUG87	1.05 1
Prosis	Daniel	25JUL04	1.16 1	Phillips	Charles	19MAY89	6.06 1
Procise	Daniel	04JUN05	1.15 11	Phillips	Charles	02AUG90	1.08 1
Persise	Daniel	13JUN06	1.18 1	Phillips	Charles	21JUN91	2.08 1
Procise	Daniel	20MAY07	1.20 1	Phillips	Charles	25SEP92	1.10 1
Persise	Daniel	26JUL08	1.29 1	Phillips	Charles	24AUG93	3.10 1
Persise	Daniel	23MAY09	2.25 1	Phillips	Charles	22MAY94	2.11 1
Persise	Thomas	27OCT88	1.08 1	Phillips	Charles	29APR95	3.13 1
Persise	Thomas	11JUN06	1.18 1	Phillips	Charles	24JUN96	2.15 1
Persise	William	11JUN06	1.18 1	Philips	Charles	08AUG97	1.20 1
PESTORUP				Phillips	Charles	11JUL99	3.16 1
Pestorup	George	06APR97	3.24 1	Phillips	Charles	10JUL00	3.24 1
PaptisthalpJohn		22MAY97	1.19 1	Phillips	Charles	30JUL01	3.27 11
PETERS				Philips	Charles	29JUL02	3.21 11
Peters	James	24MAY95	3.14 0	Philips	Charles	10AUG03	2.25 11
Peters	John	07JUL87	1.04 1	Philips	Charles	07JUN04	4.18 11
Peters	John	13JUL87	1.04 1	Philips	Charles	21JUN05	2.25 2
Peters	John	-----93	2.04 1	Philips	Charles	31JUL06	2.29 2
Peters	William	05OCT92	1.10 1	Philips	James	24JUN00	3.23 1
Peters	William	14AUG93	3.09 1	Philips	James	06AUG02	3.21 1
Peters	William	24MAY94	2.11 1	Philips	James	05AUG03	2.25 1
PETTIT				Philips	James	12JUN04	4.18 1
Pettit	Benjamin	01DEC88	1.08 1	Phillips	John	12JUN89	6.08 1
Pettit	Benjamin	16JUN89	5.09 1	Phillips	John	20MAY90	1.08 1
Petitt	Benjamin	30MAR90	2.06 1	Phillips	John	24JUN96	2.15 1
Pettit	Benjamin	08APR91	1.07 11	Philips	John	10AUG97	1.20 1
Pettit	Benj.	29OCT92	1.10 0	Philips	John	11JUL99	3.16 1
Pettir	Benjamin	04DEC92	1.10 1	Phillips	John	10JUL00	3.24 1
Pettit	Benjamin	24OCT92	2.07 11	Phillips	John	30JUL01	3.27 1
Pettit	Benjamin	09SEP93	1.07 11	Philips	John	29JUL02	3.21 11
Pettit	Benjamin	17MAY94	1.07 1	Phillips	John	10AUG03	2.25 11
Pettit	Benj. Jr	17MAY94	1.07 1	Philips	John	07JUN04	4.18 11
Pettit	Benj. Sr	12MAY95	2.10 1	Philips	John	20JUN05	2.25 12
Pettit	Benj. Jr	11MAY95	2.10 1	Philips	John	31JUL06	2.29 12
Pettet	Benjamin	01JUN96	1.10 1	Phillips	Leonard	29JUN04	4.18 1
Pettit	Benjamin	08JUN06	1.10 1	Phillips	Leonard	07AUG04	3.15 1
Pettit	Bengamin	15JUN97	3.25 1	Philips	Leonard	12JUN05	1.15 1
Pettet	Bengamin	15JUN97	3.24 1	Philis	Leonard	13JUN05	1.16 1

surname	name	date	bk.pg	TM	surname	name	date	bk.pg	TM
Philips	Lewis	30JUN01	2.22	1	Pierce	Jeremiah	13JUN87	2.06	1
Philips	Lewis	30JUN02	1.19	1	Pierce	Jeremiah	17OCT88	1.08	1
Philips	Lewis	06JUL03	1.18	1	Pierce	Jeremiah	04AUG89	5.10	1
Phillips	Lewis	16JUN04	2.16	1	Peirce	Jeremiah	18MAY90	2.06	1
Phillips	Lewis	01JUL07	1.21	1	Pierce	Jeremiah	07APR91	1.07	1
Phillips	Lewis	30MAY09	2.25	1	Peirce	Jeremiah	01NOV92	2.07	11
Phillips	Lewis	-----11	1.63	1	Pearce	Jeremiah	06AUG93	1.07	1
Phillips	Mary	02AUG90	1.08	F	Pearce	Jeremiah	15MAY94	1.07	1
Phillips	Mary	23JUN91	2.08	F	Pierce	Jeremiah	18MAY95	2.10	1
Phillips	Mary	24AUG93	3.10	F	Pearce	Jeremiah	06JUN96	1.10	11
Phillips	Mary	09MAY94	2.11	F	Pierce	Jeremiah	20APR97	3.24	11
Philips	Mary	19APR95	3.13	F	Pierce	Jeremiah	27MAY99	1.30	11
Philips	Mary	09JUL99	3.16	F	Pierce	Jeremiah	09JUL00	2.24	1
Philips	Mary Jr	20JUN00	3.23	F	Pierce	Jeremiah	17JUL01	2.22	1
Phillips	Mary	02MAY01	3.26	F	Pearce	John	08JUL05	3.28	1
Philips	Mary	06AUG02	3.21	F	Pearce	John	18JUL07	2.29	1
Philips	Mary	05AUG03	2.25	F	Perce	John	11JUL09	1.28	1
Philips	Mary	23JUL04	4.18	F	Pierce	John	-----11	1.61	1
Philips	Mary	27JUN05	2.26	F	PIGG				
Philips	Mary	15AUG06	2.30	F	Pigg	Anderson	17AUG93	3.09	1
Phillips	Mary	18AUG07	2.28	F	Pigg	Anderson	30APR94	2.11	1
Phillips	Mary	31MAY08	2.21	F	Pigg	Anderson	26MAY95	3.14	1
Phillips	Mary	-----09	1.28	F	Pigg	Anderson	29JUL96	2.15	1
Fillips	Mary	-----11	1.24	F	Pigg	Anderson	26MAY97	1.19	1
Phillips	Polly	10JUN97	1.19	F	Pigg	Anderson	02JUL99	1.30	1
Philips	Polly	09JUL99	3.16	F	Pigg	Anderson	30JUL00	2.24	1
Philips	Polley	06AUG02	3.21	F	Pigg	Anderson	20JUL01	3.28	1
Philips	Polly	05AUG03	2.25	F	Pigg	James	14JUN03	3.20	1
Phillips	Sally	10JUN97	1.20	F	Pigg	James	04AUG04	3.15	1
Philips	Sally	09JUL99	3.16	F	Pigg	James	30MAY05	2.25	1
Philips	Sarrah	20JUN00	3.23	F	Pigg	James	22JUL06	3.27	1
Philips	Sarah	06AUG02	3.21	F	Pigg	James	31JUL07	2.27	1
Philips	Sally	05AUG03	2.25	F	Pigg	John	03APR90	2.06	1
Philips	William	08AUG97	1.20	1	Pig	John	09MAY91	3.13	1
Phillips	William	26JUN99	1.30	1	Pigg	John	04DEC92	3.16	1
Philips	William	01JUL00	3.23	M1	Pig	John	29MAY94	3.17	1
Phillips	William	26JUL00	2.24	1	Pigg	John	-----95	1.11	1
Phillips	William	30MAY01	3.28	1	Pigg	John	29JUL96	2.15	1
Phillip	William	09JUL01	3.27	1	Pigg	John	26MAY97	1.19	1
Philips	William	26JUL02	3.21	1	Pigg	John	06JUN99	1.29	1
Philips	William	17AUG02	3.22	1	Pigg	John	30JUL00	2.24	1
Phillips	William	22JUN03	2.24	1	Pig	John	29MAY01	1.13	1
Philips	William	12AUG03	2.25	1	Pigg	John	10JUN02	2.25	1
Philips	William	11JUN04	4.18	1	Pigg	John	28JUN02	1.18	1
Philips	William	18JUN05	2.25	1	Pig	John	10JUN03	1.17	1
PHIPPS					Pigg	John	05AUG03	3.20	1
Phips	George	15JUL99	1.30	1	Pigg	John	06APR04	4.17	1
Phipps	George	24JUN00	2.23	1	Pig	John	13JUN04	1.15	1
Phips	George	03JUN01	2.22	1	Pig	John	05JUN05	1.15	1
Fips	George	07JUL03	1.08	1	Pigg	John	13JUN06	1.18	1
Phipps	George	18JUL04	2.16	1	Pigg	John	19MAY07	1.20	1
Fipps	George	26JUN05	1.07	1	Pigg	John	26JUL08	1.29	1
Fips	George	20JUN06	1.08	1	Pigg	John	23MAY09	2.25	1
Fepps	George	01JUL07	1.08	1	Pigg	Lewis	22JUN05	3.28	1
PICKARD					Pigg	Lewis	22JUL06	3.27	1
Pickard	Peter	15MAY09	1.27	1	Pigg	Paul	10JUN07	2.27	1
Pickard	Peter	-----11	1.60	1	Pigg	Paul	31MAY08	2.21	1
Pickens	Ruben	22JUL01	3.28	1	Pigg	Paul	-----09	1.28	1
Pickens	Reuben	08JUL05	3.29	1	Pigg	Paul	-----11	1.61	1
PIERCE					Pigg	William	29JUN89	5.09	1
Piearce	Abraham	05DEC92	3.16	1	Pigg	William	26MAR90	2.06	11
Pierce	Ephraim	31JUL06	1.19	1	Pig	William	06APR91	1.07	11
Pierce	Hugh	27JUL97	1.20	1	Pigg	William	18OCT92	1.10	11
Pierce	James	18JUL00	2.24	1	Pigg	William	17AUG93	3.09	1
Pierce	James	25MAY01	2.22	1	Pigg	William	30APR94	2.11	11
Pierce	James	04AUG02	3.21	2	Pigg	William	28MAY95	3.14	11
Pierce	James	28MAY03	2.24	2	Pigg	William	29JUL96	2.15	11
Pierse	James	25JUL04	1.16	2	Pigg	William	26MAY97	1.19	11
Pierce	James	03AUG05	2.26	2	Pigg	William	06JUN99	1.29	21
Pierce	James	06JUN06	2.28	1	Pigg	William Sr	29JUL00	2.24	11
Pearce	James	07JUN08	1.28	1	Pigg	William	22JUL00	2.24	1
Pearce	James	07JUN08	1.28	1	Pigg	William Sr	20JUL01	3.28	11

surname	name	date	bk.pg	TM	surname	name	date	bk.pg	TM
Pigg	William Jr	20JUL01	3.28	1	Pitman	Thomas	10JUN07	2.27	1
Pegg	William	27MAY02	2.24	22	Pitman	Thomas	-----08	2.22	1
Pigg	William Jr	27MAY02	2.24	1	Pitman	Thomas	12MAY09	1.27	1
Pigg	William Sr	05AUG03	3.20	12	PLEASANT				
Pigg	William Jr	14JUN03	3.20	1	Peasant	Edward	22APR08	1.27	11
Pigg	William Sr	04AUG04	3.15	12	Pleasant	Edward	25AUG09	2.27	1
Pigg	William Jr	31JUL04	3.15	1	Pleasants	Edward	-----11	1.64	11
Pigg	William	22JUN05	3.28	11	PLUMMER				
Pigg	William Jr	22JUN05	3.28	1	Plummer	George	30JUN07	1.21	1
Pigg	William	21JUL06	3.27	11	Plummer	George	30MAY09	2.25	1
Pigg	William	20AUG06	3.28	1	Plummer	George	-----11	1.63	1
Pigg	William	22JUN07	2.28	1	Plusner	Thomas	-----95	1.11	1
Pigg	William	-----08	2.22	1	POINTER				
Pigg	William	-----09	1.28	1	Pointer	Edward	13JUL91	3.13	1
PING					Pointer	Edward	05DEC92	3.16	1
Ping	John Sr	09JUL87	3.08	1	Pointer	Edward	27APR94	3.17	1
Ping	John Jr	09JUL87	3.08	1	Pointer	Edward	-----95	1.11	1
Ping	John Sr	31OCT88	1.08	1	Pointer	Edward	-----96	4.12	1
Ping	John Jr	31OCT88	1.08	1	Pointer	Edward	-----97	2.04	1
Ping	John Sr	24JUN89	5.09	1	Poynter	Edward	13MAY99	2.16	11
Ping	John Jr	24JUN89	5.09	1	Poynter	Edward	13JUN00	1.11	1
Ping	John	03APR90	2.06	1	Pointer	Edward	16JUL03	1.19	1
Ping	John	03APR90	2.06	1	Porter	Edwin	20MAY09	2.24	1
Ping	John	30MAR91	1.07	1	Poynter	George	13JUN87	2.06	1
Ping	John	11OCT92	2.07	1	Pointer	George	14OCT88	1.08	1
Ping	John	05DEC92	3.16	1	Pointer	George	25MAY90	2.06	1
Ping	John	15AUG93	1.07	1	Pointer	George	14APR91	1.07	11
Ping	John	29MAY94	1.07	1	Pointer	George	15OCT92	2.07	1
Ping	John	30MAY94	1.07	1	Pointer	James	14APR91	1.07	1
Ping	John	-----95	1.11	1	Poynter	John	13JUN87	2.06	1
Ping	John	03JUN95	2.10	1	Poynter	John Jr	13JUN87	2.06	1
Ping	John Jr	30JUN96	1.10	11	Pointer	John	14OCT88	1.08	1
Peng	John	29MAY97	3.24	1	Pointer	John	05DEC92	3.16	1
Peng	John	29MAY97	3.24	11	Pointer	John	27APR94	3.17	1
PINKERTON					Pointer	John	-----95	1.11	1
Pinkerton	James	13MAY99	1.29	1	Pointer	John	-----97	2.04	1
Pinkerton	James	03JUN00	2.23	1	Pointer	Joseph	25MAY99	3.16	1
PIPER					Porter	Samuel	22OCT88	1.08	12
Piper	John	14JUN96	2.15	11	Porter	Samuel	16MAY90	2.06	1
PIPES					Porter	Samuel	05APR91	1.07	1
Pipes	James	21JUN05	2.25	M1	Porter	Samuel	03AUG93	1.07	1
Pipes	Silvanus	05MAY91	2.08	11	Porter	Samuel	17MAY94	1.07	1
Popes	Silvanus	24SEP92	1.10	11	Porter	Samuel	13JUN95	2.10	1
Pipes	Silvanus	19SEP93	3.10	11	Poynter	Thomas	13JUN87	2.06	1
Pipes	William	21JUN05	2.25	1	Pointer	Thomas	31OCT88	1.08	1
PITMAN					Pointer	William	09JUL87	3.08	11
Pitman	Berry	10JUN07	2.27	1	Porter	William	15OCT88	1.08	1
Pitman	Berry R.	-----08	2.22	1	Porter	William	23JUN89	5.09	1
Pitmon	Lewis	29JUN04	4.18	1	Pointer	William	12AUG89	2.11	1
Pittman	Richard B.	14AUG06	2.29	1	Pointer	William	02OCT92	2.07	1
Pitman	Richard B.	12MAY09	1.27	1	Pointer	William	15AUG93	1.07	1
Pitman	Thomas	26JUN89	6.05	1	Pointer	William	27APR94	3.17	1
Pitman	Thomas	23JUN90	1.08	11	Pointer	William	-----95	1.11	1
Pitman	Thomas	19AUG91	2.08	11	Pointer	William	02JUN95	2.10	1
Pitman	Thomas	03OCT92	1.10	11	Pointer	William	-----97	2.04	1
Pitman	Thomas	27AUG93	3.09	11	Poynter	William	13MAY99	2.16	1
PIPES					Poynter	William	13JUN00	1.11	1
Pipe	Silvenus	05AUG89	5.10	12	Porter	William	17JUN02	1.18	1
Pipes	Silvenius	30MAY90	2.06	1	Porter	William	17JUN03	2.24	1
PITMAN					Porter	William	23JUL04	1.16	1
Pitmond	Thomas	29MAY94	2.11	11	Porter	William	07JUN05	2.25	1
Pitmond	Thomas	02MAY95	3.13	1	Porter	William	28JUL06	2.29	1
Pittman	Thomas	25JUN96	2.15	1	Porter	William	22JUN07	2.28	1
Pitman	Thomas	09AUG97	1.20	1	POKE				
Pitman	Thomas	08JUL99	3.16	1	Poke	Jesse	30MAY99	2.15	1
Pitman	Thomas	05JUL00	3.24	1	POLEY				
Pitman	Thomas	02MAY01	3.26	1	Polely	Isaac	13AUG07	2.28	1
Pittman	Thomas	11AUG02	3.21	11	Polly	Isaac	-----08	2.23	1
Pittman	Thomas	29JUL03	2.25	11	Poley	Isaac	-----09	1.28	1
Pitmon	Thomas	26JUN04	4.18	11	Poley	John	18MAY91	2.08	1
Pittman	Thomas	18JUL05	2.26	11	POLLARD				
Pittman	Thomas	14AUG06	2.29	1	Pollard	Abraham	02OCT87	1.05	1

surname	name	date	bk.pg	TM	surname	name	date	bk.pg	TM
Pollard	Absalom	07AUG89	2.11	1	Pope	George	01AUG07	2.28	1
Pollard	Absolum	19APR91	3.12	1	Pope	George	-----08	2.23	1
Pollard	Absalum	30NOV92	3.16	1	Pope	George	-----09	1.28	1
Pollard	Absalom	27APR94	3.17	1	Pope	George	-----11	1.60	1
Pollard	Absalom	-----95	1.11	1	Pope	Henry	13JUL87	1.04	1
Pollard	Absalom	-----96	4.12	1	Pope	Henry	14MAY89	6.05	1
Pollard	James	01JUL89	2.11	1	Pope	Henry	03APR90	1.08	1
Pollard	James	06OCT92	1.10	1	Pope	Henry	19APR91	2.08	1
Pollard	James	24AUG93	3.09	1	Pope	Henry	08OCT92	1.10	1
Pollard	James	27APR94	3.17	1	Pope	Henry	16AUG93	3.09	1
Pollard	James	08APR95	3.13	1	Pope	Henry	30APR94	2.11	1
Pollard	James	03JUN96	2.15	1	Pope	Henry	28MAY95	3.14	1
Pollard	James	20JUN97	1.20	1	Pope	Henry	21JUN96	2.15	1
Pollard	James	28JUN99	1.30	1	Pope	Henry	22MAY97	1.19	1
Pollard	James	26JUL00	2.24	1	Pope	Henry	03JUL99	3.16	1
Pollard	James	27MAY01	3.28	1	Pope	Henry	28JUN00	3.23	11
Polard	James	12AUG02	2.25	1	Pope	Henry	07JUL01	3.27	11
POLSTON					Pope	Henry	13AUG02	3.22	D1
Poulson	Thomas	22AUG04	3.16	1	Pope	Henry	13AUG02	3.22	DS
Polston	Thomas	08JUL05	3.29	1	Pope	Henry	22JUN03	2.24	D
Polston	Thomas	19AUG06	3.28	1	Tax paid by George Pope				
POPE					Pope	Henry	17JUL06	2.23	
Pope	Abraham	22JUN03	2.24	1	Michael Mires - Guardian				
Pope	Alexander	09JUL87	3.08	1	Pope	Henry	-----11	1.62	1
Listed with Thomas Pope					Pope	Humphrey	27JUN89	2.11	1
Pope	Alexander	01JUL89	2.11	1	Pope	Humphrey	08NOV92	3.15	1
Pope	Elix	09MAY91	3.13	1	Pope	Humphrey	23MAY94	3.16	1
Pope	Allemander	01DEC92	3.16	1	Pope	Humphrey	-----95	1.11	1
Pope	Allimander	27APR94	3.17	1	Pope	Humphrey	22JUL96	2.15	1
Pope	Alexander	-----95	1.12	1	Pope	Humphrey	11JUL97	1.20	1
Pope	Alexander	-----96	4.13	1	Pope	Humphrey	29JUN99	1.29	1
Pope	Eve	28JUL04	4.18	F	Pope	John	13JUL91	3.13	11
Pope	Gasper	08JUN89	6.05	1	Pope	John Jr	08NOV92	3.15	1
Pope	Gasper	03APR90	1.08	1	Pope	John	27APR94	3.17	1
John Lorger listed with him					Pope	John	-----95	1.11	1
Pope	Gasper	20APR91	2.08	1	Pope	John	-----96	4.13	1
Pope	Gasper	08OCT92	1.10	1	Pope	John	23MAY97	1.19	1
Pope	Gasper	16AUG93	3.09	1	Pope	John	03JUL99	3.16	1
Pope	Gasper	23APR94	2.12	1	Pope	John	30JUN00	3.23	1
Pope	Gasper	28MAY95	3.14	1	Pope	John	09JUL01	3.27	1
Pope	Gasper	21JUN96	2.15	1	Pope	John	30JUN02	3.20	1
Pope	Gasper	23MAY97	1.19	1	Pope	John Jr	03JUL02	3.20	1
Pope	Casper	04JUL99	3.16	1	Pope	John	17JUN03	2.24	1
Pope	Casper	28JUN00	3.23	1	Pope	John *	17JUN03	2.24	1
Pope	Gasper	09JUL01	3.27	1	Pope	John	28JUL04	4.18	1
Pope	Gasper	17AUG02	3.22	1	Pope	John	07JUN05	2.25	1
Pope	Jasper	28JUL04	4.18	1	Pope	John	25JUL05	2.26	1
Pope	Gasper	25JUL05	2.26	1	Pope	John	24APR06	2.28	1
Pope	Gasper	15JUL06	2.28	1	Pope	John	15JUL06	2.28	11
Pope	George	26JUN87	1.04	1	Pope	John	30JUL07	2.28	1
Pope	George	14MAY89	6.05	1	Pope	John	-----08	2.23	1
Pope	George	03APR90	1.08	1	Pope	John	-----09	1.28	1
Pope	George	19MAY91	2.08	1	Pope	John	-----11	1.60	1
Pope	George	08OCT92	1.10	1	Pope	Obe	22JUN03	2.24	00
Pope	George	16AUG93	3.09	1	Pope	Obe	23JUL05	2.26	00
Pope	George Sr	30APR94	2.11	1	Pope	Robert	02AUG06	1.20	1
Pope	George Jr	30APR94	2.11	1	Pope	Robert	09JUN07	1.20	1
Pope	George Sr	28MAY95	3.14	1	Pope	Robert	16JUN09	2.26	1
Pope	George Jr	28MAY95	3.14	0	Pope	Thomas	09JUL87	3.08	1
Pope	George	21JUN96	2.15	1	Listed with Alexander Pope				
Pope	George Jr	21JUN96	2.15	11	Pope	Thomas	01JUL89	2.11	11
Pope	George Sr	22MAY97	1.19	1	Pope	Thomas	13JUL91	3.13	1
Pope	George Jr	22MAY97	1.19	1	Pope	Thomas Sr	08NOV92	3.15	1
Pope	George	03JUL99	3.16	1	Pope	Thomas	27APR94	3.17	1
Pope	George Sr	28JUN00	3.23	1	Pope	Thomas	-----95	1.11	1
Pope	George	07JUL01	3.27	1	Pope	Thomas	-----96	4.12	1
Pope	George	13AUG02	3.22	1	Pope	Thomas	03AUG05	2.26	1
Pope	George	22JUN03	2.24	1	Pope	Thomas	06JUN06	2.28	1
Paid tax for Henry Pope					Pope	Thomas	22JUN07	2.28	1
Pope	George	28JUL04	4.18	1	Pope	Thomas	22JUN07	2.28	1
Pope	George	23JUL05	2.26	1	Pope	Thomas	-----11	1.62	1
Pope	George	18JUL06	2.29	1	Pope	William	26JUN87	2.06	1

surname	name	date	bk.pg	TM	surname	name	date	bk.pg	TM
Pope	William	03JUN90	2.06	1	Potts	Andrew	07JUN03	3.19	1
Pope	William	18OCT92	2.07	1	Potts	Andrew	22AUG04	3.16	1
Pope	William	14AUG93	1.07	1	Potts	Andrew	08JUL05	3.29	1
PORTMAN					Potts	Andrew	20AUG06	3.28	1
Portman	George	11MAY96	2.14	2	Potts	Isaiah	22JUL05	2.26	M1
Portman	George	18JUL97	1.20	2	Potts	Jacob	07JUN03	3.19	1
Portman	George	01JUL99	1.30	2	Potts	Jeremiah	05JUL00	3.24	1
Portman	George	31JUL00	2.24	1	Potts	Jeremiah	28JUL03	2.24	1
Portman	George	22JUL01	3.28	1	Potts	John	29JUL02	3.21	1
Portman	George	12AUG02	2.25	1	Pots	Samuel	14JUN03	1.18	1
Portman	George	06JUN03	3.19	1	Pots	Samuel	01AUG04	1.16	1
Portman	George	24AUG04	3.16	1	Pots	Samuel	29JUL05	1.17	1
Portman	George	08JUL05	3.28	1	Pots	Samuel	19JUN06	1.19	1
Portman	George	01AUG06	3.27	1	Pots	Samuel	17JUN07	1.19	1
Portman	John Jr	11MAY96	2.14	1	Potts	Samuel	07JUN08	1.28	1
Portman	John	14JUL97	1.20	1	Potts	Samuel	13JUN09	2.26	1
Portman	John	01MAY99	1.29	1	Potts	Stephen	30JUN96	1.10	1
Portman	John Sr	31JUL00	2.24	1	Pots	Stephen	12JUN99	2.16	1
Portman	John	27JUN00	2.23	1	Pots	Stephen	22JUN00	1.11	11
Portman	John	22JUL01	3.28	1	Pots	Stephen	23JUN01	1.14	11
POSEY					Potts	Stephen	20JUN02	1.18	11
Posey	Humphrey	19MAY91	2.10		Pots	Stephen	14JUN03	1.18	11
Listed with John Thurmond					Pots	Stephen	01AUG04	1.16	11
Poesy	Humphrey	08AUG93	3.09	1	Potts	Stephen	29JUL05	1.17	11
Posey	Humphrey	19APR94	2.11	1	Pots	Stephen	19JUN06	1.19	11
Posey	Humphrey	23MAY96	2.15	1	Pots	Stephen	17JUN07	1.19	1
Posey	Humphrey	12MAY97	1.19	1	Potts	Stephen	07JUN08	1.28	1
Posey	Humphrey	26JUL99	3.17	1	Potts	Stephen	12JUN09	2.25	1
Posey	Humphrey	25JUN00	3.23	1	Pots	William	17JUN07	1.19	1
Posey	Humphrey	18MAY01	3.26	1	Potts	William	07JUN08	1.28	1
POTTLE					Potts	William	13JUN09	2.26	1
Pottle	Benjamin	26JUL04	1.16	1	POWELL				
POTTER					Powell	Edmund	07JUL87	1.04	1
Potter	Benjamin Sr	03AUG05	2.26	1	Powel	Edmond	12JUN89	6.08	1
Potter	Benjamin Jr	30JUL05	2.26	12	Powel	Edmond	15APR90	1.08	1
Potter	Benjamin Sr	08MAY06	2.28	1	Powel	Edmond	19APR91	2.08	1
Potter	Benjamin Jr	08MAY06	2.28	11	Powel	Edmond	14AUG93	3.09	11
Potter	Benjamin	22JUN07	2.28	1	Powel	Edmond	09MAY94	2.11	1
Potter	Benjamin *	22JUN07	2.28	1	Powel	Edmond	21MAY95	3.13	11
Potter	Benjamin	26JUL08	1.29	1	Powel	Edmond	12MAY96	2.15	11
Potter	Benjamin *	26JUL08	1.29	1	Powell	Edmund	25MAY97	1.19	11
Potter	Benjamin	16AUG09	2.27	1	Powell	Edmond	07JUN99	1.29	11
Potter	Benjamin *	-----11	1.62	1	Powell	Edmond	12AUG00	2.24	1
Potter	Benjamin	-----11	1.62	1	Powell	James	12AUG00	2.24	1
Potter	John	27JUN97	1.19	1	Powell	John	22JUN07	2.28	1
Potter	Lemul	-----11	1.62	1	Powell	Joshua	13JUN87	2.06	M1
Potter	Lewis	17OCT88	1.08	1	Powel	Lindsey	12MAY96	2.11	1
Potter	Lewis	07AUG89	5.10	1	Powell	Lindsey	25MAY97	1.19	1
Potter	Lewis	01JUN90	2.06	1	Powel	Lindsey	25JUN99	1.29	1
Potter	Lewis	21OCT92	2.07	1	Powell	Lindsey	29JUL00	2.24	1
Potter	Lewis	20AUG93	1.07	1	Powell	Linsey	21JUL01	3.28	1
Potter	Lewis	20MAY94	1.07	1	Powell	Linsey	27MAY02	2.24	1
Potter	Lewis	22MAY95	2.10	1	Powell	Linsey	04AUG03	3.20	1
Potter	Lewis	15JUN96	1.10	1	Powell	Lindsey	04AUG04	3.15	1
Potter	Lewis	07APR97	3.24	1	Powall	Linsey	19JUN05	3.28	1
Potter	Moses	27JUN05	2.25	1	Powell	Linsey	22JUL06	3.27	1
Potter	Moses	08MAY06	2.28	1	Powel	Thomas	14OCT88	1.08	11
Potter	Moses	08JUN07	2.27	1	Powel	Thomas	23JUN89	5.09	11
Potter	Moses	-----08	2.22	11	Powel	William	24AUG87	1.05	1
Potter	Moses	10MAY09	1.27	1	Powell	William	12JUN89	6.08	1
Potter	Moses	-----11	1.62	1	Powell	William	13AUG90	1.08	1
Potter	Rubin	14MAY94	1.07	1	Powell	William	24JUN91	2.08	1
Potter	Thomas	17OCT88	1.08	11	Powel	William	25SEP92	1.10	1
Potter	Thomas	27JUN05	2.25	1	Powel	William	25SEP92	1.10	11
Potter	Thomas	08MAY06	2.28	1	Powel	William	12AUG93	3.09	1
Potter	Thomas	22JUN07	2.28	1	Powel	William	13MAY94	2.11	1
Potter	Thomas	-----08	2.22	1	Powel	William	29APR95	3.13	1
Potter	Thomas	-----11	1.62	1	Powel	William	05JUL96	2.15	1
Potter	William	17MAY94	1.07	1	Powel	William	02MAY97	3.24	1
POTTS					Powell	William	08AUG97	1.20	1
Potts	Andrew	29MAY01	3.28	1	POWERS				
Potts	Andrew	03AUG02	2.25	1	Powers	Hallamy	08JUN96	1.10	1

surname	name	date	bk.pg	TM	surname	name	date	bk.pg	TM
PRATHER					Price	John	22JUL06	3.27	1
Prator	John	18JUL06	2.29	1	Price	Moses	08JUL87	3.08	1
Prather	John	10JUN07	2.27	1	Price	Moses	31OCT88	1.08	1
PRATT					Price	Moses	20JUN89	5.09	1
Pratt	James	-----11	1.63	1	Price	Moses	03JUN90	2.06	1
PRESTON					Price	Moses	18OCT92	2.07	1
Preston	Daniel	-----97	2.04	1	Price	Moses	29MAY94	3.17	1
Presston	Daniel	18JUN00	1.11	1	Price	Nathaniel	02JUN97	3.24	1
Preston	Daniel	02JUN01	1.13	1	Price	Richard	29MAY97	3.24	1
Preston	Daniel	08AUG04	3.15	1	Price	Richard	29MAY97	3.24	11
Preston	Daniel	20AUG06	3.28	1	Price	Robert	12AUG02	2.25	1
Preston	John	12AUG89	2.11	12	Price	Robert	21JUN03	3.20	1
Preston	John	29MAY94	3.17	1	Price	Robert	09AUG04	3.16	1
Preston	John Sr	-----95	1.11	1	Price	Robert	08JUL05	3.29	1
Preston	John	-----96	4.12	11	Price	Robert	20AUG06	3.28	1
Preston	John	-----97	2.04	1	Price	Samuel	28JUN87	3.08	1
Preston	John	30MAY97	3.24	1	Price	Samuel	31OCT88	1.08	1
Presston	John	16JUN00	1.11	1	Price	Samuel	17JUL91	3.13	1
Preston	John	31JUL00	2.25	12	Price	Samuel	29MAY94	3.17	1
Preston	John	02JUN01	2.22	22	Price	Samuel	-----95	1.11	1
Preston	John	30JUN02	1.18	11	Price	Samuel	31MAY97	3.24	1
Presston	Moses	24JUN00	1.11	1	Price	William	28JUN87	3.08	1
Preston	Moses	23JUN01	1.14	1	PRIDMORE				
Presston	Moses	23JUN03	1.18	1	Pridmore	John	-----11	1.63	1
Preston	Moses	18JUN04	1.15	1	PRIEST				
Preston	William	29MAY94	3.17	1	Priest	Nathan	30JUL07	2.28	1
Preston	William	-----96	4.12	1	PRINCE				
Preston	William	-----97	2.04	1	Prince	Adam	25JUL05	1.17	1
Preston	William	17JUN99	2.16	1	Prince	Adam	23JUN06	1.19	1
Presston	William	22JUN00	1.11	1	Prince	Adam	20JUN07	1.21	1
Presston	William	24JUN01	1.14	1	Prince	Adam	02JUN08	1.27	1
Preston	William	23JUN02	1.18	1	Prince	Adam	15AUG09	2.27	1
Presston	William	23JUN03	1.18	1	Prince	George	20JUN07	1.21	M1
Presston	William	02AUG04	1.16	1	Prince	George	23APR08	1.27	1
Presston	William	31JUL05	1.17	1	Prince	George	21JUN09	2.26	1
Preston	William	02AUG06	1.19	1	Prince	Kottlif	25JUL05	1.17	11
Preston	William	06JUN07	1.19	1	Prince	Cutliff	23JUN06	1.19	11
Preston	William	07JUN08	1.28	1	PRINKLE				
Preston	William	14JUN09	2.26	1	Prinkle	John	12JUN99	2.16	1
Preston	William	16JUN09	2.26	1	PRINTY				
PRICE					Printy	Robert	28MAY95	3.14	1
Price	Abraham	08JUL87	3.08	1	PROCTER				
Price	Abraham	12AUG89	2.11	1	Proctor	James	22JUN03	1.18	1
Price	Abraham Sr	29MAY94	3.17	1	Proctor	James	31JUL06	1.19	1
Price	Abraham Jr	29MAY94	3.17	1	Proctor	James	06JUN07	1.20	1
Price	Abraham	-----95	1.11	1	Proctor	James	14JUN09	2.26	1
Price	Abraham	-----96	4.12	1	Procter	Jeremiah	24MAY99	2.14	1
Price	Abraham	-----97	2.04	1	Procter	Jeremiah	16JUN00	1.11	1
Price	Abram	13JUN97	1.19	1	Procter	Jeremiah	03JUN01	1.13	1
Price	Ann	08MAY95	2.23	F	Procter	Micajah	05DEC92	3.16	1
Price	Elizabeth	08JUL87	3.08	F	Procter	Micajah	27APR94	3.17	1
(widow)					Procter	Micajah	-----95	1.11	11
Price	Isaac	12AUG89	2.11	1	Proctor	Micajah	-----96	4.12	21
Price	Isaac	17JUL91	3.13	1	Procter	Micagah	-----97	2.04	21
Price	Isaac	29MAY94	3.17	1	Procter	Micagah	24MAY99	2.14	1
Price	Isaac	-----95	1.11	1	Procter	Michajah	16JUN00	1.11	1
Price	Isaac	-----96	4.12	1	Proctor	Robert	05DEC92	3.16	M1
Price	Isach	24MAY99	2.14	1	Procter	Robert	-----95	1.11	1
Price	Isack	19JUN00	1.11	1	Procter	Robert	24MAY99	2.14	1
Price	Isiah	04JUN01	1.13	1	Procter	Robert	16JUN00	1.11	1
Price	Isaac	03JUN02	1.16	1	Procter	Robert	03JUN01	1.13	1
Prise	Isaac	15JUN03	1.18	1	Procter	William	-----95	1.11	1
Price	Isaac	18JUN04	1.15	1	PROTZMAN				
Prise	Isaac	06JUN05	1.15	1	Proutzman	Jacob	01JUL00	3.24	1
Prise	Isaac	11JUN06	1.18	1	Protzman	Jacob	20MAY01	3.26	1
Prise	Isaac	09JUN07	1.20	1	Protzman	Jacob	14AUG02	3.22	1
Price	Isaac	26JUL08	1.29	1	Protzmon	Jacob	26JUL04	4.18	1
Price	Isaac	09JUN09	2.25	1	Sprotzman	Jacob	23JUL05	2.31	1
Price	Isaac	-----11	1.65	1	Protzman	John	29MAY99	3.16	1
Price	James	19JUN00	3.22	1	Proutzman	John	01JUL00	3.24	1
Price	James	25JUL01	2.22	1	Protzman	John	20MAY01	3.26	1
Price	James	-----08	2.22	1	Protzman	John	14AUG02	3.22	1

surname	name	date	bk.pg	TM		surname	name	date	bk.pg	TM
Sproteman	John	25JUL03	2.28	1		Quinton	William	08JUL05	3.29	1
Protzmon	John	26JUL04	4.18	1		Quinton	William	23AUG06	3.26	1
Sprotzman	John	23JUL05	2.31	1		RAGAN				
Sprotsman	John	28MAR06	2.31	1		Ragan	Amos	27JUN87	1.05	1
PROVIN						Ragen	Amos	16JUL89	6.06	1
Provin	John	27JUN89	2.11	1		Ragen	Amos	16JUL89	6.08	1
PROVO						Ragon	Michael	08JUN96	1.10	1
Prevo	John	19JUN00	2.23	1		Ragan	Oen	13JUN05	1.17	1
Prevo	John	31JUL01	2.22	1		Ragan	Oen	19JUN06	1.21	1
Provo	John	12AUG02	2.25	1		Ragan	Owen	02JUN07	1.22	1
PRUITT						Ragan	Owen	18APR08	1.29	1
Pruet	Archibald	21APR97	3.25	1		Ragan	Owen	29MAY09	2.27	1
Pruett	Archibald	29MAY99	1.30	1		Ragan	Owen	-----11	1.66	1
Pruitt	Archibald	16JUN00	2.23	1		RAGLAND				
Pruitt	Archibald	03JUL02	3.20	1		Ragland	John	26JUN89	6.06	1
Pruitt	Archibald	11JUN03	2.24	1		Ragland	John	03NOV92	1.11	1
Prewit	Archey	28JUL04	4.18	1		Ragland	John	27AUG93	3.10	1
Pruitt	Joseph	-----08	2.23	1		Ragland	John	02MAY95	3.14	1
PURCIFIELD						Raglin	John	23JUN96	2.16	1
Purcifield	Valentine	02JUN01	1.13	1		Ragland	John	10AUG97	1.21	1
Puriafield	Valentine	23JUN02	1.18	1		Ragland	John	10JUL99	3.17	1
Purcifield	William	02JUN01	1.13	1		Ragland	John	09JUL00	3.26	1
PURDOM						Ragland	John	31JUL01	3.29	1
Purtun	Edward	17JUN07	1.19	1		Raglen	John	12JUL02	3.22	1
Purdom	Hezekiah	15AUG06	2.29	1		Raglen	John	09AUG03	2.27	1
Purdom	Hezekiah	20JUN07	2.27	1		Ragland	John	08JUN04	4.19	1
Purdom	William	22JUN05	3.28	1		Raglin	John	19JUN05	2.27	1
Purdon	William	22JUL06	3.27	1		Raglen	John	28JUL06	2.31	1
Purdom	William	20JUN07	2.27	1		RAINEY				
Pardorm	William	-----09	1.28	1		Rainey	James	31JUL06	1.21	1
Purdom	William	-----11	1.61	1		Raney	James	05MAY07	1.22	1
Purdom	Zederkiah	-----11	1.61	1		Raney	James	07JUN08	1.30	1
PURNALL						Reany	Joseph	13JUN96	2.16	1
Purnal	Lemual	04JUN07	1.20	1		Reaney	Joseph	05JUN97	1.20	1
Purnell	Lemual	-----11	1.64	1		RAMSEY				
Purnall	Susannah	12JUN02	1.18	F		Ramsey	Francis	18MAY07	1.22	1
Purnel	Suzanah	30JUN03	1.18	F1		Ramsey	Francis	07JUN08	1.30	11
Purnell	Susanah	12AUG04	2.16	F1		Ramsey	Francis	13JUN09	2.28	1
Purnel	Suzannah	17JUN05	1.16	F1		Ramsey	John	11MAY99	2.17	1
Purnel	Suzannah	20JUN06	1.19	F		Ramsey	John	24JUL00	1.13	1
Purnall	Susanna	02JUN07	1.20	F		Ramsey	John	01JUN01	1.14	1
Purnell	Susannah	27APR08	1.27	F		Ramsey	Larkin	07JUL87	3.08	11
Purnal	Susannah	31MAY09	2.25	F		Ramsey	Markin	28MAY91	3.14	1
Purnell	Sussanna	-----11	1.64	F		Ramsey	Larkin	05DEC92	3.17	1
Purnal	William	20OCT88	1.08	1		Ramsey	Larkin	28APR94	3.18	1
Purnall	William	24JUN89	5.09	1		Ramsey	Larken	-----95	1.12	1
Purnell	William	02JUN90	2.06	1		Ramsey	Larking	-----96	4.13	21
Parnal	William	20MAR91	1.07	1		Ramsey	Larkin	-----97	2.04	21
Pernal	William	30MAR91	1.07	1		Ramsey	Larkin	11MAY99	2.16	1
Purnel	William	18OCT92	2.07	1		Ramsey	Larken	09JUN00	1.12	1
Purnal	William	20AUG93	1.07	1		Ramsey	Larken	01JUN01	1.14	1
Purnal	William	27MAY94	1.07	1		Ramsey	Seth	30JUN89	5.11	1
Purnal	William	02JUN95	2.10	1		R---sey	Thomas	05DEC92	3.17	1
Purnal	William	28JUN96	1.10	1		Ramsey	Thomas	-----96	4.13	1
Purnel	William	24APR97	3.24	1		Ramsey	Thomas	-----97	2.04	1
Purnell	William	18MAY99	1.29	11		Ramsey	Thomas	11MAY99	2.17	1
Purnell	William	17JUN00	2.23	1		Ramsey	Thomas	11MAY99	2.17	1
Purnell	William	04JUN01	2.22	1		Ramsey	Thomas	09JUN00	1.12	1
QUEEN						Ramsey	Thomas	23JUN00	1.12	1
Queen	John	03AUG93	1.07	1		Ramsey	Thomas	01JUN01	1.14	1
Queen	John	17MAY94	1.07	1		Ramsey	Thomas	09JUN01	1.15	11
Queen	John	16JUN96	1.10	1		RANDALL				
Queen	John	07APR97	3.25	1		Randall	Richard	15AUG93	1.08	1
QUIN						RANDOLPH				
Quin	John	14JUN09	2.27	1		Randolph	Joseph	16MAY99	3.17	1
QUINTON						Randolph	Joseph	21JUN00	3.25	1
Quinton	William	29JUN99	1.30	1		Randolph	Joseph	17JUN01	3.29	1
Quinton	William	23JUL00	2.24	1		Randolph	Nathaniel	12AUG07	2.30	1
Quinton	William	27MAY01	3.28	1		RANKIN				
Quinton	William	03AUG02	2.26	1		Ranken	Samuel	14JUN00	2.24	1
Quinton	William	20MAY03	3.21	1		RASS				
Quinton	William	09AUG04	3.16	1		Rass	Thomas	18APR08	1.29	1

surname	name	date	bk.pg	TM		surname	name	date	bk.pg	TM
Rass	Thomas	16JUN09	2.28	1		Rayburn	Robert	01AUG01	2.23	1
RATEKIN						Rayburn	Robert	27MAY02	2.26	1
Radekin	James	07JUN08	1.30	1		Rayburn	Robert	11JUL03	3.21	1
Ratekin	William	11JUN06	1.20	1		Rayburn	Robert	24APR04	3.17	11
Radekin	William	07JUN08	1.30	1		Reburn	Robert	07AUG05	3.30	11
RATLIFF						RAYDER				
Ratliff	Richard	07AUG89	5.12	1		Rayder	John	18MAY91	2.08	1
Ratliff	Richard	20APR91	3.13	1		READY				
Ratliff	Richard	26NOV92	3.16	1		Ready	Isam	08AUG03	3.21	1
Ratliff	Richard	28APR94	3.18	1		Ready	Isham	09APR04	4.19	1
Ratliff	Richard	-----95	1.12	1		Ready	Isham	18JUN05	2.27	1
Radcliff	Richard	-----96	4.13	1		Ready	William	24MAY99	1.31	1
RAULSTON						Ready	William	17JUN00	2.25	1
Raulston	George	-----11	1.66	1		Ready	William	28MAY01	2.23	
RAY						One lott in Standford				
Ray	Andrew	14APR97	3.26	1		Ready	William	03JUN02	3.22	
Ray	Daniel	11JUN05	1.17	1		One lott in Standford				
Ray	Eligah	16MAY99	1.31	1		Ready	William	18MAY03	2.26	
Ray	Elijah	20JUN04	1.17	1		1/2 Lott in Standford				
Ray	Elijah	15JUN05	1.17	1		Redy	William	23JUL04	1.17	1
Ray	Elijah	16JUN06	1.20	1		Ready	William	24MAY05	2.26	1
Ray	Elijah	11MAY07	1.22	1		One lott in Standford				
Ray	Elijah	07JUN08	1.30	1		Ready	William	06APR06	2.30	1
Ray	Elijah	08JUN09	2.27	1		One lott in Standford				
Ray	George	03AUG04	2.16	1		Ready	William	13JUL07	2.29	1
Ray	George	13JUN05	1.17	1		Ready	William	07JUN08	1.30	1
Ray	George	18JUN06	1.20	1		Ready	William	16AUG09	2.28	1
Ray	George	22JUN07	1.22	1		Ready	William	-----11	1.67	1
Ray	Isaac	02AUG06	1.21	1		REDICK				
Wray	Isaac	12JUN07	1.29	1		Redick	John	21JUN99	2.18	1
Ray	Isaac	04MAY08	1.30	1		REED				
Ray	Isaac	16AUG09	2.28	1		Reed	Daniel	12JUN05	1.17	1
Wray	Isaac	-----11	1.88	1		Read	Davidson	-----11	1.67	22
Ray	John	13JUN97	1.21	1		Reed	Downey	04OCT92	2.07	1
Ray	John	-----11	1.68	1		Reed	Elizabeth	10AUG01	3.30	F
Wray	Joseph	-----11	1.84	1		Reed	Frances	30JUL04	2.16	1
Ray	Moses	16MAY99	1.31	1		Reed	Fraces S.	25JUL05	1.18	1
Ray	Moses	17JUN00	2.25	1		Ried	Francis ()	06APR06	2.30	1
Ray	Moses	25JUL01	2.23	1		One lott in Standford				
Ray	Moses	10JUN02	1.19	1		Reed	Frances S.	15JUN07	2.29	1
Ray	Moses	04JUL03	1.20	1		Reed	Francis L.	07JUN08	1.30	1
Ray	Moses	07AUG04	2.17	1		Reed	Francis	30JUN09	2.28	1
Ray	Moses	17JUN05	1.17	11		Reed	George	24JUN99	2.16	1
Ray	Moses	20JUN06	1.21	11		Reed	George	16JUN00	1.12	1
Ray	Moses	22JUN07	1.22	11		Reed	George	04JUN01	1.15	1
Ray	Moses	07JUN08	1.30	1		Reed	Jacob	10JUN01	1.15	1
Wray	Moses	13JUL09	1.34	21		Reed	James	27JUN89	5.11	1
Ray	Moses	-----11	1.66	1		Reed	James	12JUN99	2.17	1
Ray	Nathaniel	30MAY08	2.23	11		Reed	James	23JUN01	1.15	1
Ray	Nathaniel	27JUN09	1.29	1		Reed	James	20JUN02	1.19	1
Ray	Nathan	-----11	1.68	1		Reed	James	13JUN03	1.20	1
Ray	Thomas	20MAY96	1.11	11		Reed	James	01SEP04	1.17	1
Ray	Thomas	20JUN96	1.11	1		Reed	James	12JUN05	1.17	1
Ray	Thomas Sr	13JUN97	1.21	11		Reed	James	22JUL05	1.18	1
Ray	Thomas Jr	13JUN97	1.21	1		Reed	James	19JUN06	1.21	1
Ray	William	02OCT87	1.05	1		Reed	John	07JUL87	3.08	1
Wray	William	26JUN89	6.07	1		Reed	John	06OCT87	1.06	1
Ray	William	11MAY07	1.22	11		Reed	John	27JUN89	5.11	1
Ray	William	-----11	1.69	2		Reed	John Jr	18JUL89	6.06	1
RAYBURN						Reed	John	10AUG90	1.09	1
Raybourn	Robert	26JUN87	2.06	1		Reed	John Jr	30MAR90	1.08	1
Rayburn	Robert	14OCT88	1.08	1		Reed	John Sr	23JUN91	2.08	1
Reyburn	Robert	11JUN89	6.06	1		Reed	John Jr	23JUL91	2.08	1
Rayburn	Robert	25MAR91	1.07	1		Reed	John	10OCT92	1.11	1
Rayburn	Robert	02NOV92	2.07	1		Reed	John	21AUG93	3.10	1
Reburn	Robert	12AUG93	1.08	1		Reed	John	16APR94	2.12	1
Reburn	Robert	21MAY94	1.08	1		Reed	John	28APR94	3.18	1
Raburn	Robert	28MAY95	2.11	1		Reid	John	21APR95	3.14	1
Rayburn	Robert	27JUN96	1.10	1		Reed	John Sr	13AUG96	2.16	1
Raybirn	Robert	10MAY97	3.26	1		Reed	John	-----96	4.13	1
Rayburn	Robert	16MAY99	3.17	1		Reed	John	-----97	2.04	1
Rayburn	Robert	21JUN00	3.25	1		Reed	John	29MAY97	1.22	1

surname	name	date	bk.pg	TM	surname	name	date	bk.pg	TM
Reed	John	12JUN99	2.17	1	Reed	William	25JUN00	3.25	1
Reed	John	29JUN99	3.17	1	Reed	William	18MAY01	3.29	1
Reed	John	27JUN00	3.26	1	Ried	William	12AUG02	3.23	1
Reed	John	21JUL00	1.12	1	Ried	William	27JUL03	2.26	1
Reed	John	10AUG01	3.30	1	Reed	William	27JUN04	4.19	1
Reed	John	20JUN02	1.19	1	Reid	William	29MAY05	2.27	1
Ried	John	12AUG02	3.23	1	Reid	William	18JUL06	2.31	1
Reed	John	13JUN03	1.20	1	Ried	William	18JUL06	2.31	1
Ried	John	27JUL03	2.26	1	Reed	William	15JUL07	2.30	1
Reed	John	14JUN04	1.16	1	REEDER				
Reed	John	19JUN04	1.17	1	Reeder	Elijah	07JUN00	1.12	1
Reed	John	27JUL04	4.20	1	REES				
Reed	John	11JUN05	1.17	11	Rees	David	27JUN96	2.16	1
Reed	John	22JUL05	1.18	1	Rees	David	12MAY97	1.21	1
Ried	John	22JUL05	2.27	1	Reas	John	21JUN99	2.18	11
Reed	John	16JUN06	1.20	1	REEVES				
Reid	John	18JUL06	2.31	1	Reeves	James	12JUL02	3.22	1
Reed	John	25MAY07	1.22	1	Reves	James	10AUG03	2.27	1
Reed	John	15JUL07	2.30	1	Reeves	James	08JUN04	4.19	1
Reed	John	12JUN09	2.28	1	Reves	James	20JUN05	2.27	1
Reed	Jonathan	29JUN99	3.17	1	Reves	James	30JUL06	2.31	1
Reed	Jonathan	25JUN00	3.25	1	RENFROW				
Reed	Jonathen	09MAY01	3.29	1	Rentfro	Absolam	15MAY97	3.26	1
Ried	Jonathan	12AUG02	3.23	1	Renfrow	Absalom	12JUN99	2.17	1
Ried	Jonathan	27JUL03	2.26	1	Renfrow	Absalom	22JUL00	1.13	1
Reed	Jonathan	24JUL04	4.19	1	Rentfrow	Absalom	23JUN01	1.15	1
Ried	Jonathan	22JUL05	2.27	1	Rentfrow	Absalom	20JUN02	1.19	1
Reid	Jonathan	18JUL06	2.31	1	Rentfrow	Absalom	21JUN03	1.20	1
Reed	Jonathen	15JUL07	2.30	1	Rentfrow	Absalom	01AUG04	1.17	1
Reed	Jonathen	-----08	2.24	1	Rentfrow	Absalom	29JUL05	1.18	1
Reed	Jonathan	09JUN09	1.29	1	Rentfrow	Absalom	30JUL06	1.21	1
Reed	Jonathan	-----11	1.65	1	Rentfrow	Absolom	05MAY07	1.21	1
Reed	Joseph	28MAR91	1.08	11	Rentfrow	Absalom	07JUN08	1.30	1
Reid	Joseph	13OCT92	2.07	1	Rentfrow	Absalom	13JUN09	2.28	1
Reed	Joseph	13AUG93	1.08	1	Rentfrow	Bartlet	28JUN03	1.20	1
Reed	Joseph	29MAY94	1.08	1	Rentfro	Isaac	15MAY97	3.26	1
Reed	Joseph	30MAY96	1.11	11	Rentfrow	Isaac Sr	21JUN03	1.20	11
Reed	Joseph	12JUN99	2.17	1	Rentfrow	Isaac	21JUN03	1.20	1
Reed	Joseph	23JUN01	1.15	1	Rentfrow	Isaac	01AUG04	1.17	1
Reed	Joseph	20JUN02	1.19	11	Rentfrow	Isaac	29JUL05	1.18	1
Reed	Joseph	13JUN03	1.20	11	Rentfrow	Isaac	30JUL06	1.21	1
Reed	Joseph	01AUG04	1.17	11	Rentfrow	Isaac	05MAY07	1.22	1
Reed	Joseph	22JUL05	1.18	1	Rentfrow	Isaac	07JUN08	1.30	1
Reed	Joseph Sr	19JUN06	1.21	1	Rentfro	Isaac Sr	19AUG09	2.28	1
Reed	Joseph	19JUN06	1.21	1	Rentfro	Isaac Jr	13JUN09	2.28	1
Reed	Joseph	25MAY07	1.22	1	Rentfro	Isaac	16JUN09	2.28	1
Reed	Joseph Jr	04MAY07	1.21	1	Rentfroe	Isaac	-----11	1.68	12
Reed	Margaret	-----08	2.24	F	Rentfro	James	15MAY97	3.26	1
Reed	Peggy	08JUN09	1.29	F	Rentfro	James	15MAY97	3.26	11
Reid	Michael	19APR97	3.26	1	Renfrow	James	12JUN99	2.17	1
Reed	Michael	28MAY99	1.31	1	Renfrow	James Jr	12JUN99	2.17	1
Reed	Michael	08JUL00	2.25	1	Renfrow	James	22JUL00	1.12	1
Reed	Michael	30JUN01	2.23	1	Renfrow	James Jr	22JUL00	1.13	1
Reed	Michael	21JUL02	2.26	1	Rentfrow	James Sr	23JUN01	1.15	D
Reed	Michael	12JUL03	3.21	1	James Rentfrow Jr - Exec.				
Reed	Michael	18JUN04	2.16	1	Rentfrow	James Jr	23JUN01	1.15	1
Reed	Michiel	08JUL05	3.29	1	Exec. for James Sr Rentfrow				
Reed	Michael	24JUL06	3.29	1	Rentfrow	James	20JUN02	1.19	1
Reed	Michael	05AUG07	2.30	1	Rentfrow	James	21JUN03	1.20	1
Reed	Michael	30MAY08	2.23	1	Rentfrow	James	01AUG04	1.17	1
Reed	Michael	07JUL09	1.29	1	Rentfrow	James	29JUL05	1.18	1
Reed	William	04AUG87	1.05	1	Rentfrow	James	30JUL06	1.21	1
Reed	William	18JUL89	6.06	1	Rentfrow	James	05MAY07	1.22	1
Reed	William	10AUG90	1.09	1	Renfrow	Jesse	13JUN97	1.21	1
Reed	William	25AUG91	2.08	1	Ranfro	John	17JUN05	3.29	M1
Reed	William	06DEC92	1.10	1	Rentfrow	John	18APR08	1.29	1
Reed	William	-----93	3.10	1	Rentfro	John	16JUN09	2.28	1
Reed	William	17APR94	2.12	1	Renfrow	Lewis	12JUN99	2.17	1
Reid	William	18MAR95	3.15	1	Renfrow	Lewis	22JUL00	1.13	1
Reed	William	20MAY96	2.16	1	Rentfrow	Lewis	23JUN01	1.15	1
Reed	William	29MAY97	1.21	1	Rentfrow	Lewis	21JUN02	1.20	1
Reed	William	13MAY99	3.18	1	Rentfrow	Lewis	29JUL05	1.18	1

surname	name	date	bk.pg	TM	surname	name	date	bk.pg	TM
Rentfrow	Lewis	31JUL06	1.21	1	Renick	William	-----95	2.26	
Rentfro	Lewis	13JUN09	2.28	1	One lot in Stanford				
Rentfrow	Mark	21JUN03	1.20	11	Renick	William *	09MAY95	2.11	1
Rentfrow	Mark	01AUG04	1.17	11	Renick	William	09MAY95	2.11	11
Rentfrow	Mark	29JUL05	1.18	1	Renick	William	10JUN95	2.10	1
Rentfrow	Mark	30JUL06	1.21	11	Renick	William	27MAY96	1.11	1
Rentfrow	Mark	08MAY07	1.22	11	Renick	William	13JUN97	3.26	11
Rentfrow	Mark	07JUN08	1.30	2	Renick	William	13JUN97	3.33	
Renfro	Mark	30JUN09	2.28	21	Two town lots in Stanford				
Rentfro	Thomas	13JUN09	2.28	1	REYNIORSON				
Renfrow	Turpin	12JUN99	2.17	1	Reynierson	Christopher	24MAY99	3.17	1
Renfrow	Turpen	22JUL00	1.13	1	Reynearson	Christopher	12JUL00	3.26	1
Rentfrow	Turpen	23JUN01	1.15	1	Reyniorson	Christopher	29JUL01	3.29	1
Rentfrow	Turner	20JUN02	1.19	1	Reyniorson	Christopher	02JUL02	2.26	1
Rentfrow	Turpen	21JUN03	1.20	1	Rincarson	Christopher	05AUG03	3.21	1
RENICK					Rineyarson	Christopher	26APR04	4.19	1
Rennix	Henry	16JUN89	6.06	1	Reighneson	Christopher	07AUG05	3.30	1
Renick	Henry	31MAR90	2.06	1	Reighnerson	Christopher	11AUG06	3.29	1
Renix	Henry	12APR91	1.07	1	Ryenerson	Isaac	-----11	1.65	1
Renick	Henery	09OCT92	2.07	1	REYNOLDS				
Ranick	Henry	30AUG93	1.08	1	Reynolds	Amos	-----11	1.65	1
Renox	James	04AUG87	1.05	1	Reynolds	Charles	10JUN89	6.06	1
Renex	James	23MAY89	6.08	1	Reynolds	Charles	14MAY90	1.09	1
Rennix	James	24MAY90	1.09	1	Runnels	Charles	01AUG91	2.08	1
Rennix	James	03OCT92	1.11	1	Runnels	Charles	22SEP92	1.10	1
Rennick	James	13AUG93	3.10	1	Rennals	Charles	20AUG93	3.10	1
Renix	James	11JUN94	2.12	1	Reynolds	Charles	10JUN94	2.12	1
Rennicks	James	15APR95	3.14	1	Reynolds	Charles	10JUN94	2.12	1
Renix	James	11JUN96	2.16	1	Reynolds	Fountain	-----11	1.66	1
Renick	James	23JUN97	1.20	1	Rennalds	George	06AUG93	3.10	1
Renick	James	30JUL00	2.25	1	Rynolds	George	10MAY94	2.12	1
Rannack	James	20JUN01	3.30	1	Reynolds	George	10APR95	3.14	1
Ranex	James	01JUN02	2.26	1	Runnels	George	-----96	4.13	1
Reynox	James	14JUN03	3.21	11	Renolds	George	19MAY96	2.16	1
Renicks	James	15AUG04	3.17	11	Ranoalds	George	22MAY97	1.21	1
Ranax	James	22JUN05	3.30	11	Rannols	Isham	20JUN07	2.29	1
Ranuck	James	16JUL06	3.28	12	Rannels	James	10JUN07	2.29	1
Rannak	James	13JUL07	2.29	1	Ranolds	James	30MAY08	2.23	1
Rannax	James	30MAY08	2.23	1	Raynolds	James	28JUN09	1.29	1
Rennix	James	11JUL09	1.30	1	Reynolds	James	-----11	1.68	1
Renick	James	-----11	1.67	1	Reynolds	John	22MAY89	6.06	1
Renick	John	21MAY94	1.11	1	Reynolds	John	13MAY90	1.08	1
Ranels	John	28JUL04	2.16	11	Ronnalds	John	24JUN00	2.25	1
Ranax	John	13JUL07	2.29	12	Ronnalds	John	03JUN01	2.23	1
Rannax	John	30MAY08	2.23	1	Rennels	John	30JUN02	1.20	1
Rennix	John	11JUL09	1.30	1	Rennels	John	07JUL03	1.21	1
Renick	John	-----11	1.67	1	Rennels	John	26JUL05	1.18	1
Rennix	Robert	09JUN91	2.08	1	Rennels	John	15JUL06	1.21	11
Rennix	Robert	28SEP92	1.11	1	Reanolds	John	07JUN08	1.30	12
Renick	Robert	31MAY94	1.07	1	Reanolds	John	29MAY09	2.27	1
Renick	Robert	-----95	2.26		Reynolds	John	-----11	1.66	12
One lot in Stanford					Reynolds	Joseph	-----11	1.67	1
Renick	Robert	10JUN95	2.10	1	Reynolds	Perry	-----11	1.66	1
Renick	Robert	27MAY96	1.11	11	Ranoalds	Richard	22MAY97	1.21	1
Renick	Robert	27JUN96	1.13		Renolds	Roberts	13JUL07	2.29	12
One town lot in Stanford					Ranolds	Robert	30MAY08	2.23	12
Renick	Samuel	09MAY95	2.11	1	Raynolds	Robert	30JUN09	1.29	2
Renicks	William	27JUN87	1.05	11	Reynolds	Robert	-----11	1.68	1
Renex	William Sr	23MAY89	6.08	1	Reynolds	Robert	-----11	1.68	12
Rennix	William	16JUN89	6.06	1	Rynolds	Samuel	10MAY94	2.12	M1
Renick	William	26MAR90	2.06	11	Runnels	Samuel	-----96	4.13	1
Renix	William Jr	15APR90	1.09	1	Reynolds	Samuel	29JUN96	2.16	1
Rennix	William	02JUN90	1.08	1	Ranoalds	Samuel	31MAY97	1.21	1
Renix	William	25MAR91	1.07	1	Reynolds	Thomas	-----11	1.65	1
Renix	William	12APR91	1.08	11	Ronnalds	William	24JUN00	2.25	1
Renick	William Sr	09OCT92	2.07	12	Reanolds	William	04MAR08	1.30	1
Renick	William Jr	09OCT92	2.07	1	Runnels	William	29MAY09	2.27	1
Rennick	William Sr	30AUG93	1.08	12	Reynolds	William	-----11	1.65	1
Rennick	William Jr	30AUG93	1.07	1	RICE				
Renick	William Sr	31MAY94	1.07	11	Rice	Anderson	18MAY91	2.08	1
Renick	William	31MAY94	1.07	1	Rice	Anderson	10OCT92	1.11	1
Renick	William Sr	09MAY95	2.11	11	Rice	Anderson	21AUG93	3.10	1

surname	name	date	bk.pg	TM	surname	name	date	bk.pg	TM
Rice	Anderson	30APR94	2.12	1	Richards	Leonard Sr	06AUG04	3.17	1
Rice	Anderson	04APR95	3.14	1	Richards	Leonard Jr	07AUG04	3.17	1
Rice	Anderson	16AUG96	2.16	1	Richards	Lenard	07AUG05	3.30	1
Rice	Anderson	23MAY97	1.21	1	Richards	Lenard	05AUG05	3.30	1
Rice	Anderson	03JUL99	3.17	1	Richards	Leonard Sr	04AUG06	3.29	11
Rice	Andrewson	01JUL00	3.26	1	Richards	Leonard Jr	04AUG06	3.29	1
Rice	Anderson	19JUL01	3.29	1	Richards	William	31JUL05	2.28	1
Rice	Anderson	17AUG02	3.23	1	Richards	William	28JUL06	3.29	1
Rice	Anderson	22JUN03	2.26	1	Richards	William	11JUN07	2.29	1
Rice	Anderson	27JUL04	4.20	1	Richards	William	30MAY08	2.23	1
Rice	Anderson	25JUL05	2.27	1	Richards	William	28JUN09	1.29	1
Rice	Anderson	16JUL06	2.30	1	RICHARDSON				
Rice	Anderson	14AUG07	2.30	1	Richardson	Amos	23APR94	2.12	12
Rice	Anderson	-----08	2.24	1	Richardson	Daniel	23APR94	2.12	1
Rice	Anderson	22JUN09	1.29	1	Richeson	David	15JUL99	3.17	1
Rice	Anderson	-----11	1.68	1	Richerson	David	25JUN00	3.25	1
Rice	Charles	07JUL87	3.08	1	Richardson	David	18MAY01	3.29	1
Rice	Charles	13AUG89	5.12	1	Richarson	David	12AUG02	3.23	1
Rise	Charles	12SEP91	3.14	1	Richardson	David	28JUL03	2.26	1
Rice	Charles	05DEC92	3.17	1	Richardson	David	28JUN04	4.19	1
Rice	Charles	21MAY94	3.18	1	Richardson	David	29MAY05	2.27	1
Rice	Charles	-----95	1.12	1	Richardson	David	13AUG06	2.31	1
Rice	Charles	-----96	4.13	1	Richison	David	12AUG07	2.30	1
Rice	Charles	16AUG96	2.16	1	Richeson	David	30MAY08	2.23	1
Rice	Charles	23MAY97	1.21	1	Richardson	David	09JUN09	1.29	1
Rice	Francis	30APR94	2.12	F	Richardson	David	-----11	1.67	1
Rice	Matthew	21AUG93	3.10	1	Richardson	Elijah	08JUN09	1.29	1
Rice	Matthew	30APR94	2.12	1	Richardson	Elijah	-----11	1.65	1
Rice	Matthew	04APR95	3.14	1	Richason	Felix	-----11	1.68	1
Rice	Matthew	16AUG96	2.16	1	Richardson	James	28JUN90	1.09	1
Rice	Matthew	23MAY97	1.21	1	Richardson	Jessey	07JUL87	3.09	1
Rice	Matthew	03JUL99	3.17	1	Ritcherson	Jesse	31OCT88	1.08	1
Rice	Matthew	01JUL00	3.26	1	Richardson	Jesse	13AUG89	5.12	1
Rice	Matthew	19JUL01	3.29	1	Ritchorson	Jesse	12SEP91	3.14	1
Rice	Mathew	17AUG02	3.23	1	Ritcherson	Jesse	05DEC92	3.17	1
Rice	Mathew	22JUN03	2.26	1	Richardson	Jesse	-----93	2.04	1
Rice	Matthew	27JUL04	4.20	1	Ritcheson	Jesse	29MAY94	1.08	1
Rice	Mathew	25JUL05	2.27	1	Richardson	Jesse	-----95	1.12	1
Rice	Mathew	16JUL06	2.30	1	Richardson	Jessee	-----96	4.13	1
Rice	Matthew	03AUG07	2.30	1	Richardson	Jesse	-----97	2.04	1
Rice	Mathew	-----08	2.24	1	Richason	Jesse	09JUL99	2.18	12
Rice	Mathew	22JUN09	1.29	1	Richardson	John	19AUG93	3.10	1
Rice	Matthew	-----11	1.68	11	Richardson	John	23APR94	2.12	1
Rice	Roalit	30APR94	2.12	11	Richardson	John	-----11	1.66	1
Rice	Rowlet	16AUG96	2.16	1	Ritcherson	Jonathan	05DEC92	3.17	1
RICHARDS					Richardson	Jonathan	-----93	2.04	1
Richards	Felix	31JUL05	2.28	1	Richardson	Jonathan	-----96	4.13	1
Richards	Phelex	28JUL06	3.29	1	Richardson	Jonathan	14MAY99	1.31	1
Richards	Felex	11JUN07	2.29	1	Richardson	Joseph	02OCT87	1.05	1
Richards	Felex	30MAY08	2.23	1	Richardson	Joseph	26JUN89	6.06	1
Richards	Phelix	28JUN09	1.29	1	Richardson	Joseph	03NOV92	1.11	1
Richards	John	24JUL00	2.25	1	Richason	Joseph	12JUN00	1.12	1
Richards	John	28MAY01	3.29	1	Richardson	Lande	21APR96	2.15	1
Richards	John	12AUG02	2.26	1	Richardson	Landy	27MAY96	1.11	M1
Richard	John	07JUL03	3.21	1	Richardson	Robert	16JUN09	2.28	1
Richards	John	07AUG04	3.17	1	Richardson	Thomas	-----95	1.12	1
Richards	John	08JUL05	3.29	1	Richardson	Thomas	-----97	2.04	1
Richard	John	07AUG05	3.30	1	Richason	Thomas	11MAY99	2.17	1
Richards	John	14JUL06	3.28	1	Richason	Thomas	09JUN00	1.12	1
Richards	John	28JUL06	3.29	1	Richason	Timothy	13JUN89	6.06	1
Richards	John	11JUN07	2.29	1	Richason	Timothy	31MAR91	2.08	1
Richards	John	30MAY08	2.23	11	Richardson	William	07JUL87	3.09	11
Richards	John	28JUN09	1.29	1	Richardson	William	30JUN89	5.11	11
Richards	John	-----11	1.68	11	Ritcherson	William	05DEC92	3.17	1
Richards	Leonard	27JUN99	1.31	11	Richardson	William	21MAY94	3.18	1
Richards	Leonard	24JUL00	2.25	11	Richardson	William	-----95	1.12	11
Richards	Lenard Sr	28MAY01	3.29	1	Richardson	William	-----96	4.13	1
Richards	Lenard Jr	28MAY01	3.29	1	Richardson	William	-----97	2.04	11
Richards	Leonard	12AUG02	2.26	1	Richason	William	13MAY99	2.17	1
Richards	Leonard Jr	12AUG02	2.26	1	Richason	William	12AUG00	1.13	1
Richard	Leonard Sr	07JUL03	3.21	11	Richason	William	01JUN01	1.15	1
Richard	Leonard Jr	07JUL03	3.21	1	RICHEY				

surname	name	date	bk.pg	TM	surname	name	date	bk.pg	TM
Richie	Alexander	26JUN87	1.05	1	Ridgeway	William	30MAY08	2.23	11
Richey	James	29JUN96	2.16	11	RIFFE				
Richey	James	29JUN97	1.20	1	Rife	Abraham	24MAY94	2.12	1
Richey	James	21MAY99	3.17	1	Rife	Abraham	16APR95	3.14	1
Richey	James	04JUL00	3.26	1	Rife	Abraham	17MAY96	2.16	1
Ritchey	James	16JUL06	2.30	1	Rife	Abraham	13JUL97	1.21	1
Richey	James	12AUG07	2.30	1	Rife	Abram	27JUN99	1.31	11
Richey	John	29JUN97	1.20	1	Rife	Abraham	24JUL00	2.25	11
Richey	Thomas	28JUN97	1.21	M1	Riffe	Abraham	27MAY01	3.29	11
Richey	Thomas	21MAY99	3.17	1	Riffe	Abraham	12AUG02	2.26	11
Richey	Thomas	09JUL00	3.26	1	Riffe	Abraham	24MAY03	3.21	11
Richey	Thomas	01MAY01	3.29	1	Rife	Abraham	07AUG04	3.17	11
Richey	Thomas	31JUL02	3.23	1	Riffe	Abraham	07AUG05	3.30	11
Richey	Thomas	28JUL03	2.26	1	Riffe	Abraham	11AUG06	3.29	11
RICKETTS					Rife	Christopher	23MAY89	6.06	1
Rickets	Ezekiel	02JUN03	3.21	1	Riffe	Christopher	13AUG90	1.09	1
Ricketts	Frances	22AUG04	2.17	1	Rife	Christopher	30APR91	2.08	1
Ricketts	Francis	31JUL05	2.27	1	Rife	Christopher	22SEP92	1.10	1
Rickits	Hezakiah	22JUL01	3.30	1	Rife	Christopher	07AUG93	3.10	1
Ricketts	Hezikiah	-----05	3.38		Rife	Christopher	24MAY94	2.12	1
1804 tax info in 1805 tax list					Rife	Christopher	16APR95	3.14	1
Ricketts	Hezikiah	-----05	3.38	1	Rife	Christopher	04JUN96	2.16	1
Ricketts	Hezekiah	05AUG05	3.30	1	Rife	Christopher	21JUN97	1.20	1
RIDDLE					Rife	Christopher	01JUL99	1.32	1
Ridgel	Anne	24JUN89	5.10	F	Rife	Christopher	24JUN00	2.25	1
Ridgal	Ann	02JUN90	2.06	F	Riffe	Christipher	30MAY01	3.30	1
Riggle	Anne	14APR91	1.08	F	Riffe	Christopher	13AUG02	2.26	1
Ridgle	Mariann	26JUN87	2.06	F	Riffe	Christopher	11JUN03	3.21	1
Riddle	Moses	30JUN87	1.05	1	Rife	Christopher	09AUG04	3.17	1
Riddle	Moses	18APR89	6.06	1	Rife	Christopher	17AUG05	3.30	1
Riddle	Moses	28APR94	3.18	1	Rife	Daniel	14JUN94	2.12	1
RIDGEWAY					Riffe	John	22AUG03	3.22	1
Ridgeway	Elijah	20JUN01	3.30	1	RIGDON				
Ridgeway	Elijah	18JUL03	3.21	1	Rikons	Aaron	03AUG87	1.05	1
Ridgeway	Elijah	04AUG04	3.17	1	Ridgeton	Stephen	05AUG06	3.29	1
Ridgeway	Elijah	17AUG05	3.30	1	Rigdon	Stephen	30MAY08	2.23	1
Ridgeway	Elijah	28JUL06	3.29	1	RIGGS				
Ridgeway	Elijah	11JUN07	2.29	1	Riggs	Daniel	21APR96	2.15	1
Ridgeway	Elijah	30MAY08	2.23	1	Riggs	Reuben	29MAY97	1.21	1
Ridgeway	Elijah	28JUN09	1.29	1	Riggs	Scoot	18JUN01	3.29	1
Ridgeway	Elijah	-----11	1.68	1	Riggs	Silas	29JUL05	1.18	1
Ridgeway	Isaac	17JUN05	3.29	1	Riggs	Silas	08MAY07	1.22	1
Ridgeway	Isaac	03AUG07	2.30	1	Riggs	Silas	18APR08	1.29	1
Ridgeway	Isaac	-----08	2.24	1	Riggs	Silas	16JUN09	2.28	1
Ridgeway	Isaac	10JUL09	1.30	1	Riggs	Thomas	31JUL02	3.23	11
Ridgeway	Isaac	-----11	1.67	1	Riggs	Tadok	21JUN97	1.20	11
Ridgwell	Jonathan	25JUL96	1.11	1	Riggs	Zaddock	16MAY99	3.17	11
Ridgeway	Jonathan	31MAY97	3.26	1	Riggs	Zadock	09JUL00	3.26	12
Ridgeway	Mary	17JUN05	3.29	F2	Riggs	Zedok	18JUN01	3.29	11
Ridgeway	Mary	21JUL06	3.28	F	Riggs	Zedor	05AUG03	2.27	1
Ridgeway	Mary	03AUG07	2.30	F2	Rigs	Zedeck	13JUN04	4.19	11
Ridgeway	Mary	10JUL09	1.30	F1	Riggs	Zedor	27JUN05	2.27	11
Ridgeway	Osbon	14JUN03	3.21	1	Riggs	Zedoe	13AUG06	2.31	11
Ridgeway	Ausburn	04AUG04	3.17	11	Riggs	Zedock	18AUG07	2.31	11
Ridgeway	Orsburn	17JUN05	3.29	1	Riggs	Zedick	30MAY08	2.23	12
Ridgeway	Osburn	21JUL06	3.29	1	Riggs	Zadock	17JUL09	1.30	2
Ridgeway	Orsburn	03AUG07	2.30	1	Riggs	Zadock	-----11	1.68	11
Ridgeway	Orsburn	30MAY08	2.23	1	RIGNEY				
Ridgeway	Osburn	10JUL09	1.30	1	Rigney	Jesse	21JUN05	2.27	1
Ridgeway	Osbern	-----11	1.67	1	Rigney	Jesse	18AUG06	2.31	1
Ridgeway	Samuel	29JUL00	2.25	1	Rigney	Jesse	15JUL07	2.29	11
Ridgeway	Samuel	20JUN01	3.30	1	Rigney	William	22AUG04	2.17	1
Ridgway	Samuel	02JUN02	2.26	1	Rigney	William	16MAY05	2.26	1
Ridgway	Samuel	14JUN03	3.21	1	Rigney	William	12AUG06	2.31	1
Ridgway	Samuel	29JUN04	4.19	1	Rigney	William	15JUL07	2.30	1
Ridgeway	Samuel	14JUN05	3.29	1	Rigney	William	30MAY08	2.23	1
Ridgeway	Samuel	21JUL06	3.28	1	Rigney	William	10MAY09	1.29	1
Ridgeway	Samuel	10JUN07	2.29	1	RILEY				
Ridgeway	Samuel	30MAY08	2.23	1	Riley	Alexander	-----11	1.65	1
Ridgeway	Samuel	30JUN09	1.29	1	Riley	Barney	26SEP92	2.07	1
Ridgeway	Samuel	-----11	1.68	1	Riley	Barnabas	30AUG93	1.08	1
Ridgeway	Thomas	-----11	1.68	1	Riley	Barnabas	31MAY94	1.07	1

surname	name	date	bk.pg	TM	surname	name	date	bk.pg	TM
Reily	Barnabas	08JUN95	2.11	1	Roberts	Jesse	28MAR91	1.07	1
Riley	Barnabas	30MAY96	1.11	1	Roberts	Jessey	11OCT92	2.07	1
Rhyley	Caleb	05DEC92	3.17	1	Roberts	Jesse	13AUG93	1.07	1
Riley	Edward	04AUG96	2.16	11	Roberds	Jesse	20AUG93	1.07	1
Riley	Edward	16MAY97	1.21	1	Robins	John	26JUN89	6.06	1
Reily	Edward	03JUL99	3.17	1	Roberts	John	10OCT92	1.11	1
Riley	Edward	30JUN00	3.25	1	Roberts	John	30JUN99	2.16	11
Ryley	George	24APR06	2.30	1	Rubarts	John	25MAY03	3.21	1
Reiley	George	12AUG07	2.30	1	Roberts	John	18AUG04	3.17	1
Reiley	George	-----08	2.24	1	Ruberts	John	05AUG05	3.30	1
Rilie	George	08JUN09	1.29	1	Roberts	John	11AUG06	3.29	1
Riley	George	-----11	1.65	1	Roberts	John	12JUN09	2.28	1
Reiley	Hugh	12AUG07	2.30	1	Roberts	Ritchardson	06MAY07	1.22	1
Railey	John	04AUG87	1.05	1	Roberts	Ritchardson	18APR08	1.29	1
Reily	John	15JUN89	6.06	1	Roberts	William	05JUN09	2.27	1
Ryley	John Sr	15JUL06	2.30	1	Roberts	William	-----11	1.67	2
Ryley	John Jr	17JUL06	2.31	1	ROBINET				
Reiley	John	14AUG07	2.30	1	Robennight	Joal	02MAY01	3.29	1
Reiley	John Jr	12AUG07	2.30	1	Robinet	Joel	12JUL02	3.22	1
Reiley	John	-----08	2.24	1	ROBINSON				
Reiley	John	-----08	2.24	1	Robinson	Daniel	24JUN99	2.16	11
Riley	John Sr	09JUN09	1.29	1	Robison	Duncan F.	09JUN09	1.29	1
Riley	John	09JUN09	1.29	1	Roberdson	Edward	18JUN96	1.11	1
Riley	John Sr	-----11	1.68	1	Robinson	Edward	10MAY97	3.26	1
Riley	John Jr	-----11	1.68	1	Robinson	George	15JUL01	2.23	1
Ryley	Lewis	24APR06	2.30	1	Robinson	George	17JUN02	3.22	1
Reiley	Lewis	12AUG07	2.30	1	Robinson	George	01JUN03	2.26	1
Reiley	Lewis	-----08	2.24	1	Robison	George	23JUL04	1.17	1
Riley	Lewis	09JUN09	1.29	1	Robinson	George	30MAY05	2.27	1
Ryley	Oley	24APR06	2.30	M1	Robertson	Hohnbee	28JUN95	2.11	1
Reiley	Oliver	14AUG07	2.30	1	Roberdson	Halcombe	18MAY96	1.11	1
Reiley	Oliver	14AUG07	2.30	1	Robinson	Haulkin	10MAY97	3.26	1
Riley	Robert	26SEP92	2.07	1	Robertson	Hannah	27JUN87	1.05	F1
Riley	Robert	30AUG93	1.08	1	Robinson	Hannah	25MAY89	6.06	F
Riley	Robert	17MAY94	1.08	1		Also lists Luke Robinson			
Reily	Robert	08JUN95	2.11	1	Robinson	Hannah	10MAY90	1.08	F
Riley	Robert	30MAY96	1.11	1		Luke Robinson also listed			
Reily	Robert	26JUN99	3.17	1	Robinson	Hannah	18MAY91	2.08	F
RIMAL					Robinson	Hannah	18SEP92	1.11	F
Rimal	Elias	24MAY94	2.12	1	Robertson	Hosea	18MAY90	2.06	1
RINER					Robinson	Holsey	20APR97	3.27	1
Riner	Jacob	07JUN08	1.30	1	Robinson	Hosea	19JUL00	2.25	1
ROACH					Robinson	Hosea	19MAY01	2.23	1
Roach	Charles	24MAY94	2.12	M1	Robinson	Hoses	27MAY02	3.22	1
Roach	Isaac	-----95	1.12	1	Robinson	Hosea	21JUN03	2.26	1
Roach	Isaac	-----96	4.13	1	Robinson	Hosea	08JUN05	2.27	11
Roach	Iaac	15JUL03	1.21	1	Robinson	Hosea	19MAY06	2.30	1
Roach	Isaac	25JUN04	1.17	1	Robinson	Hosea	-----11	1.67	1
Roach	Isaac	25JUL05	1.18	1	Robertson	James	07JUL87	3.08	1
Roatch	Isaac	23JUN06	1.21	1	Robertson	James	26NOV92	3.16	1
Roach	John	20JUN99	2.18	1	Robertson	James	10JUN94	2.12	1
Road	John	07JUN08	1.30	1	Robertson	James	03APR95	3.14	0
Road	Joseph	07JUN08	1.30	1	Robertson	James	-----96	4.13	1
ROBERT					Robertson	Joel	-----96	4.13	21
Robert	William	29MAR95	3.15	0	Robinson	John	21JUL89	5.10	1
ROBERTS					Robertson	John	18MAY90	2.06	1
Roberts	Alexander	18APR89	6.06	1	Robinson	John	07OCT91	1.07	1
Roberts	Elex.	29MAR90	2.06	1	Robinson	John	15OCT92	2.07	1
Robbins	Alexandria	28MAY91	3.14	1	Robinson	John	12AUG93	1.07	1
Roberts	Alexander	28APR94	3.18	1	Robinson	John	21MAY94	1.07	1
Roberts	Alexander	-----95	1.12	1	Robinson	John	28JUN95	2.11	1
Roberts	Alexander	19MAY95	2.11	1	Robinson	John	20JUN96	1.10	1
Roberts	Alexander	-----96	4.13	1	Robinson	John	30JUN96	1.11	1
Roberts	George	-----11	1.66	1	Robinson	John	26APR97	3.26	1
Roberts	Hiram	18APR08	1.29	1	Robinson	Luke	25MAY89	6.06	
Roberts	Hiram	05JUN09	2.27	1		Listed with Hannah Robinson			
Roberts	Jacob	30JUN09	2.28	1	Robinson	Luke	10MAY90	1.08	
Roberts	Jacob	-----11	1.66	1		Listed with Hannah Robinson			
Roberts	James	06JUN07	1.22	1	Robinson	Luke	18MAY91	2.08	1
Roberts	James	18APR08	1.29	1	Robinson	Luke	18SEP92	1.10	1
Roberts	James	30JUN09	2.28	1	Robertson	Luke	18APR94	2.12	1
Roberts	Jesse	19JUN89	5.10	1	Robertson	Luke	24MAR95	3.15	1

surname	name	date	bk.pg	TM	surname	name	date	bk.pg	TM
Roberson	Luke	13JUN96	2.16	1	Rogers	John	-----11	1.66	1
Robertson	Luke	16MAY97	1.21	1	Rodgers	William	14MAY90	1.08	M1
Roberson	Luke	02JUL99	3.17	1	Rodgers	William	01AUG91	2.08	1
Robertson	Luke	26JUN00	3.25	1	Roger	William	10MAY94	2.12	1
Robison	Luke	21MAY01	3.29	1	Rogers	William	15APR95	3.14	1
Robinson	Luke	08JUL02	3.22	1	Rogers	William	29JUN96	2.16	1
Robinson	Luke	26JUL03	2.26	1	ROLES				
Robinson	Luke	26JUL04	4.19	1	Rowls	Hardy	07JUL87	3.08	11
Robinson	Luke	22JUL05	2.27	1	Rawls	Hardy	13AUG89	5.12	11
Robinson	Luke	14JUL06	2.30	1	Rolls	Hardy	12SEP91	3.14	1
Robison	Luke	05AUG07	2.30	1	Rolls	Hardy	05DEC92	3.17	1
Robison	Luke	-----08	2.24	1	Rawls	Hardy	28APR94	3.18	1
Robison	Luke	09JUN09	1.29	1	Rolls	Hardy	-----95	1.12	1
Robinson	Luke	-----11	1.65	1	Rolls	Hardy	-----96	4.13	1
Robertson	Luke	-----11	1.67	1	Rolls	Hardy	-----97	2.04	1
Robertson	Merridath	05AUG03	3.21	1	Rauls	Hardy	24JUN99	2.16	11
Robertson	Osea	26JUN87	2.06	1	Roles	Hardy	18JUN00	1.12	11
Robinson	Ose	27NOV88	1.09	1	Rolls	Marmeduke	13AUG89	5.12	1
Robinson	Ose	16JUN89	5.10	1	ROMINE				
Robinson	Osey	11OCT92	2.07	1	Romine	Peter	28APR94	3.18	1
Robinson	Osee	05AUG93	1.08	1	Romine	Peter	-----95	1.12	1
Robinson	Oce	13MAY94	1.08	1	RONION				
Robinson	Oce	21MAY95	2.11	1	Ronion	Freeman	28MAR06	2.30	1
Robinson	Oce	08JUN96	1.10	1	RONSTSAN				
Robason	Osea	30MAY99	1.31	1	Ronstsan	Conrad	-----11	1.66	1
Robison	Osio	23JUL04	1.14	1	ROOP				
Robison	Osee	15JUL07	2.30	1	Roop	Barnabas	29MAY96	1.11	1
Robertson	Osie	07JUN08	1.30	1	Roop	Barnabas	10APR97	3.25	1
Robertson	Osey	19AUG09	2.28	1	Roop	Barnett	16MAY99	1.31	1
Robison	Richard	30JUN99	2.16	11	Roop	Barnett	18JUN00	2.25	1
Robertson	Robert Sr	-----11	1.69	12	Roope	Barnett	24JUL01	2.23	1
Robinson	Thomas	15JUL01	2.23	1	Roop	Barnet	10JUN02	1.19	1
Robinson	Thomas	08JUN02	3.22	1	Rupe	Barrett	09JUL04	2.16	1
Robinson	Thomas	01JUN03	2.26	1	Roop	Barnet	13JUN05	1.17	1
Robison	Thomas	24JUL04	1.17	1	Roop	Barnet	19JUN06	1.21	11
Robinson	Thomas	08JUN05	2.27	1	Roop	Barnabas	04JUN07	1.22	1
Robinson	Thomas	09JUN06	2.30	1	Roop	Barney	18APR08	1.29	11
Robison	Thomas	-----08	2.24	1	Roop	Barnabas	06JUN09	2.27	1
Robison	Thomas	23JUN09	1.29	1	Roupe	Barney	-----11	1.66	1
Robertson	Thomas	-----11	1.67	1	ROSE				
Robertson	Walter	-----93	2.04	1	Rose	George	19JUN99	2.18	1
Robinson	William	13JUN89	6.06	1	Rose	George	21JUL01	2.23	1
Robertson	William	01MAY94	2.12	1	Rose	George	16JUN02	1.19	1
Robertson	William	02APR95	3.14	1	Rose	George	05JUL03	3.21	1
Robertson	William	01JUN97	1.09	0	Rose	George	15JUN04	1.17	1
Tax pd by James Jr Givens					Ross	George	20JUN05	1.18	1
Robison	William	14JUN99	2.18	1	Rose	George	21JUN06	1.21	1
Robison	William	24JUL00	1.13	1	Rose	George	20JUN07	1.22	1
ROCK					Rose	John	-----93	2.04	1
Rock	James	15JUN89	6.06	1	Rose	John	-----96	4.13	1
Rock	John	10AUG02	2.26		Rose	Robert	-----11	1.67	1
A free black man					Rose	William	20JUN07	1.22	1
Rock	John	22AUG03	3.22		ROSEN				
A free mulatto above 21					Rosson	Charles	12JUN97	1.21	1
Rock	John	07AUG04	3.17		Rossin	Charles	24JUN99	1.31	11
(black)					Rosson	Charles	11AUG06	3.29	1
Rock	John	17AUG05	3.30		Rosson	William	20JUN97	1.21	1
A free black man					Rosen	William	07AUG05	3.30	1
Rock	John	11AUG06	3.29		Roseon	William	11AUG06	3.29	1
one black over 16					ROSS				
ROGERS					Ross	Daniel	07JUL87	3.08	1
Rogers	Anthony	26JUN87	2.06	1	Ross	Daniel	11JUN89	6.06	1
Roger	John	07JUL87	3.08	1	Ross	Daniel	15APR90	1.08	1
Rogers	John	04JUN01	2.23	1	Ross	Daniel*	02AUG90	1.08	1
Rogers	John	23AUG02	2.27	1	Ross	Daniel	--AUG91	2.08	1
Rogers	John	20JUL03	3.21	1	Ross	Daniel	22SEP92	1.17	1
Rodgers	John	14JUN04	2.16	1	Ross	Daniel	12AUG93	3.10	1
Rodgers	John	22JUN05	3.30	1	Ross	Daniel	29APR95	3.14	1
Rodgers	John	16JUL06	3.28	1	Ross	Daniel	01JUN96	2.16	1
Rodgers	John	01AUG07	2.30	1	Rous	Daniel	15MAY97	1.21	1
Rogers	John	30MAY08	2.23	1	Rous	Daniel	20MAY99	3.17	1
Rogers	John	16AUG09	1.29	1	Ross	Daniel	06AUG04	3.17	11

surname	name	date	bk.pg	TM	surname	name	date	bk.pg	TM
Ross	Daniel	07AUG05	3.30	1	RUBY				
Ross	Daniel	05AUG06	3.29	11	Renbry	Charles	23MAY97	1.21	1
Ross	Danniel	14JUN03	3.21	1	Reubey	Charles	18MAY99	3.17	11
Ross	Hugh	16AUG91	3.14	1	Reubey	Charles	03JUL99	3.17	1
Ross	Hugh	05DEC92	3.17	1	Ruby	Charles	01JUL00	3.26	11
Ross	Hugh	16MAY97	3.26	1	Rueby	Charles	19JUL01	3.29	1
Ross	Hugh	14JUN99	2.17	1	Rubey	Jacob	30MAY03	2.26	1
Ross	Thomas	28MAR91	1.08	1	Rubey	Jacob	23JUL05	2.27	1
Rouse	Thomas	27APR91	3.14	1	RUFFNER				
ROUNDTREE					Ruffner	David	-----11	1.67	1
Roundtree	Dudley Sr	06AUG93	1.08	1	Ruffner	Henry	-----11	1.67	1
Roundtree	Dudley	06AUG93	1.08	1	Rufner	Ruben	19JUN89	5.10	1
Roundtree	Dudly Sr	14MAY94	1.07	1	Rufman	Ruben	05JUL91	1.08	1
Roundtree	Dudley	14MAY94	1.08	1	Rufner	Ruben	21OCT92	2.07	1
Roundtree	Dudley Sr	22JUN95	2.11	1	Rufner	Robin	07AUG93	1.08	1
Roundtree	Dudley Jr	22JUN95	2.11	1	Rufner	Rubin	16MAY94	1.07	1
Roundtree	Nathaniel	06AUG93	1.08	1	Rusner	Reuben	18MAY95	2.11	12
Roundtree	Nathaniel	14MAY94	1.08	1	Rufnor	Rubin	13JUN96	1.11	1
Rountree	Nathaniel	28MAY95	3.14	1	Ruffner	Reuben	08MAY97	3.26	1
ROUT					Ruffnor	Reubin	22MAY99	1.31	11
Rout	Charles	-----95	1.12	1	Ruffner	Reuben	19JUL00	2.25	11
Rout	John	-----96	4.13	1	Ruffner	Reuben	28MAY01	2.23	11
ROUTEN					Ruffner	Rheuben	18JUN02	1.19	11
Routon	Elizabeth	08JUL06	2.30	F	Rufner	Reuben	05JUL03	1.20	11
Routen	Elizabeth	01AUG07	2.30	F	Ruffener	Rheuben	25JUN04	1.17	1
Rowton	Elizabeth	07JUN08	1.30	F	Ruffener	Rheuben	20JUN05	1.18	1
Rowton	Elizabeth	18AUG09	2.28	F	Ruffener	Rheuben	23JUN06	1.21	11
Rowton	Elizabeth	-----11	1.67	F	Ruffner	Ruben	04MAY08	1.30	11
Routon	John	20JUN03	2.26	1	Ruffner	Ruben	21AUG09	2.28	1
Rowton	Samuel	08JUN96	1.10	1	Ruffner	Ruben	21AUG09	2.29	1
Rowten	Samuel	20APR97	3.27	1	Ruffner	Reuben	-----11	1.66	11
Rowton	Samuel	28MAY99	1.31	1	RUSK				
Routon	Samuel	07JUL00	2.25	1	Rusk	Charles	04JUN00	2.24	1
Routon	Samuel	30JUN01	2.23	1	Rusk	Charles	11JUN02	1.19	1
Routon	Samuel	27MAY02	3.22	1	Rusk	Charles	15JUN02	1.19	1
Routon	Samuel	04JUN03	2.26	1	RUSSELL				
Rowten	Samuel	23JUL04	1.17	1	Rusell	Absolum	11AUG06	3.29	11
Routon	Samuel	08JUN05	2.27	1	Russel	Andrew	25JUL04	1.17	1
Routten	William	21AUG07	2.31	1	Russell	Andrew	27JUN05	2.27	1
Rowten	William	05JUN09	1.29	1	Russel	Andrew	20AUG06	2.31	1
Rowlon	William	-----11	1.66	1	Russel	Andrew	13JUL07	2.29	1
ROWE					Russel	Andrew	30MAY08	2.23	1
Rowe	John	20SEP92	1.11	1	Russel	Andrew	21AUG09	1.30	1
Row	John	10AUG93	3.10	1	Russel	Edmond	21AUG07	2.31	1
Row	John	29MAY94	2.12	1	Russell	Edmund	-----11	1.67	1
Row	John	01MAY95	3.14	1	Russell	Ephraim	05AUG03	2.27	1
Roe	John C.	29MAY96	1.11	1	Russel	Ephram	22JUN04	4.19	1
Rooe	JohnColeman	22MAY97	3.26	1	Russel	Ephrem	07AUG05	3.30	1
Rowe	John	29MAY99	1.32	1	Russell	Ephrain	31JUL06	2.31	1
Roe	Milley	30MAY96	1.11	F1	Russel	Ephrum	18AUG07	2.31	1
ROWSLEY					Russel	Ephrim	30MAY08	2.23	1
Rowsley	Thomas	03JUN90	2.06	1	Russel	Ephraim	07AUG09	1.30	1
ROYAL					Russel	John	28JUN03	1.20	1
Royal	John	26JUN87	2.06	1	Russel	John	22JUN05	3.29	M1
Royal	John	27NOV88	1.09	1	Russel	Joseph	22OCT88	1.08	1
Rial	John	08JUN02	1.19	1	Russel	Joseph	04AUG89	5.10	1
Ryall	John	28JUN03	1.20	1	Russel	Joseph	27MAR90	2.06	1
Rial	Thomas	08JUN02	1.19	1	Russel	Joseph	05APR91	1.08	1
Ryle	Thomas	20JUN03	1.20	1	Russel	Joseph	06OCT92	2.07	11
ROYALTY					Russel	Joseph	20AUG93	1.08	11
Ryalta	John	10AUG93	3.10	1	Russel	Joseph	12MAY94	1.07	12
Royalty	John	22MAY94	2.12	1	Russel	Joseph	11MAY95	2.11	1
Royalty	John	10APR95	3.14	1	Russel	Joseph	01JUN96	1.10	11
Royalty	John	11JUN96	2.16	1	Russle	Joseph	15JUN97	3.26	11
Ryalty	John	06JUN97	1.21	1	Russel	Joseph	31MAY99	1.31	2
Ryalty	John	26JUN99	3.17	1	Russel	Joseph	16JUN00	2.24	11
Rialtee	John	19JUN00	3.25	1	Russell	Joseph	04APR01	2.23	11
Royalty	John	02MAY01	3.29	1	Russell	Joseph	07JUN02	3.22	1
Royalty	John	31JUL02	3.23	1	Russell	Joseph Jr	12JUL02	3.22	M1
Royalty	John	04AUG03	2.26	1	Russell	Joseph	01JUN03	2.26	1
ROYSTON					Rusel	Joseph Jr	18MAY03	2.26	1
Royston	William	12SEP92	1.11	1	Russel	Joseph Sr	07AUG04	2.17	1

surname	name	date	bk.pg	TM	surname	name	date	bk.pg	TM
Russel	Joseph	07AUG04	2.17	M1	Reatherford	John Sr	02JUN97	1.21	1
Russell	Joseph Sr	31MAY05	2.27	1	Reatherford	John Jr	03JUL97	1.21	1
Russell	Joseph Jr	13MAY05	2.26	1	Rutherford	John	11JUN99	1.31	1
Russell	Joseph Sr	08MAY06	2.30	11	Rutherford	John Jr	28JUN99	1.31	1
Russell	Joseph Jr	08MAY06	2.30	1	Rutherford	John	24JUL00	2.25	1
Rusel	Joseph Sr	15JUL07	2.30	11	Rutherford	John	12AUG02	2.26	1
Russel	Joseph Jr	15JUL07	2.30	1	Rutherford	John	15AUG03	3.22	1
Russel	Joseph	-----08	2.24	1	Rutherford	John	07AUG05	3.30	1
Russel	Joseph	30MAY08	2.23	12	Rutherford	John	11AUG06	3.29	1
Russel	Joseph Sr	07JUN09	1.29	12	Reddiford	Joseph	26JUN87	2.06	1
Russel	Joseph Jr	07JUN09	1.29	1	Rutherford	Joseph	07JUL87	3.09	11
Russel	Samuel	28JUL06	3.29	M1	Reatherford	Joseph	28OCT88	1.08	1
Russel	Sanders	30MAY08	2.23	1	Reatherford	Joseph	27NOV88	1.09	11
Russell	Smith	-----11	1.67	1	Rutherford	Joseph Sr	01JUL89	5.12	1
Rusell	Thomas	13AUG02	2.26	M1	Rutherford	Joseph Jr	01JUL89	5.12	1
Russell	Thomas	13JUL03	3.21	M1	Ritherford	Joseph	19APR91	3.13	1
Russell	Thomas	07AUG05	3.30	1	Ritherford	Joseph *	19APR91	3.13	1
Russel	Thomas	28JUL06	3.29	1	Reatherford	Caty	03AUG89	5.10	F
Russell	William	01MAY96	1.11	1	Rutherford	Katy	01JUN90	2.06	F
Russle	William	15JUN97	3.26	1	Rotherford	Kelly	21OCT92	2.07	F
Russel	William	31MAY99	1.31	1	Rutherfore	Katy	07AUG93	1.08	F
Russell	William	05JUL00	2.25	1	Rutherford	Kety	16MAY94	1.08	F
Russell	William	04JUN01	2.23	1	Rutherford	Tandy	11AUG03	2.27	1
Russell	William	07JUN02	3.22	1	Ratherford	Tandy	04JUN04	4.19	1
Russell	William	13JUN03	2.26	1	Rutherford	Tandy	18JUN05	2.27	1
Rusel	William	23JUL04	4.19	1	Rutherford	Tandy	20JUN07	2.29	1
Russel	William	30JUL04	2.16	1	Rutherford	Tandy	30MAY08	2.23	1
Russell	William Sr	27JUN05	2.27	1	Rutherford	William	15AUG03	3.22	M1
Russel	William	08JUN05	2.27	1	RUTLEDGE				
Russel	William	07AUG05	3.30	2	Ruchladge	Joseph	05AUG05	3.30	1
Russell	William	08MAY06	2.30	1	RYAN				
Russel	William	08JUN07	2.29	1	Ryant	Henry	27APR91	3.14	1
Russel	William	17JUL09	1.30	1	Ryan	John	14APR89	6.06	1
Russell	William	-----11	1.66	1	Ryan	John	15APR90	1.08	1
RUTH					Ryan	Joshua	12AUG02	3.23	1
Ruth	Ruth	10MAY09	2.27		SALLEE				
Free Neagro					Sallee	George	-----93	2.04	1
RUTHERFORD					Sallee	George	-----96	4.15	1
Ritherford	Archible	19APR91	3.13	1	Sally	John	26APR97	3.28	1
Reatherford	Archer	26NOV92	3.16	1	Sally	John	20MAY99	1.33	1
Rutherford	Archibald	21MAY94	3.18	1	Salley	John	04JUN01	2.25	1
Rutherford	Dudley	15APR90	1.08	1	Sally	John	14JUN02	2.27	1
Rutherford	Dudley	06OCT92	1.11	1	Salley	John	17JUN03	3.23	1
Rutherford	Dudley	24AUG93	3.10	1	Sally	John	03JUN07	1.25	1
Rutherford	Dudley	12JUN94	2.12	11	Sally	John	27APR08	1.32	1
Retheford	Dudley	19APR95	3.14	1	Sally	Marget	04MAY08	1.32	F
Retherford	Dudley	11JUN96	2.16	11	Sally	Moses	03JUN07	1.25	1
Reatherford	Dudley	15JUN97	1.20	1	Sally	Moses	04MAY08	1.32	1
Rutherford	Dudley	15AUG03	3.22	11	Salley	Peter	28JUN96	1.11	1
Reatherford	James	02JUN97	1.20	1	Sally	Peter	26APR97	3.28	1
Rutherford	James	11JUN99	1.31	1	Sully	Peter	22MAY99	1.33	11
Rutherford	James	18JUN00	2.25	2	Salley	Peter	17JUN00	2.26	11
Rutherford	James	01AUG04	3.17	1	Salley	Peter	08JUN01	2.25	12
Rutherford	James	08JUL05	3.29	1	Salley	Peter	17JUN03	3.23	11
Rutherford	James	14JUL06	3.28	1	Sally	Peter	30JUL04	2.17	11
Rutherford	James	15JUL07	2.29	1	Sally	Peter	03JUN07	1.24	1
Rutherford	James	30MAY08	2.23	1	Sallee	Phillip	-----93	2.04	1
Reidiford	James	07JUL09	1.29	1	Sallay	Shadrach	21AUG04	3.19	1
Reatherford	James	-----11	1.67	1	Sallee	William	-----93	2.04	1
Reddiford	John	26JUN87	2.06	1	Sally	William	26APR97	3.28	1
Reatherford	John	28OCT88	1.08	1	Salley	William	04JUN01	2.25	1
Rutherford	John	13JUN89	6.06	1	SALMON				
Reatherford	John	03AUG89	5.10	1	Salmon	John	14APR94	3.19	1
Rutherford	John	15APR90	1.08	1	SALYERS				
Rutherford	John	18MAR91	2.08	1	Sallers	Benjamin	12AUG05	3.33	1
Rutherford	John	23JUN91	2.08	1	Salyers	Benjamin	04AUG06	3.31	1
Rutherford	John	06OCT92	1.11	1	Salliers	Deen	-----95	1.12	1
Rutherford	John	17AUG93	3.10	1	SAMPLE				
Rutherford	John Sr	05MAY94	2.12	1	Sample	James	26JUN87	1.05	1
Rutherford	John Jr	11JUN94	2.12	1	SAMPSON				
Retherford	John	22MAR95	3.14	1	Sampson	Benjamin	17AUG93	3.11	1
Retherford	John	02JUN96	2.16	11	Samson	Benjamin	28JUN96	2.17	11

surname	name	date	bk.pg	TM	surname	name	date	bk.pg	TM
Sampson	Benjamin	24MAY97	1.22	11	Sawyers	Absalom	07JUN08	1.31	1
Sampson	Benjamin	10JUL99	3.19	11	Sawyers	Absalom	16JUN09	2.31	1
Sampson	Benjamin	04JUL00	3.28	11	Sawyers	Isaac	19APR08	1.31	1
Sampson	Benjamin	10AUG01	3.34	1	Sawyers	Isaac	16JUN09	2.31	1
Sampson	Benjamin	06AUG02	3.25	1	Sawyers	John	03AUG04	1.19	1
Sampson	Isaac	24JUL04	1.18	1	Sawyers	John	30JUL05	1.21	1
Sampson	James	10JUL99	3.19	1	Sawyers	John	31JUL06	1.23	1
Sampson	James	10AUG01	3.34	1	Sawyers	John	26MAY07	1.24	1
Sampson	James	06JUN04	4.21	1	Sawyers	John	07JUN08	1.31	1
Sampson	William	20JUN95	2.11	1	Sawyers	John	16JUN09	2.31	1
Samson	William	28JUN96	2.17	1	Sawyers	Robert	07APR97	3.27	1
Sampson	William	10AUG97	1.24	1	Sayers	Robert	21MAY99	1.33	1
Sampson	William	06JUL99	3.19	1	Sawyers	Robert	07JUL00	2.26	1
Sampson	William	20JUN00	3.27	1	SAYERS				
Sampson	William	02MAY01	3.30	2	Sayers	Stepen	12JUL02	2.27	M1
Sampson	William	06AUG02	3.25	1	SCARBROUGH				
Sampson	William	04AUG03	2.29	1	Sartrough	William	02AUG04	1.19	1
Sampson	William	05AUG07	2.33	1	Sarborgh	William	29JUL05	1.20	1
Sampson	William	-----08	2.25	1	Scarbrow	William	31JUL06	1.23	1
Sampson	William	08JUN09	1.30	1	Scarbrough	William	05MAY07	1.23	1
SANDERS					Scarbrough	William	31MAY08	1.34	1
Sanders	George	30JUN96	1.11	1	Scarbrough	William	14JUN09	2.31	1
Sanders	George	18JUL96	1.12	1	SCOFIELD				
Saunders	George	12APR97	3.27	1	Scofield	John	05AUG02	2.28	1
Saunders	James	15MAY09	1.30	1	Scofield	John	15JUL03	3.24	1
Sunders	James	-----11	1.77	2	SCONCE				
Saunders	Joseph	11MAY09	1.30	1	Sconts	John	26JUN87	3.09	1
Sanders	Suthy	25MAY99	2.18	1	Scons	Robert	29MAY96	2.17	00
Sanders	Suthy	17JUN00	1.14	1	Sconce	Robert	08AUG97	1.11	0
SANDRIDGE						Tax Pd by Stephen Huston			
Sandidge	John	12AUG02	2.29	1	SCOTT				
Sandidge	John	-----08	2.25	1	Scott	Bartlett	-----11	1.76	1
Sandridge	John	15AUG09	1.32	1	Scott	Benjamin	13JUL97	1.24	1
Sandridge	John	-----11	1.70	1	Scott	Benjamin	27JUN99	1.35	11
Sandridge	Joshua	03JUL09	1.31	1	Scott	Benjamin	24JUL00	2.27	11
Sandridge	Larken	12JUL02	2.27	00	Scoot	Benjamin	28MAY01	3.33	11
Sandridge	Larken	13JUN03	3.22	1	Scoot	Benjamin	03AUG02	2.28	11
Sandridge	Larken	22AUG04	2.17	1	Scott	Benjamin	25JUL03	3.24	1
Sandridge	Larken	12AUG05	3.33	1	Scott	Benjamin	06AUG04	3.18	1
Sandadge	Larken	14JUL06	3.30	1	Scott	Benjamin	06AUG05	3.32	1
Sandadge	Larken	10AUG07	2.33	1	Scott	Benjamin	20AUG06	3.32	1
Sandridge	Larken	-----08	2.25	1	Scott	Cosby	09JUN95	2.11	1
Sandridge	Larkin	15AUG09	1.32	1	Scott	Causby	-----96	4.14	1
Sandridge	Larkin	-----11	1.69	2	Scott	Isaac	13JUN96	1.11	1
Sandridge	L.	-----11	1.09		Scott	Isaac	17APR97	3.27	1
	Adm for Charles Baen				Scott	Isaac	22JUL05	2.31	1
SANDIFER					Scott	James	08AUG93	3.11	1
Sandefer	Samuel	01AUG06	3.31	M1	Scott	James	09MAY94	2.14	1
Sandipher	Samuel	22AUG07	2.34	1	Scott	James	18APR95	3.15	1
Sandipher	William	05AUG02	2.28	1	Scott	James	-----96	4.14	1
Sandeford	William	15JUL03	3.23	1	Scott	James	11MAY96	2.16	1
Sandifer	William	15AUG04	2.17	1	Scott	James	25MAY97	1.23	1
Sandipher	William	29MAY05	3.31	1	Scott	James	24JUN99	1.35	1
Sandipher	William	29MAY05	3.31	1	Scott	James	22JUL00	2.27	1
Sandefer	William	01AUG06	3.31	1	Scoot	James	22JUL01	3.34	1
Sandifer	William	15MAY09	1.30	1	Scoot	James	26MAY02	2.27	1
SAPP					Scoot	James	02JUN02	2.27	1
Sapp	Caleb	29JUN99	1.35	1	Scott	James	14JUL03	3.23	1
Sapp	Caleb	23JUL00	2.27	1	Scott	James	06AUG03	3.24	1
Sapp	Caleb	27MAY01	3.33	1	Scott	James	04AUG04	3.18	1
Sapp	Caleb	12AUG02	2.28	1	Scott	James	13JUL05	3.32	1
Sapp	Caleb	20MAY03	3.22	1	Scott	James	07AUG06	3.31	1
Sapp	Caleb	06AUG04	3.18	1	Scott	James	18AUG07	2.34	1
Sapp	Caleb	12AUG05	3.33	1	Scott	James	30MAY08	2.24	1
Sapp	Caleb	04AUG06	3.31	1	Scott	James	11MAY09	1.30	1
SARTIN					Scott	James	-----11	1.75	1
Sertain	Elizabeth	01NOV92	2.08	F	Scott	Jesse	04JUN95	2.12	1
Sartin	Elizabeth	15MAY94	1.08	F	Scott	Jesse	-----96	4.14	1
Sarten	John	-----95	1.13	1	Scott	Jesse	-----97	2.05	1
SASSIMORE					Scott	Jesse	14JUN99	2.19	1
Sassimore	Richard	14APR97	3.21	1	Scott	Jesse	24JUL00	1.14	1
SAWYERS					Scott	Jesse	26JUN01	1.17	1

surname	name	date	bk.pg	TM	surname	name	date	bk.pg	TM
Scott	Jessee	23JUN02	1.22	1	Secat	Peter	17JUL06	3.30	1
Scott	Jessee	23JUN03	1.21	1	Seacott	Peter	29JUN07	1.26	1
Scott	Jesse	03AUG04	1.20	1	Seacot	Peter	04MAY08	1.32	1
Scott	Jessee	31JUL05	1.21	1	Seacat	Peter	05JUL09	2.32	1
Scott	Jessee	02AUG06	1.24	1	Seacat	Peter	-----11	1.72	1
Scott	Jesse	26MAY07	1.24	11	SEARS				
Scott	Jesse	19APR08	1.31	11	Seers	James	01JUN97	3.34	1
Scott	Jesse	17JUN09	2.31	1	SELCH				
Scott	John	30OCT88	1.09	1	SaLch	Nicholas	12AUG07	2.33	1
Scott	John	23JUN89	5.10	1	Salch	Nicholas	24AUG08	2.26	1
Scott	John	14APR91	1.08	1	Salsh	Nicholas	08JUN09	1.30	1
Scott	John	13AUG93	1.08	1	Selch	Nicholas	-----11	1.77	1
Scott	John	29MAY94	1.08	1	SELF				
Scott	John	03JUN95	2.12	1	Self	Jesse	23AUG05	3.34	1
Scott	John	20APR97	3.29	1	SELLERS				
Scott	John	16MAY99	3.18	11	Sellers	James	06AUG89	2.13	1
Scott	John	29JUL00	2.27	11	Sellers	James	22JUN91	3.15	1
Scott	John	18JUN01	3.32	2	Sellers	James	17NOV92	3.17	1
Scoot	John	02JUN02	2.27	1	Sellars	James	05MAY94	3.19	1
Scott	John	14JUN03	3.22	1	Sellers	James	-----95	1.12	1
Scott	John	25JUL03	3.24	M1	Sellers	James	-----96	4.15	1
Scott	John	31JUL04	3.18	1	Sellers	John	30JUN87	3.09	1
Scott	John	06AUG04	3.18	1	Sellers	John	06AUG89	2.13	1
Scott	John	06AUG05	3.32	1	Sellers	John	02JUN91	3.15	1
Scott	John	04AUG06	3.31	1	Sellers	John	27NOV92	3.18	1
Scott	Robert	-----95	1.12	1	Sellars	John	05MAY94	3.19	1
Scott	Robert	-----96	4.14	1	Sellers	Joseph	30JUN87	3.09	
Scott	Sabert	04AUG06	3.31	1	Listed with Nathaniel Sellers				
Scott	Samuel	15JUN96	1.11	1	Sellers	Joseph	06AUG89	2.13	1
Scott	Samuel	07APR97	3.28	1	Sellers	Nathaniel	30JUN87	3.09	
Scott	Samuel	17MAY99	1.32	1	Joseph Sellers listed with him				
Scott	Thomas	-----96	4.14	1	Sellers	Nathaniel	06AUG89	2.13	11
Scott	Thomas	17MAY97	1.22	11	Sellers	Nathaniel	27NOV92	3.18	1
Scott	Thomas	04JUL99	3.19	11	Sellars	Nathaniel	21MAY94	3.18	1
Scott	Thomas	30JUN00	3.28	11	Sellers	Samuel	17NOV92	3.17	1
Scott	Thomas	30MAY01	1.15	11	Sellars	Samuel	05MAY94	3.19	1
Scott	Thomas	03JUN02	1.20	11	Sellers	Samuel	-----96	4.15	1
Scott	Thomas	11JUN03	1.21	11	Sellers	William	17NOV92	3.17	M1
Scott	Thomas	14JUN04	1.17	1	Sellars	William	05MAY94	3.19	1
Scott	Thomas	05JUN05	1.19	11	Sellers	William	-----95	1.12	1
Scott	Thomas	11JUN06	1.22	11	Sellers	William	-----96	4.15	1
Scott	Thomas	18MAY07	1.24	11	SENTER				
Scott	Thomas	-----08	1.35	12	Senter	James	09JUN04	4.21	1
Scott	Thomas	23MAY09	2.29	1	Senter	James H.	19JUN05	2.29	1
Scott	Thomas	-----11	1.69	1	Senter	James H.	29JUL06	2.33	1
Scott	William	04AUG91	2.09	1	Sentre	James H.	30JUN09	1.31	1
Scott	William	22SEP92	1.12	1	Sentor	James H.	-----11	1.75	1
Scott	William	10AUG93	3.10	1	SERGANT				
Scott	William	15JUN96	1.11	1	Segant	Dabney	25JUL04	4.21	1
Scott	William	07APR97	3.28	1	Sergant	Dabney	23JUL05	2.31	1
Scott	William	17MAY99	1.32	11	SERVANT				
Scott	William	29MAY00	2.26	11	Survant	William	28NOV88	1.10	1
Scott	William	27JUN00	3.28	1	Servant	William	23MAY89	6.08	1
Scott	William	02JUN01	1.16	1	Servant	William	10APR90	1.09	1
Scott	William	21JUL01	2.25	11	Servant	William	17MAY91	2.09	1
Scott	William	17JUN02	1.21	11	Sevant	William	07DEC92	3.19	1
Scott	William	05JUL03	1.22	1	Survan	William	09AUG93	1.08	1
Scott	William Jr	05JUL03	1.22	1	Servant	William	20MAY94	1.08	1
Scott	William	15JUN04	1.17	11	Servant	William	-----11	1.70	1
Scott	William	15AUG04	3.19	1	SHACKLEFORD				
Scott	William Sr	08AUG05	3.33	1	ShacklefordAndrew		13MAY05	2.28	1
Scott	William Jr	08AUG05	3.33	1	ShacklefordBennett C.		28JUL02	3.24	1
Scott	William	05JUN05	1.19	1	ShacklefordBennett		16JUN03	3.22	M1
Scott	William	06JUN06	2.33	1	ShacklefordBennet		31JUL04	3.18	1
Scott	William	07AUG06	3.31	1	ShacklefordBenett		08JUL05	3.32	1
Scott	William	20AUG06	3.32	11	ShacklefordBenett		14JUL06	3.30	1
Scott	William	20MAY07	1.24	1	ShacklefordBennett		-----11	1.78	1
Scott	William	-----11	1.74	1	ShackelfordEdmond		08JUL05	3.32	M1
SCRUGGS					ShackelfordEdmond		31MAY06	2.32	1
Scruggs	William	18MAY06	2.32	1	ShackelfordEdmond		03AUG07	2.33	1
Scruggs	William	18MAY07	1.24	1	Shackeford Edmond		02AUG08	2.26	1
SEACAT					ShackelfordEdmund		11JUL09	1.31	1

surname	name	date	bk.pg	TM	surname	name	date	bk.pg	TM
ShacklefordEdmund		-----11	1.74	1	ShacklefordSamuel Sr		13MAY97	1.22	11
ShacklefordEdward		26JUN87	3.09	1	ShacklefordSamuel Jr		13MAY97	1.23	1
ShacklefordEdward		13SEP91	3.15	1	ShacklefordSamuel		25MAY99	3.18	2
ShacklefordEdward		04DEC92	3.18	1	ShacklefordSamuel		07JUN99	1.35	1
ShacklefordEdward		05MAY94	3.24	1	ShacklefordSamuel		28JUN00	2.26	1
ShacklefordGeorge		06SEP87	1.05		ShacklefordSamuel		04JUL00	3.28	11
Listed with Samuel Shackleford					ShacklefordSamuel Sr		19JUN01	3.32	11
ShacklefordGeorge		14MAY90	1.09		ShacklefordSamuel		18JUN01	3.34	1
Listed with Samuel Shackleford					ShacklefordSamuel		01JUN02	2.27	1
ShacklefordGeorge		24JUN91	2.10		ShacklefordSamuel		28JUL02	3.24	11
Listed with Samuel Shackleford					ShacklefordSamuel		31MAY03	3.22	11
ShacklefordJames Jr		26JUN87	3.09	1	ShacklefordSamuel		09AUG03	2.30	1
ShacklefordJames Sr		26JUN87	3.09	1	ShacklefordSamuel		23JUL04	4.21	1
ShacklefordJames		21MAY99	1.33	1	ShackelfordSamuel		31JUL04	3.18	11
ShacklefordJames		23JUN00	2.26	1	ShackelfordSamuel		19JUN05	3.31	1
ShacklefordJames		04JUL00	3.28	1	ShacklefordSamuel		28JUN05	2.30	1
ShacklefordJames		08AUG01	2.25	1	ShacklefordSamuel		14JUL06	3.30	1
ShacklefordJames		12JUN02	1.20	1	ShacklefordSamuel		01AUG06	2.34	1
ShacklefordJames		20MAY03	3.22	1	ShackelfordSamuel		22JUN07	2.32	1
ShacklefordJames		04JUL03	1.21	1	ShacklefordSamuel		01AUG08	2.26	1
ShacklefordJames		25AUG03	3.24	1	ShacklefordSamuel		10JUL09	1.31	1
ShackelfordJames		31JUL04	3.18	1	ShacklefordSamuel		-----11	1.74	1
ShackelfordJames		07AUG04	3.18	1	ShacklefordSarah		17JUN05	1.19	F1
ShackelfordJames		08JUL05	3.32	1	ShacklefordSarah		20JUN06	1.22	F1
ShacklefordJames		16AUG06	2.35	1	ShacklefordSarey		27APR08	1.32	F
ShacklefordJ. (heirs)		-----11	1.44	D	ShacklefordThomas		17APR91	1.08	1
Tax paid by Hugh Lawrence					ShacklefordThomas		21MAY94	3.19	1
ShacklefordJohn		03AUG90	1.10	1	ShacklefordThomas		-----95	1.12	1
ShacklefordJohn		24JUN91	2.10	1	ShackelfordThomas		-----96	4.14	1
ShacklefordJohn		20MAY94	1.08	1	ShacklefordWilliam		29MAR90	2.06	1
ShacklefordJohn		27MAY99	1.34	1	ShacklefordWilliam		16APR94	2.14	1
ShacklefordJohn		18JUL00	2.26	1	ShackelfordWilliam		29JUN95	2.11	1
ShacklefordJohn		29JUN01	2.25	1	ShacklefordWilliam		13JUN96	1.12	1
ShacklefordJohn		12JUL02	3.24	1	ShacklefordWilliam		19APR97	3.27	1
ShacklefordJohn		18JUN03	2.28	1	ShacklefordWilliam		27MAY99	1.34	1
ShacklefordJohn		25JUL04	1.19	1	ShacklefordWilliam		26JUN00	2.26	1
ShacklefordJohn		13MAY05	2.28	D	ShacklefordWilliam		03JUN02	3.23	1
ShacklefordNancy		30MAY08	2.24	F	ShacklefordWilliam		18JUN03	2.28	1
ShacklefordPolley		31MAY06	2.32	1	ShacklefordWilliam		25JUL04	1.19	1
ShacklefordRichard		12SEP91	3.15	1	ShacklefordWilliam		13MAY05	2.28	1
ShackelfordRichard		09OCT92	2.08	1	ShacklefordWilliam		18MAY06	2.32	1
ShacklefordRichard		07AUG93	1.09	1	ShacklefordZachariah		14JUN87	2.06	1
ShacklefordRichard		16MAY94	1.08	1	ShackelfordZachariah		29OCT88	1.09	11
ShackelfordRichard		18JUN95	2.11	1	ShackelfordZachariah		06AUG89	5.11	1
ShacklefordRichard		13JUN96	1.11	1	ShacklefordZachariah		03APR90	2.06	1
ShacklefordRichard		09MAY97	3.28	1	ShackelfordZachariah		07APR91	1.08	12
ShacklefordRichard		22MAY99	1.34	1	ShacklefordZacarrah		02NOV92	2.08	12
ShacklefordRichard		27MAY01	3.33	1	ShackelfordZachariah		15AUG93	1.08	12
ShacklefordRichard		12JUL02	2.27	1	ShackelfordZacariah		16MAY94	1.08	11
ShacklefordRichard		11JUN03	2.27	1	ShackelfordZechariah		22APR95	2.12	11
ShackelfordRichard		05AUG05	3.32	1	ShacklefordZacarias		13JUN96	1.12	1
ShacklefordRichard		04AUG06	3.31	1	ShacklefordZacarias		13JUN96	1.12	11
ShacklefordSally		01AUG04	2.18	F	ShacklefordZacheriah		19APR97	3.27	11
ShackelfordSally		03JUN07	1.25	F1	ShacklefordZach. Sr		29JUN99	1.35	1
ShacklefordSamuel		06SEP87	1.05	1	ShacklefordZach. Jr		27MAY99	1.34	1
George Shackleford listed with hi					ShacklefordZachariah		21JUN00	2.26	1
ShacklefordSamuel		12JUN89	6.07	1	ShacklefordZach. Jr		26JUN00	2.26	11
ShacklefordSamuel		14MAY90	1.09	21	ShacklefordZachariah		04APR01	2.24	1
George Shackleford listed with hi					ShacklefordZechariah		28MAY01	3.33	11
ShacklefordSamuel		24JUN91	2.10	2	ShacklefordZachariah		04AUG02	2.28	11
George Shackleford listed with hi					ShacklefordZacheriah		20MAY03	3.22	1
ShacklefordSamuel		05OCT92	1.12	1	ShackelfordZachariah		06AUG04	3.18	1
ShacklefordSamuel		23AUG93	3.11	1	ShackelfordZack		05AUG05	3.32	1
ShacklefordSamuel		23AUG93	3.11	1	ShackelfordZackery		04AUG06	3.31	1
ShacklefordSamuel Sr		10JUN94	2.13	1	SHADDOCK				
ShacklefordSamuel Jr		10JUN94	2.13	1	Shaddock	John	12JUN87	2.06	1
ShacklefordSamuel		-----95	2.26		Shadock	John	12AUG89	2.13	1
One lot in Stanford					Shaddock	John	13SEP91	3.15	1
ShacklefordSamuel		29APR95	3.15	1	Shaddock	John	13OCT92	2.08	1
ShackelfordSamuel		19JUN95	2.11	1	SHAFFER				
ShacklefordSamuel Sr		12MAY96	2.16	11	Shapher	Abigal	20JUN00	3.27	F
ShacklefordSamuel		05JUL96	2.17	1	Sheffer	Abigal	02MAY01	3.31	F

surname	name	date	bk.pg	TM	surname	name	date	bk.pg	TM
Shaver	David	29MAR90	2.06	1A	Shennon	Absolom	20JUN07	2.32	1
Shaver	David	03NOV92	2.08	1	Shannon	Absolom	-----08	2.25	1
Shaver	David	30JUL01	2.17	1	Shannon	Absalom	16AUG09	1.32	1
David Logan paid tax					Shannon	Absalom	-----11	1.69	1
Shefner	Henry	28JUN96	2.17	1	Shannon	Betcey	08MAY06	2.32	F
Shefner	Henry	10AUG97	1.25	1	Shannon	Hugh	30JUN87	1.05	1
Shiffer	Jacob	26JUN99	3.18	3	Hannon	Hugh	04AUG89	5.11	1
Shaver	John	09JUN96	1.11	1	Shanon	Hugh	30MAR90	2.06	1
Shiffer	John	26JUN99	3.18	1	Shannon	Hugh	05APR91	1.08	1
Shapher	John	20JUN00	3.27	1	Shannon	Hugh	29OCT92	2.08	1
Shaffer	John	02MAY01	3.31	1	Shannon	Hugh	05AUG93	1.09	1
Shiffer	John	08JUN09	1.30	1	Shanan	Hugh	17JUN94	1.08	1
Shaver	Peter	17JUN89	5.10	1	Shannon	Hugh	02JUN95	2.11	1
Shaver	Peter	03NOV92	2.08	1	Shannan	Hugh	01JUN96	1.12	1
Shaver	Samuel	02MAY01	3.30	1	Shannan	Hugh	22APR97	3.29	1
Shaver	Shadrick	09JUN96	1.11	1	Shannon	Hugh	18MAY99	1.33	1
SHANKLIN					Shannon	Hugh	17JUN00	2.26	1
Shanklin	Andrew	30JUN87	1.05	1	Shannon	Hugh	07JUL01	3.32	1
Shanklin	Andrew	25NOV92	1.11	1	Shanon	Hugh	08JUN02	3.23	1
Shanklin	Andrew	15AUG93	3.11	1	Shannon	Hugh	17JUN03	2.28	1
Shanklin	Andrew	31MAY94	1.08	1	Shannon	Hugh	22AUG04	2.18	1
Shanklin	Andrew	11MAY95	2.12	1	Shannon	Hugh	01AUG05	2.31	1
Shanklin	Andrew	06JUN96	1.12	1	Shannon	Hugh	08MAY06	2.32	1
Shanklin	Andrew	27JUN01	2.25	1	Shannon	Hugh	22JUN07	2.32	1
Shanklin	Andrew	07JUN02	3.23	1	Shannon	James	-----08	2.25	1
Shanklin	Andrew	04JUN03	2.27	1	Shannon	Polley	08MAY06	2.32	F
Shanklen	Andrew	06AUG04	2.18	1	Shannon	Thomas	03JUL87	1.05	1
Shanklin	Andrew	05AUG06	2.34	1	Shannon	Thomas	23MAY89	6.07	1
Shanklin	Andrew	03AUG07	2.33	1	Shannon	Thomas	15APR90	1.09	1
Shanklin	Andrew	07JUN09	1.30	1	Shannon	Thomas	19APR91	2.09	1
Shanklen	John	22AUG04	2.18	1	Shannon	Thomas	14SEP92	1.12	1
Shanklen	John	23AUG05	3.34	1	Shannon	Thomas	14AUG93	3.11	1
SHANKS					Shannon	Thomas	10MAY94	2.13	11
Shanks	Archabald	22JUN07	1.25	1	Shannon	Thomas	10APR95	3.16	11
Shanks	Archibold	22APR08	1.32	M1	Shannon	Thomas	05JUL96	2.17	11
Shanks	Archabald	21JUN09	2.31	1	Shannon	Thomas	31MAY97	1.23	11
Shanks	David	21JUN06	1.22	1	Shannon	Thomas	21MAY99	3.18	1
Shanks	David	22JUN07	1.25	1	Shannon	Thomas	21JUN00	3.27	1
Shanks	David	31MAY08	1.33	1	Shannon	Thomas	01MAY01	3.30	1
Shanks	David	21JUN09	2.31	1	Shanon	Thomas	27JUL02	3.24	1
Shanks	David	-----11	1.73	1	Shannon	Thomas	11AUG03	2.30	1
Pd tax for John Shanks (deceased)					Shannon	Thomas	05JUN04	4.20	11
Shanks	James	06AUG04	2.18	1	Shannon	Thomas	18JUN05	2.29	11
Shanks	James	21JUN06	1.22	1	Shannon	Thomas	01AUG06	2.34	1
Shanks	John	30JUL04	2.17	1	Shennon	Thomas	15JUL07	2.32	11
Shanks	John	19JUN05	1.19	1	Shannon	Thomas	-----08	2.25	11
Shanks	John	21JUN06	1.22	1	Shannon	Thomas	15AUG09	1.32	1
Shanks	John	22JUN07	1.25	1	Shannon	Thomas	-----11	1.69	21
Shanks	John	-----08	1.35	1	SHARP				
Shanks	John	15AUG09	2.32	1	Sharp	Benjamin	24MAY97	1.22	11
Shanks	John	-----11	1.73	D	Sharp	George	12MAY89	6.07	1
Taxes paid by David Shanks					Sharp	George	10APR90	1.09	1
Shanks	William	20MAY99	1.33	12	Sharp	George	01AUG91	2.09	1
Shanks	William	04JUN00	2.26	12	Sharp	George	20SEP92	1.12	1
Shanks	William	28MAY01	2.24	12	Sharp	George	29OCT93	3.11	1
Shanks	William	16JUN02	1.20	12	Sharp	William	18JUL91	2.09	1
Shanks	William	05JUL03	1.22	12	Sharp	William	02OCT92	1.12	1
Shanks	William	31JUL04	2.18	12	Sharp	William	09AUG93	3.10	1
Shanks	William	19JUN05	1.19	11	Sharp	William	28APR94	2.14	2
Shanks	William	11AUG06	1.25	1	Sharp	William	01MAY95	3.15	1
Shanks	William	22JUN07	1.25	1	Sharp	William	27MAY96	2.17	1
Shanks	William	22APR08	1.32	13	Sharp	William	28JUN97	1.24	1
Shanks	William	22JUN09	2.31	1	Sharp	William	26JUN99	1.35	1
Shanks	William	-----11	1.72	1	Sharp	William	25JUL00	2.27	1
SHANNON					Sharp	William	29MAY01	3.33	1
Shannon	Absolom	21MAY99	3.18	1	Sharp	William	03AUG02	2.27	1
Shannon	Absalum	21JUN00	3.27	1	Sharp	William	24AUG03	3.24	1
Shannon	Absolam	27JUL02	3.24	1	Sharp	William	06AUG04	3.18	1
Shannon	Absalom	11AUG03	2.30	1	Sharp	William	08AUG05	3.33	1
Shannon	Absalom	21MAY04	4.20	1	Sharp	William	20AUG06	3.32	1
Shannon	Absolam	27JUN05	2.29	1	SHAUNTY				
Shannon	Absolam	01AUG06	2.34	1	Slonty	Henry	07MAY91	3.14	1

surname	name	date	bk.pg	TM	surname	name	date	bk.pg	TM
Shonty	Henry	21NOV92	3.17	1	Paid tax for heirs of Evan Shelby				
Shontee	Henry	14APR94	3.19	1	Shelby	Isaac	21AUG09	1.32	1
Shaunty	Henry	-----96	4.14	1	Pd tax for Evan Shelby (deceased)				
SHAW					Shelby	Isaac	21AUG09	1.32	
Shaw	Daniel	29JUN96	2.17	1	Paid tax for John McFarland				
Shaw	Daniel	28JUN97	1.24	1	Shelby	Isaac	-----11	1.77	2
Show	John	08JUN05	2.28	1	SHELTON				
Show	John	18MAY06	2.32	1	Shelton	Aesop	07AUG06	3.32	1
Shaw	John	10JUN09	1.31	1	Shelton	Anderson	12AUG05	3.33	1
Shaw	Thomas	14JUN87	2.06	1	Shelton	Anderson	20AUG06	3.32	1
Shaw	Thomas	28OCT88	1.09	1	Shelton	Ezekiah	06AUG05	3.33	11
Shaw	Thomas	16JUN89	5.10	1	Shelton	James	29JUL96	2.18	1
Shaw	Thomas	18MAR90	2.06	1	Shelton	James	27JUN99	1.35	1
SHEEKS					Shelton	James	24JUL00	2.27	11
Sheeks	David	19JUN00	1.14	1	Shelton	James	27MAY01	3.33	11
Sheeks	George	19JUN00	1.14	1	Shelton	James	12AUG02	2.29	11
SHELBY					Shelton	James	21JUN03	3.23	11
Shelby	E. (heirs)	06JUN95	3.15	D	Shelton	James	08AUG04	3.19	11
Shelby	Evan	07AUG02	3.26	D	Shelton	James	06AUG05	3.32	1
Tax paid by Isaac Shelby					Shelton	James	06AUG05	3.32	11
Shelby	Evan	29JUL03	2.29	D	Shelton	James	20AUG06	3.32	1
Tax paid by Isaac Shelby					Shelton	James	13JUL97	1.24	11
Shelby	Evan	28JUN04	4.22	D	Shelton	Mark	20AUG06	3.32	1
Shelby	Evan(heirs)	18JUL05	2.30	D	Shelton	Peter	27JUN99	1.35	1
Shelby	Evan	19AUG06	2.35	D	Shelton	Peter	23JUL00	2.27	1
Shelby	Evan(D)	19AUG06	2.35		Shelton	Peter	27MAY01	3.33	1
Tax paid by Isaac Shelby					Shelton	Peter	12AUG02	2.28	1
Shelby	Even	12JUL07	2.33	D	Shelton	Peter	09AUG04	3.19	1
Tax paid by Isaac Shelby					Shelton	Peter	06AUG05	3.32	1
Shelby	Evan	-----08	2.25	D	Shelton	Peter	20AUG06	3.32	1
Tax pd for heirs by Isaac Shelby					Shelton	Peter	13JUL97	1.24	1
Shelby	Evan	12AUG09	1.32	1	Shelton	Thomas	28MAY91	3.15	1
Shelby	Evan	21AUG09	1.32	D	Shelton	Vardiman	29JUL96	2.18	1
Shelby	Evan	21AUG09	1.32	D	Shelton	Verdiman	13JUL97	1.24	1
Paid tax for John McFarland					Shelton	Vardiman	27JUN99	1.35	1
Shelby	Evan	21AUG09	1.32		Shelton	Vardiman	24JUL00	2.27	1
Tax paid by Isaac Shelby					Shelton	Verdiman	27MAY01	3.33	1
Shelby	Isaac	04OCT87	1.06	1	Shelton	Verdiman	12AUG02	2.29	1
Shelby	Isaac	19MAY89	6.06	1	Shelton	Vardy	25MAY03	3.22	1
Shelby	Isaac	13MAY90	1.09	1	Shelton	Vardiman	08AUG04	3.19	1
Shelby	Isaac	23APR91	2.10	1	Shelton	Vardiman	06AUG05	3.32	1
Shelby	Isaac	02OCT92	1.12	1	Shelton	Vardiman	20AUG06	3.32	1
Shelby	Isaac	05AUG93	3.11	1	Shelton	William	05AUG03	2.29	11
Shelby	Isaac Esq	14JUN94	2.13	1	Shelton	William	09JUN04	4.21	11
Shelby	Isaac	06JUN95	3.15		Shelton	William	29JUN05	2.30	11
Paid tax for J. McFarland					SHEPHERD				
Shelby	Isaac Esq	06JUN95	3.15	1	Shepherd	John	26JUN87	3.09	1
Shelby	Isaac Esq	22JUL96	2.18	1	Shepherd	John	27JUN89	2.12	1
Shelby	Isaac	13JUN97	1.22	1	Shepherd	John	27APR91	3.14	1
Shelby	Isaac	15JUL99	3.20	1	Shepheard	John	14OCT92	3.17	1
Shelby	Isaac	05JUL00	3.29	11	Shepherd	John	05MAY94	3.19	1
Shelby	Isaac	11MAY01	3.31	1	Shephard	John	-----95	1.13	1
Shelby	Isaac	07AUG02	3.26	11	Shepherd	John	-----96	4.14	1
Pd tax for Evan Shelby (deceased)					Shephard	Nicholas	06APR91	1.08	1
Shelby	Isaac	29JUL03	2.29	11	Shepherd	Samuel	23JUN90	1.09	1
Paid tax for Evan Shelby (D)					Shepherd	Sweeney	05JUN99	1.35	1
Shelby	Isaac	29JUL03	2.29		SHERLEY				
Paid tax for John McFarland (0)					Shurley	George	19JUN99	2.19	1
Shelby	Isaac	28JUN04	4.22	12	Sherley	Michael	20MAY97	3.28	1
Paid tax for John McFarland					Shurley	Michal	19JUN99	2.19	1
Shelby	Isaac	18JUL05	2.30	1	SHERROON				
Paid tax for John McFarland					Sherroon	Isaiah	10AUG97	1.25	1
Shelby	Isaac	16AUG06	2.35		SHERWOOD				
Paid tax for John McFarland					Sherwood	Thomas	27JUN99	1.35	1
Shelby	Isaac	19AUG06	2.35	1	Sherwood	Thomas	24JUL00	2.27	1
Pd tax for Evan Shelby (deceased)					Shearwood	Thomas	28MAY01	3.33	1
Shelby	Isaac	12JUL07	2.33	1	Shearwood	Thomas	12AUG02	2.28	1
Pd tax for Even Shelby - deceased					Sherwood	Thomas	07JUL03	3.23	1
Shelby	Isaac	12AUG07	2.33	1	Sherwood	Thomas	07AUG04	3.18	1
Shelby	Isaac	-----08	2.25	11	Shearwood	Thomas	06AUG05	3.33	1
Paid tax for John McFarland					Shearwood	Thomas	20AUG06	3.32	1
Shelby	Isaac	-----08	2.25		Sheill	Ann	30JUN87	1.05	F

surname	name	date	bk.pg	TM	surname	name	date	bk.pg	TM
Sheltz	Barbara	02NOV92	1.11	F	SHOULS				
Shields	Joseph	01AUG06	1.24	1	Shouls	David	05MAY94	3.24	1
Shealds	Joseph	31MAY08	1.34	1	Shools	David	-----95	1.13	1
Shealds	Joseph	14JUN09	2.31	1	SHOWERS				
Shield	Patrick	27NOV88	1.10	1	Showers	Rheuben	19JUN99	2.19	1
Shiells	Patrick	15APR90	1.10	1	Showers	William	19JUN99	2.19	12
Shiell	Patrick	19MAY91	2.09	1	SHUCK				
Shiell	Paddy	09OCT92	1.11	1	Shuck	Andrew	09AUG91	2.09	12
Shiell	Patrick	17AUG93	3.11	1	Shuck	Andrew	13OCT92	1.12	11
Sheals	Patrick	18APR94	2.14	1	Shuck	Andrew	11NOV93	3.11	11
Sheels	Patrick	18MAR95	3.16	1	Shuck	Andrew Sr	29MAY94	2.14	3
Shelts	William	21JUN05	3.32	1	Shough	Andrew Sr	01MAY95	3.15	2
SHIPLEY					Shuck	Andrew	19MAY96	2.16	1
Shipley	Thomas	-----11	1.75	1	Shuck	Andrew	29JUN97	1.24	1
SHIPMAN					Shook	John	13AUG90	1.10	1
Shepmon	Nicholas	06AUG89	5.11	1	Shook	John	30APR91	2.09	1
Shipman	Stephen	27NOV88	1.09	1	Shook	John	03OCT92	1.12	1
Shepmon	Stephen	06AUG89	5.11	1	Shuck	John	06AUG93	3.10	1
Shipman	Stephen	06APR91	1.08	1	Shook	John	24MAY94	2.13	1
SHOCKLEY					Shook	John	16APR95	3.16	1
Shockley	James	-----08	1.35	1	Shuck	John	04AUG96	2.18	1
Shockley	James	16AUG09	2.33	1	Shuck	John	14JUL97	1.24	1
Shockley	James	-----11	1.72	1	Shuck	John	26JUN99	1.35	1
Shockley	Levey	22AUG04	2.18	1	Shuck	John	26JUL00	2.27	1
Shockley	Levi	31MAY05	2.28	1	Shuck	John	29MAY01	3.33	1
Shockley	Levi	05AUG06	2.34	1	Shuck	John	02AUG02	2.27	11
Shockley	Levi	19AUG07	2.34	1	Shuck	John	05AUG03	3.24	11
Shockley	Levi	30MAY08	2.24	1	Shuck	John	15AUG04	3.19	12
Shockly	Levi	15JUN09	1.31	1	Shook	John	09AUG05	3.33	12
Shockley	Levi	-----11	1.73	1	Shook	John	28MAY06	3.30	11
Shockley	Willson	25JUL05	1.20	1	Shook	William	14JUL06	3.30	1
SHOEMAKER					SHY				
Shoemaker	Jessee	28SEP92	1.12	1	Shy	Samuel	30APR94	2.14	1
Shoemaker	Jessee	12AUG93	3.10	1	SIDEBOTTOM				
Shoemaker	Jesse	10MAY94	2.14	1	Sidebottom	Charles	12JUN87	2.06	1
Shoemate	John	-----11	1.75	1	Sidebottom	Charles	01NOV88	1.09	1
Shumaker	Leonard	21JUN99	2.20	1	Sidebottom	Charles	19JUN89	5.10	1
Shoemaker	Soloman	13JUL87	1.05	1	Sidebottom	Isaac	23JUL05	2.31	1
Shoemaker	Solomon	30APR91	2.09	1	Sidebottom	Peter	01NOV88	1.09	1
Shumake	Tolison	20JUN05	3.31	1	Sidebottom	Peter	19JUN89	5.10	1
Shumake	Tolison	29JUL06	3.30	1	Sidebottom	Peter	02JUN90	2.06	1
SHORT					Sidebottom	Peter	30MAR91	1.08	1
Short	Elizabeth	27APR08	1.32	F1	Sidebottom	Peter	11OCT92	2.08	1
Short	Fleming	02AUG05	2.31	1	Sidebottom	Peter	27AUG93	1.08	1
Short	Jacob	-----93	2.04	1	Sidebottom	Peter	29MAY94	1.08	1
Short	Jacob	14APR94	3.19	1	Sidebottom	Peter	03JUN95	2.12	1
Short	Jacob	-----95	1.13	1	Sidebottom	Peter	30JUN96	1.11	11
Short	Jacob	-----96	4.14	1	Sideburn	Peter	13APR97	3.27	11
Short	James	17JUL06	2.33	1	SIGALL				
Short	Joel	17NOV88	1.09	1	Sigall	William B.	23JUN02	1.22	1
Short	Joel	16JUN89	5.10	1	SILVERS				
Short	Joel	31MAR90	2.06	1	Silvers	John	10JUL99	3.19	11
Short	John	14JUN87	2.06	11	Silvers	John	09JUL00	3.19	1
Short	John	17NOV88	1.09	11	Silvers	John	31JUN01	3.33	12
Short	John	16JUN89	5.10	12	Silvers	John	28JUL02	3.25	1
Short	John	26MAR90	2.07	11	Silvers	John	05AUG03	2.29	1
Short	John	25MAR91	1.08	1	Silvers	John	09AUG03	2.30	1
Short	John	01NOV92	2.08	11	Silvers	John	05JUN04	4.20	1
Short	John	21AUG93	1.08	1	Silvers	John	19JUN05	2.29	1
Short	John	17MAY94	1.08	1	Silvers	John	29JUL06	2.33	1
Short	John	01AUG06	3.30	1	Silvers	Joseph	26JUN87	3.09	1
Short	Moses	30MAR91	1.08	1	Silvers	Joseph	27NOV88	1.09	1
Short	Moses	01NOV92	2.08	1	Silvers	Joseph	01JUL89	2.12	1
Short	Moses	03AUG93	1.08	1	Silvers	Joseph	14APR94	3.19	11
Short	Moses	17MAY94	1.08	11	Silvers	Joseph	-----95	1.13	11
Short	Obadiah	17NOV88	1.09	1	Silvers	William	13JUN04	4.21	1
Short	Obediah	25MAR91	1.08	11	Silvers	William	29JUN05	2.30	1
Short	Obediah	23OCT92	2.08	1	Silvers	William	29JUL06	2.33	1
Short	Obediah	03AUG93	1.08	1	SIMMS				
SHOTWELL					Sims	Francis	16AUG05	3.33	1
Shotwell	Daniel	02AUG04	2.18	1	Simms	Nathan	07JUN08	1.31	1
Shotwell	Henney	-----11	1.76	1	Sims	Starling	29JUN97	1.24	1

surname	name	date	bk.pg	TM	surname	name	date	bk.pg	TM
Simmons	Starling	12JUL99	3.19	1	Simpson	Robert	03JUL97	1.24	1
Simms	Starling	19JUL00	3.29	1	Simpson	Robert	21MAY99	1.33	11
Sims	Starling	06JUN01	1.16	1	Simpson	Robert	30JUN02	3.24	11
Sims	Starling	23JUN03	1.21	1	Simpson	Robert	11JUL03	3.23	1
Sims	Starlin	03AUG04	1.20	1	Simpson	Robert	29JUL03	2.28	11
Sims	Starlin	30JUL05	1.21	1	Simson	Robert	06JUN04	4.20	11
SIMPSON					Simpson	Robert	25AUG04	3.19	1
Simpson	Agness	24JUN91	2.09	F	Simpson	Robert	23AUG05	3.34	1
Simpson	Agnus	05OCT92	1.12	F	Simpson	Robert	09JUN06	3.30	1
Simpson	Agnus	07AUG93	3.11	F	Simpson	Robert	09JUN07	2.31	1
Simpson	Agness	11JUN94	2.13	F	Simpson	Robert	12AUG07	2.33	1
Simpson	David	24JUN91	2.09	1	Simpson	Robert	05AUG07	2.33	1
Simpson	David	18OCT92	1.11	1	Simpson	Robert	28JUL08	2.26	1
Simpson	David	07AUG93	3.10	1	Simpson	Robert	10JUL09	1.31	1
Simson	David	23MAY94	2.14	1	Simpson	Samuel	03JUN03	3.22	M1
Simpson	David	19MAR95	3.16	1	Simpson	Samuel	17AUG05	3.33	1
Simson	David	05JUL96	2.17	1	Simpson	Sarah	30JUN87	1.05	F
Simpson	David	13JUN97	3.29	1	Simpson	Sarah	30MAY89	6.07	F
Simpson	David	13JUN97	3.33		Simpson	Sarah	11MAY90	1.10	F
One town lot in Stanford					Simpson	Thomas	-----11	1.78	1
Simpson	David	24MAY99	1.34	11	Simpson	William	27AUG89	2.13	1
Simpson	David	24MAY99	1.40		Simpson	William	21MAY05	2.28	1
One lott in Stanford					Simpson	William	08MAY06	2.32	1
Simpson	David	14JUN00	2.26	11	Simpson	William	22AUG07	2.34	1
Simpson	David	28MAY01	2.24	11	Simpson	William	-----08	1.35	1
Simpson	David	03JUN02	3.23	2	Simpson	William	06JUL09	2.32	1
Simpson	David	08MAY03	2.27	2	Simpson	William	-----11	1.72	1
One lott in Standford					SINCLAIR				
Simpson	David	26JUN04	1.18	11	St Leair	Alexander	10JUN94	1.11	1
Simpson	David	03MAY05	2.28	1	Sincleer	Alexander	30MAY08	2.24	1
One lott in Standford					SINGLETON				
Simpson	David	06APR06	2.31	1	Singleton	Christopher	26JUN87	1.05	12
Simpson	David	15JUN07	2.31	11	Singleton	Christopher	-----96	4.14	2
Simpson	David	31MAY08	1.33	11	Singleton	Christopher	16JUL96	2.18	1
Simpson	David	24AUG09	2.33	1	Singleton	Christopher	03JUN01	2.24	11
Simpson	David	-----11	1.73	2	Singleton	Christopher	30JUN02	1.22	11
Simpson	James	24JUN91	2.09	1	Singleton	Christopher	07JUL03	1.22	11
Simpson	James	24NOV92	1.11	1	Singleton	Chris. Sr	16AUG04	2.17	1
Simpson	James	06AUG93	3.10	1	Singleton	Chris.	16AUG04	2.17	2
Simson	James	24MAY94	2.14	1	Singelton	Christopher	29MAY05	3.31	1
Simson	James	29JUL03	2.28	1	Singleton	Christopher	27JUL05	1.20	1
Simpson	Jesse	24APR06	2.32	1	Singleton	Christopher	16JUL06	1.23	2
Simpson	John	26JUN87	1.05	1	Singleton	Christopher	01AUG06	3.30	1
Simpson	John	30MAY89	6.07	1	Singelton	Christopher	28JUL08	2.26	1
Simpson	John	05APR90	1.10	1	Singleton	Christopher	14JUN09	2.29	1
Simpson	John	19MAY91	2.09	1	Singleton	Christ. Jr	08APR09	1.30	1
Simpson	John	20SEP92	1.12	1	Singleton	Chris. Sr	-----11	1.71	1
Simpson	John	11JUN94	2.13	M1	Singleton	Chris. Jr	-----11	1.71	1
Simson	John	24MAR95	3.16	1	Singleton	Daniel	22JUN02	1.21	11
Simson	John	16APR95	3.14	1	Singleton	Daniel	22JUN03	1.21	12
Simpson	John	10MAY97	3.28	1	Singleton	Daniel	02AUG04	1.19	1
Simpson	Joseph	24JUN91	2.09	1	Singleton	Daniel	30JUL05	1.20	1
Simpson	Joseph	05OCT92	1.12	1	Singleton	Daniel	31JUL06	1.24	1
Simpson	Joseph	07AUG93	3.10	1	Singleton	Daniel	05MAY07	1.23	11
Simpson	Joseph	11JUN94	2.13	1	Singleton	John	14APR94	3.19	1
Simpson	Joseph	-----11	1.76	1	Singleton	John	-----95	1.12	1
Simpson	Joshua	11MAY96	2.16	1	Singleton	John	-----96	4.14	1
Simpson	Joshua	18JUL97	1.24	1	Singleton	John	13APR97	3.27	1
Simpson	Reuben Sr	14JUL97	1.24	11	Singleton	John	13APR97	3.27	1
Simpson	Reuben Jr	14JUL97	1.24	1	Singleton	John	25MAY99	2.18	1
Simpson	Reubin Sr	01JUL99	1.36	1	Singleton	John Jr	25MAY99	2.18	1
Simpson	Reubin Jr	01JUL99	1.36	1	Singleton	John	17JUN00	1.14	1
Simpson	Reuben	22JUL00	2.27	21	Singleton	John	03JUN01	2.24	1
Simpson	Reuben Jr	26JUL00	2.27	1	Singleton	John	03JUN01	1.16	11
Simpson	Robert	24JUN91	2.10	1	Singleton	John	30JUN02	1.22	1
Simpson	Robert	18OCT92	1.11	1	Singleton	John	07JUL03	1.22	1
Simpson	Robert	17AUG93	3.11	1	Singleton	John	15JUL03	3.24	1
Simson	Robert	09MAY94	2.14	1	Singleton	John Sr	15AUG04	2.17	1
Simson	Robert	28APR95	3.15	1	Singleton	John Jr	15AUG04	2.17	1
Simson	Robert	02JUN96	2.17	1	Singelton	John	29MAY05	3.31	1
Simpson	Robert	18JUN96	1.11	1	Singleton	John	27JUL05	1.20	1
Simpson	Robert	10MAY97	3.28	1	Singelton	John	01AUG06	3.31	1

surname	name	date	bk.pg	TM	surname	name	date	bk.pg	TM
Singelton	John Jr	07AUG06	3.31	11	Skidmore	James	-----05	3.38	1
Singleton	John	30JUN07	1.26	1	Skidmore	James	03JUN05	3.31	1
Singleton	John	30JUN07	1.26	1	Skidmore	James	04AUG06	3.38	1
Singleton	John	02JUL07	1.23	1	Skidmore	James	17AUG07	1.23	1
Singleton	John	19AUG07	2.34	1	Skidmore	James	24AUG08	2.26	1
Singleton	John	-----08	2.27	1	Skidmore	James	27JUN09	1.31	1
Singleton	John	31MAY08	1.34	1	Skidmore	James	-----11	1.78	1
Singelton	John	28JUL08	2.26	1	Skidmore	John	06OCT92	1.12	1
Singleton	John Sr	08APR09	1.30	1	Skidmore	John	24AUG93	3.11	1
Singleton	John	30MAY09	2.29	1	Skidmore	Joseph	03APR90	2.06	1
Singleton	Matthias	15JUL03	3.23	1	Skidmore	Joseph	02OCT92	2.08	1
Singleton	Matthew	16AUG04	2.17	1	Skidmore	Joseph	24AUG93	3.11	1
Singelton	Matthew	29MAY05	3.31	1	Skidmore	Joseph	12JUN94	2.13	1
Singelton	Mathew	07AUG06	3.31	1	Skidmore	Joseph	28APR95	3.15	1
Singleton	Matthew	-----11	1.71	1	Skidmore	Joseph	03JUN96	2.17	1
Singleton	Middleton	22JUN03	1.21	1	Skidmore	Joseph	23JUN97	1.23	1
Singleton	Middleton	02AUG04	1.19	1	Skidmore	Joseph	06JUN99	1.34	1
Singleton	Middleton	30JUL05	1.20	1	Skidmore	Joseph	28JUN00	2.26	1
Singleton	Middleton	31JUL06	1.23	1	Skidmore	Joseph	01AUG01	2.25	1
Singleton	Philip	05JUN01	1.16	1	Skidmore	Joseph	27MAY02	2.27	1
Singleton	Philip	12JUN02	1.20	1	Skidmore	Joseph	31MAY03	3.22	1
Singleton	Phillip	02AUG04	1.19	1	Skidmore	Joseph	04MAY04	3.18	1
Singleton	Philip	30JUL05	1.20	1	Skidmore	Joseph	13JUN05	3.31	1
Singleton	Philip	31JUL06	1.24	1	Skidmore	Joseph	17JUL06	3.30	1
Singleton	Phillip	05MAY07	1.23	1	Skidmore	Joseph	14JUL07	2.32	1
Singleton	Phillip	31MAY08	1.34	1	Skidmore	Joseph	30MAY08	2.24	1
Singleton	Phillip	14JUN09	2.31	1	Skidmore	Joseph	30JUN09	1.31	1
Singleton	Polly	-----11	1.71	F	Skidmore	Joseph	-----11	1.70	11
Singleton	Richard	17JUN99	2.19	1	SKILLERN				
Singleton	Richard	23JUL00	1.14	11	Skillerin	George	29JUN96	2.17	1
Singleton	Richard	24JUN01	1.16	11	Skillern	George	05JUN97	1.24	1
Singleton	Richard	22JUN02	1.21	11	Skillern	George	13MAY99	3.18	1
Singleton	Richard	27JUL05	1.20	1	Skillern	George	19JUN00	3.27	1
Singleton	Richard	31MAY08	1.34	2	Skilleron	George	17JUN01	3.31	1
Singleton	Richard	14JUN09	2.29	1	Skillern	George	26JUL02	3.24	1
Singleton	Richard	14JUN09	2.29	1	Skillern	George	06AUG03	2.29	1
Singleton	Richard	-----11	1.71	1	Skillon	George	23JUL04	4.21	1
Singleton	Robert	30JUN87	3.09	1	Skillern	George	18JUN05	2.29	1
Singleton	Robert	25JUL89	2.12	1	Skillern	George	02AUG06	2.34	1
Singleton	Robert	13SEP91	3.15	1	Skillerun	William	05MAY94	3.24	1
Singleton	Robert	30NOV92	3.18	1	SKINEAR				
Singleton	Robert	-----93	2.04	1	Skinear	Stone	02APR95	3.16	1
Singleton	Robert	21MAY94	3.19	1	SLADE				
Singleton	Robert	-----95	1.12	1	Slade	Anne	19JUN89	5.10	F
Singleton	Robert	-----96	4.14	1	Slade	William	06AUG89	2.13	1
Singleton	Robert	16JUL06	1.23	1	Sledd	William	07SEP91	3.15	1
Singleton	Robert	02JUL07	1.23	1	Sled	William	02DEC92	3.18	1
Singleton	Robert	31MAY08	1.34	1	Sleed	William	14APR94	3.19	1
Singleton	Robert	31MAY08	1.33	11	SLAUGHTER				
Singleton	Robert	14JUN09	2.29	1	Slaughter	James	11AUG06	1.25	11
Singleton	Robert	-----11	1.69	1	Slaughter	John	21JUN99	2.20	11
Singleton	Robert	-----11	1.71	11	Slaughter	Matthew	-----11	1.74	1
SINK					SLAYTON				
Sink	Jesse	27JUN05	2.29	M1	Sleton	Arthur	27JUN96	1.12	1
SISSON					Slayton	Hugh	04AUG89	5.11	1
Sisson	Wm. Jer.	05DEC92	3.18	1	Sleton	George	20AUG06	3.32	1
Sissen	William Jr	21MAY94	3.18	1	Slaton	James	03APR90	2.06	1
Sissen	William J.	10MAY99	2.18	1	Slattan	James	25MAR91	1.08	1
Sissen	William J.	09JUN00	1.13	1	Slaten	James	17JUL06	2.33	11
SKIDMORE					Slaton	James	-----11	1.70	1
Skidmore	James	02SEP93	1.09	1	Slaton	John	25JUL05	2.31	1
Skidmore	James	21MAY94	1.08	1	Slatin	Joseph	25JUL00	2.27	1
Skidmore	James	25MAY95	2.24	1	Slaten	Joseph	28MAY01	3.33	1
Skidmore	James	25JUN95	2.11	1	Slaton	Joseph	06AUG05	3.32	1
Skidmore	James	01JUN96	1.12	1	Slaten	Joseph	20AUG06	3.32	1
Skidmore	James	21MAY99	1.33	1	Sleton	Ruben	20AUG06	3.32	1
Skidmore	James	14JUN00	2.26	1	Slayton	Samuel	-----08	2.25	1
Skidmore	James	28MAY01	2.24	1	Slatin	Samuel	08JUN09	1.30	1
Skidmore	James	12JUN02	1.20	1	Slatton	Tyra	13JUL87	1.05	1
Skidmore	James	21JUL03	3.24	1	Slanton	Tyrus	12MAY89	6.06	1
Skidmore	James	-----05	3.38		Slaton	Tyra	02AUG90	1.09	1
1804 tax info in 1805 tax list					Slaten	William	27JUL04	4.22	1

surname	name	date	bk.pg	TM	surname	name	date	bk.pg	TM
Slatin	William	25JUL05	2.31	1	Smeck	Godlep	24AUG08	2.26	1
SLEET					Smick	Godlip	23JUN09	1.31	1
Sleet	John	26JUN87	3.09	1	Smick	Godlip	-----11	1.70	1
Sleet	John	01JUL89	2.12	1	SMIDDY				
Sleet	John	19APR91	3.14	1	Smiddy	Thomas	11MAY90	1.10	1
Sleet	John	08OCT92	3.17	1	Smidda	Thomas	19MAY91	2.09	1
Sleet	John	14APR94	3.19	1	SMILEY				
Sleet	John	-----95	1.12	1	Smily	John	02AUG90	1.09	1
Sleight	John	-----96	4.14	1	Smily	John	01AUG91	2.10	1
SLOAN					Smily	John	22SEP92	1.12	1
Sloan	Alexander	23MAY89	6.08	1	Smily	John	20AUG93	3.11	1
Sloan	Alexander	20APR90	1.10	1	Smiley	John	23MAY94	2.14	1
Sloan	Alexander	21JUN91	2.10	1	Smiley	John	13JUL96	2.18	1
Sloan	Alexander	21SEP92	1.12	1	Smiley	John	05JUN97	1.24	1
Sloan	Alexander	09AUG93	3.11	1	Smiley	John	26JUN99	1.35	1
Slone	Alexander	20MAY94	2.13	1	Smiley	John	19JUN00	3.27	1
Slone	Alexander	13APR95	3.16	1	Smiley	John	29MAY01	3.33	1
Sloan	James	04JUL00	3.28	1	Smiley	John	11AUG02	2.28	1
Sloan	John	13JUL87	1.05	1	Smiley	John	25JUN03	3.23	1
Sloan	John	04SEP87	1.05	1	Smilie	John	06AUG04	3.18	1
Sloan	John	13MAY89	6.06	1	Smiley	John	05AUG05	3.32	1
Sloan	John Jr	19MAY89	6.07	1	Smiley	John	20AUG06	3.32	1
Sloan	John	21APR90	1.09	1	SMITH				
Sloan	John	30MAY97	1.22	1	Smith	Abner	-----95	1.12	M1
Sloan	John	26JUN99	3.19	1	Smith	Abner	-----96	4.14	1
Sloan	John	02MAY01	3.31	1	Smith	Abraham	23JUN99	2.18	1
Sloan	John	06AUG02	3.25	1	Smith	Abraham	14JUN02	3.24	1
Sloan	John	04AUG03	2.29	1	Smith	Abraham	10AUG03	2.30	1
Slone	John	12JUN04	4.21	1	Smith	Abraham	07APR04	4.20	1
Sloon	John	19APR08	1.31	1	Smith	Abraham	20JUN05	2.29	1
Slone	John	01JUL09	2.32	1	Smith	Abraham	31JUL06	2.34	1
Slone	John	-----11	1.74	1	Smith	Adam	23MAY97	1.23	1
Sloan	Margaret	03AUG90	1.10	F	Smith	Amos	21MAY90	1.09	1
Sloan	Margrate	21JUN91	2.10	F	Smith	Arquilla	08MAY07	1.24	1
Sloan	Mary	17JUN05	2.29	F	Smith	Arthur	21JUN99	3.18	1
Sloan	Thomas	02OCT87	1.06	1	Smith	Arthur M.	20JUN00	3.27	1
Sloan	Thomas	21SEP92	1.12	1	Smith	Arthur	01MAY01	3.30	1
Slone	Thomas	22MAY94	2.14	1	Smith	Arthur H.	04AUG02	3.25	1
Sloan	William	13JUL87	1.05	1	Smith	Arthur	06AUG03	2.29	1
Sloan	William	11JUN89	6.07	1	Smith	Arthur	13JUN04	4.21	1
Sloan	William	29MAY90	1.09	1	Smith	Arthur M.	29JUN05	2.30	1
Sloan	William	18MAR91	2.09	1	Smith	Arthur M.	14JUL06	2.33	1
Sloan	William	14SEP92	1.12	1	Smith	Arthur	14AUG07	2.33	1
Sloan	William	09AUG93	3.10	1	Smith	Arthur	24AUG08	2.26	1
Slone	William	12MAY94	2.13	1	Smith	Arthur M.	10JUN09	1.31	1
Slone	William	09MAY95	3.15	1	Smith	Arthur M.	-----11	1.74	1
Sloan	William	07JUN97	1.23	1	Smith	Caleb	20APR91	2.10	1
Sloan	William	23JUL00	2.27	1	Smith	Charles	08APR91	1.08	
SLUDER					Smith	Listed with William Smith			
Sluder	David	22JUL01	3.34	1	Smith	Charles	19MAY91	2.09	1
Sluder	David	01JUN02	2.27	1	Smith	Charters	12OCT92	2.08	11
Slader	David	09JUL03	3.23	1	Smith	Charles	13AUG93	1.08	1
Shuder	David	10JUN05	3.31	1	Smyth	Charles	29MAY94	1.08	1
Sluder	David	01AUG06	3.31	1	Smith	Charles	17MAY97	3.28	1
SMALL					Smith	Charls	17JUN99	2.19	1
Small	Barnett	29MAY05	2.28	1	Smith	Charles	24JUL00	1.14	1
SMICK					Smith	Charles	24JUN01	1.16	1
Smack	Gotlip	08OCT92	1.12	1	Smith	Charles	21JUN03	1.21	1
Smack	Gotlip	16AUG93	3.11	1	Smith	Charles	02AUG04	1.19	1
Smeck	Godlep	05MAY94	2.14	1	Smith	Charls	30JUN05	1.20	1
Shmick	Godlip	28MAR95	3.16	1	Smith	Charles	01AUG06	2.34	1
Smeck	Godlep	04AUG96	2.17	1	Smith	Charls	01AUG06	1.24	1
Smick	Godlil	23MAY97	1.23	1	Smith	Charles	06MAY07	1.23	1
Smick	Godlib	03JUL99	3.19	1	Smith	Charles	18JUN07	2.32	1
Smack	Godlip	30JUN00	3.28	1	Smith	Charles	31MAY08	1.33	1
Schmick	Godlip	07JUL01	3.32	1	Smith	Charles	24AUG08	2.26	1
Smack	Cutliff	18AUG02	3.26	1	Smith	Charles	08JUN09	1.30	1
Smack	Cutliff	21JUN03	2.28	1	Smith	Charles	14JUN09	2.30	1
Smick	Godlip	27JUL04	4.22	1	Smith	Christopher	19MAY91	2.09	1
Smack	Sutliff	25JUL05	2.31	1	Smyth	Christopher	05AUG93	1.09	1
Smach	Cutliff	15JUL06	2.33	1	Smith	Christopher	14APR94	3.19	1
Snuck	Godlep	30JUL07	2.32	1	Smith	Christopher	-----95	1.13	1

surname	name	date	bk.pg	TM
Smith	Christopher-----96	4.15	1
Smith	Christopher-----97	2.05	1
Smith	Christopher23JUN99	2.20	1
Smith	Christopher13JUN00	1.13	1
Smith	Christopher02JUN01	1.16	1
Smith	Daniel	04AUG00	2.27	M1
Smith	Daniel	08AUG01	2.25	M1
Smith	Daniel	09AUG02	3.25	1
Smith	Daniel	11JUN03	2.27	1
Smith	Edmund	19APR91	3.14	1
Smith	Edmund	16NOV92	3.17	1
Smith	Edmond	21MAY94	3.19	1
Smith	Edmond	-----95	1.12	1
Smyth	Edmond	21JUN96	1.11	1
Smith	Edmund	-----96	4.14	1
Smith	Edmond	02MAY97	3.28	1
Smith	Edward	27MAY99	1.34	1
Smith	Edmond	13JUL01	2.25	1
Smith	Edmond	04AUG02	3.25	1
Smith	Edmonds	13JUN03	2.28	1
Smith	Edmonds	-----05	2.36	1
Smith	Edmonds	02AUG05	2.31	1
Smith	Edmond	06JUN06	2.32	1
Smith	Elias	30JUN02	3.24	1
Smith	Elias	28MAY03	2.27	1
Smith	Elias	25JUL04	1.19	1
Smith	Elias	08JUN05	2.29	1
Smith	Elias	06JUN06	2.32	1
Smith	Elias	20JUN07	2.32	1
Smith	Elijah	12AUG89	2.13	1
Smith	Elijah	05MAY94	3.24	1
Smith	Elijah	-----95	1.13	1
Smith	Elijah	11MAY96	2.16	M1
Smith	Elijah	30MAY97	3.29	1
Smith	Elijah	08MAY07	1.24	1
Smith	Elijah	18APR08	1.31	1
Smith	Elijah	16JUN09	2.31	1
Smith	Elizabeth	21JUN05	2.29	F
Smith	Enoch	30JUN97	1.24	1
Smith	Ephragm	-----08	1.35	M1
Smith	Ephrame	-----11	1.74	1
Smith	Fleming	05JUL03	1.22	1
Smith	Fleming	06AUG04	2.18	1
Smith	George	13MAY89	6.06	1
Smith	George	15APR90	1.09	1
Smith	George	06AUG91	2.10	1
Smith	George	14SEP92	1.12	1
Smith	George	-----93	2.04	1
Smith	George	10AUG93	3.10	1
Smith	George	10MAY94	2.14	1
Smith	George	10APR95	3.15	1
Smith	Hannah	03JUL99	3.19	F
Smith	Hannah	-----11	1.75	F
Smith	Hubbard	17JUL00	2.27	1
Smith	Hubbard	08JUN01	2.25	1
Smith	Hubbard	14JUN02	3.24	1
Smith	Hubbard	28MAY03	2.27	1
Smith	Hubbard	24JUL05	2.31	1
Smith	Hubbard	06JUN06	2.32	1
Smith	Hubbert	25JUL04	1.19	1
Smith	Hubbert	-----08	1.35	1
Smith	Isaac	15AUG93	3.11	31
Smyth	Isaac	21MAY94	1.08	11
Smith	Isaac	29JUN03	2.28	1
Smith	Isaac	04AUG04	3.18	1
Smith	Isaac	20JUN05	2.29	1
Smith	Isaac	31JUL06	2.34	1
Smith	Jackman	16JUL96	2.17	1
Smith	Jackman	23MAY97	1.23	1
Smith	Jackman	29JUN99	3.19	1
Smith	Jacob	21MAY99	3.18	1
Smith	Jacob	24AUG08	2.26	1

surname	name	date	bk.pg	TM
Smith	James	14MAY89	6.06	1
Smith	James	18MAY90	1.09	1
Smith	James	18MAY90	1.10	1
Smith	James	07MAY91	2.09	1
Smith	James	21SEP92	1.12	
Listed with Mary Smith as minor				
Smith	James	04DEC92	3.18	1
Smith	James	-----93	2.04	1
Smith	James	10AUG93	3.10	
Listed with Mary Smith				
Smith	James	14APR94	3.19	11
Smyth	James	12MAY94	1.08	1
Smith	James	22MAY94	2.13	1
Smith	James	09APR95	3.15	1
Smith	James	01MAY95	3.15	11
Smith	James	11MAY96	2.16	1
Smith	James	26MAY97	1.23	1
Smith	James	30MAY97	3.29	1
Smith	James	14JUL97	1.24	1
Smith	James	26JUN99	1.33	1
Smith	James	19JUN00	3.27	1
Smith	James	25JUL00	2.27	1
Smith	James	02MAY01	3.31	1
Smith	James	30MAY01	3.33	1
Smith	James	31JUL02	3.25	1
Smith	James	03AUG02	2.28	1
Smith	James	06JUN03	3.22	1
Smith	James	06AUG03	2.30	1
Smith	James	12JUN04	4.21	1
Smith	James	06AUG04	3.18	1
Smith	James	23AUG05	3.34	1
Smith	James	01AUG06	2.34	1
Smith	James	-----11	1.72	11
Smith	Jesse	26JUN87	1.05	1
Smith	Jesse	30MAY89	6.07	1
Smith	Jesse	11MAY90	1.09	1
Smith	Jessee	18MAY91	2.09	1
Smith	Jessey	21MAY94	3.19	1
Smith	Jesse	10MAY94	2.14	1
Smith	Jesse	-----95	1.13	1
Smith	Jesse	29APR95	3.15	1
Smith	Jesse	-----96	4.14	1
Smith	Jesse	13JUL96	2.17	1
Smith	Jesse	02MAY01	3.31	1
Smith	Jesse	31JUL02	3.25	1
Smith	Jesse	09AUG03	2.30	1
Smith	Jesse	08JUN04	4.21	1
Smith	Jesse	03JUN05	3.31	11
Smith	Jesse	18JUN05	2.29	M1
Smith	Jesse	22AUG08	2.26	1
Smith	John	30JUN87	3.09	1
Smith	John	20MAY89	6.06	1
Smith	John	11JUN89	6.07	1
Smith	John	06APR90	1.09	1
Smith	John	18MAR91	2.10	1
Smith	John	28SEP92	1.12	1
Smith	John	09AUG93	3.10	1
Smith	John	21AUG93	3.11	1
Smith	John	01MAY94	2.13	1
Smith	John	07JUN94	2.13	1
Smith	John	07JUN94	2.13	1
Smith	John	02APR95	3.16	11
Smith	John Colman	10JUN95	2.12	1
Smyth	John	27JUN96	1.12	1
Smyth	John	27JUN96	1.13	
One town lot in Stanford				
Smith	John	04AUG96	2.18	1
Smith	John	23MAY97	1.23	1
Smith	John	16JUN97	3.29	1
Smith	John	15JUL99	3.19	1
Smith	John	26JUN00	3.28	1
Smith	John	27JUN00	3.28	1

surname	name	date	bk.pg	TM	surname	name	date	bk.pg	TM
Smith	John	19MAY01	3.31	1	Smith	Reuben	02AUG05	2.31	11
Smith	John	10AUG01	3.34	1	Smith	Reuben	06JUN06	2.32	11
Smith	John	17AUG02	3.25	1	Smith	Reuben	30JUL07	2.32	11
Smith	John	28JUL03	2.28	1	Smith	Ruben	-----08	1.35	1
Smith	John	24JUL04	4.21	1	Smith	Ruben	24AUG09	2.33	1
Smith	John	18JUL05	2.31	1	Smith	Reuben	-----11	1.73	1
Smith	John	16JUL06	2.33	1	Smith	Samuel	17JUN05	1.19	1
Smith	John	13AUG06	2.34	1	Smith	Scarlet	26JUN87	1.05	1
Smith	John	07MAY07	1.24	1	Smith	Scarlet	30MAY89	6.07	1
Smith	John	22JUL07	2.32	1	Smith	Scarlott	11MAY90	1.10	1
Smith	John	22JUL07	2.32	1	Smith	Scarlet	18MAY91	2.09	1
Smith	John	30JUL07	2.33	1	Smith	Scarlet	10OCT92	1.11	1
Smith	John	-----08	1.35	1	Smith	Scarlet	21AUG93	3.11	1
Smith	John	04MAY08	1.32	1	Smith	Scarlet	01MAY94	2.13	1
Smith	John	24AUG08	2.26	1	Smith	Scarlot	01APR95	3.16	1
Smith	John	15MAY09	1.30	1	Smith	Scarlot	16JUL96	2.17	1
Smith	John	10JUN09	1.31	1	Smith	Scarlet	23MAY97	1.23	1
Smith	John	15JUN09	2.31	1	Smith	Scarlet	03JUL99	3.19	1
Smith	John	-----11	1.77	1	Smith	Scarlet	01JUL00	3.28	1
Smith	John(lame)	-----11	1.70	1	Smith	Scarlet	07JUL01	3.32	1
Smith	Joseph	12AUG02	2.28	1	Smith	Scarlett	17AUG02	3.26	1
Smith	Joseph	06JUN03	3.22	1	Smith	Scarlett	22JUN03	2.28	1
Smith	Joseph	07AUG04	3.19	1	Smith	Scarlett	27JUL04	4.21	1
Smith	Joseph	17AUG05	3.33	1	Smith	Scarlett	25JUL05	2.31	1
Smith	Joseph	01AUG06	3.31	1	Smith	Scarlett	15JUL06	2.33	1
Smith	Martin	04AUG91	2.09	1	Smith	Scarlett	14AUG07	2.33	1
Smith	Martin	14SEP92	1.13	1	Smith	Scarlett	24AUG08	2.26	1
Smith	Martin	06AUG93	3.10	11	Smith	Scarlett	22JUN09	1.31	1
Smith	Martin	10JUN94	2.13	11	Smith	Scarlett	-----11	1.70	11
Smith	Martin	14APR95	3.16	11	Smith	Semion	02JUN91	3.15	1
Smith	Martin	14JUL97	1.24	1	Smith	Simion	08NOV92	3.17	1
Smith	Martin	26JUN99	1.35	1	Smith	Solomon	22JUL05	2.31	1
Smith	Martin	26JUL00	2.27	11	Smith	Solomon	05AUG06	2.34	1
Smith	Martin	30MAY01	3.33	11	Smith	Solomon	05AUG07	2.33	1
Smith	Martin	12JUL02	2.27	11	Smith	Solomon	-----08	2.27	1
Smith	Martin	11JUN03	3.22	12	Smith	Solomon	10JUN09	1.31	1
Smith	Martin	06AUG04	3.18	11	Smith	Solomon	-----11	1.75	1
Smith	Martin	23AUG05	3.33	11	Smith	Stephen	18JUL07	2.32	1
Smith	Martin	07AUG06	3.32	11	Smith	Thomas	14JUN87	2.07	1
Smith	Marshall	12JUN07	1.25	1	Smith	Thomas	26JUN87	1.05	1
Smith	Mary	21SEP92	1.12	F1	Smith	Thomas	30JUN87	3.09	1
James Smith listed with her					Smith	Thomas	28NOV88	1.10	1
Smith	Mary	10AUG93	3.10	F1	Smith	Thomas	09MAY89	6.07	1
James Smith listed with her					Smith	Thomas	30MAY89	6.07	1
Smith	Mary	12MAY96	2.16	21	Smith	Thomas	25JUL89	2.12	1
SMITH					Smith	Thomas	04AUG89	5.11	1
Smith	Matthew	16MAY99	1.32	1	Smith	Thomas	05APR90	1.09	1
Smith	Matthew	08JUL00	2.26	1	Smith	Thomas	11MAY90	1.09	1
Smith	Peter	06AUG04	2.18	1	Smith	Thomas	30MAY90	2.06	1
Smith	Peter	17JUN05	1.19	1	Smith	Thomas	05APR91	1.08	1
Smith	Peter	07MAY07	1.23	11	Smith	Thomas	18MAY91	2.09	2
Smith	Peter	27APR08	1.32	11	Thomas Jr Smith listed with him				
Smith	Peter	15JUN09	2.31	1	Smith	Thomas	26AUG91	3.15	1
Smith	Robert	28JUN99	3.19	1	Smith	Thomas Jr	18MAY91	2.09	
Smith	Ruben	14JUN87	2.06	1	Listed with Thomas Smith				
Smith	Ruben	17NOV88	1.09	1	Smith	Thomas	10OCT92	1.11	1
Smith	Ruben	04AUG89	5.11	1	Smith	Thomas	23OCT92	2.08	1
Smith	Rubin	08MAY90	2.06	1	Smith	Thomas	30NOV92	3.18	1
Smith	Rubin	02JUN91	3.15	1	Smith	Thomas Sr	21AUG93	3.11	1
Smith	Ruben	22OCT92	2.08	1	Smith	Thomas Jr	21AUG93	3.11	1
Smith	Rubin	20AUG93	1.08	11	Smith	Thomas	05AUG93	1.09	1
Smyth	Rubin	15MAY94	1.08	11	Smith	Thomas	01MAY94	2.13	2
Smith	Reuben	22MAY95	2.24	1	Smith	Thomas	01APR95	3.16	1
Smith	Reuben	22MAY95	2.12	11	Smith	Thomas	19MAY95	3.15	1
Smyth	Rubin	21JUN96	1.11	11	Smith	Thomas	27MAY96	2.17	1
Smith	Reubin	02MAY97	3.28	12	Smith	Thomas	16JUL96	2.17	1
Smith	Reubin	27MAY99	1.34	12	Smith	Thomas Jr	16JUL96	2.17	1
Smith	Reuben	17JUL00	2.27	11	Smith	Thomas Sr	23MAY97	1.23	1
Smith	Reuben	17JUL01	2.25	11	Smith	Thomas Jr	23MAY97	1.23	1
Smith	Reuben	24MAY02	3.23	1	Smith	Thomas Jr	29JUN99	3.19	1
Smith	Reuben	13JUN03	2.27	1	Smith	Thomas Sr	03JUL99	3.19	1
Smith	Rheuben	25JUL04	1.19	11	Smith	Thomas R.	24MAY97	1.23	1

surname	name	date	bk.pg	TM	surname	name	date	bk.pg	TM
Smith	Thomas	12AUG02	2.29	1	Smith	William C.	18MAY90	1.10	1
Smith	Thomas	08JUN05	2.28	1	Smith	William C.	30APR91	2.09	1
Smith	William	14JUN87	2.06	1	Smith	William C.	14SEP92	1.13	1
Smith	William	13JUL87	1.05	12	Smith	William C.	07AUG93	3.11	1
Smith	William	17NOV88	1.09	1	Smith	William	14MAY95	3.15	1
Smith	William	13MAY89	6.06	1	Smith	William	05JUL96	2.17	1
Smith	William	23MAY89	6.07	1	Smith	William	31MAY97	1.23	1
(Shoemaker)					Smith	William	20MAY99	3.18	0
Smith	William	04AUG89	5.11	11	Tax pd by Jacob Spears				
Smith	William	08MAY90	2.06	1	Smith	William	21JUN00	3.27	1
Smith	William	02AUG90	1.10	11	Smith	William	21JUN00	3.27	1
Smith	William	18MAR91	2.09	12	Smith	William C.	17JUN01	3.32	11
Smith	William	08APR91	1.08	22	Smith	William	21JUN00	3.27	1
Charles Smith listed with him					Smith	William C.	27JUL02	3.24	1
Smith	William	22OCT92	2.08	11	Smith	William C.	11AUG03	2.30	1
Smyth	William	06AUG93	1.09	11	Smith	William	05JUN04	4.20	1
Smyth	William	15MAY94	1.08	11	Smith	William C.	18JUN05	2.29	1
Smith	William Sr	26MAY95	2.24	1	Smith	William C.	01AUG06	2.34	1
Smith	William Jr	06JUN95	2.23	1	Smith	William C.	22AUG07	2.34	1
Smith	William	22MAY95	2.10	1	Smith	William C.	-----08	2.25	1
Smith	William	22MAY95	2.10	1	Smith	William C.	12JUL09	1.32	1
Smyth	William	10JUN96	1.11	1	Smith	Winston	20MAY89	6.06	1
Smith	William	20APR97	3.29	1	Smith	Winston	09AUG93	3.10	1
Smith	William	20APR97	3.27	1	Smith	Winston	13JUL96	2.17	1
Smith	William	17MAY97	3.28	1	Smith	Winston	24MAY97	1.22	1
Smith	William	27MAY99	1.34	1	SNEED				
Smith	William Jr	27MAY99	1.34	1	Sneed	John	14AUG06	2.34	11
Smith	William	17JUN99	2.19	1	Sneed	John	22JUL07	2.32	11
Smith	William Sr	09JUL00	2.26	1	Sneed	John	-----08	2.25	2
Smith	William Jr	09JUL00	2.26	1	Sneed	John	13MAY09	1.30	21
Smith	William	10JUL00	3.29	M1	Sneed	William	01JUL96	1.12	1
Smith	William	24JUL00	1.14	1	Sneed	William	18MAY97	3.28	1
Smith	William Sr	17JUL01	2.25	1	Sneed	William	19JUN99	2.19	1
Smith	William Jr	17JUL01	2.25	1	SNIDER				
Smith	William	24JUN01	1.16	1	Snider	Harmon	03MAY89	6.07	1
Smith	William Sr	30JUN02	3.24	1	Snider	Harm	05APR90	1.09	1
Smith	William Jr	30JUN02	3.24	1	Snider	Harmon	18MAY91	2.09	1
Smith	William	22JUN02	1.21	1	Snider	Harmond	20SEP92	1.12	1
Smith	William	29JUL02	3.25	M1	Snider	Harmond	19AUG93	3.11	1
Smith	William Sr	12MAY03	2.27	1	Snider	Harmond	01MAY94	2.14	1
Smith	William	18JUN03	3.23	M1	Snider	Harmon	03APR95	3.16	1
Smith	William	22JUN03	1.21	1	Snider	Harmon	22JUL96	2.18	1
Smith	William	10AUG03	2.30	M1	Snider	Joseph	01JUL00	3.28	1
Smith	William Sr	25JUL04	1.19	1	Snider	Joseph	09JUL01	3.32	1
Smith	William Jr	25JUL04	1.19	1	Snider	Joseph	08JUL02	3.24	1
Smith	William	20JUN04	1.18	1	Snider	Joseph	26JUL03	2.28	1
Smith	William	--AUG04	1.19	1	Snider	Joseph	27JUL04	4.22	1
Smith	William	01AUG04	2.18	1	Snider	Joseph	23JUL05	2.31	1
Smith	William Sr	02AUG05	2.31	1	Snider	Joseph	09JUN09	1.31	1
Smith	William	20JUN05	2.29	1	SNODGRASS				
Smith	William	30JUN05	1.20	1	Snodgrass	Isaac	30JUL03	2.29	1
Smith	William	02AUG05	2.31	1	Snodgrass	Isaac	28JUN04	4.21	1
Smith	William	23AUG05	3.34	1	Snodgrass	Isaac	27JUN05	2.29	1
Smith	William Sr	06JUN06	2.33	1	Snodgrass	Isaac	04AUG06	3.31	1
Smith	William	06JUN06	2.32	1	SNOW				
Smith	William	31JUL06	1.24	1	Snow	Frostin	11JUN07	2.31	12
Smith	William	04AUG06	3.31	1	Snow	Frostin	30MAY08	2.24	12
Smith	William Sr	30JUL07	2.32	1	Snow	Frostin	28JUN09	1.31	1
Smith	William Jr	30JUL07	2.32	1	Snow	Frostin	-----11	1.70	1
Smith	William	06MAY07	1.23	1	Snow	James	30MAY08	2.24	1
Smith	William	11JUN07	1.25	1	Snow	James	28JUN09	1.31	1
Smith	William	-----08	1.35	1	Snow	James	-----11	1.70	1
Smith	William Jr	-----08	1.35	1	Snow	John	11JUN07	2.31	1
Smith	William	30MAY08	2.24	1	Snow	John	12JUL09	1.32	1
Smith	William	31MAY08	1.34	1	Snow	John	-----11	1.74	1
Smith	William	24AUG08	2.26	1	Snow	Leonard	02AUG05	2.31	1
Smith	William Sr	24AUG09	2.33	1	Snow	Leonard	06JUN06	2.32	1
Smith	William Jr	24AUG09	2.33	1	Snow	Lenard	11JUN07	2.31	1
Smith	William	07JUN09	1.30	1	Snow	Lenard	30MAY08	2.24	1
Smith	William	14JUN09	2.30	1	Snow	Leonard	28JUN09	1.31	1
Smith	William Sr	-----11	1.74	1	Snow	Leonard	-----11	1.70	1
Smith	William Jr	-----11	1.73	1	Snow	Nicodemus	06JUN06	2.32	1

surname	name	date	bk.pg	TM	surname	name	date	bk.pg	TM
Snow	Nichodemus	20JUN07	2.32	1	Sowder	Peter	30JUL05	1.21	1
Snow	Nichodemus	-----08	2.25	1	Sowder	Peter	01AUG06	1.24	1
Snow	Nicodemus	12JUL09	1.31	1	Sowder	Peter	08MAY07	1.24	1
Snow	Nichodemus	-----11	1.74	1	Sowder	Peter	07JUN08	1.31	1
Snow	Noah	-----11	1.77	1	Srowder	Peter	16JUN09	2.31	1
Snow	Samuel	29JUL06	2.33	1	SOWELL				
Snow	Samuel	22JUL07	2.32	1	Sowell	Edmond	-----11	1.72	1
Snow	Samuel	-----08	2.25	1	SPANN				
Snow	Samuel	29JUN09	1.31	1	Spann	Elizabeth	10AUG97	1.24	F
Snow	Samuel	-----11	1.70	1	Spann	John	10AUG97	1.24	1
Snow	Siles A.	02AUG08	2.26	1	Spann	Thomas	10AUG97	1.24	1
Snow	William	06AUG03	2.30	1	SPARKS				
SOCKRIS					Sparks	Benjamin	-----93	2.04	1
Sockris	Frederick	27JUL04	4.22	1	Sparks	Robert	30JUL07	2.32	1
SOJURNER					Sparks	Robert	-----08	1.35	1
Sogurner	Hardy	12JUN99	2.19	1	Sparks	Robert	23AUG09	2.33	1
Sojurner	Hardy	18JUN00	1.14	1	Sparks	Robert	-----11	1.74	1
Sogurner	Lewis	18JUN99	2.19	M1	Sparks	Thomas	12JUN87	2.06	1
SOUTHARD					Sparks	Thomas	01NOV88	1.09	1
Southard	John	-----11	1.75	1	Sparks	Thomas	19JUN89	5.10	1
SOUTHERN					Sparkes	Thomas	18MAY90	2.07	1
Souther	David	03JUN90	2.06	1	Sparks	Thomas	15AUG93	1.08	1
Southren	William	25JUL89	2.12	1	Sparks	Thomas	29MAY94	1.08	1
SOWDER					Sparks	Thomas	03JUN95	2.12	1
Sowder	David	11OCT92	2.08	1	SPEARS				
Sowder	David	28MAY94	1.08	1	Speers	Christianah	02AUG08	2.26	F
Souder	David	03JUN95	2.12	1	Spears	Christena	12JUL09	1.32	F
Souder	David	22MAY97	3.28	1	Spears	Christena	-----11	1.69	F
Sowder	David	14JUN99	2.19	1	Spears	David	16MAY99	3.18	0
Souder	David	22JUL00	1.14	1	Speers	David	28JUL02	3.25	1
Souder	David	23JUN01	1.16	1	Spears	David	11AUG03	2.30	1
Sowder	David	23JUN02	1.21	1	Speers	David	25JUN04	4.21	1
Sowder	David	22JUN03	1.21	1	Spears	David	28JUN05	2.30	1
Sowder	David	03AUG04	1.19	1	Spears	David	29JUL06	2.33	1
Sowder	David	31JUL05	1.21	1	Speers	David	10JUN07	2.31	1
Sowder	David	01AUG06	1.24	1	Speers	David	22AUG08	2.26	1
Sowder	David	08MAY07	1.24	1	Spears	David	12JUL09	1.32	1
Sowder	David	07JUN08	1.31	1	Spears	David	-----11	1.69	1
Sowder	David	24AUG09	2.33	1	Spears	George	15APR90	1.10	1
Souders	Henry	24AUG08	2.26	1	Spears	George	04AUG91	2.09	1
Sowder	Jacob	13JUN99	2.19	1	Spears	George	06AUG93	3.10	1
Souder	Jacob	22JUL00	1.14	1	Spears	George Sr	22MAY94	2.14	0
Souder	Jacob	24JUN01	1.16	1	Spears	George	24MAY94	2.13	1
Sowder	Jacob	23JUN02	1.21	1	Spears	George Sr	17APR95	3.16	D
Sowder	Jacob	03AUG04	1.19	11	Spears	George	16APR95	3.16	1
Sowder	Jacob	31JUL05	1.21	11	Spears	George	16APR95	3.16	1
Sowder	Jacob	01AUG06	1.24	11	Spears	George	09APR04	4.20	1
Sowder	Jacob	26MAY07	1.24	11	Spears	George	28JUN05	2.30	1
Sowder	Jacob	19APR08	1.31	11	Speer	Jacob	06SEP87	1.06	1
Souder	Jacob	01JUL09	2.32	1	Spears	Jacob	23MAY89	6.07	1
Sowder	John	28MAY94	1.08	1	Spears	Jacob	13MAY90	1.09	1
Sowder	Michael	28MAY94	1.08	1	Spears	Jacob	24JUN91	2.09	1
Souder	Michael	22MAY97	3.29	1	Spears	Jacob	13SEP92	1.12	1
Sowder	Michal	13JUN99	2.19	1	Spears	Jacob	22AUG93	3.11	1
Souder	Michael	22JUL00	1.14	1	Spears	Jacob	24MAY94	2.14	1
Souder	Michael	24JUN01	1.16	1	Spears	Jacob	17APR95	3.16	1
Sowder	Michael	23JUN02	1.21	00	Spears	Jacob	05JUL96	2.17	1
Sowder	Michael	22JUN03	1.21	1	Spears	Jacob	21JUN97	1.23	1
Sowder	Michael	03AUG04	1.19	1	Spears	Jacob	16MAY99	3.18	11
Sowder	Michael	31JUL05	1.21	1	Paid tax for William Smith				
Sowder	Michael	01AUG06	1.24	1	Spears	Jacob	19JUL00	3.29	11
Sowder	Michael	08MAY07	1.24	1	Speers	Jacob	18JUN01	3.32	12
Sowder	Michael	07JUN08	1.31	1	Spears	Jacob	28JUL02	3.25	1
Sowder	Michael	01JUL09	2.32	1	Spears	Jacob	11AUG03	2.30	12
Sowder	Peter	28MAY94	1.08	1	Spears	Jacob	05APR04	4.20	11
Souder	Peter	03JUN95	2.12	1	Spears	Jacob	28JUN05	2.30	11
Souder	Peter	22JUL00	1.14	1	Spears	Jacob	29JUL06	2.33	2
Souder	Peter	23JUN01	1.16	1	Speers	Jacob Sr	22AUG07	2.34	1
Souder	Peter	23JUN02	1.21	1	Spears	Jacob Jr	22AUG07	2.34	1
Sowder	Peter	23JUN03	1.21	1	Spears	Jacob	01AUG08	2.26	1
Sowder	Peter	23JUN03	1.21	1	Speers	Jacob	22AUG08	2.26	1
Sowder	Peter	02AUG04	1.19	1	Spears	Jacob Sr	12JUL09	1.31	1

surname	name	date	bk.pg	TM	surname	name	date	bk.pg	TM
Spears	Jacob Jr	12JUL09	1.32	1	Sponimore	Adam	29MAY01	2.24	1
Spears	Jacob	-----11	1.74	11	Spohnamore	Adam	17JUN02	1.21	1
Spears	James	08JUN09	1.30	1	Sponomore	Adam	14JUL03	1.22	1
Spears	James	-----11	1.75	1	Sponomore	Adam	25JUN04	1.18	1
Pd tax for William Martin (dec)					Sponomore	Adam	04JUN05	1.19	1
Spears	Moses	08JUL03	3.23	M1	Sponomore	Adam	13JUN06	1.22	1
Speer	Moses	-----05	3.38		Sponomore	Adam	13JUL07	1.23	1
1804 tax info in 1805 tax list					Sponomore	Adam	31MAY08	1.33	1
Speer	Moses	-----05	3.38	11	Spoonamore	Adam	-----11	1.76	1
Speer	Moses	22AUG05	3.33	M1	Spoonamor	Fredrick	15JUN96	1.11	1
Speers	Moses	17JUL06	3.30	1	Sponomore	Fredrick	22MAY99	1.33	1
Speer	Richard	26JUN99	1.35	1	Spoonimore	Frederick	29MAY00	2.25	1
Speer	Richard	25JUL00	2.27	1	Sponimore	Frederick	29MAY01	2.24	1
Speers	Richard	29MAY01	3.33	1	Spohnamore	Frederick	17JUN02	1.21	1
SPEED					Sponomore	Frederick	10JUN03	1.21	1
Speed	John	06APR04	4.20	1	Sponomore	Frederick	25JUN04	1.18	1
Speed	John	20JUN05	3.31	1	Sponomore	Frederick	13JUN06	1.22	1
Speed	Matthias	24MAY99	3.18	11	Shonomore	Frederick	20JUN07	1.25	1
Speed	Matthew	11JUL00	3.29	11	Sponomore	Fredrick	31MAY08	1.33	1
Speed	Matthias	19JUN01	3.32	12	Sponomore	Fredrick	15AUG09	2.33	1
Speed	Matthias	10JUN02	2.27	11	Spoonamore	Frederick	-----11	1.72	1
Speed	Mathias	11JUL03	3.23	12	Sponamore	Henry	07APR97	3.28	1
Speed	Mathew	06APR04	4.20	11	Sponamore	Henry	22MAY99	1.34	1
Speed	Matthias	20JUN05	3.31	11	Sponimore	Henry	29MAY01	2.24	1
Speed	Mathias	29JUL06	3.30	1	Spohnamore	Henry	17JUN02	1.21	1
Speed	Mathias Jr	29JUL06	3.30	1	Sponomore	Henry	18JUL03	1.23	1
SPELCE					Sponomore	Henry	25JUN04	1.18	1
Spelce	Joseph	11MAY96	2.16	1	Sponomore	Henry	20JUN05	1.20	1
SPENCER					Sponomore	Henry	13JUN06	1.22	1
Spencer	Edward	02JUN95	2.24	1	Shonomore	Henry	20JUN07	1.25	1
Spencer	George	23MAY89	6.07	1	Sponomore	Henry	31MAY08	1.33	1
Spencer	Jephthah	21MAY99	3.18	1	Spoonimore	Jacob	19JUL00	2.27	1
Spencer	Jephthah	19JUL00	3.29	1	Sponimore	Jacob	29MAY01	2.24	1
Spencer	Jeptha	31JUL01	2.25	1	Spohnamore	Jacob	17JUN02	1.21	1
Spenser	John	03AUG04	1.19	1	Sponomore	Jacob	15JUL03	1.23	1
Spencer	John	29JUL05	1.20	1	Sponomore	Jacob	25JUN04	1.18	1
Spencer	John	16JUN06	1.22	1	Sponomore	Jacob	20JUN05	1.20	1
Spencer	John	12MAY09	2.29	1	Sponomore	Jacob	13JUN06	1.22	1
Spencer	John	-----11	1.69	1	Spoonamore	Jacob	-----11	1.76	1
Spencer	Noadiah	29JUN97	1.23	1	Spoonemer	Phillip	03AUG89	5.11	11
Spencer	Noadiah	21MAY99	3.18	1	Spoonamore	Phillip	03APR90	2.06	1
Spencer	Naodiah	24JUN00	3.27	1	Shunamer	Phillip	05JUL91	1.08	11
Spencer	Noadiah	01MAY01	3.30	2	Spoonimer	Phillip	08OCT92	2.08	1
SPILLMAN					Spoonimore	Phillip	08OCT92	2.07	1
Spilman	Francis	18MAY91	2.09	1	Spoonamore	Phillip Sr	09AUG93	1.08	12
Spilman	Frank	11OCT92	1.11	1	Spoonamore	Phillip	09AUG93	1.08	1
Spilman	Frank	13SEP93	3.11	1	Spoonamor	Phillip	16MAY94	1.08	1
Spilman	Francis	20MAY94	2.14	1	Spoonamore	Phillip	16MAY94	1.08	11
Spelman	Francis	19MAR95	3.16	1	Spoonamore	Philip	22JUN95	2.11	1
Spillman	Nathaniel	26JUN87	1.05	1	Spoonamore	Philip	26JUN95	2.11	12
Spilman	Thomas	26SEP92	1.11	1	Spoonamore	Phillip	15JUN96	1.11	1
Spilman	Thomas	13SEP93	3.11	1	Spoonamore	Phillip	15JUN96	1.11	13
Spilman	William	10OCT92	1.11	1	Sponamore	Phillip	07APR97	3.27	1
Spilman	William	21AUG93	3.11	1	Sponamore	Phillip	07APR97	3.28	12
Spelman	William	30APR94	2.14	1	Sponamore	Phillip Sr	22MAY99	1.34	11
Spelman	William	19MAR95	3.16	11	Sponomore	Phillip	23MAY99	1.33	1
Spelman	William	20MAY96	2.17	12	Spoonimore	Phillip Sr	19JUL00	2.27	1
Spilman	William	30MAY97	1.22	12	Spoonimore	Phillip Jr	19JUL00	2.27	1
SPIRES					Sponimore	Philip	29MAY01	2.24	1
Spires	John	-----11	1.70	1	Sponimore	Philip Jr	29MAY01	2.24	1
Shier	John	-----11	1.77	1	Spohnamore	Philip Jr	17JUN02	1.21	1
Spires	William	30JUL04	2.17	1	Sponomore	Philip	15JUL03	1.23	1
Spires	William	17JUL06	3.30	1	Spoonemore	Phillip	26JUL03	3.24	1
Spires	William	14AUG06	3.37	1	Sponomore	Philip Sr	25JUN04	1.18	1
Spyers	William	30JUN07	1.26	1	Spoonamore	Phillip	15AUG04	3.19	1
Shyers	William	-----08	1.35	1	Sponomore	Philip	20JUN05	1.20	1
Spires	William	30MAY09	2.29	1	Spoonimore	Philip	08AUG05	3.33	1
Spires	William	-----11	1.70	1	Spoonimore	Phillip	20AUG06	3.32	1
SPOONAMORE					SPRAGGINS				
Sponamore	Adam	07APR97	3.27	1	Sasseen	Francis	-----96	4.14	1
Sponamore	Adam	22MAY99	1.34	1	Spragens	Frances	22APR97	3.29	F
Spoonimore	Adam	19JUL00	2.27	1					

surname	name	date	bk.pg	TM	surname	name	date	bk.pg	TM
Spragens	Francis	01JUN99	1.32	F	Sprowl	Joseph	01JUN09	2.30	1
Spraggins	Frances	04AUG00	2.27	01	Sproul	Joseph	-----11	1.76	1
Spraggins	James	27JUL02	3.24	M1	Sprowl	Oliver	20JUN04	1.18	1
Spraggens	James	14JUN05	3.31	1	Sprowl	William	18APR97	3.27	1
Spraggans	James	30JUL06	3.30	1	SPURGON				
Spragan	James	30MAY08	2.24	1	Spurgon	Eli	-----11	1.75	1
Spraggins	Jesse	16JUN00	2.26	1	SQUIRE				
Spraggins	Jesse	04APR01	2.24	1	Squire	Samuel	07JUL01	3.32	1
Spraggins	Jesse	03JUN02	3.23	1	SRONTS				
Spraggens	Jesse	28MAY03	2.27	1	Stront	Henry	-----95	1.13	1
Spraggan	Jesse	07APR04	4.20	1	Shrons	Nicholas	20MAY99	1.33	1
Spraggins	Jesse	31JUL05	2.28	1	Sronch	Nicholas	24JUN00	2.26	1
Spraggens	Jesse	08MAY06	2.32	1	Sronch	Nicholas	03JUN01	2.24	1
Spraggon	Jesse	22JUN07	2.32	11	Sronce	Nicolas	30JUN02	1.22	1
Spragons	Jesse	-----08	2.25	11	Sronce	Nicholas	07JUL03	1.22	1
Pd tax for Joel Atkinson (decd)					Swance	Nicholas	16AUG04	2.17	1
Spraggens	Jesse	07JUN09	1.30	1	Sronts	Nicholas	27JUL05	1.20	1
Spragens	Jesse	-----11	1.73	1	Sronce	Nicholas	20JUN06	1.22	1
Sasseen	Lewis	-----96	4.14	1	Seronts	Nicholes	01JUL07	1.23	1
Souseen	Lewis	30JUL01	1.17	1	Sronts	Nicholas	30MAY09	2.29	1
Spragens	Nathaniel	29MAY99	1.33	1	Serounce	Nicholas	-----11	1.71	1
Spraggins	Nathaniel	21JUN00	2.26	1	STACY				
Spraggans	Nathaniel	29JUL01	3.32	1	Stacy	Benjamin	26JUN99	3.18	11
Spraggins	Nathaniel	10JUN02	2.27	1	Stacy	Benjamin	06AUG02	3.25	1
Spraggins	Nathaniel	04AUG03	3.24	1	Stacy	Benjamin	29JUL03	2.28	1
Spraggin	Nathaniel	07APR04	4.20	1	Stacy	Benjamin	27JUN04	4.21	1
Spraggens	Nathaniel	20JUN05	3.31	1	Stacy	Benjamin	11JUL09	1.31	1
Spraggans	Nathaniel	29JUL06	3.30	1	Stagg	Ephraim	28JUN97	1.24	1
Spragins	Nathaniel	31MAY08	1.33	1	Staggs	Ephraim	12JUL99	3.19	1
Spragan	William	01JUN96	1.12	1	Stagg	Ephraim P.	05JUL00	3.29	1
Spragons	William	24MAY99	3.18	1	STANLEY				
Spragins	William	11JUL00	3.29	1	Stanley	Anderson	13MAY09	1.30	1
Spraggans	William	29JUL01	3.32	1	Stanley	Jonathan	19AUG07	2.34	1
Spraggins	William	03JUN02	3.23	1	STANTON				
Spraggens	William	28MAY03	2.27	1	Stanton	Matthew	31JUL06	1.23	1
Spraggins	William	18JUN05	2.29	1	Staunton	Mathew	06MAY07	1.23	1
Spraggins	William	02AUG06	2.34	1	Stanton	Richard	13MAY99	3.18	1
SPRATT					Stanton	Thomas	13MAY99	3.18	1
Sprat	Andrew	21MAY94	3.18	1	STAR				
Spratt	Andrew	-----95	1.13	1	Star	John	25MAY99	2.18	1
Sprat	Andrew	-----97	2.05	1	STEELE				
Sprat	Andrew	13MAY99	2.18	1	Steel	Paul	25MAY89	6.06	1
Sprat	Andrew	13JUN00	1.13	1	Steele	William	21AUG90	1.12	1
Sprat	Andrew	04JUN01	1.16	1	Steel	William	25JUN91	2.09	1
Sprat	William	27AUG89	2.13	1	Steel	William	26SEP92	1.11	1
Sprat	William	22JUN91	3.15	1	Steel	William	17AUG93	3.11	1
Spratt	William	07DEC92	3.19	1	Steel	William	28APR94	2.14	1
Sprat	William	21MAY94	3.18	1	Steel	William	26MAR95	3.16	1
Spratt	William	-----95	1.13	1	Steel	William	20MAY96	2.17	1
Sprot	William	-----96	4.15	1	Steel	William	20JUN96	2.17	1
Spratt	William	29JUN03	2.28	1	Steel	William	17MAY97	1.23	1
Spratt	William	24JUL04	1.19	1	Steele	William	30MAY97	1.22	11
Spratt	William	20MAY05	2.28	11	Steel	William	28JUN99	3.19	1
Spratt	William	06APR06	2.31		Steele	William	28JUN00	3.28	1
One 1/4 lott in Standford					Steel	William	07JUL01	3.32	1
Spratt	William	22JUN07	2.32	11	Steel	William	17JUN02	3.24	1
Sprat	William	31MAY08	1.33	11	Steel	William	20JUN03	2.28	1
Sprat	William	06JUL09	2.32	1	Steal	William	28JUL04	4.22	1
Spratt	William	-----11	1.73	1	STEMMONS				
SPRINGATE					Stemman	Henry	10OCT92	1.11	1
Springate	William	14MAY89	6.06	1	Stemans	Henry	18NOV93	3.11	1
Springate	William	05APR91	1.08	1	Stemmons	Stephen	28OCT92	2.08	1
Springgate	William	27OCT92	2.08	1	Stemans	Steven	05AUG93	1.09	1
Springate	William	05AUG93	1.08	1	Stemans	Stephen	21MAY94	1.08	1
SPROWL					STEPHENS				
Sproule	Joseph	30JUN03	1.21	1	Stephens	Abraham	14JUN87	2.07	1
Sprowl	Joseph	20JUN04	1.18	1	Stevens	Abraham	17NOV88	1.09	1
Sprowl	Joseph	19JUN05	1.19	1	Stevens	Abraham	04AUG89	5.11	1
Sprowl	Joseph	21JUN06	1.22	1	Stephenson	Abrim	01JUN90	2.06	1
Sprowl	Joseph	29JUN07	1.26	1	Stephens	Abraham	22OCT92	2.08	1
Sprowl	Joseph	29JUN07	1.26	1	Stevens	Abraham	07AUG93	1.09	1
Sprowl	Joseph	31MAY08	1.32	1	Stavens	Abraham	15MAY94	1.08	1

surname	name	date	bk.pg	TM	surname	name	date	bk.pg	TM
Stephen	Abraham	18MAY95	2.12	1	Stepp	Elijah	26JUL04	1.19	1
Stephens	Abraham	13JUN96	1.11	1	Stapp	Elijah	08JUN05	2.29	1
Stephens	Abram	20APR97	3.27	1	Stepp	Elijah	18MAY06	2.32	1
Stevinston	David	23JUN89	5.10	1	Stepp	Golston	28MAY91	3.15	1
Stephenson	David	30MAR90	2.06	1	Stepp	Grafton	04DEC92	3.18	1
Stephenson	David	25MAR91	1.08	1	Step	Gholsten	11JUN99	2.18	1
Stephenson	David	02OCT92	2.07	1	Stapp	James	28NOV88	1.10	12
Stephenson	David	12AUG93	1.08	1	Stapp	James	04AUG89	5.11	11
Stephenson	David	21MAY94	1.08	1	Stepp	James	02JUN91	3.15	1
Stephenson	David	28JUN95	2.11	1	Stepp	Joseph	28MAY91	3.15	1
Stephenson	David	18JUN96	1.12	1	Step	Joseph	09JUL99	2.20	1
Stephenson	David	10MAY97	3.28	1	Stepp	Joseph	21JUN00	2.26	1
Stephenson	David	22MAY99	1.33	11	Stepp	Joseph	17JUL01	2.25	1
Stephenson	David/heirs-----11		1.26	D	Step	Lucy	09JUL99	2.20	F
Tax paid by William Finley					Stepp	Stepp	03JUL09	1.31	
Stephenson	Edith	04JUN00	2.26	F	A free negroe				
Stephens	Francis	31MAY97	3.29	1	Stapp	William	28NOV88	1.10	1
Stephens	Jacob	12JUN87	2.06	1	Stapp	William	04AUG89	5.11	1
Stephens	Jacob	29JUN87	1.05	1	Step	William	07APR91	1.08	1
Stavens	Jacob	31OCT88	1.09	1	Stepe	William	27OCT92	2.08	1
Stephens	Jacob	12MAY89	6.06	1	Step	William	09JUN00	1.13	1
Stephens	Jacob	21APR90	1.09	1	Stepp	William	08JUN01	1.16	1
Stephens	Jacob	20JUN91	2.09	1	Steward	Alexander	19JUN99	2.19	11
Stephens	Jacob	13SEP92	1.12	1	Stewart	Benjamin	18APR08	1.31	1
Stephens	Jacob	07AUG93	3.11	1	Stewart	Benjamin	01JUL09	2.32	1
Stephens	Jacob	12MAY94	2.13	1	Stewart	Charles	31JUL05	1.21	1
Stephens	Jacob	12MAY94	2.13	1	Stewert	Charls	01AUG06	1.24	1
Stephens	Jacob	09MAY95	3.15	1	Stewart	Charles	09MAY07	1.24	1
Stephens	Jacob	16JUN96	2.17	1	Stewart	Charles	07JUN08	1.31	1
Stephens	Jacob	07JUN97	1.23	1	Stewart	Charles	01JUL09	2.32	1
Stephens	Jacob	21MAY99	3.18	1	Pd tax for Bethlaham Garrat heirs				
Stephenson	Jacob	20JUN00	3.27	1	Stewart	Gibson	-----11	1.76	1
Stephens	Jacob	01MAY01	3.30	1	Stewert	Jiles	18JUN00	1.14	1
Stephens	Jacob	06AUG02	3.25	11	Stewart	Giles	05JUN01	1.16	1
Stephens	Jacob	05AUG03	2.29	11	Stewart	Jiles	03JUN02	1.20	1
Stephens	Jacob	09JUN04	4.21	12	Stewart	Giles	14JUN03	1.21	1
Stephens	Jacob	29JUN05	2.30	13	Stewart	Isaiah	06AUG04	3.18	1
Stephenson	James	22MAY89	6.06	1	Steward	Isiah	12AUG05	3.33	1
Stephenson	James	23MAY89	6.08	1	Stewart	James	11JUL00	3.29	1
Stephenson	James	12AUG93	1.08	1	Stewart	James	29JUL01	3.32	1
Stephenson	James	25JUN95	2.11	1	Stuart	James	30JUL02	3.15	1
Stephenson	James	18MAY99	1.33	1	Stewart	James	10AUG03	2.30	1
Stevenson	James	28JUN99	3.19	1	Stuart	James	07APR04	4.20	1
Stephenson	James	13JUL01	2.25	1	Stuart	James	20JUN05	2.29	1
Stephenson	James	02AUG02	2.27	1	Stewart	James	31JUL05	1.21	1
Stephenson	James	01AUG04	2.18	1	Stewart	James	31JUL06	2.34	1
Stephenson	James	19AUG05	3.33	1	Stewert	James	01AUG06	1.24	1
Syephenson	John	04JUN96	2.17	1	Stewart	James	09MAY07	1.24	1
Stephens	John	04AUG02	2.28	1	Stewart	James	19APR08	1.31	1
Stevens	John	15JUL03	3.23	1	Stewart	James	01JUL09	2.32	1
Stever	John	17JUL06	3.30	11	Stewart	John	14MAY94	3.24	1
Stephens	John	02JUN07	1.24	11	Stewart	John	-----95	1.13	1
Stepher	John	06JUN09	2.30	1	Steward	John	-----96	4.15	1
Stevens	John	-----11	1.76	2	Stewart	John	-----97	2.05	1
Stephens	Luis	24MAR95	3.16	1	Stewerd	John	14MAY99	2.19	1
Stevinston	Robert	30JUN89	5.11	1	Steward	John	21MAY99	1.33	1
Stephenson	Robert	03APR90	2.06	1	Steward	John	19JUN99	2.19	11
Stephenson	Robert	31MAR91	1.08	1	Stuart	John	29MAY00	2.25	1
Stephenson	Robert	10AUG93	1.08	1	Stewert	John	18JUN00	1.14	1
Stephenson	Robert	21MAY94	1.08	1	Stewart	John	11JUN05	1.19	1
Stephenson	Robert	13JUN05	1.19	1	Stewart	John	29MAY07	1.24	1
Stephenson	Robert	18JUN06	1.22	1	Stewart	John	-----08	1.35	1
Stevenson	Thomas	28OCT88	1.09	1	Stewart	John	08JUN09	2.30	1
Stevinston	Thomas	16JUN89	5.10	1	Stewart	Mary	04AUG01	1.17	F1
Stephenson	Thomas	02JUN90	2.06	1	Stewert	Mary	03JUN02	1.20	F1
Stephenson	Thomas	04OCT92	2.07	1	Stewart	Mary	15JUN03	1.21	F2
STEPP					Stewart	Mary	14JUN04	1.17	F2
Stapp	Elijah	11JUN99	1.35	1	Stewart	Mary	07JUN05	1.19	F2
Stepp	Elijah	18JUL00	2.26	1	Stewert	Mary	11JUN06	1.22	F2
Stepp	Elijah	19MAY01	2.24	1	Stewart	Mary	29APR07	1.23	F2
Stepp	Elijah	27MAY02	3.23	1	Stewart	Mary	27JUL08	1.35	F
Stepp	Elijah	28MAY03	2.27	1	Stewart	Mary	10MAY09	2.29	F

surname	name	date	bk.pg	TM	surname	name	date	bk.pg	TM
Stewart	Mary	-----11	1.69	F	Stockdale	Shadrick	31MAY97	3.29	1
Stewart	Reuben	-----95	1.12	1	STOGDON				
Sturret	Steward	06NOV88	1.09	1	Stogdon	Hargate	13JUL97	1.24	1
Sterret	Steward	21MAY90	1.09	1	Stogdon	Thomas	28JUL97	1.24	11
Stewart	Thomas	01JUL09	2.32	1	STOKES				
Stewart	Washington	04AUG01	1.17	1	Stokes	Joel	03JUN03	3.22	1
Stewart	Washington	03JUN02	1.20	1	Stokes	Joel	09AUG04	3.19	1
Stewart	Washington	15JUN03	1.21	1	Stokes	Joal	05AUG05	3.32	1
Stewart	Washington	14JUN04	1.17	1	Paid tax for John Right heirs				
Stewart	Washington	11JUN05	1.19	1	Stokes	Joal	05AUG06	3.31	1
Stewert	Washington	02AUG06	1.25	1	STONE				
Stewart	Washington	29MAY07	1.24	1	Stone	Elias	-----11	1.70	1
Steward	William	26NOV92	3.17	1	Stone	Isiah	18AUG07	2.34	1
Sterus	William	22MAY97	3.28	1	Stone	John	01JUL00	3.28	1
Stewerd	William	20JUN99	2.19	1	Stons	John	19AUG07	2.34	1
Stewart	William	06MAY07	1.23	1	Stone	John	-----08	1.35	1
STIGALL					Stone	John	23AUG09	2.33	1
Steagal	George	11JUN99	1.32	1	Stone	Josiah	05JUN04	4.20	1
Stagall	George	31MAY00	2.26	1	Stone	Josiah	27JUN05	2.29	1
Stigall	George	26JUN01	1.17	1	Stone	Josiah	18AUG06	2.35	1
Stigall	George	23JUN02	1.22	1	Stone	Josiah	30MAY08	2.24	1
Stigall	George	23JUN03	1.21	1	Stone	Josiah	08AUG09	1.32	1
Stigal	George	06AUG04	1.20	1	Stone	Levi	28JUN05	2.30	1
Stigall	George	31JUL05	1.21	1	Stone	Levi	01AUG06	2.34	1
Stigall	George	02AUG06	1.24	1	Stone	Levi	18AUG07	2.34	1
Stygall	George	26MAY07	1.24	1	Stone	Levi	-----08	2.25	1
Stygall	George	19APR08	1.31	1	Stone	Levi	16AUG09	1.32	1
Stygall	George	21JUN09	2.31	1	Stone	Levi	-----11	1.70	1
Stigate	Thomas	-----11	1.75	1	Stone	Smith	22JUN09	1.31	1
Stygall	William	21JUN09	2.31	1	Stone	Spencer	26JUN87	1.05	1
Stygall	Zacheriah	12MAY09	2.29	1	Stone	Spencer	30MAY89	6.07	1
STINE					Stone	Spencer	05APR90	1.09	1
Stine	Jacob	18MAY91	2.09	1	Stone	Spencer	18MAY91	2.09	1
Stine	Jacob	08OCT92	1.12	1	Stone	Spencer	10OCT92	1.11	1
Stine	Jacob	21AUG93	3.11	1	Stone	Spencer	21AUG93	3.11	1
Stine	Jacob	23APR94	2.14	1	Stone	Spencer	01MAY94	2.13	1
Stine	Jacob	02APR95	3.16	1	Stone	Spencer	16JUL96	2.17	11
Stine	Jacob	04AUG96	2.18	1	Stone	Spencer	23MAY97	1.23	11
Stine	Jacob	15MAY97	1.22	1	Stone	Spencer	03JUL99	3.19	11
Stine	Jacob	28JUN99	3.19	1	Stone	Spencer	01JUL00	3.28	1
Stine	Jacob	27JUN00	3.28	1	Stone	Spencer	09JUL01	3.32	1
Stine	Jacob	21MAY01	3.31	11	Stone	Spensor	17AUG02	3.25	11
Stine	Jacob	08JUL02	3.24	11	Stone	Spensor	22JUN03	2.28	11
Stine	Jacob	25JUL03	2.28	11	Stone	Spencer	27JUL04	4.21	11
Stones	Jacob	25JUL04	4.21	11	Stone	Spencer	25JUL05	2.31	12
Stine	Jacob	22JUL05	2.31	11	Stone	Spencer	15JUL06	2.33	13
Stine	Jacob	18MAY06	2.32	11	Stone	Spencer	14AUG07	2.33	12
Stine	Jacob	30JUL07	2.32	2	Stone	Spencer	24AUG08	2.26	12
Stine	Jacob	-----08	1.35	2	Stone	Spencer	22JUN09	1.31	1
Stine	Jacob Sr	18AUG09	2.33	1	Stone	Spencer	-----11	1.70	11
Stine	Jacob Jr	18AUG09	2.33	1	Stone	Thomas	05AUG89	5.11	11
Stine	Jacob Sr	-----11	1.74	1	Stone	Thomas	18MAY91	2.09	1
Stine	Jacob Jr	-----11	1.74	1	Stone	William	12JUN87	2.06	1
Stean	James	20APR90	1.09	1	Stone	William	14NOV88	1.09	1
Stein	William	07AUG89	2.13	1	Stone	William	24JUN89	5.10	1
Steen	William	30NOV92	3.18	1	Stone	William	08MAY90	2.06	1
Steene	William	14APR94	3.19	1	Stone	William	14APR91	1.08	1
Steen	William	-----95	1.12	1	Stone	William	18OCT92	2.08	1
Steen	William	-----96	4.15	1	Stone	William	12AUG93	1.08	1
STINNET					Stone	William	26MAY94	1.08	1
Stinnet	Joel	07APR95	3.15	1	Stone	William	29MAY95	2.10	1
Stinnot	Reubin	-----96	4.15	1	Stone	William	09JUN96	1.11	1
Stinnot	William	-----96	4.15	1	Stone	William	14JUN96	2.17	1
STINSON					Stone	William	24APR97	3.28	1
Stinson	Henry	10OCT92	2.08	1	STOTT				
Stincen	James	17JUN03	3.23	1	Stotes	John	08OCT92	2.08	1
Stinson	Robert	03NOV92	2.08	1	Stots	John	10AUG93	1.08	1
Stinson	Robert	03NOV92	2.08	1	Stots	John	28JUN96	1.11	1
Stinson	Thomas	12JUN87	2.06	11	Stotts	John	24APR97	3.28	1
STOCKDALE					Staff	Solomon	15NOV88	1.09	11
Stockdale	Richard	31MAY97	3.29	1	Stott	Solomon	30JUN89	5.11	11
Stockdale	Samuel	31MAY97	3.29	1	Stotts	Usley	02JUN90	2.06	11

surname	name	date	bk.pg	TM	surname	name	date	bk.pg	TM
Stotes	Uzhy	08OCT92	2.08	F	Stilts	John	15JUL03	3.23	1
Stots	Elsley	12AUG93	1.08	F	Stull	John	23JUL04	1.18	1
STOW					Stull	John	03JUN05	3.31	1
Stoo	Joel	19MAY97	3.28	1	Stull	John	24APR06	2.32	1
Stow	Joal	22JUN99	2.20	1	Stults	William	10AUG97	1.24	1
STOWERS					Stolts	William	29JUL02	3.25	1
Stowers	John	29MAY05	2.28	1	Stutts	William	09AUG03	2.30	1
Stowers	John	09JUN06	2.33	1	Stults	William	05APR04	4.20	1
Stowers	John	12AUG07	2.33	1	Stuls	William	29JUL06	3.30	1
Stowers	John	14AUG07	2.33	1	STUMP				
STRAND					Stump	Jacob	20AUG87	1.05	1
Strand	Thomas	24MAR95	3.16	1	Stump	Jacob	23MAY89	6.07	1
STRANGE					Stump	Jacob	13MAY90	1.10	1
Strange	Cornal	16MAY97	1.22	1	Stump	Jacob	23JUN91	2.09	1
Strange	Cornwell	29MAY99	1.34	1	Stump	Jacob	14SEP92	1.13	1
Strange	William	26MAY07	1.24	1	STURGEL				
STRATIN					STURGIS				
Stratin	William	30MAY05	2.28	11	Sturgis	George	10JUN05	2.29	1
STREET					STYLEE				
Street	Murray	08OCT92	1.12	1	Stylee	William	09AUG93	1.08	1
Street	Nathaniel	08OCT92	1.12	1	SUBLETT				
Street	Nathaniel	21AUG93	3.11	1	Sublett	Abram	20MAY99	1.33	1
Street	Nathaniel	01MAY94	2.14	1	Sublett	Abraham	04JUN00	2.26	1
Sreet	Nathaniel	01APR95	3.16	1	Sublett	Abraham	04JUN01	2.25	1
Street	Nathaniel	16JUL96	2.18	1	Sublet	Abraham	12JUN02	1.20	1
Street	Nathaniel	17MAY97	1.22	1	Sublet	Abraham	04JUL03	1.22	11
Street	Nathaniel	04JUL99	3.19	1	Sublet	Abraham	02AUG04	2.18	11
Street	Nathaniel	01JUL00	3.28	1	Sublet	Abraham	15JUN05	1.19	11
Street	Nathaniel	19MAY01	3.31	1	Sublet	Abraham	20JUN06	1.22	11
Street	Nathaniel	14AUG02	3.25	1	Sublet	Abraham	03JUN07	1.25	1
Street	Nathaniel	25JUL03	2.28	1	Sublet	Abraham	27APR08	1.32	1
Street	Nathaniel	26JUL04	4.21	1	Sublet	Abraham Jr	27APR08	1.32	M1
Street	Nathaniel	23JUL05	2.31	1	Sublet	Abraham	-----11	1.72	11
Street	Nathaniel	17JUL06	2.33	1	Sublett	Abraham			
Street	Nathaniel	14AUG07	2.33	1	Sublet	Allen	22AUG04	2.17	1
Street	Nathaniel	-----08	2.27	1	Sublet	Allen	25JUL05	1.20	1
Street	Nathaniel	22JUN09	1.31	1	Sublet	Benjamin	22JUN07	1.25	1
Street	Nathaniel	-----11	1.70	1	Sublet	Benjamin	27APR08	1.32	1
STRINGER					Sublet	Benjamin	31MAY09	2.29	1
Stringer	Limeledge	13AUG89	2.13	1	Sublet	Branch	25JUL05	1.20	1
Stringer	Lemledy	13SEP91	3.15	1	Sublett	George A.	30MAY08	2.24	1
Stringer	Simeledge	21MAY94	3.19	1	Sublett	Geo. Allen	05JUN09	1.30	11
Stringer	Limeledger	-----95	1.13	1	Sublett	George A.	-----11	1.73	1
Stringer	Limly	-----96	4.14	1	Sublet	Philip A.	29MAY09	2.18	1
Stringer	Limeledge	-----97	2.05	1	Sublet	Philip A.	12AUG00	1.14	1
Stringer	Limeledg	13MAY99	2.19	1	Sublett	Phillip A.	08JUN09	2.30	1
Stringer	Limeledge	12JUN00	1.13	1	Sublett	Philip A.	-----11	1.76	1
Stringer	Limeledge	02JUN01	1.16	1	Sublett	Valentine	19JUN00	2.26	1
Stringer	William	30JUN87	3.09	1	Sublett	Vallentine	28MAY01	2.24	12
Stringer	William	13AUG89	2.13	1	Sublet	Valentine	18JUN00	1.21	11
Stringer	William	13SEP91	3.15	1	Sublet	Valentine	11JUL03	1.22	11
Stringer	William	-----95	1.13	1	Sublet	Valentine	22AUG04	2.17	11
Stringer	William	-----96	4.14	1	Sublet	Valentine	25JUL05	1.20	11
Stringer	William	-----97	2.05	1	Sublet	William	03JUN07	1.25	1
Stringer	William	18MAY99	2.19	1	Sublick	William	22APR08	1.32	1
Stringer	William	16JUN00	1.14	1	Sublet	William	01JUN09	2.30	1
Stringer	William	02JUN01	1.16	1	Sublett	William	-----11	1.76	1
STUCK					SUDDETH				
Stuck	John	11JUN05	1.19	1	Suddeth	Samuel	-----11	1.69	1
Stuck	John	10JUN06	1.21	1	SUGG				
Stuck	John	25MAY07	1.24	1	Sugg	Thomas	20JUN97	1.23	1
STUCKLER					SULLIVAN				
Stickler	Jacob	23JUL96	2.18	1	Sulavan	Manoah	24AUG08	2.26	1
Stukley	Jacob	26MAY97	1.23	1	Sullivan	Manoa	08JUN09	1.30	1
Stickley	Jacob	02JUL99	3.19	1	Sulivan	Mary	-----08	2.27	F
Stuckler	Jacob	26JUN00	3.28	1	Sullivan	Mary	08JUN09	1.30	F1
STULTS					Sullivan	Mary	-----11	1.74	F1
Stuts	George	20JUN96	2.17	2	Sulivan	William	-----08	2.27	1
Stults	George	10AUG97	1.25	1	SUMMERS				
Stills	John	24JUN00	2.26	1	Summers	Jesse	08MAY06	2.32	1
Stilts	John	03JUN01	2.25	1	Summers	Jesse	15JUL07	2.32	1
Stilts	John	05AUG02	2.28	1	Summers	Jesse	15JUL07	2.32	1

surname	name	date	bk.pg	TM	surname	name	date	bk.pg	TM
Summers	John	30JUN87	3.09	1	Sutton	Benjamin	28MAY91	3.14	1
Summers	John	30JUN87	3.10	1	Sutton	Benjamin	26NOV92	3.17	1
Summers	John	25JUL89	2.12	1	Sutton	Benjamin	21MAY94	3.18	1
Summers	John	02JUN91	3.15	1	Sutton	Bengamin	-----95	1.12	1
Summers	John	27NOV92	3.17	1	Sutton	Benjamin	-----96	4.14	1
Summers	John	21MAY94	3.18	1	Sutton	Christopher	14JUN87	2.07	11
Summers	Thomas	30JUN87	3.10	1	Sutton	Christopher	28NOV88	1.10	1
Summers	Thomas	02JUL89	2.13	1	Sutton	Christopher	05AUG89	5.11	11
Summers	Thomas	26AUG91	3.15	1	Sutton	Christopher	06APR91	1.08	11
Summers	Thomas	27NOV92	3.18	M1	Sutton	Edmond	08JUN05	2.28	1
Summers	William	31OCT88	1.09	1	Sutton	Edmond	06JUN06	2.33	1
SUMPTER					Sutton	Edmand	30JUL07	2.32	1
Sumpter	William	27APR08	1.32	1	Sutton	Edman	-----08	1.35	1
Sumpter	William	31MAY09	2.29	1	Sutton	Edmund	23AUG09	2.33	1
SUNN					Sutten	James	18MAY90	2.07	1
Sunn	Abraham	25JUL89	2.12	1	Sutton	James	28OCT92	2.08	1
SURVAY					Sutton	James	20AUG93	1.08	1
Survay	Christopher	09AUG05	3.33	1	Sutton	James	21MAY94	3.18	0
Surver	Christopher	15JUL07	2.32	1	Sutton	James	14MAY94	1.08	1
Survay	Christopher	30MAY08	2.24	1	Sutton	James	09JUN96	1.11	1
SUTHERLAND					Sutton	James	20APR97	3.27	1
Sutherland	Enos	30JUN07	1.26	1	Sutton	James	27MAY99	1.34	1
Sutherland	Enos	31MAY08	1.33	11	Sutton	James	21JUN00	2.26	1
Sutherland	Enos	30MAY09	2.29	1	Sutton	James	28JUL01	2.25	1
Sutherland	Enos	-----11	1.71	11	Sutton	James	12JUL02	3.24	1
Sutherland	Fendal	30MAY01	3.34	1	Sutton	James	21JUN03	2.28	1
Sutherland	Fendal	10AUG02	2.28	1	Sutton	James	07AUG04	1.20	1
Sutherland	Fendal	25JUN03	3.23	1	Sutton	James	08JUN05	2.28	1
Sutherland	Fendon	16AUG04	3.19	1	Sutton	James	06JUN06	2.33	1
Sutherland	Fendal	22AUG05	3.33	1	Sutton	James	12JUN07	1.25	11
Sutherland	Fendal	01AUG06	3.31	1	Sutton	James	30JUL07	2.32	1
Sutherland	George	22AUG05	3.33	M1	Sutton	James	-----08	1.35	1
Sutherland	George	07AUG06	3.32	1	Sutton	James	22AUG09	2.33	1
Sutherland	Mary	16AUG04	3.19	F1	Sutton	James	-----11	1.74	1
Sutherland	Owen	08JUL03	3.23	1	Sutton	James R.	31MAY08	1.34	1
Sutherland	Owen	16AUG04	3.19	1	Sutton	James R.	-----11	1.76	1
Sutherland	Owen	22AUG05	3.33	1	Sutton	Jeremiah	16MAY99	1.32	1
Sutherland	Owen	19AUG06	3.32	1	Sutton	Jeremiah	17JUN00	2.26	1
Sutherland	Rebecca	07AUG04	3.18	F	Sutton	Jeremiah	04JUN01	2.25	1
Sutherland	Rebecka	06AUG05	3.32	F1	Sutton	John	26JUN87	3.09	1
Sutherland	Rebecka	20AUG06	3.32	F1	Sutton	John	27JUN89	2.12	1
Sutherland	Uriah	12MAY89	6.06	1	Sutton	John	20APR91	3.14	1
Southerland	Uriah	14MAY90	1.09	1	Sutton	John	02DEC92	3.18	1
Sutherland	Uriah	30APR91	2.09	1	Sutton	John	21MAY94	3.18	1
Sutherland	Uriah	14SEP92	1.12	1	Sutton	John	-----95	1.13	1
Sutherland	Uriah	07AUG93	3.11	1	Sutton	John	-----96	4.15	11
Sutherland	Uriah	24MAY94	2.14	1	Sutton	John	-----11	1.70	1
Sutherland	Uriah	14APR95	3.16	1	Sutton	Jonas	31MAY08	1.32	1
Sutherland	Uriah	05JUL96	2.17	1	Sutton	Jonas	12MAY09	2.29	1
Sutherland	Uriah	13JUL97	1.24	1	Sutton	Jonas	-----11	1.75	1
Southerland	Uriah	28JUN99	1.35	1	Sutton	Joseph	12JUN07	1.25	1
Sutherland	Uriah	24JUL00	2.27	1	Sutton	Joshua	06JUN09	2.30	1
Sutherland	Uriah	27MAY01	3.33	1	Sutton	Joshua	-----11	1.76	1
Sutherland	Uriah	12AUG02	2.28	1	Sutton	Rolin	14JUN87	2.07	1
Southerland	Uriah	07JUL03	3.23	1	Sutton	Rolland	28MAY91	3.15	1
Southerland	William	07DEC92	3.19	1	Sutton	Rowland	02DEC92	3.18	1
Sutherland	William Sr	30MAY01	3.34	11	Sutton	Rowland	14APR94	3.19	1
Sutherland	William Jr	30MAY01	3.34	1	Sutton	Roland	-----95	1.13	1
Sutherland	William	10AUG02	2.28	21	Sutton	Rooling	-----96	4.15	1
Sutherland	William Jr	10AUG02	2.28	1	Sutton	Sarah	14MAY94	1.08	F
Southerland	William Sr	25JUN03	3.23	11	Sutton	Sarah	20JUN95	2.11	F
Southerland	William	25JUN03	3.23	1	Sutton	Sarah	09JUN96	1.11	F
Sutherland	William	30MAY08	2.24	1	Sutton	Sarah	20APR97	3.27	F
Sutherland	William	-----11	1.69	1	Sutton	Sarah	27MAY99	1.34	F
SUTTELS					Sutton	Sarah	18JUL00	2.26	F
Suttle	Jesse	30MAY05	2.28	1	Sutton	Sarah	12JUL02	3.24	F
Sutter	Jesse	15AUG06	2.34	1	Sutton	William	01DEC88	1.10	1
Suttels	Jesse	20JUN07	2.32	1	Sutten	William	06AUG89	5.11	11
Suttles	Jesse	08JUN09	1.30	1	Sutton	William	18MAY90	2.06	1
SUTTON					Sutton	William	29OCT92	2.08	1
Sutton	Benjamin	26JUN87	3.09	1	Sutton	William	21JUN03	2.28	1
Sutton	Benjamin	27JUN89	2.12	1	SWAN				

surname	name	date	bk.pg	TM
Swan	James	30OCT88	1.09	1
Swan	James	24JUN89	5.11	1
Swan	Samuel	27MAY96	2.17	M1
SWEENEY				
Swinna	Charles	11JUN89	6.07	
Listed with Joseph Swinna				
Swinny	Charles	02AUG90	1.09	1
Sweeney	Charles	29JUN99	1.35	1
Swiney	Charles	26JUN00	2.26	1
Sweney	Charles	27MAY01	3.33	1
Sweney	Charles	04AUG02	2.28	1
Sweeney	Charles	20MAY03	3.22	1
Sweney	Charles	06AUG04	3.18	1
Sweney	Charles	06AUG05	3.32	1
Sweney	Charles	04AUG06	3.31	1
Sweeney	Daniel	21JUN00	3.27	1
Sweney	Daniel	24JUL01	3.34	1
Sweney	Daniel	27MAY02	2.27	1
Sweeney	Danniel	02JUN03	3.22	1
Swinny	Edmond	24MAY90	1.09	1
Sweeney	Edmond	17APR95	3.15	1
Sweeney	Edward	10MAY97	1.23	1
Sweeney	Edward	02JUL99	1.36	1
Swiney	Edward	23JUL00	2.27	1
Sweney	Edward	24JUL01	3.34	1
Sweney	Edward	27MAY02	2.27	1
Sweeney	Edmond	02JUN03	3.22	1
Sweeney	Edward	03MAY04	3.18	1
Swenney	Edward	17AUG05	3.33	1
Sweeney	Edward	17JUL06	3.30	1
Sweney	Edward	18AUG07	2.34	1
Sweeney	Edward	-----08	2.27	1
Sweney	Edmund	13JUL09	1.32	1
Sweeney	Job	26JUN99	1.35	1
Swiney	Job	23JUL00	2.27	1
Sweney	Job	28MAY01	3.33	1
Sweney	Job	11AUG02	2.28	1
Sweeney	Job	25JUN03	3.23	1
Sweeney	Job	06AUG04	3.18	1
Sweney	Job	06AUG05	3.32	1
Swenny	Job	20AUG06	3.32	1
Swiney	John	28MAR06	2.31	1
Sweney	John	22JUL07	2.32	1
Sweney	John	01AUG08	2.26	1
Swinna	Joseph	11JUN89	6.07	1
Charles Swinna listed with him				
Swinny	Joseph	14MAY90	1.09	1
Swinna	Joseph	24JUN91	2.09	1
Swenna	Joseph	04DEC92	1.11	1
Swiney	Moses	02AUG87	1.05	12
Swinna	Moses	11JUN89	6.07	1
Swinny	Moses	02AUG90	1.10	11
Swinna	Moses	20APR91	2.09	1
Swinna	Moses	22SEP92	1.12	1
Swinna	Moses	10AUG93	3.10	11
Swinney	Moses	22MAY94	2.13	11
Sweeny	Moses	07MAY95	3.15	12
Swiney	Moses	13JUL96	2.17	11
Sweeney	Moses	06JUN97	1.23	11
Sweeney	Moses	15JUL99	3.19	11
Sweeney	Moses	20JUN00	3.27	1
Sweeney	Moses	02MAY01	3.31	1
Swiney	Moses	31JUL02	3.25	11
Swiney	Moses	06AUG03	2.29	11
Sweeney	Moses	09JUN04	4.21	11
Swiney	Moses	18JUN05	2.29	11
Swiney	Moses	02AUG06	2.34	11
Swiney	Moses	05AUG06	2.34	1
Sweney	Moses	20JUN07	2.32	2
Sweney	Moses	18JUL07	2.32	1
Sweney	Moses	-----08	2.25	1
Sweeney	Moses	30MAY08	2.24	1
Sweney	Moses	19JUN09	1.31	2
Silvenny	Moses	-----11	1.69	2
Swenney	Shephard	12JUN94	2.13	1
Sweeney	Sheppard	20JUN97	1.23	1
Swiney	Shepard	22JUL00	2.27	1
Sweney	Stephen	24JUL01	3.34	1
Sweney	Shepard	27MAY02	2.27	1
Sweeney	Shepherd	21JUN03	3.23	1
Sweeney	Shepherd	08AUG04	3.19	1
Swenny	Sheppard	20AUG06	3.32	1
SWIGGETT				
Swigget	James	28MAY01	3.33	1
Swigget	James	12AUG02	2.28	1
Swigget	James	25JUN03	3.23	1
Swigget	James	06AUG04	3.18	1
Swiggett	James	08AUG05	3.33	1
Swigget	James	20AUG06	3.32	1
SWISHER				
Swisher	Henry	23JUL00	2.27	1
Swisher	Henry	18JUN01	3.32	1
Swisher	Henry	28JUL02	3.24	1
Swisher	Henry	11AUG03	2.30	1
Swisher	Henry	05JUN04	4.20	1
Swisher	Henry	28JUN05	2.30	1
Swisher	Henry	29JUL06	2.33	1
SWOPE				
Swope	Benedict Sr	27AUG89	2.13	1
Swope	Benedict Jr	27AUG89	2.13	1
Swope	Benedick Sr	19APR91	3.14	1
Swope	Benedick	19APR91	3.14	1
Swope	Benedick Sr	04DEC92	3.18	1
Swope	Benedick	04DEC92	3.18	1
Swope	Benedict Sr	12MAY94	3.24	1
Swope	Benedict Jr	12MAY94	3.24	1
Swope	Benedick Sr	-----95	1.13	1
Swope	Benedick Jr	-----95	1.13	1
Swope	Benedick	-----96	4.14	1
Swope	David	19APR91	3.14	1
Swope	David	04DEC92	3.18	1
Swope	David	05MAY94	3.24	1
Swope	David	-----95	1.13	1
Swope	David	-----96	4.14	1
Swope	David	-----97	2.05	1
Swope	David	10MAY99	2.18	1
Swope	David	06JUN00	1.13	1
Swope	David	30MAY01	1.15	1
Swope	David	18JUN02	1.21	1
Swope	David	10JUN03	1.21	1
Swope	David	14JUN04	1.17	1
Swope	David	04JUN05	1.19	1
Swope	David	13JUN06	1.22	1
Swop	David	18MAY07	1.24	1
Swope	David	-----11	1.76	1
Swope	George	14JUN87	2.07	1
Swope	George	17NOV88	1.09	1
Swope	George	23JUN89	5.10	1
Swope	George	03APR90	2.06	1
Swope	George	24OCT92	2.08	1
Swope	George	09AUG93	1.08	1
Swope	George	20MAY94	1.08	1
Swope	George	19MAY95	2.12	1
Swope	George	15JUN96	1.11	11
Swope	George	22APR97	3.29	11
Swope	Jacob	08OCT92	2.07	1
Swope	Jacob	10JUN96	1.11	1
Swope	Jacob	07APR97	3.27	1
Swope	Jacob	30MAY99	1.32	1
Pd for Grenaugh Majors (3 tracts)				
Swope	Jacob	29MAY00	2.25	1
Swope	Jacob	29MAY01	2.24	1
Swope	Jacob	30JUN02	1.22	1
Swope	Jacob	18JUL03	1.23	1

surname	name	date	bk.pg	TM	surname	name	date	bk.pg	TM
Swope	Jacob	25JUN04	1.18	1	Taps	John	30JUN09	2.34	1
Swope	Jacob	04JUN05	1.18	1	TARDIVAN				
Swope	Jacob	17JUL06	1.23	1	Tardavan	Peter	17APR94	2.15	1
Swop	Jacob	30JUN07	1.26	1	Tardevou	Peter	09JUL96	2.19	1
Swop	Jacob	30JUN07	1.26	1	Tardivean	Peter	27JUN97	1.25	1
Swop	Jacob	31MAY08	1.33	1	Tardivean	Peter	29JUN99	3.20	1
Swop	Jacob	15AUG09	2.32	1	Tardevau	Peter	26JUN00	3.30	1
Swope	Jacob	-----11	1.72	1	Tardiveau	Peter	27JUL04	4.23	1
SWORD					Tardeveau	Peter	24AUG08	2.28	1
Sword	Henry	14AUG93	1.08	1	TARRANT				
Sword	Henry	30JUN96	1.12	1	Tarrant	Reubon	05JUN04	4.23	12
Sword	Henry	16JUN00	1.14	1	TATE				
Sworde	Henry	02JUN01	1.16	1	Tate	Charles	30JUL00	2.28	1
Sword	Henry	22APR08	1.32	1	Tate	Stephen	05APR91	1.08	1
SWORTS					Tate	Stephen	17MAY94	1.08	1
Sworts	John	05DEC92	3.18	1	Tate	Stephen	28JUN95	2.12	1
Swarts	John	10MAY99	2.18	1	Tate	Stephen	31MAY03	3.24	1
Swartson	John	29MAY00	2.25	1	Tate	Stephen	31JUL04	3.20	1
Swarts	John	15JUN04	1.18	1	Tate	Stephen	16MAY05	2.32	1
Swarts	John	16JUN06	1.22	1	Tate	Stephen	05AUG06	2.36	1
TADLOCK					Tate	Stephen	05AUG06	2.36	1
Tadlock	Elisha	-----11	1.81	1	Tate	Stephen	09MAY07	1.26	1
TALBOTT					Tate	Stephen	10JUN08	1.37	1
Talbot	Richard	30MAY96	2.18	1	Tate	Stephen	17JUN09	2.33	1
Talbot	Richard	30MAY97	1.25	1	Tate	William	23MAY94	2.15	21
Talbot	Richard	16JUL99	3.21	1	Tate	William	16APR95	3.17	2
Tolbott	Richard C.	20JUN00	3.30	1	Tate	William	06JUL96	2.18	2
Talbot	Richard	02MAY01	3.34	1	Tate	William	22JUN97	1.26	2
Tolbert	Richard C.	07AUG02	3.27	1	Tate	William	14JUN99	1.36	2
Tolbert	Richard C.	04AUG03	2.32	1	Tate	William	30JUL00	2.28	1
Talbot	Richard	13JUN04	4.23	1	Tate	William	21JUL01	3.35	1
Tolbert	Richard	17JUN05	2.32	11	Tate	William	27MAY02	2.29	1
Talbert	Richard	18AUG06	2.36	11	Tate	William	10JUN03	3.24	1
Tolbart	Richard	15JUN07	2.35	11	Tate	William	03AUG04	3.20	1
Tolbott	Richard	04AUG08	2.28	11	Tate	William	17JUN05	3.34	1
Tolbert	Richard	13JUL09	1.34	1	Tate	William	22JUL06	3.33	1
Talbott	Richard	-----11	1.81	11	Tate	William	30JUL07	2.35	1
TANNER					Tate	William	02JUN08	2.27	1
Tanner	Jacob	30JUN00	3.30	1	Tate	William	11JUL09	1.33	1
Tanner	Martin	26AUG93	1.09	1	Tate	William	-----11	1.81	1
Tanner	Martin	10JUN95	2.12	1	TATEM				
Tanner	Martin	15JUN96	1.12	1	Tatem	Isham B.	12MAY94	1.09	1
Tanner	Martin	09MAY97	3.30	1	Tatern	Isham	10JUN95	2.12	1
Tanner	Martin	01JUN99	1.36	1	Tally	Isom	02JUN98	2.18	1
Tanner	Martin	02JUN01	2.26	1	TAYLOR				
Tanner	Martin	02JUN01	2.26	1	Taylor	George	27JUN05	2.32	1
Tanner	Martin	17JUN02	1.23	1	Taylor	Jackson	19MAY01	3.35	1
Tanner	Martain	11JUN03	1.23	1	Taylor	Jackson	11AUG02	3.27	1
Tanner	Martin	10JUN08	1.36	1	Taylor	Jackson	28JUL03	2.31	1
Tanner	Martin	12MAY09	2.33	1	Taylor	James G.	30JUN87	1.06	1
Tanner	Martin	-----11	1.79	1	Taylor	James	-----96	4.18	1
Tanner	William	13OCT92	2.08	1	Taylor	Jiles	19JUL05	2.32	1
Tanner	William	10AUG93	1.09	1	Taylor	John	15APR90	1.10	1
Tanner	William	21MAY94	1.08	1	Taylor	John M.	19AUG91	2.10	1
Tanner	William	11JUN95	2.12	1	Taylor	John	31JUL00	2.28	M1
Tanner	William	16AUG96	1.12	1	Taylor	John	07JUL01	3.35	1
Tanner	William	19AUG97	3.35	1	Taylor	John	26JUN02	1.23	1
Tanner	William	15JUL99	1.36	1	Taylor	John	01JUL02	3.26	1
Tanner	William	24JUN00	2.28	1	Taylor	John	20JUN03	2.31	1
Tanner	William	02JUN01	2.26	1	Taylor	John	28JUN03	1.23	1
Tanner	William	20JUL03	3.24	1	Taylor	John	26JUL04	4.23	1
Tanner	William	14JUN04	2.18	1	Taylor	John	03AUG04	1.20	1
Tanner	William	14JUN04	2.18	1	Taylor	John	-----05	2.36	1
Tanner	William	29MAY05	3.34	1	Taylor	John	18JUN05	2.32	1
Tanner	William	07AUG06	3.33	1	Taylor	John	20JUL05	2.32	1
Tanner	William	10JUN08	1.36	1	Taylor	John	31JUL05	1.22	1
Tanner	William	30MAY09	2.33	1	Taylor	John	31JUL05	1.22	1
Tanner	William	-----11	1.80	1	Taylor	John	28MAR06	2.35	1
TANZEY					Taylor	John	16JUN06	1.25	1
Tanzey	Joshua	07JUN97	1.25	1	Taylor	John	29JUL06	2.36	1
Tanzey	Nathan	07JUN97	1.25	1	Taylor	John	01AUG06	1.26	1
TAPS					Taylor	John	09MAY07	1.26	1

surname	name	date	bk.pg	TM	surname	name	date	bk.pg	TM
Taylor	John	09JUN07	2.34	1	Templin	John	24JUL00	2.28	1
Taylor	John	30JUL07	2.35	1	Templin	John	18JUL01	2.26	1
Taylor	John Sr	02AUG08	2.28	1	Templin	John	18JUL01	2.26	1
Taylor	John	18APR08	1.36	1	Templin	John	12AUG02	3.27	1
Taylor	John	29JUN08	2.27	1	Templin	John	01AUG03	2.32	1
Taylor	John(heirs)	10JUN08	1.36	0	Templen	John	23JUN04	1.20	1
Tax paid by Walter Taylor					Templin	John	03AUG05	2.33	1
Taylor	John	21JUN09	1.33	1	Templen	John	22JUL07	2.35	1
Taylor	John	30JUN09	2.34	1	Templeman	John	07JUN09	1.33	1
Taylor	John	02JUL09	1.33	1	Templeman	John	-----11	1.79	1
Taylor	John	-----11	1.80	1	Templin	Martha	23AUG09	2.34	F
Taylor	John	-----11	1.81	11	Templen	Martha	-----11	1.80	F
Taylor	Jonathan	15JUL87	3.10	1	Templin	Mathew	10JUN08	1.37	0
Taylor	Jonathan	03APR89	2.13	1	TERRELL				
Taylor	Jonathan	13SEP91	3.16	1	Terill	Joseph	14JUN87	2.07	1
Taylor	Jonathan	05DEC92	3.19	1	Terrel	Joseph	31OCT88	1.10	1
Taylor	Jonathan	23APR94	3.21	1	Terrel	Robert	24AUG08	2.28	1
Taylor	Jonathan	-----95	1.13	1	TETER				
Taylor	Jonathan	-----96	4.15	1	Teter	Samuel	15JUL87	3.10	1
Taylor	Jonathan	-----97	2.05	1	THACKER				
Taylor	Jonathan	16MAY99	2.20	1	Thacker	John	-----11	1.79	2
Taylor	Jonathan	13JUN00	1.15	1	THARP				
Taylor	Jonathan	08JUN01	1.17	1	Tharp	Terry	10AUG02	3.27	1
Taylor	Leonard	11JUN04	4.23	00	Tharp	Terry	28JUL03	2.31	1
Taylor	Leonard	20JUN05	2.32	1	THOMAS				
Taylor	Leonard	30JUL06	2.36	11	Thomas	David	21MAY90	1.10	1
Taylor	Moreman	23APR94	3.21	1	Thomas	Edward	08NOV92	3.19	1
Taylor	Moreman	-----95	1.13	1	Thomas	Hamlett	22JUL07	2.35	1
Taylor	Moorman	-----96	4.15	1	Thomas	Hamilton	10JUN08	1.36	1
Taylor	Robert	27JUN05	2.32	M1	Thomas	Hardin	22JUN95	3.16	1
Taylor	Stephen	-----95	1.13	1	Thomas	Hardin	12JUL96	2.19	1
Taylor	Stephen	17MAY97	3.30	1	Thomas	Hardin	31MAY97	1.25	1
Taylor	Walter	01JUL96	1.12	1	Thomas	Hardin	28JUN99	1.18	1
Taylor	Walter	14JUN97	3.30	11	Thomas	Hardin	26MAY01	3.35	1
Taylor	Walter	13AUG99	1.40	1	Thomas	Hardin	27MAY02	2.29	11
Taylor	Walter	31JUL00	2.28	1	Thomas	Hardin	21JUN03	3.24	12
Taylor	Walter	22JUL01	2.26	2	Thomas	Hardin	06AUG04	3.20	11
Taylor	Walter	22JUL01	2.26	2	Thomas	Harden	17JUN05	3.34	11
One lott in Lancaster					Thomas	Harden	04AUG06	3.33	11
Taylor	Walter	15JUN02	1.22	1	Thomas	James	01JUN95	2.12	1
Taylor	Walter	28JUN03	1.23	1	Thomas	James	04JUL00	3.31	1
Taylor	Walter	15JUN04	1.20	1	Thomas	James	09MAY01	3.34	11
Taylor	Walter	20JUN05	1.21	1	Thomas	James	11AUG02	3.27	11
Taylor	Walter	16JUN06	1.25	1	Thomas	James	28JUL03	2.31	11
Taylor	Walter	06AUG07	1.27	1	Thomas	John	14AUG93	1.09	1
Taylor	Walter	10JUN08	1.36	1	Thomas	John	24MAY94	2.14	1
Paid tax for John Taylor heirs					Thomas	John Sr	07APR95	3.16	1
Taylor	Walter	24AUG09	2.34	1	Thomas	John Jr	07APR95	3.16	1
Taylor	Walter	-----11	1.79	1	Thomas	John Sr	11JUL96	2.18	1
Taylor	William	31OCT88	1.10	1	Thomas	John Jr	11JUL96	2.18	1
Taylor	William	14MAY89	6.07	1	Thomas	John	17MAY97	3.30	12
Taylor	William	02APR90	1.10	1	Thomas	John	08JUN97	1.25	1
Taylor	William	30MAY94	1.09	1	Thomas	John	25JUN99	3.20	1
Taylor	William	24MAY99	2.20	1	Thomas	John	19JUN00	3.30	1
Taylor	William	19JUN00	2.28	1	Thomas	John	18MAY01	3.34	1
Taylor	William	10AUG01	2.26	1	Thomas	John	30AUG02	3.27	1
Taylor	William	27MAY02	2.29	1	Thomas	John	16AUG03	2.32	1
Taylor	William	17JUN03	3.24	1	Thomas	John	09JUN04	4.23	1
Taylor	William	09JUN06	3.33	1	Thomas	John	31MAY05	2.32	1
Taylor	William	30JUL07	2.35	1	Thomas	John	02AUG06	2.36	1
Taylor	William	24AUG08	2.28	1	Thomas	John	20MAY07	1.26	1
TEBO					Thomas	John	29JUN08	2.27	1
Teboe	George	10APR90	1.10	1	Thomas	John	13JUL09	1.34	1
Tebo	George	10OCT92	1.12	1	Thomas	John	-----11	1.81	1
Teboe	George	17AUG93	3.12	1	Thomas	John W.	20JUL05	2.32	M1
Tebo	George	17APR94	2.15	1	Thomas	John W.	08MAY06	2.35	M1
Tebo	George	18MAR95	3.17	1	Thomas	Obidiah	04AUG06	3.33	1
TEDLERSON					Thomas	Obediah	30JUL07	2.35	1
Tedlerson	Lewis	31OCT88	1.10	1	Thomas	Ruben	21JUN03	3.24	1
TEMPLIN					Thomas	Reubin	07AUG04	3.20	1
Templin	John	18APR97	3.29	1	Thomas	Reuben	17JUN05	3.34	1
Templin	John	24MAY99	1.36	1	Thomas	Reuben	23JUL06	3.33	1

surname	name	date	bk.pg	TM	surname	name	date	bk.pg	TM
Thomas	Robert	22MAY94	2.15	11	Thompson	John	26JUN00	3.30	1
Thomas	Robert	07APR95	3.16	11	Thompson	John	19MAY01	3.35	1
Thomas	Robert	12JUL96	2.19	1	Thompson	John	11AUG02	3.27	1
Thomas	William	17JUN05	3.34	1	Thompson	John	25JUL03	2.31	1
Thomas	William	08AUG06	3.33	1	Tompson	John	25JUL04	4.23	1
Thomas	William	30JUN09	2.34	1	Tompson	John	26JUL04	4.23	1
THOMPSON					Thompson	John	23JUL05	2.32	1
Thompson	Alex.	26JUN87	1.06	1	Tomplin	John	18MAY06	2.35	1
Thompson	Alexander	09JUN89	6.07	1	Thompson	John	16JUL06	2.36	1
Thompson	Alexander	11MAY90	1.10	1	Thompson	John	09JUN07	2.34	1
Thompson	Alexander	18MAY91	2.10	1	Thompson	John	30JUL07	2.35	1
Thompson	Alexander	10OCT92	1.12	1	Thompson	John	25JUN08	2.27	1
Thompson	Alexander	20AUG93	3.11	1	Thompson	John	19MAY09	1.32	1
Thomson	Alexander	01MAY94	2.15	1	Thompson	John	08JUN09	1.33	1
Thomson	Alexander	02APR95	3.17	1	Thompson	John	-----11	1.79	1
Thomson	Alexander	16JUL96	2.19	1	Thompson	Joseph	22MAY99	1.36	1
Thomson	Alexander	17MAY97	1.25	1	Thompson	Joseph	17JUN00	2.28	1
Thompson	Alexander	02JUL99	3.21	1	Thompson	Joseph	24JUL01	2.26	1
Thompson	Alexander	01JUL00	3.30	1	Tompson	Joseph	10JUN02	1.22	1
Thompson	Alexander	09JUL01	3.35	1	Thompson	Joseph	29JUN03	1.24	1
Thompson	Alexander	17JUN02	3.26	1	Thompson	Joseph	24JUL04	2.19	1
Thompson	Alexander	25JUL03	2.31	1	Tompson	Joseph	12JUN05	1.21	1
Thompson	Alexander	26JUL04	4.23	1	Thompson	Joseph	18JUN06	1.25	1
Thompson	Alexander	10JUN05	2.32	1	Thomson	Lewis	23JUN96	2.18	F1
Thompson	Alexander	12MAY06	2.35	1	Thomson	Lucy	10AUG97	1.26	F1
Thompson	Alexander	30JUL07	2.35	1	Tompson	Mariday	31JUL05	1.22	1
Thompson	Alexander	04AUG08	2.28	1	Thompson	Meriday	01SEP06	1.25	1
Thompson	Alexander	09JUN09	1.33	1	Tompson	Mirida	09MAY07	1.26	1
Thomson	Balim	23JUN96	2.18	1	Tompson	Merideth	18APR08	1.36	1
Thomson	David	13SEP91	3.16	1	Thompson	Meredith	01JUL09	2.34	1
Thompson	David	-----96	4.18	1	Thompson	Nelson A.	15JUN07	2.35	1
Thompson	David	18JUN04	2.19	1	Thompson	Nelson A.	22AUG08	2.28	1
Tompson	David	25JUN05	1.22	1	Thompson	Nelson A.	29JUN09	1.33	1
Thompson	Frances	19AUG07	2.36	1	Thompson	Nelson	-----11	1.80	1
Thomson	George	01MAY94	2.15	M1	Thomson	Samuel	23JUN96	2.18	1
Thompson	George	02JUL99	3.21	1	Thomson	Samuel	10AUG97	1.26	1
Thompson	George	01JUL00	3.30	1	Thompson	Samuel	-----11	1.80	1
Thompson	George	09JUL01	3.35	1	Thompson	Sarah	22AUG08	2.28	F
Thompson	George	11AUG02	3.27	1	Thompson	Sarah	30JUN09	1.33	F
Thompson	George	25JUL03	2.31	1	Thompson	Sarah	-----11	1.80	F
Thompson	George	26JUL04	4.23	1	Thompson	William	09JUN89	6.07	1
Thompson	George	23JUL05	2.33	1	Thompson	William	11MAY90	1.10	1
Thompson	George	16JUL06	2.36	1	Thompson	William	11MAY90	1.10	m
Thompson	George	30JUL07	2.35	1	Thompson	William Jr	11MAY90	1.10	
Thompson	George	04AUG08	2.28	1		Listed with William Thompson			
Thompson	George	09JUN09	1.33	1	Thompson	William	18MAY91	2.10	1
Thompson	James	15JUL87	3.10	1	Thompson	William	18MAY91	2.10	11
Thompson	James	25JUL89	2.14	1	Thompson	William	10OCT92	1.12	11
Thompson	James	26AUG91	3.16	1	Thompson	William	10OCT92	1.12	1
Thompson	James	20SEP92	3.19	1	Thompson	William Sr	21AUG93	3.12	11
Thompson	James	04DEC92	3.19	1	Thompson	William	21AUG93	3.12	1
Thompson	James	-----93	2.05	1	Thomson	William	01MAY94	2.15	1
Thompson	James	09AUG93	1.09	1	Thomson	William	01MAY94	2.15	1
Thompson	James	14MAY94	3.20	1	Thomson	William Jr	02APR95	3.17	1
Thompson	James	23MAY94	1.08	1	Thomson	William	16JUN96	2.18	1
Thompson	James	-----95	1.13	1	Thomson	William	07JUN97	1.25	1
Thompson	James	02JUN95	2.12	1	Thompson	William	07MAY01	3.34	1
Thompson	James	-----96	4.16	1	Thompson	William	06AUG02	3.27	1
Thompson	James	16JUN96	1.12	1	Thompson	William	05AUG03	2.32	11
Thompson	James	04AUG06	2.36	1	Thompson	William	13JUN04	4.23	11
Thompson	James	18APR08	1.36	1	Thomeson	William	14JUN04	1.20	1
Thompson	James H.	30JUL07	2.35	1	Thompson	William	21JUN05	2.32	11
Thompson	James H.	24AUG08	2.28	1	Thompson	William	13AUG06	2.36	1
Thompson	James H.	13JUL09	1.34	1	Thompson	William	13AUG06	2.36	11
	One lott in town of Standford				Thompson	William	22JUL07	2.35	1
Thompson	James H.	-----11	1.80	1	Thompson	William	19MAY09	1.32	1
Thompson	John	26JUN87	1.06	1	Thompson	William	01JUL09	2.34	1
Thompson	John	11JUN95	2.12	1	THORNTON				
Thompson	John	-----97	2.05	1	Thornton	George	25JUN08	2.27	1
Thomson	John	15MAY97	1.25	1	Thornton	Peter	24AUG07	2.36	1
Thomson	John	30MAY97	1.25	1	Thornton	Peter	25JUN08	2.27	1
Thompson	John	31MAY97	3.30	12	Thornton	Peter	30JUN09	1.33	1

surname	name	date	bk.pg	TM	surname	name	date	bk.pg	TM
THURMAN					Thurmon	Philip	09AUG04	4.24	1
Thermon	Benjamin	28JUN03	1.24	1	Thurman	Philip	31MAY05	2.32	1
Thurman	Bennett	01AUG08	2.27	1	Thurman	Philip	09AUG06	2.36	1
Thurman	Burnett	-----11	1.79	11	Thurman	Phillip	15AUG07	2.36	1
Thurman	Charles	24AUG08	2.28	1	Thurman	Philip	02AUG08	2.28	1
Thurman	Charles	07JUN09	1.33	1	Thurman	Philip	07JUN09	1.33	1
Thorton	Charles	-----11	1.79	1	Thurman	Phillip	-----11	1.79	1
Thurman	David	14JUN87	2.07	1	Thurmon	Richard	-----95	1.13	1
Thurman	David	06NOV88	1.10	1	Thurman	Richard	10JUN08	1.37	1
Turney	David	10JUL89	2.14	1	Thurmond	Fanny	21APR96	2.18	F
Thurman	David	27MAR90	2.07	1	Thurman	William	16APR90	1.10	1
Thirmon	David	28OCT92	2.08	1	Thurmond	William	17MAY91	2.10	1
Therman	David	09AUG93	1.09	1	Thurmond	William	12OCT92	1.12	1
Therman	David	26MAY95	2.12	1	Thurmond	William	17AUG93	3.11	1
Tharman	David	15JUN96	1.12	1	Thurmond	William	21APR94	2.14	1
Thyrman	David	11APR97	3.29	1	Thurmond	William	20MAR95	3.17	1
Thyrman	David	17MAY99	1.36	1	Thurmond	William	09MAY96	2.18	1
Thurman	David	29JUL00	2.28	1	Thrumond	William	12MAY97	1.25	1
Thermon	David	20JUN05	1.22	1	Thurmond	William	28JUN99	3.20	1
Thurman	David	20JUN07	1.26	1	Thurman	William	25JUN00	3.30	1
Thurman	David	18APR08	1.36	1	Thurman	William	18MAY01	3.35	1
Therman	David	16AUG09	2.34	1	Thurman	William	01JUL02	3.26	1
Thurmond	Jesse	28MAR95	3.17	1	Thurman	William	01JUL03	2.31	1
Thurmond	John	02APR90	1.10	12	Thurmon	William	09AUG04	4.24	1
Thurmond	John/John	17MAY91	2.10	3	Thurman	William	31MAY05	2.32	1
Humphrey Posey listed also					Thurman	William	09AUG06	2.36	1
Thurmond	John	10OCT92	1.12	1	Thurman	William	18JUN07	1.26	1
Thurmond	John	20OCT92	1.12	1	Thurman	William	15AUG07	2.36	1
Thurmond	John Sr	08AUG93	3.12	2	Thurman	William	24AUG08	2.28	1
Thurmond	John Sr	26APR94	2.15	2	Thurman	William	07JUN09	1.33	11
Thurmond	John Sr	26MAR95	3.17	11	Thurman	William	-----11	1.79	1
Thurmond	John Jr	26MAR95	3.17	1	THURSBY				
Thurmond	John	30MAR95	3.17	1	Thursbey	Edward	18JUL06	2.04	1
Thurmond	John Sr	23MAY96	2.18	11	Thursby	Edward	17AUG07	2.05	0
Thurmond	John Jr	23MAY96	2.18	1	Tax paid by John L. Bredger				
Thurmond	John Sr	12MAY97	1.25	1	Thursby	Edward	17AUG07	2.05	
Thurmond	John Jr	12MAY97	1.25	1	Two town lotts in Danville				
Thrumond	John	12MAY97	1.25	1	Thursby	Edward	29JUN08	2.02	0
Thurmond	John	27JUN99	3.20	1	Tax pd by John L. Bridges				
Thurmond	John	28JUN99	3.20	1	THURSTON				
Thurman	John Sr	25JUN00	3.30	1	Thurston	Bartlett	-----11	1.79	1
Thurman	John Jr	25JUN00	3.30	1	TIBBS				
Thurman	John	21MAY01	3.35	1	Tibbs	Duskin	23JUN96	2.18	1
Thurman	John	01JUL02	3.26	1	Tibbs	Fanny	04AUG08	2.28	F
Thurman	John Jr	08AUG02	3.27	1	Tibbs	Fanny	19JUN09	1.33	F
Thermon	John	28JUN03	1.23	1	Tibbs	Fanny	-----11	1.79	F
Thurman	John	01JUL03	2.31	1	Tebbs	Foushee	04AUG87	1.06	1
Thurman	John	27JUL03	2.31	1	Tibbs	Foushee	09JUN89	6.07	1
Thurmon	John	28JUN04	4.23	1	Tebbs	Foushee	10APR90	1.10	1
Thurmon	John	28JUN04	4.23	11	Tebbs	Foushee	13MAY91	2.10	1
Thurman	John	29MAY05	2.32	1	Tebbs	Foushee	20OCT92	1.12	1
Thurmon	John	30MAY05	2.32	11	Tebbs	Foushee	17AUG93	3.12	1
Thermon	John	15JUN05	1.21	11	Tibbs	Foushee	17APR94	2.15	1
Thermon	John	18JUN06	1.25	11	Tibbs	Foushee	19MAR95	3.17	1
Thurman	John	09AUG06	2.36	11	Tibbs	Foushee	09JUL96	2.19	1
Therman	John	10JUN07	1.26	12	Tibbs	Foushee	10MAY97	2.18	1
Thurman	John	15AUG07	2.36	2	Tibbs	Foushee	15JUL99	3.21	1
Therman	John	10JUN08	1.36	11	Tebb	Foushee	25JUN00	3.30	1
Therman	John	24AUG09	2.34	1	Tibs	Foshee	07MAY01	3.34	1
Thurman	John	-----11	1.79	11	Tibbs	Foushee	09AUG02	3.27	1
Thurman	John C.	10JUN08	1.37	1	Tibbs	Foushee	11JUL03	2.31	1
Therman	John C.	06JUL09	2.34	1	Tibs	Feushy	24JUL04	4.23	1
Thurman	John C.	-----11	1.80	1	Tebbs	Foushee	29MAY05	2.32	1
Turney	Michael	10JUL89	2.14	1	Tibbs	Foushee	04AUG06	2.36	1
Thurman	Molly	07JUN09	1.33	F	Tubbs	Fushee	30JUL07	2.35	1
Thurmond	Nathaniel	30APR95	3.16	1	Tubbs	William	-----97	2.05	1
Thurman	Phillip	20JUN87	2.07	1	Tub	William	15MAY99	2.20	1
Thurmond	Philip	12MAY97	1.25	1	Tubb	William	12JUN00	1.14	1
Thurmond	Philip	27JUN99	3.20	1	Tubb	William	03JUN01	1.17	1
Thurman	Phillip	25JUN00	3.30	1	Tibbs	William	11JUL03	2.31	1
Thurman	Phillip	18MAY01	3.35	1	Tibs	William	28JUN04	4.23	1
Thurman	Philip	01JUL03	2.31	1	Tibbs	William	29MAY05	2.32	1

surname	name	date	bk.pg	TM	surname	name	date	bk.pg	TM
TIDWELL					Tisdale	John	-----11	1.79	1
Tidwell	Francis	26APR97	3.30	1	Tisdale	William	10JUN08	1.37	1
Tidwell	George	26APR97	3.29	1	Tisdel	William	01JUL09	2.34	1
TIERNEY					Tisdale	William	-----11	1.79	1
Tierney	Mathew	25JUN08	2.27	12	TITOUS				
TIG					Titous	Ebenezar	10JUN94	1.11	1
Tig	William	20JUN03	1.23	1	TODD				
TILFORD					Todd	Thomas	18MAY89	6.07	1
Tilford	John	26JUL06	3.33	1	Todd	Thomas	20APR90	1.10	1
Tilford	William	29MAY05	3.34	1	Todd	Thomas	18JUL91	2.10	1
Tilford	William	07AUG06	3.33	1	Todd	Thomas	18OCT92	1.12	1
Talford	William	06APR09	1.32	1	TOMPKINS				
Talford	William	-----11	1.81	1	Tomlinson	Archer	20SEP92	3.19	1
TILMAN					Tomlinson	Archibald	14MAY94	3.20	1
Tilman	Rice	28MAY95	2.12	1	Tompkins	Edward	15JUL87	3.10	11
TIMBERLAKE					Tompkins	Edward	27JUN89	2.13	1
Timberlake	William	14MAY99	1.36	1	Tomlinson	Edward	26AUG91	3.15	1
TIMRELL					Tomlinson	Edward	08NOV92	3.19	1
Timrell	Robert	-----11	1.81	1	Tomlinson	Edward	14MAY94	3.20	1
TINDLE					Tompkins	Edward	-----95	1.13	1
Tindel	John	19AUG07	2.36	1	Tomkins	Edward	-----96	4.15	1
Tindel	John	25JUN08	2.27	1	Tompkins	Edward	-----97	2.05	1
Tindle	John	30JUN09	1.33	1	Tompkins	Edward	12MAY99	2.20	1
Tindle	John	-----11	1.80	1	Tomkins	Edward	07JUN00	1.14	1
Tindle	Samuel	17JUL06	1.26	11	Tomkins	Edward	29MAY01	1.17	1
Tindel	Samuel Sr	19AUG07	2.36	1	Tompkins	Edward	26JUN02	1.23	1
Tindel	Samuel	22JUL07	2.35	1	Tomkins	Edward	10JUN03	1.23	1
Tindel	Samuel	25JUN08	2.27	1	Tomkins	Edward	26JUL04	1.20	1
Tindel	William	02JUN08	2.27	1	Tomkins	Edward	04JUN05	1.21	1
Tindle	William	06APR09	1.32	1	Tomkins	Edward	13JUN06	1.25	1
Tindle	William	-----11	1.81	1	Tompkins	Edward	20MAY07	1.26	1
TINKERSLEY					Tomkins	Edward	10JUN08	1.37	1
Tinkersley	Joseph	24AUG08	2.28	1	Tomkins	Edward	24MAY09	2.33	1
TINKLE					Tompkun	Edward	-----11	1.80	1
Tinkle	George	15JUN90	2.07	1	Tomlinson	Hamblin	08NOV92	3.19	1
TINSLEY					Tomlinson	Hamlin	14MAY94	3.20	1
Truby	Christopher	17JUN89	5.11	1	Tomkins	Hamblin	-----96	4.15	1
Tinsley	David	08AUG02	3.27	1	Tompkins	Hamlin	26JUN02	1.23	1
Tinsly	David	26JUN04	4.23	1	Tomkins	Hamlin	10JUN03	1.23	1
Tinsly	James	13OCT92	1.12	1	Tomkins	Hamlin	26JUL04	1.20	1
Tensly	James	17AUG93	3.12	1	Tomkins	Hamlin	04JUN05	1.21	1
Tinley	James	28MAY94	2.15	1	Tomkins	Hamlin	13JUN06	1.25	1
Tinsly	James	11APR95	3.16	1	Tompkins	Hamlen	20MAY07	1.26	1
Tinsley	James	25MAY96	2.18	1	Tomkins	Hamlin	10JUN08	1.37	1
Tinsley	James	15MAY97	1.25	1	Tomkins	Hamlin	24MAY09	2.33	1
Tinsley	James	28JUN99	3.20	1	Tomlinson	James	20SEP92	3.19	1
Tinsley	James	28JUN00	3.30	11	Tomlinson	James	14MAY94	3.20	1
Tinsley	James	07JUL01	3.35	11	TOMS				
Tinsley	James	08JUL02	3.26	1	Toms	Ambrose	-----11	1.81	1
Tinsley	James	11JUL03	2.31	1	Toms	Jesse	-----11	1.80	1
Tinsley	James	06AUG04	4.24	12	Tombs	Nathen	24JUL04	2.19	M1
Tinsley	James	29MAY05	2.32	21	Tombs	Salley	17JUN05	3.34	F1
Tinsley	James	12AUG06	2.36	21	Toms	Thomas	17JUN03	3.24	1
Tinsley	James	30JUL07	2.35	21	Toms	William	24MAY94	2.14	1
Tinsley	James	04AUG08	2.28	22	Tombs	William	16APR95	3.17	1
Tinsley	James	10JUN09	1.33	2	Toms	William	20AUG00	2.28	1
Tinsley	James	-----11	1.79	11	Toms	William	17JUL01	2.26	1
Tinsley	Thomas	-----95	1.13	1	Toms	William	07JUN02	3.26	1
Tinsley	William	28JUL03	2.31	M1	Toms	William	01AUG03	2.31	1
Tinsley	William	10JUN09	1.33	1	Tombs	William	18JUN04	2.19	1
TIPTON					Tombs	William	12JUL05	3.34	1
Tipton	William	13SEP91	3.16	1	Tombs	William	18JUL06	3.33	1
Tipton	William	05DEC92	3.19	1	Tombs	William	15JUN07	2.35	1
Tipton	William	14MAY94	3.20	1	Toms	William	02JUN08	2.27	1
Tipton	William	-----95	1.13	1	Tombs	William	07JUN09	1.33	1
Tipton	William	-----96	4.15	1	Tombs	William	07JUN09	1.33	1
Tipton	William	-----97	2.05	1	Tombs	William	07JUN09	1.33	1
Tipton	William	12MAY99	2.20	1	Tombs	William	07JUN09	1.33	1
Tipton	William	13JUN00	1.14	11	Toms	William	-----11	1.81	1
TISDALE					TONEY				
Tizdale	John	24AUG08	2.28	1	Toney	Alexander	06AUG89	2.14	1
Tisdel	John	01JUL09	2.34	1	Toney	Alexandria	26AUG91	3.16	1

surname	name	date	bk.pg	TM	surname	name	date	bk.pg	TM
Toney	Alexander	08NOV92	3.19	1	TROUP				
Toney	Alexander	14MAY94	3.20	1	Troup	Jacob	20JUN02	1.23	1
Toney	Alex.	-----95	1.13	1	Troup	Jacob	21JUN03	1.23	1
Toney	Alexander	-----96	4.15	1	Troup	Jacob	05MAY07	1.26	1
TOTTISMAN					Troup	Jacob	10JUN08	1.37	1
Tottesman	John	24AUG08	2.28	1	Troup	Jacob	14JUN09	2.33	1
Tattisman	Matthias	18MAY91	2.10	1	Troup	Mary	22JUL00	1.15	F1
Tattisman	Matthis	08OCT92	1.12	1	Troup	Mary	23JUN01	1.17	F1
Tallisman	Matthias	20AUG93	3.11	1	Troup	Mary	20JUN02	1.23	F
Tatisman	Matthias	04JUL96	2.19	11	Troup	Mary	30JUN07	1.26	F
Tadderman	Matthias	03JUL99	3.21	1	Troup	Mary	10JUN08	1.36	F
Tottisman	Mathias	01JUL00	3.30	1	TROUTMAN				
Tottisman	Matthias	09JUL01	3.35	1	Troutman	Joana	28MAY01	2.26	F
Tottisman	Matthias	11AUG02	3.27	11	Four lotts in Standford				
Tollisman	Matthias	22JUN03	2.31	11	Troutman	John	26AUG93	1.09	1
Toddesman	Matthias	27JUL04	4.23	11	Troutman	John	23MAY94	1.08	1
Tottisman	Mathias	16JUL06	2.36	11	Troutman	John	-----95	2.26	
Tottisman	Matthias	30JUL07	2.35	1	Four lots in Stanford				
Tottesman	Matthias	04AUG08	2.28	1	Troughtman	John	10JUN95	2.12	1
Tottisman	Mathias	21JUN09	1.33	1	Troughtman	John	27JUN96	1.12	1
TOWNSEND					Troughtman	John	27JUN96	1.13	
Tounsin	Jabus	14JUN87	2.07	1	4 town lots in Stanford				
Townsend	Jabez	16AUG90	1.12	1	Troutman	John	13JUN97	3.35	1
Townsend	Jabus	26OCT92	2.08	1	Troutman	John	13JUN97	3.33	
Townsend	Jabes	03AUG93	1.09	1	3 town lots in Stanford				
Townsend	Jabus	13MAY94	1.08	1	Troutman	John	24MAY99	1.36	11
Townsend	Jabus	29JUN95	2.12	1	Troutman	John	24MAY99	1.39	
Townsend	John	20MAY95	2.24	1	Four lotts in Stanford				
TRAP					Troutman	John	08JUL00	2.28	1
Trap	John	29MAY97	3.30	1	Four lotts in Standford				
Trap	Martin	15JUL87	3.10	1	Troutman	Peter	25OCT92	2.08	1
Trap	Martin	24JUL96	1.12	11	TROWBRIDGE				
Trap	Martin	29MAY97	3.30	1	Strawbridge	Isaac	17MAY99	1.33	1
Trap	Mary	01OCT92	2.09	F	Strowbridge	Isack	11JUN00	1.13	1
TRAVIS					Strowbridge	Isaac	21JUL01	2.25	1
Travis	Edward	10JUN94	1.11	1	Strowbridge	Isach	16JUN02	1.20	1
TRESNER					Strawbridge	Isaac	05JUL03	1.22	1
Tressner	Jacob	25JUN04	1.20	1	Strowbridge	Isaac	15JUN04	1.18	1
Tresner	Jacob	21JUN09	1.33	1	Strowbridge	Isaac	23JUL05	2.31	1
Trusner	Jacob	-----11	1.80	1	Trobridge	Isaac	08AUG06	3.33	1
TRIPLETTE					Strawbridge	Jonathan	17MAY99	1.32	1
Triplette	Francis	-----93	2.06	1	Trowbridge	Jonathan	30JUL00	2.28	1
Triplette	Reuben	-----93	2.06	1	TROWSEL				
Triplette	Simon	-----93	2.05	1	Trowsel	Jonathon	12JUN05	1.21	1
TROCKSEL					TROYER				
Trocksel	Chris.	28JUL97	1.25	1	Troyer	Adam	30MAR90	2.07	1
Trocksel	Daniel	13JUN97	1.25	1	TRUELOVE				
Trocksel	Jacob	13JUN97	1.25	1	Truelove	William	02JUN08	2.27	1
Trocksel	Peter	13JUN97	1.25	1	Truelove	William	03JUL09	1.33	1
TROTTER					TRUMBALL				
Trotter	Elijah	21JUN06	1.26	1	Trumball	Robert	-----93	2.05	1
Trotter	Elijah	18APR08	1.36	1	TRUMBOW				
Trotter	Elijah	12MAY09	2.33	1	Trumbow	George	12AUG89	2.14	1
Trotter	John	05APR91	1.08	1	TRUMP				
Trotter	John	23OCT92	2.08	1	Trump	Frederick	02MAY05	2.32	1
Troter	John	03AUG93	1.09	1	Trump	Frederick	31MAY06	2.36	1
Troter	John	20MAY94	1.09	1	Triumph	Fredrick	17AUG07	2.36	11
Trotter	John	26JUN95	2.12	1	Trump	Frederick	10JUN08	1.36	1
Troter	John	15JUN96	1.12	1	Trump	Fredrick	15JUL09	2.34	1
Trotter	John	07APR97	3.30	1	Trump	Frederick	-----11	1.80	1
Trotter	John	17MAY99	1.36	1	TUCKER				
Trotter	John	29JUL00	2.28	1	Tucker	Berny	28JUN04	4.23	1
Trotter	John	29MAY01	1.17	1	Tucker	Berry	30JUL07	2.35	1
Trotter	John	11JUN02	1.22	1	Tucker	Dandridge	02JUL09	1.33	1
Trotter	John	26JUN04	1.20	11	Tucker	Drury	21JUN95	3.16	0
Trotter	John	21JUN06	1.25	1	Tucker	Henry	12APR97	3.29	1
Trotter	John	18JUN07	1.26	1	Tucker	Henry	10MAY99	2.20	1
Trotter	John	18APR08	1.36	1	Tucker	Henry	23JUN01	1.17	1
Trotter	John	30JUN09	2.33	1	Tucker	Henry	04JUN02	1.22	1
TROTTY					Tucker	Henry	30JUN03	1.24	1
Trotty	Abner	10AUG02	3.27	1	Tucker	Henry	03AUG04	2.19	1
Trotty	Abner	28JUL03	2.31	1	Tucker	Henry	18JUN06	1.25	1

surname	name	date	bk.pg	TM	surname	name	date	bk.pg	TM
Tucker	Henry	12JUN07	1.26	1	Turner	Anne	04AUG08	2.28	F
Tucker	James H.	09JUN07	2.34	1	Turner	Anne	26JUN09	1.33	F
Tucker	John	23JUL87	1.06	1	Turner	Ann	-----11	1.81	F
Tucker	John	11JUN89	6.09	1	Turner	Caleb	30MAY99	1.36	1
Tucker	John	02AUG90	1.10	1	Turner	Caleb	17JUL00	2.28	1
Tucker	John	20APR91	2.10	1	Turner	Caleb	17JUL01	2.26	1
Tucker	John	12MAY96	2.18	1	Turner	Caleb	27MAY02	3.26	1
Tucker	Littleberry	09AUG06	2.36	1	Turner	Caleb	11JUN03	2.31	1
Tucker	Littleberry	07JUN09	1.33	1	Turner	Caleb	26JUL04	1.20	1
Tucker	Littleberry	-----11	1.80	1	Turner	Calip	04JUN05	1.21	1
Tucker	Matthew	17JUN05	3.34	1	Turner	Calip	13JUN06	1.25	1
Tucker	Mathew	31JUL06	2.36	1	Turner	Caleb	20MAY07	1.26	1
Tucker	Matthew	09JUN07	2.34	1	Turner	Caleb	10JUN08	1.37	1
Tucker	Philip	04JUN95	2.12	1	Turner	Caleb	23AUG09	2.34	1
Tucker	Phillip	29JUN96	1.12	1	Turner	Caleb	-----11	1.80	1
Tucker	Phillip	14APR97	3.29	1	Turner	George	06AUG89	2.14	1
Tucker	Philip	29MAY99	2.20	1	Turner	James	13JUN95	2.24	1
Tucker	Phillip	10JUN00	2.28	1	Turner	Jeremiah	31JUL01	2.26	1
Tucker	Philip	24JUL01	2.26	1	Turner	John	20APR95	3.16	1
Tucker	Philip	24JUL01	2.26	1	Turner	Joseph	20MAY99	1.36	1
Tucker	Philip	04JUN02	1.22	1	Turner	Joseph	24JUL01	2.26	1
Tucker	Philip	30JUN03	1.24	1	Turner	Joseph	17JUN02	1.23	1
Tucker	Phillip	03AUG04	2.19	1	Turner	Joseph	10JUN03	1.23	1
Tucker	Philip	15JUN05	1.21	1	Turner	Joseph	25JUN04	1.20	1
Tucker	Philip	19JUN06	1.25	1	Turner	Joseph	04JUN05	1.21	1
Tucker	Phillip	25JUN07	1.27	1	Turner	Joseph	13JUN06	1.25	1
Tucker	Phillip	18APR08	1.36	11	Turner	Joseph	20MAY07	1.26	1
Tucker	Phillip	07JUN09	2.33	1	Turner	Joseph	10JUN08	1.37	1
Tucker	Phillip	-----11	1.79	1	Turner	Josiah	24AUG08	2.28	1
Tucker	Pleasant	01JUL03	2.31	1	Turner	Josiah	26JUN09	1.33	M1
Tucker	Pleasant	28JUN04	4.23	1	Turner	Josiah	-----11	1.79	1
Tucker	Pleasant	15MAY06	2.35	1	Turner	Mary	10JUN08	1.37	F
Tucker	Plesent	30JUL07	2.35	1	Turner	Mary	23AUG09	2.34	F
Tucker	Plesant	01AUG08	2.27	1	Turner	Mary	-----11	1.80	F
Tucker	Pleasent	07JUN09	1.33	1	Turner	Stephen	22MAY95	2.12	1
Tucker	Pleasant	-----11	1.80	1	Turner	Stephen	10JUN96	1.12	1
Tucker	Robert	24JUN00	3.30	1	Turner	Stephen	20APR97	3.29	12
Tucker	Robert	19JUN01	3.35	1	Turner	Stephen	30MAY99	1.36	1
Tucker	Robert	27AUG02	3.27	1	Turner	Stephen	21JUN00	2.28	1
Tucker	Robert	15AUG03	2.32	1	Turner	Stephen	17JUL01	2.26	1
Tucker	Robert	04JUN04	4.23	1	Turner	Stephen	17JUL01	2.26	1
Tucker	Robert	13MAY05	2.32	1	Turner	Stephen	27MAY02	3.26	1
Tucker	Robert	12MAY06	2.35	1	Turner	Stephen	28MAY03	2.31	1
Tucker	Robert	09JUN07	2.34	1	Turner	Stephen	26JUN04	1.20	1
Tucker	Robert	25JUN08	2.27	1	Turner	Stephen	03AUG05	2.33	1
Tucker	Robert	13JUL09	1.34	1	Turner	Stephen	06JUN06	2.36	1
Tucker	Robert	-----11	1.80	1	Turner	Stephen	30JUL07	2.35	1
Tucker	Zacheriah	10AUG02	3.11	0	TURPIN				
Tax paid by John W. Gilbert					Turpen	George	-----95	1.13	1
Tucker	Zachariah	30JUL03	2.12	0	Turpin	George	-----96	4.15	1
Tax paid by John W. Gilbert					Turpen	Hezekiah	-----95	1.13	1
Tucker	Zachariah	28JUN04	4.23	1	Turpin	Hezekiah	-----96	4.15	1
Tucker	Zachariah	24MAY05	2.32	1	Turpin	Hezekiah	-----97	2.05	1
Tucker	Zachariah	15MAY06	2.35	1	Tirpin	Jerimiah	04DEC92	3.19	1
Tucker	Zack	17AUG07	2.36	1	Turpin	Jeremiah	14MAY94	3.20	1
Tucker	Zachery	01AUG08	2.27	2	Turpin	Jeremiah	-----95	1.13	1
Tucker	Zachariah	07JUN09	1.32	1	Turpin	Jeremiah	-----96	4.15	1
Ticker	Zachariah	-----11	1.79	1	Turpin	Martin	12MAY99	2.20	1
TULL					TWIDWELL				
Tull	John	22JUN03	2.31	1	Twidwell	William	-----11	1.79	1
TUNGATE					TYLER				
Tunget	Jeremiah	-----96	4.18	11	Tylor	Frank	20MAY89	6.07	1
Tunget	John	-----96	4.18	1	Tyler	Francis	16APR90	1.10	1
TUNSTELL					Tylor	Francis	18MAR91	2.10	1
Tunstell	John	20JUN04	1.20	1	Tyler	John	-----93	2.06	1
TURNER					ULREY				
Turner	Anne	24MAY02	2.29	F	Ulery	Peter	30MAY89	6.07	1
Turner	Ann	13JUL03	3.24	F	Ulery	Peter	05APR90	1.10	1
Turner	Anne	18JUN04	2.19	f	Ulery	Peter	17MAY91	2.10	1
Turner	Anne	14JUN05	3.34	F1	Ulery	Peter	09OCT92	1.13	1
Turner	Ann	18JUL06	3.33	F	Ulrey	Peter	17AUG93	3.12	1
Turner	Anne	09JUN07	2.34	F	Ulrey	Peter	05MAY94	2.15	1

surname	name	date	bk.pg	TM	surname	name	date	bk.pg	TM
Ulrey	Peter	03JUN95	3.17	1	Vandiver	Charles	16AUG04	3.20	1
UNDERWOOD					Vandiver	Charles Sr	22AUG05	3.35	1
Underwood	Cohee	16AUG06	1.26	1	Vandiver	Charles	12JUN05	3.35	1
Underwood	John	18APR89	6.07	1	Vandiver	Charles	22AUG05	3.35	11
Underwood	John	10MAY90	1.10	1	Vandiver	Charles	22JUL06	3.30	11
Underwood	John	17MAY91	2.10	1	Vandiver	Charles Jr	22JUL06	3.30	1
Underwood	Joseph	28JUN87	1.06	1	Vandever	George	25JUN99	1.37	1
Underwood	Rheuben	18AUG06	1.26	1	Vandiver	George	23JUL00	2.28	1
Underwood	William	07JUL99	1.36	1	Vandiver	George	30MAY01	3.36	1
UPTON					Vandiver	George	13AUG02	2.29	1
Upton	Edward	16JUN96	1.12	1	Vandever	George	20MAY03	3.25	1
Upton	Edward	07APR97	3.30	1	Vandiver	George	06AUG04	3.20	1
USERY					Vandiver	George	05AUG05	3.35	1
Usery	Bob	23JUL96	1.12	1	Vandiver	George	22JUL06	3.30	1
Usery	Phillip	13JUN96	1.12	1	Vandever	John Jr	04AUG03	3.25	1
Ussery	Phillip	03JUN97	3.30	1	Vandever	John Sr	04AUG03	3.25	11
Usary	Richard	02JUN95	2.13	1	VANDYKE				
Usery	Richard	23JUL96	1.12	1	Vandike	John	22JUL06	3.30	1
Ussery	Richard	27JUL97	1.26	1	VANMETER				
Usery	William	23JUL96	1.12	1	VanMeter	Isaac	25JUN87	3.10	1
Usery	William Jr	23JUL96	1.12	1	VanMeter	Isaac	06MAY90	1.11	1
Ussery	William	24APR97	3.30	1	VanMeter	Isaac	09JUN91	2.10	1
Ussery	William	03JUN97	3.30	1	VanMeter	Joshua	18JUL87	3.04	1
Ussery	William	03JUN97	3.30	1	Listed with Samuel Gill				
UTMAN					VanMetre	Joshua	-----93	2.06	1
Utman	Andrew	24JUN91	3.16	1	VanMeter	Joshua	23APR94	3.21	1
Utman	Joseph	25JUN87	3.10	1	VanMeter	Morgan	23APR94	3.21	01
Utman	Joseph	10JUL89	2.14	1	VANTREESE				
Utman	Joseph	27APR91	3.16	1	Vantreese	Jacob	07JUN08	2.28	1
Utman	Peter	25JUN87	3.10	1	Vantress	Jacob	30JUN09	1.34	1
Utman	Peter	27JUN89	2.14	1	Vontreese	Jacob	-----11	1.82	1
Utman	Peter	24JUN91	3.16	1	Vantreese	Samuel	07JUN08	2.28	1
VANASDALE					Vantress	Samuel	13JUL09	1.34	1
Vanisdale	Isaac	16AUG02	3.27	1	Vontreese	Samuel	-----11	1.82	1
Venasdale	Isaac	26JUN03	2.32	1	Vantress	William	28NOV88	1.10	1
VANCOUNTY					Vontress	William	05AUG89	5.11	1
Fincounty	Joseph	14MAY89	6.03	1	Vantreece	William	30MAY90	2.07	1
Vancounty	Joseph	03APR90	1.10	1	VanTreece	William	05APR91	1.09	1
VanCounty	Joseph	20APR91	2.10	1	Fantrees	William	27OCT92	2.03	1
VanCounter	Joseph	07MAY91	3.16	1	Fantrees	William	05AUG93	1.04	1
VanCounty	Joseph	16AUG93	3.12	1	Fantrees	William	13MAY94	1.04	1
Funcounty	Joseph	23APR94	2.05	1	Fantrees	William	20MAY95	2.05	1
Funcounty	Joseph	03APR95	3.07	1	Fantrees	William	08JUN96	1.04	1
Finncounty	Joseph	22JUN96	2.07	1	Vantreez	William	21APR97	3.31	1
Vencounty	Joseph	16MAY97	1.26	1	Vantress	William	16MAY99	1.37	1
Vancounty	Joseph	04JUL00	3.31	11	Vantress	William	07JUL00	2.28	1
Funcounty	Joseph	12AUG02	3.09	1	Vantress	William	19MAY01	1.26	11
Wincounty	Joseph	06JUN04	4.24	1	Vantress	William	24MAY02	3.27	11
VANDIVER					Vantress	William	30MAY03	2.32	12
Vendevere	Ashbury	14JUL97	1.26	1	Vantrase	William	25AUG04	3.20	12
Vandever	Ashbury	25JUN99	1.37	1	Vantreece	William	04JUN05	3.35	12
Vandiver	Ashberry	26JUL00	2.29	1	Vantrise	William	16JUL06	3.30	21
Vandiver	Ashbury	30MAY01	3.36	1	Vantreece	William	03AUG07	2.36	2
Vandiver	Ashbury	03AUG02	2.29	1	Vantreese	William	07JUN08	2.28	1
Vandever	Ashberry	25JUN03	3.25	1	Vantress	William	13JUL09	1.34	1
Vandiver	Ashbury	06AUG04	3.20	1	Vontreese	William	-----11	1.82	1
Vandiver	Ashberry	22AUG05	3.35	1	VANWINKLE				
Vandiver	Ashbury	22JUL06	3.30	2	VanWinkle	Abraham	18JUN96	1.12	1
Vendevere	Charles Sr	14JUL97	1.26	1	VanWinkle	Abram	12JUN97	3.31	1
Vendevere	Charles Jr	14JUL97	1.26	1	VanWinkle	Michael	25MAY89	6.07	1
Vandever	Charles	25JUN99	1.37	1	VanWinkle	Michael	14MAY91	2.10	1
Vandever	Charles Jr	25JUN99	1.37	1	VanWinkle	Michael	02NOV92	1.13	11
Vandiver	Charles Sr	26JUL00	2.28	1	VANCE				
Vandiver	Charles	22JUL00	2.28	11	Vance	Elener	08MAY07	1.27	F1
Vandiver	Charles	30MAY01	3.36	1	Vance	Elener	04MAY08	1.37	F1
Vandiver	Charles	10AUG02	2.29	1	Vance	Elener	15JUN09	2.35	F
Vandiver	Charles Jr	10AUG02	2.29	1	Vance	George	25MAY89	6.07	1
Vandever	Charles Sr	25JUN03	3.25	1	Vance	George	21APR90	1.11	1
Vandever	Charles Jr	25JUN03	3.25	1	Vance	George	12APR91	1.09	1
Vandever	Charles	25JUN03	3.25	1	Vance	George	26SEP92	1.13	1
Vandiver	Charles Sr	06AUG04	3.20	1	Vance	George	23APR94	3.21	1
Vandiver	Charles Jr	24AUG04	3.20	1	Vance	George	-----95	1.14	1

surname	name	date	bk.pg	TM	surname	name	date	bk.pg	TM
Vance	George	-----96	4.18	11	Vardiman	John	04JUN02	1.23	1
Vance	George	25JUL05	2.33	1	Vardiman	John	28JUN03	1.24	1
Vance	George	24JUN07	2.36	1	Vardimon	John	20JUN04	1.20	1
Vance	George	04MAY08	1.38	1	Vardimon	John	12JUN05	1.22	1
Vance	George Jr	13JUL09	1.34	1	Vardimon	John	16JUN06	1.26	1
Vance	George	-----11	1.82	1	Vardiman	John	04JUN07	1.27	1
Vance	John	08MAY07	1.27	1	Vardaman	John	04MAY08	1.37	1
Vance	John	-----11	1.82	1	Vardaman	John	15MAY09	2.34	1
Vance	Joseph	-----95	1.14	1	Vardeman	John	-----11	1.82	1
Vancel	Samuel	14JUN99	2.21	1	Vardiman	Morgan	03JUN90	2.07	1
Vancel	Samuel	05MAY07	1.27	1	Vardiman	Morgan	11OCT92	2.09	1
Vance	Samuel	04MAY08	1.37	1	Vardiman	Morgan	14AUG93	1.09	1
Vansil	Samuel	16JUL09	2.35	1	Vardiman	Morgan	29MAY94	1.09	1
VANDICRAFT					Vardiman	Morgan	03JUN95	2.13	1
Vandicraft	Samuel	20JUL05	2.33	1	Vardiman	Morgan	03JUN95	2.25	1
VANN					Vardiman	Morgan	30JUN96	1.12	1
Vann	Jesse	26MAY95	2.13	1	Vardeman	Morgan	12JUN97	3.30	1
VARDEMAN					Vardiman	Morgan	14MAY99	1.37	1
Vardiman	Amm	20JUN87	2.07	1	Vardiman	Morgan	19JUN00	1.15	1
Vardimon	Ameziah	30JUN89	5.11	1	Vardiman	Morgan	10JUN01	1.17	1
Verdiman	Amaziah	25MAR91	1.09	1	Vardiman	Morgan	04JUN02	1.23	1
Vardiman	Amaziah	11OCT92	2.09	1	Vardiman	Morgan	23JUN03	1.24	1
Vardiman	Amaziah	14AUG93	1.09	1	Vardiman	Morgan	20JUN04	1.20	1
Vardiman	Amaziah	30MAY94	1.09	1	Vardiman	Morgan	12JUN05	1.22	1
Vardiman	Amaziah	03JUN95	2.13	1	Vardiman	Morgan	18JUN06	1.26	1
Vardiman	Amariah	30JUN96	1.12	1	Vardaman	Morgan	13JUN07	1.27	1
Vardeman	Amaziah	12JUN97	3.30	1	Vardaman	Morgan	04MAY08	1.37	1
Vardiman	Amaziah	19JUN00	1.15	1	Vardaman	Morgin	08JUN09	2.35	1
Vardiman	Ammeziah	10JUN01	1.17	1	Vardeman	Morgan	-----11	1.82	1
Vardiman	Ammeziah	04JUN02	1.23	1	Vardimon	William	04NOV88	1.10	1
Vardiman	Ammeziah	28JUN03	1.24	1	VAUGHN				
Vardimon	Ammeziah	20JUN04	1.20	1	Vawn	Allen	15JUN05	1.22	1
Vardimon	Ammeziah	12JUN05	1.22	1	Vaughn	Allen	13JUN07	1.27	1
Vardimon	Ammeziah	16JUN06	1.26	1	Vaughn	Allen	27APR08	1.37	1
Vardiman	Amaziah	04JUN07	1.27	1	Vaughn	Allen	05AUG09	2.35	1
Vardaman	Amaziah	04MAY08	1.37	1	Vaughn	Allen	-----11	1.82	1
Vardaman	Ameziah	29MAY09	2.34	1	Vaughn	Elisha	19JUN06	1.26	1
Vardeman	Amaziah	-----11	1.82	1	Vaughn	Elisha	02JUN07	1.27	1
Vardeman	Jeremiah	12JUN97	3.30	1	Vaughn	Elisha	04MAY08	1.37	1
Vardimon	Jeremiah	29MAY99	2.20	1	Vaughn	Elisha	29MAY09	2.34	1
Vardiman	Jeremiah	05AUG02	3.27	1	Vaughn	Elisha	-----11	1.82	1
Vardiman	Jeremiah	04AUG03	2.32	1	Vaun	James	20JUN87	2.07	1
Vardymon	Jeramiah	23JUL04	4.24	1	Vaughn	James	15NOV88	1.10	1
Vardiman	Jeremiah	03JUN05	3.35	1	Vaughn	James	14APR91	1.09	1
Vardiman	Jeremiah	16JUL06	3.30	1	Vaughn	James	26OCT92	2.09	1
Vardiman	Jar.	24JUN07	2.36	1	Vaughn	James	12AUG93	1.09	1
Vardiman	Jeremiah	07JUN08	2.28	1	Vaughn	James	20MAY94	1.09	1
Vardiman	Jeremiah	13JUL09	1.34	1	Vaughn	James	02AUG04	2.19	1
Vardiman	John Sr	20JUN87	2.07	11	Vawn	James	19JUN05	1.22	1
Vardiman	John Jr	20JUN87	2.07	1	Vaughn	James	13JUN07	1.27	1
Vardimon	John Sr	30OCT88	1.10	11	Vaughn	James	04MAY08	1.38	1
Vardimon	John Jr	01NOV88	1.10	1	Vaughn	James	23AUG09	2.35	1
Vardimon	John Sr	19JUN89	5.11	1	Vaugh	James	-----11	1.82	1
Vardimon	John Jr	19JUN89	5.11	11	Vaun	John	20JUN87	2.07	1
Vardiman	John Jr	03JUN90	2.07	1	Vaughn	John	04NOV88	1.10	1
Vardiman	John	30MAR91	1.09	11	Vaughn	John	16JUN89	5.11	11
Vardiman	John Sr	11OCT92	2.09	11	Vaughn	John	21APR90	2.07	11
Vardimon	John Jr	11OCT92	2.09	1	Vaughn	John	05OCT92	2.09	11
Vardiman	John Sr	14AUG93	1.09	11	Vaughn	John	20AUG93	1.09	11
Vardiman	John Jr	14AUG93	1.09	1	Vaughn	John	18MAY94	1.09	11
Vardiman	John Sr	30MAY94	1.09	11	Vaughn	John	28MAY95	2.24	1
Vardiman	John Jr	30MAY94	1.09	1	Vaughn	John	28MAY95	2.12	11
Vardiman	John Sr	03JUN95	2.13	11	Vaughn	John	02JUN95	2.13	1
Vardiman	John Jr	03JUN95	2.13	1	Vawn	Johnston	15JUN05	1.22	1
Vardiman	John	03JUN95	2.24	1	Vaughn	Nancy	-----05	3.38	F
Vardiman	John	30JUN96	1.12	11	Vaughn	Nancy	-----05	3.38	F
Vardiman	John	15JUL96	1.12	1	Vaughn	Nancy	11JUN05	3.35	F
Vardeman	John	31MAY97	3.31	1	Vaun	Nancy	22JUL06	3.30	F
Vardeman	John	12JUN97	3.30	1	Vaught	Nancy	19AUG07	2.36	F
Vardimon	John	29MAY99	2.20	1	Vaughn	Nancy	28JUN08	2.28	F
Vardiman	John	19JUN00	1.15	1	Vaughn	Nancy	13JUL09	1.34	F
Vardiman	John	11JUN01	1.17	1	Vaughn	Nancy	-----11	1.82	F

surname	name	date	bk.pg	TM	surname	name	date	bk.pg	TM
Vaughn	Philip	07JUN02	3.27	1	Vorrus	Garrard	22JUL06	3.30	1
Vaughn	Thomas	15NOV88	1.10	1	VOTAW				
Vaughn	Thomas	25JUN89	5.11	1	Vanton	Aaron	24JUN07	2.36	1
Vaughn	Thomas	18MAY90	2.07	1	Vawtre	Aaron	04MAY08	1.38	1
Vaughn	Thomas	29OCT92	2.09	1	Vaughtes	Aaron	23AUG09	2.35	1
Vaughn	Thomas	12AUG93	1.09	1	Votta	Henry	21MAY94	1.09	1
Vaughn	Thomas	27MAY94	1.09	1	Votaw	Henry	28MAY95	2.13	1
Vaughn	Thomas	28MAY95	2.12	1	Vattaw	John	03APR90	2.07	1
Vaughn	Thomas	28MAY95	2.24	1	Votau	John	25MAR91	1.09	1
Vaughn	Thomas	28JUN96	1.12	1	Votta	John	26MAY94	1.09	1
Vaughen	Thomas	24APR97	3.31	1	WADDEL				
Vaughen	Thomas	16MAY99	1.37	11	Waddle	David	07JUL89	2.15	1
Vaughn	Thomas	17JUN00	2.28	11	Waddle	David	05JUL91	1.09	1
Vaughn	Thomas	24JUL01	2.26	12	Waddel	David	04OCT92	2.09	1
Vaughn	Thomas	10JUN02	1.23	12	WADE				
Vaughn	Thomas	11JUL03	1.24	13	Waid	James	10AUG07	2.39	1
Vaughn	Thomas	02AUG04	2.19	12	Wade	James	-----08	2.30	1
Vaughn	Thomas	08JUL05	1.22	12	Wade	Jeremiah	-----11	1.86	1
Vaughn	Thomas	19JUN06	1.26	11	Wade	John	26JUL03	2.34	M1
Vaughn	Thomas	02JUN07	1.27	11	Wade	John	29JUN04	4.25	1
Vaughn	Thomas	27APR08	1.37	11	Wade	John	13MAY05	2.33	1
Vaughn	Thomas	29MAY09	2.35	1	Waid	John	17AUG07	2.39	1
Vaughn	Thomas	-----11	1.82	1	Wade	Perce	20SEP92	1.14	1
Vaughn	William	20AUG93	1.09	1	Wade	Pearce	08AUG93	3.12	1
Vaughn	William	23MAY94	1.09	1	Wade	Pearce	16APR94	2.16	1
Vaughn	William	28JUN96	1.12	1	Wade	Pearce	18MAR95	3.18	1
Vaughen	William	15APR97	3.31	1	Wade	Pearce	23APR96	2.19	1
VAZY					Wade	Pierce	15MAY97	1.26	1
Vazy	Samuel	12SEP92	1.13	1	Wade	Pierce	04JUL99	3.22	11
VEACH					Wade	Pierce	25JUN00	3.31	1
Veach	John	15MAY89	6.07	1	Wade	Parce	07MAY01	3.36	11
VEST					Wade	Pierce	08JUL02	3.28	11
Vest	Elias	13JUL09	1.34	1	Wade	Pierce	26JUL03	2.34	12
Vest	Robert	08JUN02	3.27	1	Wade	Pierce	29JUN04	4.25	11
Vest	Robert	17JUN03	2.32	1	Wade	Pierce	29MAY05	2.33	1
Vest	Robert	07AUG04	2.19	1	Wade	Pierce	02AUG06	2.38	1
Vest	Robert	20JUN05	1.22	11	Waid	Perce	10AUG07	2.39	1
Vest	Robert	22JUL06	3.30	11	Waid	Parce	-----08	2.30	11
Vest	Robert	03AUG07	2.36	11	Wade	Pearce	25AUG08	2.04	
Vest	Robert	27JUN08	2.28	11	Paid tax for William Baker				
Vest	Robert	13JUL09	1.34	1	Wade	Pearce	10JUN09	1.35	1
Vest	Robert	-----11	1.82	11	Wade	Pierce Sr	-----11	1.86	11
VIGUS					Wade	William	17JUN02	3.28	11
Vigus	Zacariah	15AUG96	1.13	1	Wade	William	26JUL03	2.34	12
Vigers	Zachariah	29JUN99	1.37	1	Wade	William	29JUN04	4.25	11
Vigrus	Zachariah	30JUL00	2.29	1	Wade	William	29MAY05	2.33	11
Vigus	Zechariah	21JUL01	3.36	1	Wade	William	30MAY05	2.34	1
VILEZATT					Wade	William	19JUN06	2.38	11
Valuzatt	Francas	10MAY99	2.20	1	Waid	William	12AUG07	2.39	1
Valuzatt	Francis	11JUN00	1.15	1	Wade	William	-----08	2.29	1
Vilezatt	Anna	20MAY06	2.37	F	Wade	William	10JUN09	1.35	1
Valuzat	Frances	04AUG07	2.36	1	Wade	William	13JUL09	1.34	1
Viluzette	Francis	04MAY08	1.37	1	Wade	William	-----11	1.86	1
Vellezette	Francis	23AUG09	2.35	1	Wade	William	-----11	1.86	12
Vilezat	John F.B.	24MAY02	3.27	1	WAGGONER				
Vilezat	John F.B.	30MAY03	2.32	1	Waggoner	John	14APR91	2.11	1
Vilezatt	John B.F.	04AUG06	2.37	1	Waggoner	John	08OCT92	1.13	1
Viluzott	John F.B.	-----11	1.82	1	Waggoner	John	15AUG93	3.12	1
VINEGARDEN					Waggonner	John	23APR94	2.15	1
Vinegarden	John	29JUN04	4.24	1	Waggoner	John	03JUN95	2.13	1
Vinegarden	John	30MAY05	2.33	11	Wagonar	John	30JUN96	1.13	1
Vinegarden	John Jr	30MAY05	2.33	1	Waggoner	John	12JUN97	3.32	1
Vinegarden	John	15AUG06	2.37	11	Waggoner	John	01JUN99	1.38	1
Vinegarden	John Jr	15AUG06	2.37	11	Wagoner	John	01AUG00	2.30	1
VINEYARD					Waggoner	John	23JUL01	2.27	1
Vineyard	William	18JUN07	2.36	1	Wagner	John	14JUN02	2.30	1
VINSON					Waggoner	John	12JUL03	3.26	1
Vinson	John	18JUN06	1.26	1	Wagner	John	06AUG04	2.20	1
VORRUS					Wagner	John	03JUN05	3.35	1
Vorus	Garret	10AUG02	2.29	1	Wagner	John	18JUL06	3.34	1
Voris	Gerret	07AUG04	3.20	1	Wagner	John	03AUG07	2.39	1
Vorrus	Garrard	22AUG05	3.35	1	Wagner	John	31MAY08	2.29	11

surname	name	date	bk.pg	TM	surname	name	date	bk.pg	TM
Waggoner	John	07JUL09	1.36	1	Wallace	Andrew	04JUN01	2.27	12
WAIN					Wallace	Andrew	03JUN02	3.28	12
Wain	Adam	30JUN87	1.06	1	Wallace	Andrew	18JUN03	2.33	21
WALD					Wallace	Andrew	13AUG04	2.20	2
Wald	John	11MAY90	1.11	1	Wallace	Andrew	10JUN05	2.34	2
WALDON					Wallace	Andrew	24JUL06	2.38	11
Walden	James	25JUN87	3.11	1	Wallace	Andrew	16JUL07	2.37	11
Waldon	John	16NOV92	3.20	1	Walles	Andrew	31MAY08	2.29	11
Waldon	John	11JUN05	1.23	1	Wallace	Andrew	21AUG09	1.36	1
WALES					Wallace	Andrew	-----11	1.86	1
Wales	James	04DEC92	3.20	1	Wallace	Caleb	-----11	1.87	1
WALKER					Wallace	Ezekiel	15JUN07	2.37	1
Walker	Alexander	18NOV88	1.11	1	Wallace	James	05AUG05	2.35	1
Walker	Alexander	24JUN89	5.12	1	Wallace	James	05MAY06	2.37	1
Walker	Elexander	22MAR90	2.07	1	Wallace	James	15JUN07	2.37	11
Walker	Alexander	04MAY08	1.38	1	Wallace	James	31MAY08	2.29	1
Walker	Eliz.	05AUG93	1.10	F1	Wallace	James	08AUG09	1.36	1
Walker	Eliz.	14MAY94	1.09	F	Wallace	James	-----11	1.86	1
Walker	Eliz.	20MAY95	2.13	F	Wallace	Joseph	24JUL06	2.38	1
Walker	Elizabeth	20MAY95	2.25	F	Wallis	Joseph	03AUG07	2.39	1
Walker	Elmore	04MAY07	1.27	1	Walace	Joseph	-----08	2.30	1
Walker	Isaac	01JUN96	1.13	1	Wallace	Joseph	08AUG09	1.36	1
Walker	Isaac	18APR97	3.31	1	Wallace	Joseph	-----11	1.86	1
Walker	James	-----97	2.06	1	Wallace	Richard	05AUG05	2.35	1
Walker	James	25JUN99	2.21	1	Wallace	Richard	24JUL06	2.38	1
Walker	James	20JUN00	1.16	1	Wallace	Richard	08AUG09	1.36	1
Walker	Jesse	18APR97	3.31	1	Wallace	Richard	-----11	1.86	1
Walker	Jesse	27MAY99	1.38	1	Wallace	Robert	14AUG05	3.37	1
Walker	Jessee	29MAY01	1.17	1	Wallen	Robert	08AUG06	3.36	1
Walker	Jessee	28JUN02	1.25	1	Wallace	Samuel	25JUN87	3.10	1
Walker	Jessee	13JUL03	3.26	1	Wallace	Samuel	05MAY91	3.16	1
Walker	Jesse	07AUG04	2.20	1	Wallace	Samuel	17NOV92	3.20	1
Walker	Jesse	03JUN05	3.35	1	Wallace	Samuel	23APR94	3.21	1
Walker	Jesse	08AUG06	3.36	1	Wallace	Samuel	-----95	1.14	1
Waken	Jesse	16JUL07	2.37	1	Wallace	Samuel	14JUN96	1.13	1
Walker	Jesse	31MAY08	2.29	1	WAMUCK				
Walker	Jesse	03JUL09	1.36	1	Wamuck	Jesse	24MAY02	3.28	1
Walker	Jesse	-----11	1.86	1	Wamuch	Jesse	26JUL03	2.33	1
Walker	John	04MAY07	1.27	1	Wamuck	Jesse	13MAY05	2.33	1
Walker	John	12JUN09	2.36	1	Wamuck	William	29JUL06	2.38	1
Walker	Thomas	-----96	4.19	1	WARD				
Walker	Thomas	25JUN99	2.21	1	Ward	Barney	16SEP91	3.17	1
Walker	Walter	21JUL01	2.27	1	Ward	Bernard	-----96	4.18	1
Walker	Walter	18JUN02	1.24	1	Ward	Barnabas	03JUL97	1.28	1
Walker	William	13JUL91	3.16	1	Ward	Barney	-----08	2.30	1
Walker	William	-----11	1.87	1	Word	Cuthburt	12JUN00	1.15	1
Walker	Willis	29MAY05	2.34	1	Word	Cuthbert	01JUN01	1.18	1
WALKUP					Ward	Demey	19JUN89	5.11	11
Walkup	Samuel	14MAY90	1.11	1	Ward	James	17SEP91	3.17	1
Walkup	Samuel	17MAY91	2.11	1	Ward	John	13MAY94	1.09	1
Walkup	Samuel	12SEP92	1.13	1	Ward	John	27MAR95	3.18	1
WALL					Ward	John	03JUN95	2.13	1
Wall	Francis	19JUL03	3.26	1	Ward	John	04JUN96	2.20	1
Walls	Francis	06AUG04	3.21	1	Ward	John	30JUN96	1.13	1
Wall	Frances	12JUN05	3.35	1	Ward	John	06APR93	3.32	1
Wall	Frances	26JUL06	3.35	1	Ward	Peter	13MAY94	1.09	1
Wall	Gabriel	26JUL06	3.35	1	Ward	Peter	03JUN95	2.13	1
Wall	Jacob	24JUL01	3.39	11	Ward	Thomas	01AUG89	2.15	1
Wall	Jacob	05AUG02	2.30	11	Ward	Thomas	07DEC92	3.20	1
Wall	Jacob	19JUL03	3.26	2	Ward	Thomas	15MAY99	2.21	1
Walls	Jacob	06AUG04	3.21	1	Ward	Thomas	12JUN00	1.15	1
Wall	Jacob	12JUN05	3.35	21	Ward	William	-----08	1.39	1
Wall	James	22JUN09	1.35	M1	Ward	William	10MAY09	2.35	1
Wall	James	-----11	1.87	1	WARDEN				
Wall	Robert	05AUG02	2.30	1	Warden	John	05JUL09	2.37	1
Wall	Robert	31MAY08	2.29	1	Warden	William	04MAY07	1.27	11
Wall	Robert	13JUL09	1.34	1	Warden	William	30JUN09	2.37	1
Wall	Robert	-----11	1.87	1	WARE				
Walls	Suttle	06AUG04	3.21	1	Ware	Dudley	25JUN87	3.11	1
Wall	Isaac S.	26JUL06	3.35	2	Weir	Dudley	-----11	1.87	1
Wall	Thomas	20JUN07	2.37	1	Wear	Philip	30JUN89	5.12	1
WALLACE					Wear	Phillip	03APR90	2.07	1

surname	name	date	bk.pg	TM	surname	name	date	bk.pg	TM
Weire	William	23JUL01	3.39	1	Warran	Charles	04JUN95	2.13	11
Ware	William	22JUN02	1.25	1	Warran	Charles	30JUN96	1.13	1
Ware	William	23JUN03	1.25	1	Warren	Charles	30JUN96	1.13	1
Ware	William	02AUG04	2.20	1	Warren	Charles	13APR97	3.31	1
WARNER					Warren	Charles	13APR97	3.31	1
Warner	David	-----08	1.40	1	Warren	Charles	30JUN99	2.21	1
Warner	Jacob	15JUL06	2.37	1	Warren	Charles Jr	30JUN99	2.21	1
Warner	Jacob	06JUN09	2.36	1	Warren	Charles	20JUN00	1.15	11
Warner	John	24JUL04	4.26	1	Warren	Charles Jr	20JUN00	1.15	1
Warner	John	20JUL05	2.35	1	Warren	Charles Sr	10JUN01	1.18	11
Warner	John	15JUL06	2.37	1	Warren	Charles Jr	10JUN01	1.18	1
Warner	John	-----08	1.40	1	Warren	Charles	08JUN02	1.24	11
Warner	John	19AUG09	2.37	1	Warren	Charles Jr	08JUN02	1.24	1
Woner	Peter	09JUN89	6.07	1	Warren	Charles	20JUL03	1.24	11
Woner	Peter	05APR90	1.11	1	Warren	Charles Jr	20JUL03	1.24	1
Warner	Peter	06APR91	1.10	1	Warren	Charles Sr	19JUN04	1.21	1
Warner	Peter	26OCT92	2.09	1	Warren	Charles	19JUN04	1.21	1
Warner	Peter	06AUG93	1.09	1	Warren	Charles Sr	11JUN05	1.22	1
Worner	Peter	14MAY94	1.09	1	Warren	Charles	11JUN05	1.22	1
Worner	Peter	21MAY95	2.13	1	Warren	Charles	16JUN06	1.26	1
Worner	Peter	09JUN96	1.13	1	Warren	Charles	26MAY07	1.28	1
Warner	Peter	29MAY99	1.38	11	Warren	Charles	-----08	1.39	1
Warner	Peter	21JUN00	2.29	1	Warren	Charles	01JUL09	2.37	1
Warner	Peter	28JUL01	2.27	12	Warren	David	20AUG87	1.06	1
Warner	Peter	30JUN02	3.28	11	Warren	David	16MAY89	6.07	
Warner	Peter	30MAY03	2.32	11	Listed with James Warren				
Warner	Peter	31JUL05	2.35	11	Warren	David	20APR90	1.11	1
Warner	Peter	15JUL06	2.37	1	Warren	David	19APR91	2.11	1
Warner	Peter	31JUL07	2.39	1	Warren	Gabriel	08JUN02	1.24	1
Warner	Peter	-----08	1.40	1	Warren	Gabriel	20JUL03	1.24	1
Warner	Peter	19AUG09	2.37	1	Warren	Gabriel	18JUN04	1.21	1
Warner	Peter	-----11	1.87	1	Warren	Gabriel	12JUN05	1.23	1
WARREN					Warren	Gabriel	10MAY09	2.35	1
Warren	Benjamin	08JUN02	1.24	1	Warren	Gabriel	-----11	1.87	1
Warren	Benjamin	20JUL03	1.24	1	Weron	Jacob	24JUN00	2.29	11
Warren	Benjamin	20JUN04	1.21	1	Weron	Jacob	03JUN01	2.27	12
Warren	Benjamin	03AUG04	1.22	1	Warren	Jacob	11JUN02	1.23	11
Warren	Benjamin	11JUN05	1.23	1	Warren	James	29JUN87	1.06	1
Warren	Benjamin	16JUN06	1.26	1	Warren	James	16MAY89	6.07	1
Warren	Benjamin	28MAY07	1.28	1	David Warren listed with him				
Warren	Benjamin	04MAY08	1.38	1	Warren	James	20APR90	1.11	1
Warren	Benjamin	05JUN09	2.35	1	Warren	James	19APR91	2.11	11
Warren	Benjamin	-----11	1.85	1	Warren	James	12SEP92	1.13	11
Warren	Burress	25JUN87	3.11	1	Warrin	James	05AUG93	3.12	11
Warren	Burress	13AUG89	2.14	1	Warren	James	13MAY94	2.15	11
Warrin	Burris	17SEP91	3.17	1	Warren	James	08APR95	3.17	11
Warren	Burris	29MAY94	3.21	1	Warren	James Sr	16JUL96	2.19	1
Warren	Burrus	-----95	1.14	1	Warren	James Jr	16JUL96	2.19	1
Warren	Burrus	-----96	4.19	1	Warren	James	30JUN96	1.13	11
Warren	Burrus	13APR97	3.31	1	Warren	James Sr	08JUN97	1.27	1
Warren	Burress	-----97	2.05	1	Warren	James Jr	08JUN97	1.27	1
Warren	Burres	09JUL99	2.22	1	Warren	James	13APR97	3.31	1
Warren	Burres	25JUL00	1.16	1	Warren	James	21MAY99	3.21	11
Warren	Burres	08JUN01	1.18	11	Warren	James	19JUN00	1.15	1
Warren	Burres Jr	10JUN01	1.18	1	Warren	James	26JUN00	3.32	11
Warren	Burres	14JUN02	1.24	1	Warren	James	01MAY01	3.36	11
Warren	Burres	20JUN03	1.25	1	Warren	James	08JUN02	1.24	1
Warren	Burres Jr	03AUG04	1.22	1	Warren	James	05AUG02	3.29	11
Warren	Burres	22JUL05	1.24	1	Warren	James Jr	14JUN02	1.24	1
Warren	Burres	16JUN06	1.26	1	Warren	James	20JUN03	1.25	1
Weiren	Burres	28MAY07	1.28	1	Warren	James	20JUL03	1.24	1
Warren	Burres	-----08	1.40	1	Warren	James	20JUL03	1.24	11
Warren	Burres	05JUN09	2.36	1	Warren	James	05AUG03	2.35	1
Warren	Burris	-----11	1.85	1	Warran	James	13JUN04	4.25	1
Warren	Charles	12JUN87	2.07	1	Warran	James	24JUL04	4.25	0
Warren	Charles	31OCT88	1.10	11	Tax paid by William Sr Warran				
Warren	Charles	19JUN89	5.12	11	Warren	James	06AUG04	2.20	1
Warren	Charles	18MAY90	2.07	1	Warren	James	12JUN05	1.23	1
Warring	Charles	30MAR91	1.09	1	Warren	James	29JUN05	2.34	1
Warren	Charles	12OCT92	2.09	11	Warren	James	13AUG06	2.39	1
Warran	Charles	14AUG93	1.09	11	Warren	James	28MAY07	1.28	1
Warran	Charles	30MAY94	1.09	11	Warren	James	28MAY07	1.28	1

surname	name	date	bk.pg	TM	surname	name	date	bk.pg	TM
Warren	James	18AUG07	2.39	1	Warren	Martin	08JUN97	1.27	1
Warren	James	-----08	1.40	1	Wearen	Michael	12JUN07	1.29	1
Warren	James	-----08	2.29	1	Wearen	Michael	-----08	1.39	1
Warren	James	31MAY08	2.29	1	Warring	Ruben	30MAR91	1.09	1
Warren	James	07JUL09	1.36	1	Warran	Ruben	12OCT92	2.09	1
Warren	James Jr	30JUN09	2.37	1	Warran	Rubin	14AUG93	1.09	1
Warren	James	09AUG09	1.36	1	Warran	Rubin	30MAY94	1.09	1
Warren	James	-----11	1.85	1	Warran	Reuben	04MAY95	2.13	1
Warren	James	-----11	1.88	1	Warren	Rubin	30JUN96	1.13	1
Warren	James	-----11	1.88	11	Warren	Reubin	13APR97	3.31	1
Warren	John	31OCT88	1.10	1	Warren	Rheuben	30JUN99	2.21	1
Warren	John	21JUL89	5.12	1	Warren	Reuben	20JUN00	1.16	1
Warren	John	20APR90	1.11	1	Warren	Rheuben	13JUN01	1.19	1
Warren	John	18MAY90	2.07	1	Warren	Rheuben	08JUN02	1.24	1
Warren	John	29MAR91	1.09	1	Warren	Rheuben	20JUL03	1.24	1
Warren	John	19AUG91	2.11	1	Warren	Rheuben	19JUN04	1.21	1
Warran	John	14AUG93	1.10	12	Warren	Rheuben	11JUN05	1.22	1
Warrin	John	27AUG93	3.12	1	Warran	Samuel	24JUL04	4.25	0
Warren	John	17APR94	2.16	1	Tax paid by William Sr Warran				
Warran	John	30MAY94	1.09	12	Warren	Samuel	-----11	1.83	1
Warren	John	20APR95	3.17	2	Warran	Thomas	03JUN95	2.13	1
Warren	John	03JUN95	2.13	11	Warren	Thomas	30JUN96	1.13	1
Warren	John	28JUN96	2.20	1	Warren	Thomas	13APR97	3.31	1
Warren	John	30JUN96	1.13	12	Warran	Thomas	24JUL04	4.25	0
Warren	John	13APR97	3.31	1	Tax paid by William Sr Warran				
Warren	John	13APR97	3.31	11	Warren	Thomas	28MAY07	1.28	1
Warren	John	22MAY97	1.27	1	Warren	Thomas	-----08	1.40	1
Warren	John	29JUN99	3.22	1	Warren	Thomas Jr	-----08	1.40	1
Warren	John	30JUN99	2.21	1	Warren	Thomas	10MAY09	2.35	1
Warren	John Jr	29JUN99	3.22	1	Warren	Thomas	05JUN09	2.35	1
Warren	John	20JUN00	1.15	1	Warren	Veter	26JUL04	1.22	11
Warran	John	05JUL00	3.32	1	Warren	William	06OCT87	1.06	1
Warren	John	07MAY01	3.36	1	Warren	William	09JUN89	6.07	1
Warren	John	07MAY01	3.36	1	Warren	William	10APR90	1.11	11
Warren	John	10JUN01	1.18	1	Warren	William	18JUL91	2.11	11
Warren	John	10JUN01	1.18	12	Warren	William	14SEP92	1.14	1
Warren	John Jr	11JUN01	1.18	1	Warren	William	05NOV92	1.14	1
Warren	John	14JUN02	1.24	1	Warrin	William Sr	01OCT93	3.12	1
Warren	John	10AUG02	3.29	1	Warrin	William Jr	27AUG93	3.12	1
Warren	John Jr	14JUN02	1.24	1	Warren	William Sr	18APR94	2.15	1
Warren	John Jr	24JUN02	1.25	1	Warren	William Sr	17JUN94	2.15	1
Warren	John	20JUL03	1.24	1	Warren	William Jr	18APR94	2.15	1
Warren	John	20JUL03	1.24	1	Warren	William Sr	19APR95	3.17	11
Warran	John	28JUL03	2.35	1	Warren	William	20MAY96	2.19	1
Warren	John Jr	20JUN03	1.25	1	Warren	William Sr	24MAY97	1.26	11
Warran	John	28JUN04	4.25	11	Warren	William Jr	24MAY97	1.26	1
Warran	John	03AUG04	1.22	1	Warren	William Sr	29JUN99	3.22	1
Warren	John	13AUG04	2.20	1	Warren	William Sr	29JUN99	3.21	11
Warran	John Jr	03AUG04	1.22	1	Warren	William Sr	05JUL00	3.33	11
Warren	John	11JUN05	1.22	1	Warren	William Jr	26JUN00	3.32	1
Warren	John	12JUN05	1.23	1	Warren	William Sr	06MAY01	3.36	1
Warran	John	20JUL05	2.35	1	Warren	William Jr	06MAY01	3.36	1
Warran	John	22JUL05	1.23	1	Warren	William Jr	12AUG02	3.29	1
Warren	John Jr	22JUL05	1.24	1	Warren	William Jr	12AUG02	3.29	1
Warren	John Sr	16JUN06	1.26	11	Warren	William	28JUL03	2.34	1
Warran	John	16JUN06	1.24	1	Warran	William	05AUG03	2.35	M1
Warren	John	15AUG06	2.39	1	Warran	William Jr	28JUL03	2.35	1
Warren	John Sr	28MAY07	1.28	11	Warran	William Sr	24JUL04	4.25	1
Warren	John Jr	28MAY07	1.28	1	Paid tax for James Warran				
Warren	John	16JUL07	2.37	1	Warran	William Sr	24JUL04	4.25	
Warren	John Sr	-----08	1.40	12	Paid tax for Samuel Warran				
Warren	John	-----08	2.29	1	Warran	William Sr	24JUL04	4.25	
Warren	John	24APR08	1.38	1	Paid tax for Thomas Warran				
Warren	John Sr	30JUN09	2.37	1	Warran	William	12JUN04	4.25	1
Warren	John	08JUN09	1.35	1	Warran	William	24JUL04	4.25	1
Warren	John	12JUN09	2.36	1	Warran	William	29JUN05	2.34	1
Warren	John Sr	-----11	1.85	1	Warran	William	20JUL05	2.34	1
Warren	John Jr	-----11	1.85	1	Warran	William Jr	29MAY05	2.34	1
Warren	John	-----11	1.83	1	Warran	William Sr	15AUG06	2.39	1
Warren	Martin	02APR90	1.11	1	Warran	William	13AUG06	2.39	1
Warren	Martin	08APR95	3.17	1	Warran	William	18AUG06	2.39	1
Warren	Martin	16JUL96	2.19	1	Warran	William Sr	16JUL07	2.37	1

surname	name	date	bk.pg	TM	surname	name	date	bk.pg	TM
Warren	William Jr	16JUL07	2.37	1	Waters	Samuel	17JUN05	2.34	1
Warren	William	18AUG07	2.39	1	Waters	Samuel	08AUG06	2.39	1
Warren	William	-----08	2.31	1	Waters	Samuel	16AUG09	1.36	1
Warren	William	-----08	2.30	1	Waters	Samuel	-----11	1.88	1
Warren	William	31MAY08	2.29	1	WATKINS				
Warren	William	08JUN09	1.35	1	Watkins	Berryman	28MAY95	2.13	1
Warren	William	19JUN09	1.35	1	Watkins	George	04AUG03	3.26	M1
Warren	William	09AUG09	1.36	1	Watkins	George	07APR04	4.24	1
Warren	William Sr	-----11	1.83	1	Watkins	George	26JUL06	3.35	1
Warren	William	-----11	1.85	1	Watkins	George	09MAY07	1.28	1
Warren	William	-----11	1.83	1	Watkins	George	04MAY08	1.38	1
Warren	William	-----11	1.88	1	Watkins	George	01JUL09	2.37	1
WARTON					Watkins	James	10JUN02	2.30	1
Warton	James	05APR91	1.09	1	Watkins	James	04AUG03	3.26	1
WASH					Watkins	James	07APR04	4.24	1
Wash	Benj.	23MAY89	6.07	1	Watkins	James	20JUN05	3.36	1
Wash	Benj.	03AUG90	1.11	1	Watkins	James	26JUL06	3.35	1
Wash	Benj.	01AUG91	2.11	1	Watkins	John	03JUN02	3.28	M1
Wash	Benj.	14SEP92	1.14	1	Watkins	John	04AUG03	3.26	1
Wash	Benj.	14AUG93	3.12	1	Watkins	John	05APR04	4.24	1
Wash	Benj.	10MAY94	2.15	11	Watkins	John	20JUN05	3.36	1
Wash	Benj.	10MAY95	3.17	11	Watkins	John	26JUL06	3.35	1
Wash	Benj.	05JUL96	2.20	1	Watkins	Robert	21MAY94	3.22	1
Wash	Benj. Sr	06JUN97	1.27	1	Watkins	Robert	-----95	1.14	1
Wash	Benj. Jr	06JUN97	1.27	1	Watkins	Robert	-----96	4.18	1
WASSEN					Watkins	Stephen	10JUN02	2.30	12
Wason	Henry	26JUN96	1.13	1	Watkins	Stephen	04AUG03	3.26	11
Wassen	Henry	30MAY97	3.32	1	Watkins	Stephen	05APR04	4.24	11
Wassen	John	30MAY97	3.32	1	Watkins	Stephen	20JUN05	3.36	11
Wassen	William	30MAY97	3.32	1	Watkins	Stephen	26JUL06	3.35	11
WATERS					Watkins	Willis	30MAR91	1.09	1
Water	Aaron	19JUN06	2.38	1	WATLEY				
Waters	Adamson	19JUN00	2.29	1	Watley	Wiley	18MAY95	3.17	1
Waters	Adamson	31JUL01	2.28	1	WATSON				
Waters	Adamson	07AUG02	3.29	1	Watson	James	08AUG06	3.37	1
Waters	Adamson	12JUL03	3.26	1	Watson	Michael	12JUN07	1.29	1
Waters	Adamson	22AUG04	2.20	1	Watson	Michael	05JUL09	2.37	1
Waters	Adamson	27JUN05	2.34	1	Watson	Thomas	14JUN02	1.23	1
Waters	Isaac	26JUN99	3.21	11	WATTS				
Waters	Isaac	20JUN00	3.31	1	Watts	John	-----93	2.06	1
Waters	Isaac	02MAY01	3.36	1	Watt	John	19JUN00	1.15	1
Waters	Isaac	05AUG02	3.29	1	Wats	John	13MAY09	2.35	1
Waters	John	25MAR91	1.09	1	WEATHERFORD				
Waters	John	21JUN00	3.31	M1	WeatherfordAbel		01JUN03	2.33	1
Waters	John	05AUG02	3.29	1	WeatherfordAbel		20MAY05	2.33	1
Waters	John	04AUG03	2.35	1	WeatherfordAbel		20MAY05	2.33	1
Watters	John	08JUN04	4.25	1	WeatherfordAbell		06APR06	2.37	1
Waters	John	17JUN05	2.34	1	WeatherfordAbel		15JUN07	2.37	1
Waters	John	18AUG06	2.39	11	Weather Abel		-----08	1.39	1
Waters	John	20JUN07	2.37	1	WeatherfordAbel		06JUL09	2.37	1
Waters	John	31MAY08	2.29	1	WeatherfordAbel		-----11	1.86	1
Waters	John	16AUG09	1.36	1	Wetherford Archebald		12MAY94	1.09	1
Waters	Joseph	25JUN99	3.21	1	WeatherfordArchibald		20MAY95	2.13	1
Waters	Joseph	23JUL00	2.29	1	Watherford Archebald		08JUN96	1.13	1
Waters	Joseph	27MAY01	3.38	1	WeatherfordArchibald		19APR97	3.31	1
Waters	Joseph	03AUG02	2.30	1	WeatherfordArchibald		08JUL00	2.29	1
Waters	Joseph	20MAY03	3.25	1	WeatherfordArchibald		28MAY01	2.27	1
Waters	Joseph	07AUG04	3.21	1	WeatherfordArchibald		14JUN02	3.28	12
Waters	Joseph	05AUG05	3.36	1	WeatherfordArchibald		13JUN03	2.33	12
Waters	Joseph	08AUG06	3.36	1	WeatherfordArchabald		-----08	1.40	11
Waters	Martha	17JUN05	2.34	F	WeatherfordArchabold		20AUG09	2.37	1
Waters	Martha	20JUN07	2.37	F	WeatherfordArchibald		-----11	1.87	3
Waters	Martha	-----08	2.30	F	Wetherford Ardhibald		11JUN09	1.38	1
Waters	Martha	16AUG09	1.36	F	WeatherfordDavid		28JUN03	1.25	1
Waters	Nathen	16JUL07	2.37	1	WeatherfordDavid		19JUN04	1.21	1
Waters	Nathen	31MAY08	2.29	1	WeatherfordElijah		-----08	1.40	1
Waters	Nathaniel	16AUG09	1.36	1	WeatherfordElijah		20AUG09	2.37	1
Waters	Patey	04AUG03	2.35	F	WeatherfordGeorge		04AUG00	2.30	1
Waters	Samuel	05JUN01	3.37	1	WeatherfordGeorge		27JUN01	2.27	1
Waters	Samuel	07AUG02	3.29	1	WeatherfordGeorge		03JUN02	3.28	1
Waters	Samuel	04AUG03	2.35	1	WeatherfordGeorge		17JUN03	2.33	1
Waters	Samuel	28JUN04	4.25	1	WeatherfordGeorge		06APR04	4.24	1

surname	name	date	bk.pg TM	surname	name	date	bk.pg TM
Wetherford	George	20JUN05	3.36 1	Weldon	John	26JUL05	1.24 1
Weatherford	George	26JUL06	3.35 1	Wheeldon	John	12JUN07	1.29 1
Weatherford	Hardin	01JUN03	2.33 11	Weldon	John	30MAY09	2.35 1
Weatherford	Harden	-----11	1.87 1	Wheldon	John	-----11	1.87 M1
Weather	James	-----93	2.06 1	Welden	Josiah	24JUN99	1.37 1
Weatherford	Joel	-----08	1.39 11	WELLS			
Wetherford	John	01JUN99	1.38 1	Wells	Anthony	30JUL03	2.35 1
Weatherford	John	24MAY00	2.29 1	Welles	John	13JUN97	3.32 1
Weatherford	John	04APR01	2.27 11	Wells	John	24MAY02	3.28 1
Weatherford	John	07JUN02	3.28 1	Wells	Sittleberry	-----96	4.19 1
Weatherford	John	18JUL03	1.26 1	Wells	William	03APR90	2.07 1
Wetherford	John	12JUN04	2.19 11	Wells	William	26JUL02	3.28
Weatherford	John	03JUN05	3.35 11	Exempt from county leavy			
Weatherford	John	18JUL06	3.34 11	WELSH			
Wetherford	John	31MAY08	2.29 11	Welch	Ephrem	10AUG02	2.30 1
Watherford	Money	01JUN96	1.13 1	Welsh	George	17SEP91	3.17 1
Wetherford	Money	12JUN97	3.32 1	Welch	George	16NOV92	3.20 1
Weatherford	Money	24MAY99	3.21 1	Welch	George	21MAY94	3.22 1
Weatherford	Money	24MAY00	2.29 1	Welch	George	10MAR95	1.15
Weatherford	Money	04APR01	2.27 1	"Gone to Franklin County"			
Weatherford	Money	17JUN02	3.28 1	Welch	James	11JUN89	6.09 1
Weatherford	Money	01JUN03	2.33 1	Welch	James	30JUL90	1.11 1
Wetherford	Money	13AUG04	2.20 1	Welch	James	18MAR91	2.11 1
Weatherford	Money	29JUN05	2.34 1	Welch	James	22SEP92	1.13 1
Weatherford	Money	18MAY06	2.37 1	Welsh	James	10AUG93	3.12 1
Weather	William	-----93	2.06 1	Wellch	James	14JUN94	2.15 1
Weatheringt	William	24JUL04	4.26 1	Wellch	James	10APR95	3.18 1
WEBB				Welsh	James	02AUG06	2.38 1
Webb	Isaac	-----08	2.30 1	Welsh	James	12JUN07	1.29 1
Webb	Isaac	22JUN09	1.35 1	Welsh	James	24APR08	1.38 1
Webb	Jesse	03AUG02	2.30 1	Welsh	James	08JUN09	2.36 1
Webb	Jessee	06JUN03	3.25 11	Welsh	James	-----11	1.84 1
Webb	Jesse	22AUG04	3.22 11	Welch	John	10JUN95	2.13 1
Webb	Jesse	14AUG05	3.37 1	Welch	John	27JUN96	1.13
Webb	Jesse	04AUG06	3.36 11	One town lot in Stanford			
Webb	Joel	07JUL03	3.25 1	Walch	John+4com	27JUN96	1.13 42
Webb	Joel	06AUG04	3.21 1	One retail store			
Webb	Joal	14AUG05	3.37 1	Welsh	John/Cox	13JUN97	3.33
Webb	Joal	04AUG06	3.36 1	One town lot in Frankfort			
Webb	Townsend	14AUG05	3.37 M1	Welsh	John/Cox	13JUN97	3.33
Webb	Townend	08AUG06	3.36 1	One town lot in Stanford			
WEBER				Welsh	John	13JUN97	3.33 1
Weber	Phillip	14AUG93	1.10 1	Welsh	John	10JUN03	3.25 1
Webber	Phillip	29MAY94	1.09 1	Welsh	John	24AUG04	3.22 1
WEBSTER				Walsh	John	17JUN05	3.17
Webster	William	03NOV92	1.14 1	Pd tax for John Barnett (heirs)			
Webster	William	28AUG03	3.12 1	Welsh	John	09AUG05	3.37 1
Webster	William	12JUN94	2.15 1	Welsh	John	18JUL06	3.35 1
Webster	William	21APR95	3.17 1	Welsh	John	02AUG06	2.38 1
Webster	William	17MAY96	2.19 1	Walsh	John	23AUG06	3.18
Webster	William	29JUN97	1.27 1	Admin. for John Barnett (decd)			
Webster	William	11JUL99	3.22 1	Welsh	John	11JUN07	2.36 1
Webster	William	10JUL00	3.33 1	Welsh	John	12JUN07	1.29 1
Webster	William	30JUL01	3.37 1	Walsh	John	22JUN07	2.16
Webster	William	29JUL02	3.28 1	Paid tax for John Barnett (Decd)			
Webster	William	10AUG03	2.35 1	Wals	John	-----08	1.39 1
Webster	William	08JUN04	4.25 1	Welsh	John	24APR08	1.38 1
Webster	William	21JUN05	2.34 1	Welsh	John	31MAY08	2.29 1
Webster	William	30JUL06	2.38 11	Walsh	John	18JUL08	2.14
WELAND				Paid tax for John Barnett (decd)			
Weland	Joshua	15AUG07	2.39 1	Walsh	John	05JUN09	1.17
Wyland	Josiah	-----08	2.30 2	Paid tax for John Barnett (decd)			
Weeland	Joshua	09JUN09	1.35 1	Welsh	John	08JUN09	2.36 1
WELDON				Welsh	John	11JUL09	1.36 1
Welldon	Cornelias	10JUN02	1.24 1	Welsh	John	-----11	1.85 1
Welldon	Cornelias	29JUN03	1.25 1	Welsh	John	-----11	1.88 1
Welden	John	24JUN99	1.37 1	Welsh	Jos./Thos.	14JUN00	2.29 2
Weldon	John	14JUN00	2.29 1	One lott in Frankford			
Weldon	John	24JUL01	2.27 1	Welsh	Jos./Thos.	14JUN00	2.29
Welldon	John	10JUL02	1.24 1	Two lotts in Standford			
Weldon	John	07JUL03	1.26 1	Welsh	Joseph/Thos	28MAY01	2.27 2
Weldon	John	28JUL04	2.19 1	Half lott in Frankfort			

surname	name	date	bk.pg	TM	surname	name	date	bk.pg	TM
Welsh	Joseph/Thos	28MAY01	2.27		Wite	David	26NOV92	3.20	1
One lott in Standford					White	David	21MAY94	3.22	1
Welsh	Jos./Thos.	17JUN02	1.24	2	White	David	-----95	1.14	1
Welch	Jos./Thos.	11JUL03	1.26	2	White	David	-----96	4.18	11
Welsh	Jos./Thos.	18JUN04	2.19	2	White	George	25JUN87	3.11	1
Weltch	Jos./Thos.	20AUG05	1.24	2	White	George	02OCT87	1.06	1
Welsh	Jos./Thos.	12JUN07	1.29	2	White	George	26MAY89	6.07	1
Welsh	Jos./Thos.	23AUG09	2.38	2	White	George	27JUN89	2.14	1
Welsh	Jos./Thos.	-----11	1.86	2	White	George	18JUN90	1.11	1
Welch	Joseph	10MAY94	2.16	1	White	George	16APR91	2.11	1
Wellch	Joseph	10APR95	3.18	1	White	George	03NOV92	1.14	1
Welch	Joseph	10JUN95	2.13	1	White	George	27AUG93	3.12	1
Welch	Joseph	27JUN96	1.13	1	White	George	02MAY95	3.17	1
Welch	Joseph	05JUL96	2.20	2	White	George	10AUG97	1.28	11
Welsh	Joseph	31MAY97	1.27	1	White	George	10JUL99	3.22	11
Welsh	Joseph	13JUN97	3.33	1	White	George	09JUL00	3.33	11
Welsh	Joseph	13MAY99	3.21	1	White	George	31JUL01	3.37	1
Welsh	Joseph	24MAY99	1.38	2	White	George	29JUL02	3.28	1
Welsh	Joseph	24MAY99	1.39		White	George	09AUG03	2.35	1
one lott in Stanford					White	George	06JUN04	4.24	1
Welsh	Joseph	18JUN00	3.31	11	White	George	19JUN05	2.34	1
Welsh	Joseph	17JUN01	3.37	11	White	George	30JUL06	2.38	1
Welsh	Joseph	27JUL02	3.28	11	White	James	13JUL96	2.19	1
Welsh	Joseph	12AUG03	2.35	1	White	James	16MAY97	1.27	1
Welch	Joseph	05JUN04	4.24	1	White	James	09AUG03	2.35	1
Welsh	Joseph	27JUN05	2.34	11	White	James	06JUN04	4.24	1
Welsh	Joseph	02AUG06	2.38	11	White	James	19JUN05	2.34	1
Welsh	Joseph	20JUN07	2.37	12	White	James	30JUL06	2.38	1
Welsh	Joseph	31MAY08	2.29	11	White	Jesse	11JUN89	6.07	1
Welsh	Joseph	13JUL09	1.36	12	White	Jesse	23JUN91	2.11	1
Welsh	Joseph	-----11	1.86	1	White	John	03AUG90	1.11	1
Welch	Nicholas	18JUN95	2.25	1	White	Randolph	10JUL99	3.22	1
Welsh	Shared	-----11	1.88	1	Whight	Randolph	10JUL00	3.33	1
Welch	Thomas	10JUN95	2.13	1	White	Randolph	31JUL01	3.37	1
Welch	Thomas	27JUN96	1.13	1	White	Randolph	29JUL02	3.28	1
Welsh	Thomas	13JUN97	3.33	1	White	Randolph	09AUG03	2.35	1
Welsh	Thos./James	-----08	1.39	2	White	Randolph	08JUN04	4.25	1
Welsh	William	16JUL06	3.34	1	White	Randolph	10JUN05	2.34	1
Walsh	William	17AUG07	2.39	1	White	Randolph	30JUL06	2.38	1
Welsh	William	-----08	2.30	1	White	William	22JUN99	2.22	1
Welsh	William	31MAY08	2.29	1	White	William	31MAY08	2.29	1
WESE					White	William	26JUN09	1.36	1
Wese	Zillip	25MAR91	1.09	1	White	William	-----11	1.88	1
WEST					White	Wilson	13JUL07	2.37	1
West	Jepthee	16JUN06	1.26	1	WHITEHEAD				
West	Jeptath	11JUN07	1.29	1	Whitehead	Robert	30MAY97	3.32	1
West	Joseph	19APR91	3.16	1	Whitehead	William	11JUL99	3.22	1
West	Joseph	16NOV92	3.20	1	Whitehead	William	11JUL00	3.33	1
West	Joseph	29MAY94	3.21	1	Whitehead	William	30JUL01	3.37	1
West	Joseph	-----95	1.14	1	Whitehead	William	29JUL02	3.29	1
West	Joseph	-----96	4.19	1	Whitehead	William	10AUG03	2.35	1
West	William	26JUL06	3.35	1	Whitehead	William	08JUN04	4.24	1
West	William	13JUL09	1.34	11	Whitehead	William	20JUN05	2.34	1
West	William	-----11	1.88	11	Whitehead	William	30JUL06	2.38	1
WESTERVILL					WHITEHOUSE				
Westervill	James	-----93	2.06	1	Whitehouse	Thomas	31MAY08	2.29	1
WHELAN					WHITESIDES				
Wheeland	William	11JUN07	2.37	1	Whitesides	Jean	18AUG07	2.39	F1
WHEELER					Whiteside	John	23MAR90	2.07	1A
Wheeler	James	-----08	2.30	1	Whiteside	John	02OCT92	2.09	1
WHELES					Whiteside	John	30AUG93	1.09	1
Wheles	Thomas	17JUN97	3.33	1	Whiteside	John	21MAY94	1.09	1
WHITAKER					Whiteside	John	01JUN95	2.13	1
Whitticar	Abraham	07JUL03	3.25	1	Whiteside	John	15MAY97	3.32	1
Whitaker	Abraham	22AUG04	3.22	1	Whitesides	John	14JUN99	2.22	1
WHITE					Whiteside	John	24JUL00	1.16	1
White	Andrew	30MAR90	2.07	1	Whitesides	John	26JUN01	1.19	1
White	Benjamin	18AUG07	2.39	1	Whitesides	John	23JUN02	1.25	1
White	Benjamin	-----08	1.40	1	Whitesides	John	22JUN03	1.25	1
White	Dabney	21MAY99	1.38	1	Whitesides	John	02AUG04	1.22	1
White	Daniel	25MAR90	2.07	1	Whitsid	Thomas	27MAY94	1.09	1
White	David	19APR91	3.16	1	Whiteside	Thomas	05MAY07	1.27	11

surname	name	date	bk.pg	TM	surname	name	date	bk.pg	TM
Whitesides	William	02AUG04	1.22	1	Whittle	John	08AUG06	3.36	1
Whiteside	William	-----08	2.30	1	Whittle	John Jr	04AUG06	3.36	1
WHITLEY					Whittle	Ninion	30JUN97	1.28	1
Whitley	Andrew	12JUN07	1.29	1	Whittle	Vincent	05AUG06	3.36	1
Whitley	Andrew	24APR08	1.38	1	WHITTON				
Whitley	James	22JUN89	5.12	1	Whitton	Anna	14MAY90	1.11	F1
Whitley	James	22MAY90	2.07	1	Whitton	Ann	21JUN91	2.11	F
Whitley	James	14APR91	1.09	1	Whitton	Elijah	23MAY94	2.15	1
Whitley	James	21JUN05	2.34	1	Whitten	Elijah	17MAY95	3.18	1
Whitley	James	30JUL06	2.38	1	Whitten	Elijah	05JUL96	2.20	1
Wheetley	Nicholas	08AUG06	3.36	1	Whitten	Elisha	05JUN97	1.28	1
Whitley	Solomon	11JUN01	1.19	1	WIGGASON				
Whitley	Solomon	02AUG04	2.20	1	Wiggason	Peter	12MAY99	2.21	1
Whitley	Solomon	22JUL05	1.23	1	Wiggason	Peter	01JUN01	1.18	1
Whitley	Solaman	12JUN07	1.29	1	WILBURN				
Whitley	Solaman	24APR08	1.38	1	Wilburn	Samuel	14JUN03	3.25	1
Whitley	Solaman	08JUN09	2.36	1	Wilburn	Samuel	07AUG04	3.21	1
Whitley	Solomon	-----11	1.85	1	Wilburn	Samuel	14AUG05	3.37	1
Wheatley	Thomas	25JUN87	3.11	1	Wilburn	Samuel	08AUG06	3.37	1
Whitley	Thomas	13AUG89	2.14	1	WILCHER				
Whitley	Thomas	02JUN91	3.16	1	Wilcher	Charles	19JUN04	1.21	1
Whitley	Thomas	07DEC92	3.20	1	Wilcher	Charles	11JUN05	1.23	1
Whitley	Thomas	21MAY94	3.22	1	Welcher	Charles	11JUN07	1.29	1
Whitley	William	12JUN87	2.07	1	Welcher	Charles	-----08	1.40	1
Whitley	William	04NOV88	1.11	1	Welcher	Charles	05JUN09	2.35	1
Whitley	William	04JUL89	5.12	1	Welcher	John	11JUN07	1.29	1
Whitley	William	22MAY90	2.07	1	Welcher	John	-----08	1.40	1
Whitley	William	14APR91	1.09	1	Welcher	John	05JUN09	2.35	1
Whitley	William	14OCT92	2.09	11	Wilcher	John	-----11	1.85	1
Whitley	William	13AUG93	1.10	11	Welcher	Joseph	19JUN04	1.21	11
Whitley	William	29MAY94	1.09	11	Wilcher	Joseph	11JUN05	1.23	1
Whitley	William	04JUN95	2.13	1	Wilcher	Joseph	18MAY07	1.28	1
Whitley	William	29JUN96	1.13	1	Welcher	Joseph	-----08	1.39	1
Whitley	William	15MAY97	3.32	11	Welcher	Joseph	05JUN09	2.35	1
Whitley	William	29JUN99	2.21	12	Wilcher	Joseph	-----11	1.85	1
Whitley	William	19JUN00	1.15	12	WILCOTT				
Whitley	William	11JUN01	1.18	11	Wilcot	Barnibas	18JUN04	2.19	1
Whitley	William	14JUN02	1.23	12	Wilcott	Barnibas	03JUN05	3.35	1
Whitley	William	28JUN03	1.25	12	Wilcot	Barnibas	26JUL06	3.35	11
Whitley	William	02AUG04	2.20	11	WILCOX				
Whitley	William Jr	02AUG04	2.20	1	Wilcox	George	20JUN87	2.07	1
Whitley	William	22JUL05	1.23	11	Wilcox	Isaac	20JUN87	2.07	1
Whitley	William Jr	22JUL05	1.23	1	Wilcock	John	23MAY94	3.21	1
Whitley	William	29MAY07	1.28	1	Wilcock	John	-----95	1.14	1
Whitley	William	12JUN07	1.29	1	WILEY				
Whitley	William	-----08	1.41	1	Wiley	Aquilla	26JUN87	1.06	1
Whitley	William	24APR08	1.38	1	Wiley	Aquilla	18APR89	6.07	1
Whitley	William Sr	08JUN09	2.36	1	Wylie	Aquilla	10APR90	1.11	1
Whitley	William Jr	06JUN09	2.36	1	Wilye	Acquilla	17MAY91	2.11	1
Whitley	William Sr	-----11	1.85	1	Wilye	Acquilla	12SEP92	1.13	1
Whitley	William Jr	-----11	1.85	1	Wilye	Aquilla	08AUG93	3.12	1
WHITTING					Wiley	Aquiley	17APR94	2.16	1
Whitting	Charles	06AUG89	5.12	1	Wiley	Equiley	19MAR95	3.18	1
WHITTLE					Wiley	Equily	20APR96	2.19	1
Whittle	John	22MAY94	2.15	11	Wyle	Aquilla	30MAY97	1.27	1
Whittle	John	29APR95	3.17	11	Wyle	Aquilla	15JUL99	3.22	1
Whittle	John	13JUL96	2.20	21	Wiley	Aquila	25JUN00	3.32	1
Whittle	John	30JUN97	1.27	1	Willey	Aquilla	07MAY01	3.36	1
Whittle	John	30JUN97	1.27	11	Wiley	Aquilla	12AUG02	3.29	1
Whittle	John Sr	14MAY99	3.21	1	Wiley	Aquila	26JUL03	2.34	1
Whittle	John Jr	13MAY99	3.21	1	Wiley	Quiller	24JUL04	4.26	1
Whittle	John Sr	18JUN00	3.31	12	Wiley	Aquilla	29MAY05	2.34	1
Whittle	John Sr	27MAY01	3.38	11	Wiley	Aquila	02AUG06	2.38	2
Whittle	John	17JUN01	3.37	1	Wiley	Aquila	03AUG07	2.39	2
Whittle	John Sr	10AUG02	2.31	11	Wilye	Benj.	12SEP92	1.13	1
Whittle	John Jr	10AUG02	2.30	1	Listed as	"son of William Wilye"			
Whittle	John Sr	11JUL03	3.26	12	Wilye	Ben.	08AUG93	3.12	1
Whittle	John Jr	25JUN03	3.26	1	Listed as	"son of William Wilye"			
Whittle	John Sr	06AUG04	3.21	11	Wiley	Ben.	16APR94	2.16	1
Whittle	John Jr	07AUG04	3.21	1	Listed as	"son of William Wiley"			
Whittle	John Sr	05AUG05	3.36	1	Wiley	Benj.	16OCT87	1.06	1
Whittle	John	05AUG05	3.36	1	Wiley	Benj.	16MAY89	6.09	1

surname	name	date	bk.pg	TM
Wiley	Benj.	26JUN89	6.07	1
Wylie	Benj.	21APR90	1.11	1
Wylie	Benj.	21MAY90	1.11	21
Joshua Wylie listed with him				
Wylie	Benj. Jr	02AUG90	1.11	1
Wilye	Benj.	17MAY91	2.11	1
Wilye	Benj.	17MAY91	2.11	1
Wilye	Benj.	12SEP92	1.13	1
Wilye	Benj. Jr	12SEP92	1.13	1
Wilye	Benj. Sr	08AUG93	3.12	1
Wilye	Benj. Jr	08AUG93	3.12	1
Wiley	Benj. Sr	17APR94	2.16	1
Wiley	Benj. Jr	17APR94	2.16	1
Wiley	Benj. Sr	19MAR95	3.18	1
Wiley	Benj. Jr	18APR95	3.17	1
Wiley	Benj.	20MAY96	2.19	1
Wiley	Benj.	16JUL96	2.20	1
Wyle	Benj.	30MAY97	1.26	1
Wyle	Benj. Sr	15JUL99	3.22	1
Wyle	Benj. Jr	15JUL99	3.22	1
Wiley	Benj. Sr	25JUN00	3.31	11
Wiley	Benj. Jr	25JUN00	3.31	1
Willey	Benjamin	07MAY01	3.36	2
Wiley	Benjamin	10AUG02	3.29	1
Wiley	Benjamin	26JUL03	2.34	2
Wylie	James	21MAY90	1.11	
Listed with William Wylie				
Wiley	James	10APR94	2.15	1
Wiley	James	18MAR95	3.18	1
Wiley	John	28MAR91	1.09	1
Wiley	John	01NOV92	2.09	11
Wiley	John	15AUG93	1.09	11
Willey	John	23MAY94	1.09	11
Wyley	John	13JUN96	1.13	1
Wyle	John	15MAY97	1.26	1
Wyle	John	12JUL99	3.22	1
Wiley	John	10AUG02	3.29	1
Wiley	John	05JUN04	4.24	1
Wiley	John	28JUN05	2.34	1
Wiley	John	24JUL05	2.35	1
Wiley	John	18JUL06	2.37	1
Wiley	John	18JUL06	2.38	1
Wiley	John	13AUG07	2.38	1
Wiley	John	-----08	2.30	11
Wyley	John	23AUG09	2.37	1
Wiley	John	-----11	1.87	1
Wylie	Joshua	21MAY90	1.11	
Listed with Benj. Wylie				
Wilye	Joshua	25JUN91	2.11	1
Wilye	Joshua	12SEP92	1.13	1
Wilye	Joshua	08AUG93	3.12	1
Wiley	Joshua	18APR94	2.16	1
Wiley	Joshua	10MAR95	3.18	1
Wiley	Joshua	20MAY96	2.19	1
Wyle	Joshua	15MAY97	1.27	1
Wyle	Joshua	30MAY97	1.26	1
Wyle	Joshua	15JUL99	3.22	1
Wiley	Joshua	25JUN00	3.31	1
Wiley	Joshua	12AUG02	3.29	1
Wiley	Joshua	14AUG07	2.39	1
Wiley	Josiah	13JUN96	1.13	1
Wylie	Luke	21MAY90	1.11	1
Wilye	Walter	17MAY91	2.11	1
Wilye	Walter	21SEP92	1.14	1
Wilye	Walter	09AUG93	3.12	1
Wiley	Walter	05MAY94	2.16	1
Wiley	Walter	09APR95	3.18	1
Wiley	Walter	15JUL96	2.19	11
Wyle	Walter	30MAY97	1.26	1
Wyle	Walter	16JUL99	3.23	1
Wiley	Walter	05JUL00	3.32	1
Wiley	William	12MAY89	6.07	1

surname	name	date	bk.pg	TM
Wylie	William	21MAY90	1.11	3
James Wylie listed with him				
Wylie	William	21MAY90	1.11	
William Wylie listed with him				
Wilye	William	12SEP92	1.13	
Father of Benj. Wilye				
Wilye	William	08AUG93	3.12	
Father of Ben. Wilye				
Wiley	William	16APR94	2.16	
Father of Ben. Wiley				
Wylie	Zachariah	21MAY90	1.11	1
WILHOIT				
Wilhite	Aaron	16JUL07	2.37	11
Wilhite	Aaron	-----08	2.30	12
Willhoit	Aaron	08JUN09	1.35	1
Wilhort	Joseph	18JUL06	2.37	1
Wilhite	Joseph	-----08	2.30	1
Willhoit	Joseph	08JUN09	1.35	1
Wilhoit	Joseph	-----11	1.86	11
Witthorst	Lewis	25JUL03	2.33	1
Willhite	Lewis	27JUL04	4.24	1
Willhoit	Lewis	13MAY05	2.33	1
Willhort	Lewis	22MAR06	2.37	1
Wilhite	Lewis	-----08	2.30	11
Willhoit	Lewis	13JUL09	1.34	11
Wilhoit	Louis	-----11	1.88	11
Wilhite	Samson	04AUG96	2.20	1
WILKERSON				
Wilkerson	John	20JUN87	2.07	1
Wilkerson	John	06NOV88	1.11	1
Wilkins	John	26JUN89	6.07	1
Wilkerson	John	30JUN89	5.12	1
Wilkins	John	20APR90	1.11	1
Wilkinson	John	01JUN90	2.07	1
Wilkins	John	31MAR91	2.11	1
Wilkeson	John	10OCT92	2.09	1
Wilkens	John	13OCT92	2.09	1
Wilkinson	John	20AUG93	1.09	1
Wilkans	John	20AUG93	1.09	11
Wilkenson	John	28MAY94	1.09	1
Wilkins	John	29MAY94	3.21	1
Wilkenson	John	29MAY94	1.09	1
Wilkinson	John	03JUN95	2.13	1
Wilkinson	John	16JUN96	1.13	1
Wilkison	John	06APR97	3.32	1
Wilkison	John	17JUN99	1.37	11
Wilkinson	John	30MAY00	2.29	11
Wilkinson	John	22JUL01	2.27	11
Wilkenson	John	15JUN02	1.24	1
Wilkinson	John	04JUL03	1.26	1
Wilkenson	John	15JUN04	1.21	11
Wilkenson	John	17JUN05	1.23	11
Wilkerson	John	10JUN07	1.28	1
Wilkerson	John	10JUN07	1.28	11
Wilkerson	John	-----08	1.39	1
Wilkerson	John	05JUL09	2.37	1
Wilkerson	John	-----11	1.84	1
Wilkerson	William	-----08	1.39	1
Wilkerson	William	-----11	1.84	1
WILLIAMS				
Williams	Beverly	06AUG90	1.11	1
Williams	Burd	04AUG03	3.26	1
Williams	Bird	06APR04	4.24	1
Williams	Bird	26JUL06	3.35	1
Williams	Charles	20AUG87	1.06	1
Williams	Charles	12MAY89	6.07	1
William	Charles	21MAY90	1.11	1
Williams	Charles	17MAY91	2.11	1
Williams	Charles	12SEP92	1.13	1
Williams	Charles	05AUG93	3.12	1
Williams	Charles	05MAY94	2.16	1
Williams	Charles	31MAR95	3.18	1

surname	name	date	bk.pg	TM	surname	name	date	bk.pg	TM
Williams	Charles	04MAY96	2.19	1	Williams	John	-----97	2.06	1
Williams	Charles	24JUN00	3.31	11	Williams	John	01JUN97	3.32	1
Williams	Charles	07MAY01	3.36	11	Williams	John	22JUN97	1.27	1
Williams	Charles	10AUG02	3.29	11	Williams	John	18MAY99	2.22	1
Williams	Charles	30JUL03	2.35	11	Williams	John	25JUN99	1.38	1
Williams	Charles	29JUN04	4.25	1	Williams	John	23JUN00	1.16	1
Williams	David	12JUN89	6.08	1	Williams	John	29JUL00	2.30	11
Williams	David	13MAY90	1.11	12	Williams	John	02JUN01	1.18	1
Williams	David	24JUN91	2.11	11	Williams	John	21JUL01	3.38	11
Williams	David	05OCT92	1.14	11	Williams	John	11JUN02	2.30	11
Williams	David	20AUG93	3.12	12	Williams	John	05AUG03	3.26	11
Williams	David	12JUN94	2.15	21	Williams	John	03AUG04	3.20	1
Williams	David	28APR95	3.17	11	Williams	John	11JUN05	1.22	1
Williams	David	12MAY96	2.19	2	Williams	John	22JUN05	3.36	1
Williams	David Sr	20JUN97	1.27	11	Williams	John	10JUN06	1.26	1
Williams	David	05JUN99	1.38	1	Williams	John(decd)	22JUL06	3.34	D
Williams	David Sr	22JUL00	2.29	1	Tax paid by Isaac Williams				
Williams	David Jr	22JUL00	2.29	1	Williams	John	06JUN07	1.28	1
Williams	David Sr	20JUL01	3.38	1	Williams	John	-----08	1.40	1
Williams	David Jr	20JUL01	3.38	1	Williams	John	08MAY09	2.35	1
Williams	David Sr	01JUN02	2.29	1	Williams	John	-----11	1.85	1
Williams	David Jr	01JUN02	2.29	1	Williams	John	-----11	1.86	1
Williams	David Sr	31MAY03	3.25	1	Williams	Joseph	25JUN00	2.29	1
Williams	David Jr	31MAY03	3.25	1	Williams	Joseph	13JUL01	3.38	1
Williams	David	11JUN03	3.25	1	Williams	Joseph	05AUG02	2.30	1
Williams	David Sr	01AUG04	3.20	1	Williams	Joseph	16JUL03	3.26	1
Williams	David Jr	01AUG04	3.20	1	Williams	Joseph	16JUN04	2.19	1
William	David	14JUN05	3.35	1	Williams	Joseph	13AUG05	3.37	1
Williams	David	14JUN05	3.36	1	Williams	Joseph	07AUG06	3.36	1
Williams	David Sr	16JUL06	3.34	1	Williams	Mary	16SEP91	3.17	F
Williams	David Sr	20JUN07	2.37	12	Williams	Mary	31MAY97	3.32	F1
Williams	David Jr	20JUN07	2.37	1	Williams	Ralph	-----96	4.18	1
William	David Sr	31MAY08	2.29	1	Williams	Ralph	-----97	2.06	1
Williams	David	30MAY08	2.29	1	Williams	Ralph	25JUN99	2.21	1
Williams	David Sr	30JUN09	1.36	1	Williams	Robert	01JUN97	3.32	1
Williams	David	26JUN09	1.35	1	Williams	Robert	05AUG02	2.30	1
Williams	David Sr	-----11	1.88	1	Williams	Robet	07AUG04	2.20	1
William	David	-----11	1.88	1	Williams	Robert	17JUN05	1.23	1
Williams	Elijah	07JUL89	2.15	1	Williams	Samuel	01JUN97	3.32	1
Williams	Elijah	02JUN91	3.16	1	Williams	Samuel	20JUN97	1.27	1
Williams	Elijah	10OCT92	3.20	1	Williams	Samuel	20JUL01	3.38	1
Williams	Elijah	23MAY94	3.21	1	Williams	Samuel	14JUN02	2.30	1
Williams	Elijah	-----95	1.14	1	Williams	Samuel	31MAY03	3.25	1
Williams	Isaac	25SEP92	1.14	1	Williams	Samuel	04AUG04	3.21	1
Williams	Isaac	17AUG93	3.12	1	Williams	Samuel	10JUN05	3.35	1
Williams	Isaac	04AUG04	3.20	1	Williams	Samuel	18JUL06	3.34	1
Williams	Isaac	22JUN05	3.36	1	Williams	Samuel	03AUG07	2.39	1
Williams	Isaac	22JUL06	3.34	1	Williams	Samuel	-----08	2.30	1
Paid tax for John(decd) Williams					Williams	Samuel	10JUL09	1.36	1
Williams	Isaac	13JUL09	1.34	1	Williams	Samuel	-----11	1.86	1
Williams	Isaac	13JUL09	1.34	1	Williams	Thomas Sr	25JUN87	3.10	1
Williams	Isaac	-----11	1.87	1	Williams	Thomas Jr	25JUN87	3.10	1
Williams	James	12APR97	3.31	1	Williams	Thomas Sr	13AUG89	2.14	1
Williams	James	01JUN97	3.32	1	Williams	Thomas Jr	13AUG89	2.14	1
Williams	James	09AUG03	2.35	1	Williams	Thomas	16SEP91	3.17	1
Williams	James	07APR04	4.24	1	Williams	Thomas	07DEC92	3.20	1
Williams	James	20JUN05	3.36	1	Williams	Thomas	-----93	2.06	1
Williams	James	26JUL06	3.35	1	Williams	Thomas	29MAY94	3.21	1
Williams	John	25JUN87	3.10	1	Williams	Thomas	-----95	1.14	1
Williams	John	13AUG89	2.14	1	Williams	Thomas	-----96	4.18	1
Williams	John	13AUG89	2.14	1	Williams	Thomas	-----97	2.06	1
Williams	John	05MAY91	3.16	1	Williams	Thomas	22JUN97	1.27	1
Williams	John	16SEP91	3.17	1	Williams	Thomas	24MAY99	3.21	1
Williams	John	26NOV92	3.20	1	Williams	Thomas	25JUN99	1.38	1
Williams	John	01DEC92	3.20	1	Williams	Thomas	09JUL99	2.22	11
Williams	John	07DEC92	3.20	1	Williams	Thomas	17JUN00	1.15	11
Williams	John	-----93	2.06	1	Williams	Thomas	11JUL00	3.33	1
Williams	John	21AUG93	1.10	1	Williams	Thomas	29JUL00	2.30	1
Williams	John	29MAY94	3.21	1	Williams	Thomas	04JUN01	1.18	11
Williams	John	-----95	1.14	1	Williams	Thomas	21JUL01	3.38	1
Williams	John	28MAY95	2.13	1	Williams	Thomas	30JUL01	3.37	1
Williams	John	-----96	4.18	1	Williams	Thomas	10JUN02	2.29	1

surname	name	date	bk.pg	TM	surname	name	date	bk.pg	TM
Williams	Thomas	12JUL02	2.30	1	Willibough	William	29APR95	3.17	1
Williams	Thomas	05AUG03	3.26	1	Willibough	William	05JUL96	2.20	1
Williams	Thomas	05AUG03	3.26	1	Willoughby	William	05JUN97	1.27	1
Williams	Thomas	06APR04	4.24	1	Willoughby	William	25MAY99	3.21	1
Williams	Thomas	29JUN04	4.25	1	Willeby	William	18JUN00	3.31	1
Williams	Thomas	15AUG04	3.22	1	Willoughby	William	19JUN01	3.37	1
Williams	Thomas	20JUN05	3.36	1	Willoughby	William	28JUL02	3.28	1
Williams	Thomas	22JUN05	3.36	1	Willoughby	William	12AUG03	2.35	1
Williams	Thomas	29JUN05	2.34	1	Williby	William	05JUN04	4.24	1
Williams	Thomas	26JUL06	3.35	1	Willoughby	William	28JUN05	2.34	1
Williams	Thomas	26JUL06	3.35	1	Willoughby	William	30JUL06	2.38	1
Williams	Thomas Jr	26JUL06	3.35	1	Willoby	William	09JUN07	2.36	1
Williams	Walter	-----95	1.14	M1	Willoughby	William	31MAY08	2.29	11
Williams	Walter	-----96	4.18	1	Willoby	William	13JUL09	1.36	11
Williams	Walter	-----97	2.06	1	Willoughsby	William	-----11	1.85	2
Williams	Walter	18MAY99	2.22	M1	WILSON				
Williams	Walter	17JUN00	1.15	1	Willson	Abraham	18JUL97	1.28	1
Williams	Walter	02JUN01	1.18	1	Wilson	Abram	01JUL99	1.39	1
Williams	William	18SEP92	1.13	1	Wilson	Abraham	27JUN00	2.29	1
Williams	William	09AUG93	3.12	1	Wilson	Abraham	30MAY01	3.38	1
Williams	William	25JUN96	1.13	1	Wilson	Abraham	13AUG02	2.31	1
William	William	24MAY97	1.28		Wilson	Abraham	19JUL03	3.26	1
(A negro)					Wilson	Abraham	07AUG04	3.21	1
Williams	William	01JUN97	3.32	1	Wilson	Abraham	14AUG05	3.37	1
Williams	William	01JUN97	3.32	11	Wilson	Abraham	26JUL06	3.35	1
William	William	15JUL99	3.22		Wilson	Abraham	29JUN09	1.36	1
A black man					Wilson	Abraham	-----11	1.88	1
William	William	26JUN00	3.33		Wilson	Allin	27JUN87	1.06	1
A free black over 21 years old					Wilson	Elizabeth	05AUG02	2.30	F
WILLIAMSON					Wilson	George	20JUN87	2.07	1
Williamson	James	29MAY94	3.21	1	Wilson	George	06NOV88	1.11	1
Williamson	John	13JUL09	1.34	1	Wilson	George	07AUG89	5.12	1
Williamson	John	-----11	1.84	1	Wilson	George	31MAR90	2.07	1
Williamson	Thomas	03AUG07	2.39	1	Wilson	George	13APR91	1.09	1
Williamson	Thomas	31MAY08	2.29	1	Wilson	George	09OCT92	2.09	1
Williamson	Thomas	13JUL09	1.34	11	Wilson	George	30AUG93	1.09	1
Williamson	Thomas	-----11	1.87	1	Wilson	George	30MAY94	1.09	1
WILLIS					Wilson	George	29MAY95	2.13	1
Willis	Joel	26JUN87	1.06	1	Wilson	George	23MAY96	1.13	1
Willis	John	07JUL87	1.06	1	Wilson	George	12JUN97	3.33	1
Willis	John	11JUN89	6.07	1	Wilson	George	03JUN99	1.38	1
Willis	John	16JUL89	6.08	1	Wilson	George	19JUN00	2.29	1
Willis	John	07MAY91	2.11	1	Wilson	George Jr	21JUN00	2.29	M1
Willis	John	17SEP92	1.13	1	Wilson	George	19MAY01	2.27	1
Willis	John	03AUG93	1.09	1	Wilson	George	01AUG01	2.28	1
Willis	John	14JUN96	1.13	1	Wilson	George	11JUN03	2.33	1
Willis	John	06JUN99	1.38	1	Wilson	George	16JUL07	2.39	1
Willes	John	25JUL00	2.30	1	Wilson	Isaac	12AUG02	3.29	1
Willis	John	28MAY01	3.38	1	Wilson	Isaac	26JUL03	2.34	1
Willis	John	10AUG02	2.31	1	Wilson	Isaac	22AUG04	3.22	1
Willis	Major	16OCT87	1.06	1	Wilson	Isaac	09AUG05	3.37	1
Willis	Major	10JUN89	6.07	1	Wilson	Isaac	05AUG06	3.36	1
Willis	Major	29MAR90	2.07	1	Wilson	Isaac	11JUN07	2.37	1
Willis	Major	05APR91	1.09	1	Willson	Isaac	31MAY08	2.29	1
Willis	Major	06OCT92	2.09	1	Wilson	James	16OCT87	1.06	1
Willis	Majors	20AUG93	1.10	1	Wilson	John	20SEP91	1.09	1
Willis	Matthew	13MAY97	1.27	1	Wilson	John	06AUG93	1.09	1
Wiles	Thomas	31OCT88	1.10	1	Wilson	John	07AUG93	1.09	1
Wiles	Thomas	30MAR91	1.09	1	Wilson	John	21---94	1.09	1
Wiles	Thomas	19OCT92	2.09	1	Wilson	John	14MAY94	1.09	1
Wyles	Thomas	15AUG93	1.10	1	Wilson	John	22MAY95	2.13	1
Wyles	Thomas	28MAY94	1.09	1	Wilson	John	28MAY95	2.13	1
Wyler	Thomas	02JUN95	2.13	1	Wilson	John	02JUN96	1.13	1
Wyles	Thomas	29JUN96	1.13	12	Wilson	John	18JUN96	1.13	1
Wiles	Thomas	07AUG06	3.36	11	Wilson	John	27MAY02	3.28	1
Willis	William	24JUL96	2.20	1	Wilson	John	23AUG02	2.31	1
Willes	William	30MAY03	2.32	1	Wilson	John	28JUN03	2.32	1
Willis	William	13JUN04	1.21	1	Wilson	John	24JUL04	1.21	1
WILLOUGHBY					Willson	John	17JUN05	1.23	1
Willoughby	William	13SEP92	1.13	1	Wilson	John	17JUN05	1.23	1
Willoughby	William	12AUG93	3.12	1	Wilson	Jonas	13JUN99	2.22	1
Willoughby	William	11MAY94	2.16	1	Wilson	Jonas	23JUL00	1.16	1
					Wilson	Jonas	23JUN01	1.19	1

surname	name	date	bk.pg	TM	surname	name	date	bk.pg	TM
Wilson	Jonas	23JUN02	1.25	1	Wilson	Samuel	03NOV92	1.14	1
Wilson	Jonas	22JUN03	1.25	1	Wilson	Samuel	28AUG93	3.12	1
Wilson	Jonas	03AUG04	1.22	1	Wilson	Spencer	28NOV88	1.11	1
Willson	Jonas	31JUL05	1.24	1	Wilson	Stephen	23JUN02	1.25	1
Wilson	Jonas	09MAY07	1.28	1	Wilson	Stephen	22JUN03	1.25	1
Wilson	Jonas	24APR08	1.38	1	Wilson	Stephen	03AUG04	1.22	1
Wilson	Jonas	04MAY08	1.38	1	Willson	Stephen	31JUL05	1.24	1
Wilson	Joseph	13JUN99	2.22	1	Wilson	Stephen	09MAY07	1.28	1
Wilson	Joseph	24JUN01	1.19	1	Wilson	Stephen	24APR08	1.38	1
Willson	Joseph	22JUN03	1.25	1	Wilson	Stephen	01JUL09	2.37	1
Wilson	Joseph	02AUG04	1.22	1	Wilson	Thomas	25MAY95	2.13	1
Willson	Joseph	30JUL05	1.24	1	Wilson	Thomas	18JUN96	1.13	1
Wilson	Joseph	08MAY07	1.27	1	Wilson	Thomas	09MAY97	3.32	1
Wilson	Joseph	04MAY08	1.38	1	Wilson	Thomas	20MAY99	1.37	1
Wilson	Joseph	16JUN09	2.36	1	Wilson	Thomas	04JUN00	2.29	1
Wilson	Joshua	13JUN99	2.22	1	Wilson	Thomas	24JUL01	2.27	1
Wilson	Joshua	23JUL00	1.16	1	Wilson	Thomas	11JUN02	1.23	1
Wilson	Joshua	23JUL00	1.16	1	Wilson	Thomas	18JUL03	1.26	1
Wilson	Joshua	24JUN01	1.19	1	Wilson	Thomas	30JUL03	2.35	1
Wilson	Joshua	23JUN02	1.25	1	Wilson	Thomas	13JUN04	4.25	1
Wilson	Joshua	22JUN03	1.25	1	Wilson	Thomas	30JUL04	2.20	1
Wilson	Joshua Jr	22JUN03	1.25	1	Willson	Thomas	19JUN05	1.23	11
Wilson	Joshua Sr	03AUG04	1.22	1	Wilson	Thomas	12JUN07	1.29	11
Wilson	Joshua	03AUG04	1.22	1	Wilson	Thomas	-----08	1.40	11
Willson	Joshua Sr	31JUL05	1.24	1	Wilson	Thomas	21JUN09	2.36	2
Willson	Joshua	31JUL05	1.24	1	Wilson	Thomas	-----11	1.87	2
Wilson	Joshua	09MAY07	1.28	1	Wilson	William	06AUG93	1.10	1
Wilson	Joshua	24APR08	1.38	1	Wilson	William	20MAY95	2.13	1
Wilson	Joshua	16JUN09	2.36	1	Wilson	William	02JUN96	1.13	1
Wilson	Martin	11JUN03	2.33	M1	WINANT				
Wilson	Martin	06JUN06	2.37	1	Wynant	John	24APR08	1.38	1
Wilson	Martin	16JUL07	2.39	1	Wenant	John	29MAY09	2.35	1
Wilson	Martin	-----08	1.40	1	Winant	John	-----11	1.85	1
Wilson	Martin	23AUG09	2.36	1	WINEGARDNER				
Wilson	Martin	-----11	1.87	1	Winegardner	John Sr	15AUG07	2.39	11
Wilson	Mathias	27NOV88	1.11	11	Winegardner	John Jr	15AUG07	2.39	1
Wilson	Matthew	06AUG89	5.12	11	Winegardner	John	31MAY08	2.29	1
Wilson	Mathew	01JUN90	2.07	11	Winegarden	John	13JUL09	1.34	1
Wilson	Mathew	06APR91	1.09	11	WINFORD				
Wilson	Mathew	01NOV92	2.09	12	Winford	Joshua	12JUN02	1.24	1
Wilson	Mathew	06AUG93	1.10	1	WINFREY				
Wilson	Mathew	14MAY94	1.09	1	Winfrey	Henry	03JUL96	2.19	1
Wilson	Matthew	22MAY95	2.13	11	Winfrey	Henry	21JUN03	3.26	1
Willson	Mathew	10JUN96	1.13	11	Winfree	Henry	08AUG04	3.21	1
Wilson	Matthew	30MAY99	1.38	1	Winfrey	Henry	07AUG05	3.36	11
Wilson	Matthew	21JUN00	2.29	11	Winfrey	Henry	05AUG06	3.36	1
Wilson	Mathew	17JUL01	2.27	11	Wenfrey	John Sr	14APR95	3.18	11
Wilson	Mathew Jr	17JUL01	2.27	1	Winfrey	John Jr	14APR95	3.18	1
Wilson	Mathew Sr	27MAY02	3.28	11	Winfrey	John	03JUL96	2.19	12
Wilson	Mathew Jr	27MAY02	3.28	1	Winfrey	John Sr	21JUN03	3.26	1
Wilson	Mathew Jr	11JUN03	2.33	1	Winfree	John	08AUG04	3.21	1
Wilson	Matthew Sr	26JUL04	1.22	1	Winfrey	John	07AUG05	3.36	1
Wilson	Matthew Jr	26JUL04	1.22	1	Winfrey	John	08AUG06	3.36	1
Wilson	Mathew Sr	03AUG05	2.35	1	Winfrey	Phillip	03JUL96	2.19	1
Wilson	Mathew	08JUN05	2.34	1	Winfrey	Philip	18JUL97	1.28	1
Wilson	Mathew	06JUN06	2.37	1	Winfree	William	07AUG04	3.21	1
Wilson	Mathew Jr	06JUN06	2.37	1	Winfrey	William	07AUG05	3.36	1
Wilson	Mathews	16JUL07	2.37	1	Winfrey	William	08AUG06	3.36	1
Wilson	Mathew Sr	-----08	1.40	1	WINKLE				
Wilson	Mathew	-----08	1.40	1	Winkle	David	03AUG96	2.20	1
Wilson	Mathew	23AUG09	2.38	1	WINSCOT				
Wilson	Mathew Jr	18AUG09	2.37	1	Winscot	Isaac	23MAY94	1.09	1
Wilson	Matthew	-----11	1.87	1	WINTEM				
Wilson	Moses	12JUN99	2.21	1	Wintem	Joseph	06AUG04	3.21	11
Wilson	Moses	19JUL00	2.29	1	WINTERS				
Wilson	Moses	29MAY01	2.27	1	Winters	Obadiah	28JUL03	2.35	1
Wilson	Moses	18JUN02	1.25	11	Winters	William	03AUG02	2.30	1
Wilson	Moses	18JUL03	1.26	11	WISE				
Wilson	Rebecka	23AUG02	2.31	F	Wise	John	17AUG07	2.39	1
Wilson	Samuel	26JUN89	6.07	1	Wise	John	18AUG09	2.37	1
Wilson	Samuel	23JUN90	1.11	1	WISER				
Wilson	Samuel	18AUG91	2.11	1	Wiser	Philip	11JUL00	3.33	1

surname	name	date	bk.pg	TM	surname	name	date	bk.pg	TM
Werzer	Phillip	30JUL01	3.37	1	1802 tax info in 1805 tax list				
Wizer	Phillip	10JUN02	2.29	1	Witt	Charles	18JUN03	3.25	11
Wiser	Phillip	04AUG03	3.26	1	Witt	Charles	30JUL04	2.19	11
Wisor	Philip	06APR04	4.24	1	Witt	Charles	07JUN05	3.36	1
Wyzer	Philip	20JUN05	3.36	1	WOLF				
Wizer	Phillip	26JUL06	3.35	1	Wolf	Jacob	03AUG89	5.12	1
WISHER					Wolfe	Jacob	05JUL91	1.09	1
Wisher	John	29JUL96	2.20	1	WOODALL				
WITHAM					Woodall	Charles	13JUN02	1.23	11
Withum	Peter	18MAY07	1.28	1	Woodall	Charles	14JUL03	1.24	12
Witham	Peter	-----08	1.40	1	Woodall	Charles	18JUN04	1.21	11
WITHEROE					Woodall	Charles	07JUN05	1.22	11
Witherow	John	31MAY08	2.29	1	Woodall	Charles Jr	07JUN05	1.22	1
Witheroe	John	13JUL09	1.36	1	Woodall	Charles	10JUN06	1.26	11
Withroe	William	13JUL09	1.36	1	Woodall	Charles	06JUN07	1.28	1
WITHERS					Woodall	Charles Jr	06JUN07	1.28	1
Withers	Cain	31JUL07	2.39	1	Woodall	John	06JUN07	1.28	1
Weithers	Garland	16AUG02	3.29	1	Woodall	John	-----08	1.39	1
Withers	Garland	13MAY05	2.33	1	Woodall	John	10MAY09	2.35	1
Weithers	Garland	08MAY06	2.37	1	Woodall	John	10MAY09	2.35	1
Withers	Garland	03AUG07	2.39	1	Woodall	John	-----11	1.84	1
Withers	Garland	-----08	2.30	1	Woodall	John	-----11	1.85	1
Withers	Garland	09JUN09	1.35	1	Woodall	William	12JUN02	1.23	1
Withers	Garland	-----11	1.83	1	Woodall	William	14JUL03	1.24	1
Wethers	George	02APR90	1.11	1	Woodall	William	18JUN04	1.21	1
Withers	Gideon	14JUN04	1.21	1	Woodall	William	07JUN05	1.22	1
Weathers	James	-----96	4.19	00	Woodall	William	10JUN06	1.26	1
Withers	James	-----97	2.05	1	Woodall	William	06JUN07	1.28	1
Withers	James	10MAY99	2.21	1	Woodall	William	-----08	1.39	1
Withers	James	11JUN99	1.38	1	Woodall	William	10MAY09	2.35	1
Withers	James	09JUN00	1.15	1	Woodall	William	-----11	1.84	1
Werthers	James	18JUL00	2.29	1	WOODFIN				
Withers	James	30MAY01	1.17	1	Woodfin	Samuel	-----93	2.06	1
Weithers	James	29JUL01	2.28	1	WOODFORK				
Weithers	James	27MAY02	3.28	1	Woodfork	Joseph H.	12AUG07	2.39	1
Withers	James	26JUN02	1.25	1	Woodfork	Joseph H.	10JUN09	1.35	1
Weathers	James	18JUN03	2.33	1	WOODRUF				
Weithers	James	26JUL03	2.34	1	Woodruf	John	10OCT92	2.09	1
Withers	James	25JUL04	1.21	1	WOODRUM				
Werthers	James	25JUL05	2.35	1	Woodram	Drury	01DEC92	3.20	1
Weithers	James	18MAY06	2.37	1	Woodrum	James	18NOV88	1.11	1
Withers	James	31JUL07	2.39	1	Woodrom	James	08OCT91	1.09	1
Weathers	James	-----08	1.40	1	Woodrum	James	01NOV92	2.09	1
Weathers	James	10JUN09	2.36	1	Woodrum	John	01JUN99	1.38	1
Withers	James	19AUG09	2.37	1	Woodrum	John	31JUL00	2.30	1
Withers	James	-----11	1.87	1	Woodrum	John	04APR01	2.27	1
Withers	James	-----11	1.84	1	Woodrum	John	08JUN02	3.28	1
Withers	John	29JUN87	1.06	1	Woodram	John	17JUN03	2.33	1
Weathers	John	31OCT88	1.10	1	Woodrum	John	24JUL04	1.21	1
Weathers	John	18AUG89	5.12	1	Woodrum	William	27OCT92	2.09	1
Weathers	John	15JUN90	2.07	1	Woodram	William	31MAY94	1.09	1
Weathers	John	09JUL99	3.22	1	Woodram	William	08MAY95	2.13	1
Withers	John	27JUN00	3.32	1	Woodram	William	30JUN96	1.13	1
Withers	John	20MAY01	3.37	1	Woodrum	William	01JUN99	1.38	1
Weithers	John	16AUG02	3.30	1	Woodrum	William	05JUL00	2.29	1
Weathers	John	24JUL04	4.26	1	Woodrum	William	28MAY01	2.27	1
Withers	John	20JUL05	2.35	1	Woodrum	William	03JUN02	3.28	1
Weithers	John	18JUL06	2.37	1	Woodrum	William	17JUN03	2.33	1
Withers	John	03AUG07	2.39	1	Woodrum	William	07AUG04	2.20	1
Withers	John	-----08	2.30	1	Woodrum	William	24JUL05	2.35	1
Withers	John	09JUN09	1.35	1	Woodrum	William	08MAY06	2.37	1
Withers	John	-----11	1.83	1	Woodrum	William	12AUG07	2.39	1
Withers	William	26JUN87	1.06	1	Woodram	William	13JUL09	1.34	1
Withors	William	21MAY94	3.22	1	Woodram	William	-----11	1.87	1
Withers	William	-----95	1.14	1	WOODS				
Weathers	William	-----96	4.18	1	Wood	Abraham	06AUG04	3.21	1
Withers	William	-----97	2.05	1	Wood	Abraham	08AUG05	3.37	1
WITT					Wood	Abraham	04AUG06	3.36	1
Witt	Charles	17MAY99	1.37	1	Wood	Absolom	03JUL99	3.22	1
Witt	Charles	03JUN00	2.29	1	Wood	Absalum	01JUL00	3.32	1
Witt	Charles	04JUN01	2.27	1	Woods	Andrew	26JUL04	1.22	1
Witt	Charles	-----05	2.38	1	Wood	Caldwell	-----11	1.84	21

surname	name	date	bk.pg	TM	surname	name	date	bk.pg	TM
Wood	David	24JUN96	2.20	11	WOODSON				
Wood	David	10AUG97	1.28	11	Woodson	David	-----96	4.19	1
Wood	David	10JUL99	3.22	1	Woodson	Tarlton	31JUL05	2.35	1
Wood	David	09JUL00	3.33	11	WOODWARD				
Wood	David	31JUL01	3.37	11	Woodward	Peter	12JUN97	3.32	1
Wood	David	29JUL02	3.28	11	WOOLFORK				
Woods	David	09AUG03	2.35	1	Woolford	John	-----96	4.19	1
Woods	David	08JUN04	4.25	1	Woolfork	Joseph H.	-----11	1.86	1
Woods	David	20JUN05	2.34	1	Woollen	Leonard	14JUN00	2.29	M1
Woods	David	30JUL06	2.38	1	Woollen	Leonard	04APR01	2.27	1
Wood	Edmund	23JUN97	1.27	1	Woolen	Leonard	02AUG02	3.29	1
Woods	Edmond	27JUN99	1.39	11	Woolen	Leonard	04JUN03	2.33	1
Wood	Edmond	25JUL00	2.30	11	Woolen	Leonard	09AUG04	3.21	1
Wood	Edmund	28MAY01	3.38	11	Woolen	Leonard	05AUG05	2.35	1
Wood	Edmond	10AUG02	2.31	11	WOOLSEY				
Woode	Edmond	26JUL03	3.26	11	Woolsey	George	25JUN87	3.11	1
Wood	Edmund	06AUG04	3.21	1	Woolsey	Jacob	25JUN02	1.25	1
Wood	Edmond	08AUG05	3.37	1	Woolsey	James	-----11	1.83	1
Wood	Edmond	08AUG06	3.36	1	Woolsey	Joseph	20JUN02	1.25	1
Wood	Edward	06AUG89	5.12	1	Woolsey	Joseph	21JUN03	1.25	1
Woods	Francis	08JUN04	4.25	1	Woolsey	Joseph	01AUG04	1.22	1
Woods	James	12JUN94	2.15	1	Woolsey	Joseph	29JUL05	1.24	1
Woods	James	29APR95	3.17	1	Woolsey	Joseph	04MAY07	1.27	1
Wood	James	21JUL00	3.06	1	Woolsey	Nathaniel	01AUG04	1.22	1
Tax pd by agent-Robert Barnett					Woolsey	Nathaniel	29JUL05	1.24	1
Woods	James	26JUL04	1.22	1	Woolsey	Richard	20JUN02	1.25	11
Woods	Jeremiah	26JUN99	1.39	1	Woolsey	Richard	21JUN03	1.25	11
Wood	Jeremiah	25JUL00	2.30	1	Woolsey	Richard	01AUG04	1.22	1
Wood	Jeremiah	28MAY01	3.38	1	Woolsey	Richard	29JUL05	1.24	1
Wood	Jeremiah	10AUG02	2.30	1	Woolsey	Richard	04MAY07	1.27	11
Woode	Jeremiah	25JUN03	3.26	1	Woolsey	Richard	-----08	1.39	11
Wood	Jeremiah	06AUG04	3.21	1	WORLEY				
Wood	Jeremiah	08AUG05	3.36	1	Worley	Joshua	30MAY05	2.34	1
Wood	Jeremiah	04AUG06	3.36	1	Worley	William	15JUN03	2.33	1
Wood	John	28NOV88	1.11	1	Worley	William	15JUN03	2.33	)
Wood	John	05AUG89	5.12	1	Worley	William	23JUL04	1.21	1
Wood	John	30MAY90	2.07	1	Worley	William	20MAY05	2.33	1
Wood	John	20AUG93	1.09	1	Eight lotts in Standford				
Wood	John	14MAY94	1.09	1	Worley	William	20MAY05	2.33	
Wood	John	16MAY94	1.09	1	Three lotts in Columbia				
Wood	John	19MAY97	3.32	1	WORNELL				
Wood	John	23JUN97	1.27	1	Wornell	Richard	12AUG89	2.14	1
Wood	John	25JUN99	2.22	1	WORSER				
Woods	John	27JUN99	1.39	1	Worser	Peter	17JUN01	3.37	
Wood	John	25JUL00	2.30	1	A free black man				
Wood	John	29MAY01	3.38	1	WORTHAM				
Wood	John	03AUG02	2.30	1	Wortham	Bartholomew	10AUG97	1.28	1
Woode	John	26JUL03	3.26	1	WORTHINGTON				
Wood	John	06AUG04	3.21	1	Worthington	Charles	12AUG07	2.39	1
Wood	John	08AUG05	3.37	1	Worthington	Charles	-----08	2.30	1
Wood	John	04AUG06	3.36	1	Worthington	Edward	30JUN87	1.06	1
Woods	John	08JUN09	2.36	1	Worthington	Edward	10JUN89	6.07	1
Woods	Mark	26JUL03	2.34	1	Worthington	Edward	06APR90	1.11	1
Woods	Mark D.	24JUL04	4.26	1	Warthington	Edward	23JUN91	2.11	1
Woods	Mark J./S.	28JUN05	2.34	1	Worthington	Edward	17SEP92	1.14	1
Woods	Michael	12JUN87	2.07	1	Worthington	Edward	26MAY96	2.19	1
Woods	Michael D.	11JUL03	2.33	1	Worthington	Edward	11JUL97	1.26	1
Wood	Richard	12JUN97	1.27	11	Worthington	Edward	28JUN99	3.23	1
Wood	Richard	04JUN99	1.38	1	Worthington	Edward	02JUL00	3.32	1
Wood	Thomas	05AUG89	5.12	1	Worthington	Edward	10AUG01	3.38	1
Wood	Thomas	01JUN90	2.07	1	Worthington	Edward	12AUG02	3.29	1
Wood	Thomas	24APR08	1.38	1	Worthington	Edward	26JUL03	2.34	1
Wood	Thomas	-----11	1.85	1	Worthington	Edward	12JUN04	4.25	1
Wooddy	William	23MAY94	3.21	1	Worthington	Edward	02AUG06	2.39	M1
Wood	William	20JUL96	2.20	1	Worthington	Edward	12AUG07	2.39	1
Wood	William	17JUL97	1.27	1	Worthington	Edward	12AUG07	2.39	D
Wood	William	04JUN99	1.38	1	Worthington	Edward	-----08	2.30	1
Wood	William	03JUL99	3.22	1	Worthington	Edward	10JUN09	1.35	M1
Wood	William	30JUN00	3.32	1	Worthington	Eliza.	20JUL05	2.35	F
Wood	William	09JUL01	3.37	1	Worthington	Eliza.	02AUG06	2.39	F
Woods	William	17AUG02	3.30	1	Worthington	Eliz.	12AUG07	2.39	F
Wood	William	22JUN03	2.33	1	Worthington	Eliz.	-----08	2.30	F

surname	name	date	bk.pg	TM	surname	name	date	bk.pg	TM
WorthingtonJames T.		31MAY00	2.29	1	Right	James	10JUN02	1.19	1
WorthingtonJames F.		28JUL01	2.27	12	Wright	James	31MAY03	3.25	1
WorthingtonJames T.		12JUN02	1.24	1	Wright	James	17JUN03	3.25	1
WorthingtonJames		28JUN03	1.25	1	Right	James	30JUN03	1.20	1
WorthingtonJames T.		20JUN04	1.21	11	Wright	James	01AUG04	3.20	1
WorthingtonJames T.		15JUN05	1.23	1	Wright	James	13JUN05	3.35	1
WorthingtonJames T.		16JUN06	1.26	1	Right	James	19JUN05	1.18	1
Worthing James L.		05JUN07	1.28	1	Right	James	19JUN06	1.21	1
WorthingtonJames T.		-----08	1.39	1	Wright	James	16JUL06	3.34	11
WorthingtonJames T.		23AUG09	2.38	1	Wright	James	10JUN07	2.36	11
WorthingtonJames		-----11	1.84	1	Wright	James	25JUN07	1.28	1
WorthingtonWilliam		18APR89	6.07	1	Wright	James	31MAY08	2.29	11
WorthingtonWilliam		10MAY90	1.11	1	Wright	James	27JUN09	1.36	1
WarthingtonWilliam		04MAY91	2.11	1	Wright	James	-----11	1.88	1
WorthingtonWilliam		17SEP92	1.14	1	Wright	James W.	16MAY97	1.26	1
Wuthington William		10AUG93	3.12	1	Wright	Jeremiah	03AUG96	2.20	1
WorthingtonWilliam		16APR94	2.15	1	Wright	Jeremiah	17JUL97	1.27	1
WorthingtonWilliam		18MAR95	3.18	1	Wright	Jessee	13JUL87	1.06	1
WorthingtonWilliam		21APR96	2.19	1	Wright	Jesse	02AUG90	1.11	1
WorthingtonWilliam		15MAY97	1.27	1	Wright	Jessee	28SEP92	1.14	1
WorthingtonWilliam		28JUN99	3.21	1	Wright	Jessey	12AUG93	3.12	1
WorthingtonWilliam		27JUN00	3.32	1	Wright	Jesse	22MAY94	2.15	1
WorthingtonWilliam		21MAY01	3.37	1	Wright	Jesse	09JUN07	2.36	1
WorthingtonWilliam		08JUL02	3.28	1	Wright	Joel	-----11	1.88	1
WorthingtonWilliam		26JUL03	2.34	1	Wright	John	18MAY95	3.17	1
WorthingtonWilliam		20JUL05	2.35	1	Wright	John	10MAY96	2.19	1
WorthingtonWilliam		31MAY06	2.37	1	Wright	John	16JUL96	2.20	1
WorthingtonWilliam		03AUG07	2.39	1	Wright	John	24JUN99	1.38	1
WorthingtonWilliam		-----08	2.30	1	Wright	John	09JUL99	3.22	1
WorthingtonWilliam		10JUN09	1.35	1	Wright	John	26JUN00	3.32	1
WREN					Wright	John Sr	21JUL01	3.38	1
Ren	John	-----95	1.12	1	Wright	John Jr	22JUL01	3.39	1
Ren	John	30MAY99	2.16	1	Wright	John	07MAY01	3.36	1
Ren	John	16JUN00	1.12	1	One lot in the town of Danville				
Renn	John	05JUN01	1.15	1	Wright	John	07MAY01	3.36	
Ren	John	11JUN02	1.19	1	One retail store				
Ren	John	18JUN04	1.17	1	Wright	John	19MAY01	3.36	1
Ren	John	06JUN05	1.17	1	Wright	John	11JUN02	2.30	1
Ren	John	01JUL07	1.22	1	Wright	John	16AUG02	3.30	1
Renn	John	12MAY09	2.27	1	Wright	John	23AUG02	2.31	1
Ren	John	-----11	1.66	1	Wright	John Sr	10JUN03	3.25	11
WRENCH					Wright	John Jr	10JUN03	3.25	1
Rench	Michael	24MAR90	2.06	1	Wright	John	03JUN03	3.25	1
WRIGHT					Rite	John	06JUL03	2.26	1
Wright	Aaron	21JUN97	1.28	1	Right	John	25JUL04	4.19	1
Wright	Aaron	16MAY99	3.21	1	Wright	John	09AUG04	3.22	1
Rite	Aaron	29JUL00	2.25	1	Rite	John	16MAY05	2.26	1
Wright	Aaron	29JUL01	3.39	1	Wright	John	09AUG05	3.37	11
Wright	Bennett	-----11	1.86	1	Right	John(heirs)	05AUG05	3.32	
Right	Chris.	26SEP87	1.05	1	Tax paid by Joal Stokes				
Wright	Esau	01JUN02	2.29	1	Wright	Jonathan	23MAY96	2.19	1
Wright	Ezekiel	24APR08	1.38	1	Rite	Jonathan	11MAY97	1.21	1
Right	George	18APR08	1.29	11	Rite	Jonathan	29JUL00	2.25	1
Wright	Isaac	20JUN07	2.37	1	Wright	Jonathan	27JUN01	2.27	1
Wright	J!mes	14NOV88	1.11	1	Wrigh4	Jonathan	11JUN02	2.30	1
Wright	J!mes	21JUL89	5.12	1	Wri'ht	Jonathan	04AUG03	3.26	1
Ri'ht	Jam%s	30MAR90	2.06	1	Wrigh4	Jonathan	04AUG04	3.21	1
Wright	James	05APR91	1.09	1	Wright	Jonathen	08JUL05	3.36	1
Wright	James	26OCT92	2.09	1	Wright	Jonathen	18JUL06	3.35	1
Wright	James	03AUG93	1.10	1	Wright	Jonathen	17AUG07	2.39	1
Wright	James	12MAY94	1.09	1	Wright	Jonathen	31MAY08	2.29	1
Wright	James	11MAY95	2.13	1	Wright	Jonathan	11JUL09	1.36	1
Wright	James	03AUG96	2.20	1	Wright	Jonathan	-----11	1.86	1
Right	James	20JUN97	1.21	1	Wright	Joseph	02MAR95	3.18	1
Wright	James	16MAY99	3.21	1	Wright	Joseph	27MAY02	2.29	1
Wright	James	05JUN99	1.38	1	Wright	Joseph	14JUL03	3.26	1
Wright	James	21JUN00	3.31	1	Wright	Joseph	31JUL04	3.20	1
Rite	James	22JUL00	2.25	1	Rite	Joseph	19JUL05	2.27	1
Wright	James	20JUL01	3.38	1	Rite	Joseph	18JUL06	2.31	1
Wright	James	01AUG01	2.28	1	Wright	Joseph	16JUL07	2.37	1
Wright	James	10MAY02	2.29	1	Wright	Joseph	-----08	2.29	1
Wright	James	27MAY02	2.29	1	Right	Joseph	09JUN09	1.29	1

surname	name	date	bk.pg	TM	surname	name	date	bk.pg	TM
Wright	Lazarous	28MAR95	3.18	1	Wyatt	Rex	20JUN04	1.21	1
Right	Levy	13JUN05	1.17	1	Wyatt	Rex	12JUN05	1.23	1
Wright	Levi	25JUN07	1.28	1	Wyatt	Rex	28MAY07	1.28	1
Wright	Linsey	09JUN07	2.36	1	Wyatt	William	13AUG93	1.10	1
Wright	Linsey	31MAY08	2.29	1	Wyatt	William	28MAY94	1.09	1
Wright	Lindsay	30JUN09	1.36	1	Wyette	William	26APR97	3.32	1
Right	Lindsey	-----11	1.67	1	Wiatt	William	11JUN01	1.19	1
Right	Lindsey	-----11	1.67	1	YAGER				
Right	Morris	13JUL09	1.30	1	Yeager	Absolam	27JUN87	1.06	1
Wright	Morris	-----11	1.85	1	Yegor	Cornales	10JUN94	2.16	0
Wright	Philbard	11JUN02	2.30	1	Yager	Frederick	16JUL06	2.39	1
Wright	Phillip	11JUL03	3.26	1	Yager	Fredrick	30JUL07	2.39	1
Right	Robert	23JUL00	1.13	1	Yager	Fredrick	-----08	2.31	1
Wright	Ruben	11JUN07	1.29	11	Yager	Frederick	22JUN09	1.36	1
Wright	Samuel	-----11	1.84	1	Yager	Frederick	-----11	1.89	1
Right	Susannah	30JUN09	1.29	F	Yeager	Joseph	28MAR95	3.18	1
Wright	William	12JUN87	2.07	1	Yagor	Joseph	03AUG96	2.20	1
Wright	William	14NOV88	1.11	1	Yeager	Joseph	17MAY97	1.28	1
Wright	William	24JUN89	5.12	1	Yeager	Joseph	04JUL99	3.23	1
Right	William	26JUN89	6.06	1	Yager	Joseph	30JUN00	3.33	1
Wright	William	23JUN90	1.11	1	Yager	Joseph	08JUL02	3.30	1
Wright	William	28MAR95	3.18	1	Yager	Joseph	25JUL03	2.35	1
Wright	William	03AUG96	2.20	11	Yager	Joseph	28JUL04	4.26	1
Wright	William	17JUL97	1.27	11	Yager	Joseph	24JUL05	2.36	1
Wright	William	30JUN00	3.32	11	Yager	Joseph	24APR06	2.39	1
Wright	William	08JUL01	3.37	11	Yeger	Joseph	-----08	2.31	1
Wright	William	12JUN07	1.29	1	Yager	Joseph	21JUN09	1.36	1
Wright	William	16JUL07	2.37	1	Yager	Joseph	-----11	1.89	11
Wright	William	16JUL07	2.37	1	Yager	Lewis	30JUL07	2.39	1
Wright	William	-----08	1.39	1	Yager	Lewis	09JUN09	1.36	1
Wright	Windfield	13JUN99	1.37	12	Yager	Lewis	-----11	1.89	1
Rite	Winfield	30JUL00	2.25	21	Yager	Peter	28JUL03	2.36	1
Right	Winfield	02JUN01	1.15	11	YANCY				
Right	Winfield	10JUN02	1.19	11	Yancey	Austin	25JUN00	2.30	1
Right	Winfield	28JUN03	1.20	11	Yency	Austen	10JUN02	2.31	1
Wright	Winfield	02AUG04	2.20	12	Yancey	Auston	04AUG03	3.27	1
Right	Winfield	13JUN05	1.17	11	Yansey	Auston	06APR04	4.26	1
Right	Winfield	18AUG06	1.20	12	Yancy	Austen	14AUG05	3.37	1
Wright	Wingfield	25JUN07	1.28	12	Yancy	Austin	08AUG06	3.37	1
Wright	Wingfield	-----08	1.39	1	YANTES				
WYATT					Yantes	George	04DEC92	3.20	1
Wyatt	James	29JUN03	1.25	1	Yantes	Henry	04DEC92	3.20	1
Wyatt	James	02AUG04	2.20	1	Yandeirs	Jacob	21MAY94	3.22	1
Wyatt	James	12JUN05	1.23	1	Yeandus	Jacob	-----95	1.14	1
Wyatt	John	19JUN89	5.11	1	Yantus	Jacob	-----96	4.19	1
Wyett	John	03JUN90	2.07	1	Yantes	Jacob	-----97	2.06	11
Wayet	John	30MAR91	1.09	1	Yantice	Jacob	10MAY99	2.22	11
Wyatt	John	14OCT92	2.09	1	Yantice	Jacob	06JUN00	1.16	11
Wyatt	John	13AUG93	1.10	1	Yantice	Jacob	12JUN01	1.19	11
Wyatt	John	29MAY94	1.09	11	Yantice	Jacob	28JUN02	1.25	11
Wyett	John	03JUN95	2.13	11	Yantise	Jacob	10JUN03	1.26	1
Wyatt	John	29JUN96	1.13	1	Yantise	Jacob	13JUN04	1.22	1
Wyette	John	26APR97	3.31	12	Yantise	Ruth	04JUN05	1.24	F1
Wyatt	John	29JUN99	2.21	1	Yantes	Ruth	18MAY07	1.29	F
Wiatt	John	11JUN01	1.19	1	Yantes	Ruth	-----08	1.41	F
Wyatt	John	14JUN02	1.23	1	YARBROUGH				
Wyatt	John	28JUN03	1.25	1	Yarberer	James	05JUN89	5.12	1
Wyatt	John	20JUN04	1.21	1	Yarberer	Randel	05JUN89	5.12	1
Wyatt	John	06JUN05	1.22	1	Yarbrough	Randolph	21MAY94	3.22	1
Wyatt	John	28MAY07	1.28	1	Yarborough	Randolph	-----95	1.14	1
Wyatt	John	24APR08	1.38	1	Yarborough	Randolph	-----96	4.19	1
Wyatt	John	08JUN09	2.36	1	YATES				
Wyatt	John	-----11	1.84	11	Yates	Charles	14NOV88	1.11	1
Wyatt	Penellipe	14OCT92	2.09	F	Yates	Charles	02JUN90	2.07	1
Wyatt	Penelipy	13AUG93	1.10	F1	Yates	Charles	14APR91	1.09	1
Wyatt	Rebecka	02AUG04	2.20	1	Yates	Charles	02SEP92	2.09	1
Wyatt	Rebeckah	11JUN05	1.23	F	Yeats	Charles	20AUG93	1.10	1
Wyatt	Rebekah	12JUN07	1.29	F	Yates	Lias	25JUL04	4.26	1
Wyatt	Rebekah	06JUN09	2.36	F	Yates	Elias	30JUL07	2.39	1
Wyatt	Rebecca	-----11	1.85	F	Yates	Elias	-----08	2.31	1
Wyatt	Ricks	04JUN02	1.24	1	Yates	Jesse	25JUL04	4.26	1
Wyatt	Rex	28JUN03	1.25	1	Yates	Jesse	20JUL05	2.36	1

surname	name	date	bk.pg	TM	surname	name	date	bk.pg	TM
Yates	Jesse	07AUG06	2.40	1	Young	John	28JUN87	1.06	11
Yates	John	29MAY97	3.33	1	Young	John	15MAY89	6.08	1
Yates	John	25JUL04	4.26	11	Young	John	16JUN89	5.12	1
Yates	John	20JUL05	2.35	1	Young	John	15MAY90	1.11	11
Yates	John	07AUG06	2.40	1	Young	John	-----91	2.11	1
Yates	John	30JUL07	2.39	1	Young	John	08OCT92	1.14	1
Yates	Mary	29JUN05	2.35	F1	Young	John	15OCT93	3.13	11
Yates	Samuel	30JUL07	2.39	1	Young	John	20MAY94	2.16	1
Yates	Stephen	29APR07	1.29	1	Young	John	01MAY95	3.18	1
Yates	Stephen	-----08	1.41	1	Young	John	19MAY96	2.20	1
Yates	Stephen	03MAY09	2.38	1	Young	John	28JUN97	1.28	1
Yates	Thomas	20JUL05	2.35	1	Young	John	08JUL99	3.23	1
Yates	Thomas	16JUL06	2.39	1	Young	John	14JUL00	3.33	1
Yates	Thomas	30JUL07	2.39	1	Young	John	09MAY01	3.39	1
Yates	Thomas	10JUN09	1.36	1	Young	John	11AUG02	3.30	1
Yates	William	20JUL05	2.35	1	Young	John	29JUL03	2.36	11
Yates	William	07AUG06	2.40	1	Yongue	John	27JUN04	4.26	11
Yates	William	10JUN09	1.36	1	Young	John	18JUN05	2.35	11
Yates	William	-----11	1.89	1	Young	John	14AUG06	2.40	11
YEARY					Young	John	03JUL07	2.39	11
Yearry	Benedict	22JUL02	1.26	1	Young	John	28JUN08	2.31	2
Yeary	Benedict	03AUG04	1.22	1	Young	John	11MAY09	1.36	2
Yeary	Benedic	31JUL05	1.24	1	Young	John	-----11	1.89	2
Yerry	Benedict	09MAY07	1.29	1	Young	Joseph	10MAY99	2.22	1
Yeary	Benedict	-----08	1.41	1	Young	Joseph C.	19JUN05	2.35	1
Yeary	Benedick	03MAY09	2.38	1	Young	Leah	12JUL03	3.27	F
Yeary	David	23JUN01	1.19	1	Young	Lear	07JUL09	1.36	F
Yearry	David	28JUN02	1.25	1	Young	Peter	15MAY89	6.07	1
Yearry	David	22JUL02	1.26	1	Young	Peter	01JUN89	6.09	1
Yeary	David	03AUG04	1.22	1	Young	Peter	11MAY90	1.11	1
Yerry	David	26MAY07	1.29	1	Young	Peter	03AUG90	1.11	1
Yeary	David	-----08	1.41	1	Young	Peter	-----91	2.11	1
Yearly	William	28JUN87	2.07	1	Young	Peter	-----91	2.11	1
Yerry	William	27MAY07	1.29	1	Young	Peter	16SEP92	1.14	1
YOCUM					Young	Peter	13OCT92	1.14	1
Yocum	Henry Sr	16JUN04	2.20	1	Young	Peter	15AUG93	3.13	1
Yocum	Henry	16JUN04	2.20	1	Young	Peter	29AUG93	3.13	1
Yocom	Henry Sr	14AUG05	3.37	1	Young	Peter	07SEP93	3.13	1
Yocom	Henry	14AUG05	3.37	1	Young	Peter	01MAY94	2.16	1
Yocum	Henry Sr	08AUG06	3.37	1	Young	Peter	28MAY94	2.16	1
Yocum	Henry	08AUG06	3.37	1	Young	Peter	21MAR95	3.18	1
Yocum	John	21AUG04	3.22	1	Young	Peter	22MAY96	2.20	1
Yocom	John	14AUG05	3.37	1	Young	Peter	25JUN96	2.20	1
Yocum	John	08AUG06	3.37	1	Young	Peter	03AUG96	2.20	1
YORK					Young	Peter	16MAY97	1.28	11
York	James	08MAY97	3.33	1	Young	Peter	30JUN97	1.28	1
YOUNG					Young	Peter	03JUL97	1.28	1
Young	Charles	01JUL03	2.35	1	Young	Peter	02JUL99	3.23	11
Yongue	Charles	06APR04	4.26	1	Young	Peter	08JUL99	3.23	1
Young	Charles	14AUG05	3.37	1	Young	Peter	04JUL00	3.33	1
Young	Charles	08AUG06	3.37	1	Young	Peter	14JUL00	3.33	1
Young	Edward	15MAY90	1.11	1	Young	Peter	01AUG00	2.30	1
Young	Edward	-----91	2.11	1	Young	Peter	07MAY01	3.39	1
Young	Edward	13OCT92	1.14	1	Young	Peter	30JUL01	2.28	1
Young	Edward	13SEP93	3.13	1	Young	Peter	12JUN02	2.31	1
Young	Edward	29MAY94	2.16	1	Young	Peter	11AUG02	2.30	1
Young	Edward	06JUN95	3.18	1	Young	Peter	09AUG03	3.27	1
Young	Isham	30MAR90	2.07	1	Young	Peter	28JUL03	2.36	1
Young	Isham	27JUN99	3.23	1	Young	Peter	18JUN04	2.20	1
Young	Isham	07JUL01	3.39	1	Yongue	Peter	27JUN04	4.26	1
Young	Isham	14AUG02	3.30	1	Young	Peter	20JUL05	2.36	1
Young	Jacob	23JUN90	1.11	1	Young	Peter	07AUG06	2.39	1
Yonders	Jacob	05JUL91	1.09	1	Young	Peter	15AUG06	2.40	1
Young	James	14NOV88	1.11	1	Young	Peter	30JUL07	2.39	1
Young	James	23MAR90	2.07	1	Young	Peter	18AUG07	2.39	1
Young	James	29APR91	3.17	11	Young	Peter	-----08	2.31	1
Young	James	12SEP92	2.09	1	Young	Peter	10JUN09	1.36	1
Young	James	29SEP92	2.09	1	Young	Peter	-----11	1.89	1
Young	James	10AUG93	1.10	1	Young	Robert	26JUN89	6.08	1
Young	James	14AUG93	1.10	1	Young	Robert	12JUN00	1.16	1
Young	James	21MAY94	1.10	1	Young	Thomas	07MAY01	3.39	1
Young	James	29MAY94	1.10	1	Young	William	25JUN87	3.11	1

surname	name	date	bk.pg	TM	surname	name	date	bk.pg	TM
Young	William	30AUG89	2.15	1					
Young	William	29APR91	3.17	1					
YOUNGER									
Younger	Joshua	01JUN90	2.07	1					
YOUNT									
Yont	George	28JUN87	1.06	1					
Yount	George	25MAY89	6.08	1					
Yount	George	10MAY90	1.11	1					
Younse	James	05DEC92	3.20	M1					
ZACHARIAS									
Zacharias	Fredrick	14AUG90	1.11	1					
Zacharias	Fredrick	-----91	2.11	1					
Zacharias	Frederick	08OCT92	1.14	1					
Zacharias	Frederick	15AUG93	3.13	1					
Zachariah	Fredrick	23APR94	2.16	1					
Zachariah	Fredrick	28MAR95	3.18	1					
Zacherias	Frederick	03AUG96	2.20	1					
Zecharias	Frederick	23MAY97	1.28	1					
Zacharias	Frederick	03JUL99	3.23	1					
Zacherias	Fredrick	30JUN00	3.33	1					
Zacheheus	Frederick	09JUL01	3.39	1					
Zacharias	Frederick	17AUG02	3.30	1					
Zachariah	Frederick	22JUN03	2.36	1					
Zacharias	Frederick	25JUL05	2.36	1					
Zacharias	Frederick	15JUL06	2.40	1					
Zackerias	Fredrick	30JUL07	2.39	1					
Zachariah	Fredrick	-----08	2.31	1					
ZEKLEDGE									
Zukledge	William	30AUG89	2.15	11					
Zeklidge	William	02JUN91	3.17	1					
ZIMMERMAN									
Zimmerman	John	-----11	1.89	1